SATURDAY AM PRESENTS...

THE MASSIVELY MULTIPLAYER WORLD OF CHOSTS

VOLUME 1

THE KING OF CHEATING

BY OSCAR FONG WITH FREDERICK L. JONES

CONTENTS

LEVEL 1
A TASTE OF POWER

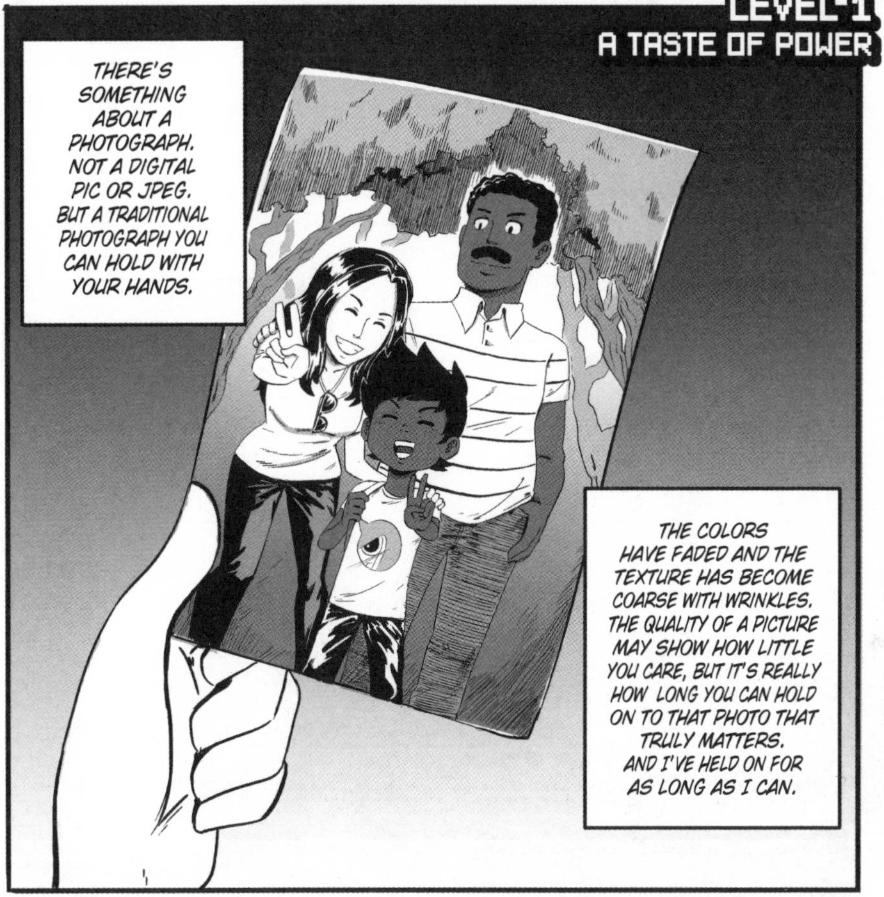

THERE'S SOMETHING ABOUT A PHOTOGRAPH. NOT A DIGITAL PIC OR JPEG. BUT A TRADITIONAL PHOTOGRAPH YOU CAN HOLD WITH YOUR HANDS.
THE COLORS HAVE FADED AND THE TEXTURE HAS BECOME COARSE WITH WRINKLES. THE QUALITY OF A PICTURE MAY SHOW HOW LITTLE YOU CARE, BUT IT'S REALLY HOW LONG YOU CAN HOLD ON TO THAT PHOTO THAT TRULY MATTERS. AND I'VE HELD ON FOR AS LONG AS I CAN.

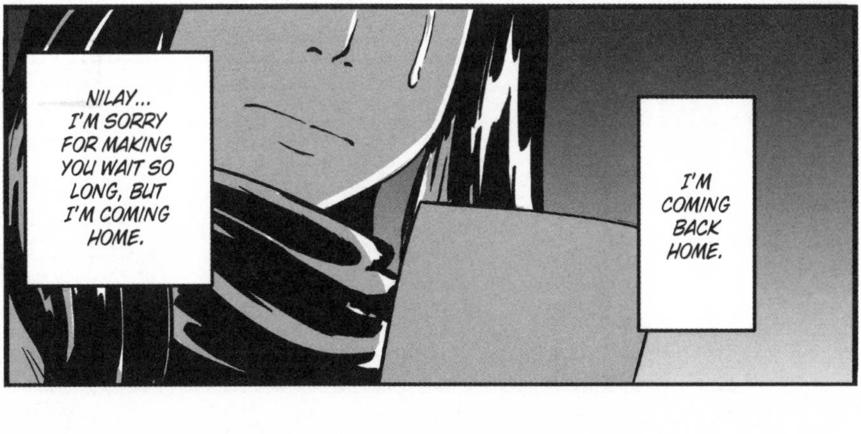

NILAY... I'M SORRY FOR MAKING YOU WAIT SO LONG, BUT I'M COMING HOME.
I'M COMING BACK HOME.

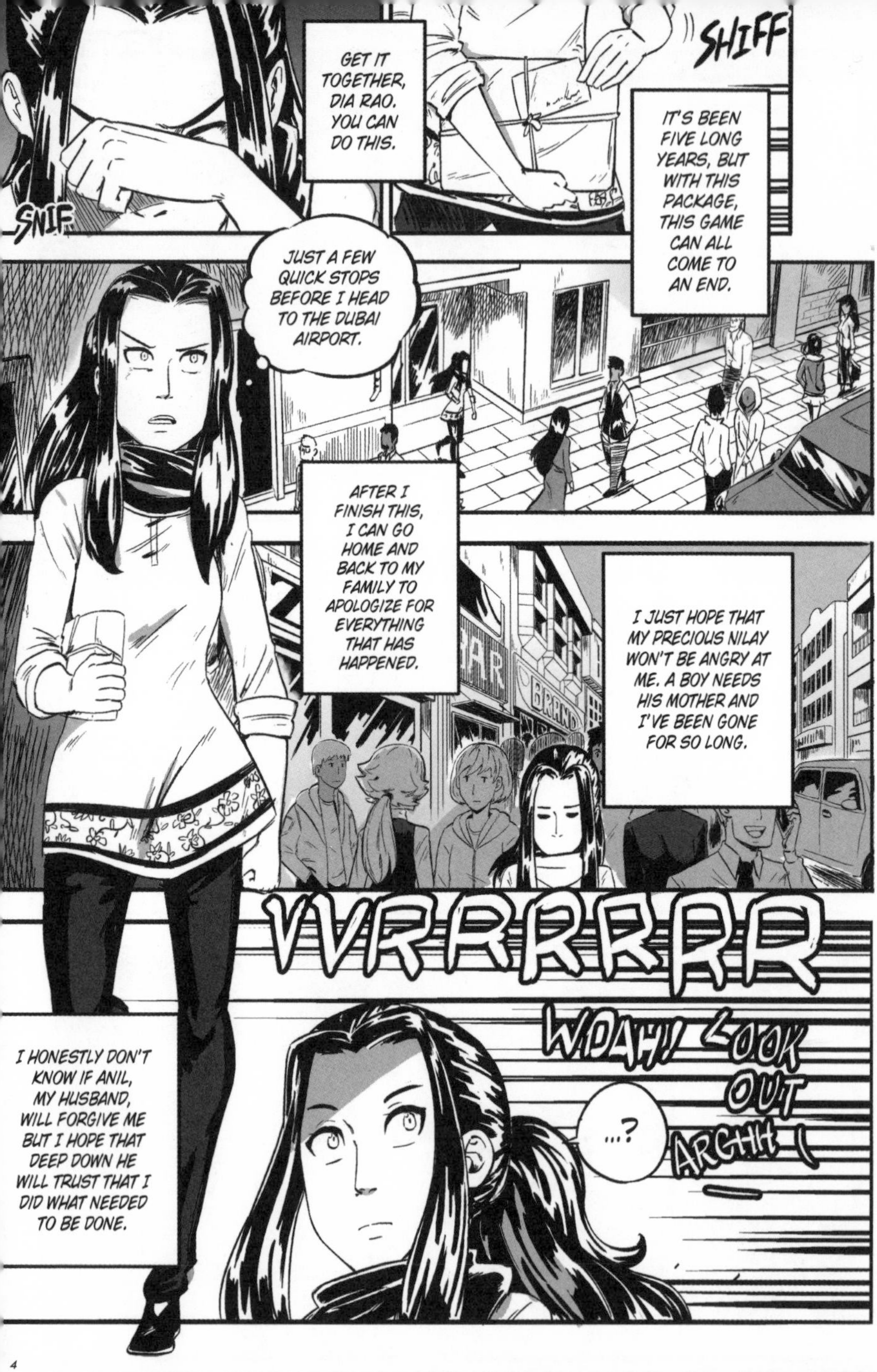
SNIF
GET IT TOGETHER, DIA RAO. YOU CAN DO THIS.
SHIFF
IT'S BEEN FIVE LONG YEARS, BUT WITH THIS PACKAGE, THIS GAME CAN ALL COME TO AN END.
JUST A FEW QUICK STOPS BEFORE I HEAD TO THE DUBAI AIRPORT.
AFTER I FINISH THIS, I CAN GO HOME AND BACK TO MY FAMILY TO APOLOGIZE FOR EVERYTHING THAT HAS HAPPENED.
I JUST HOPE THAT MY PRECIOUS NILAY WON'T BE ANGRY AT ME. A BOY NEEDS HIS MOTHER AND I'VE BEEN GONE FOR SO LONG.
VVRRRRRR
I HONESTLY DON'T KNOW IF ANIL, MY HUSBAND, WILL FORGIVE ME BUT I HOPE THAT DEEP DOWN HE WILL TRUST THAT I DID WHAT NEEDED TO BE DONE.
WOAH! LOOK OUT ARCHH !
...?

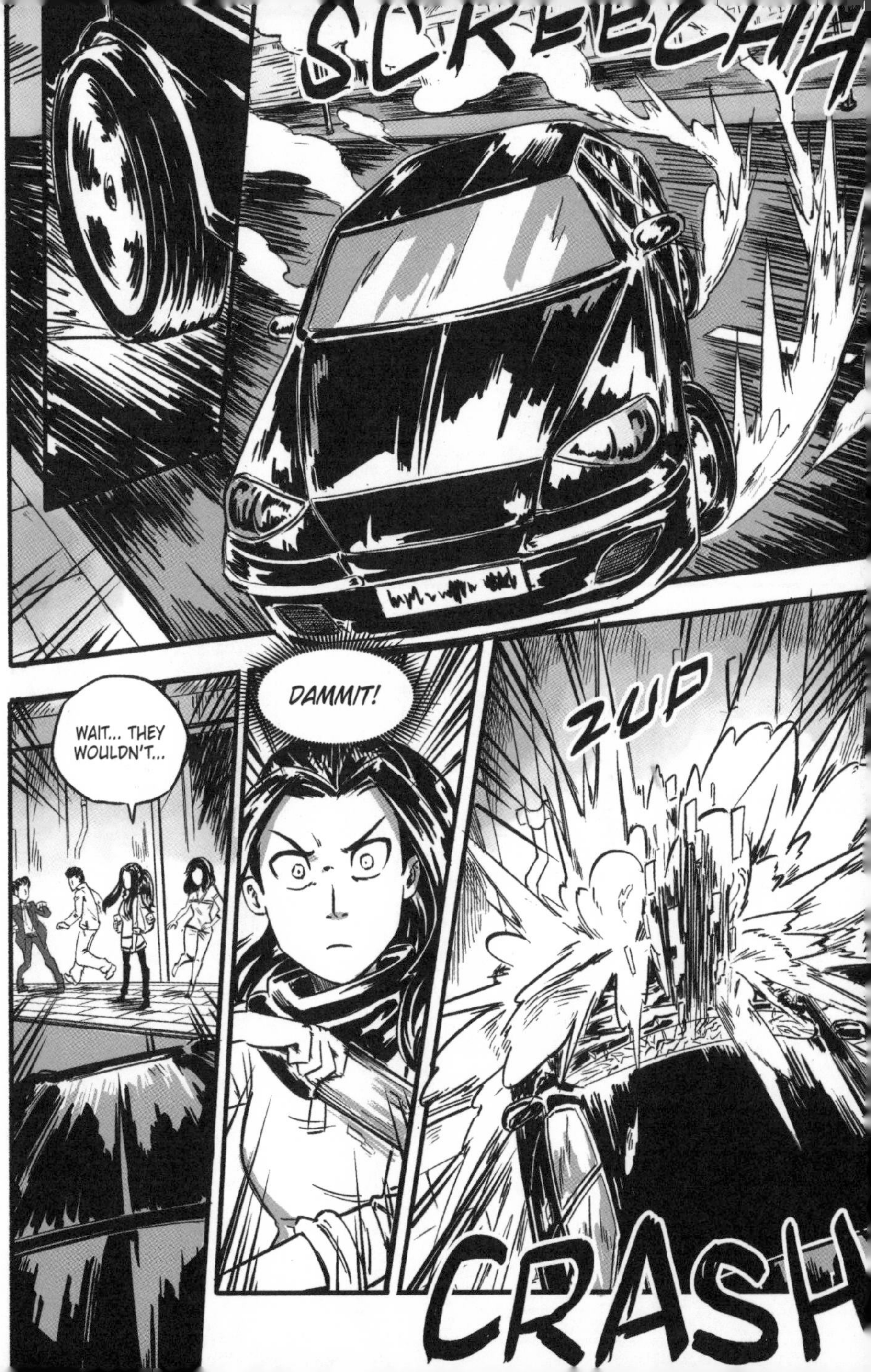
SCREECHH
WAIT... THEY WOULDN'T...
DAMMIT!
ZUD
CRASH

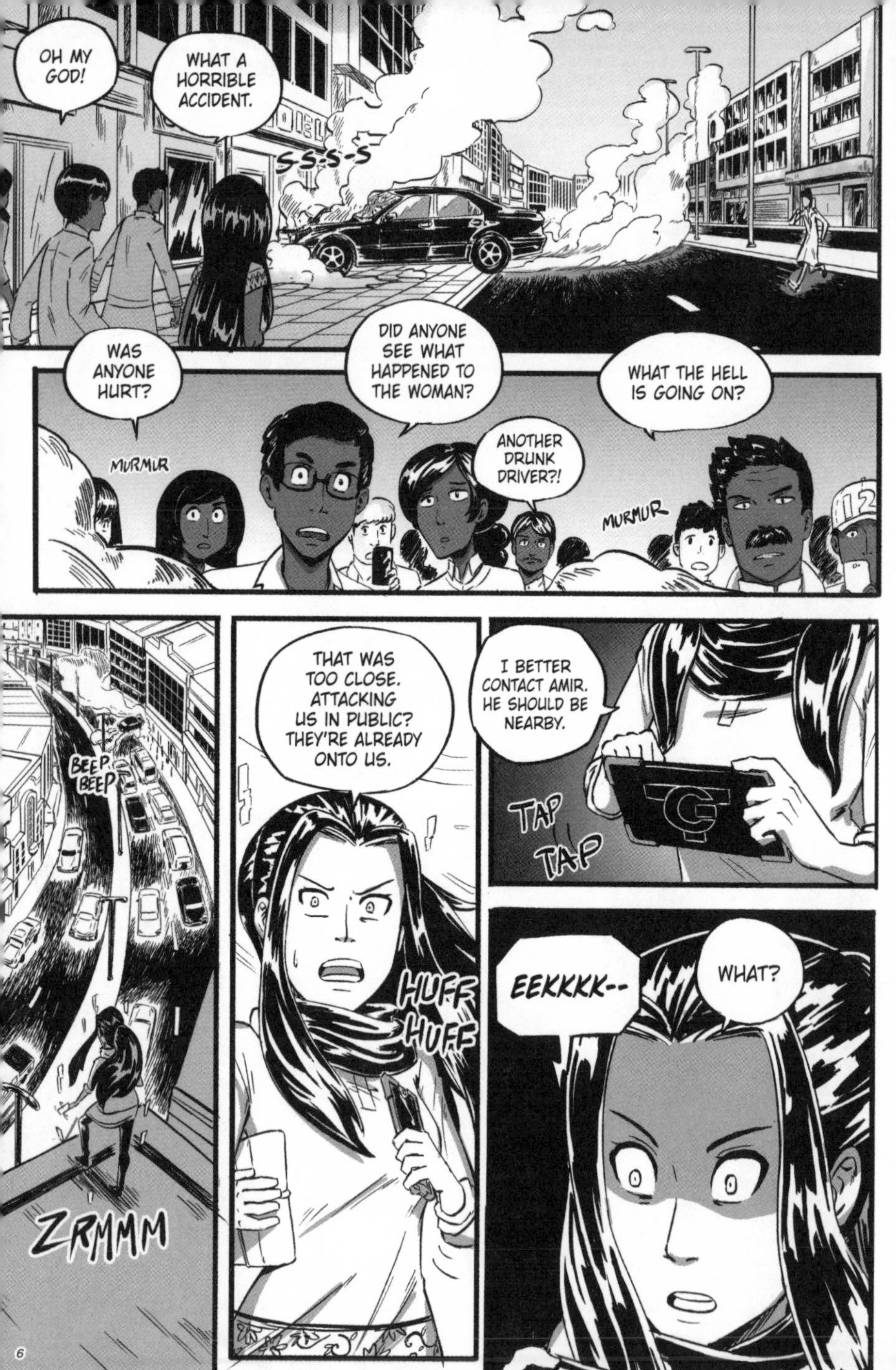
OH MY GOD!
WHAT A HORRIBLE ACCIDENT.
S-S-S-S
WAS ANYONE HURT?
DID ANYONE SEE WHAT HAPPENED TO THE WOMAN?
WHAT THE HELL IS GOING ON?
MURMUR
ANOTHER DRUNK DRIVER?!
MURMUR
BEEP BEEP
ZRMMM
THAT WAS TOO CLOSE. ATTACKING US IN PUBLIC? THEY'RE ALREADY ONTO US.
HUFF HUFF
I BETTER CONTACT AMIR. HE SHOULD BE NEARBY.
TAP TAP
EEKKKK--
WHAT?

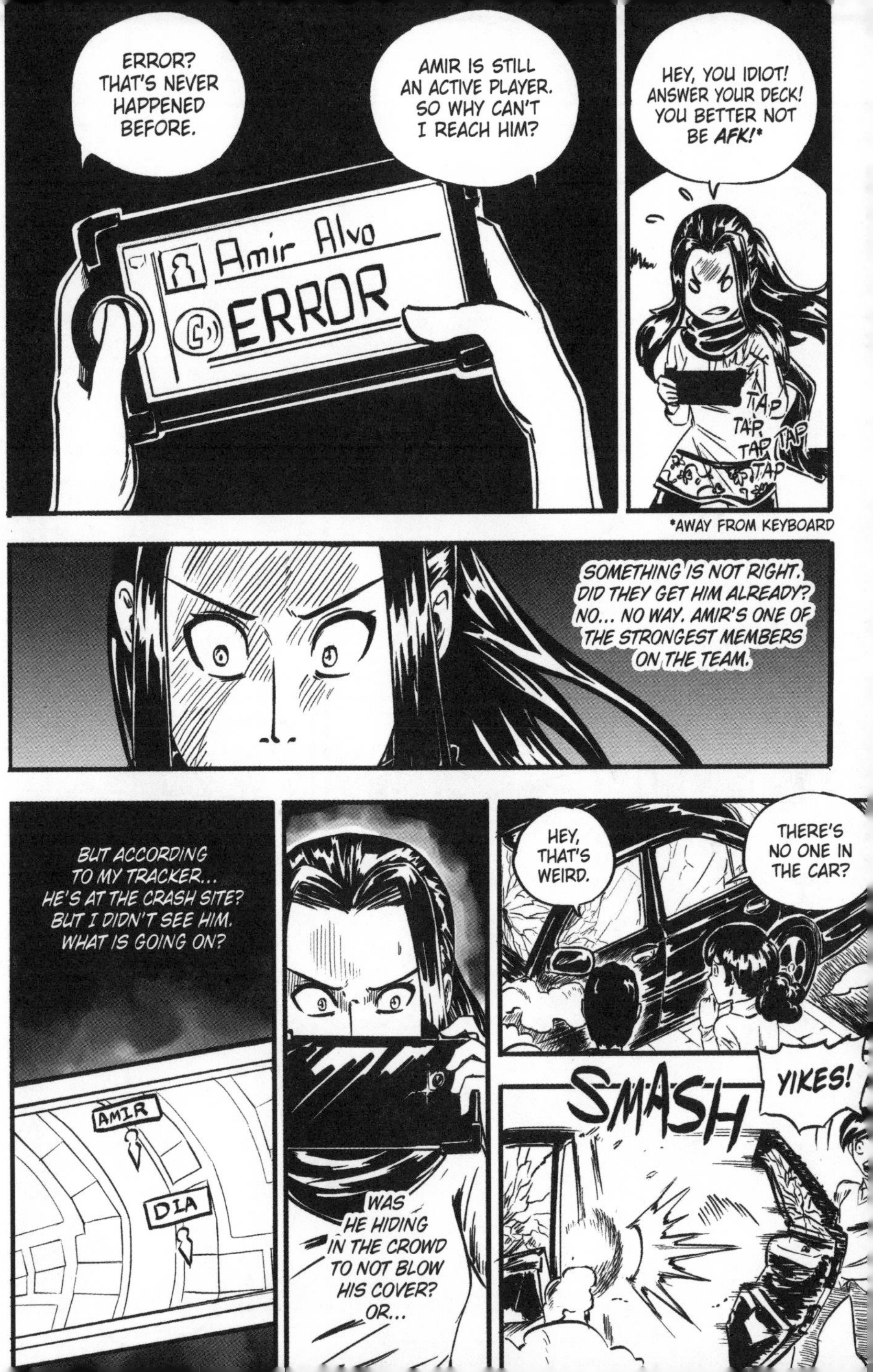
ERROR? THAT'S NEVER HAPPENED BEFORE.
AMIR IS STILL AN ACTIVE PLAYER. SO WHY CAN'T I REACH HIM?
Amir Alvo
ERROR
HEY, YOU IDIOT! ANSWER YOUR DECK! YOU BETTER NOT BE *AFK!**
TAP TAP TAP TAP TAP
*AWAY FROM KEYBOARD
SOMETHING IS NOT RIGHT. DID THEY GET HIM ALREADY? NO... NO WAY. AMIR'S ONE OF THE STRONGEST MEMBERS ON THE TEAM.
BUT ACCORDING TO MY TRACKER... HE'S AT THE CRASH SITE? BUT I DIDN'T SEE HIM. WHAT IS GOING ON?
AMIR
DIA
WAS HE HIDING IN THE CROWD TO NOT BLOW HIS COVER? OR...
HEY, THAT'S WEIRD.
THERE'S NO ONE IN THE CAR?
SMASH
YIKES!

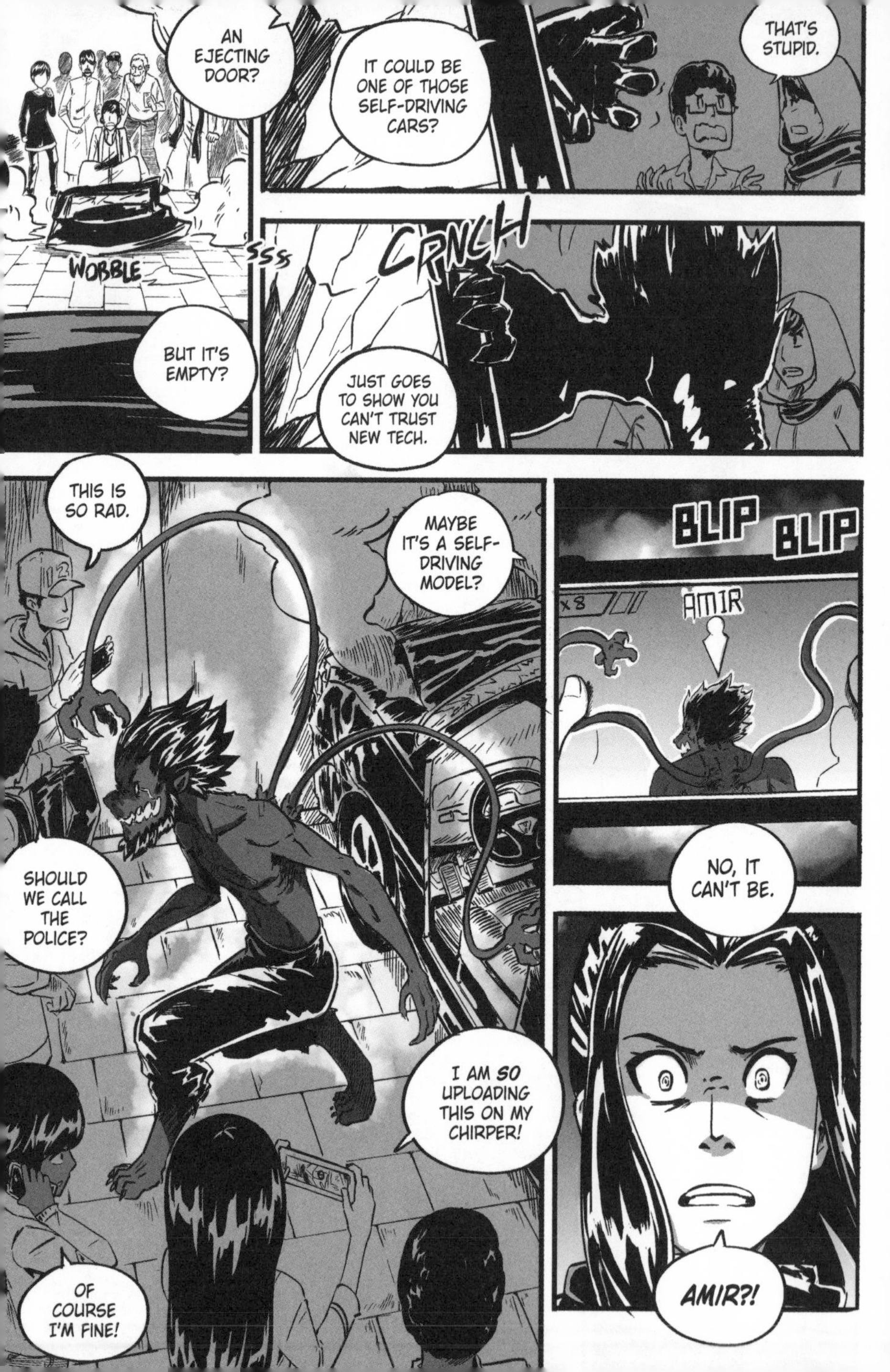
AN EJECTING DOOR?
WOBBLE
SSSS
BUT IT'S EMPTY?
IT COULD BE ONE OF THOSE SELF-DRIVING CARS?
THAT'S STUPID.
CRNCH
JUST GOES TO SHOW YOU CAN'T TRUST NEW TECH.
THIS IS SO RAD.
MAYBE IT'S A SELF-DRIVING MODEL?
SHOULD WE CALL THE POLICE?
I AM *SO* UPLOADING THIS ON MY CHIRPER!
OF COURSE I'M FINE!
BLIP BLIP
x8
AMIR
NO, IT CAN'T BE.
AMIR?!

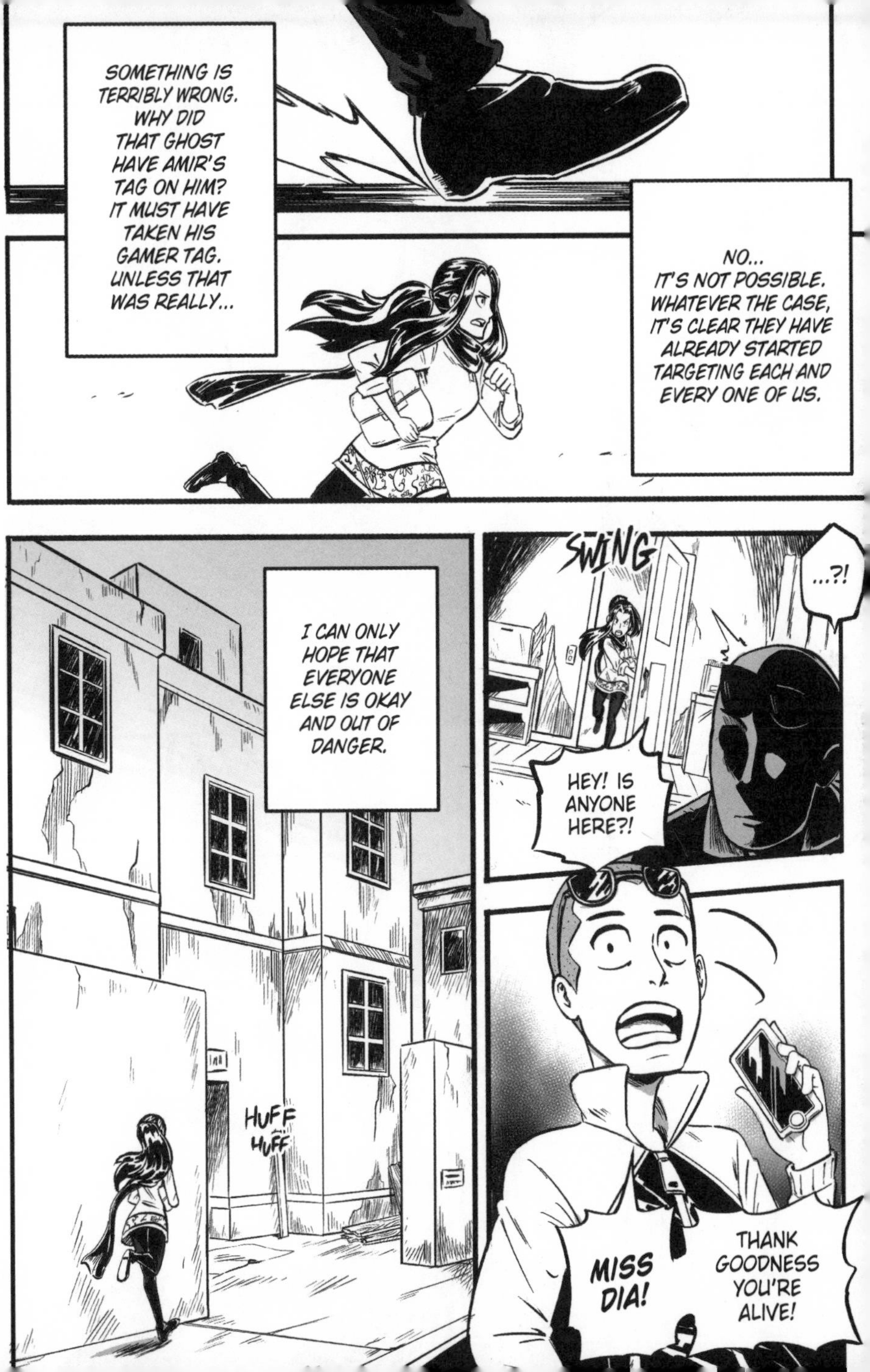
SOMETHING IS TERRIBLY WRONG. WHY DID THAT GHOST HAVE AMIR'S TAG ON HIM? IT MUST HAVE TAKEN HIS GAMER TAG. UNLESS THAT WAS REALLY...
NO... IT'S NOT POSSIBLE. WHATEVER THE CASE, IT'S CLEAR THEY HAVE ALREADY STARTED TARGETING EACH AND EVERY ONE OF US.
I CAN ONLY HOPE THAT EVERYONE ELSE IS OKAY AND OUT OF DANGER.
HUFF
HUFF
SWING
...?!
HEY! IS ANYONE HERE?!
MISS DIA!
THANK GOODNESS YOU'RE ALIVE!

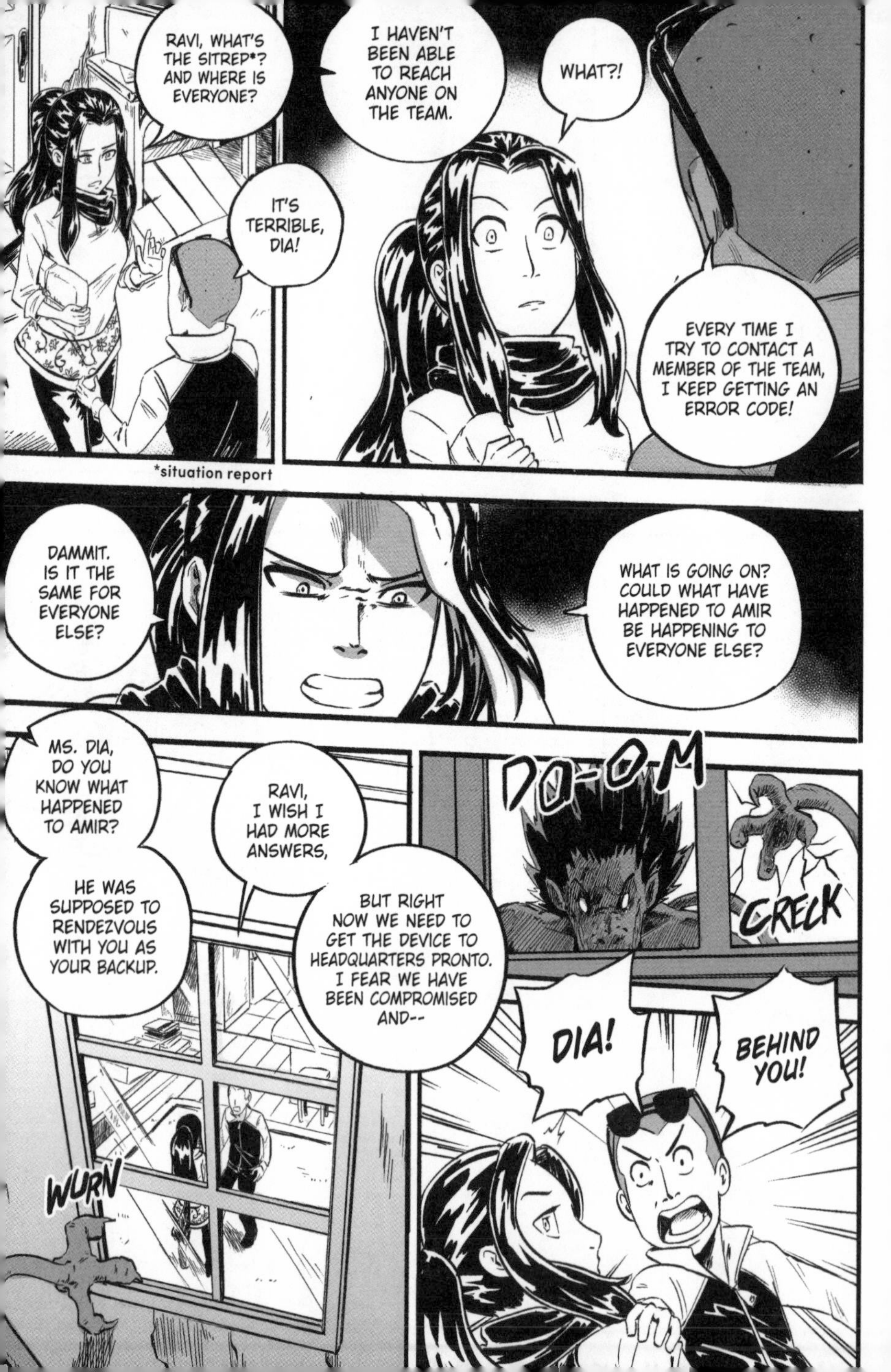
RAVI, WHAT'S THE SITREP*? AND WHERE IS EVERYONE?
IT'S TERRIBLE, DIA!
I HAVEN'T BEEN ABLE TO REACH ANYONE ON THE TEAM.
WHAT?!
EVERY TIME I TRY TO CONTACT A MEMBER OF THE TEAM, I KEEP GETTING AN ERROR CODE!
*situation report
DAMMIT. IS IT THE SAME FOR EVERYONE ELSE?
WHAT IS GOING ON? COULD WHAT HAVE HAPPENED TO AMIR BE HAPPENING TO EVERYONE ELSE?
MS. DIA, DO YOU KNOW WHAT HAPPENED TO AMIR?
HE WAS SUPPOSED TO RENDEZVOUS WITH YOU AS YOUR BACKUP.
RAVI, I WISH I HAD MORE ANSWERS,
BUT RIGHT NOW WE NEED TO GET THE DEVICE TO HEADQUARTERS PRONTO. I FEAR WE HAVE BEEN COMPROMISED AND--
WURN
DO-O-M
CRECK
DIA!
BEHIND YOU!

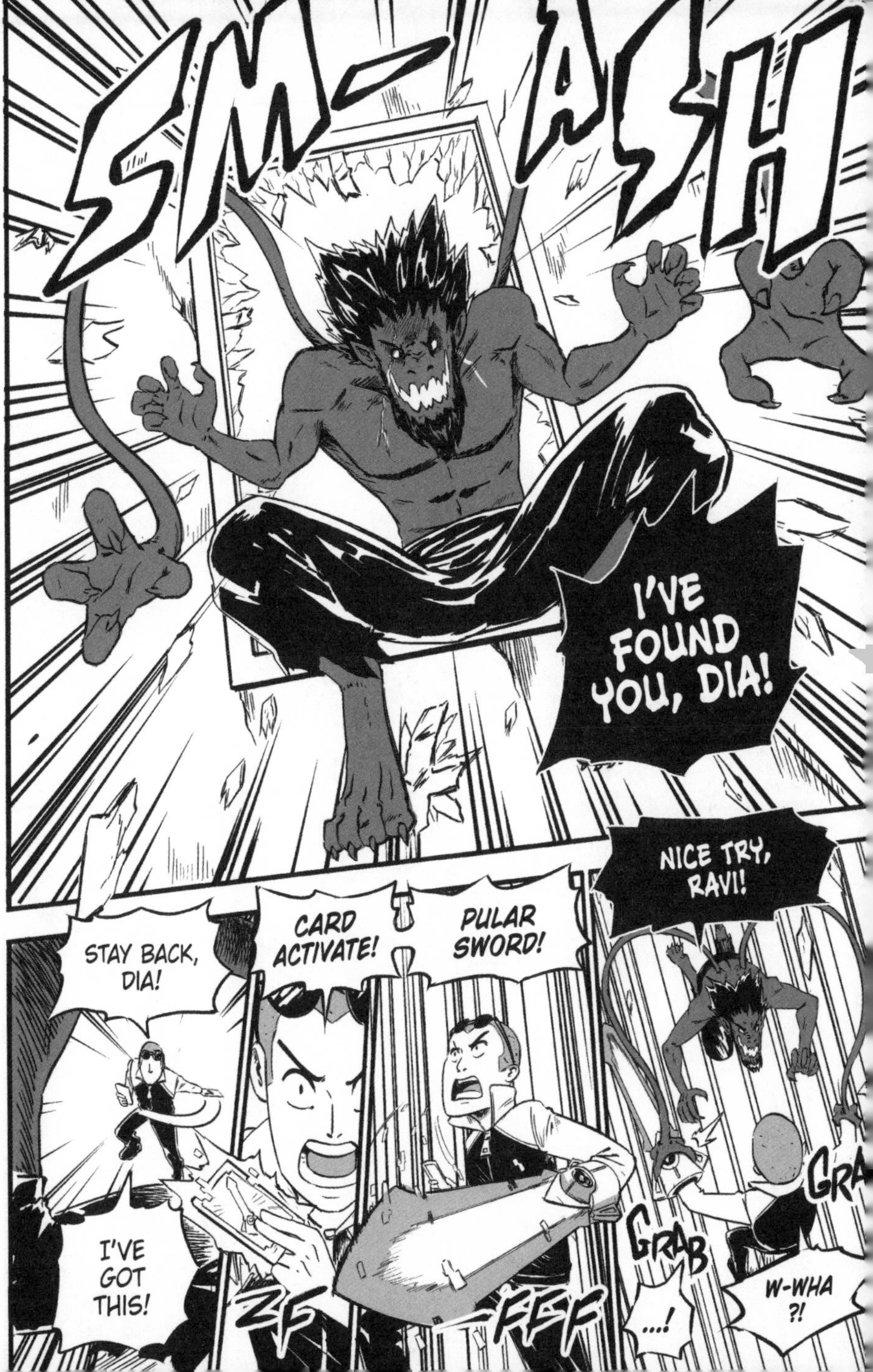
SM-ASH
I'VE FOUND YOU, DIA!
STAY BACK, DIA!
CARD ACTIVATE!
PULAR SWORD!
I'VE GOT THIS!
ZF
FFF
NICE TRY, RAVI!
GRAB
GRA
...!
W-WHA ?!

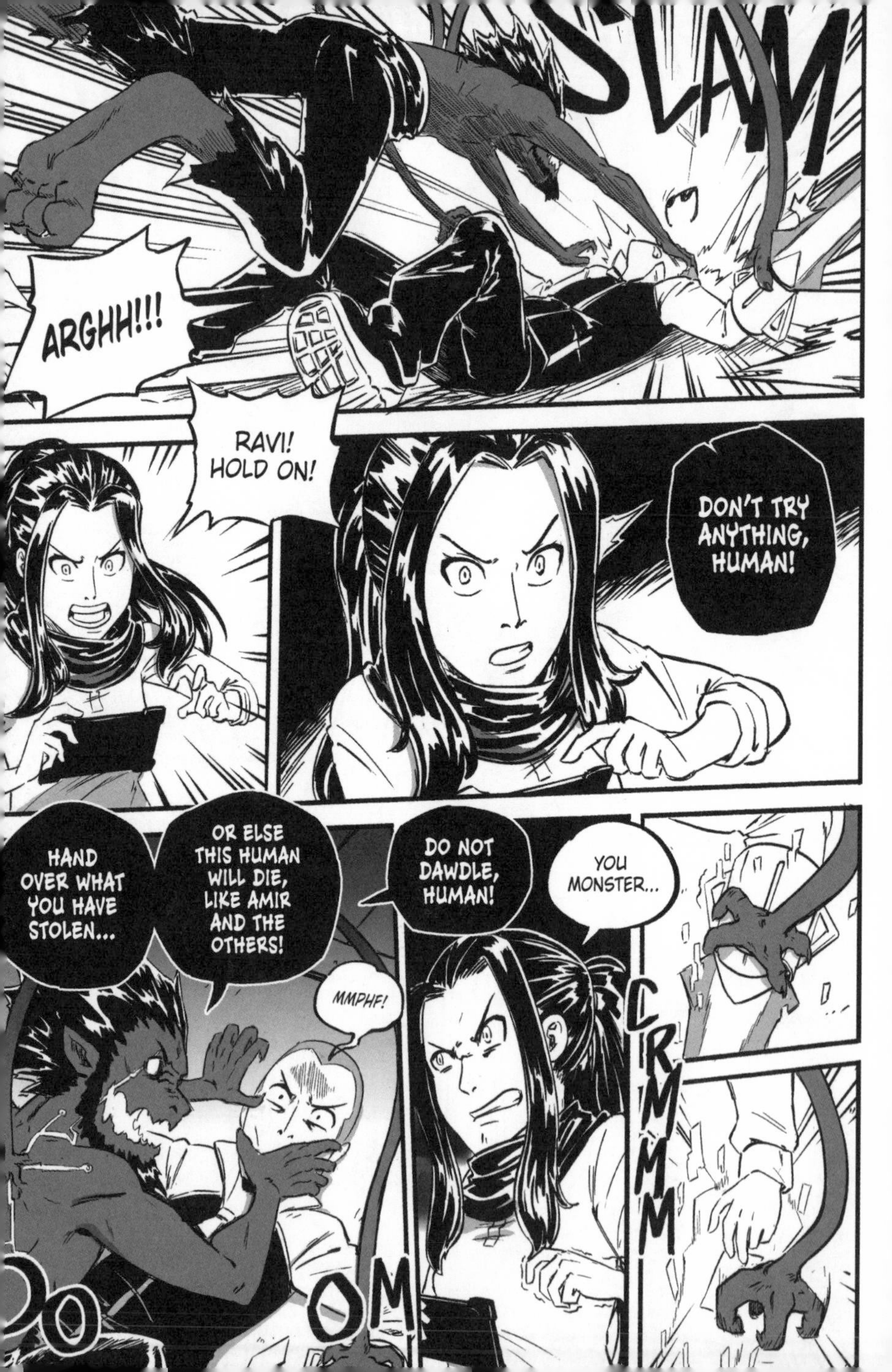
SLAM
ARGHH!!!
RAVI! HOLD ON!
DON'T TRY ANYTHING, HUMAN!
HAND OVER WHAT YOU HAVE STOLEN...
OR ELSE THIS HUMAN WILL DIE, LIKE AMIR AND THE OTHERS!
MMPHF!
DOOOM
DO NOT DAWDLE, HUMAN!
YOU MONSTER...
CRMMMM

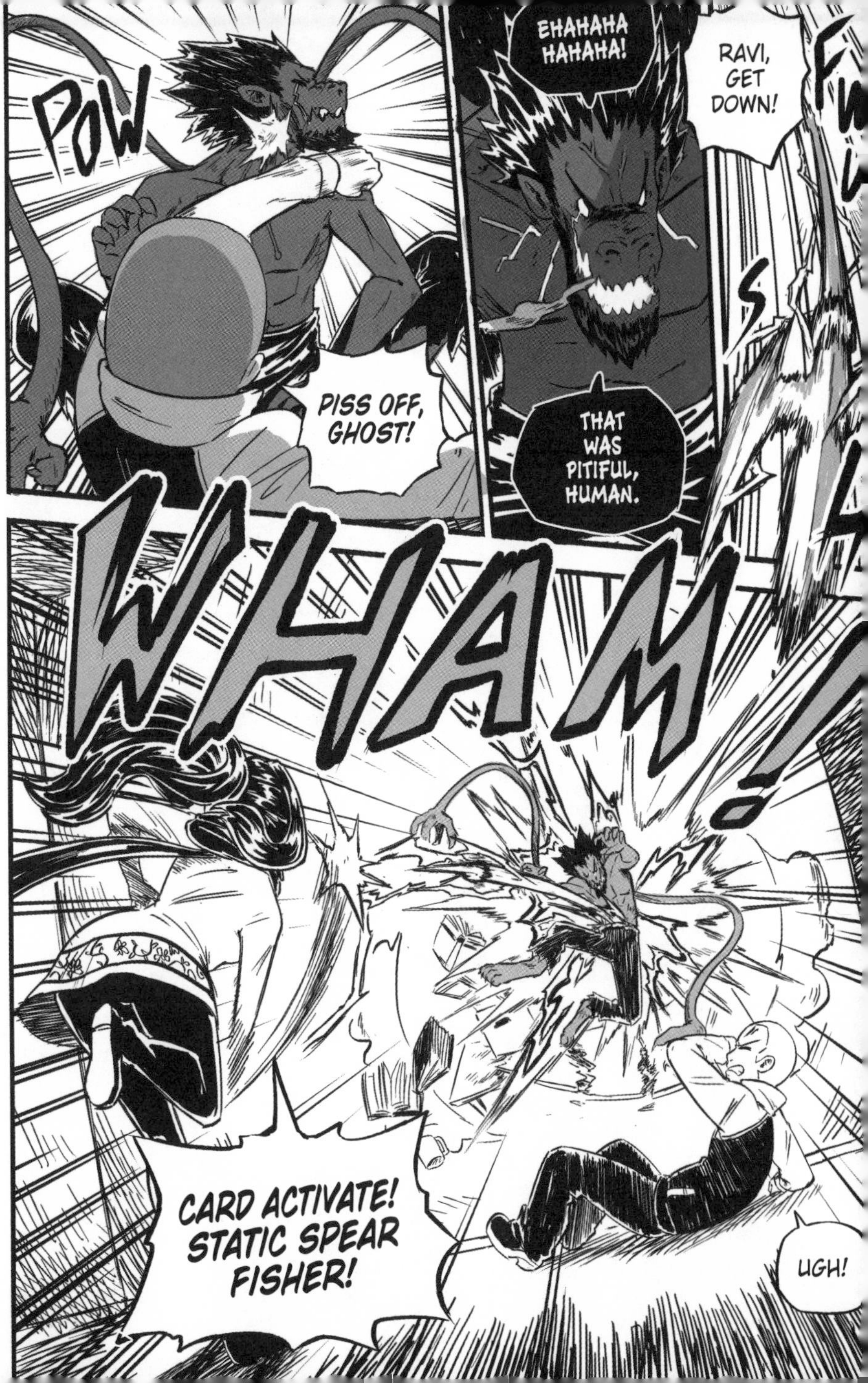
POW
PISS OFF, GHOST!
EHAHAHA HAHAHA!
THAT WAS PITIFUL, HUMAN.
RAVI, GET DOWN!
WHAM!
CARD ACTIVATE! STATIC SPEAR FISHER!
UGH!

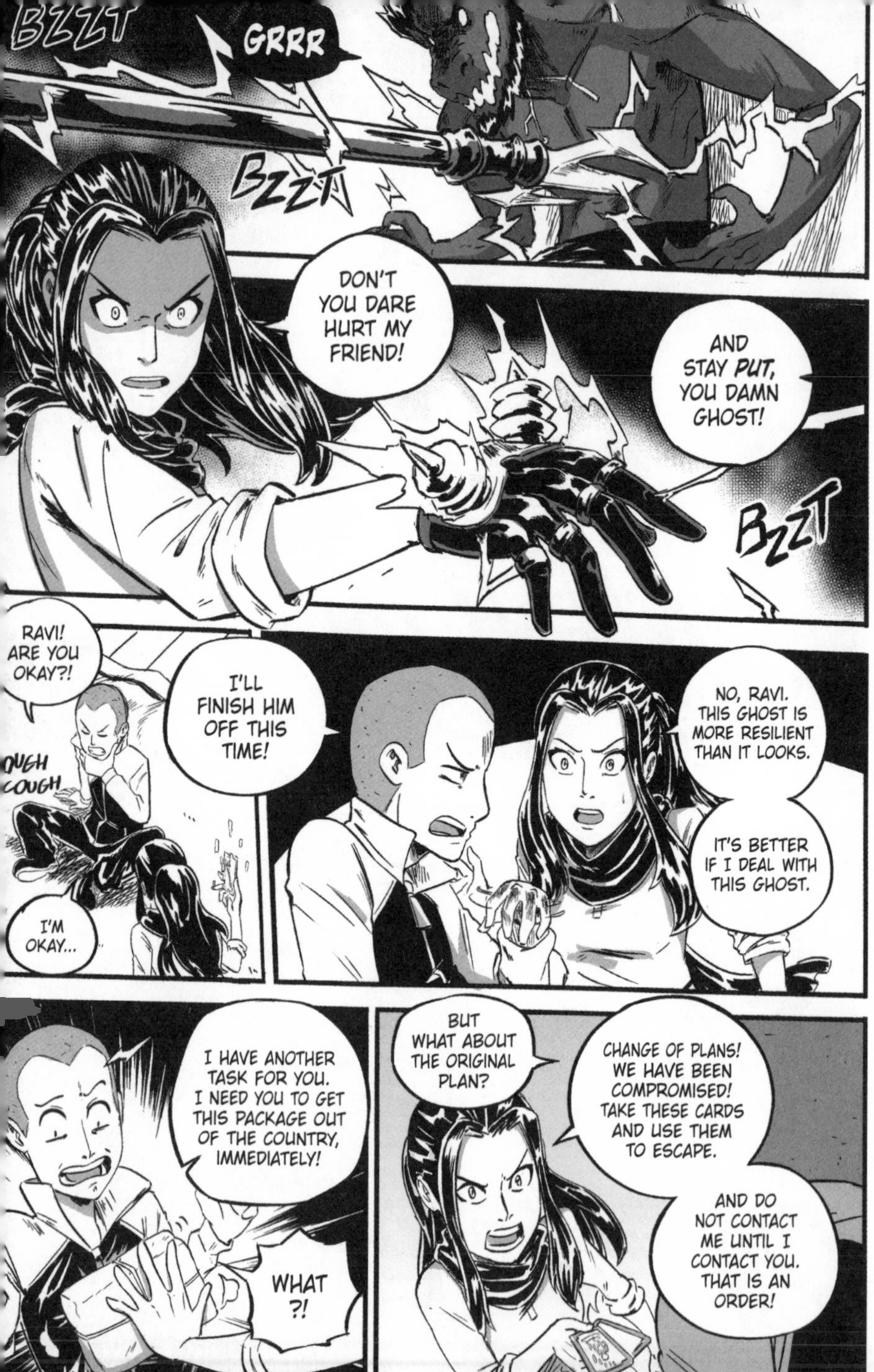

BZZT
GRRR
BZZT
DON'T YOU DARE HURT MY FRIEND!
AND STAY *PUT*, YOU DAMN GHOST!
BZZT
RAVI! ARE YOU OKAY?!
OUGH
COUGH
I'M OKAY...
I'LL FINISH HIM OFF THIS TIME!
NO, RAVI. THIS GHOST IS MORE RESILIENT THAN IT LOOKS.
IT'S BETTER IF I DEAL WITH THIS GHOST.
I HAVE ANOTHER TASK FOR YOU. I NEED YOU TO GET THIS PACKAGE OUT OF THE COUNTRY, IMMEDIATELY!
WHAT ?!
BUT WHAT ABOUT THE ORIGINAL PLAN?
CHANGE OF PLANS! WE HAVE BEEN COMPROMISED! TAKE THESE CARDS AND USE THEM TO ESCAPE.
AND DO NOT CONTACT ME UNTIL I CONTACT YOU. THAT IS AN ORDER!

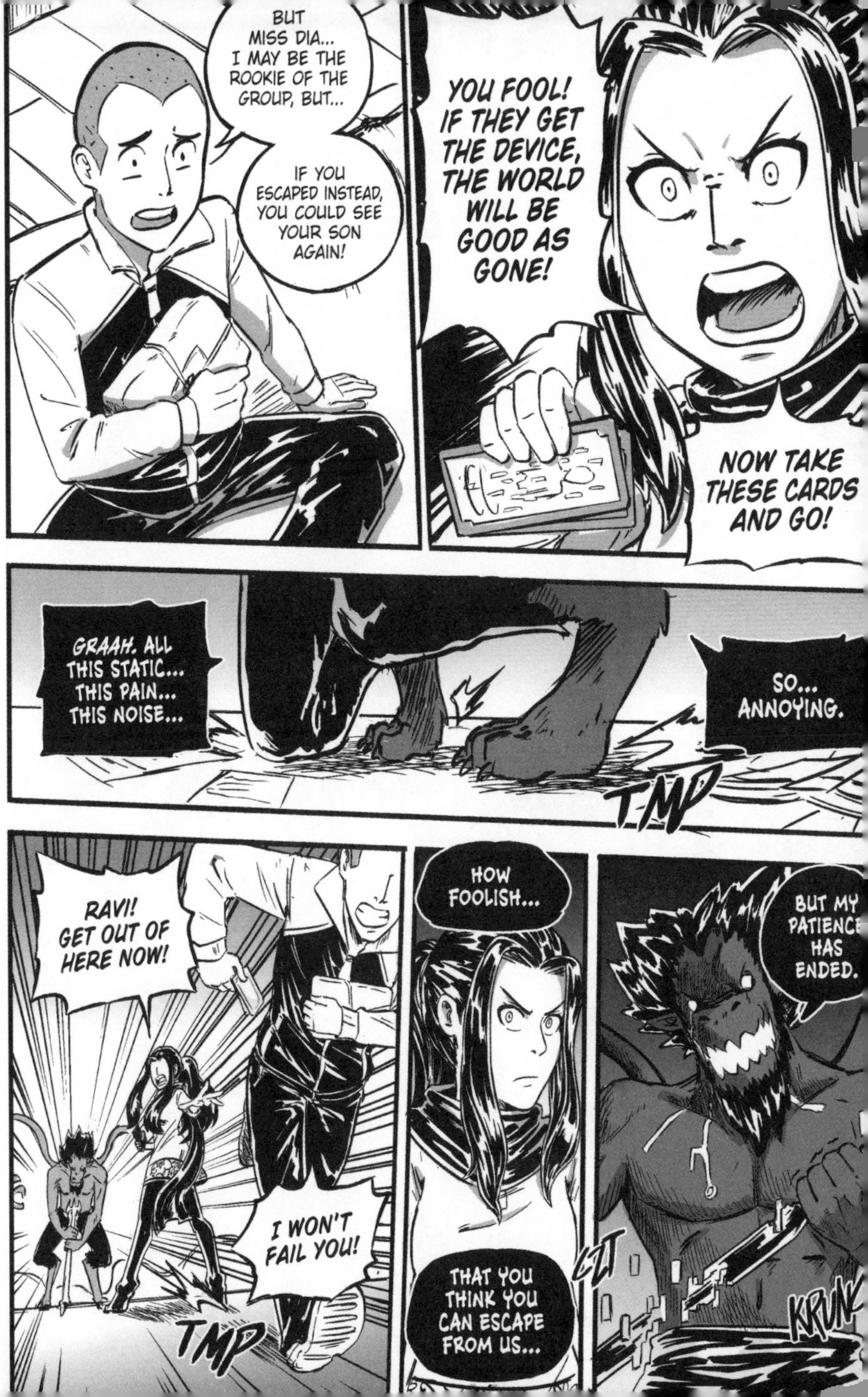
BUT MISS DIA... I MAY BE THE ROOKIE OF THE GROUP, BUT...
IF YOU ESCAPED INSTEAD, YOU COULD SEE YOUR SON AGAIN!
YOU FOOL! IF THEY GET THE DEVICE, THE WORLD WILL BE GOOD AS GONE!
NOW TAKE THESE CARDS AND GO!
GRAAH. ALL THIS STATIC... THIS PAIN... THIS NOISE...
SO... ANNOYING.
TMP
RAVI! GET OUT OF HERE NOW!
I WON'T FAIL YOU!
TMP
HOW FOOLISH...
THAT YOU THINK YOU CAN ESCAPE FROM US...
CZT
BUT MY PATIENCE HAS ENDED.
KRUNK

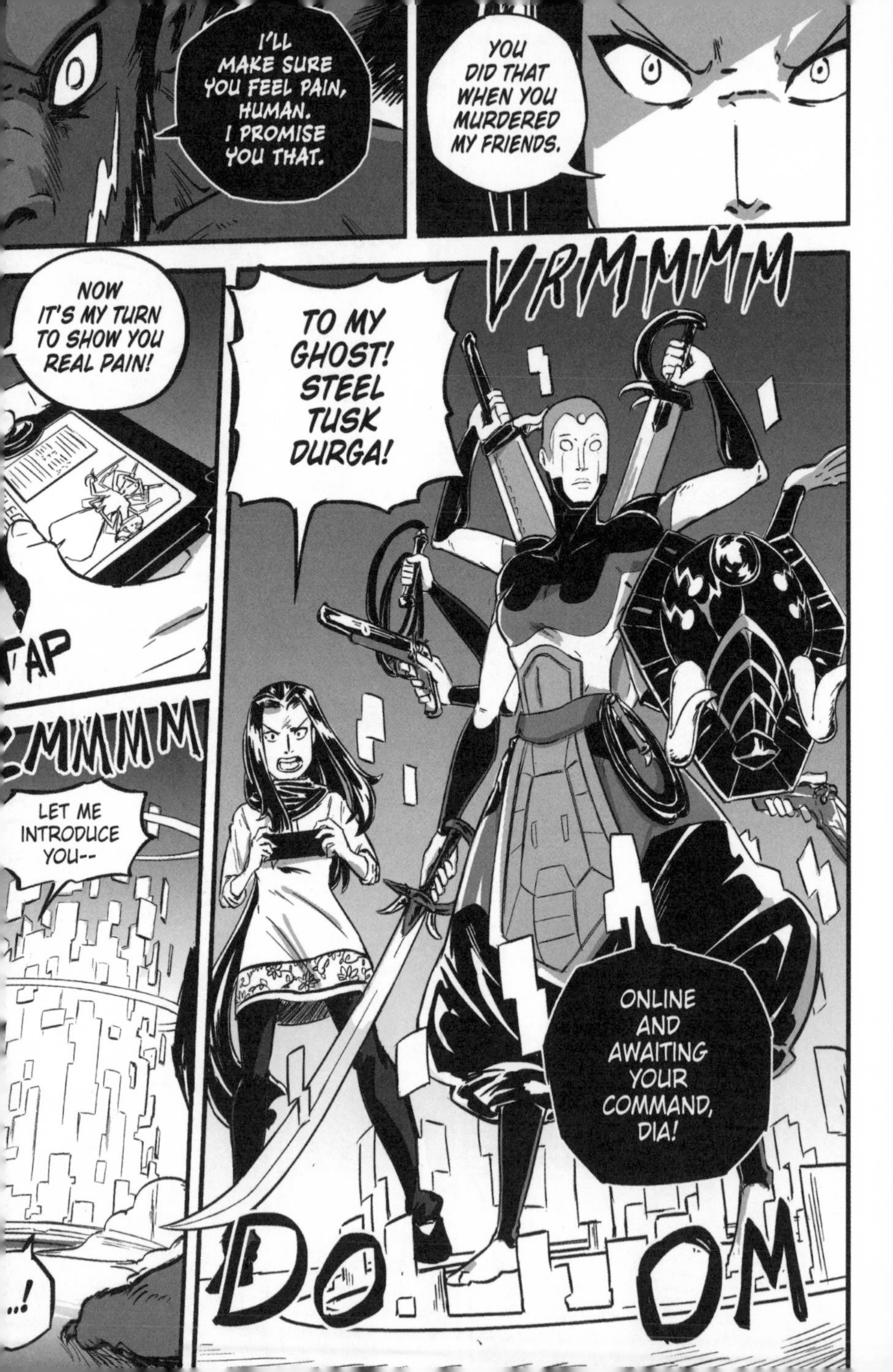
I'LL MAKE SURE YOU FEEL PAIN, HUMAN. I PROMISE YOU THAT.
YOU DID THAT WHEN YOU MURDERED MY FRIENDS.
NOW IT'S MY TURN TO SHOW YOU REAL PAIN!
TAP
MMMMM
LET ME INTRODUCE YOU--
..!
TO MY GHOST! STEEL TUSK DURGA!
VRMMMMM
ONLINE AND AWAITING YOUR COMMAND, DIA!
DO OM

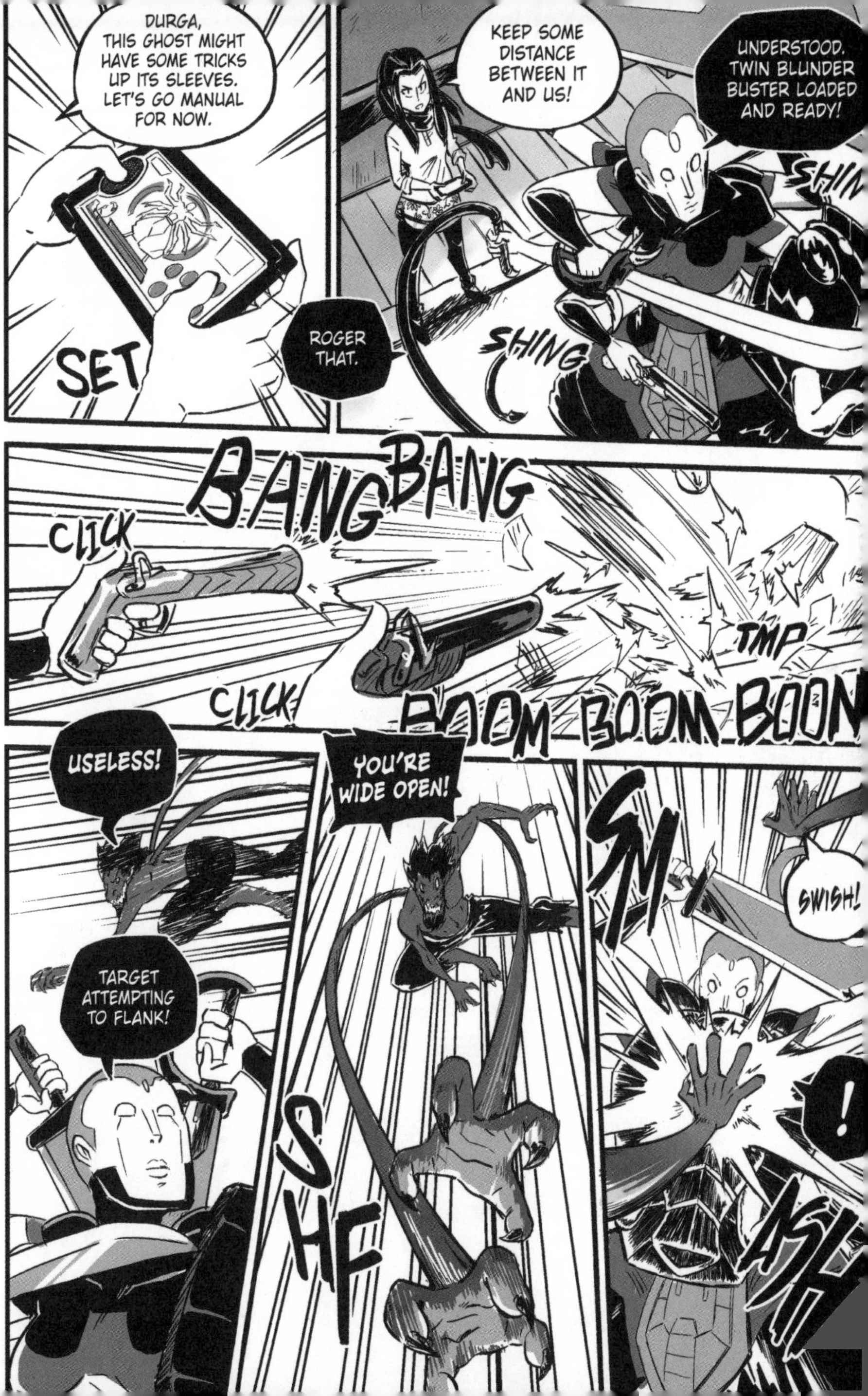
DURGA, THIS GHOST MIGHT HAVE SOME TRICKS UP ITS SLEEVES. LET'S GO MANUAL FOR NOW.
SET
ROGER THAT.
KEEP SOME DISTANCE BETWEEN IT AND US!
UNDERSTOOD. TWIN BLUNDER BUSTER LOADED AND READY!
SHIN
SHING
CLICK
BANG BANG
CLICK
TMP
BOOM BOOM BOOM
USELESS!
TARGET ATTEMPTING TO FLANK!
YOU'RE WIDE OPEN!
SHF
SM
SWISH!
!

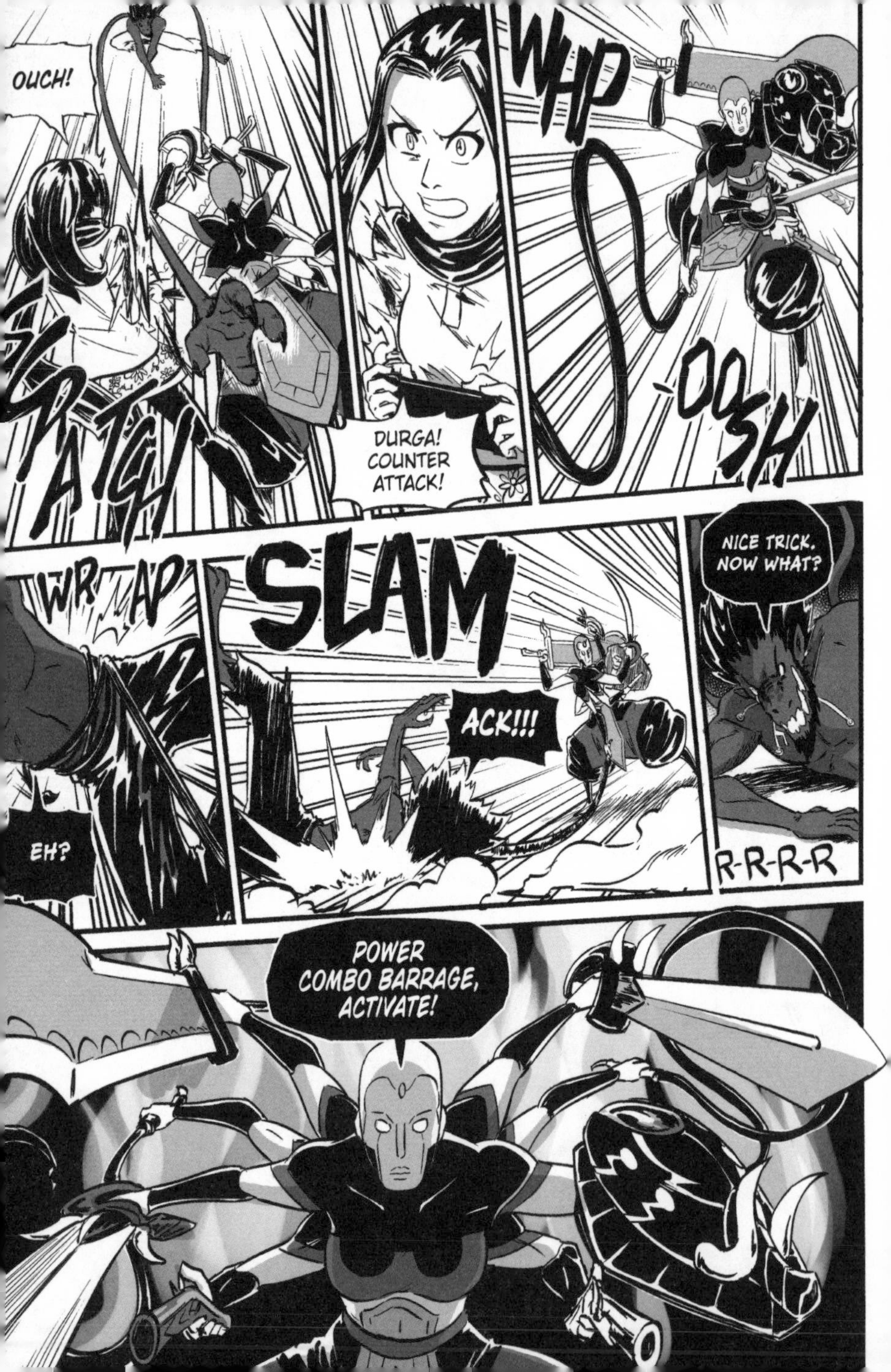

OUCH!
DURGA! COUNTER ATTACK!
WHIP
WRAP
EH?
SLAM
ACK!!!
NICE TRICK. NOW WHAT?
R-R-R-R
POWER COMBO BARRAGE, ACTIVATE!

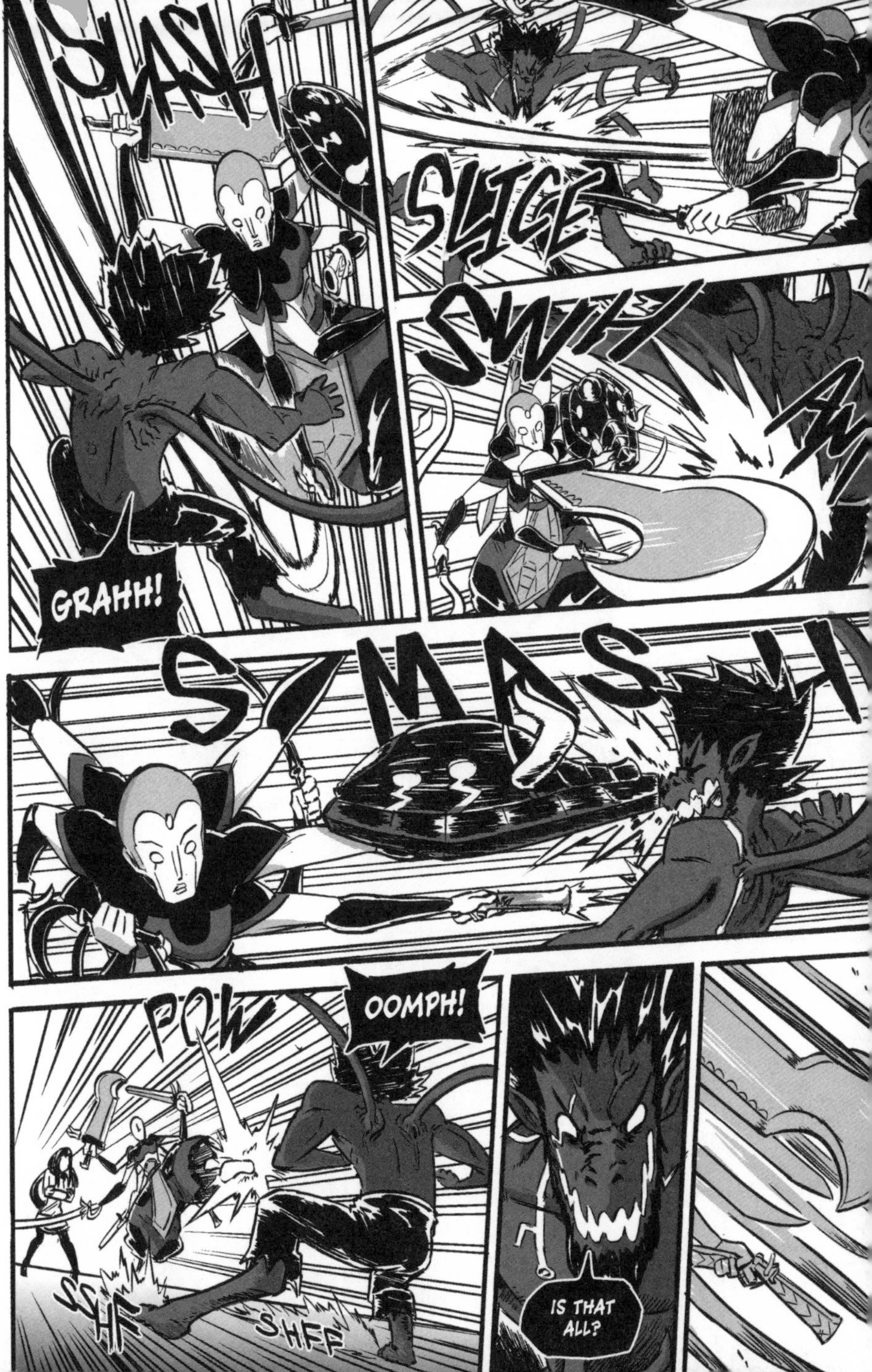
SLASH
GRAHH!
SLICE
SMASH
POW
OOMPH!
SHF
SHFF
IS THAT ALL?

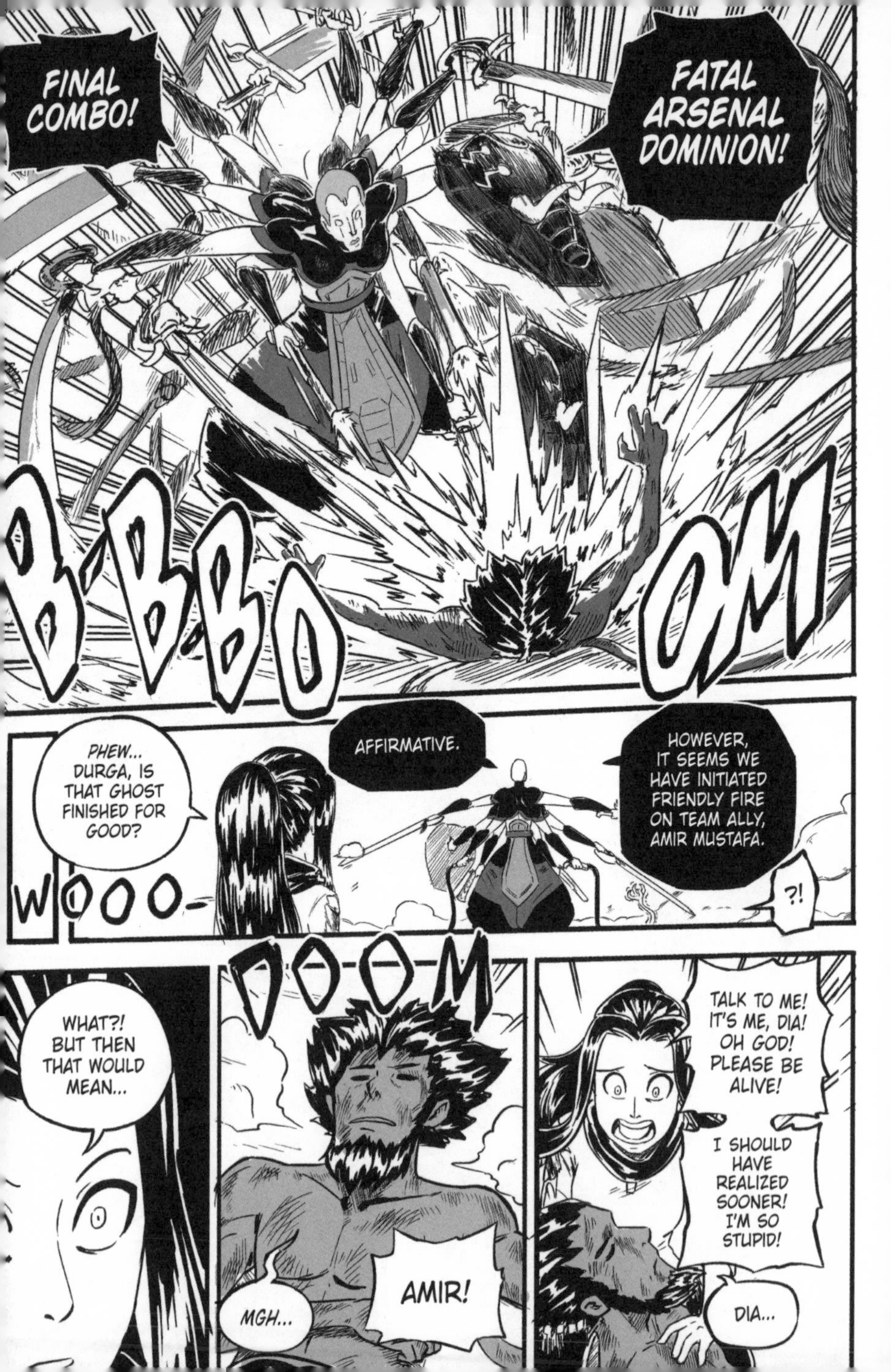
FINAL COMBO!
FATAL ARSENAL DOMINION!
B-B-BOOM
PHEW... DURGA, IS THAT GHOST FINISHED FOR GOOD?
AFFIRMATIVE.
HOWEVER, IT SEEMS WE HAVE INITIATED FRIENDLY FIRE ON TEAM ALLY, AMIR MUSTAFA.
WOOO-
?!
WHAT?! BUT THEN THAT WOULD MEAN...
DOOOM
AMIR!
MGH...
TALK TO ME! IT'S ME, DIA! OH GOD! PLEASE BE ALIVE!
I SHOULD HAVE REALIZED SOONER! I'M SO STUPID!
DIA...

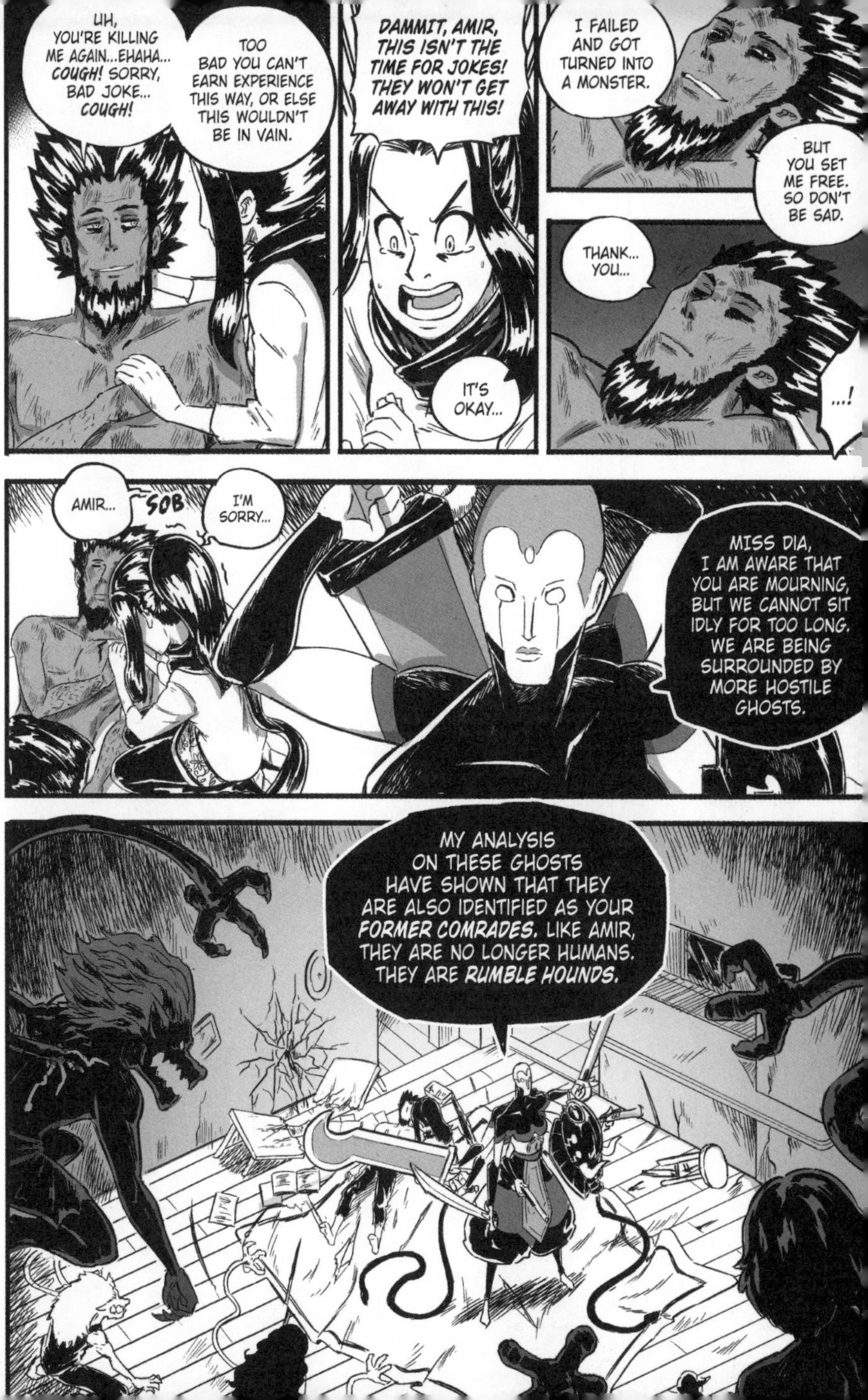

UH, YOU'RE KILLING ME AGAIN...EHAHA... COUGH! SORRY, BAD JOKE... COUGH!
TOO BAD YOU CAN'T EARN EXPERIENCE THIS WAY, OR ELSE THIS WOULDN'T BE IN VAIN.
DAMMIT, AMIR, THIS ISN'T THE TIME FOR JOKES! THEY WON'T GET AWAY WITH THIS!
IT'S OKAY...
I FAILED AND GOT TURNED INTO A MONSTER.
BUT YOU SET ME FREE. SO DON'T BE SAD.
THANK... YOU...
...!
AMIR...
SOB
I'M SORRY...
MISS DIA, I AM AWARE THAT YOU ARE MOURNING, BUT WE CANNOT SIT IDLY FOR TOO LONG. WE ARE BEING SURROUNDED BY MORE HOSTILE GHOSTS.
MY ANALYSIS ON THESE GHOSTS HAVE SHOWN THAT THEY ARE ALSO IDENTIFIED AS YOUR FORMER COMRADES. LIKE AMIR, THEY ARE NO LONGER HUMANS. THEY ARE RUMBLE HOUNDS.

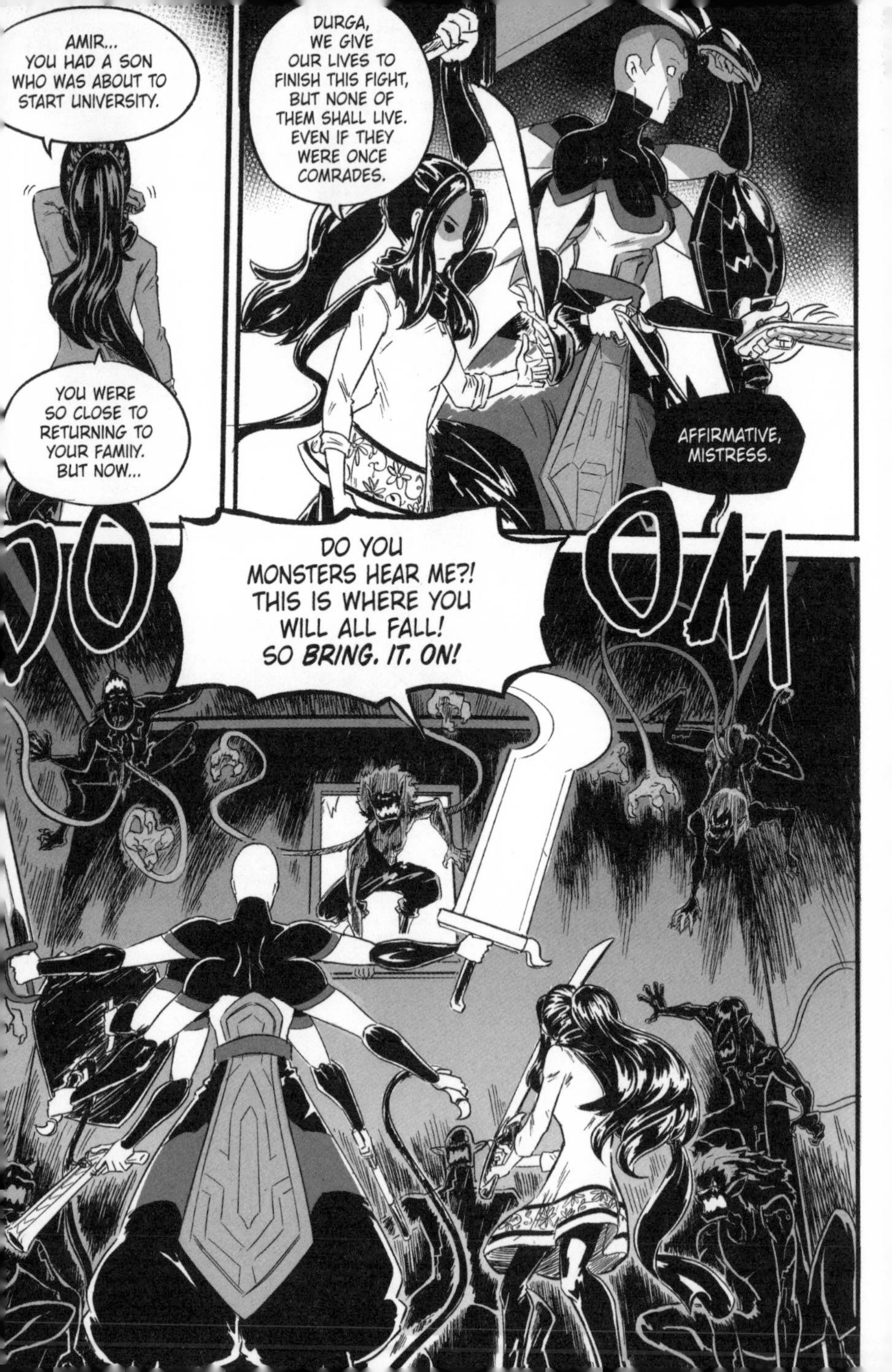
AMIR... YOU HAD A SON WHO WAS ABOUT TO START UNIVERSITY.
YOU WERE SO CLOSE TO RETURNING TO YOUR FAMIIY. BUT NOW...
DURGA, WE GIVE OUR LIVES TO FINISH THIS FIGHT, BUT NONE OF THEM SHALL LIVE. EVEN IF THEY WERE ONCE COMRADES.
AFFIRMATIVE, MISTRESS.
DOOOM
DO YOU MONSTERS HEAR ME?! THIS IS WHERE YOU WILL ALL FALL! SO *BRING. IT. ON!*

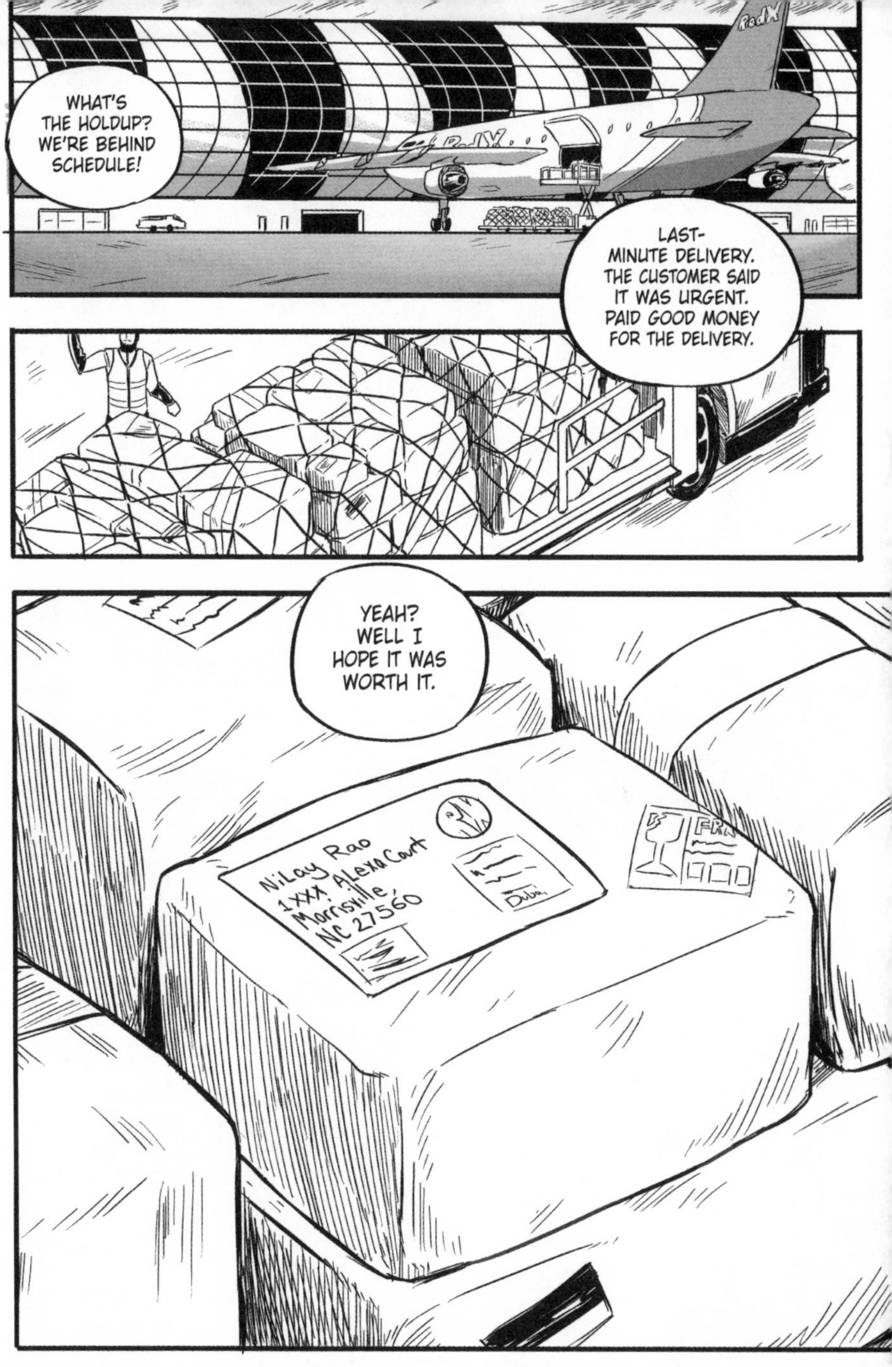
RedX
WHAT'S THE HOLDUP? WE'RE BEHIND SCHEDULE!
LAST-MINUTE DELIVERY. THE CUSTOMER SAID IT WAS URGENT. PAID GOOD MONEY FOR THE DELIVERY.
YEAH? WELL I HOPE IT WAS WORTH IT.
NiLay Rao
1XXX ALexa Court
Morrisville,
NC 27560
Dubai

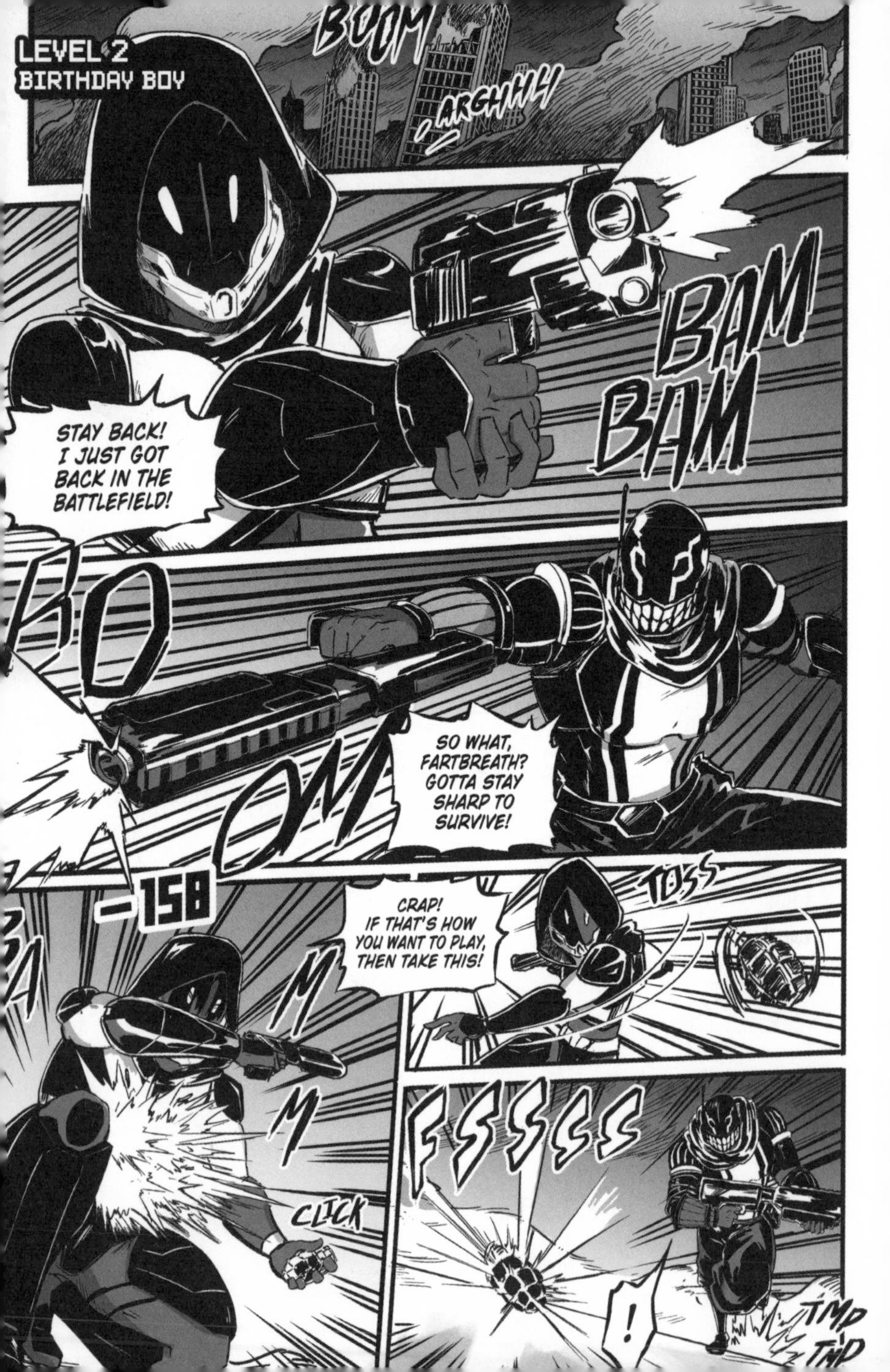
LEVEL 2
BIRTHDAY BOY
BOOM
ARGHHH
BAM
BAM
STAY BACK! I JUST GOT BACK IN THE BATTLEFIELD!
BOOM
SO WHAT, FARTBREATH? GOTTA STAY SHARP TO SURVIVE!
-158
CLICK
CRAP! IF THAT'S HOW YOU WANT TO PLAY, THEN TAKE THIS!
TOSS
FSSSSS
!
TMP
TMP

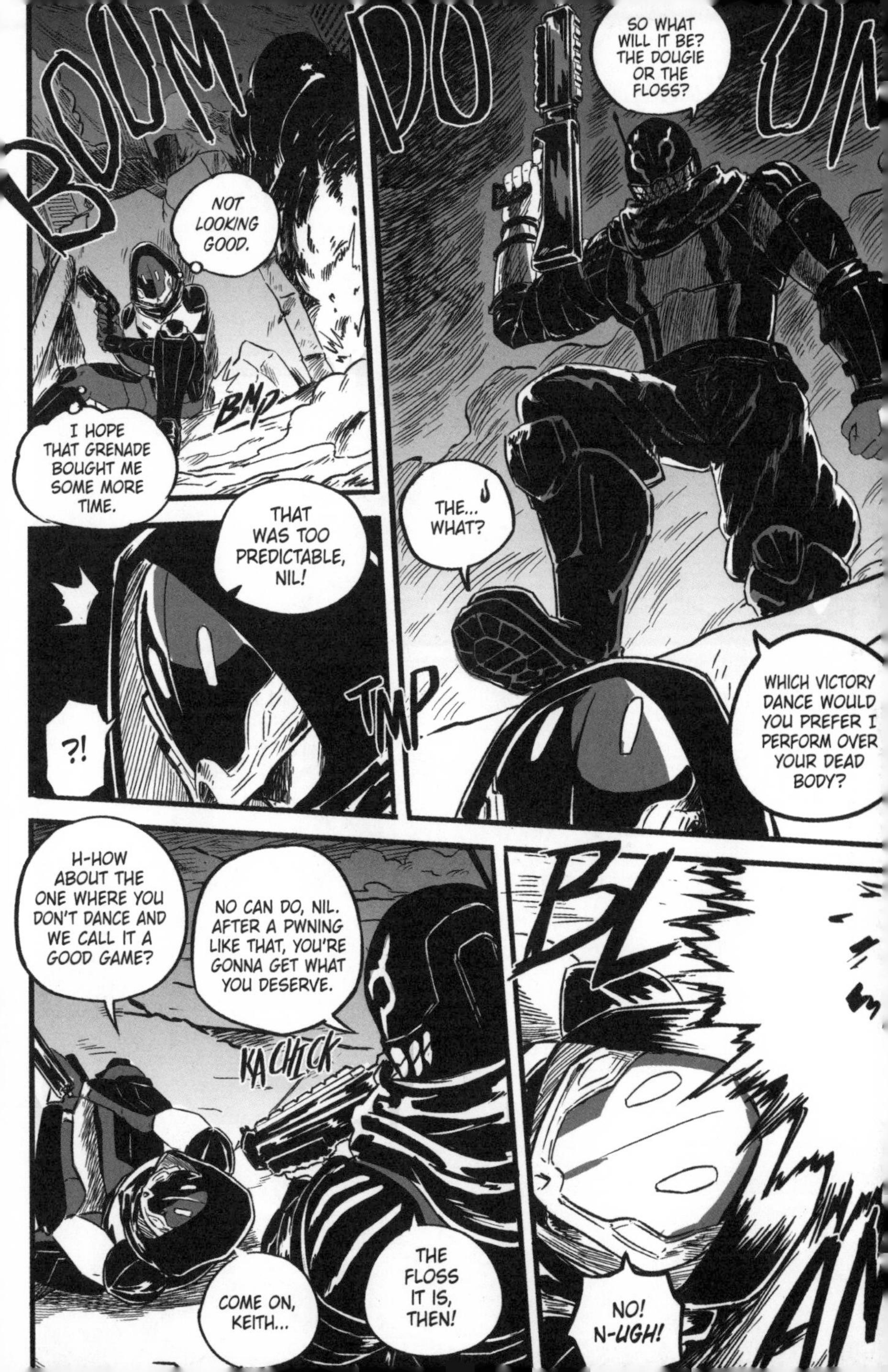
BOOM
NOT LOOKING GOOD.
BMP
I HOPE THAT GRENADE BOUGHT ME SOME MORE TIME.
THAT WAS TOO PREDICTABLE, NIL!
?!
TMP
DO
OM
SO WHAT WILL IT BE? THE DOUGIE OR THE FLOSS?
THE... WHAT?
WHICH VICTORY DANCE WOULD YOU PREFER I PERFORM OVER YOUR DEAD BODY?
H-HOW ABOUT THE ONE WHERE YOU DON'T DANCE AND WE CALL IT A GOOD GAME?
NO CAN DO, NIL. AFTER A PWNING LIKE THAT, YOU'RE GONNA GET WHAT YOU DESERVE.
KACHICK
COME ON, KEITH...
THE FLOSS IT IS, THEN!
BL
AM
NO! N-UGH!

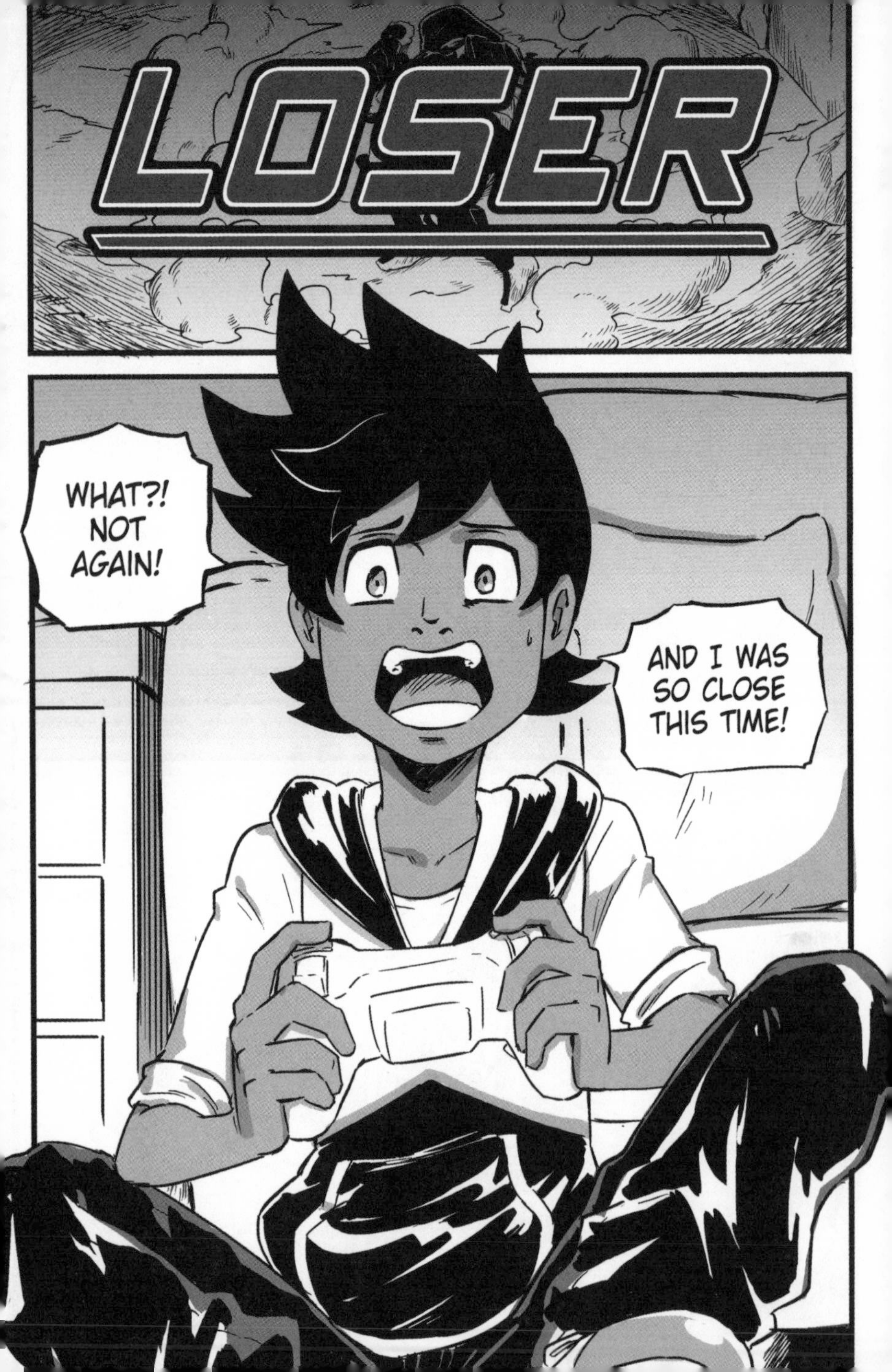
LOSER
WHAT?! NOT AGAIN!
AND I WAS SO CLOSE THIS TIME!

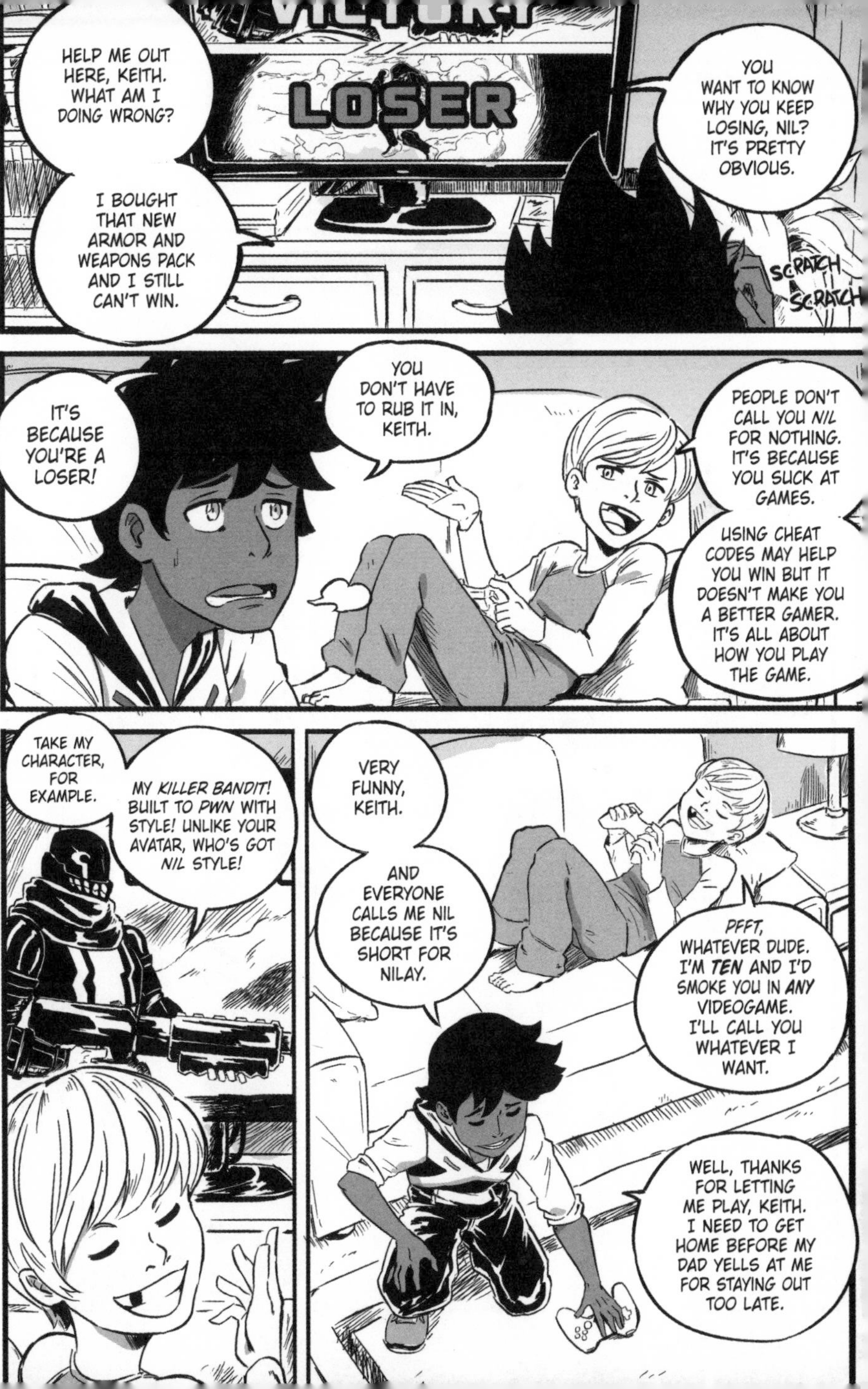
VICTORY
LOSER
HELP ME OUT HERE, KEITH. WHAT AM I DOING WRONG?
I BOUGHT THAT NEW ARMOR AND WEAPONS PACK AND I STILL CAN'T WIN.
YOU WANT TO KNOW WHY YOU KEEP LOSING, NIL? IT'S PRETTY OBVIOUS.
SCRATCH SCRATCH
IT'S BECAUSE YOU'RE A LOSER!
YOU DON'T HAVE TO RUB IT IN, KEITH.
PEOPLE DON'T CALL YOU *NIL* FOR NOTHING. IT'S BECAUSE YOU SUCK AT GAMES.
USING CHEAT CODES MAY HELP YOU WIN BUT IT DOESN'T MAKE YOU A BETTER GAMER. IT'S ALL ABOUT HOW YOU PLAY THE GAME.
TAKE MY CHARACTER, FOR EXAMPLE.
MY KILLER BANDIT! BUILT TO *PWN* WITH STYLE! UNLIKE YOUR AVATAR, WHO'S GOT *NIL* STYLE!
VERY FUNNY, KEITH.
AND EVERYONE CALLS ME NIL BECAUSE IT'S SHORT FOR NILAY.
PFFT, WHATEVER DUDE. I'M ***TEN*** AND I'D SMOKE YOU IN ***ANY*** VIDEOGAME. I'LL CALL YOU WHATEVER I WANT.
WELL, THANKS FOR LETTING ME PLAY, KEITH. I NEED TO GET HOME BEFORE MY DAD YELLS AT ME FOR STAYING OUT TOO LATE.

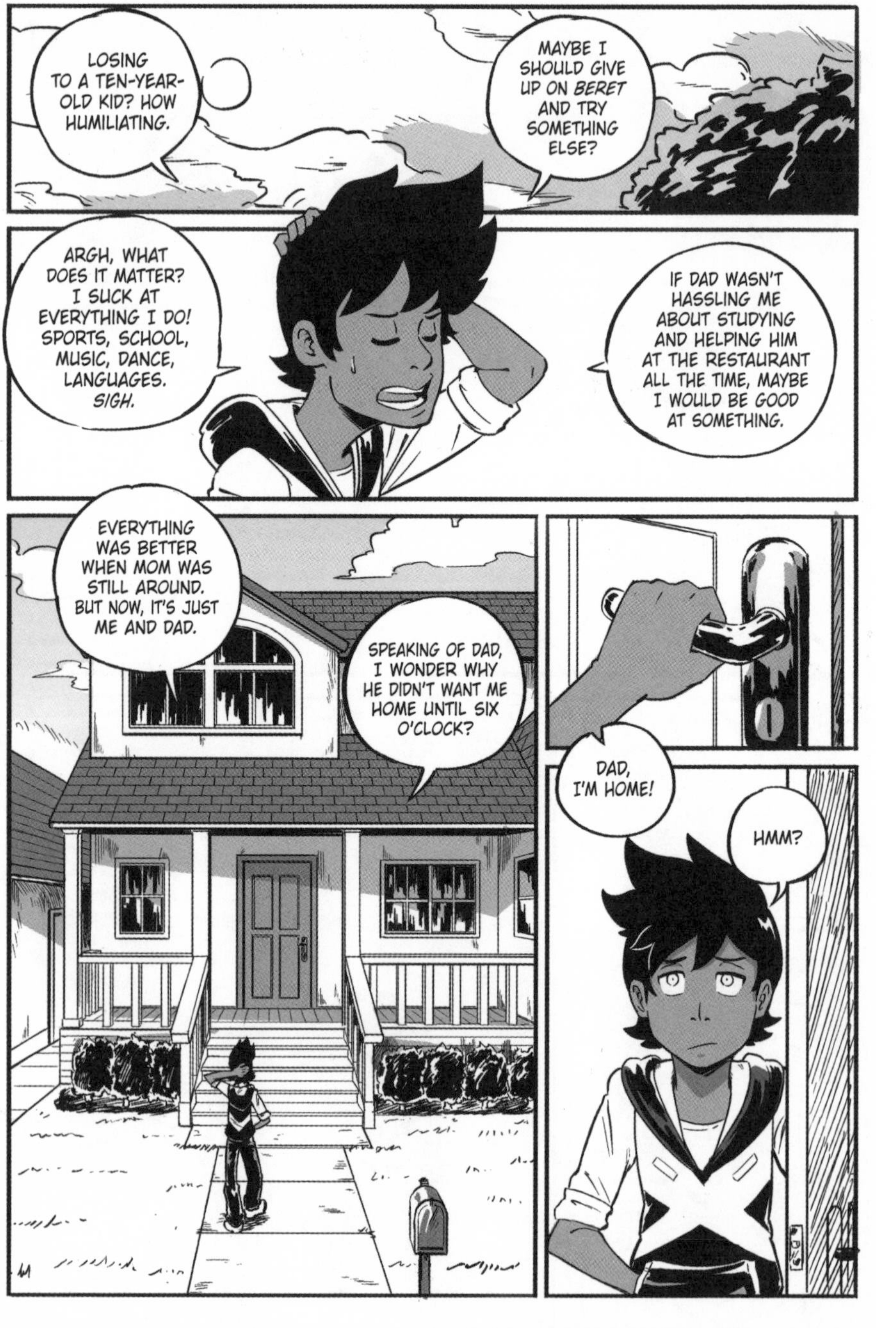
LOSING TO A TEN-YEAR-OLD KID? HOW HUMILIATING.
MAYBE I SHOULD GIVE UP ON *BERET* AND TRY SOMETHING ELSE?
ARGH, WHAT DOES IT MATTER? I SUCK AT EVERYTHING I DO! SPORTS, SCHOOL, MUSIC, DANCE, LANGUAGES. *SIGH.*
IF DAD WASN'T HASSLING ME ABOUT STUDYING AND HELPING HIM AT THE RESTAURANT ALL THE TIME, MAYBE I WOULD BE GOOD AT SOMETHING.
EVERYTHING WAS BETTER WHEN MOM WAS STILL AROUND. BUT NOW, IT'S JUST ME AND DAD.
SPEAKING OF DAD, I WONDER WHY HE DIDN'T WANT ME HOME UNTIL SIX O'CLOCK?
DAD, I'M HOME!
HMM?

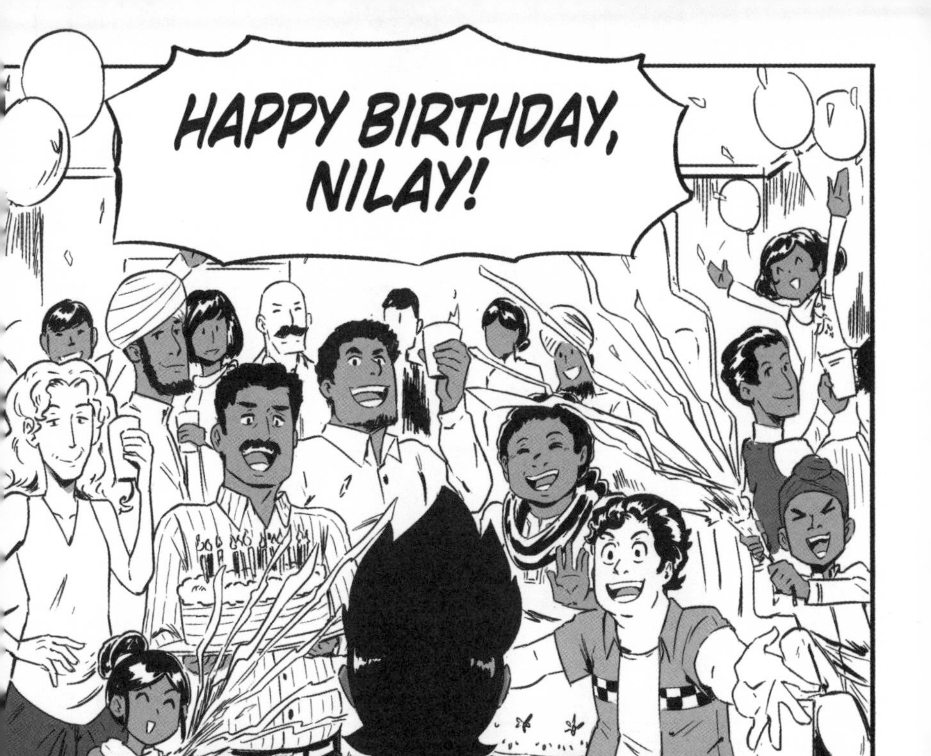
HAPPY BIRTHDAY, NILAY!

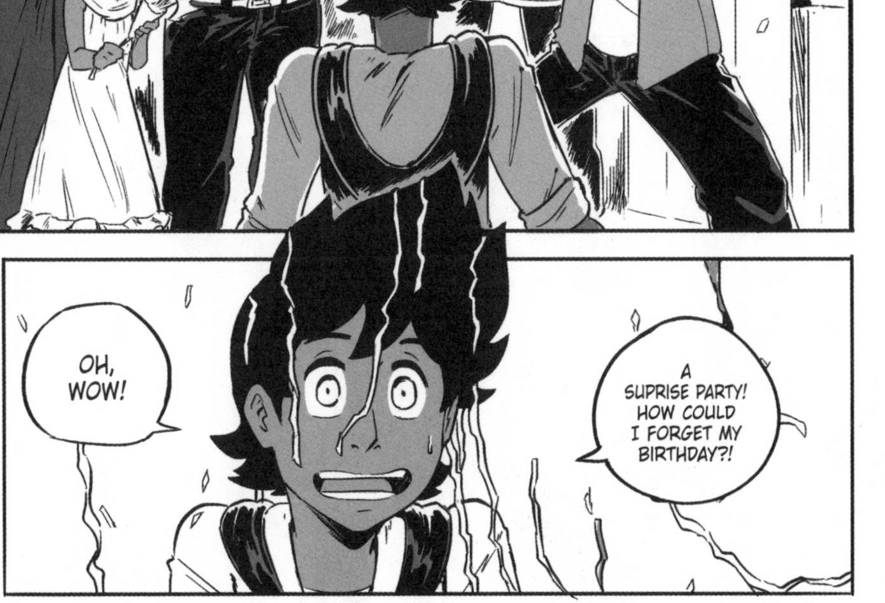
OH, WOW!
A SUPRISE PARTY! HOW COULD I FORGET MY BIRTHDAY?!

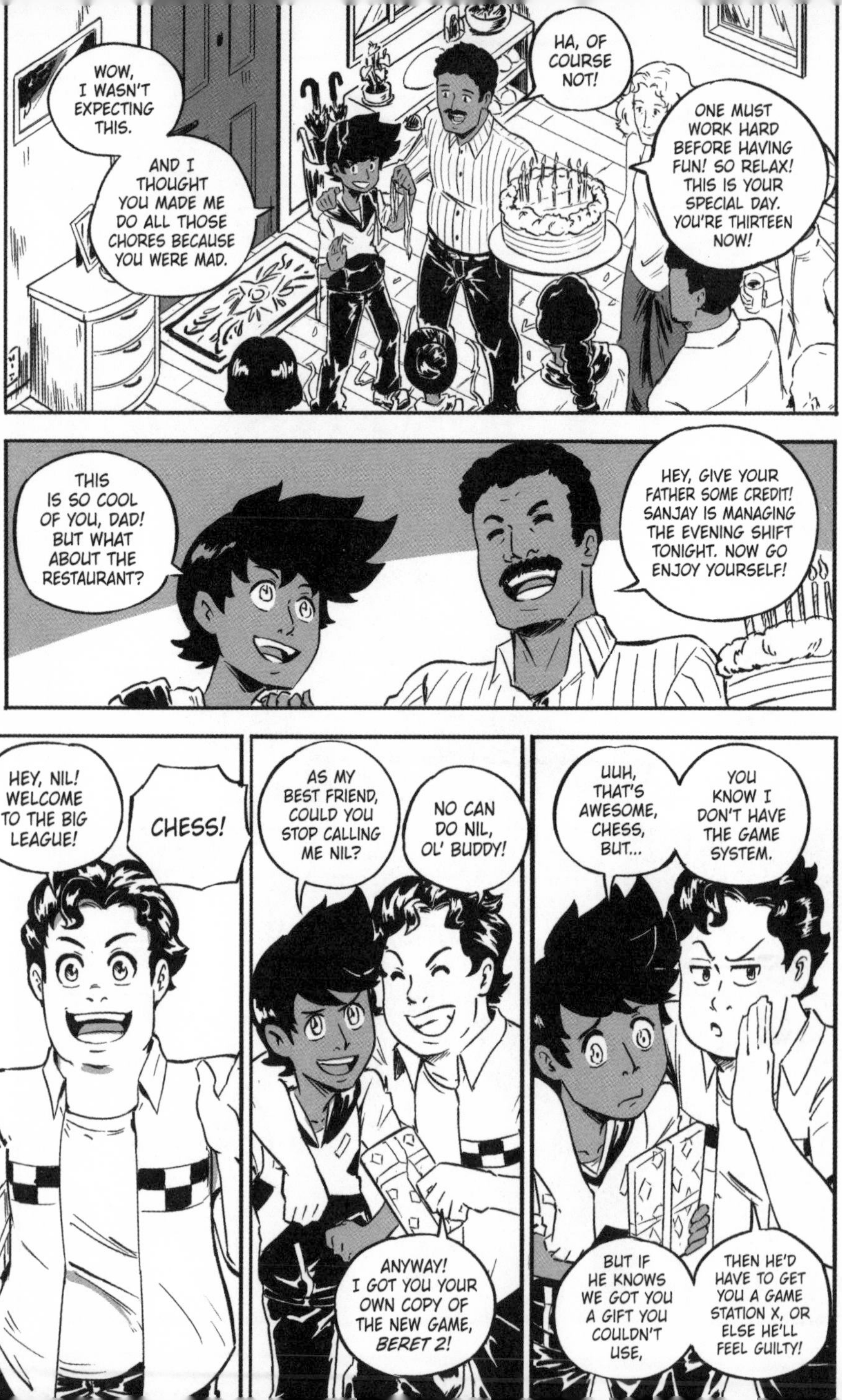
WOW, I WASN'T EXPECTING THIS.
AND I THOUGHT YOU MADE ME DO ALL THOSE CHORES BECAUSE YOU WERE MAD.
HA, OF COURSE NOT!
ONE MUST WORK HARD BEFORE HAVING FUN! SO RELAX! THIS IS YOUR SPECIAL DAY. YOU'RE THIRTEEN NOW!
THIS IS SO COOL OF YOU, DAD! BUT WHAT ABOUT THE RESTAURANT?
HEY, GIVE YOUR FATHER SOME CREDIT! SANJAY IS MANAGING THE EVENING SHIFT TONIGHT. NOW GO ENJOY YOURSELF!
HEY, NIL! WELCOME TO THE BIG LEAGUE!
CHESS!
AS MY BEST FRIEND, COULD YOU STOP CALLING ME NIL?
NO CAN DO NIL, OL' BUDDY!
ANYWAY! I GOT YOU YOUR OWN COPY OF THE NEW GAME, *BERET 2*!
UUH, THAT'S AWESOME, CHESS, BUT...
YOU KNOW I DON'T HAVE THE GAME SYSTEM.
BUT IF HE KNOWS WE GOT YOU A GIFT YOU COULDN'T USE,
THEN HE'D HAVE TO GET YOU A GAME STATION X, OR ELSE HE'LL FEEL GUILTY!

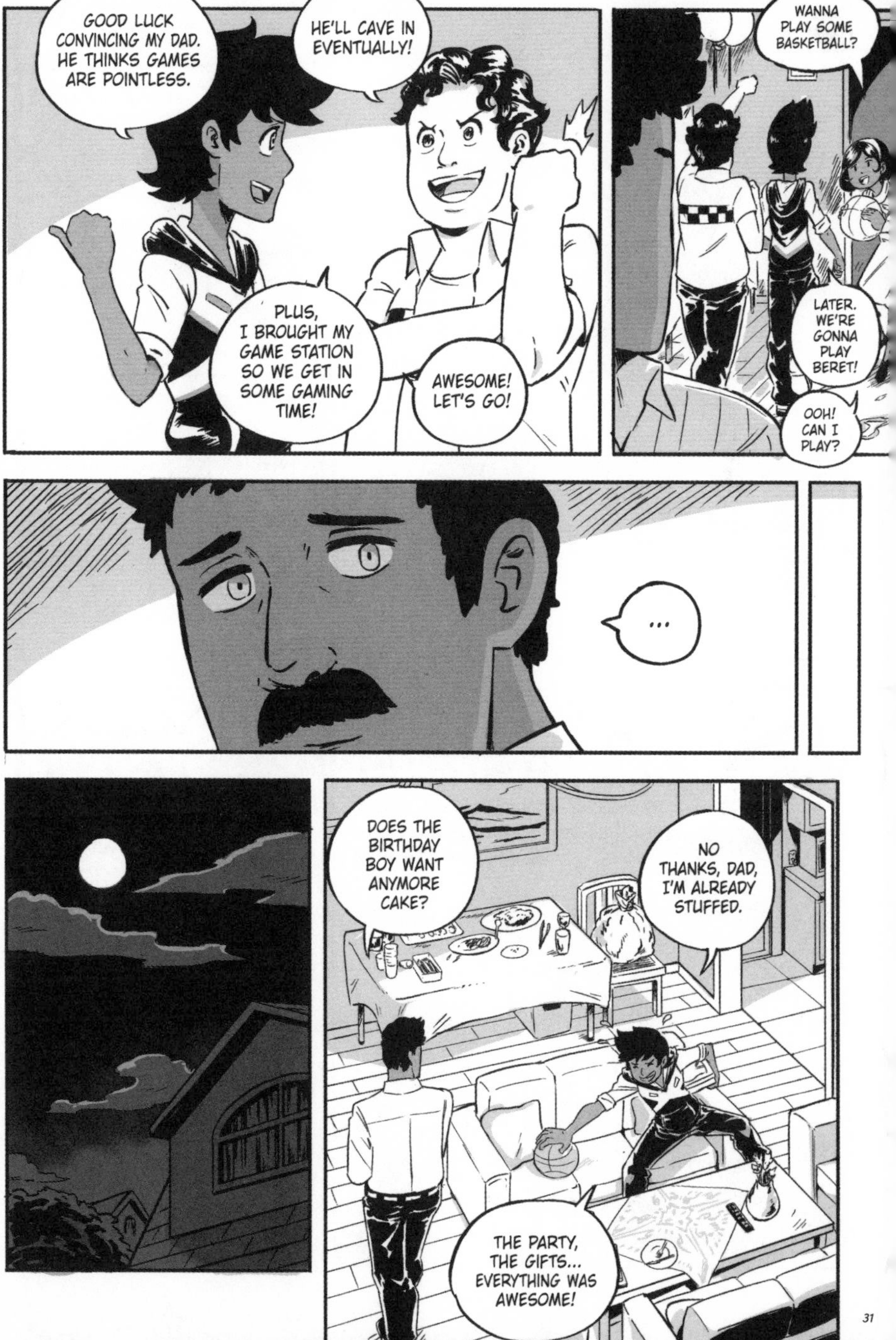
GOOD LUCK CONVINCING MY DAD. HE THINKS GAMES ARE POINTLESS.
HE'LL CAVE IN EVENTUALLY!
PLUS, I BROUGHT MY GAME STATION SO WE GET IN SOME GAMING TIME!
AWESOME! LET'S GO!
WANNA PLAY SOME BASKETBALL?
LATER. WE'RE GONNA PLAY BERET!
OOH! CAN I PLAY?
...
DOES THE BIRTHDAY BOY WANT ANYMORE CAKE?
NO THANKS, DAD, I'M ALREADY STUFFED.
THE PARTY, THE GIFTS... EVERYTHING WAS AWESOME!

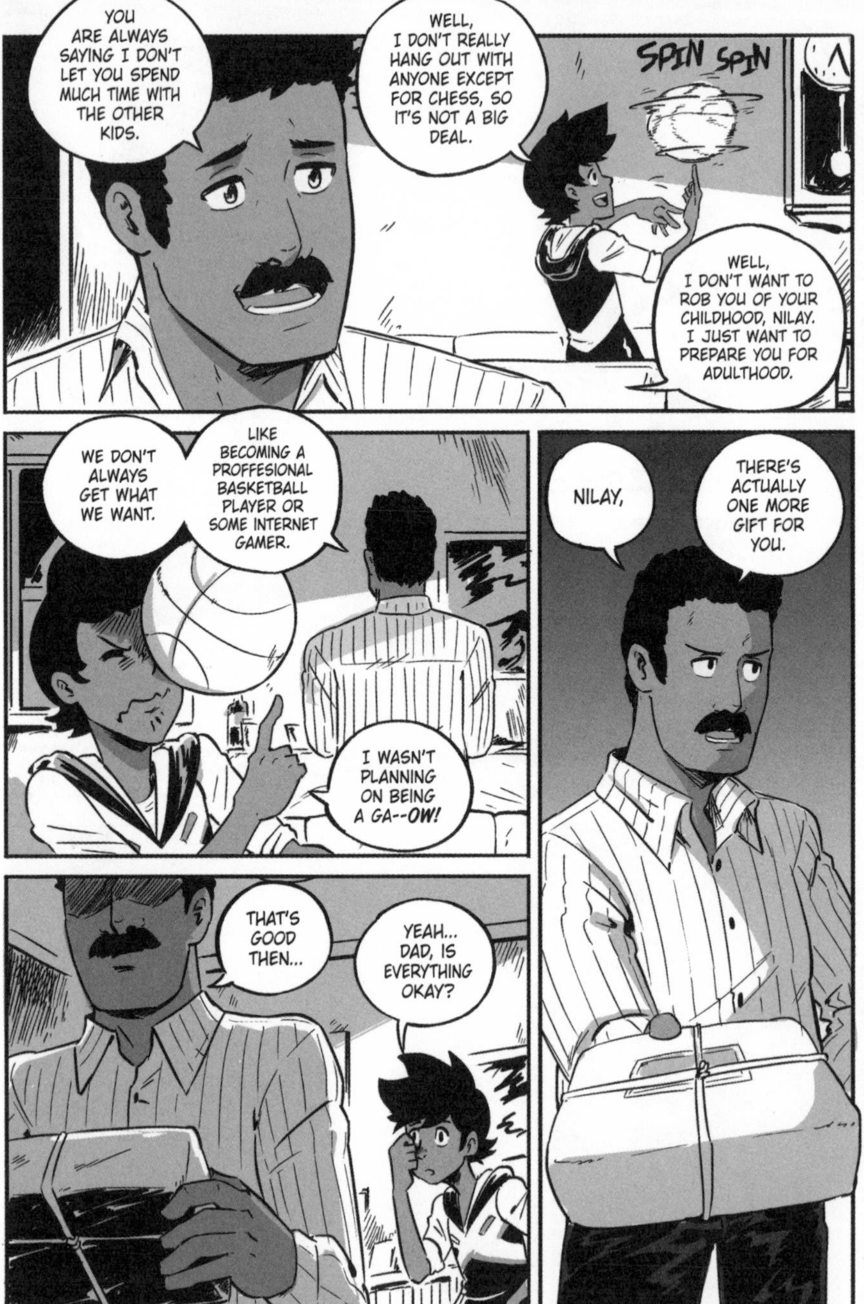
YOU ARE ALWAYS SAYING I DON'T LET YOU SPEND MUCH TIME WITH THE OTHER KIDS.
WELL, I DON'T REALLY HANG OUT WITH ANYONE EXCEPT FOR CHESS, SO IT'S NOT A BIG DEAL.
SPIN SPIN
WELL, I DON'T WANT TO ROB YOU OF YOUR CHILDHOOD, NILAY. I JUST WANT TO PREPARE YOU FOR ADULTHOOD.
WE DON'T ALWAYS GET WHAT WE WANT.
LIKE BECOMING A PROFFESIONAL BASKETBALL PLAYER OR SOME INTERNET GAMER.
I WASN'T PLANNING ON BEING A GA--OW!
THAT'S GOOD THEN...
YEAH... DAD, IS EVERYTHING OKAY?
NILAY,
THERE'S ACTUALLY ONE MORE GIFT FOR YOU.

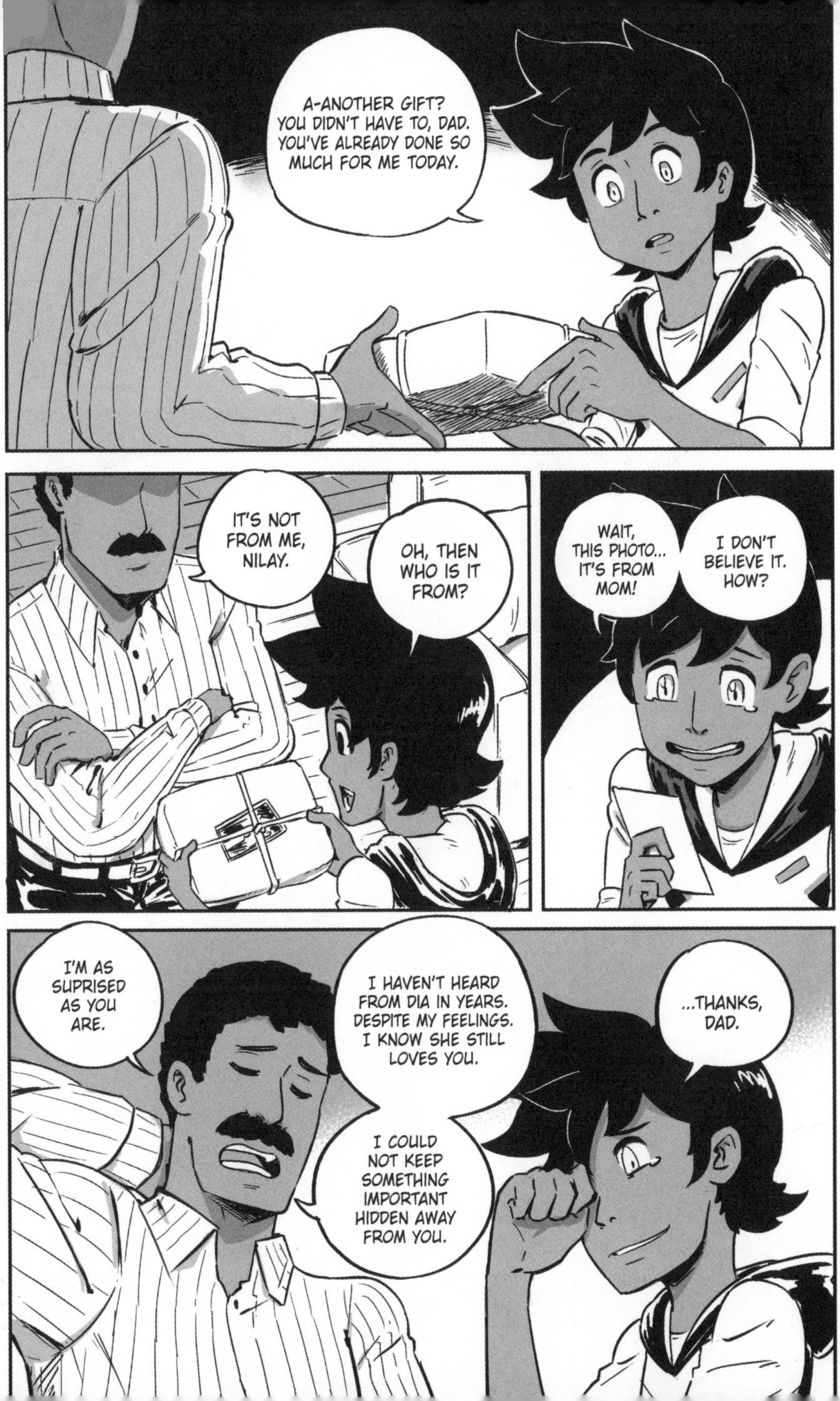
A-ANOTHER GIFT? YOU DIDN'T HAVE TO, DAD. YOU'VE ALREADY DONE SO MUCH FOR ME TODAY.
IT'S NOT FROM ME, NILAY.
OH, THEN WHO IS IT FROM?
WAIT, THIS PHOTO... IT'S FROM MOM!
I DON'T BELIEVE IT. HOW?
I'M AS SUPRISED AS YOU ARE.
I HAVEN'T HEARD FROM DIA IN YEARS. DESPITE MY FEELINGS. I KNOW SHE STILL LOVES YOU.
I COULD NOT KEEP SOMETHING IMPORTANT HIDDEN AWAY FROM YOU.
...THANKS, DAD.

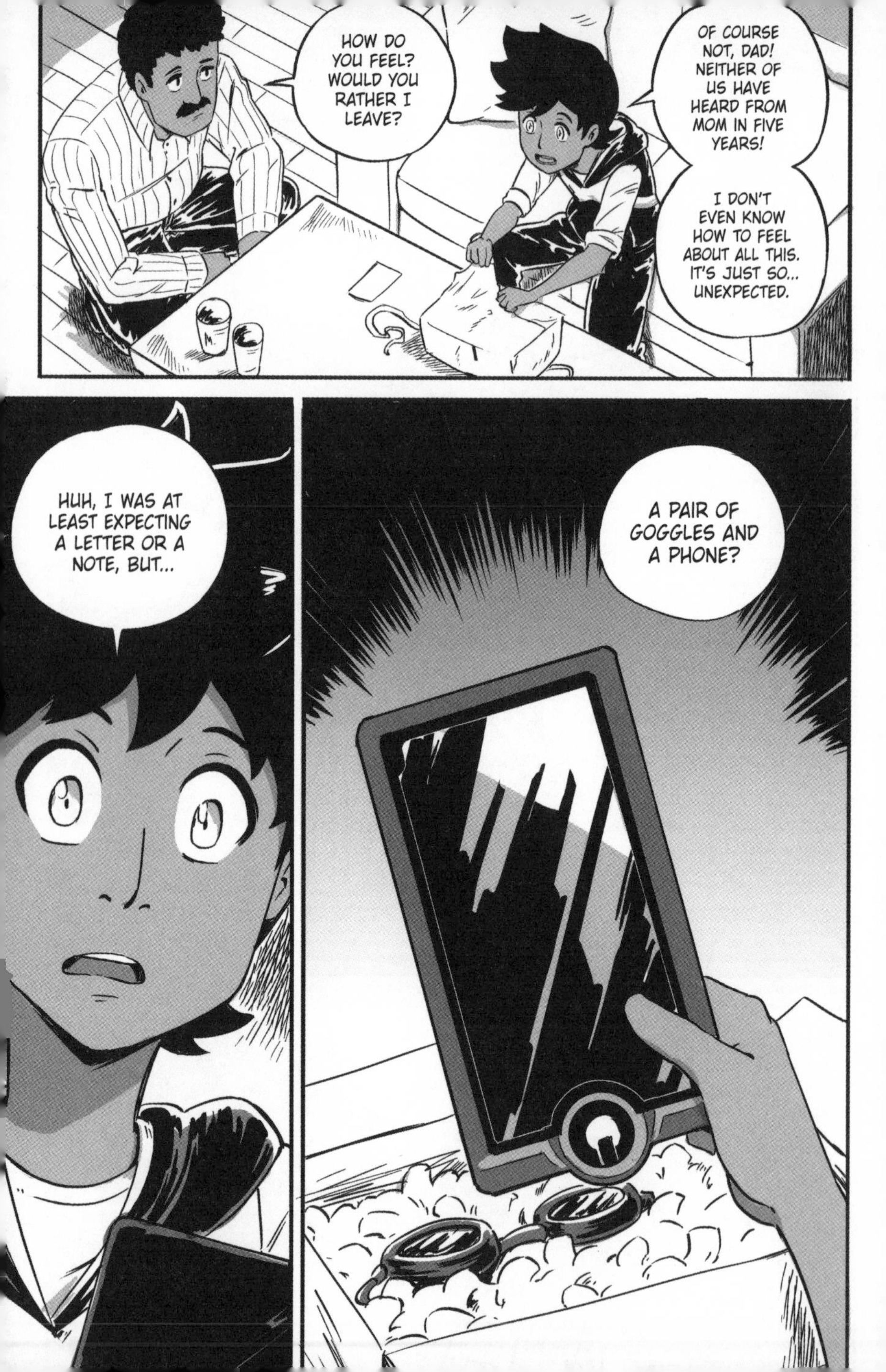
HOW DO YOU FEEL? WOULD YOU RATHER I LEAVE?
OF COURSE NOT, DAD! NEITHER OF US HAVE HEARD FROM MOM IN FIVE YEARS!
I DON'T EVEN KNOW HOW TO FEEL ABOUT ALL THIS. IT'S JUST SO... UNEXPECTED.
HUH, I WAS AT LEAST EXPECTING A LETTER OR A NOTE, BUT...
A PAIR OF GOGGLES AND A PHONE?

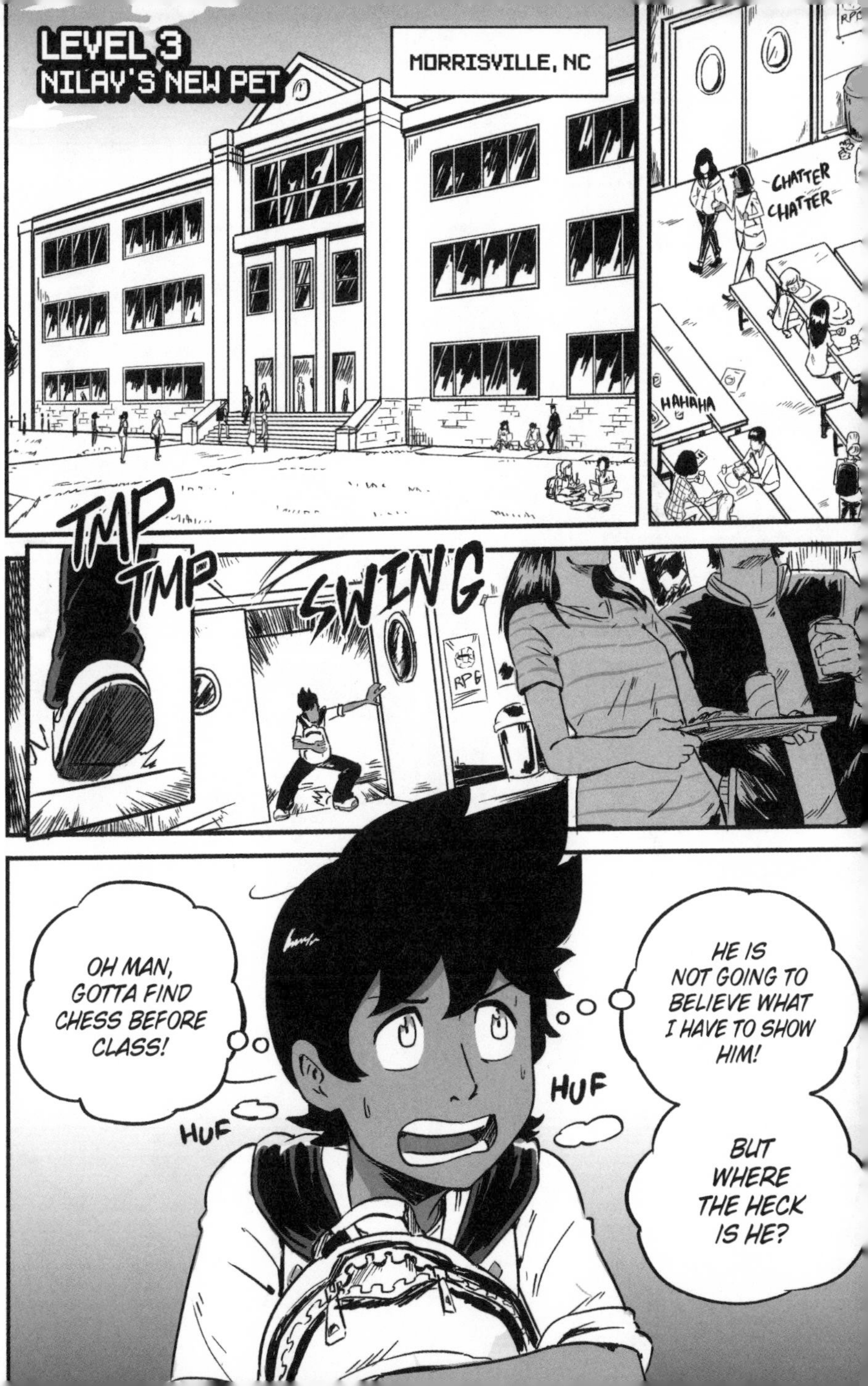
LEVEL 3
NILAY'S NEW PET
MORRISVILLE, NC
CHATTER
CHATTER
HAHAHA
TMP
TMP
SWING
RPG
OH MAN, GOTTA FIND CHESS BEFORE CLASS!
HUF
HUF
HE IS NOT GOING TO BELIEVE WHAT I HAVE TO SHOW HIM!
BUT WHERE THE HECK IS HE?

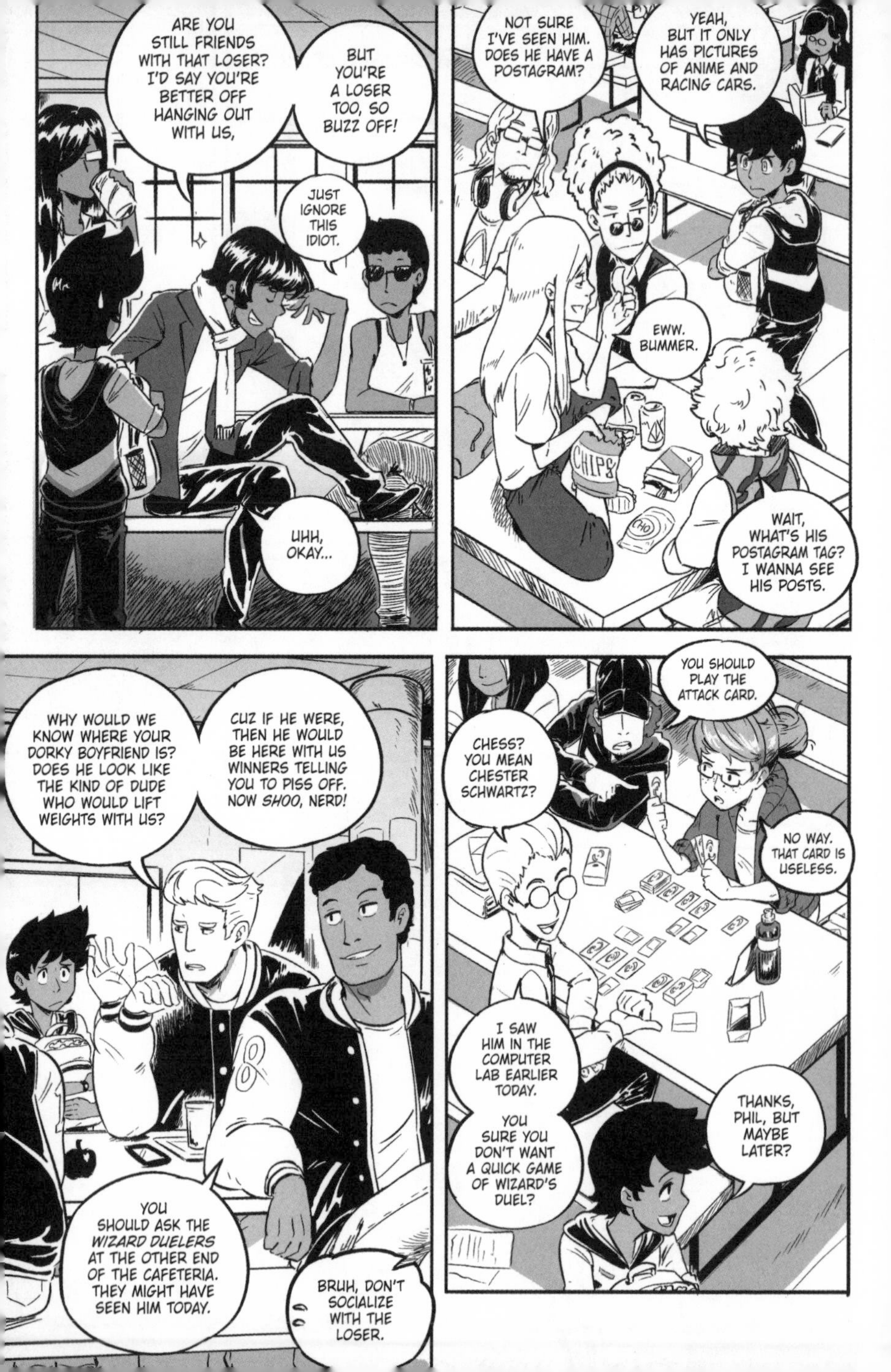
ARE YOU STILL FRIENDS WITH THAT LOSER? I'D SAY YOU'RE BETTER OFF HANGING OUT WITH US,
BUT YOU'RE A LOSER TOO, SO BUZZ OFF!
JUST IGNORE THIS IDIOT.
UHH, OKAY...
NOT SURE I'VE SEEN HIM. DOES HE HAVE A POSTAGRAM?
YEAH, BUT IT ONLY HAS PICTURES OF ANIME AND RACING CARS.
EWW. BUMMER.
CHIPS
WAIT, WHAT'S HIS POSTAGRAM TAG? I WANNA SEE HIS POSTS.
WHY WOULD WE KNOW WHERE YOUR DORKY BOYFRIEND IS? DOES HE LOOK LIKE THE KIND OF DUDE WHO WOULD LIFT WEIGHTS WITH US?
CUZ IF HE WERE, THEN HE WOULD BE HERE WITH US WINNERS TELLING YOU TO PISS OFF. NOW *SHOO*, NERD!
YOU SHOULD ASK THE *WIZARD DUELERS* AT THE OTHER END OF THE CAFETERIA. THEY MIGHT HAVE SEEN HIM TODAY.
BRUH, DON'T SOCIALIZE WITH THE LOSER.
YOU SHOULD PLAY THE ATTACK CARD.
CHESS? YOU MEAN CHESTER SCHWARTZ?
NO WAY. THAT CARD IS USELESS.
I SAW HIM IN THE COMPUTER LAB EARLIER TODAY.
YOU SURE YOU DON'T WANT A QUICK GAME OF WIZARD'S DUEL?
THANKS, PHIL, BUT MAYBE LATER?

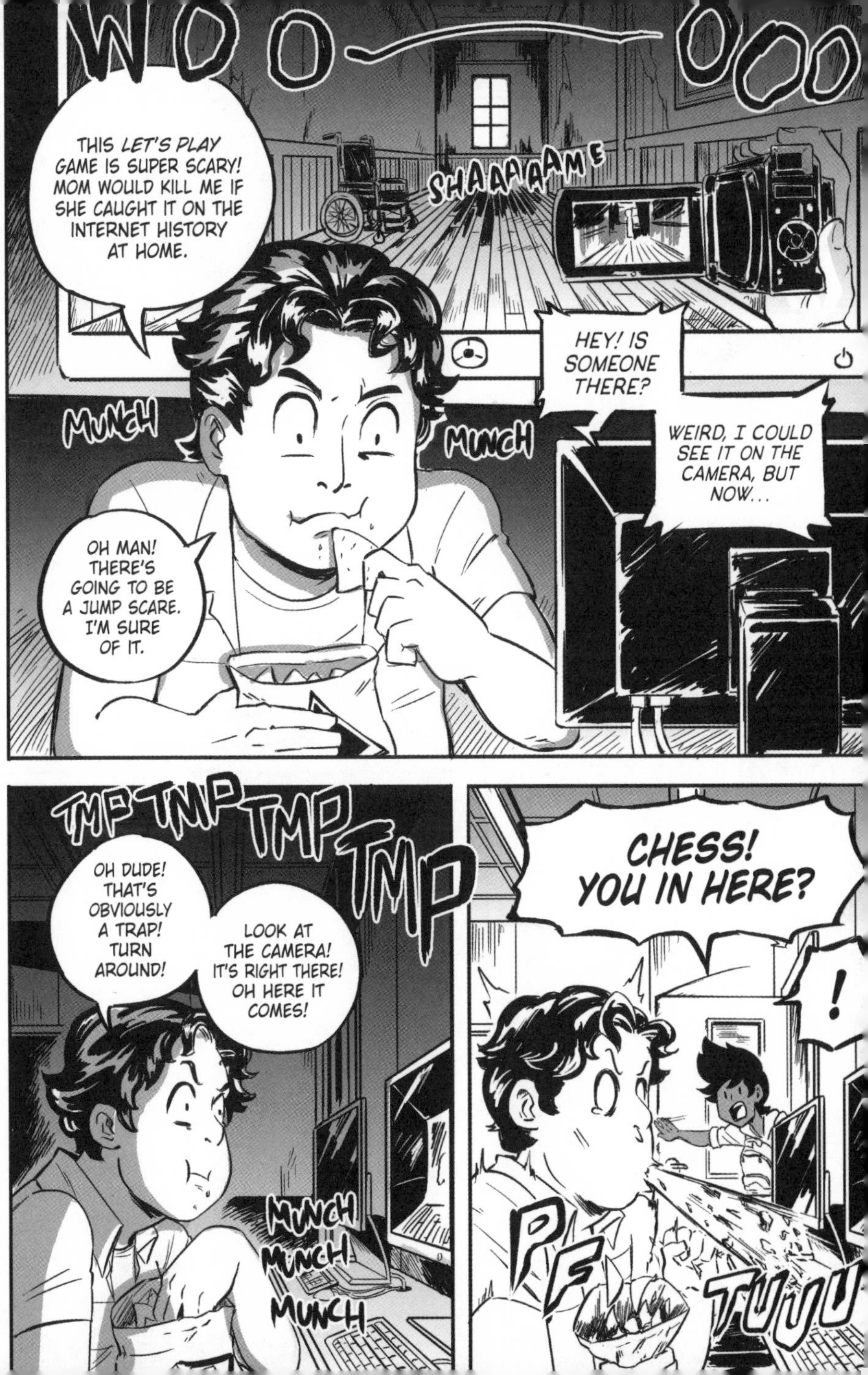
WOO———OOO
THIS LET'S PLAY GAME IS SUPER SCARY! MOM WOULD KILL ME IF SHE CAUGHT IT ON THE INTERNET HISTORY AT HOME.
SHAAAAAAME
HEY! IS SOMEONE THERE?
MUNCH
MUNCH
WEIRD, I COULD SEE IT ON THE CAMERA, BUT NOW...
OH MAN! THERE'S GOING TO BE A JUMP SCARE. I'M SURE OF IT.
TMP TMP TMP TMP
OH DUDE! THAT'S OBVIOUSLY A TRAP! TURN AROUND!
LOOK AT THE CAMERA! IT'S RIGHT THERE! OH HERE IT COMES!
MUNCH MUNCH MUNCH
CHESS! YOU IN HERE?
!
PFFTUUU

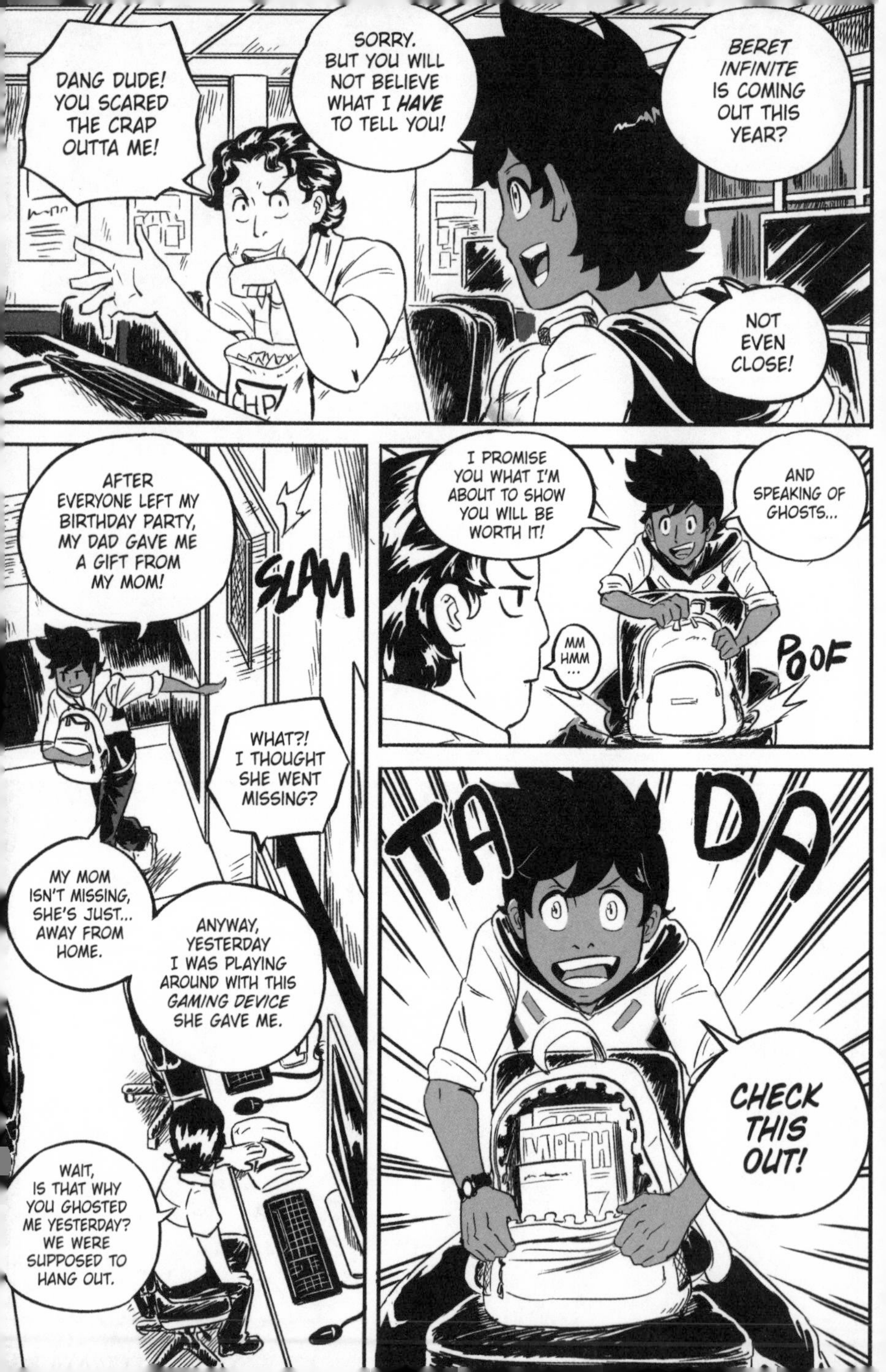
DANG DUDE! YOU SCARED THE CRAP OUTTA ME!
SORRY. BUT YOU WILL NOT BELIEVE WHAT I *HAVE* TO TELL YOU!
BERET *INFINITE* IS COMING OUT THIS YEAR?
NOT EVEN CLOSE!
AFTER EVERYONE LEFT MY BIRTHDAY PARTY, MY DAD GAVE ME A GIFT FROM MY MOM!
SLAM
WHAT?! I THOUGHT SHE WENT MISSING?
MY MOM ISN'T MISSING, SHE'S JUST... AWAY FROM HOME.
ANYWAY, YESTERDAY I WAS PLAYING AROUND WITH THIS *GAMING DEVICE* SHE GAVE ME.
WAIT, IS THAT WHY YOU GHOSTED ME YESTERDAY? WE WERE SUPPOSED TO HANG OUT.
I PROMISE YOU WHAT I'M ABOUT TO SHOW YOU WILL BE WORTH IT!
AND SPEAKING OF GHOSTS...
MM HMM ...
POOF
TA DA
MATH
CHECK THIS OUT!

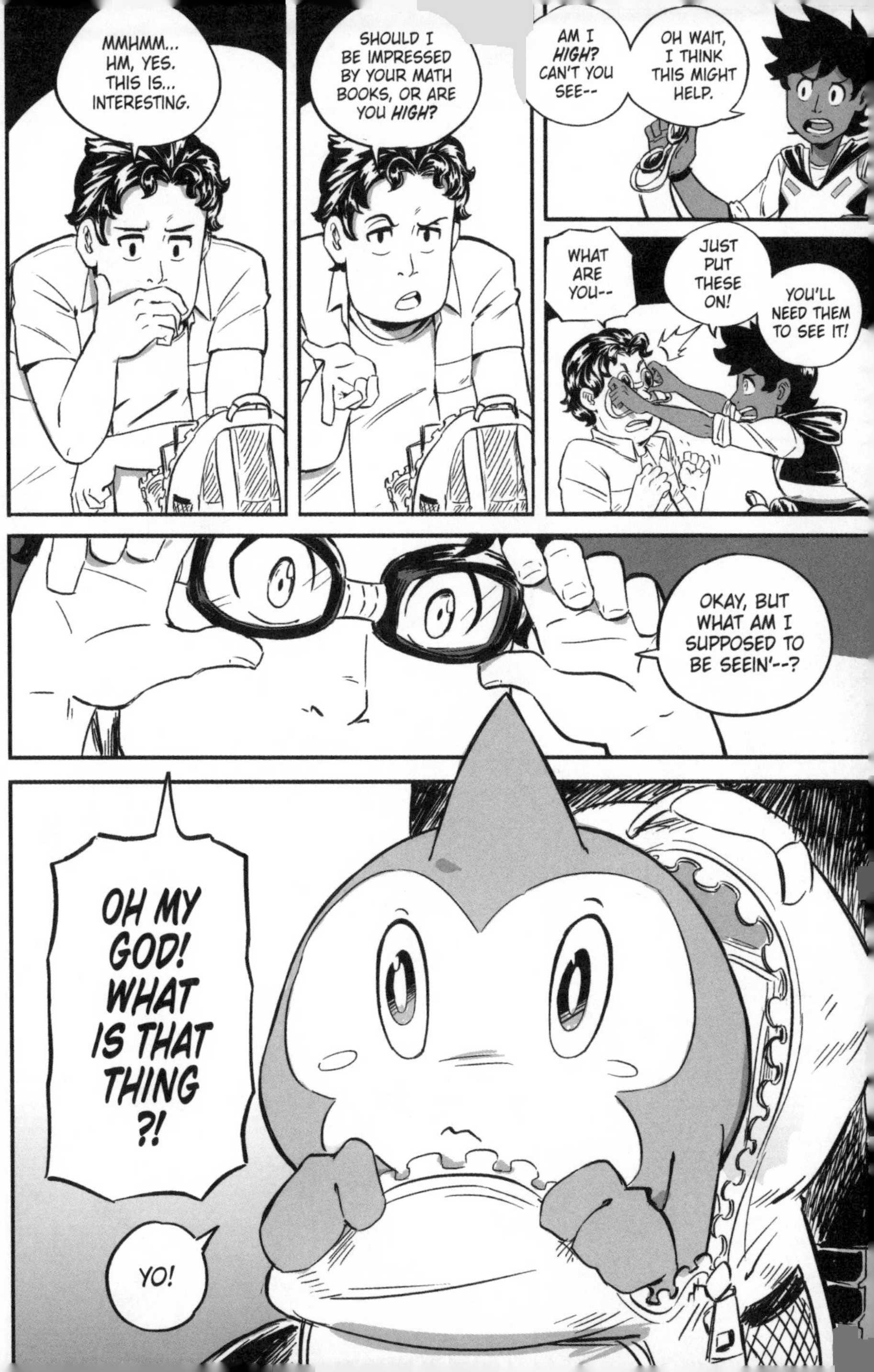
MMHMM... HM, YES. THIS IS... INTERESTING.
SHOULD I BE IMPRESSED BY YOUR MATH BOOKS, OR ARE YOU HIGH?
AM I HIGH? CAN'T YOU SEE--
OH WAIT, I THINK THIS MIGHT HELP.
WHAT ARE YOU--
JUST PUT THESE ON!
YOU'LL NEED THEM TO SEE IT!
OKAY, BUT WHAT AM I SUPPOSED TO BE SEEIN'--?
OH MY GOD! WHAT IS THAT THING ?!
YO!

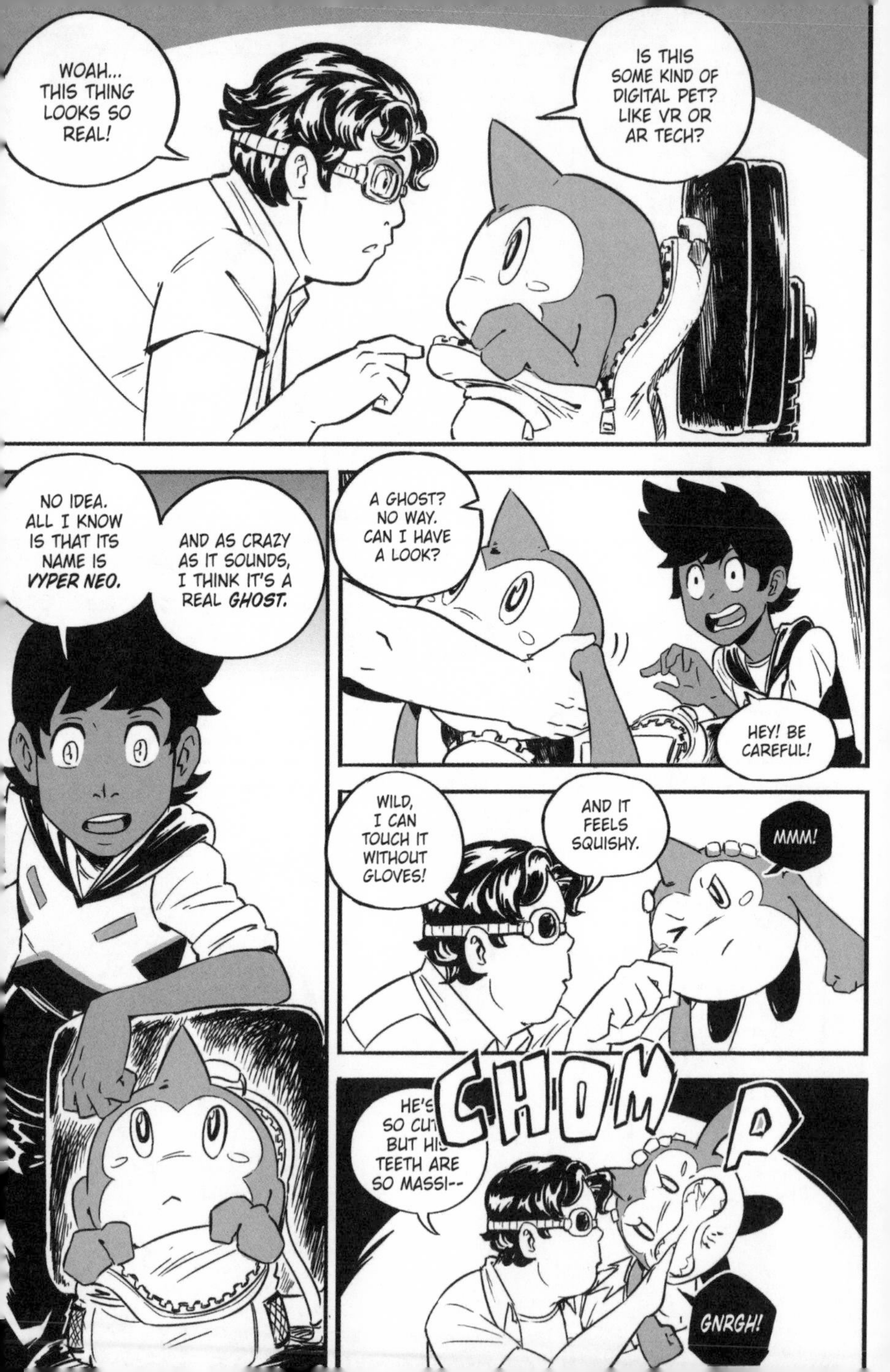
WOAH... THIS THING LOOKS SO REAL!
IS THIS SOME KIND OF DIGITAL PET? LIKE VR OR AR TECH?
NO IDEA. ALL I KNOW IS THAT ITS NAME IS VYPER NEO.
AND AS CRAZY AS IT SOUNDS, I THINK IT'S A REAL GHOST.
A GHOST? NO WAY. CAN I HAVE A LOOK?
HEY! BE CAREFUL!
WILD, I CAN TOUCH IT WITHOUT GLOVES!
AND IT FEELS SQUISHY.
MMM!
HE'S SO CUTE BUT HIS TEETH ARE SO MASSI--
CHOMP
GNRGH!

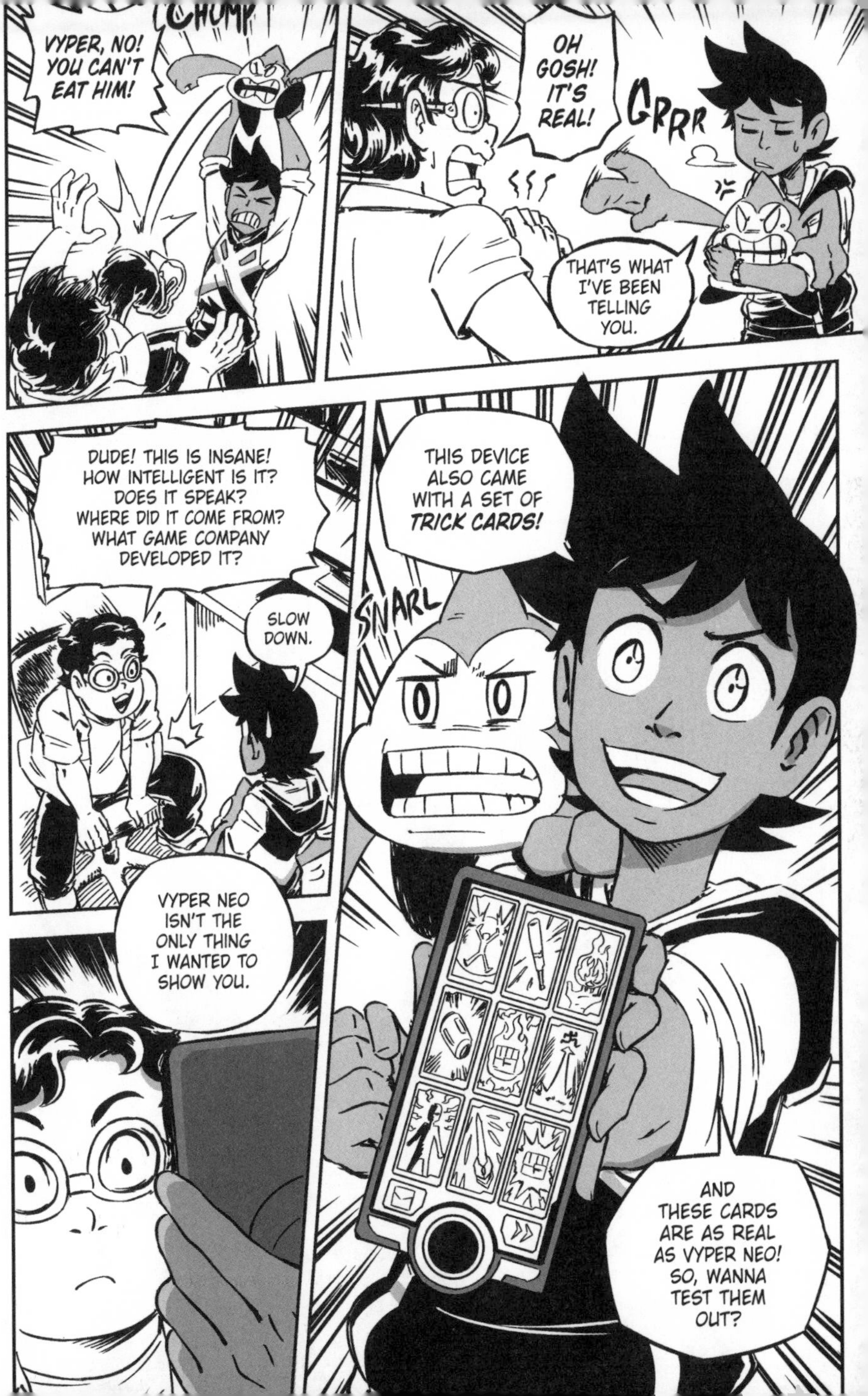
CHUMP
VYPER, NO! YOU CAN'T EAT HIM!
OH GOSH! IT'S REAL!
GRRR
THAT'S WHAT I'VE BEEN TELLING YOU.
DUDE! THIS IS INSANE! HOW INTELLIGENT IS IT? DOES IT SPEAK? WHERE DID IT COME FROM? WHAT GAME COMPANY DEVELOPED IT?
SLOW DOWN.
VYPER NEO ISN'T THE ONLY THING I WANTED TO SHOW YOU.
THIS DEVICE ALSO CAME WITH A SET OF TRICK CARDS!
SNARL
AND THESE CARDS ARE AS REAL AS VYPER NEO! SO, WANNA TEST THEM OUT?

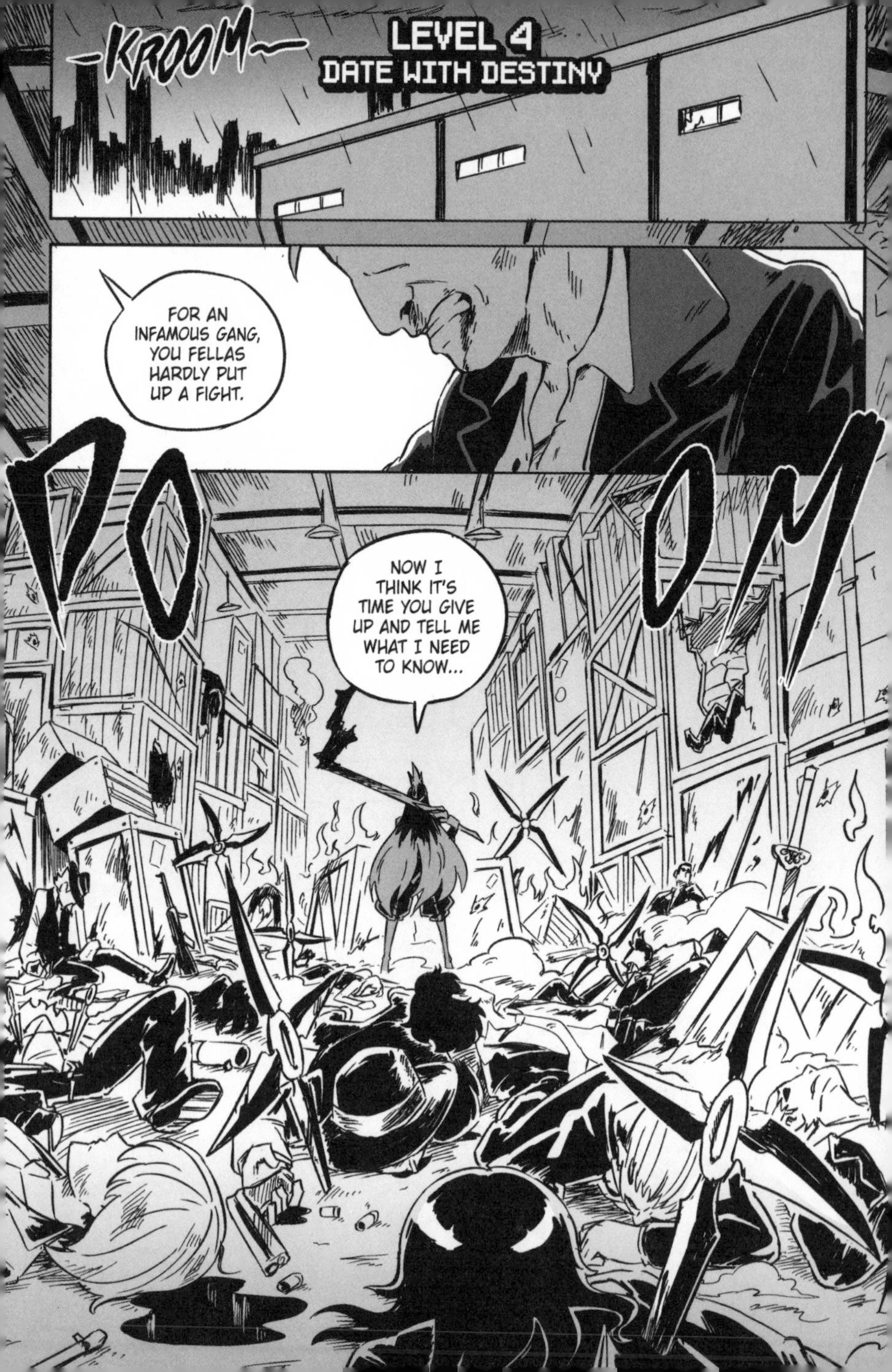
KROOM
LEVEL 4
DATE WITH DESTINY
FOR AN INFAMOUS GANG, YOU FELLAS HARDLY PUT UP A FIGHT.
DOOM
NOW I THINK IT'S TIME YOU GIVE UP AND TELL ME WHAT I NEED TO KNOW...

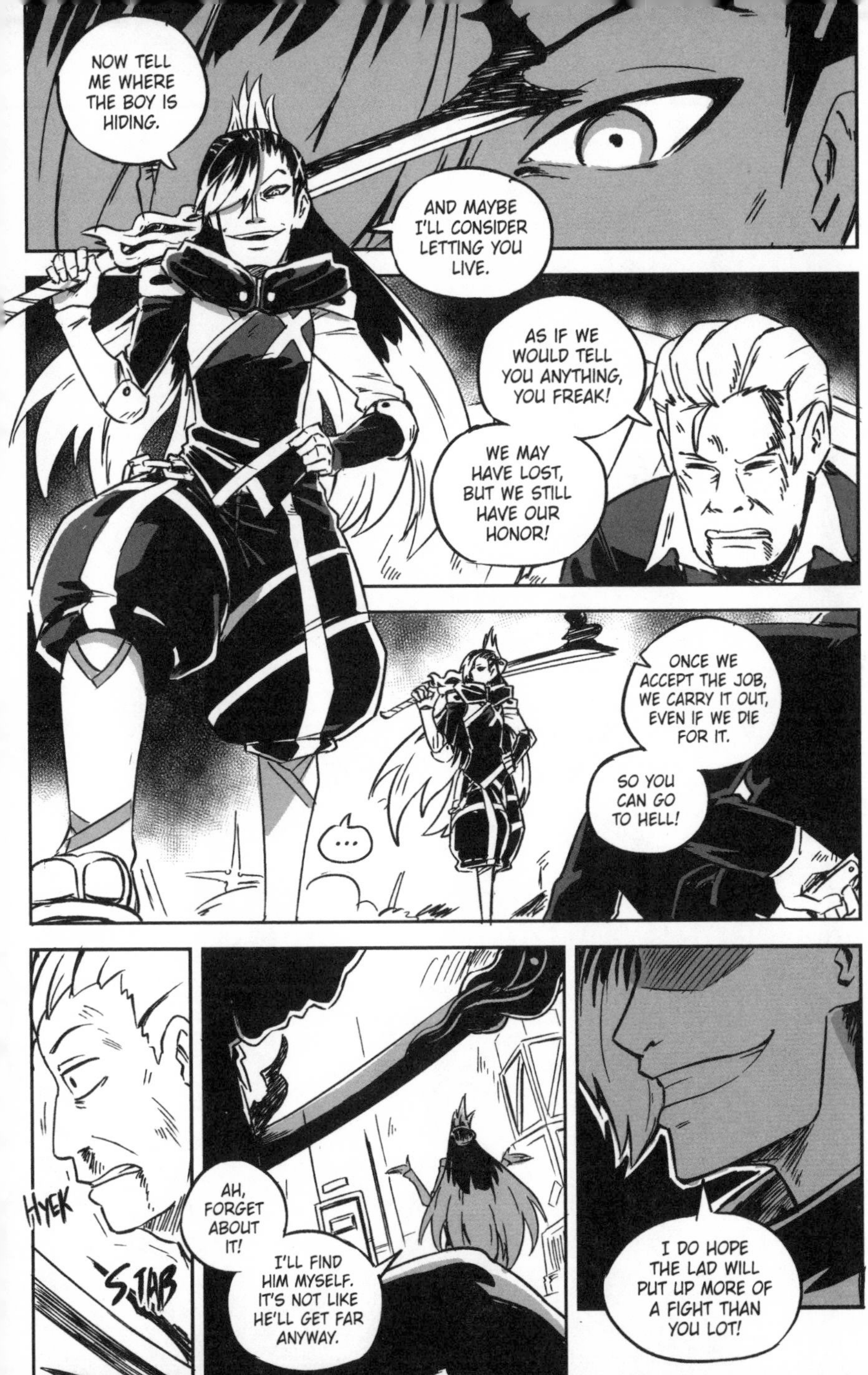
NOW TELL ME WHERE THE BOY IS HIDING.
AND MAYBE I'LL CONSIDER LETTING YOU LIVE.
AS IF WE WOULD TELL YOU ANYTHING, YOU FREAK!
WE MAY HAVE LOST, BUT WE STILL HAVE OUR HONOR!
...
ONCE WE ACCEPT THE JOB, WE CARRY IT OUT, EVEN IF WE DIE FOR IT.
SO YOU CAN GO TO HELL!
HYEK
STAB
AH, FORGET ABOUT IT!
I'LL FIND HIM MYSELF. IT'S NOT LIKE HE'LL GET FAR ANYWAY.
I DO HOPE THE LAD WILL PUT UP MORE OF A FIGHT THAN YOU LOT!

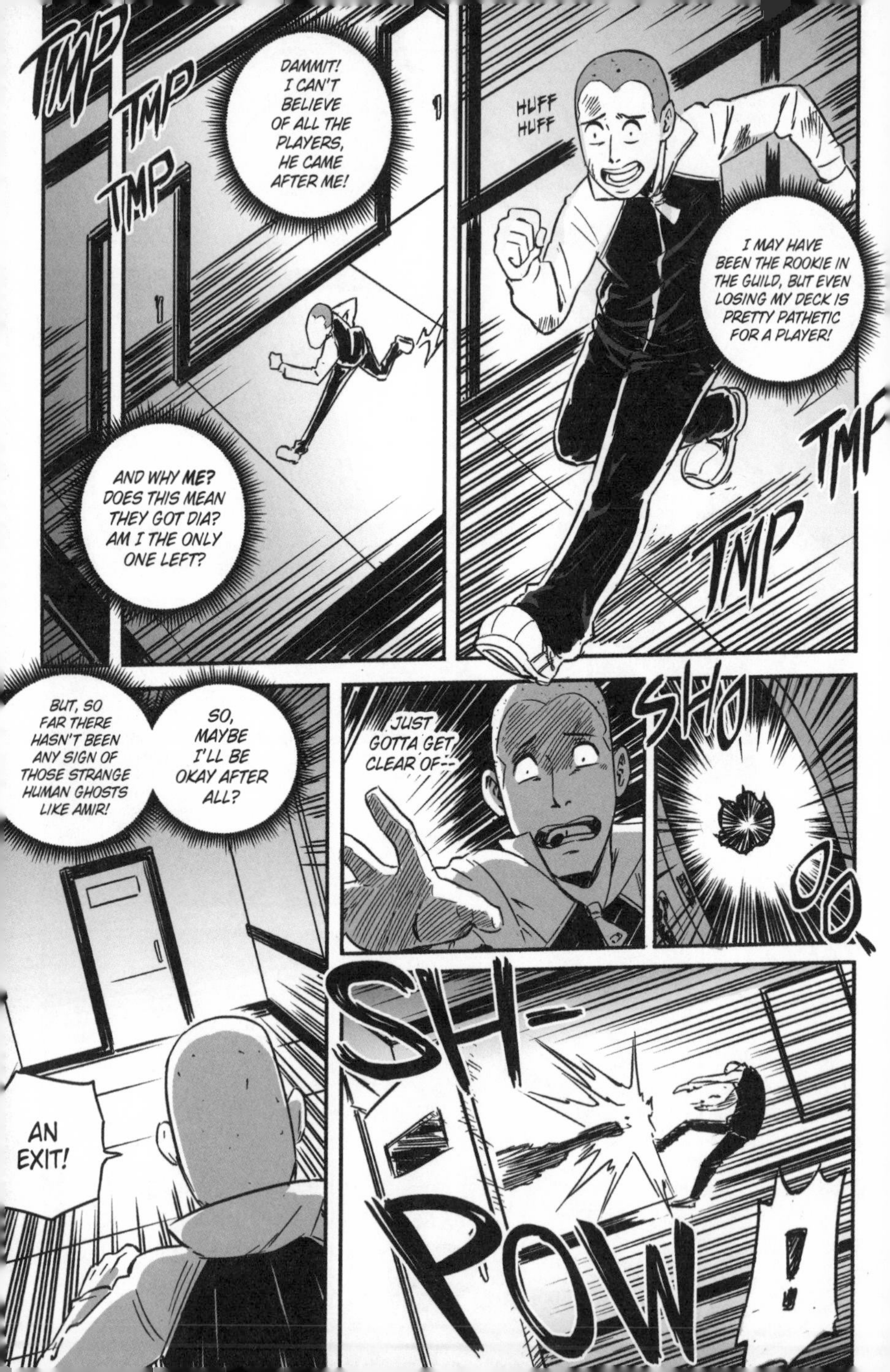
TMP TMP TMP
DAMMIT! I CAN'T BELIEVE OF ALL THE PLAYERS, HE CAME AFTER ME!
AND WHY ME? DOES THIS MEAN THEY GOT DIA? AM I THE ONLY ONE LEFT?
HUFF HUFF
I MAY HAVE BEEN THE ROOKIE IN THE GUILD, BUT EVEN LOSING MY DECK IS PRETTY PATHETIC FOR A PLAYER!
TMP TMP
BUT, SO FAR THERE HASN'T BEEN ANY SIGN OF THOSE STRANGE HUMAN GHOSTS LIKE AMIR!
SO, MAYBE I'LL BE OKAY AFTER ALL?
AN EXIT!
JUST GOTTA GET CLEAR OF--
SHOOO
SH-POW
!

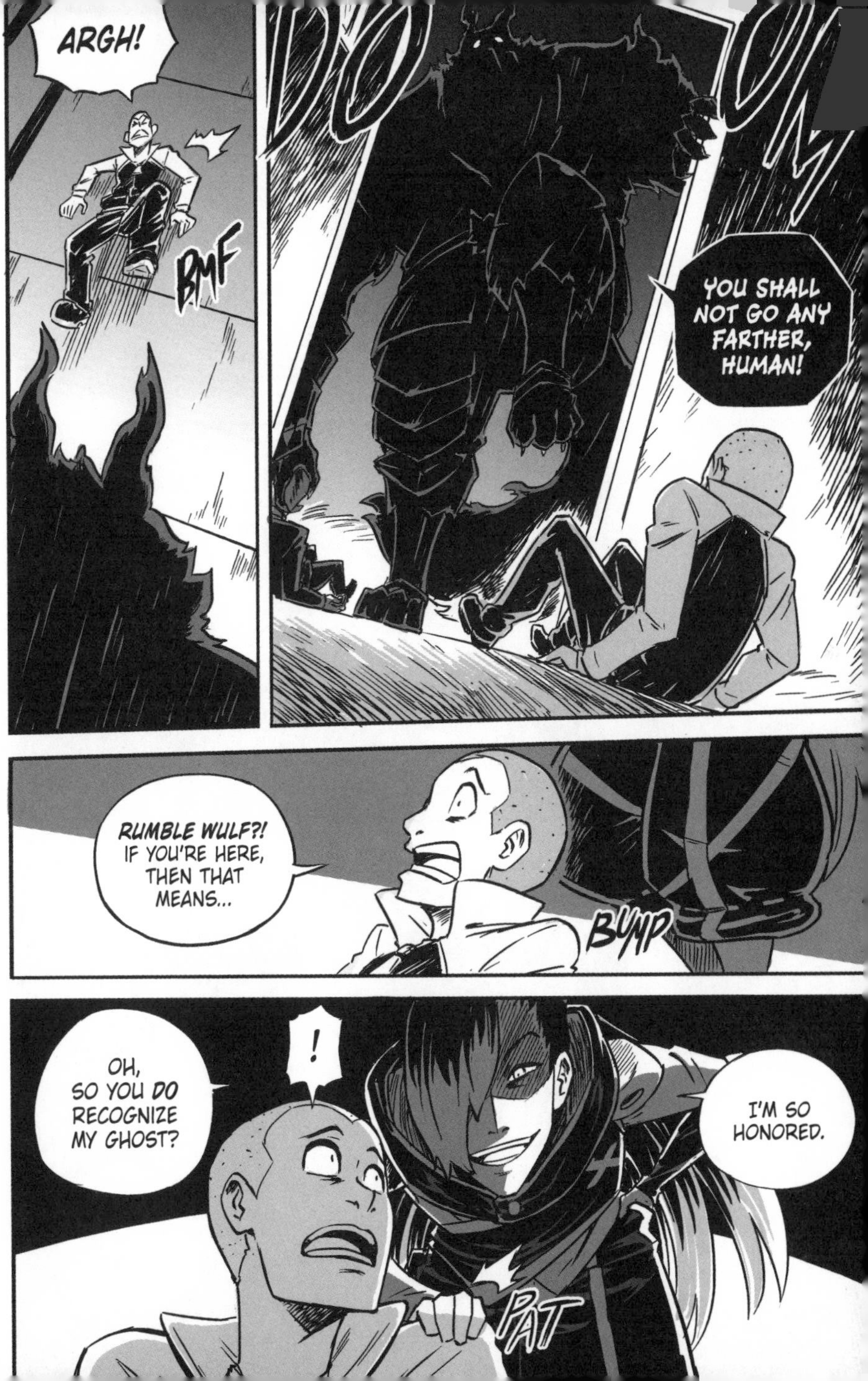
ARGH!
BMF
DOOM
YOU SHALL NOT GO ANY FARTHER, HUMAN!
RUMBLE WULF?! IF YOU'RE HERE, THEN THAT MEANS...
BUMP
!
OH, SO YOU DO RECOGNIZE MY GHOST?
I'M SO HONORED.
PAT

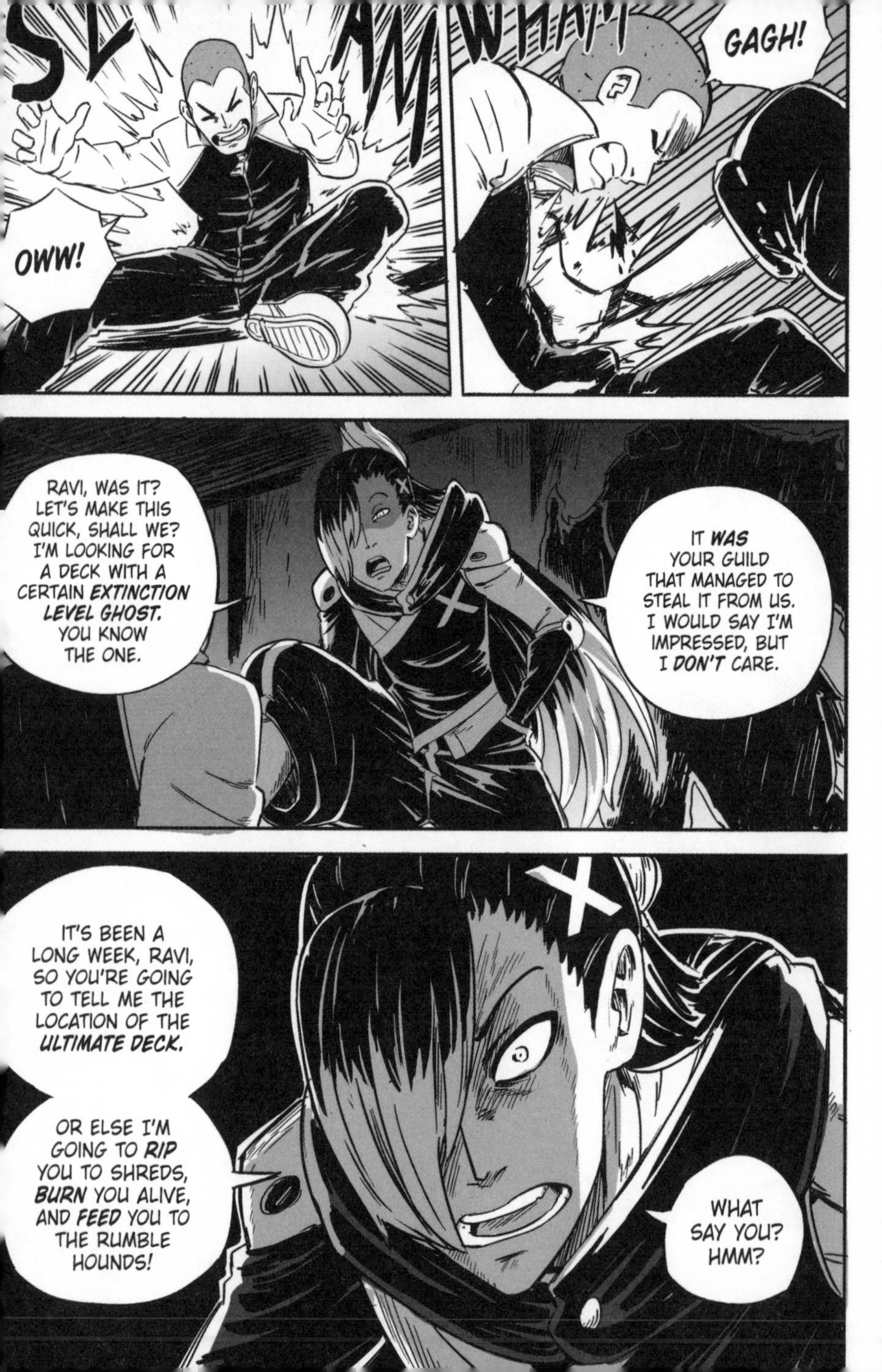
SLAM
OWW!
WHAM
GAGH!
RAVI, WAS IT? LET'S MAKE THIS QUICK, SHALL WE? I'M LOOKING FOR A DECK WITH A CERTAIN **EXTINCTION LEVEL GHOST.** YOU KNOW THE ONE.
IT **WAS** YOUR GUILD THAT MANAGED TO STEAL IT FROM US. I WOULD SAY I'M IMPRESSED, BUT I **DON'T** CARE.
IT'S BEEN A LONG WEEK, RAVI, SO YOU'RE GOING TO TELL ME THE LOCATION OF THE **ULTIMATE DECK.**
OR ELSE I'M GOING TO **RIP** YOU TO SHREDS, **BURN** YOU ALIVE, AND **FEED** YOU TO THE RUMBLE HOUNDS!
WHAT SAY YOU? HMM?

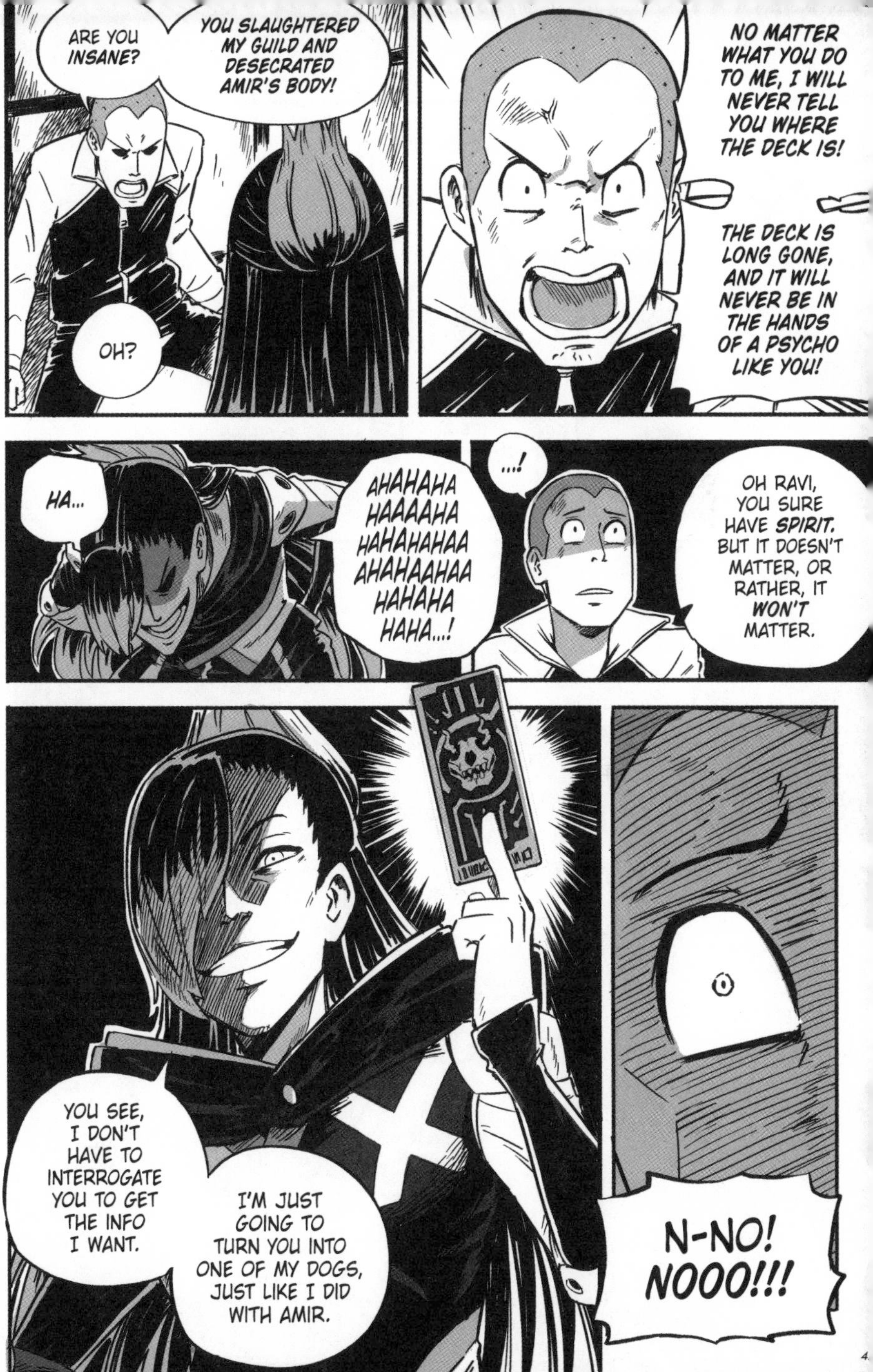
ARE YOU INSANE?
YOU SLAUGHTERED MY GUILD AND DESECRATED AMIR'S BODY!
OH?
NO MATTER WHAT YOU DO TO ME, I WILL NEVER TELL YOU WHERE THE DECK IS!
THE DECK IS LONG GONE, AND IT WILL NEVER BE IN THE HANDS OF A PSYCHO LIKE YOU!
HA...
AHAHAHA HAAAAHA HAHAHAHAA AHAHAAHAA HAHAHA HAHA...!
...!
OH RAVI, YOU SURE HAVE SPIRIT. BUT IT DOESN'T MATTER, OR RATHER, IT WON'T MATTER.
YOU SEE, I DON'T HAVE TO INTERROGATE YOU TO GET THE INFO I WANT.
I'M JUST GOING TO TURN YOU INTO ONE OF MY DOGS, JUST LIKE I DID WITH AMIR.
N-NO! NOOO!!!

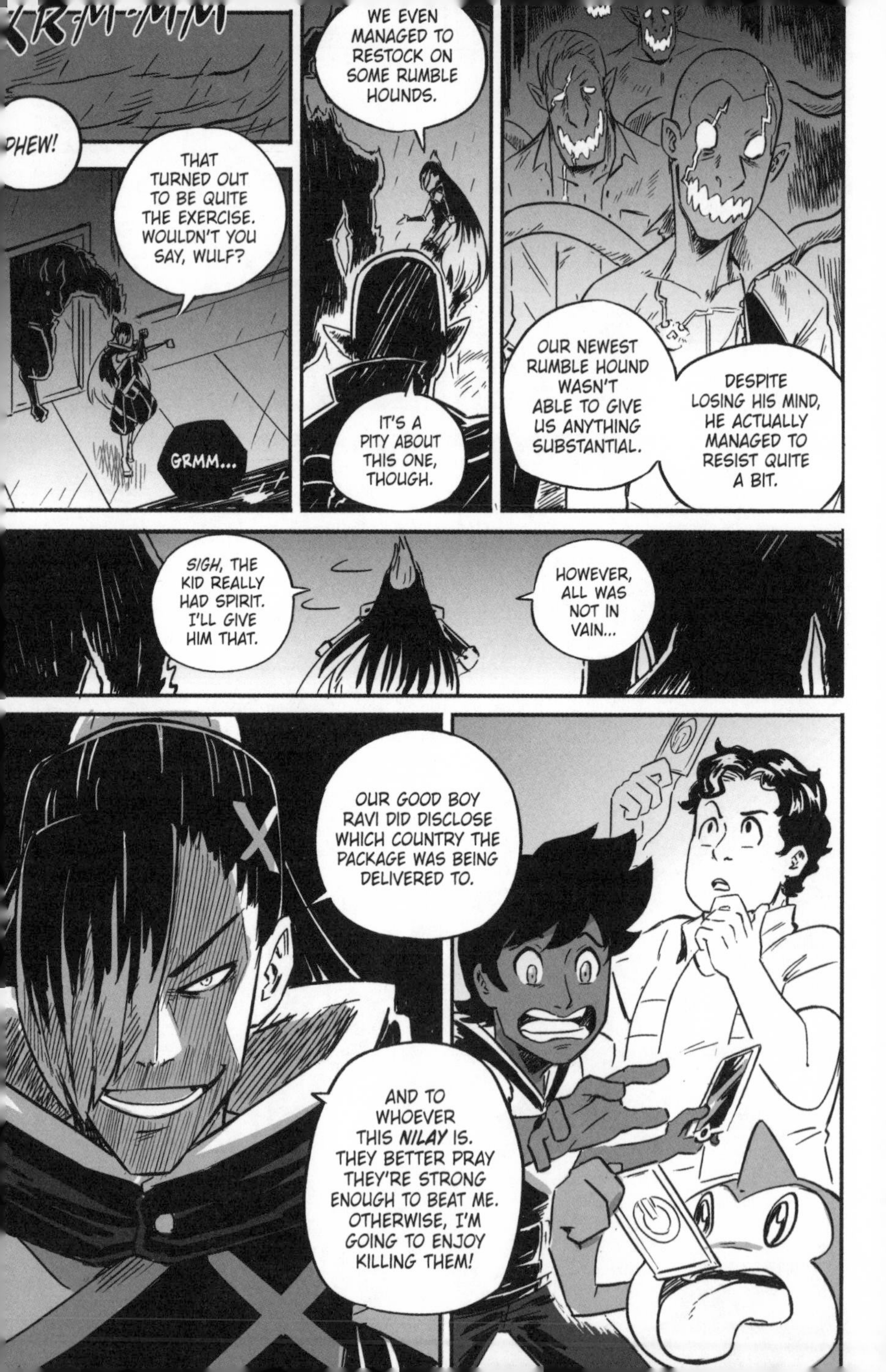
KRMMM
PHEW!
THAT TURNED OUT TO BE QUITE THE EXERCISE. WOULDN'T YOU SAY, WULF?
GRMM...
WE EVEN MANAGED TO RESTOCK ON SOME RUMBLE HOUNDS.
IT'S A PITY ABOUT THIS ONE, THOUGH.
OUR NEWEST RUMBLE HOUND WASN'T ABLE TO GIVE US ANYTHING SUBSTANTIAL.
DESPITE LOSING HIS MIND, HE ACTUALLY MANAGED TO RESIST QUITE A BIT.
SIGH, THE KID REALLY HAD SPIRIT. I'LL GIVE HIM THAT.
HOWEVER, ALL WAS NOT IN VAIN...
OUR GOOD BOY RAVI DID DISCLOSE WHICH COUNTRY THE PACKAGE WAS BEING DELIVERED TO.
AND TO WHOEVER THIS *NILAY* IS. THEY BETTER PRAY THEY'RE STRONG ENOUGH TO BEAT ME. OTHERWISE, I'M GOING TO ENJOY KILLING THEM!

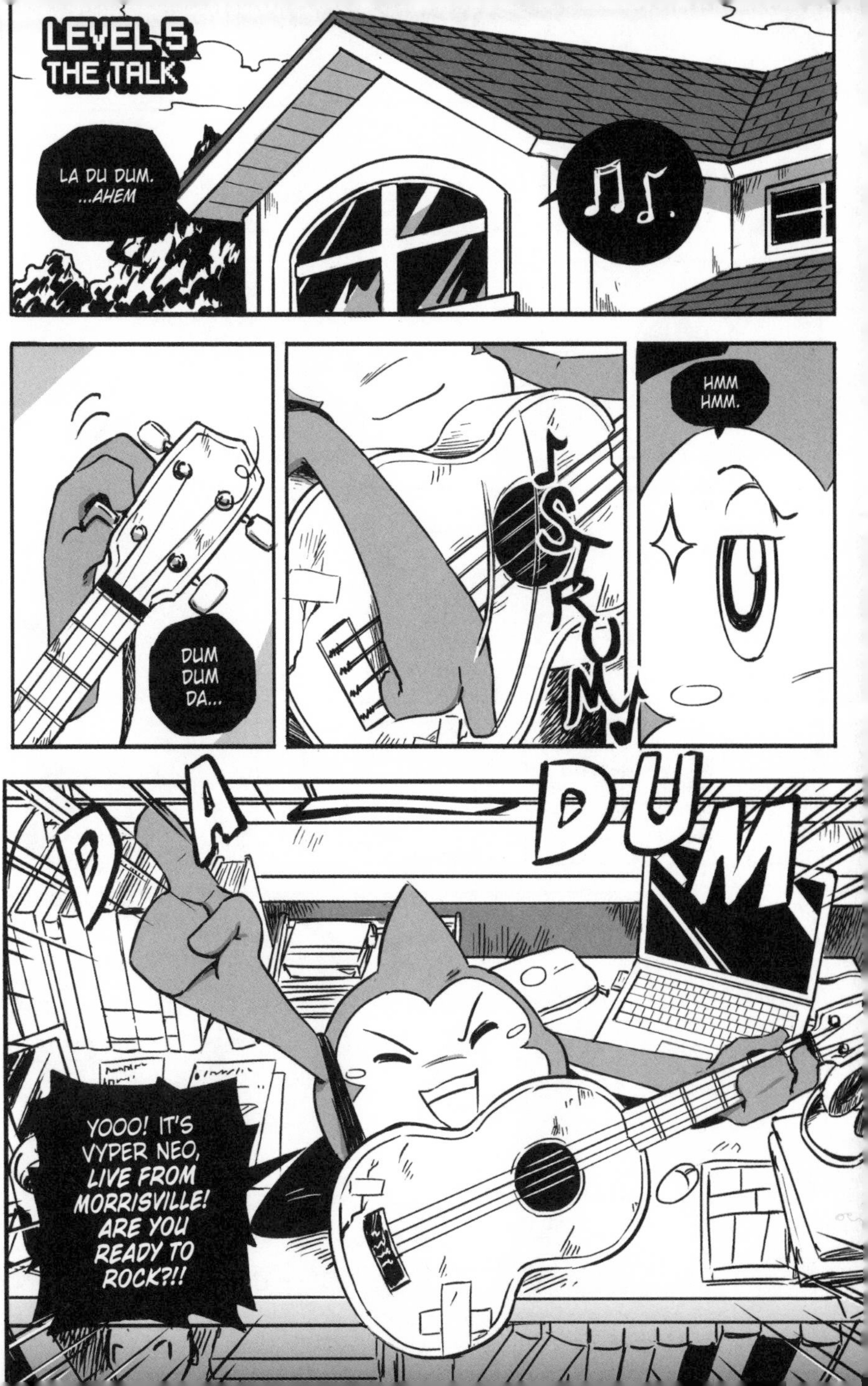
LEVEL 5
THE TALK
LA DU DUM. ...AHEM
DUM DUM DA...
STRUM
HMM HMM.
DA—DUM
YOOO! IT'S VYPER NEO, LIVE FROM MORRISVILLE! ARE YOU READY TO ROCK?!!

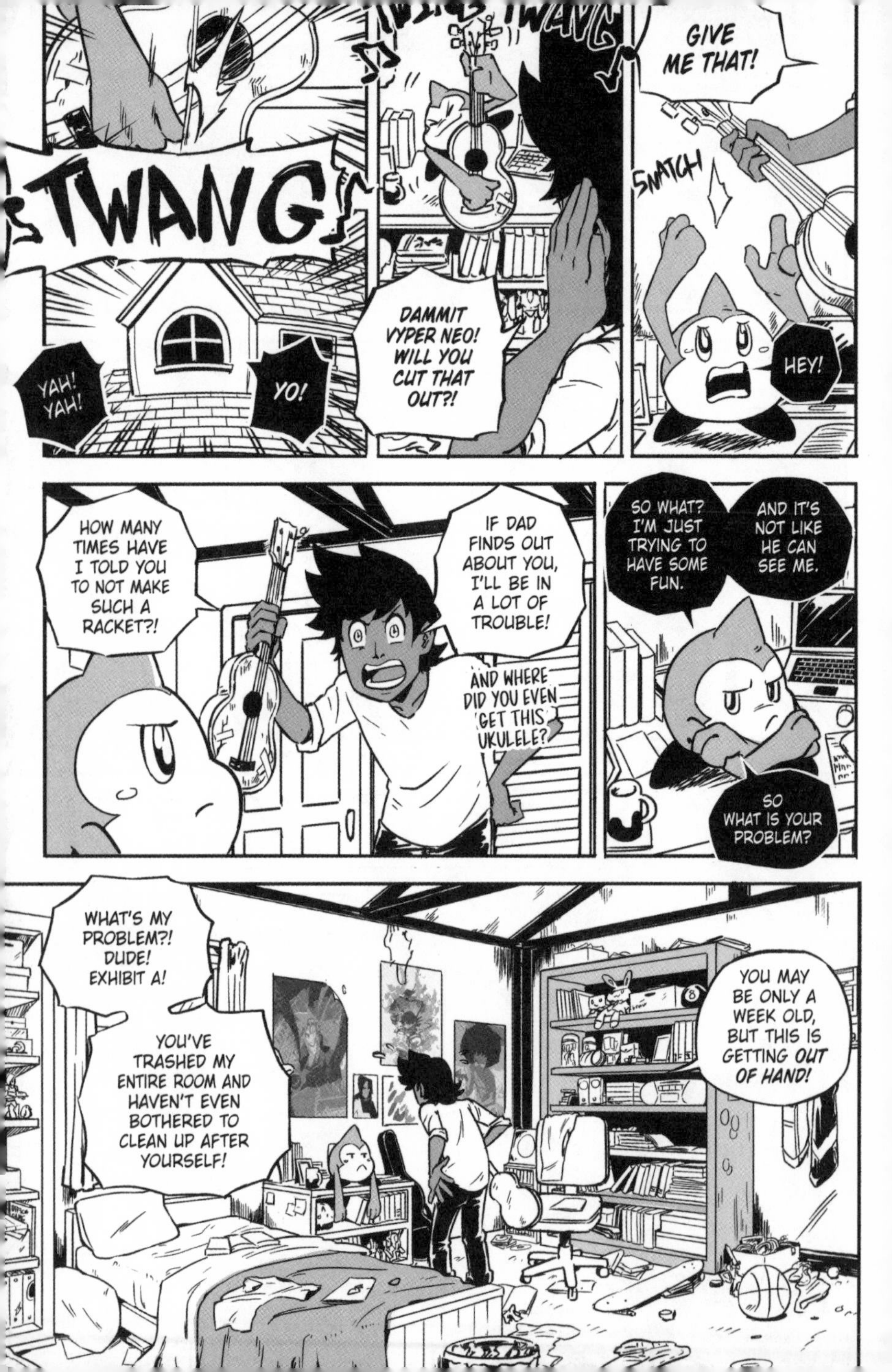
TWANG
TWANG!
YAH! YAH!
YO!
TWANG
DAMMIT VYPER NEO! WILL YOU CUT THAT OUT?!
GIVE ME THAT!
SNATCH
HEY!
HOW MANY TIMES HAVE I TOLD YOU TO NOT MAKE SUCH A RACKET?!
IF DAD FINDS OUT ABOUT YOU, I'LL BE IN A LOT OF TROUBLE!
AND WHERE DID YOU EVEN GET THIS UKULELE?
SO WHAT? I'M JUST TRYING TO HAVE SOME FUN.
AND IT'S NOT LIKE HE CAN SEE ME.
SO WHAT IS YOUR PROBLEM?
WHAT'S MY PROBLEM?! DUDE! EXHIBIT A!
YOU'VE TRASHED MY ENTIRE ROOM AND HAVEN'T EVEN BOTHERED TO CLEAN UP AFTER YOURSELF!
YOU MAY BE ONLY A WEEK OLD, BUT THIS IS GETTING OUT OF HAND!

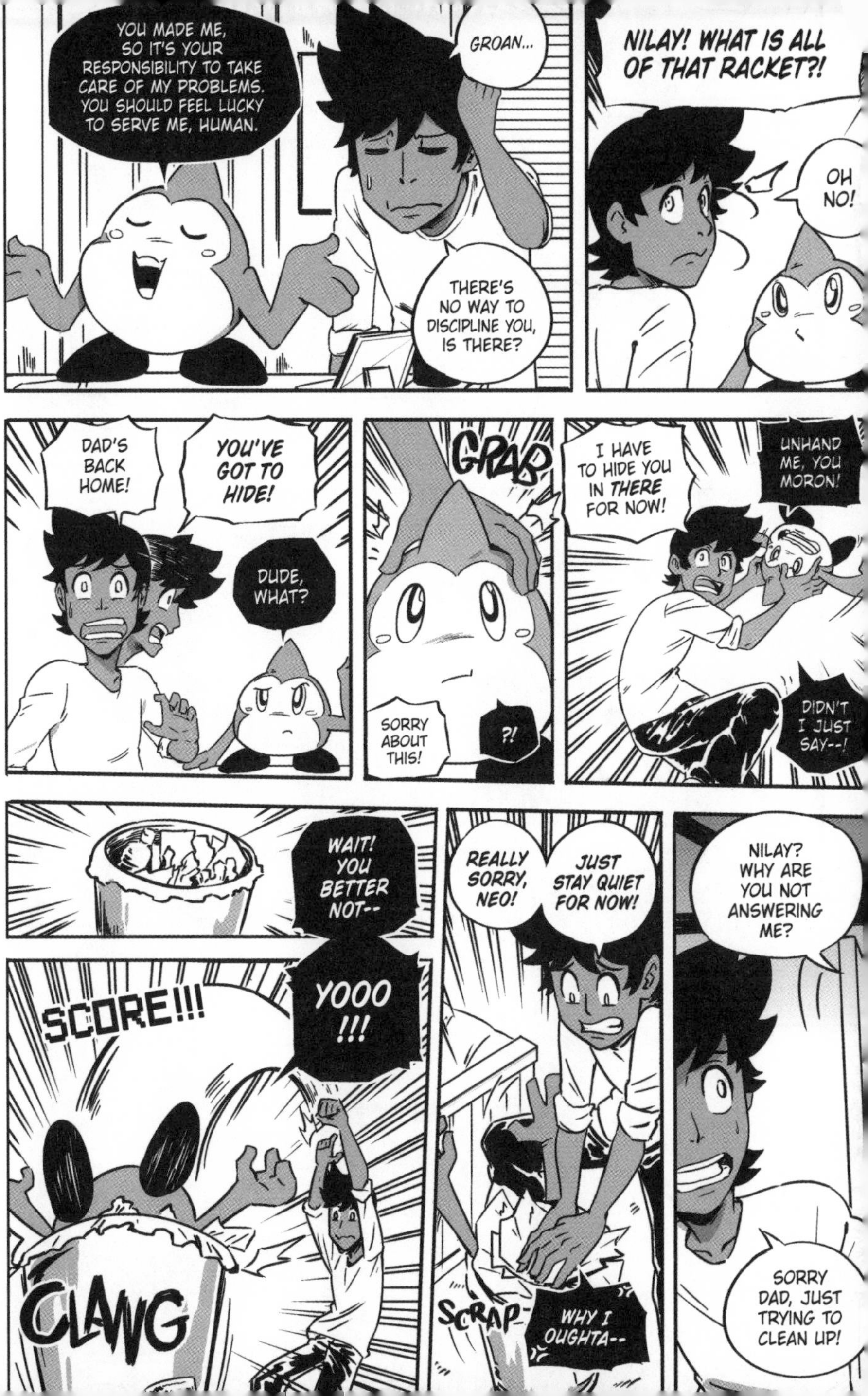
YOU MADE ME, SO IT'S YOUR RESPONSIBILITY TO TAKE CARE OF MY PROBLEMS. YOU SHOULD FEEL LUCKY TO SERVE ME, HUMAN.
GROAN...
THERE'S NO WAY TO DISCIPLINE YOU, IS THERE?
NILAY! WHAT IS ALL OF THAT RACKET?!
OH NO!
DAD'S BACK HOME!
YOU'VE GOT TO HIDE!
DUDE, WHAT?
GRAB
SORRY ABOUT THIS!
?!
I HAVE TO HIDE YOU IN THERE FOR NOW!
UNHAND ME, YOU MORON!
DIDN'T I JUST SAY--!
WAIT! YOU BETTER NOT--
SCORE!!!
YOOO !!!
CLANG
REALLY SORRY, NEO!
JUST STAY QUIET FOR NOW!
SCRAP
WHY I OUGHTA--
NILAY? WHY ARE YOU NOT ANSWERING ME?
SORRY DAD, JUST TRYING TO CLEAN UP!

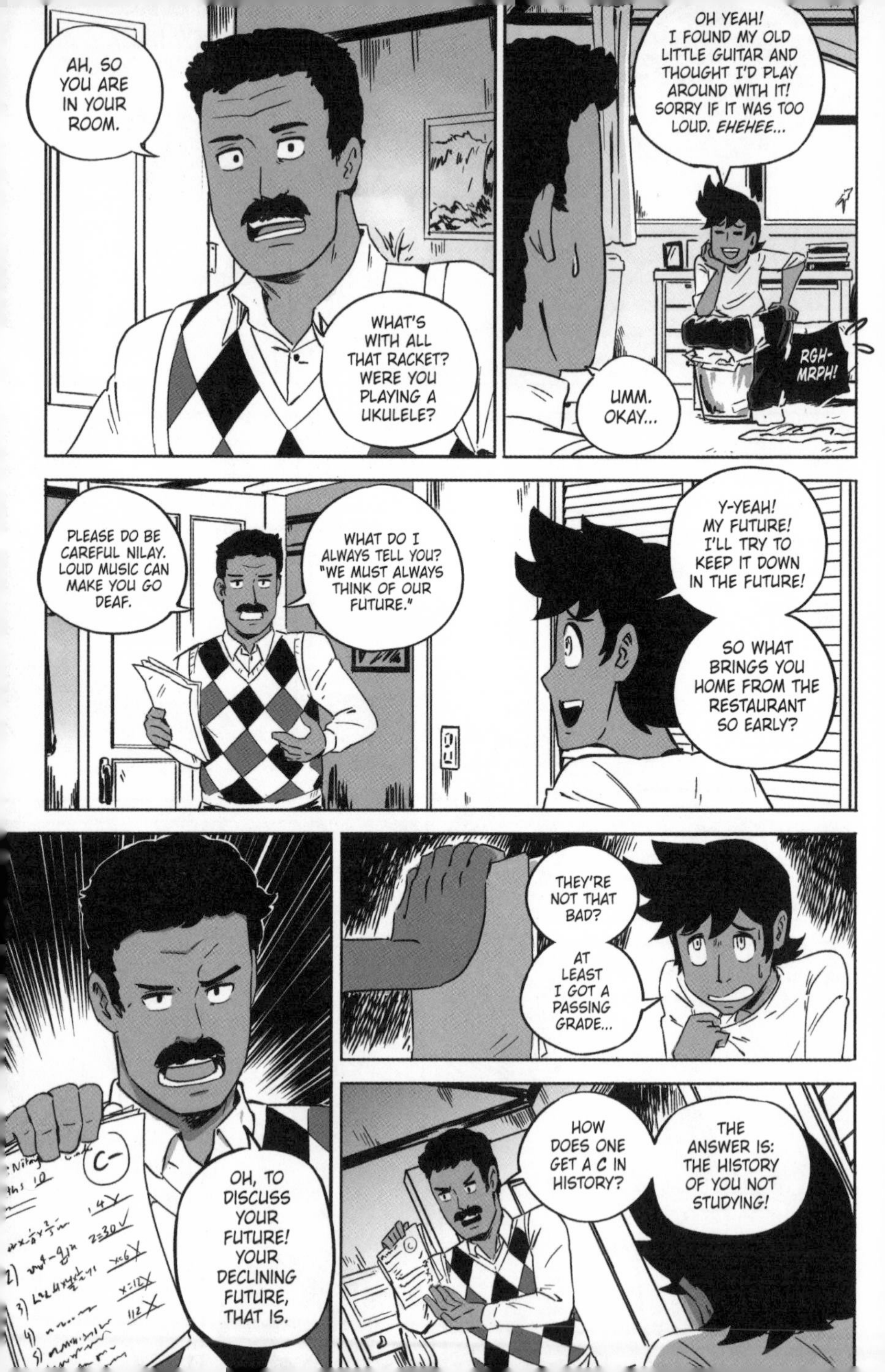
AH, SO YOU ARE IN YOUR ROOM.
WHAT'S WITH ALL THAT RACKET? WERE YOU PLAYING A UKULELE?
OH YEAH! I FOUND MY OLD LITTLE GUITAR AND THOUGHT I'D PLAY AROUND WITH IT! SORRY IF IT WAS TOO LOUD. *EHEHEE...*
UMM. OKAY...
RGH-MRPH!
PLEASE DO BE CAREFUL NILAY. LOUD MUSIC CAN MAKE YOU GO DEAF.
WHAT DO I ALWAYS TELL YOU? "WE MUST ALWAYS THINK OF OUR FUTURE."
Y-YEAH! MY FUTURE! I'LL TRY TO KEEP IT DOWN IN THE FUTURE!
SO WHAT BRINGS YOU HOME FROM THE RESTAURANT SO EARLY?
C-
OH, TO DISCUSS YOUR FUTURE! YOUR DECLINING FUTURE, THAT IS.
THEY'RE NOT THAT BAD?
AT LEAST I GOT A PASSING GRADE...
HOW DOES ONE GET A C IN HISTORY?
THE ANSWER IS: THE HISTORY OF YOU NOT STUDYING!

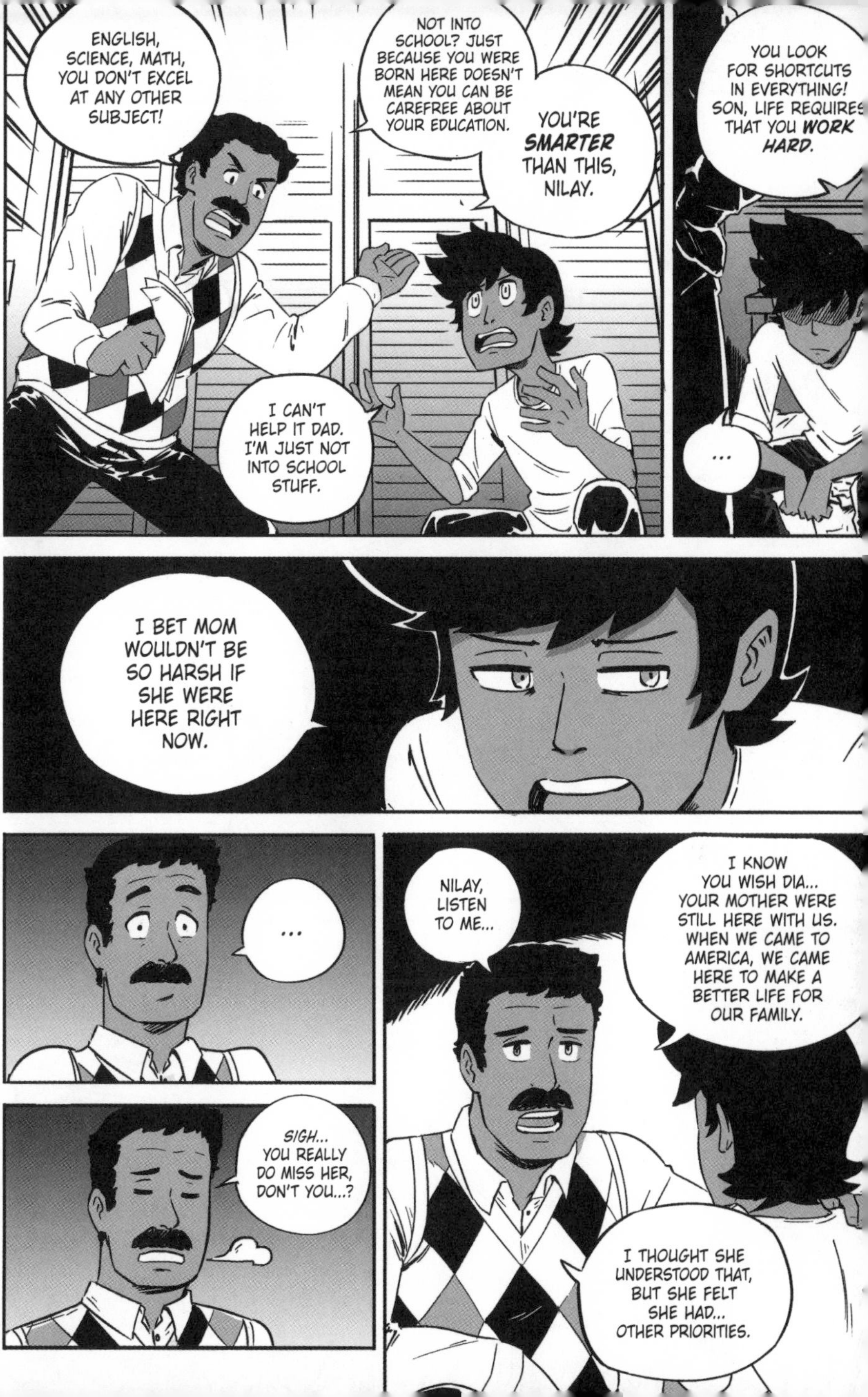

ENGLISH, SCIENCE, MATH, YOU DON'T EXCEL AT ANY OTHER SUBJECT!
I CAN'T HELP IT DAD. I'M JUST NOT INTO SCHOOL STUFF.
NOT INTO SCHOOL? JUST BECAUSE YOU WERE BORN HERE DOESN'T MEAN YOU CAN BE CAREFREE ABOUT YOUR EDUCATION.
YOU'RE *SMARTER* THAN THIS, NILAY.
YOU LOOK FOR SHORTCUTS IN EVERYTHING! SON, LIFE REQUIRES THAT YOU ***WORK HARD.***
...
I BET MOM WOULDN'T BE SO HARSH IF SHE WERE HERE RIGHT NOW.
...
SIGH... YOU REALLY DO MISS HER, DON'T YOU...?
NILAY, LISTEN TO ME...
I KNOW YOU WISH DIA... YOUR MOTHER WERE STILL HERE WITH US. WHEN WE CAME TO AMERICA, WE CAME HERE TO MAKE A BETTER LIFE FOR OUR FAMILY.
I THOUGHT SHE UNDERSTOOD THAT, BUT SHE FELT SHE HAD... OTHER PRIORITIES.

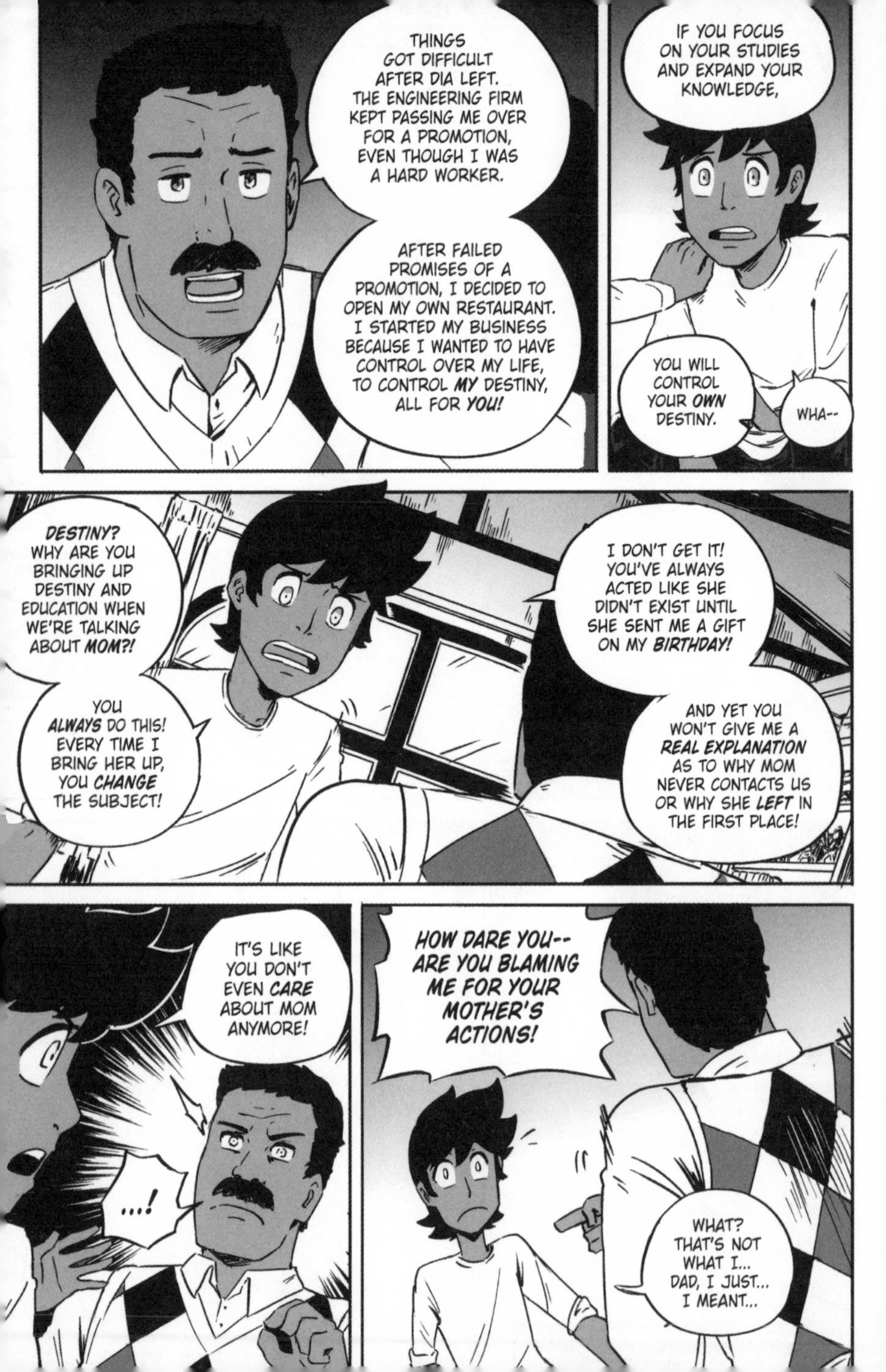
THINGS GOT DIFFICULT AFTER DIA LEFT. THE ENGINEERING FIRM KEPT PASSING ME OVER FOR A PROMOTION, EVEN THOUGH I WAS A HARD WORKER.
AFTER FAILED PROMISES OF A PROMOTION, I DECIDED TO OPEN MY OWN RESTAURANT. I STARTED MY BUSINESS BECAUSE I WANTED TO HAVE CONTROL OVER MY LIFE, TO CONTROL *MY* DESTINY, ALL FOR *YOU!*
IF YOU FOCUS ON YOUR STUDIES AND EXPAND YOUR KNOWLEDGE,
YOU WILL CONTROL YOUR *OWN* DESTINY.
WHA--
DESTINY? WHY ARE YOU BRINGING UP DESTINY AND EDUCATION WHEN WE'RE TALKING ABOUT *MOM?!*
YOU *ALWAYS* DO THIS! EVERY TIME I BRING HER UP, YOU *CHANGE* THE SUBJECT!
I DON'T GET IT! YOU'VE ALWAYS ACTED LIKE SHE DIDN'T EXIST UNTIL SHE SENT ME A GIFT ON MY *BIRTHDAY!*
AND YET YOU WON'T GIVE ME A *REAL EXPLANATION* AS TO WHY MOM NEVER CONTACTS US OR WHY SHE *LEFT* IN THE FIRST PLACE!
IT'S LIKE YOU DON'T EVEN *CARE* ABOUT MOM ANYMORE!
...!
HOW DARE YOU-- ARE YOU BLAMING ME FOR YOUR MOTHER'S ACTIONS!
WHAT? THAT'S NOT WHAT I... DAD, I JUST... I MEANT...

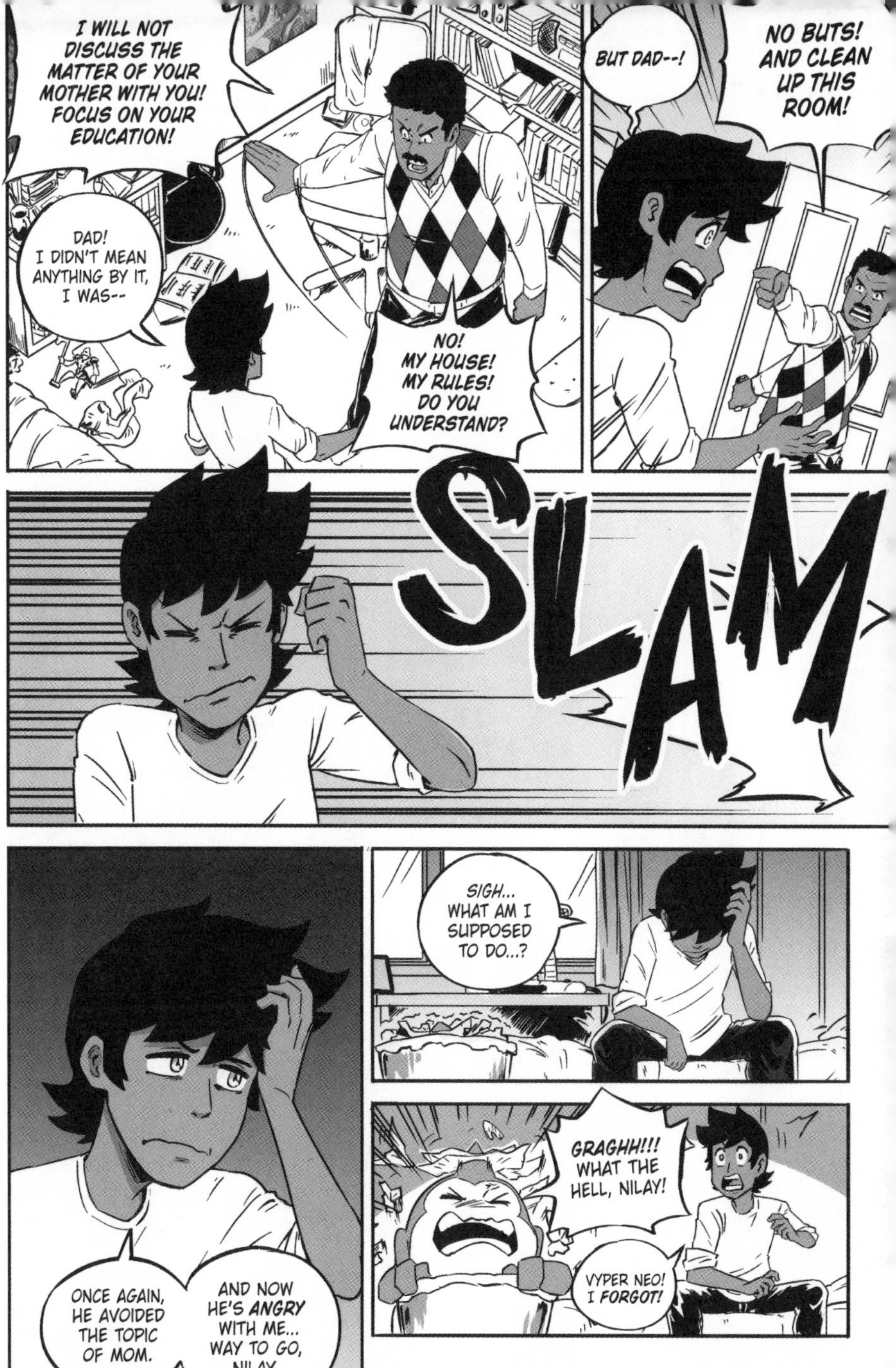
I WILL NOT DISCUSS THE MATTER OF YOUR MOTHER WITH YOU! FOCUS ON YOUR EDUCATION!
DAD! I DIDN'T MEAN ANYTHING BY IT, I WAS--
NO! MY HOUSE! MY RULES! DO YOU UNDERSTAND?
BUT DAD--!
NO BUTS! AND CLEAN UP THIS ROOM!
SLAM
ONCE AGAIN, HE AVOIDED THE TOPIC OF MOM.
AND NOW HE'S ANGRY WITH ME... WAY TO GO, NILAY.
SIGH... WHAT AM I SUPPOSED TO DO...?
GRAGHH!!! WHAT THE HELL, NILAY!
VYPER NEO! I FORGOT!

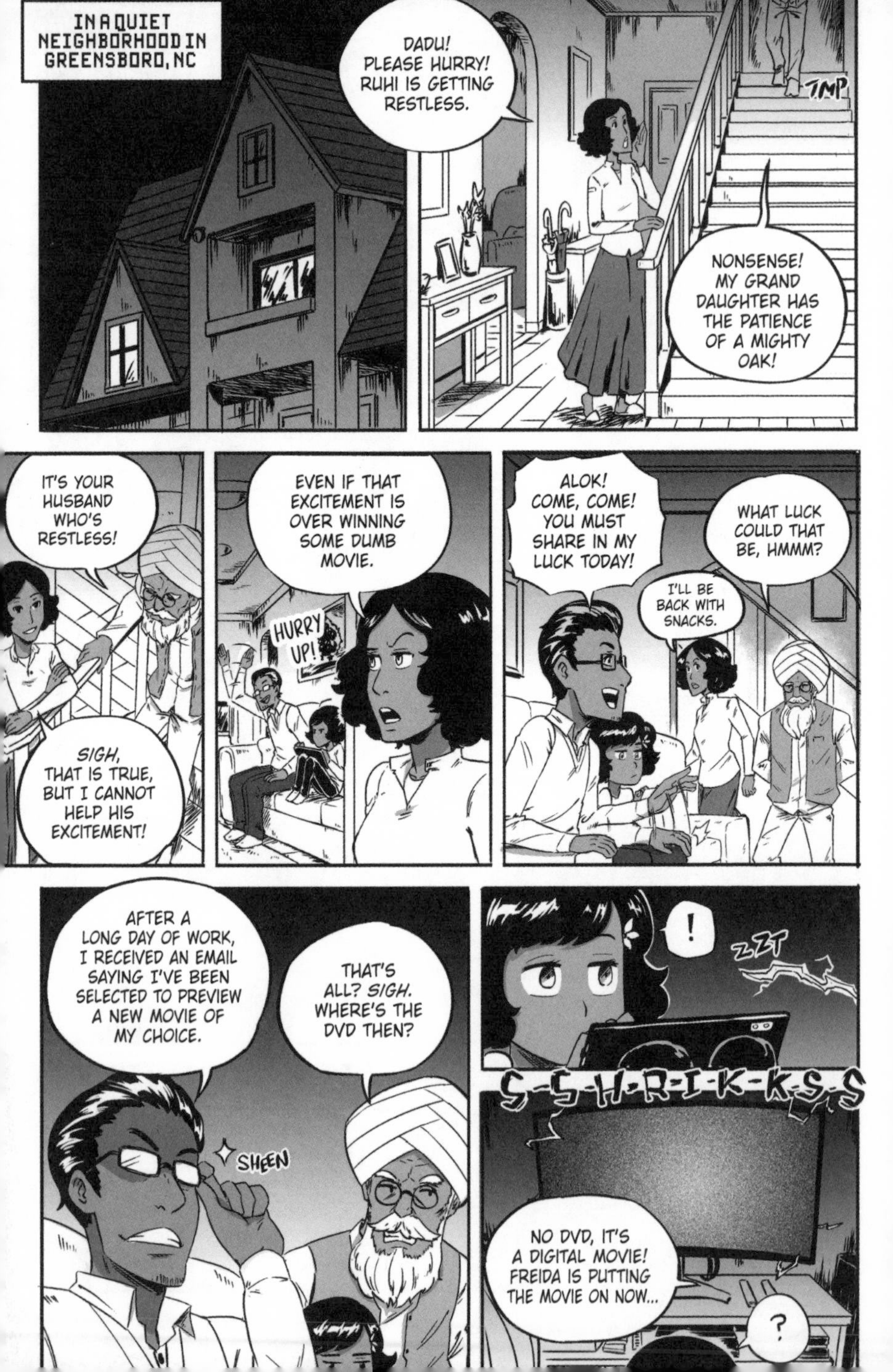
IN A QUIET NEIGHBORHOOD IN GREENSBORO, NC
DADU! PLEASE HURRY! RUHI IS GETTING RESTLESS.
TMP
NONSENSE! MY GRAND DAUGHTER HAS THE PATIENCE OF A MIGHTY OAK!
IT'S YOUR HUSBAND WHO'S RESTLESS!
SIGH, THAT IS TRUE, BUT I CANNOT HELP HIS EXCITEMENT!
EVEN IF THAT EXCITEMENT IS OVER WINNING SOME DUMB MOVIE.
HURRY UP!
ALOK! COME, COME! YOU MUST SHARE IN MY LUCK TODAY!
WHAT LUCK COULD THAT BE, HMMM?
I'LL BE BACK WITH SNACKS.
AFTER A LONG DAY OF WORK, I RECEIVED AN EMAIL SAYING I'VE BEEN SELECTED TO PREVIEW A NEW MOVIE OF MY CHOICE.
THAT'S ALL? SIGH. WHERE'S THE DVD THEN?
SHEEN
!
ZZT
S-S-H-R-I-K-K-S-S
NO DVD, IT'S A DIGITAL MOVIE! FREIDA IS PUTTING THE MOVIE ON NOW...
?

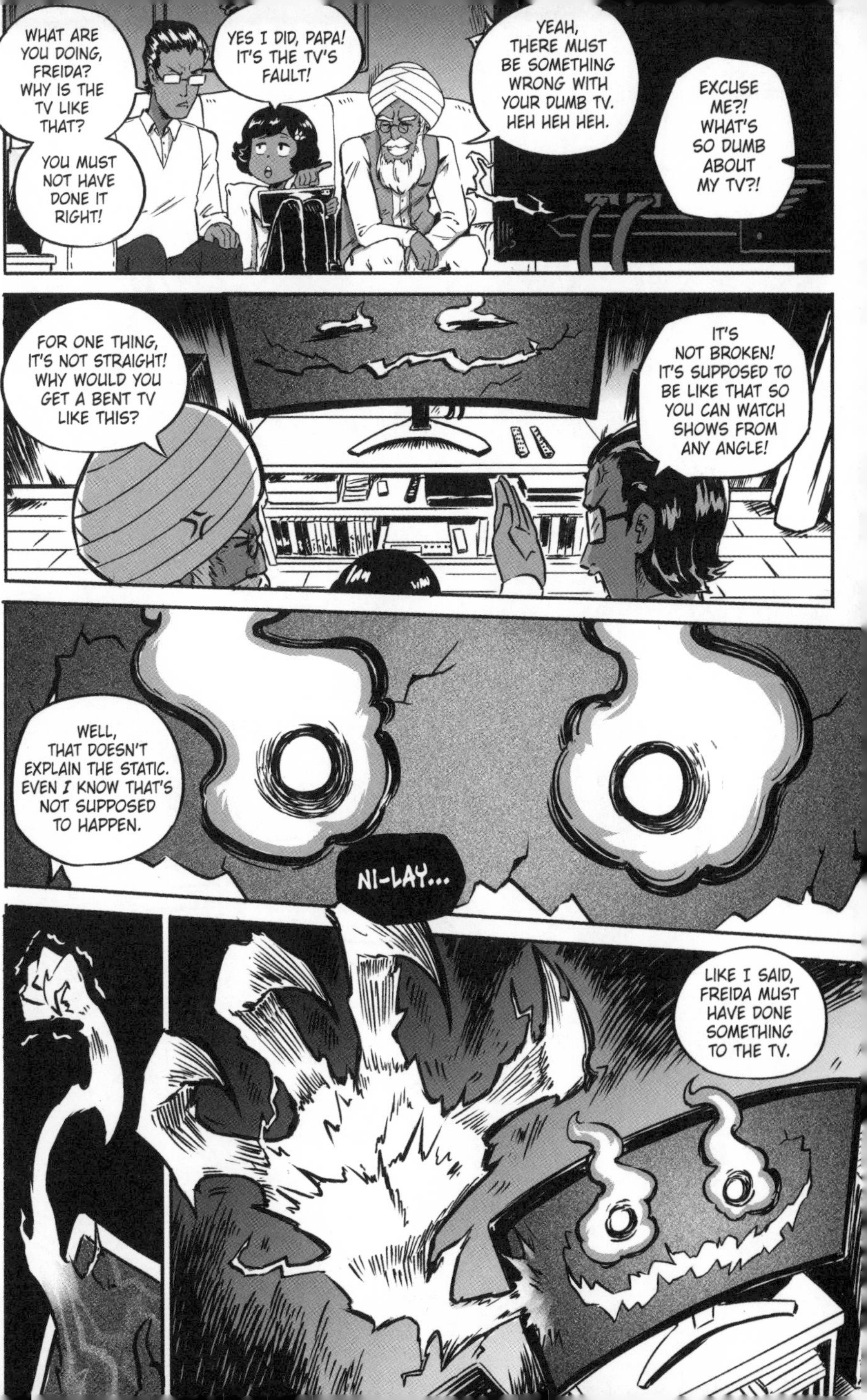
WHAT ARE YOU DOING, FREIDA? WHY IS THE TV LIKE THAT?
YOU MUST NOT HAVE DONE IT RIGHT!
YES I DID, PAPA! IT'S THE TV'S FAULT!
YEAH, THERE MUST BE SOMETHING WRONG WITH YOUR DUMB TV. HEH HEH HEH.
EXCUSE ME?! WHAT'S SO DUMB ABOUT MY TV?!
FOR ONE THING, IT'S NOT STRAIGHT! WHY WOULD YOU GET A BENT TV LIKE THIS?
IT'S NOT BROKEN! IT'S SUPPOSED TO BE LIKE THAT SO YOU CAN WATCH SHOWS FROM ANY ANGLE!
WELL, THAT DOESN'T EXPLAIN THE STATIC. EVEN I KNOW THAT'S NOT SUPPOSED TO HAPPEN.
NI-LAY...
LIKE I SAID, FREIDA MUST HAVE DONE SOMETHING TO THE TV.

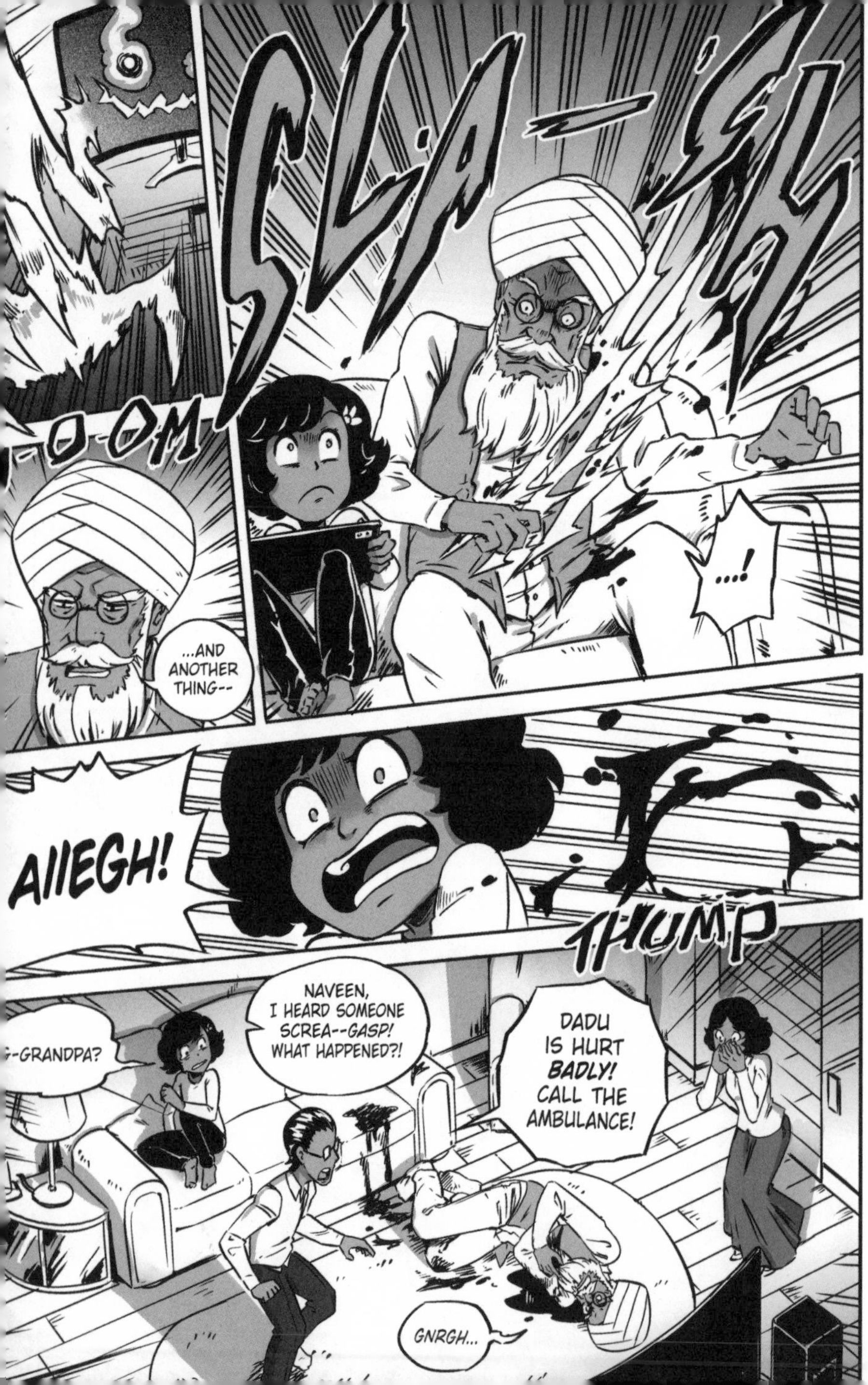
SCLA--ASH
-O-OM
...AND ANOTHER THING--
...!
AIIEGH!
THUMP
G-GRANDPA?
NAVEEN, I HEARD SOMEONE SCREA--GASP! WHAT HAPPENED?!
DADU IS HURT BADLY! CALL THE AMBULANCE!
GNRGH...

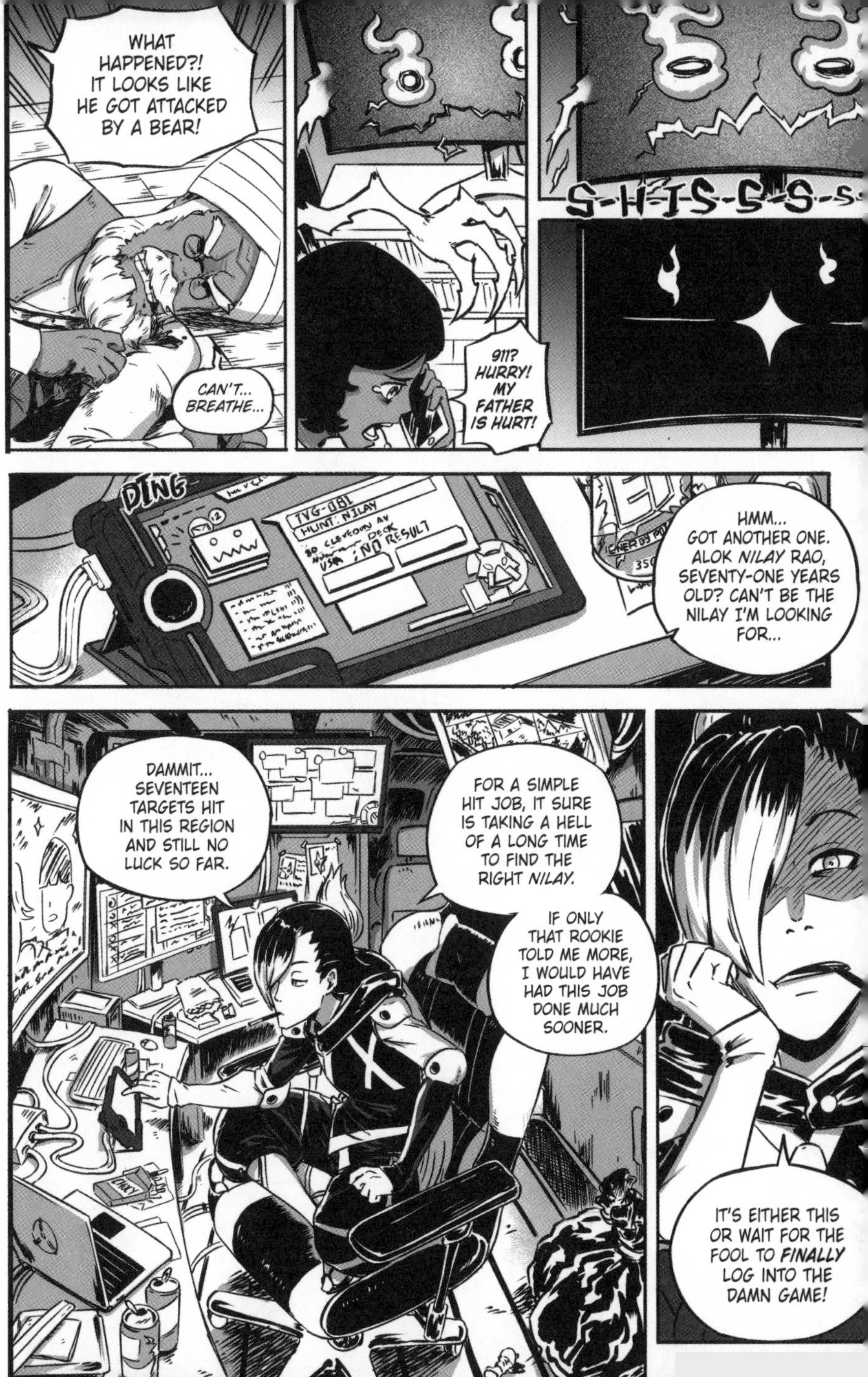
WHAT HAPPENED?! IT LOOKS LIKE HE GOT ATTACKED BY A BEAR!
CAN'T... BREATHE...
911? HURRY! MY FATHER IS HURT!
S-H-I-S-S-S-S
DING
HMM... GOT ANOTHER ONE. ALOK *NILAY* RAO, SEVENTY-ONE YEARS OLD? CAN'T BE THE NILAY I'M LOOKING FOR...
DAMMIT... SEVENTEEN TARGETS HIT IN THIS REGION AND STILL NO LUCK SO FAR.
FOR A SIMPLE HIT JOB, IT SURE IS TAKING A HELL OF A LONG TIME TO FIND THE RIGHT *NILAY*.
IF ONLY THAT ROOKIE TOLD ME MORE, I WOULD HAVE HAD THIS JOB DONE MUCH SOONER.
IT'S EITHER THIS OR WAIT FOR THE FOOL TO *FINALLY* LOG INTO THE DAMN GAME!

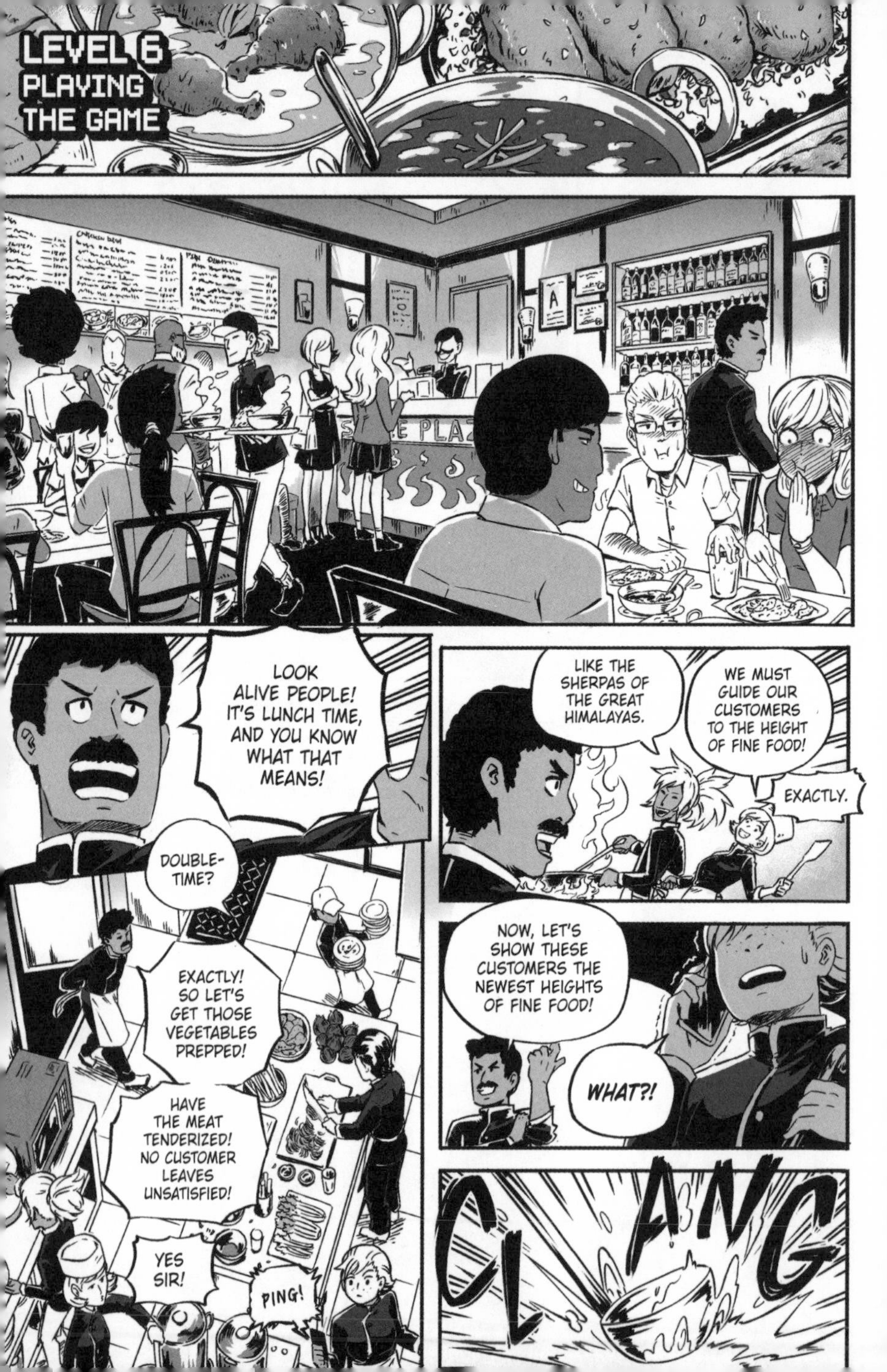
LEVEL 6
PLAYING THE GAME
LOOK ALIVE PEOPLE! IT'S LUNCH TIME, AND YOU KNOW WHAT THAT MEANS!
DOUBLE-TIME?
EXACTLY! SO LET'S GET THOSE VEGETABLES PREPPED!
HAVE THE MEAT TENDERIZED! NO CUSTOMER LEAVES UNSATISFIED!
YES SIR!
PING!
LIKE THE SHERPAS OF THE GREAT HIMALAYAS.
WE MUST GUIDE OUR CUSTOMERS TO THE HEIGHT OF FINE FOOD!
EXACTLY.
NOW, LET'S SHOW THESE CUSTOMERS THE NEWEST HEIGHTS OF FINE FOOD!
WHAT?!
CLANG

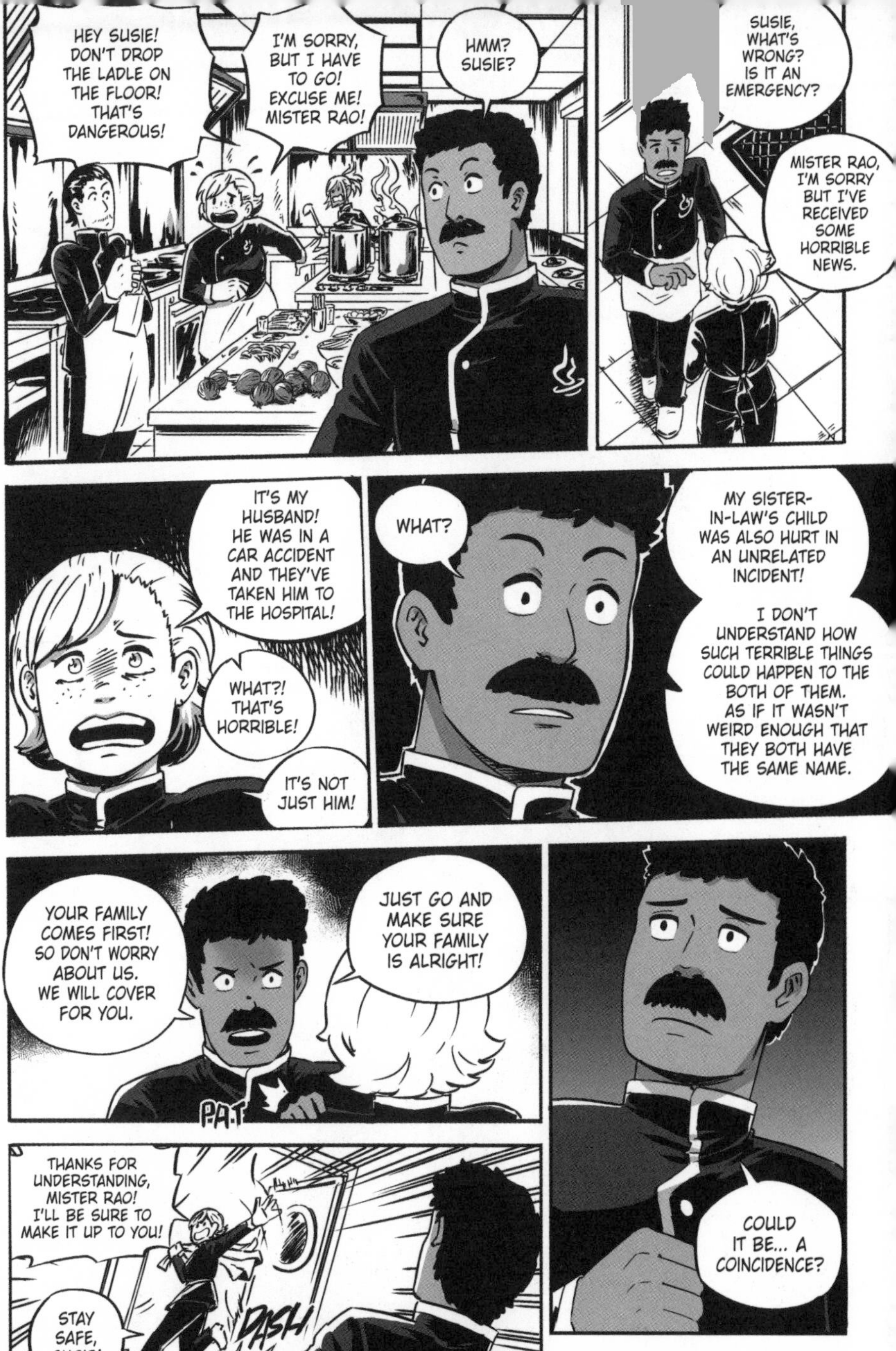
HEY SUSIE! DON'T DROP THE LADLE ON THE FLOOR! THAT'S DANGEROUS!
I'M SORRY, BUT I HAVE TO GO! EXCUSE ME! MISTER RAO!
HMM? SUSIE?
SUSIE, WHAT'S WRONG? IS IT AN EMERGENCY?
MISTER RAO, I'M SORRY BUT I'VE RECEIVED SOME HORRIBLE NEWS.
IT'S MY HUSBAND! HE WAS IN A CAR ACCIDENT AND THEY'VE TAKEN HIM TO THE HOSPITAL!
WHAT?! THAT'S HORRIBLE!
IT'S NOT JUST HIM!
WHAT?
MY SISTER-IN-LAW'S CHILD WAS ALSO HURT IN AN UNRELATED INCIDENT!
I DON'T UNDERSTAND HOW SUCH TERRIBLE THINGS COULD HAPPEN TO THE BOTH OF THEM. AS IF IT WASN'T WEIRD ENOUGH THAT THEY BOTH HAVE THE SAME NAME.
YOUR FAMILY COMES FIRST! SO DON'T WORRY ABOUT US. WE WILL COVER FOR YOU.
JUST GO AND MAKE SURE YOUR FAMILY IS ALRIGHT!
PAT
THANKS FOR UNDERSTANDING, MISTER RAO! I'LL BE SURE TO MAKE IT UP TO YOU!
STAY SAFE, SUSIE!
DASH
COULD IT BE... A COINCIDENCE?

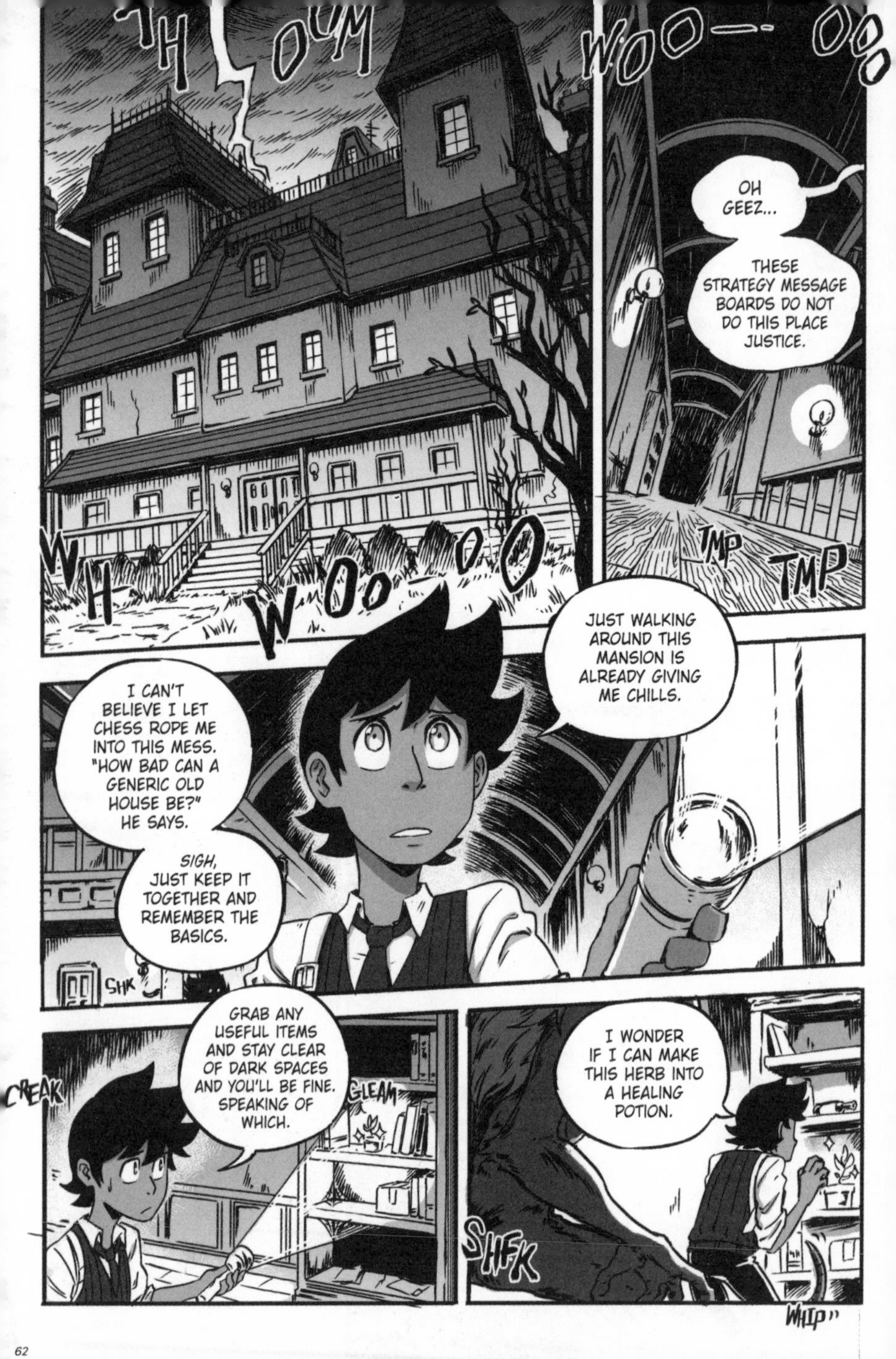
THOOM
WOO--OOO
OH GEEZ...
THESE STRATEGY MESSAGE BOARDS DO NOT DO THIS PLACE JUSTICE.
WHWOO-OO
TMP TMP
I CAN'T BELIEVE I LET CHESS ROPE ME INTO THIS MESS. "HOW BAD CAN A GENERIC OLD HOUSE BE?" HE SAYS.
JUST WALKING AROUND THIS MANSION IS ALREADY GIVING ME CHILLS.
SIGH, JUST KEEP IT TOGETHER AND REMEMBER THE BASICS.
SHK
CREAK
GRAB ANY USEFUL ITEMS AND STAY CLEAR OF DARK SPACES AND YOU'LL BE FINE. SPEAKING OF WHICH.
GLEAM
I WONDER IF I CAN MAKE THIS HERB INTO A HEALING POTION.
SHFK
WHIP

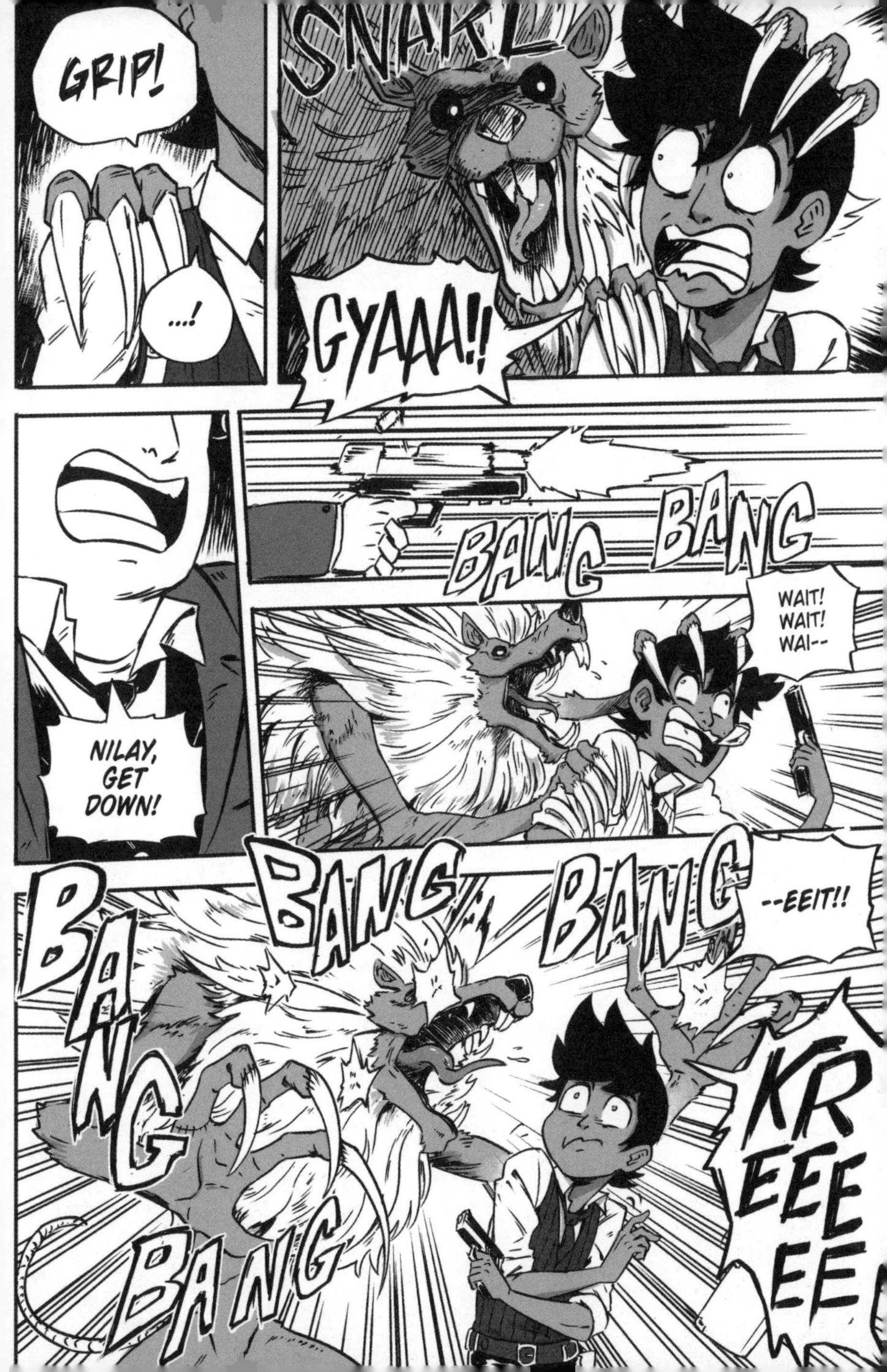
GRIP!
...!
SNARL
GYAAA!!
NILAY, GET DOWN!
BANG
BANG
WAIT! WAIT! WAI--
BANG
BANG
BANG
--EEIT!!
BANG
KREEEEEE

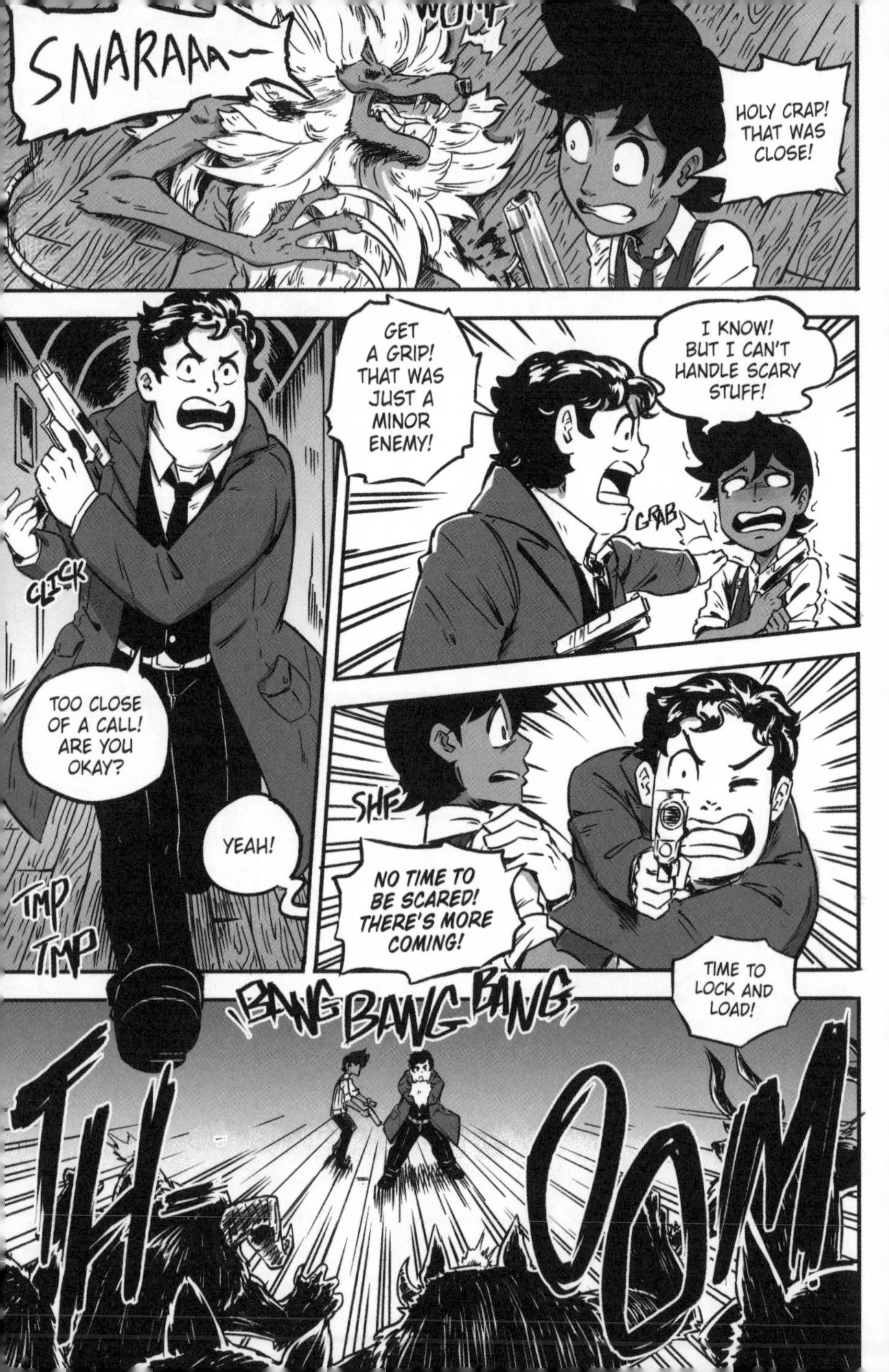
SNARAAA~
HOLY CRAP! THAT WAS CLOSE!
CLICK
TOO CLOSE OF A CALL! ARE YOU OKAY?
YEAH!
TMP TMP
GET A GRIP! THAT WAS JUST A MINOR ENEMY!
I KNOW! BUT I CAN'T HANDLE SCARY STUFF!
GRAB
SHF
NO TIME TO BE SCARED! THERE'S MORE COMING!
TIME TO LOCK AND LOAD!
BANG BANG BANG
THOOM!

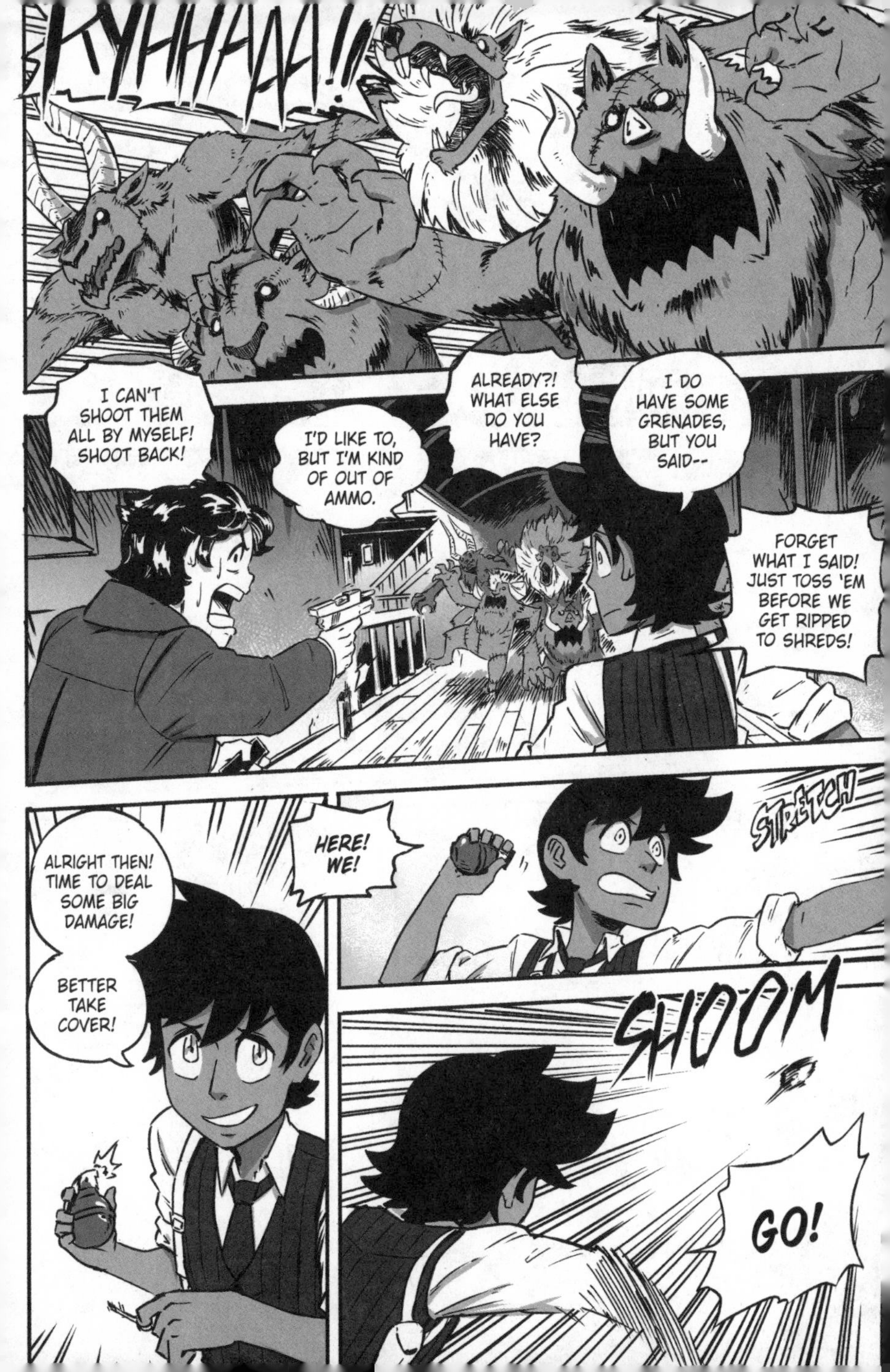
KYHHAA!!!
I CAN'T SHOOT THEM ALL BY MYSELF! SHOOT BACK!
I'D LIKE TO, BUT I'M KIND OF OUT OF AMMO.
ALREADY?! WHAT ELSE DO YOU HAVE?
I DO HAVE SOME GRENADES, BUT YOU SAID--
FORGET WHAT I SAID! JUST TOSS 'EM BEFORE WE GET RIPPED TO SHREDS!
ALRIGHT THEN! TIME TO DEAL SOME BIG DAMAGE!
BETTER TAKE COVER!
HERE! WE!
STRETCH
SHOOM
GO!

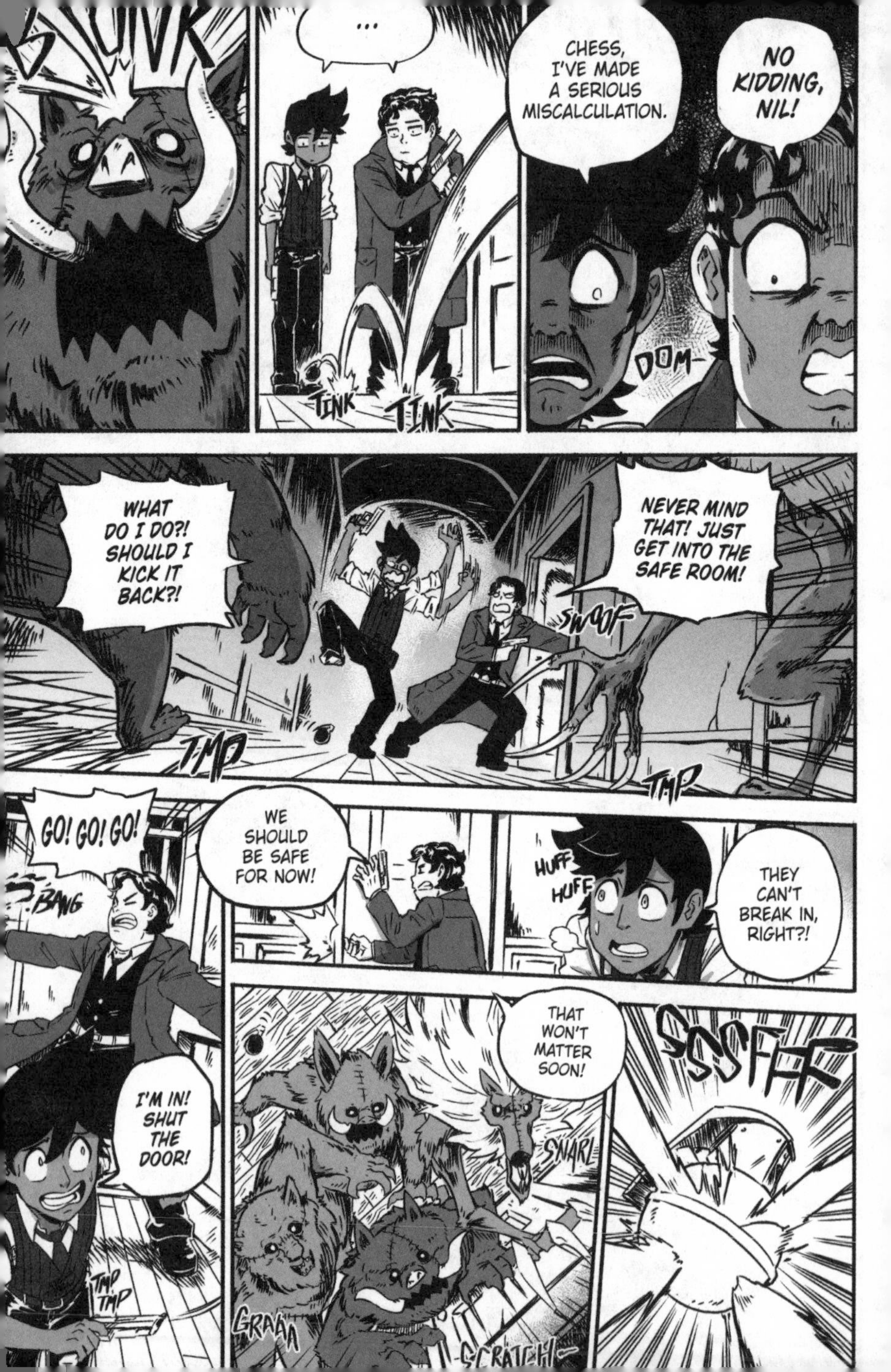
SHUNK
...
TINK
TINK
CHESS, I'VE MADE A SERIOUS MISCALCULATION.
NO KIDDING, NIL!
DOM
WHAT DO I DO?! SHOULD I KICK IT BACK?!
NEVER MIND THAT! JUST GET INTO THE SAFE ROOM!
SWOOF
TMP
TMP
GO! GO! GO!
BANG
I'M IN! SHUT THE DOOR!
TMP TMP
WE SHOULD BE SAFE FOR NOW!
HUFF HUFF
THEY CAN'T BREAK IN, RIGHT?!
THAT WON'T MATTER SOON!
SNARL
GRAAA
SCRATCH
SSSFFF

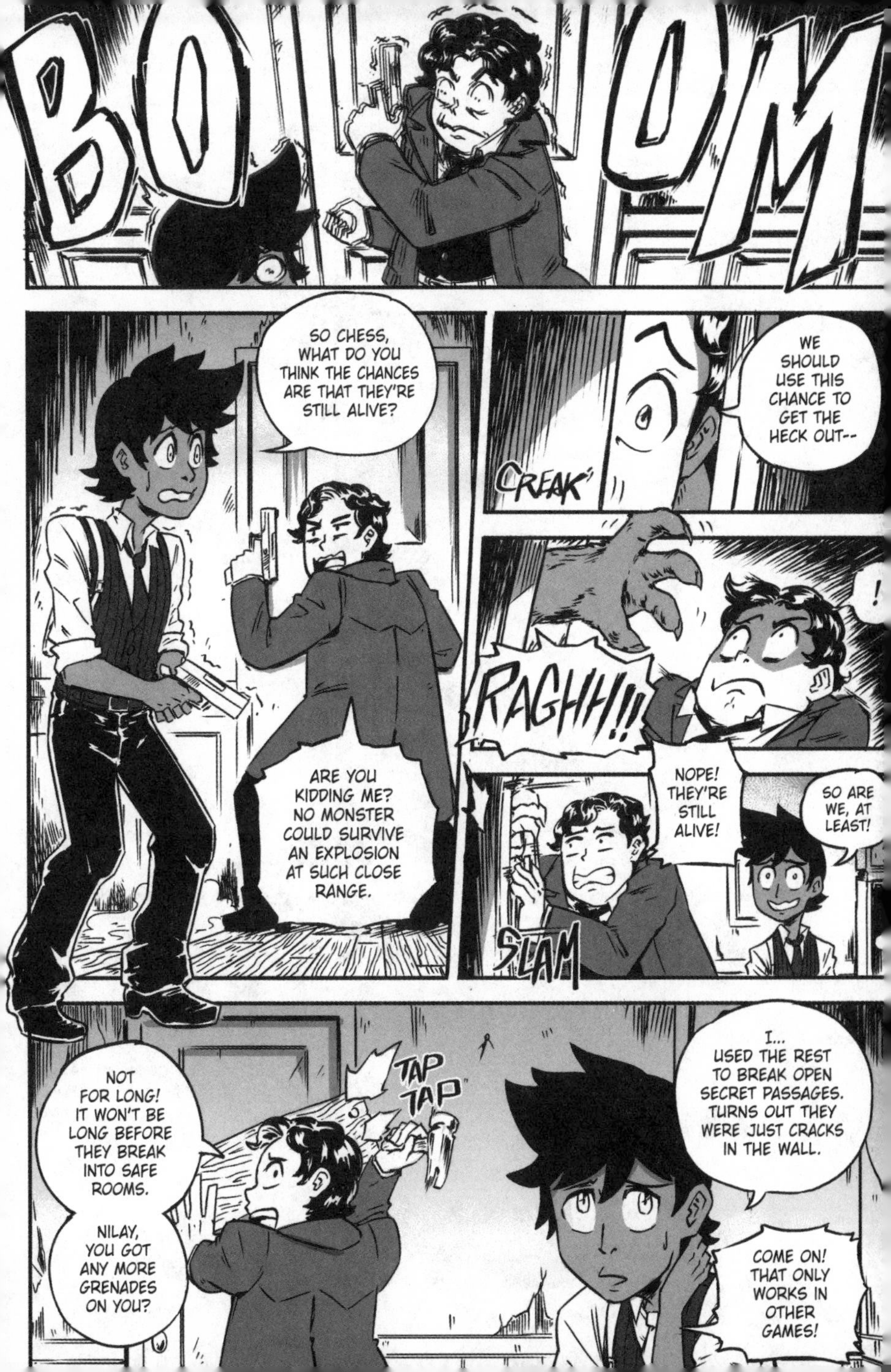
BOOOM
SO CHESS, WHAT DO YOU THINK THE CHANCES ARE THAT THEY'RE STILL ALIVE?
ARE YOU KIDDING ME? NO MONSTER COULD SURVIVE AN EXPLOSION AT SUCH CLOSE RANGE.
CREAK
WE SHOULD USE THIS CHANCE TO GET THE HECK OUT--
RAGHH!!!
!
NOPE! THEY'RE STILL ALIVE!
SLAM
SO ARE WE, AT LEAST!
NOT FOR LONG! IT WON'T BE LONG BEFORE THEY BREAK INTO SAFE ROOMS.
NILAY, YOU GOT ANY MORE GRENADES ON YOU?
TAP TAP
I... USED THE REST TO BREAK OPEN SECRET PASSAGES. TURNS OUT THEY WERE JUST CRACKS IN THE WALL.
COME ON! THAT ONLY WORKS IN OTHER GAMES!

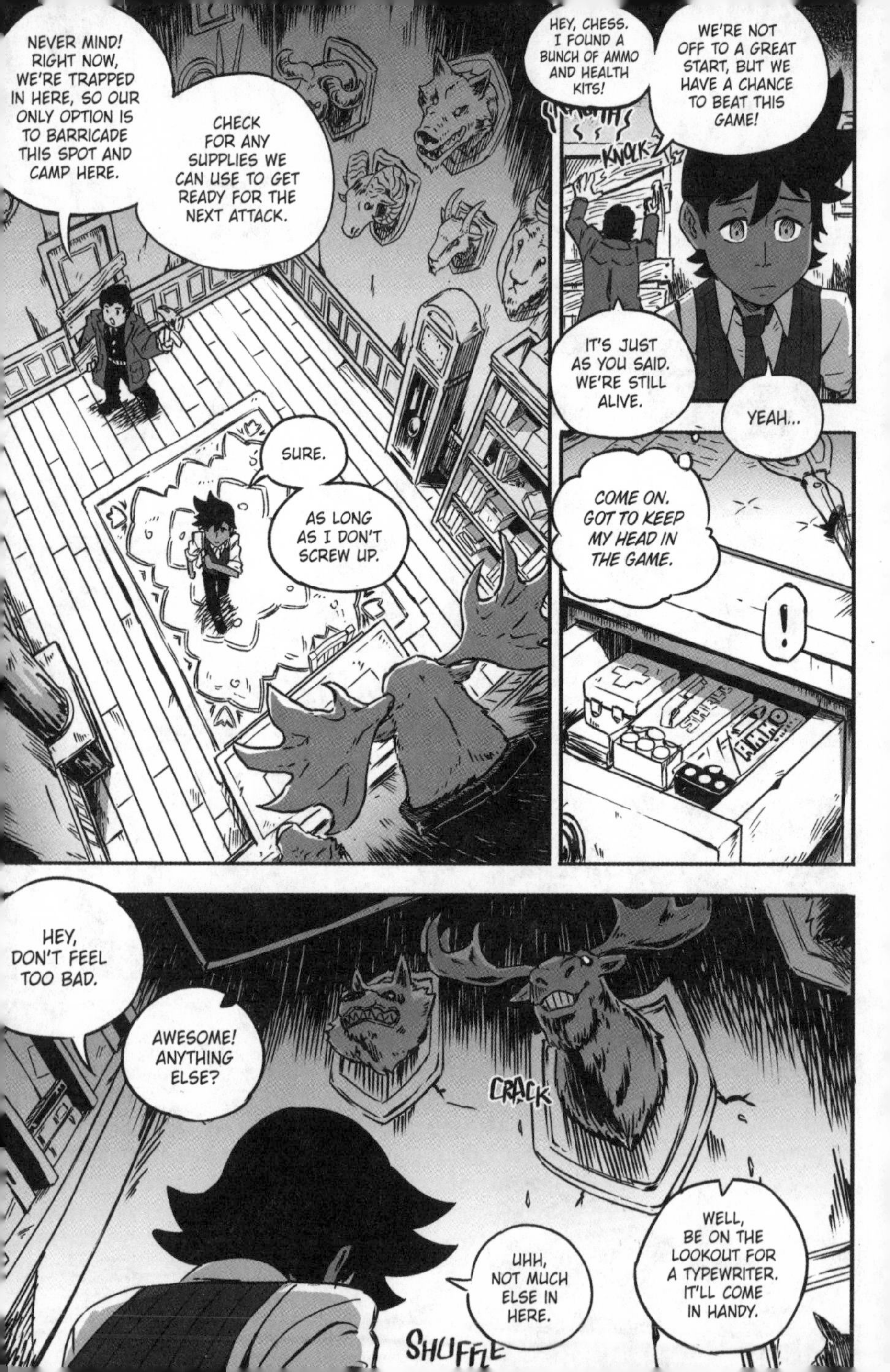
NEVER MIND! RIGHT NOW, WE'RE TRAPPED IN HERE, SO OUR ONLY OPTION IS TO BARRICADE THIS SPOT AND CAMP HERE.
CHECK FOR ANY SUPPLIES WE CAN USE TO GET READY FOR THE NEXT ATTACK.
SURE.
AS LONG AS I DON'T SCREW UP.
HEY, CHESS. I FOUND A BUNCH OF AMMO AND HEALTH KITS!
KNOCK
WE'RE NOT OFF TO A GREAT START, BUT WE HAVE A CHANCE TO BEAT THIS GAME!
IT'S JUST AS YOU SAID. WE'RE STILL ALIVE.
YEAH...
COME ON. GOT TO KEEP MY HEAD IN THE GAME.
!
AMMO
HEY, DON'T FEEL TOO BAD.
AWESOME! ANYTHING ELSE?
CRACK
UHH, NOT MUCH ELSE IN HERE.
WELL, BE ON THE LOOKOUT FOR A TYPEWRITER. IT'LL COME IN HANDY.
SHUFFLE

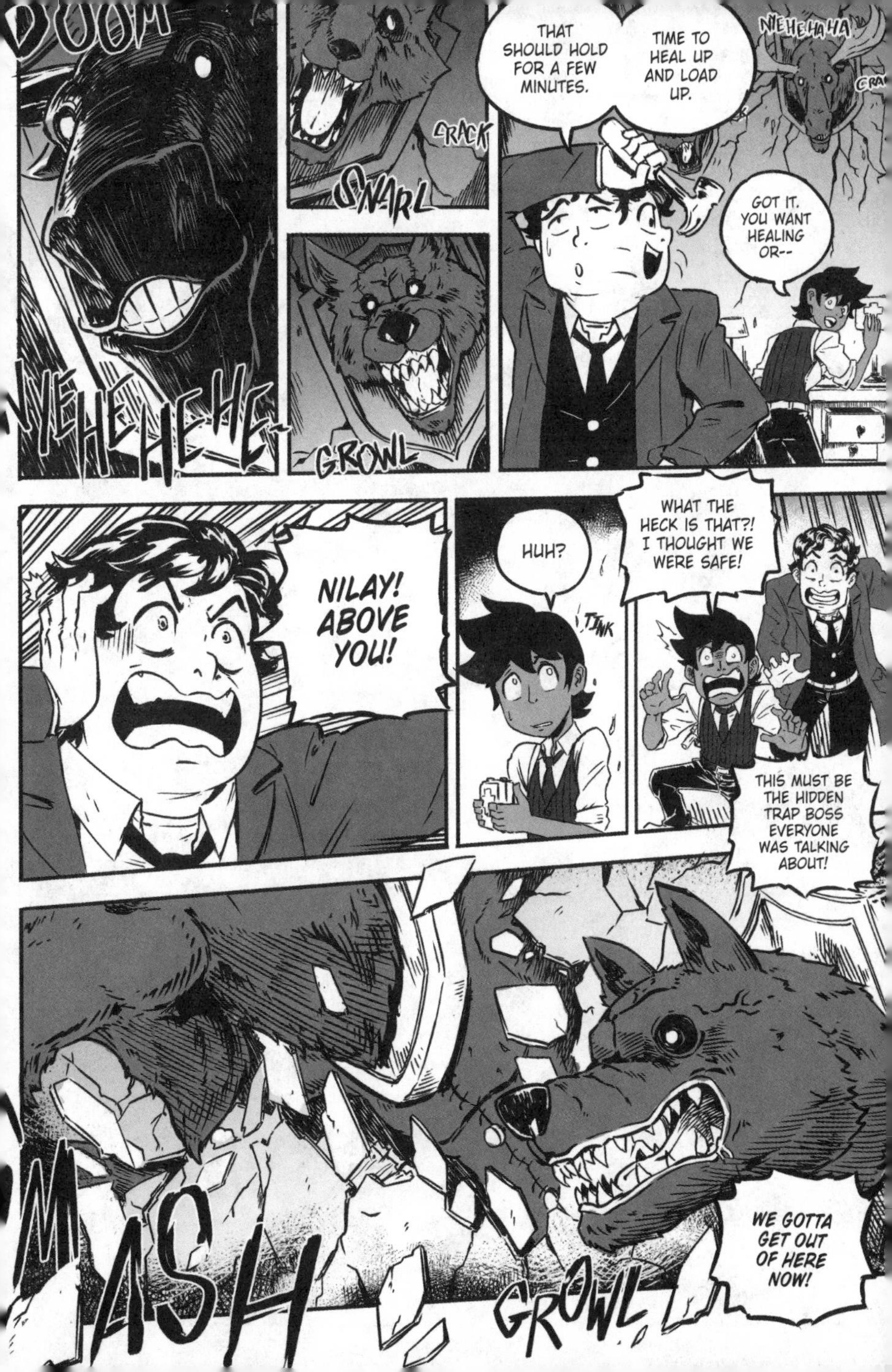
DOOM
NYEHEHEHE-
CRACK
SNARL
GROWL
THAT SHOULD HOLD FOR A FEW MINUTES.
TIME TO HEAL UP AND LOAD UP.
NYEHEHAHA
GOT IT. YOU WANT HEALING OR--
NILAY! ABOVE YOU!
HUH?
TINK
WHAT THE HECK IS THAT?! I THOUGHT WE WERE SAFE!
THIS MUST BE THE HIDDEN TRAP BOSS EVERYONE WAS TALKING ABOUT!
MASH
GROWL
WE GOTTA GET OUT OF HERE NOW!

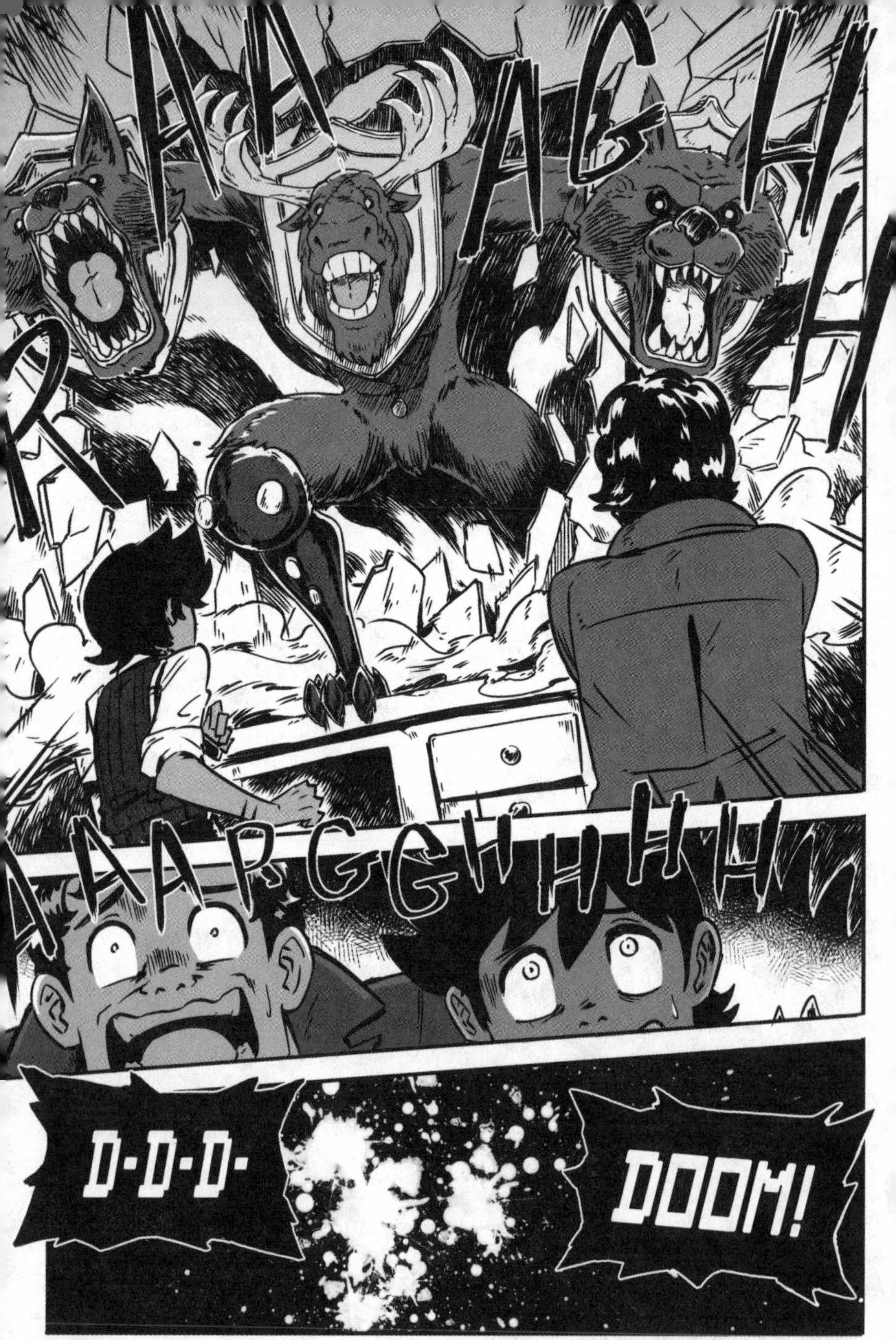
RAAAAAGHHH
AAARGGHHHHH
D-D-D-
DOOM!

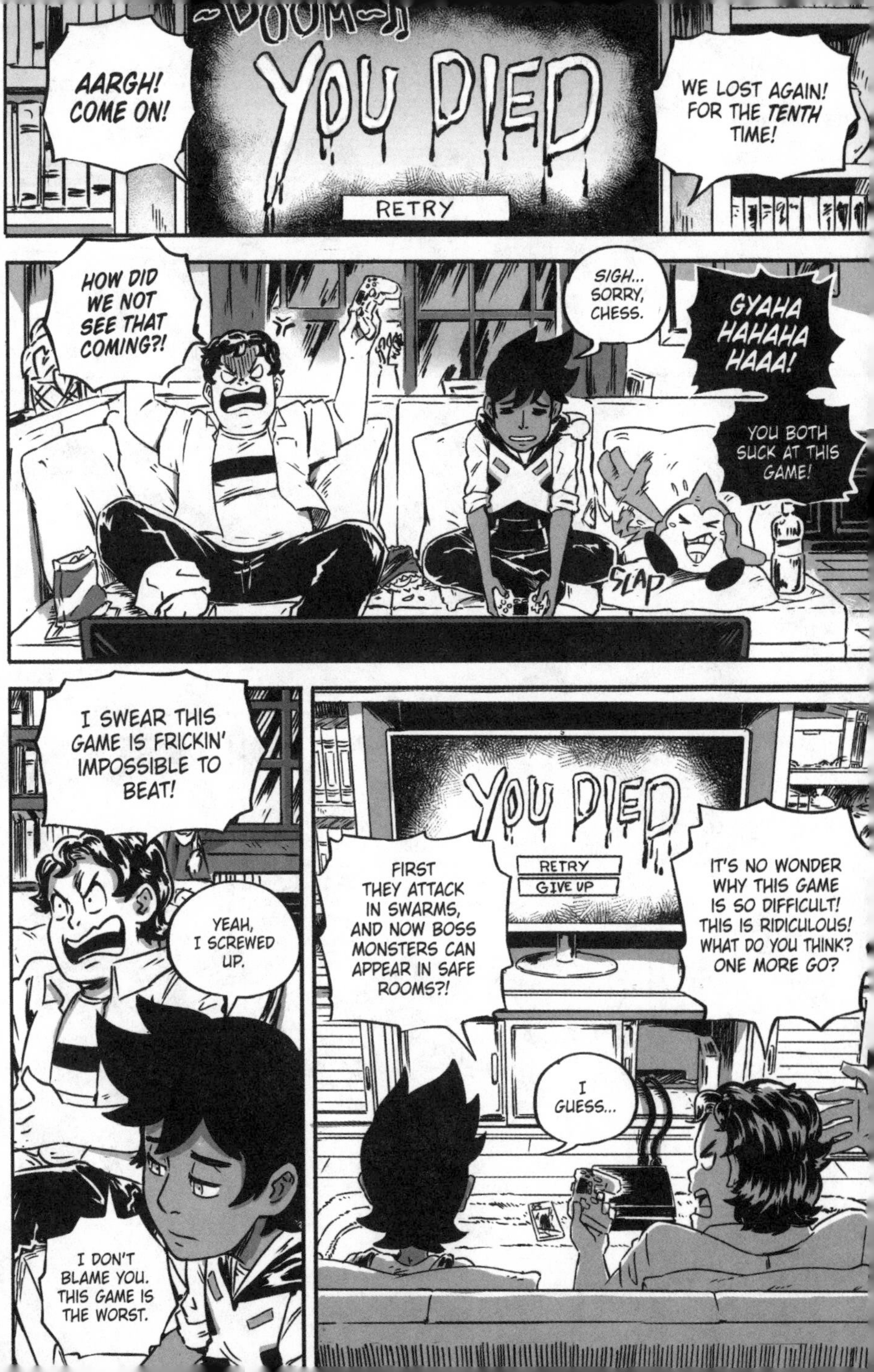

~DOOM~♪
AARGH! COME ON!
YOU DIED
RETRY
WE LOST AGAIN! FOR THE TENTH TIME!
HOW DID WE NOT SEE THAT COMING?!
SIGH... SORRY, CHESS.
GYAHA HAHAHA HAAA!
YOU BOTH SUCK AT THIS GAME!
SLAP
I SWEAR THIS GAME IS FRICKIN' IMPOSSIBLE TO BEAT!
YEAH, I SCREWED UP.
I DON'T BLAME YOU. THIS GAME IS THE WORST.
YOU DIED
RETRY
GIVE UP
FIRST THEY ATTACK IN SWARMS, AND NOW BOSS MONSTERS CAN APPEAR IN SAFE ROOMS?!
IT'S NO WONDER WHY THIS GAME IS SO DIFFICULT! THIS IS RIDICULOUS! WHAT DO YOU THINK? ONE MORE GO?
I GUESS...

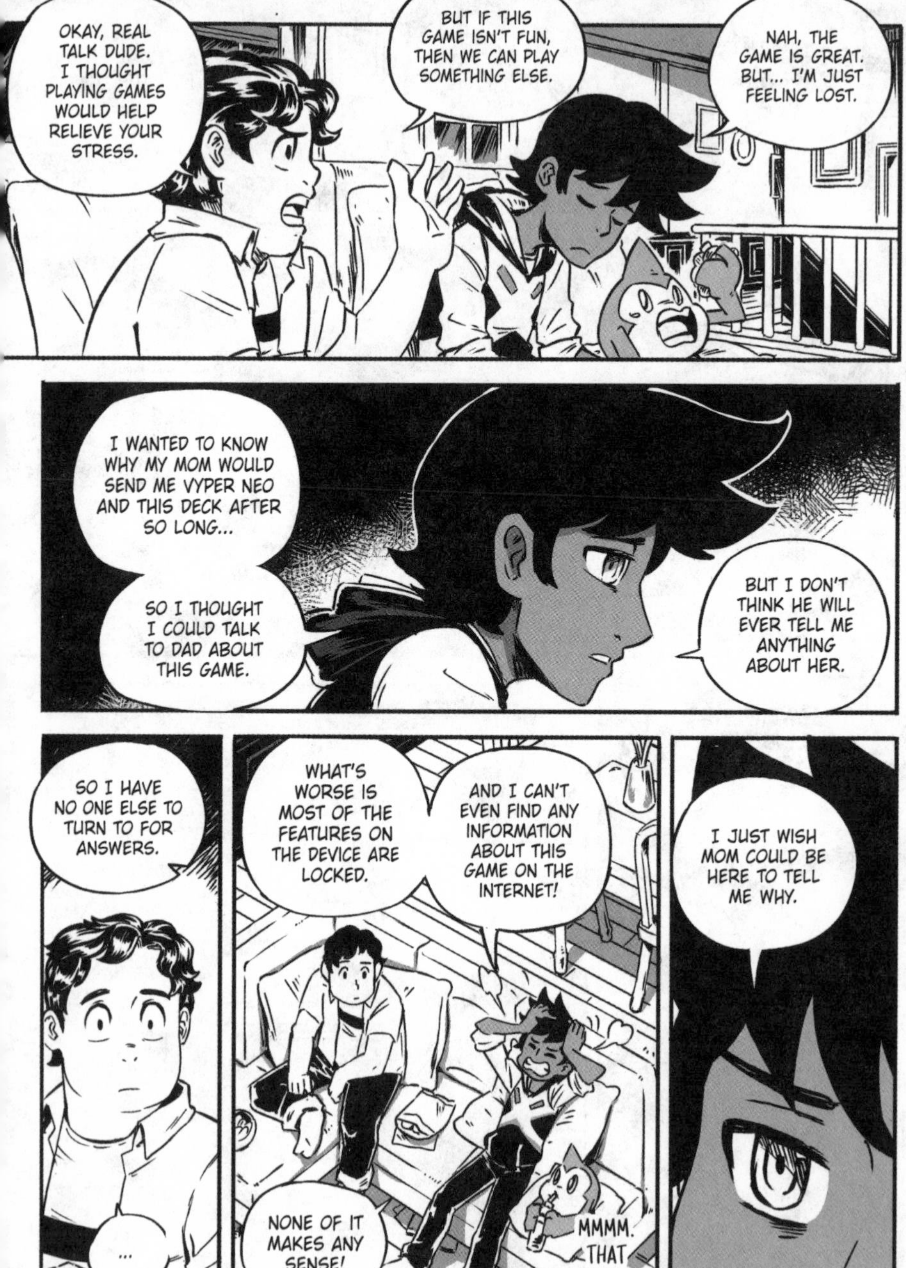
OKAY, REAL TALK DUDE. I THOUGHT PLAYING GAMES WOULD HELP RELIEVE YOUR STRESS.
BUT IF THIS GAME ISN'T FUN, THEN WE CAN PLAY SOMETHING ELSE.
NAH, THE GAME IS GREAT. BUT... I'M JUST FEELING LOST.
I WANTED TO KNOW WHY MY MOM WOULD SEND ME VYPER NEO AND THIS DECK AFTER SO LONG...
SO I THOUGHT I COULD TALK TO DAD ABOUT THIS GAME.
BUT I DON'T THINK HE WILL EVER TELL ME ANYTHING ABOUT HER.
SO I HAVE NO ONE ELSE TO TURN TO FOR ANSWERS.
...
WHAT'S WORSE IS MOST OF THE FEATURES ON THE DEVICE ARE LOCKED.
AND I CAN'T EVEN FIND ANY INFORMATION ABOUT THIS GAME ON THE INTERNET!
NONE OF IT MAKES ANY SENSE!
MMMM. THAT SUCKS.
I JUST WISH MOM COULD BE HERE TO TELL ME WHY.

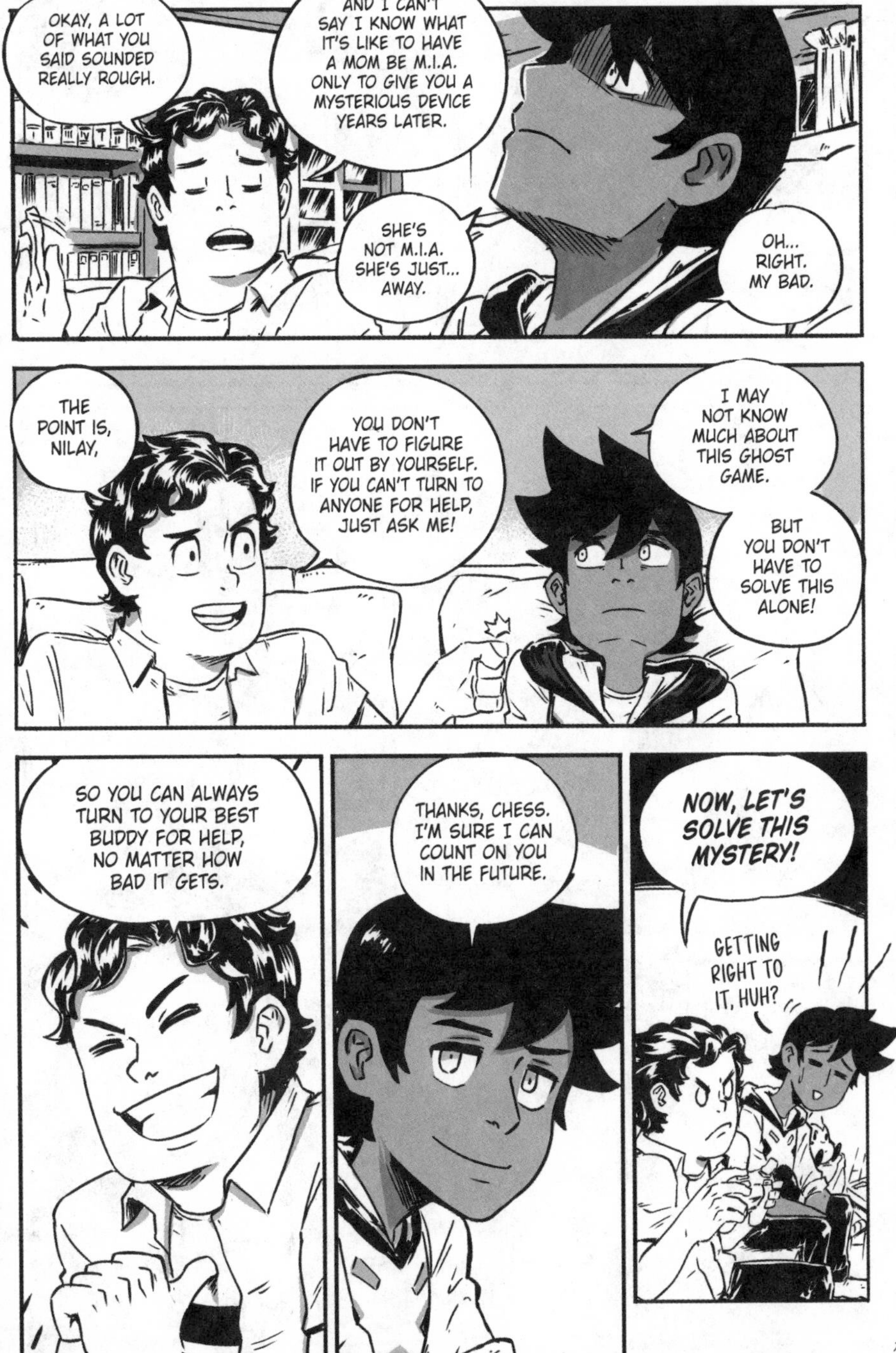
OKAY, A LOT OF WHAT YOU SAID SOUNDED REALLY ROUGH.
AND I CAN'T SAY I KNOW WHAT IT'S LIKE TO HAVE A MOM BE M.I.A. ONLY TO GIVE YOU A MYSTERIOUS DEVICE YEARS LATER.
SHE'S NOT M.I.A. SHE'S JUST... AWAY.
OH... RIGHT. MY BAD.
THE POINT IS, NILAY,
YOU DON'T HAVE TO FIGURE IT OUT BY YOURSELF. IF YOU CAN'T TURN TO ANYONE FOR HELP, JUST ASK ME!
I MAY NOT KNOW MUCH ABOUT THIS GHOST GAME.
BUT YOU DON'T HAVE TO SOLVE THIS ALONE!
SO YOU CAN ALWAYS TURN TO YOUR BEST BUDDY FOR HELP, NO MATTER HOW BAD IT GETS.
THANKS, CHESS. I'M SURE I CAN COUNT ON YOU IN THE FUTURE.
NOW, LET'S SOLVE THIS MYSTERY!
GETTING RIGHT TO IT, HUH?

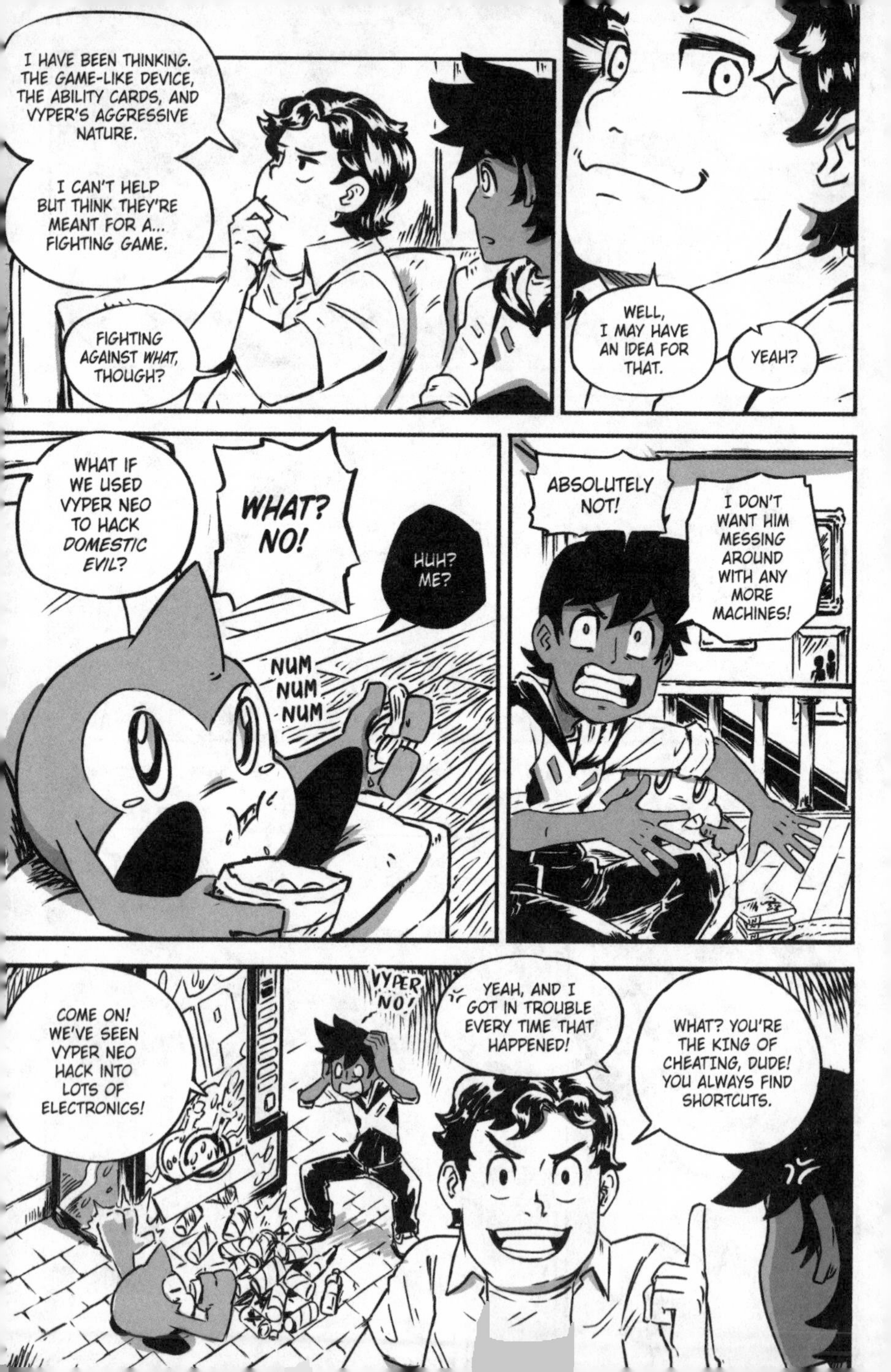
I HAVE BEEN THINKING. THE GAME-LIKE DEVICE, THE ABILITY CARDS, AND VYPER'S AGGRESSIVE NATURE.
I CAN'T HELP BUT THINK THEY'RE MEANT FOR A... FIGHTING GAME.
FIGHTING AGAINST *WHAT*, THOUGH?
WELL, I MAY HAVE AN IDEA FOR THAT.
YEAH?
WHAT IF WE USED VYPER NEO TO HACK *DOMESTIC EVIL*?
WHAT? NO!
HUH? ME?
NUM NUM NUM
ABSOLUTELY NOT!
I DON'T WANT HIM MESSING AROUND WITH ANY MORE MACHINES!
COME ON! WE'VE SEEN VYPER NEO HACK INTO LOTS OF ELECTRONICS!
VYPER NO!
YEAH, AND I GOT IN TROUBLE EVERY TIME THAT HAPPENED!
WHAT? YOU'RE THE KING OF CHEATING, DUDE! YOU ALWAYS FIND SHORTCUTS.

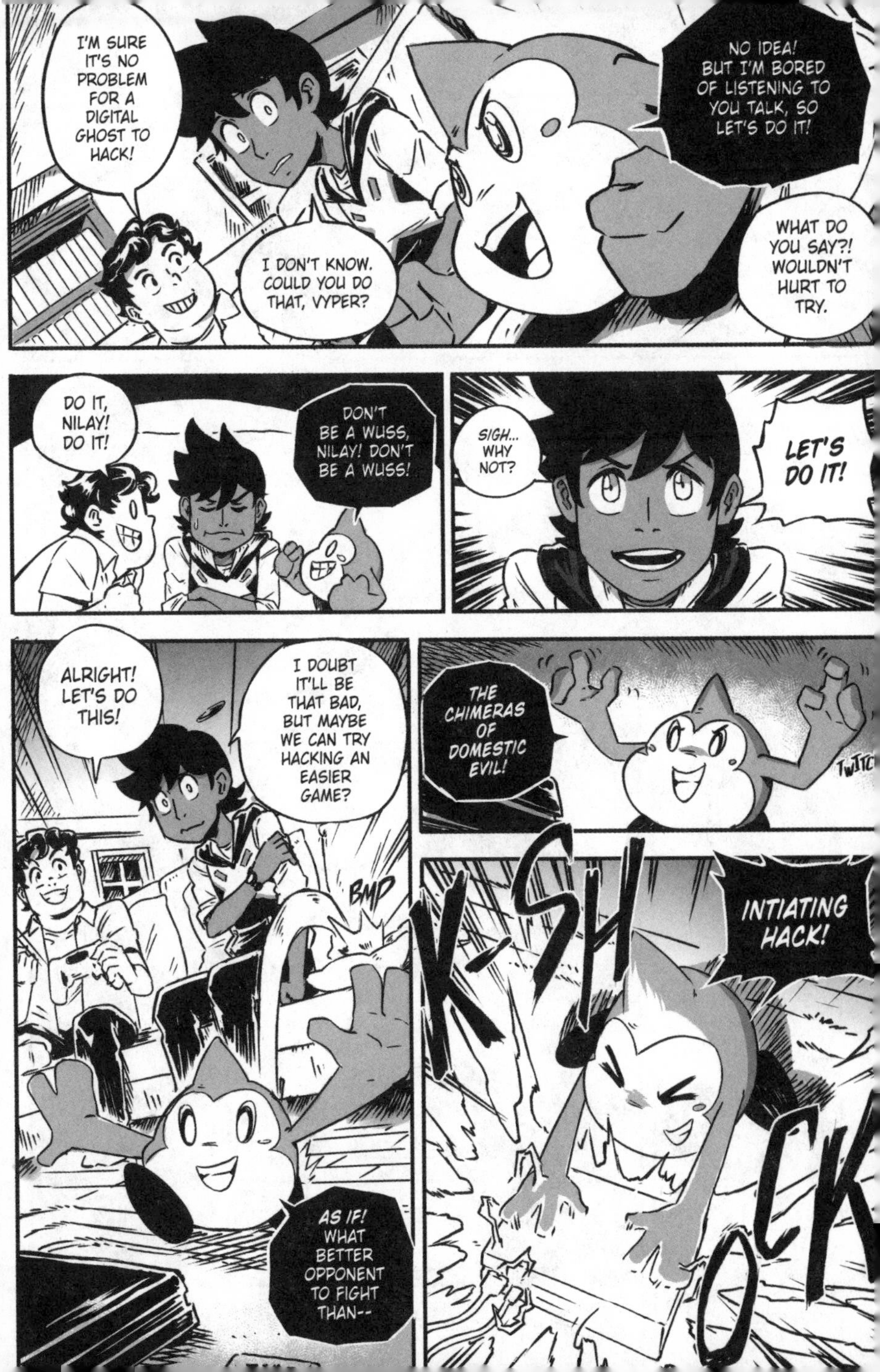
I'M SURE IT'S NO PROBLEM FOR A DIGITAL GHOST TO HACK!
I DON'T KNOW. COULD YOU DO THAT, VYPER?
NO IDEA! BUT I'M BORED OF LISTENING TO YOU TALK, SO LET'S DO IT!
WHAT DO YOU SAY?! WOULDN'T HURT TO TRY.
DO IT, NILAY! DO IT!
DON'T BE A WUSS, NILAY! DON'T BE A WUSS!
SIGH... WHY NOT?
LET'S DO IT!
ALRIGHT! LET'S DO THIS!
I DOUBT IT'LL BE THAT BAD, BUT MAYBE WE CAN TRY HACKING AN EASIER GAME?
BMP
AS IF! WHAT BETTER OPPONENT TO FIGHT THAN--
THE CHIMERAS OF DOMESTIC EVIL!
TWITC
K-SH
INTIATING HACK!
OCK

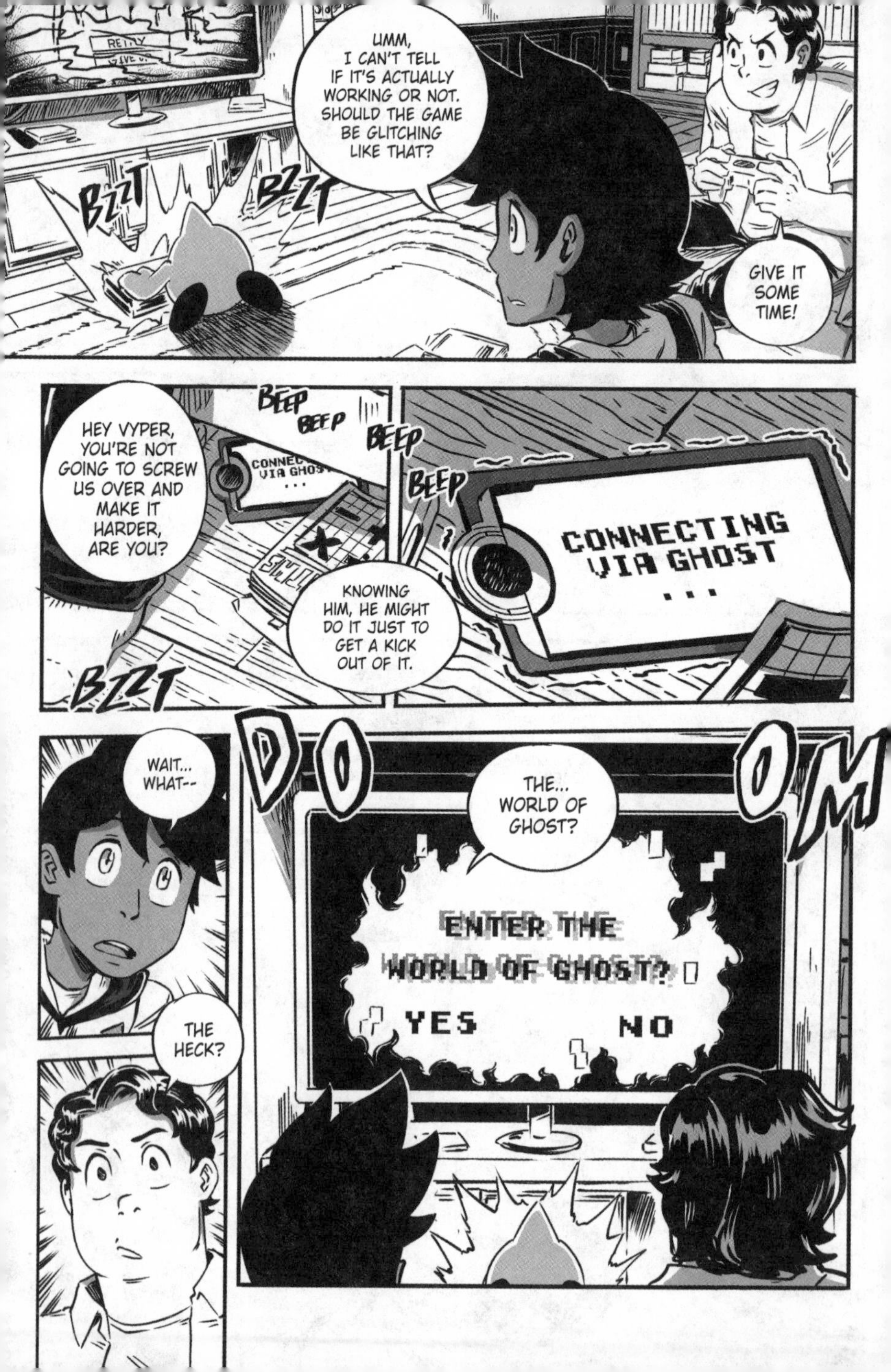
RETRY
GIVE UP
BZZT
BZZT
UMM, I CAN'T TELL IF IT'S ACTUALLY WORKING OR NOT. SHOULD THE GAME BE GLITCHING LIKE THAT?
GIVE IT SOME TIME!
BEEP
BEEP
HEY VYPER, YOU'RE NOT GOING TO SCREW US OVER AND MAKE IT HARDER, ARE YOU?
CONNEC
VIA GHOS
...
BZZT
BEEP
BEEP
CONNECTING VIA GHOST ...
KNOWING HIM, HE MIGHT DO IT JUST TO GET A KICK OUT OF IT.
DOOM
WAIT... WHAT--
THE... WORLD OF GHOST?
ENTER THE WORLD OF GHOST?
YES
NO
THE HECK?

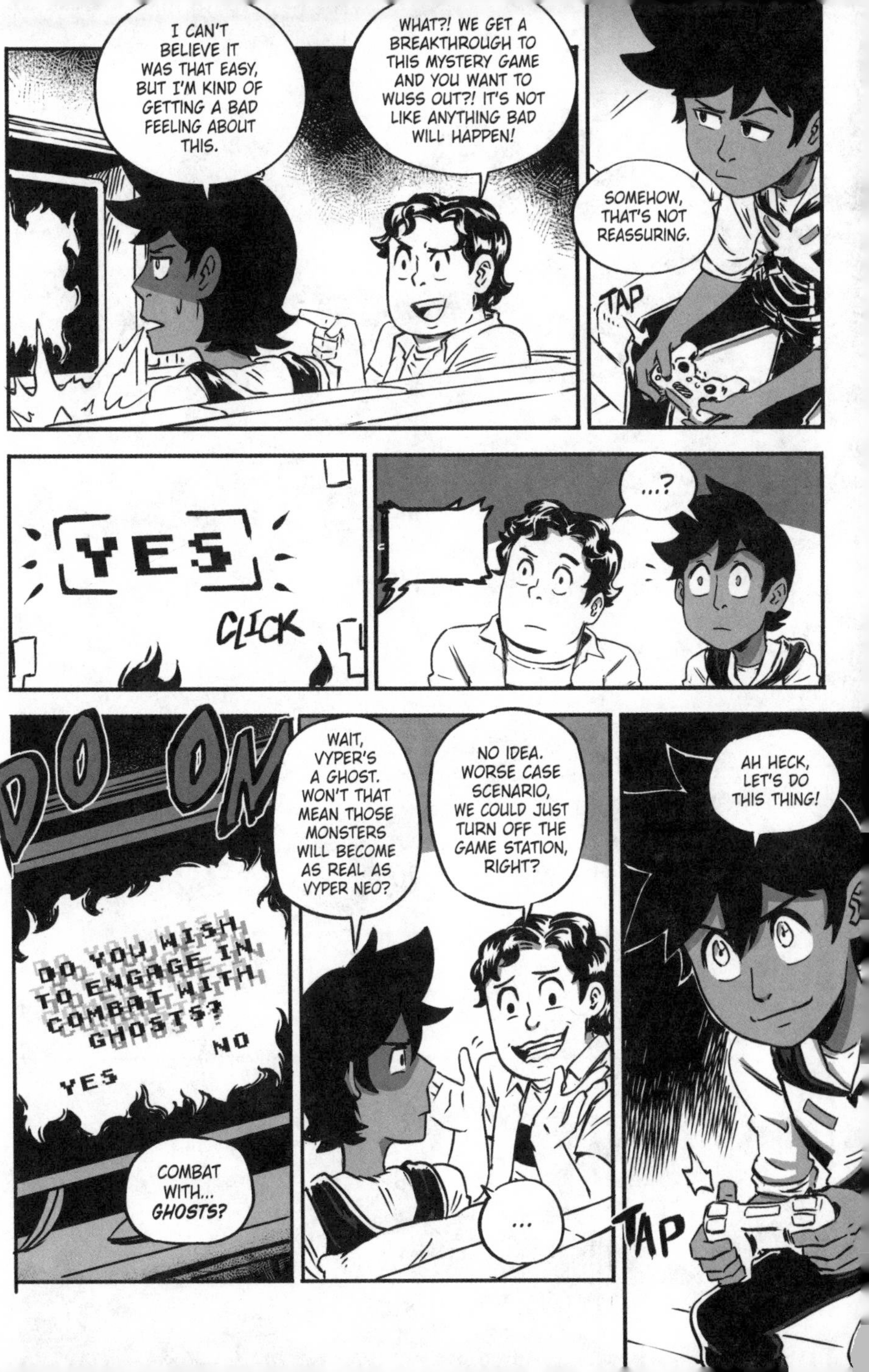
I CAN'T BELIEVE IT WAS THAT EASY, BUT I'M KIND OF GETTING A BAD FEELING ABOUT THIS.
WHAT?! WE GET A BREAKTHROUGH TO THIS MYSTERY GAME AND YOU WANT TO WUSS OUT?! IT'S NOT LIKE ANYTHING BAD WILL HAPPEN!
SOMEHOW, THAT'S NOT REASSURING.
TAP
YES
CLICK
...?
DOOM
DO YOU WISH TO ENGAGE IN COMBAT WITH GHOSTS?
NO
YES
COMBAT WITH... GHOSTS?
WAIT, VYPER'S A GHOST. WON'T THAT MEAN THOSE MONSTERS WILL BECOME AS REAL AS VYPER NEO?
NO IDEA. WORSE CASE SCENARIO, WE COULD JUST TURN OFF THE GAME STATION, RIGHT?
...
AH HECK, LET'S DO THIS THING!
TAP

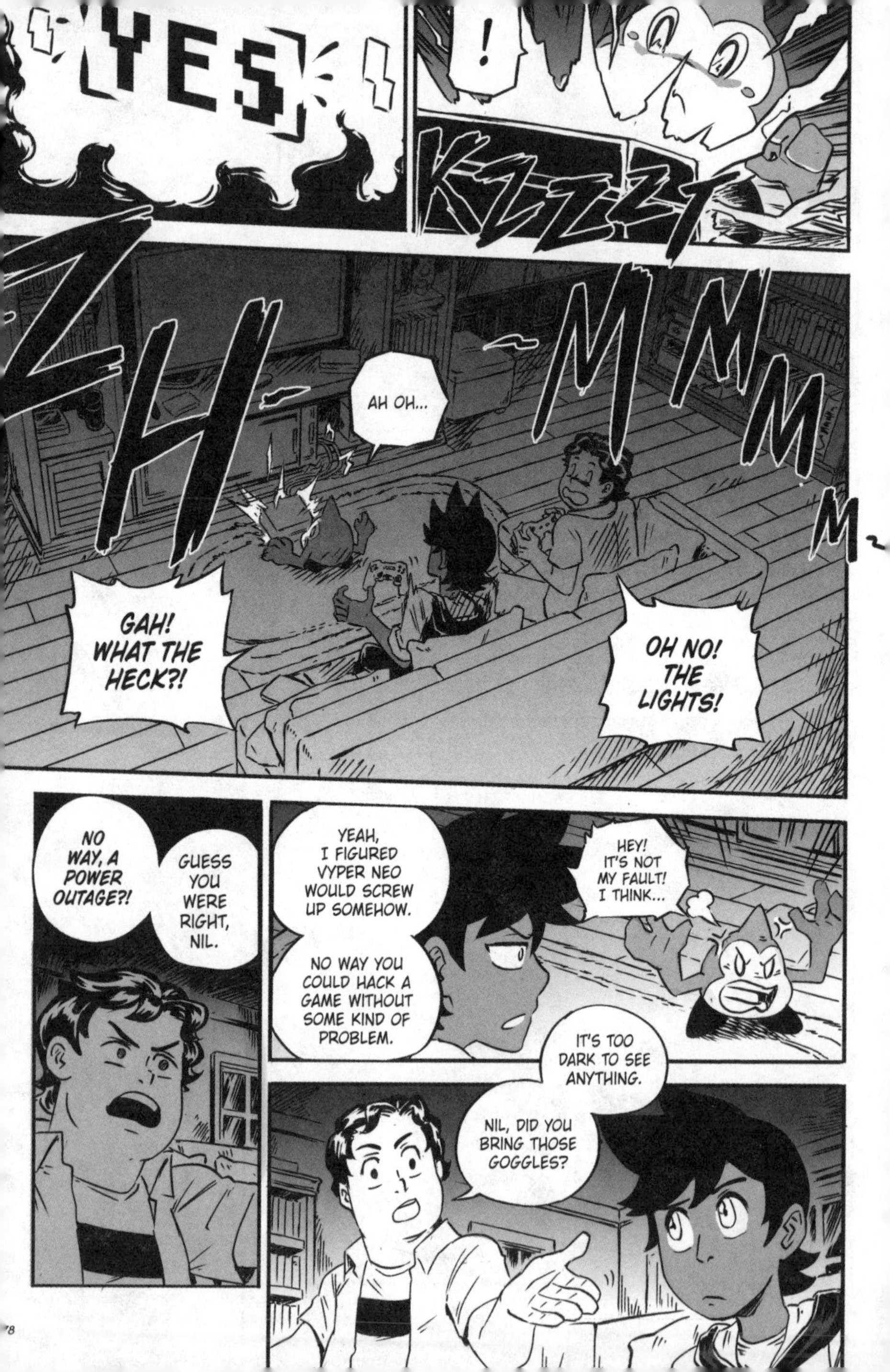

YES
!
KZZZZT
ZHH-MMMMMM
AH OH...
GAH! WHAT THE HECK?!
OH NO! THE LIGHTS!
NO WAY, A POWER OUTAGE?!
GUESS YOU WERE RIGHT, NIL.
YEAH, I FIGURED VYPER NEO WOULD SCREW UP SOMEHOW.
NO WAY YOU COULD HACK A GAME WITHOUT SOME KIND OF PROBLEM.
HEY! IT'S NOT MY FAULT! I THINK...
IT'S TOO DARK TO SEE ANYTHING.
NIL, DID YOU BRING THOSE GOGGLES?

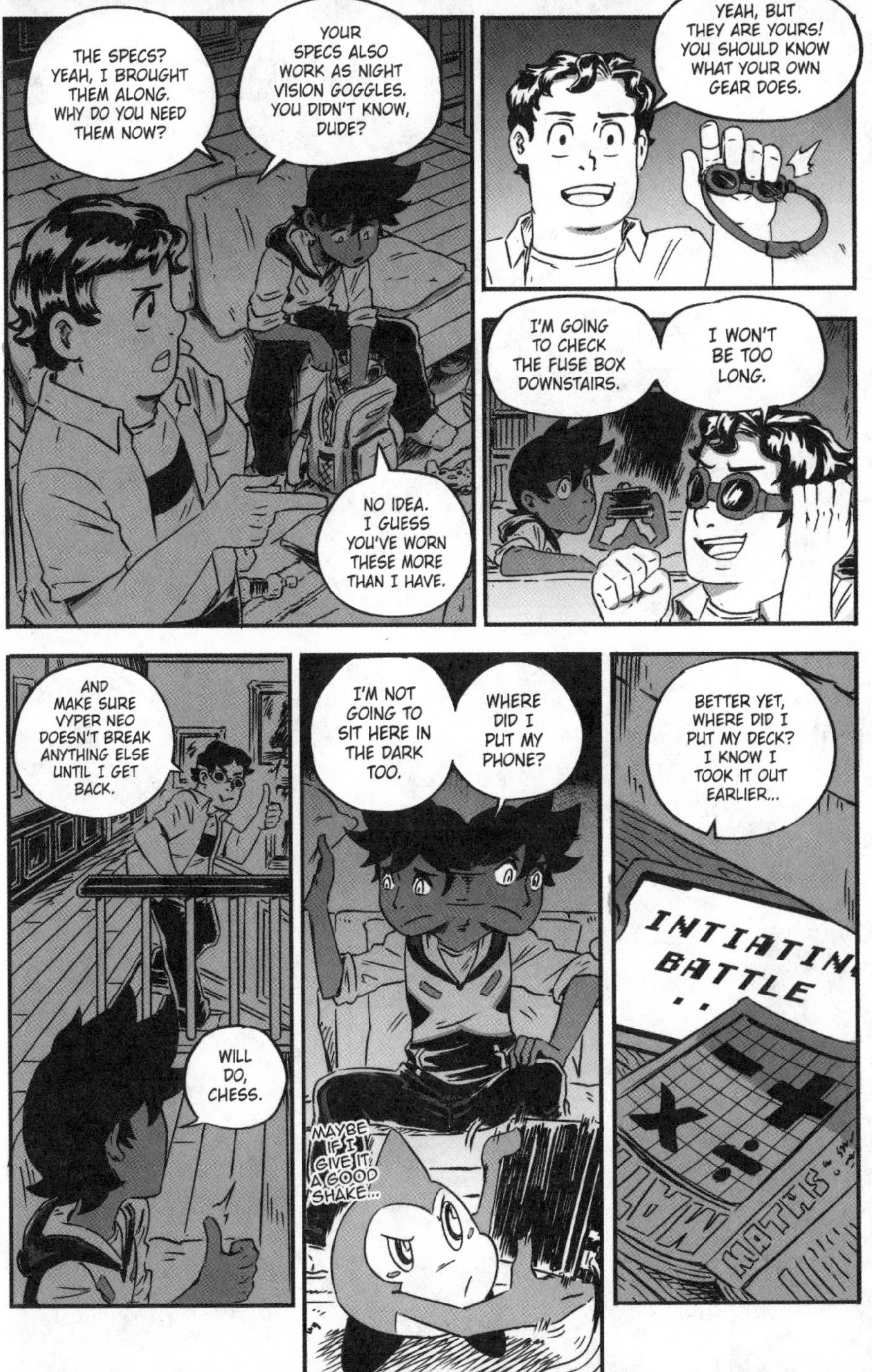
THE SPECS? YEAH, I BROUGHT THEM ALONG. WHY DO YOU NEED THEM NOW?
YOUR SPECS ALSO WORK AS NIGHT VISION GOGGLES. YOU DIDN'T KNOW, DUDE?
NO IDEA. I GUESS YOU'VE WORN THESE MORE THAN I HAVE.
YEAH, BUT THEY ARE YOURS! YOU SHOULD KNOW WHAT YOUR OWN GEAR DOES.
I'M GOING TO CHECK THE FUSE BOX DOWNSTAIRS.
I WON'T BE TOO LONG.
AND MAKE SURE VYPER NEO DOESN'T BREAK ANYTHING ELSE UNTIL I GET BACK.
WILL DO, CHESS.
I'M NOT GOING TO SIT HERE IN THE DARK TOO.
WHERE DID I PUT MY PHONE?
MAYBE IF I GIVE IT A GOOD SHAKE...
BETTER YET, WHERE DID I PUT MY DECK? I KNOW I TOOK IT OUT EARLIER...
INTIATIN
BATTLE
. .

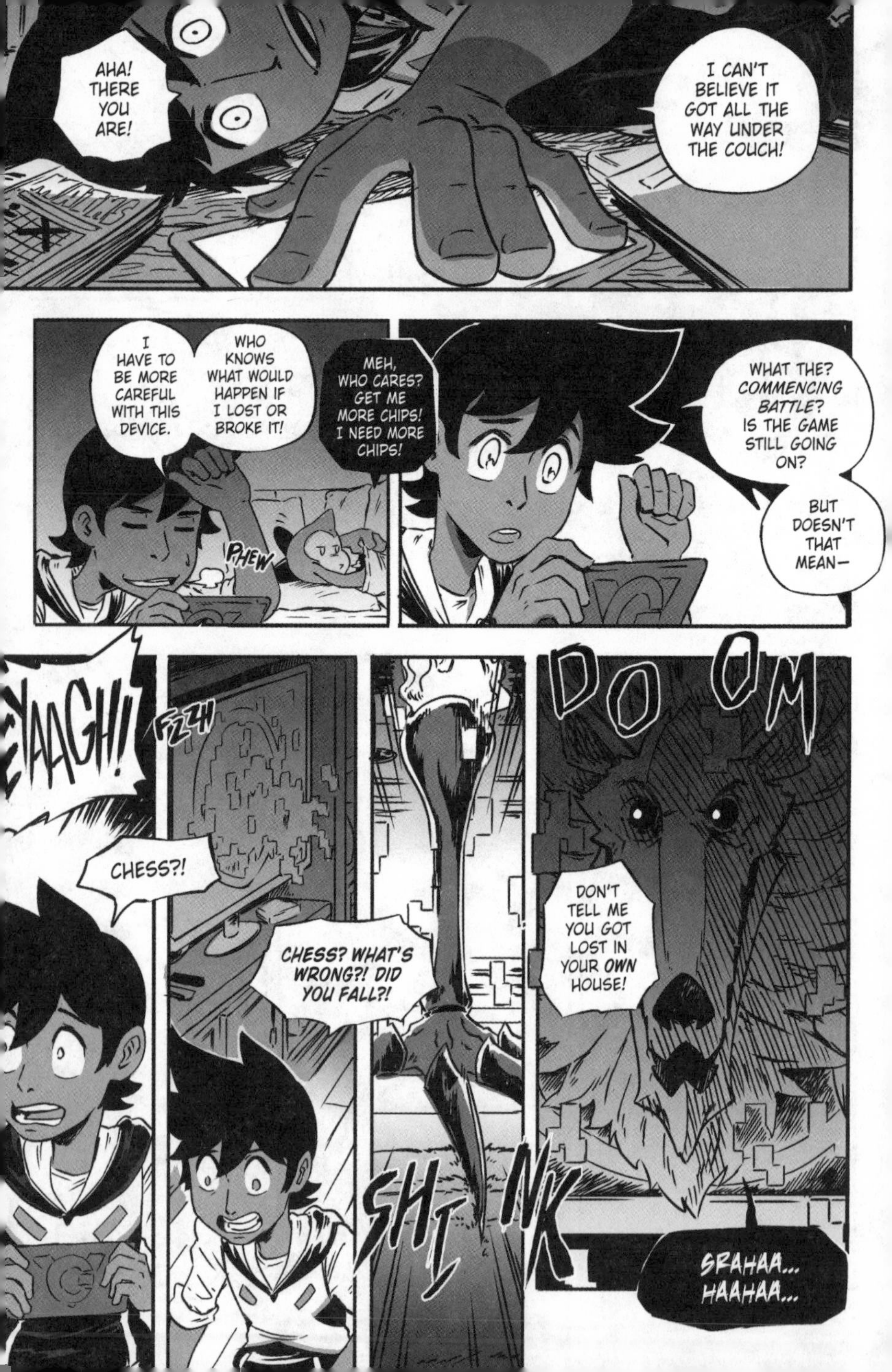
AHA! THERE YOU ARE!
I CAN'T BELIEVE IT GOT ALL THE WAY UNDER THE COUCH!
I HAVE TO BE MORE CAREFUL WITH THIS DEVICE.
WHO KNOWS WHAT WOULD HAPPEN IF I LOST OR BROKE IT!
PHEW
MEH, WHO CARES? GET ME MORE CHIPS! I NEED MORE CHIPS!
WHAT THE? COMMENCING BATTLE? IS THE GAME STILL GOING ON?
BUT DOESN'T THAT MEAN—
YAAGH!
FZZZH
CHESS?!
CHESS? WHAT'S WRONG?! DID YOU FALL?!
SHINK
DOOM
DON'T TELL ME YOU GOT LOST IN YOUR OWN HOUSE!
SRAHAA... HAAHAA...

LEVEL 7
GHOST ATTACK

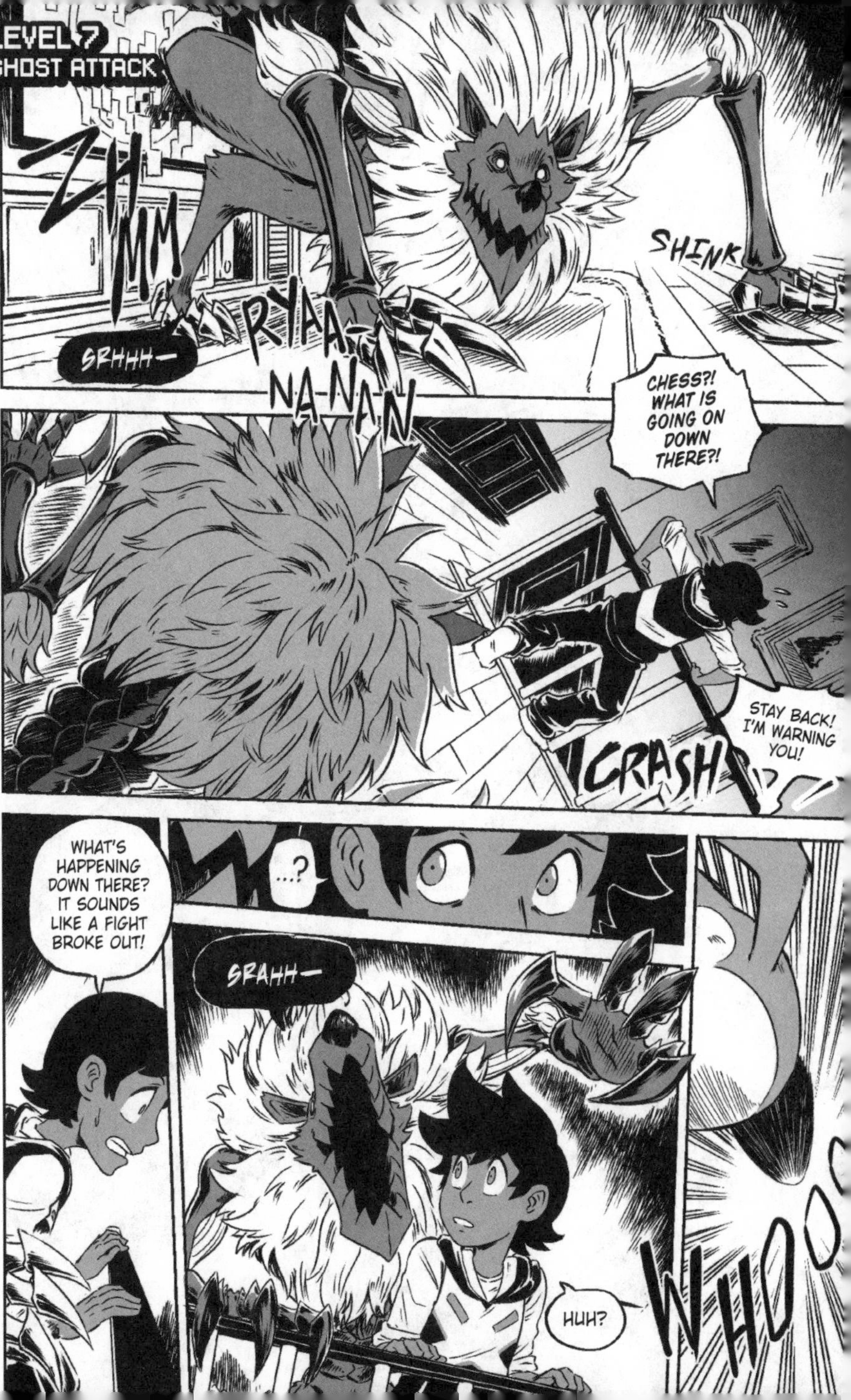
ZHMM
SHINK
SRHHH—
RYAA-NANAN
CHESS?! WHAT IS GOING ON DOWN THERE?!
STAY BACK! I'M WARNING YOU!
CRASH
WHAT'S HAPPENING DOWN THERE? IT SOUNDS LIKE A FIGHT BROKE OUT!
...?
SRAHH—
HUH?
WHOO

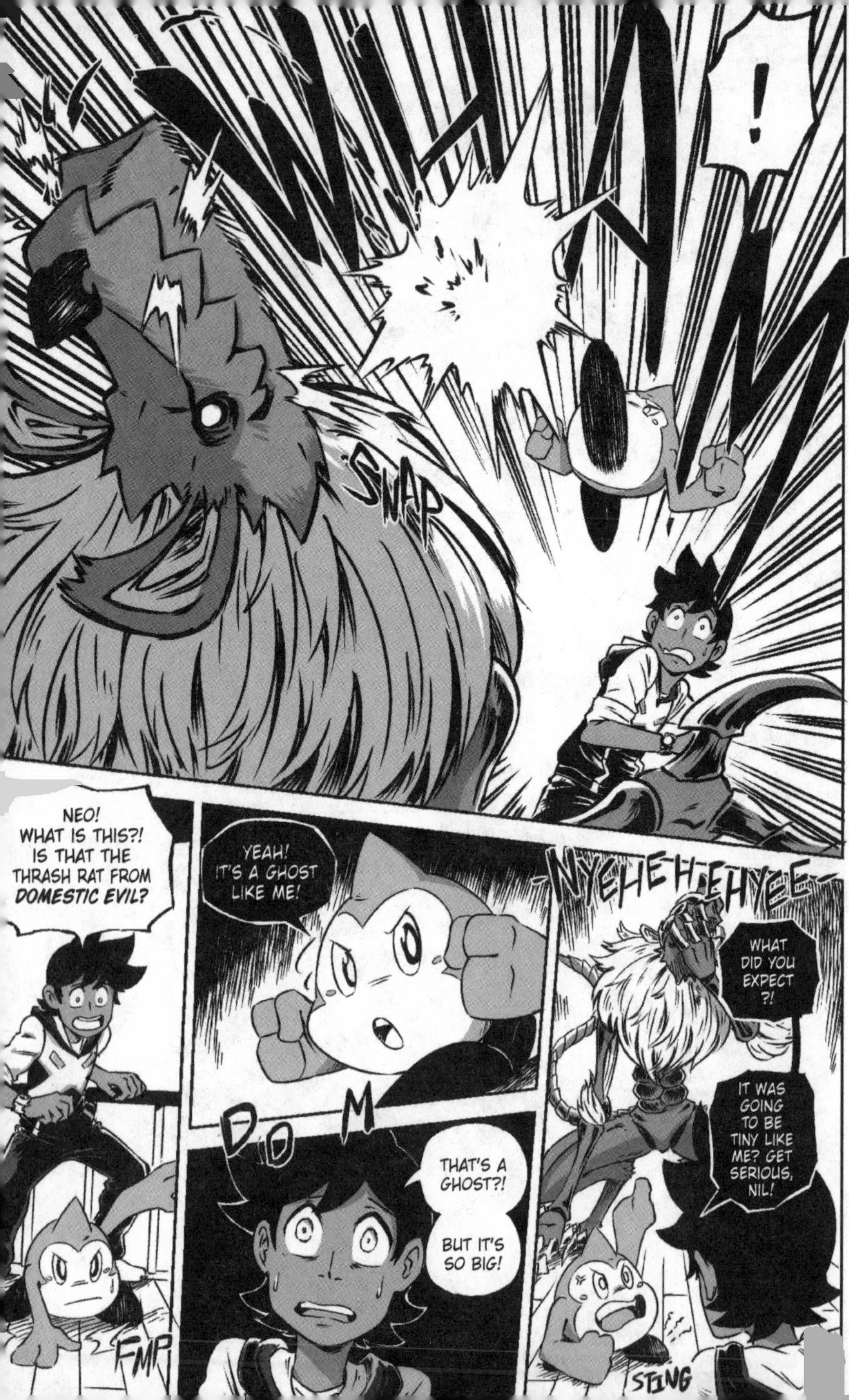
WHAM!
SNAP
NEO! WHAT IS THIS?! IS THAT THE THRASH RAT FROM DOMESTIC EVIL?
FMP
YEAH! IT'S A GHOST LIKE ME!
DOM
THAT'S A GHOST?!
BUT IT'S SO BIG!
NYEHEHEHYEE
WHAT DID YOU EXPECT ?!
IT WAS GOING TO BE TINY LIKE ME? GET SERIOUS, NIL!
STING

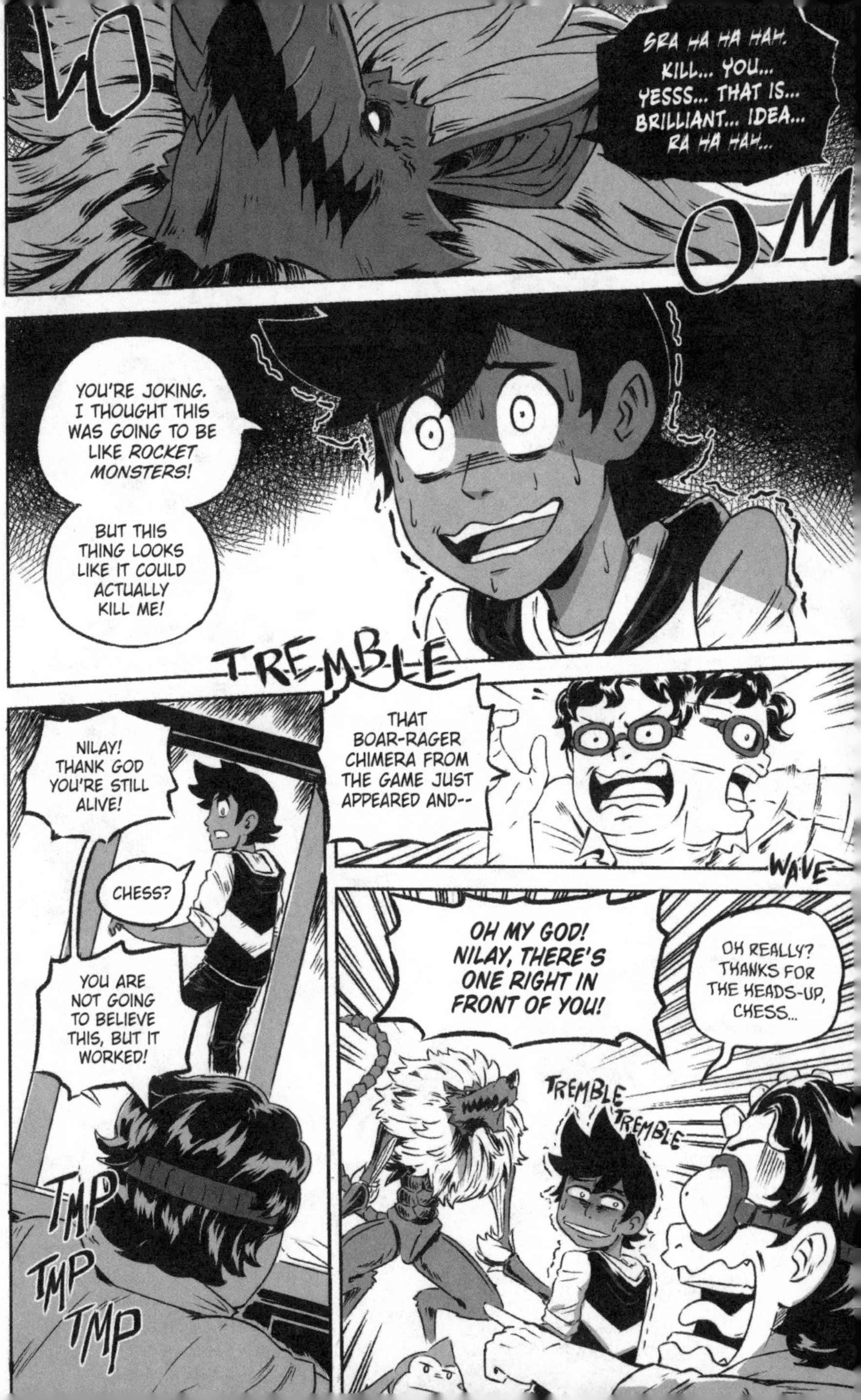
SRA HA HA HAH. KILL... YOU... YESSS... THAT IS... BRILLIANT... IDEA... RA HA HAH...
OM
YOU'RE JOKING. I THOUGHT THIS WAS GOING TO BE LIKE *ROCKET MONSTERS*!
BUT THIS THING LOOKS LIKE IT COULD ACTUALLY KILL ME!
TREMBLE
NILAY! THANK GOD YOU'RE STILL ALIVE!
CHESS?
YOU ARE NOT GOING TO BELIEVE THIS, BUT IT WORKED!
TMP
TMP
TMP
THAT BOAR-RAGER CHIMERA FROM THE GAME JUST APPEARED AND--
WAVE
OH MY GOD! NILAY, THERE'S ONE RIGHT IN FRONT OF YOU!
OH REALLY? THANKS FOR THE HEADS-UP, CHESS...
TREMBLE
TREMBLE

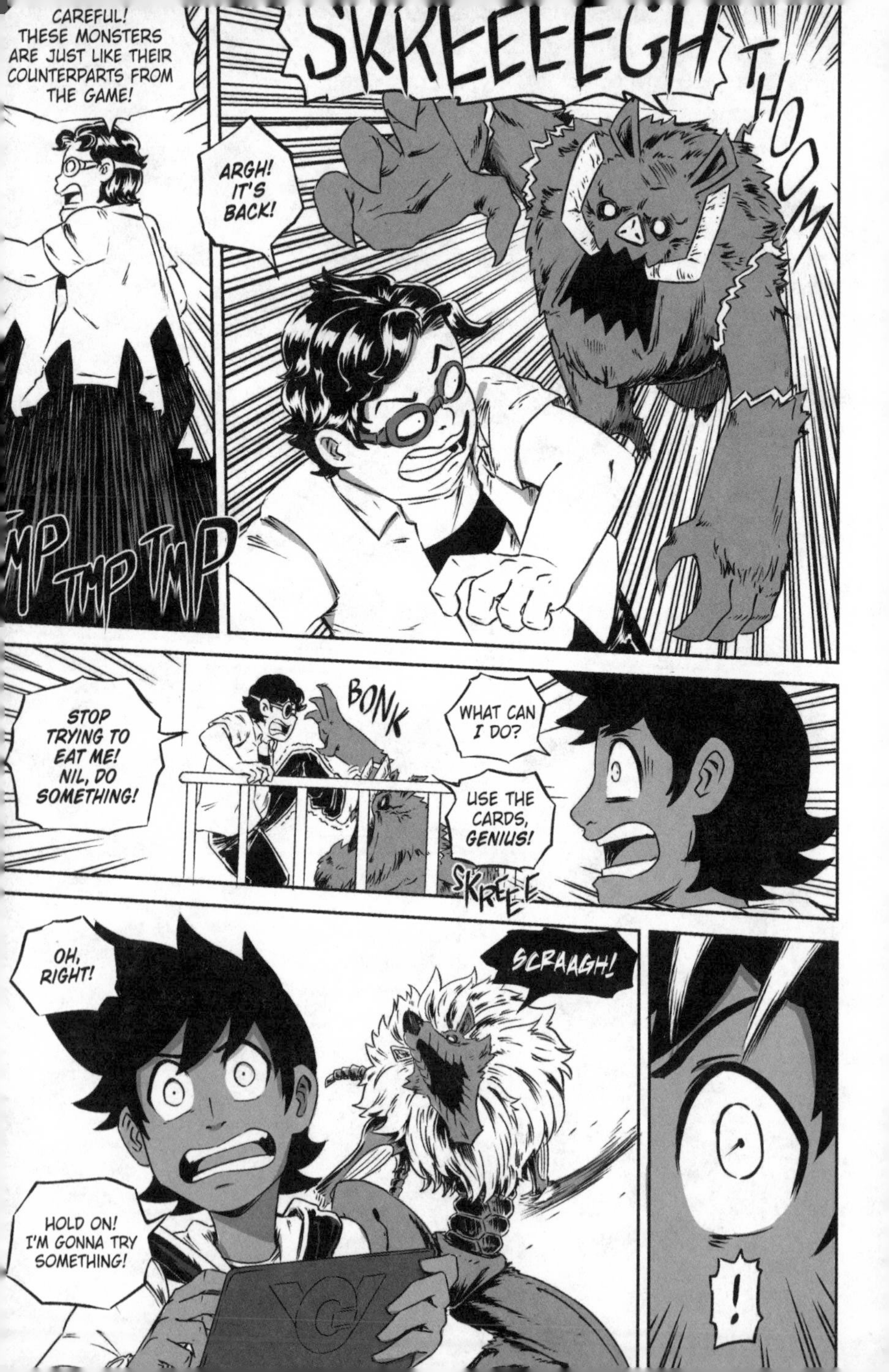
CAREFUL! THESE MONSTERS ARE JUST LIKE THEIR COUNTERPARTS FROM THE GAME!
TMP TMP TMP
SKREEEEGH
THOOM
ARGH! IT'S BACK!
STOP TRYING TO EAT ME! NIL, DO SOMETHING!
BONK
WHAT CAN I DO?
USE THE CARDS, GENIUS!
SKREEE
OH, RIGHT!
SCRAAGH!
HOLD ON! I'M GONNA TRY SOMETHING!
!

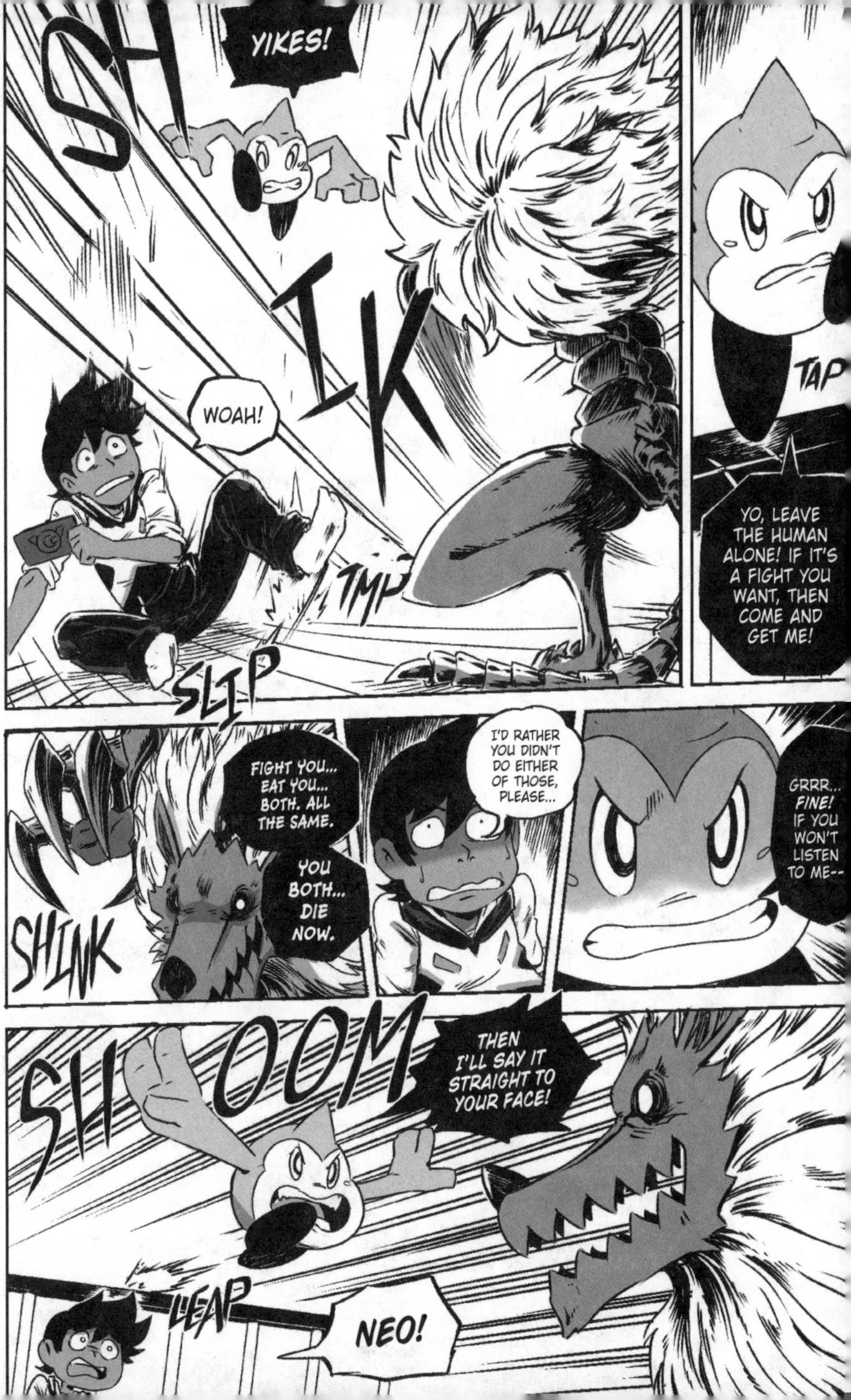
SH
YIKES!
IK
WOAH!
TMP
SLIP
TAP
YO, LEAVE THE HUMAN ALONE! IF IT'S A FIGHT YOU WANT, THEN COME AND GET ME!
FIGHT YOU... EAT YOU... BOTH. ALL THE SAME.
YOU BOTH... DIE NOW.
SHINK
I'D RATHER YOU DIDN'T DO EITHER OF THOSE, PLEASE...
GRRR... FINE! IF YOU WON'T LISTEN TO ME--
SH OOM
THEN I'LL SAY IT STRAIGHT TO YOUR FACE!
LEAP
NEO!

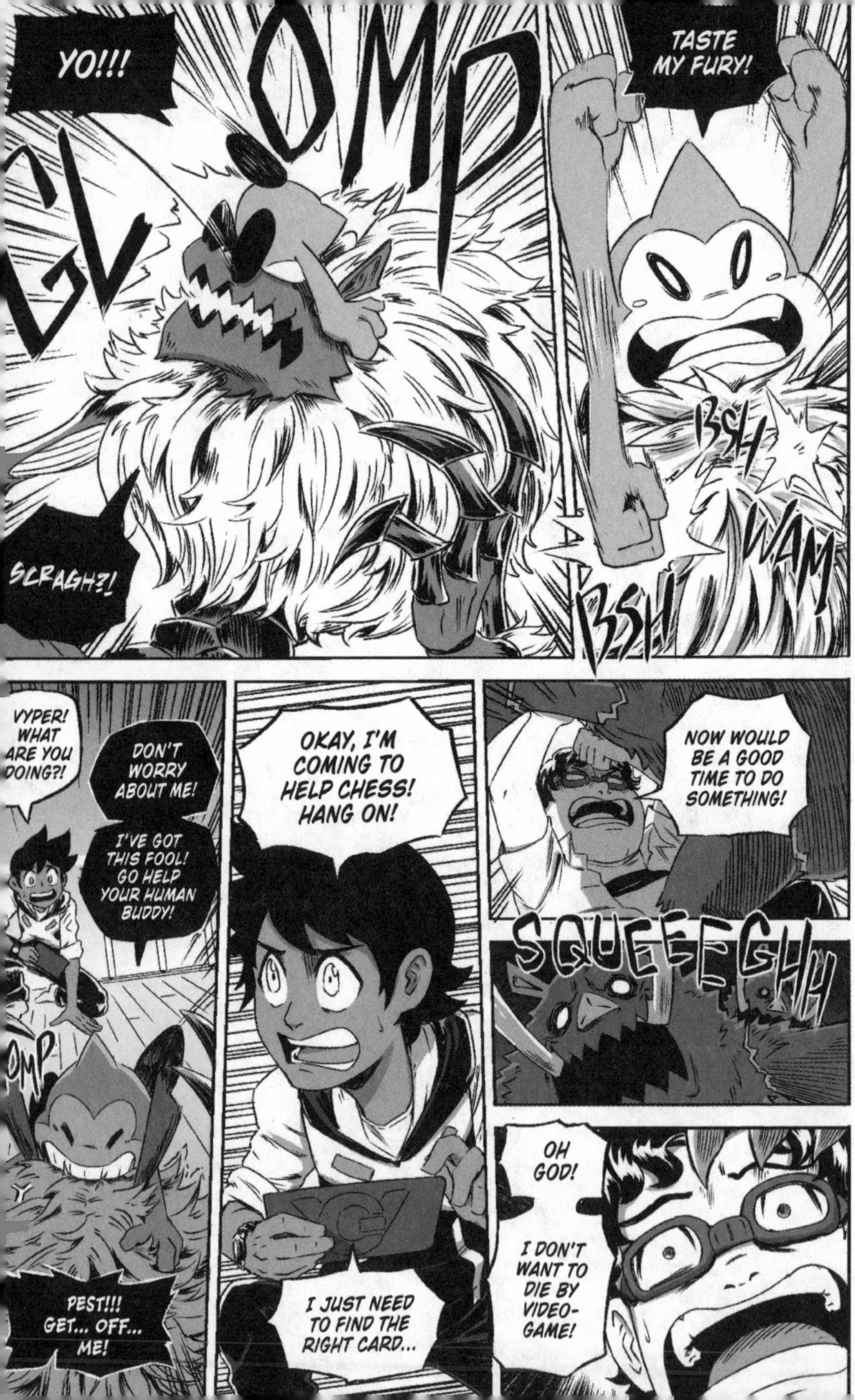
YO!!!
GL-OMP
SCRAGH?!
TASTE MY FURY!
BSH
WAM
BSH
VYPER! WHAT ARE YOU DOING?!
DON'T WORRY ABOUT ME!
I'VE GOT THIS FOOL! GO HELP YOUR HUMAN BUDDY!
OMP
PEST!!! GET... OFF... ME!
OKAY, I'M COMING TO HELP CHESS! HANG ON!
I JUST NEED TO FIND THE RIGHT CARD...
NOW WOULD BE A GOOD TIME TO DO SOMETHING!
SQUEEEGHH
OH GOD!
I DON'T WANT TO DIE BY VIDEO-GAME!

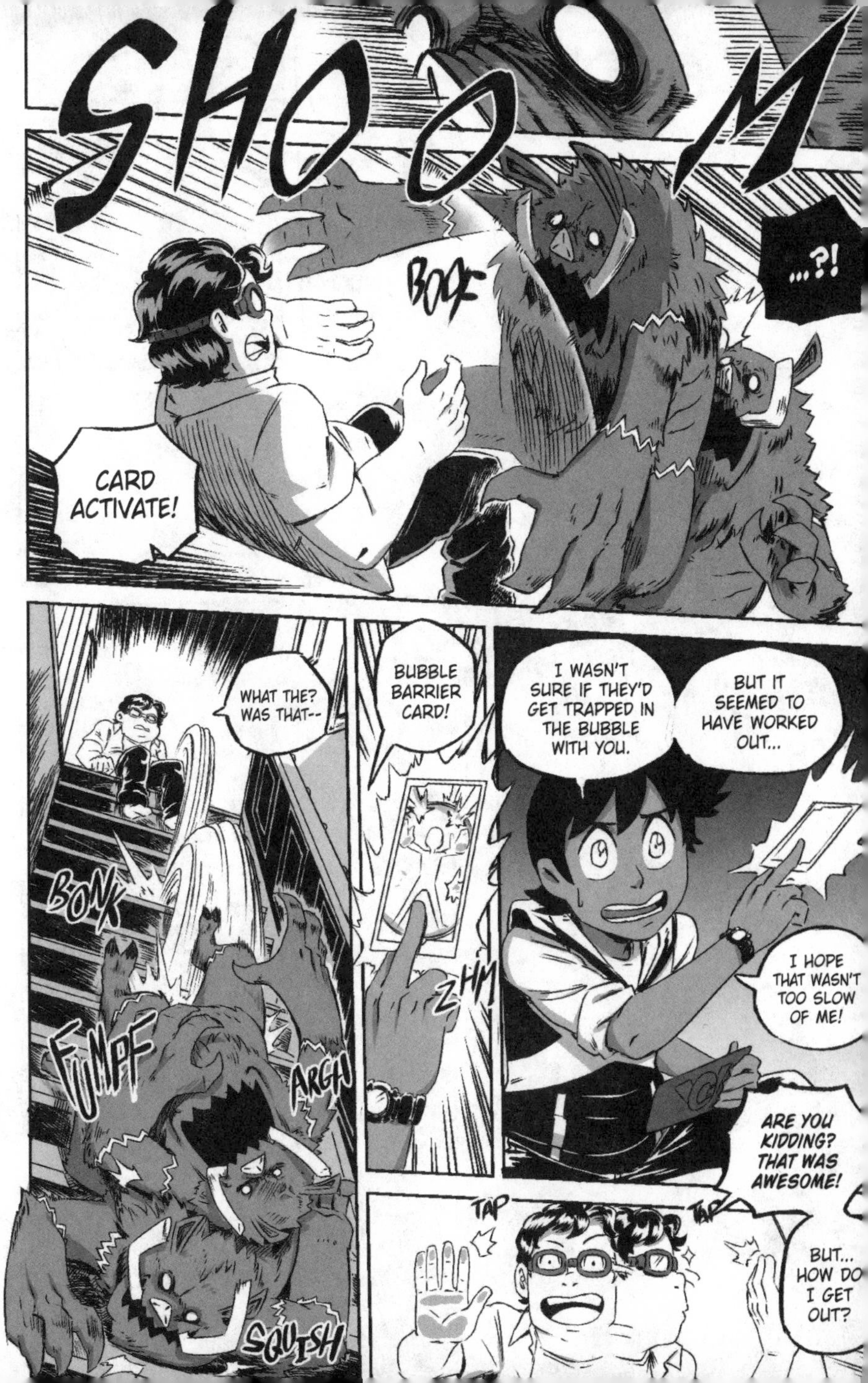
SHOOOM
BOOF
...?!
CARD ACTIVATE!
WHAT THE? WAS THAT--
BONK
FUMPF
ARGH
SQUISH
BUBBLE BARRIER CARD!
ZHM
I WASN'T SURE IF THEY'D GET TRAPPED IN THE BUBBLE WITH YOU.
BUT IT SEEMED TO HAVE WORKED OUT...
I HOPE THAT WASN'T TOO SLOW OF ME!
ARE YOU KIDDING? THAT WAS AWESOME!
TAP
TAP
BUT... HOW DO I GET OUT?

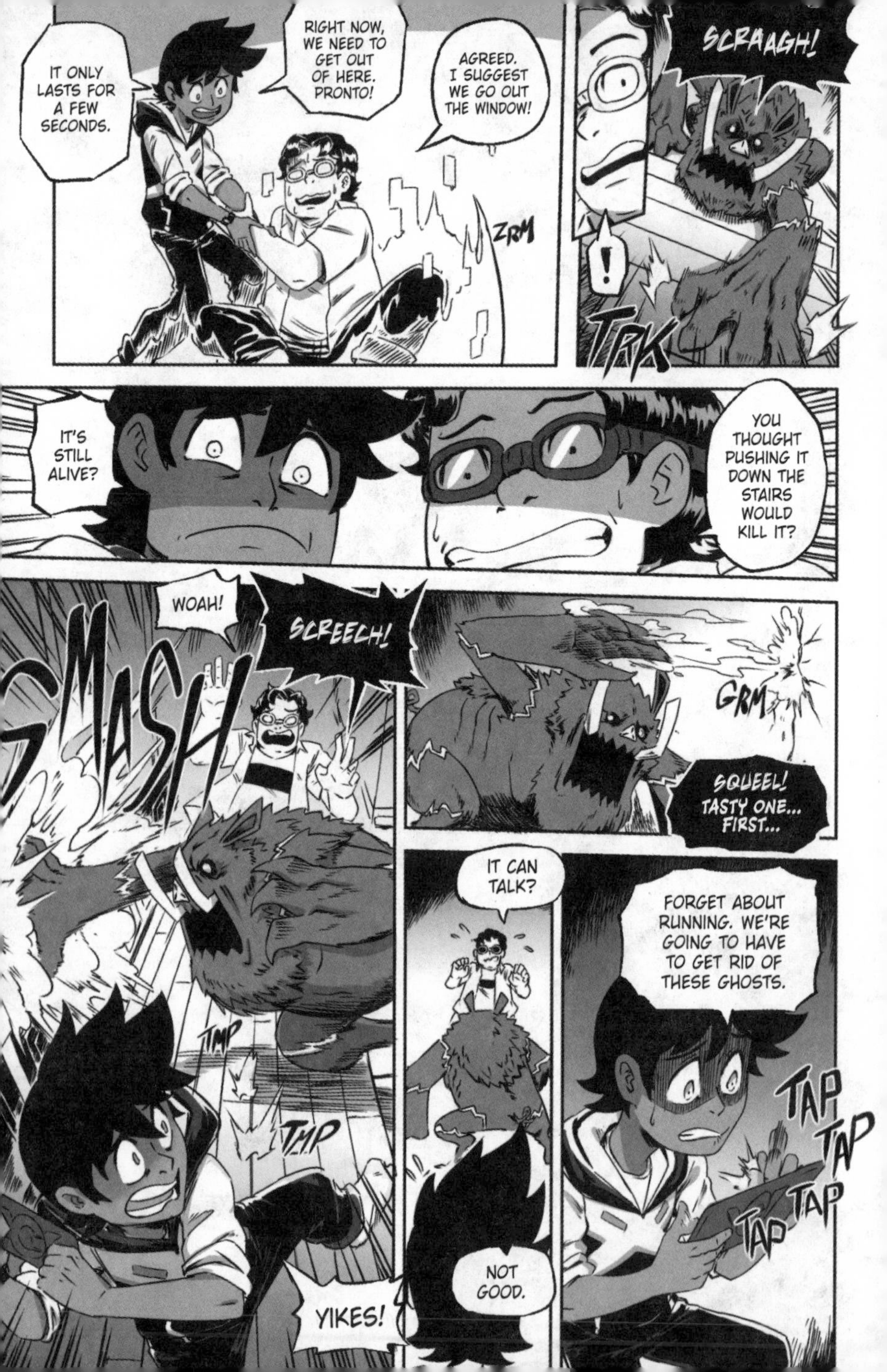
IT ONLY LASTS FOR A FEW SECONDS.
RIGHT NOW, WE NEED TO GET OUT OF HERE. PRONTO!
AGREED. I SUGGEST WE GO OUT THE WINDOW!
ZRM
SCRAAGH!
!
TRK
IT'S STILL ALIVE?
YOU THOUGHT PUSHING IT DOWN THE STAIRS WOULD KILL IT?
SMASH
WOAH!
SCREECH!
TMP
TMP
YIKES!
GRM
SQUEEL! TASTY ONE... FIRST...
IT CAN TALK?
NOT GOOD.
FORGET ABOUT RUNNING. WE'RE GOING TO HAVE TO GET RID OF THESE GHOSTS.
TAP TAP TAP TAP

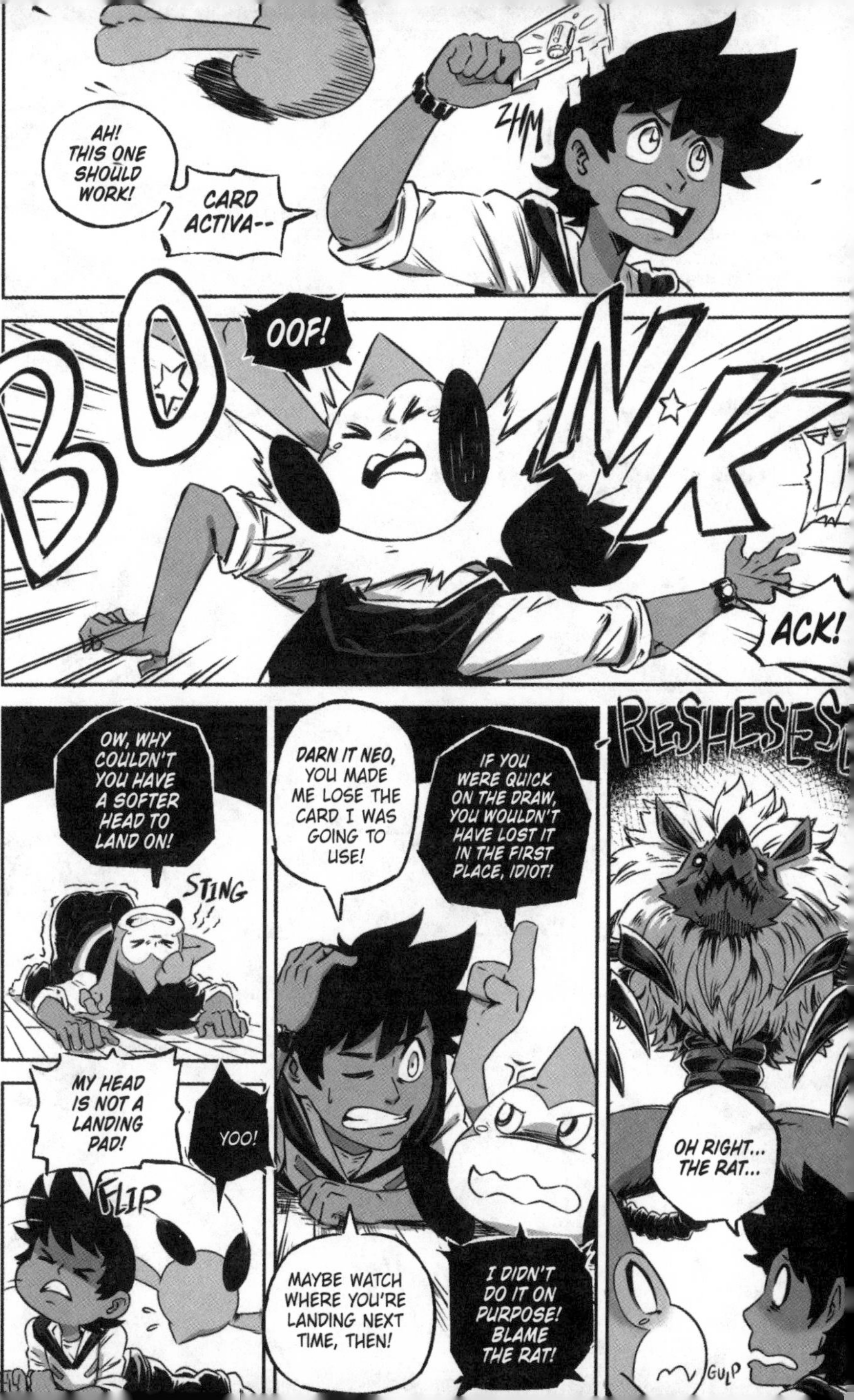

AH! THIS ONE SHOULD WORK!
CARD ACTIVA--
ZHM
BONK
OOF!
ACK!
OW, WHY COULDN'T YOU HAVE A SOFTER HEAD TO LAND ON!
STING
MY HEAD IS NOT A LANDING PAD!
YOO!
FLIP
DARN IT NEO, YOU MADE ME LOSE THE CARD I WAS GOING TO USE!
IF YOU WERE QUICK ON THE DRAW, YOU WOULDN'T HAVE LOST IT IN THE FIRST PLACE, IDIOT!
MAYBE WATCH WHERE YOU'RE LANDING NEXT TIME, THEN!
I DIDN'T DO IT ON PURPOSE! BLAME THE RAT!
RESHESESE
OH RIGHT... THE RAT...
GULP

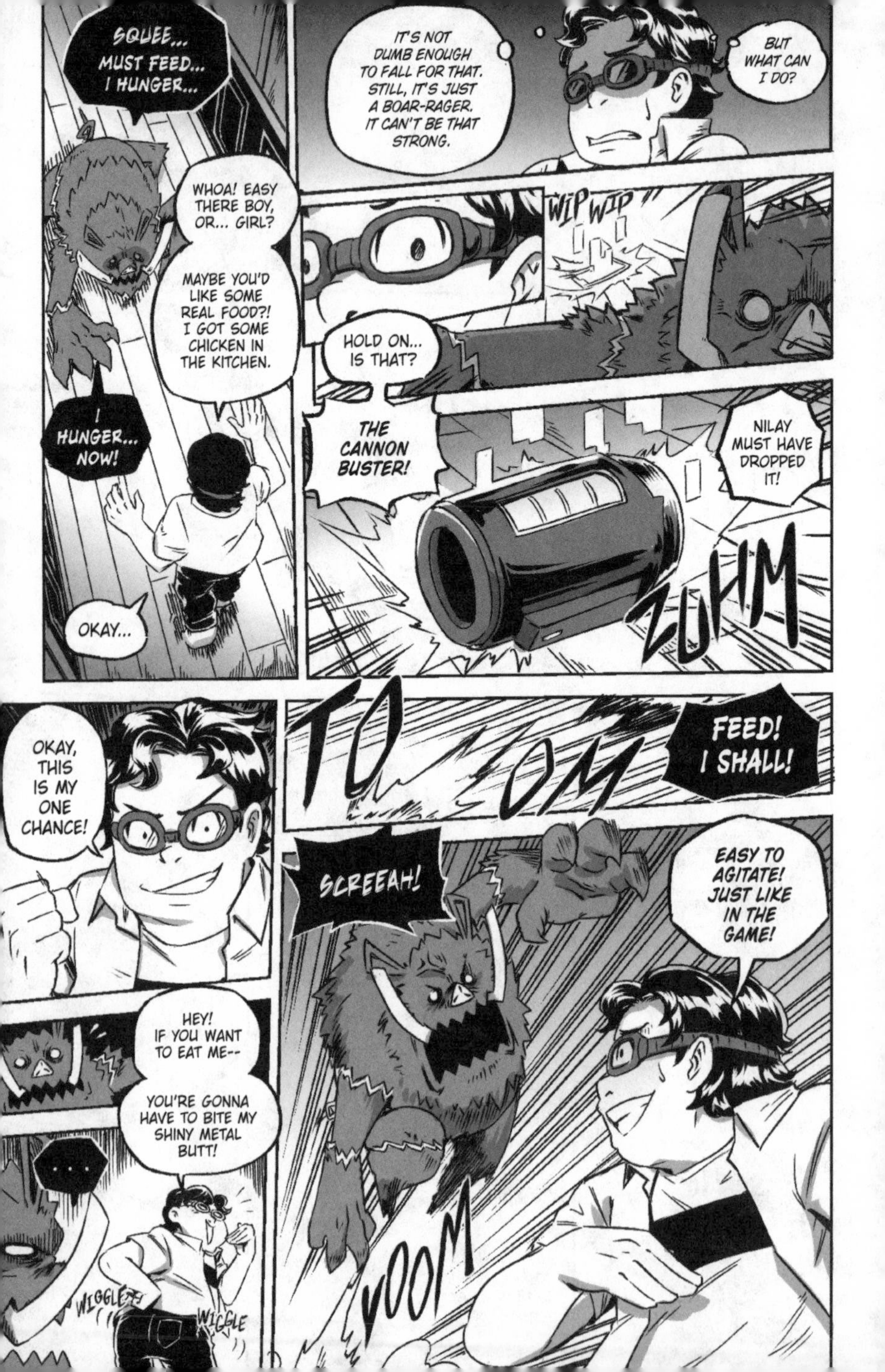
SQUEE... MUST FEED... I HUNGER...
WHOA! EASY THERE BOY, OR... GIRL?
MAYBE YOU'D LIKE SOME REAL FOOD?! I GOT SOME CHICKEN IN THE KITCHEN.
I HUNGER... NOW!
OKAY...
IT'S NOT DUMB ENOUGH TO FALL FOR THAT. STILL, IT'S JUST A BOAR-RAGER. IT CAN'T BE THAT STRONG.
BUT WHAT CAN I DO?
WIP WIP
HOLD ON... IS THAT?
THE CANNON BUSTER!
NILAY MUST HAVE DROPPED IT!
ZUHM
OKAY, THIS IS MY ONE CHANCE!
HEY! IF YOU WANT TO EAT ME--
YOU'RE GONNA HAVE TO BITE MY SHINY METAL BUTT!
...
WIGGLE
WIGGLE
TOOM
FEED! I SHALL!
SCREEAH!
EASY TO AGITATE! JUST LIKE IN THE GAME!
VOOM

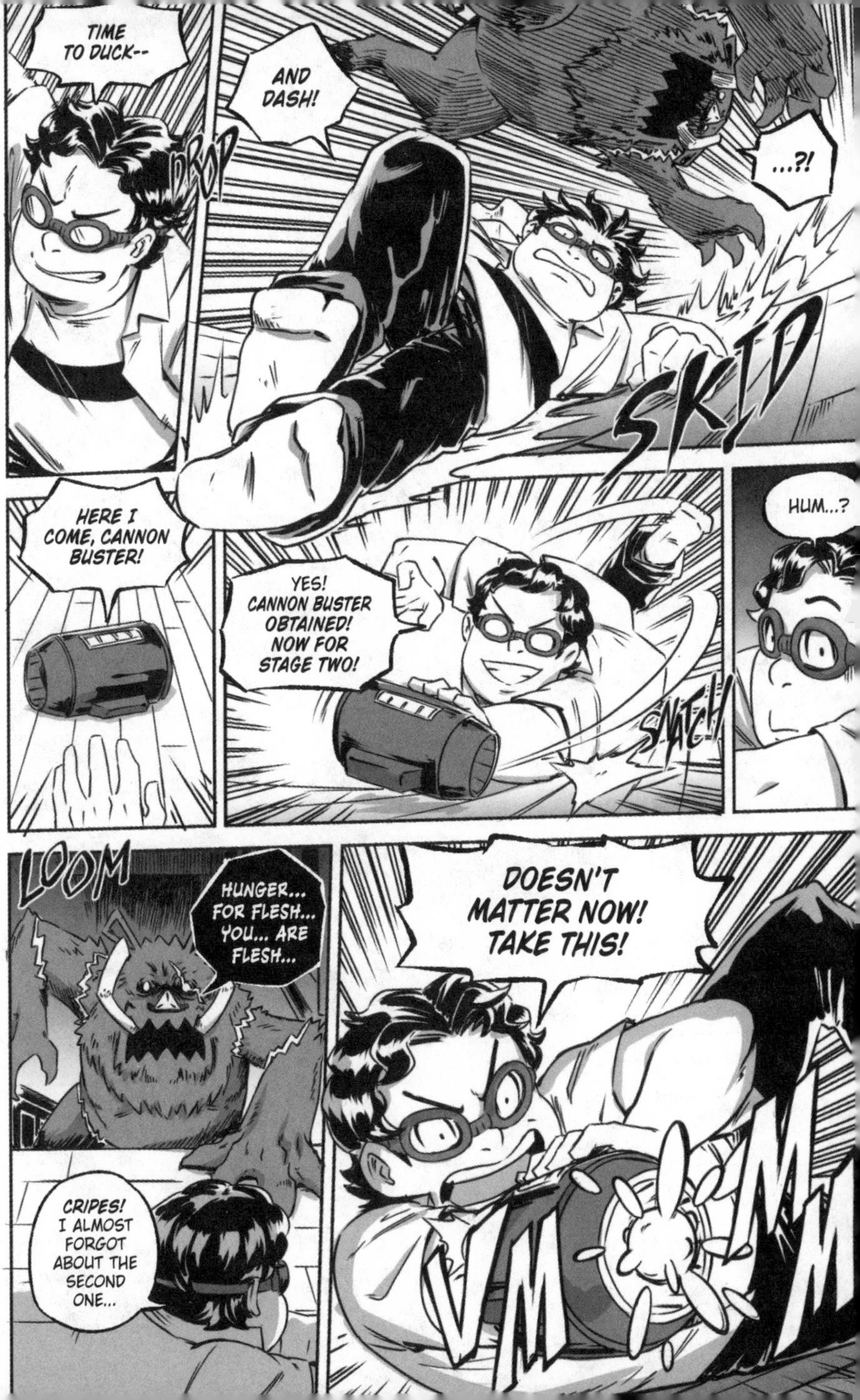
TIME TO DUCK--
DROP
AND DASH!
...?!
SKID
HERE I COME, CANNON BUSTER!
YES! CANNON BUSTER OBTAINED! NOW FOR STAGE TWO!
SNATCH!
HUM...?
LOOM
HUNGER... FOR FLESH... YOU... ARE FLESH...
CRIPES! I ALMOST FORGOT ABOUT THE SECOND ONE...
DOESN'T MATTER NOW! TAKE THIS!
VMMM

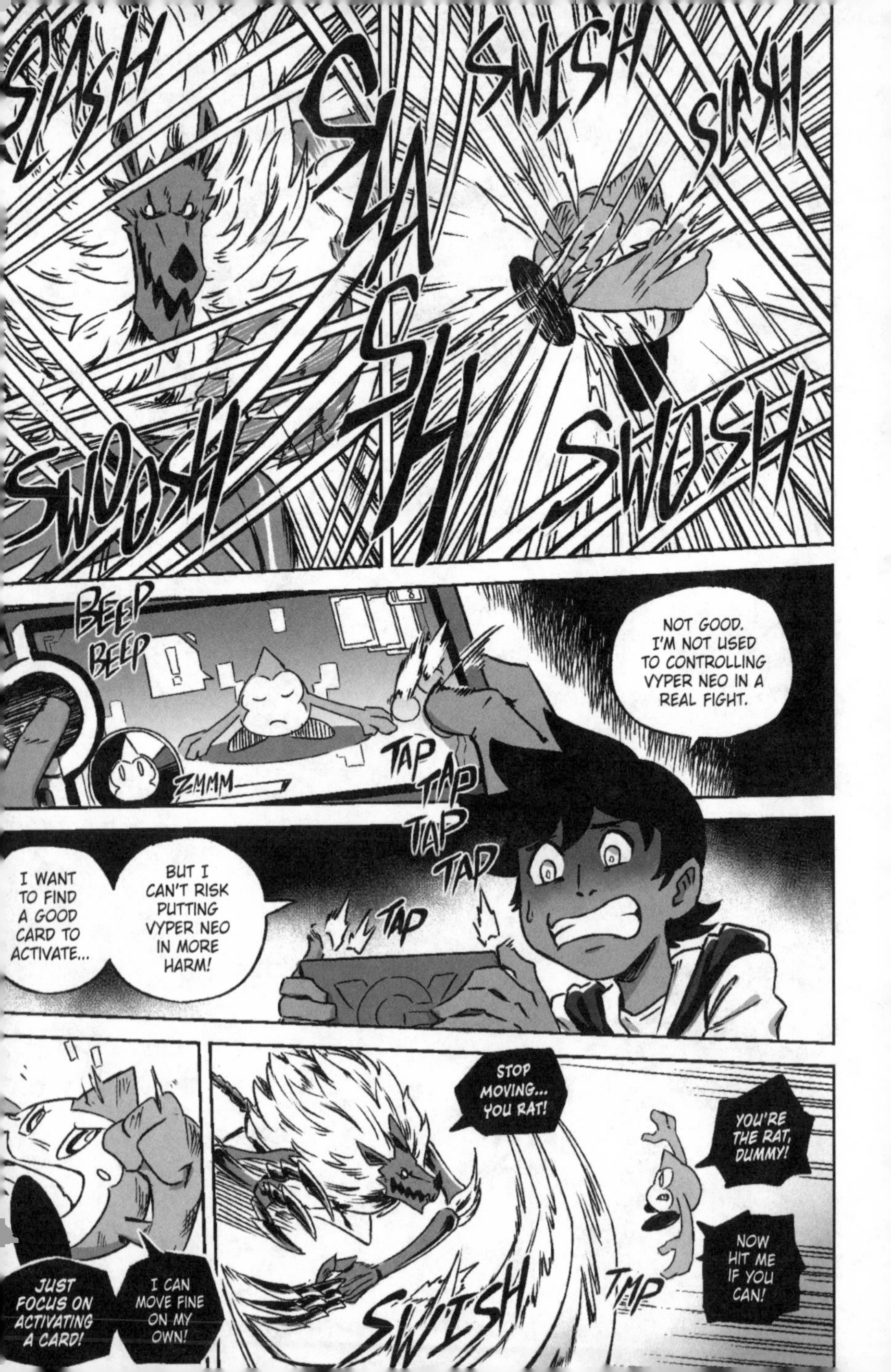
SLASH
SLASH
SWISH
SLASH
SWOOSH
SWOSH
BEEP BEEP
!
NOT GOOD. I'M NOT USED TO CONTROLLING VYPER NEO IN A REAL FIGHT.
ZMMM
TAP TAP TAP TAP TAP
I WANT TO FIND A GOOD CARD TO ACTIVATE...
BUT I CAN'T RISK PUTTING VYPER NEO IN MORE HARM!
JUST FOCUS ON ACTIVATING A CARD!
I CAN MOVE FINE ON MY OWN!
STOP MOVING... YOU RAT!
YOU'RE THE RAT, DUMMY!
NOW HIT ME IF YOU CAN!
SWISH
TMP

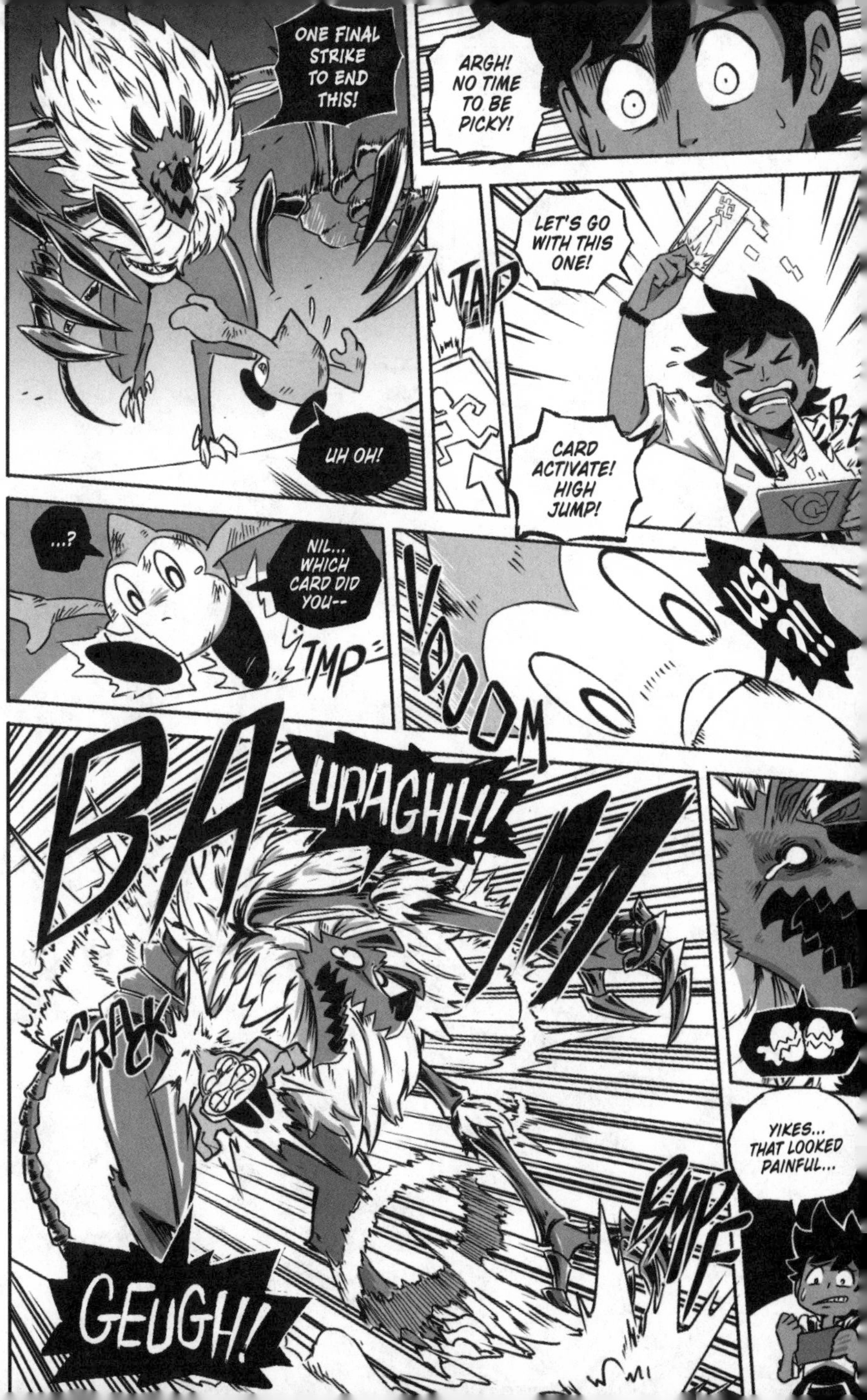

ONE FINAL STRIKE TO END THIS!
UH OH!
ARGH! NO TIME TO BE PICKY!
TAP
LET'S GO WITH THIS ONE!
CARD ACTIVATE! HIGH JUMP!
...?
NIL... WHICH CARD DID YOU--
TMP
VOOOM
USE ?!!
BAM
URAGHH!
CRACK
GEUGH!
YIKES... THAT LOOKED PAINFUL...

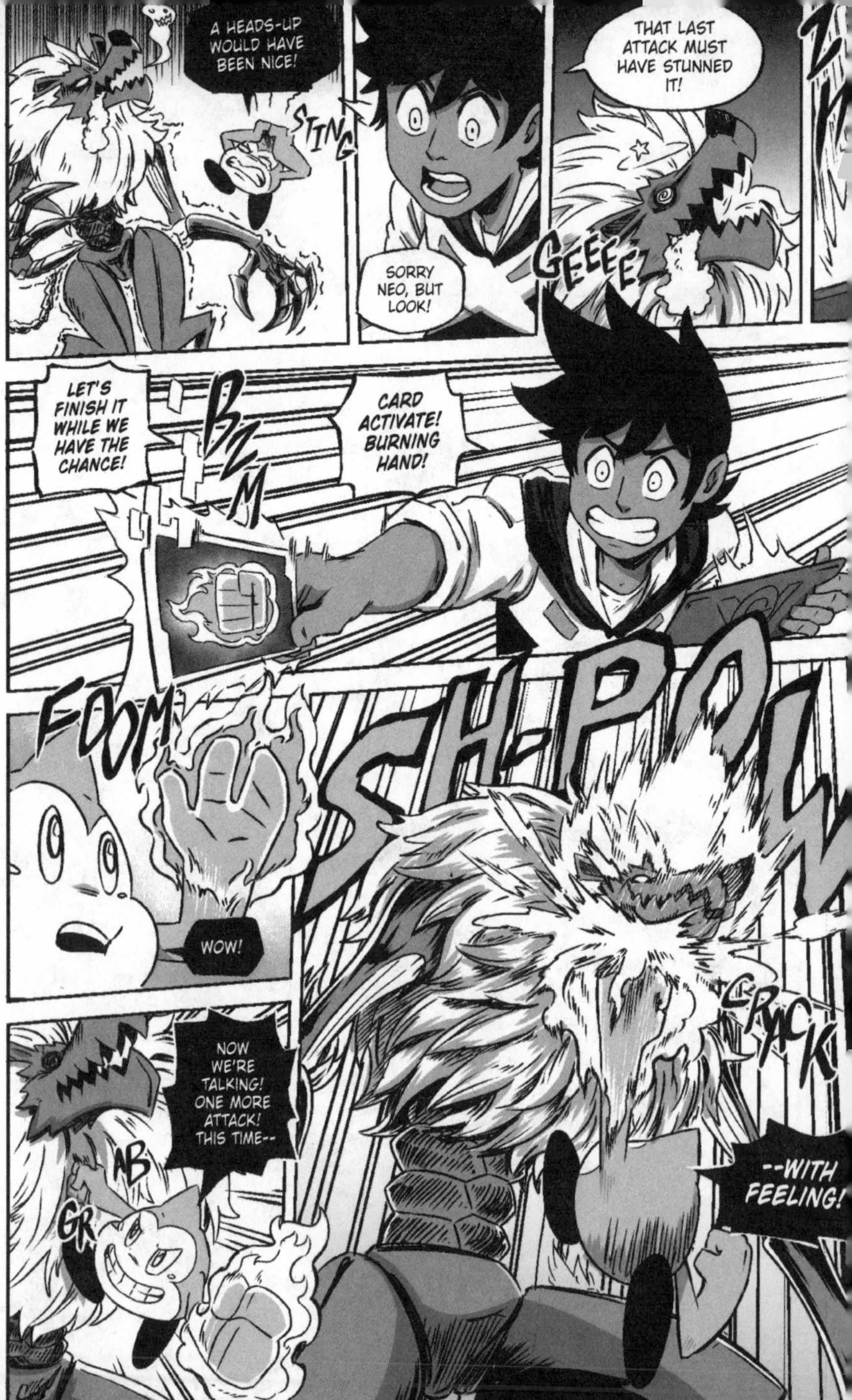
A HEADS-UP WOULD HAVE BEEN NICE!
STING
SORRY NEO, BUT LOOK!
THAT LAST ATTACK MUST HAVE STUNNED IT!
GEEEE
LET'S FINISH IT WHILE WE HAVE THE CHANCE!
BZZM
CARD ACTIVATE! BURNING HAND!
FOOM
WOW!
SH-POW
CRACK
NOW WE'RE TALKING! ONE MORE ATTACK! THIS TIME--
AB
GR
--WITH FEELING!

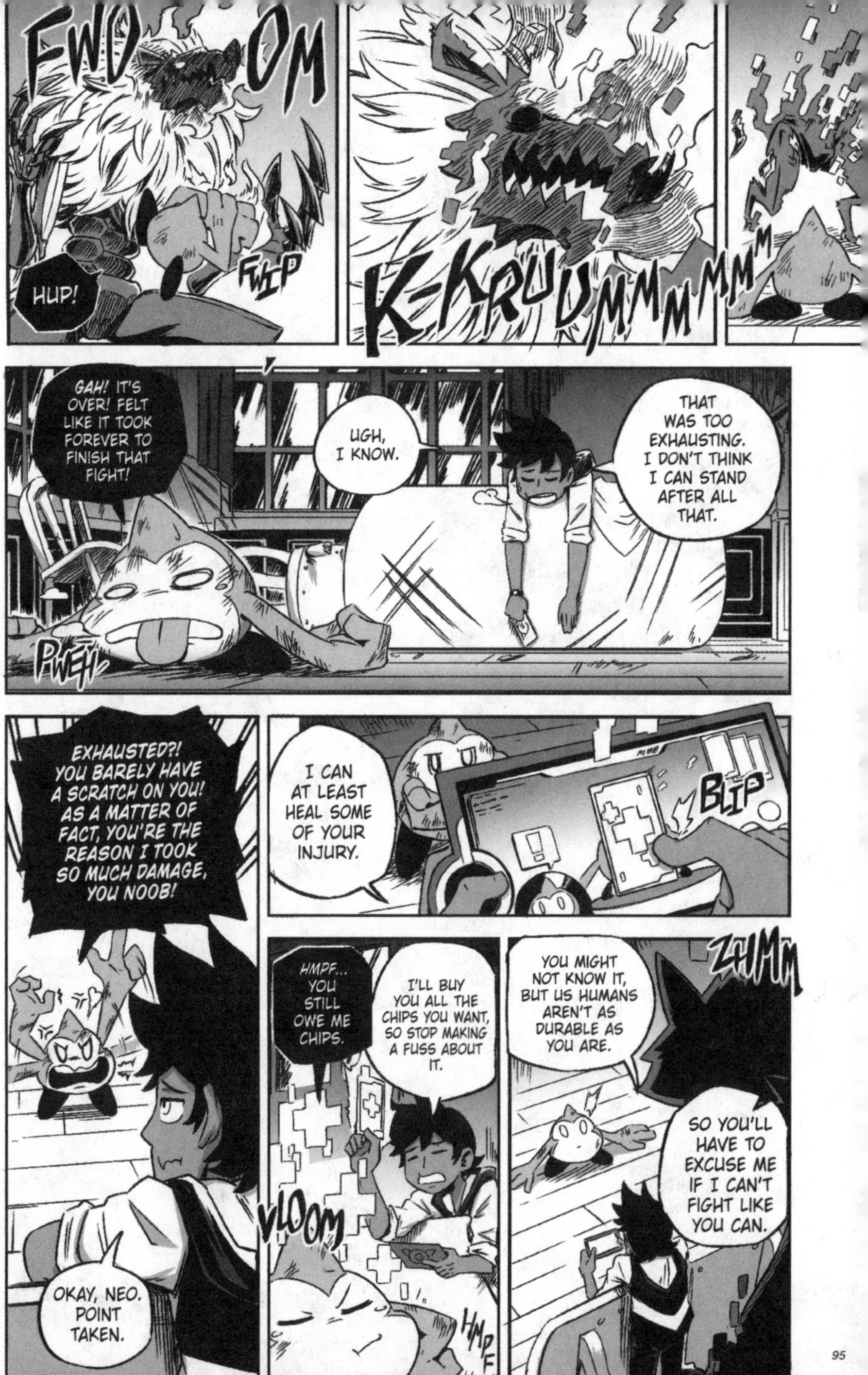
FWOOM
HUP!
FWIP
K-KRUUMMMMMMMM
GAH! IT'S OVER! FELT LIKE IT TOOK FOREVER TO FINISH THAT FIGHT!
UGH, I KNOW.
THAT WAS TOO EXHAUSTING. I DON'T THINK I CAN STAND AFTER ALL THAT.
PWEH
EXHAUSTED?! YOU BARELY HAVE A SCRATCH ON YOU! AS A MATTER OF FACT, YOU'RE THE REASON I TOOK SO MUCH DAMAGE, YOU NOOB!
I CAN AT LEAST HEAL SOME OF YOUR INJURY.
BLIP
OKAY, NEO. POINT TAKEN.
HMPF... YOU STILL OWE ME CHIPS.
I'LL BUY YOU ALL THE CHIPS YOU WANT, SO STOP MAKING A FUSS ABOUT IT.
VLOOM
HMPF
YOU MIGHT NOT KNOW IT, BUT US HUMANS AREN'T AS DURABLE AS YOU ARE.
ZHMM
SO YOU'LL HAVE TO EXCUSE ME IF I CAN'T FIGHT LIKE YOU CAN.

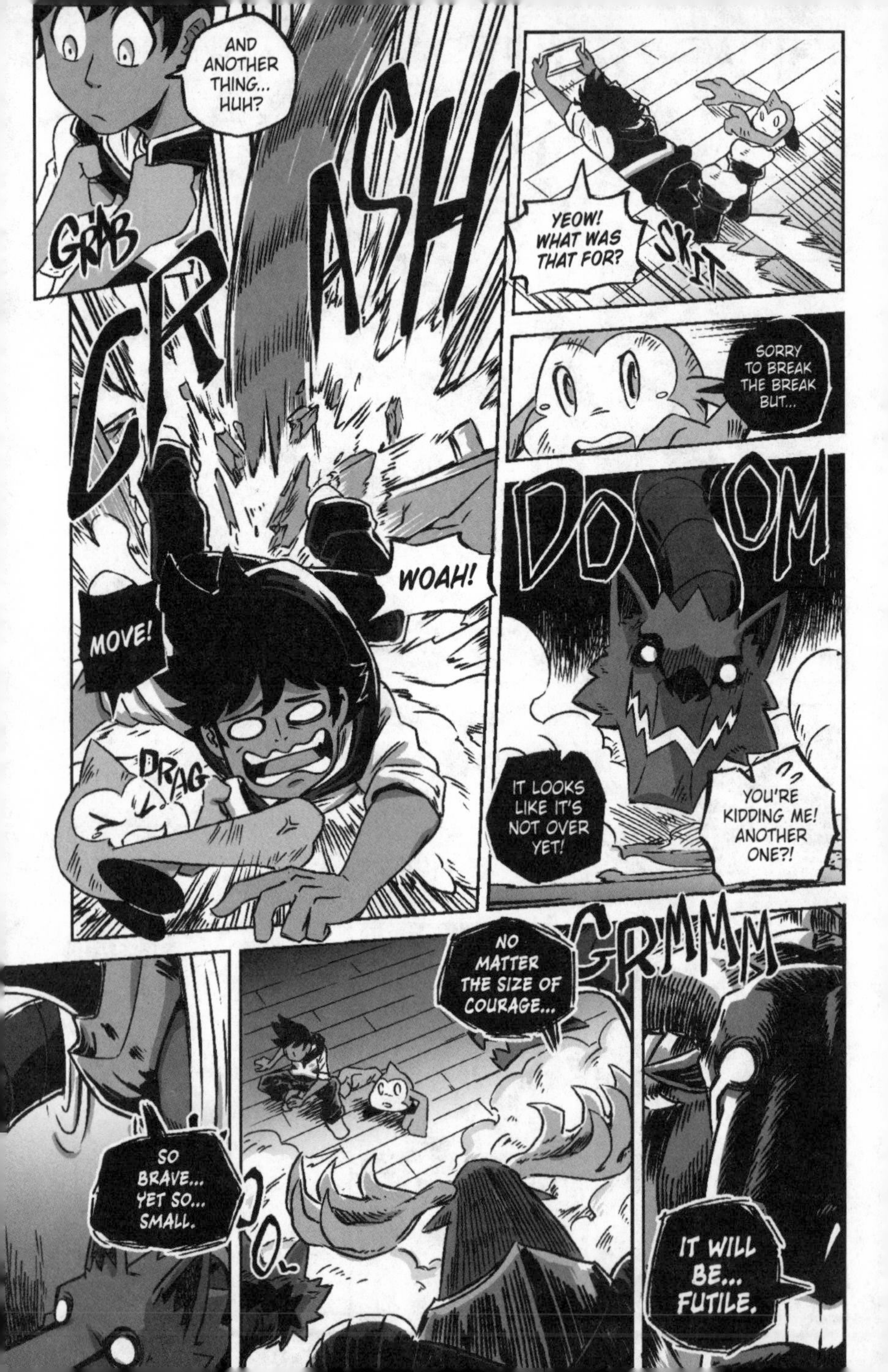
AND ANOTHER THING... HUH?
GRAB
CRASH
WOAH!
MOVE!
DRAG
YEOW! WHAT WAS THAT FOR?
SKIT
SORRY TO BREAK THE BREAK BUT...
DOOOM
IT LOOKS LIKE IT'S NOT OVER YET!
YOU'RE KIDDING ME! ANOTHER ONE?!
GRMMM
SO BRAVE... YET SO... SMALL.
NO MATTER THE SIZE OF COURAGE...
IT WILL BE... FUTILE.

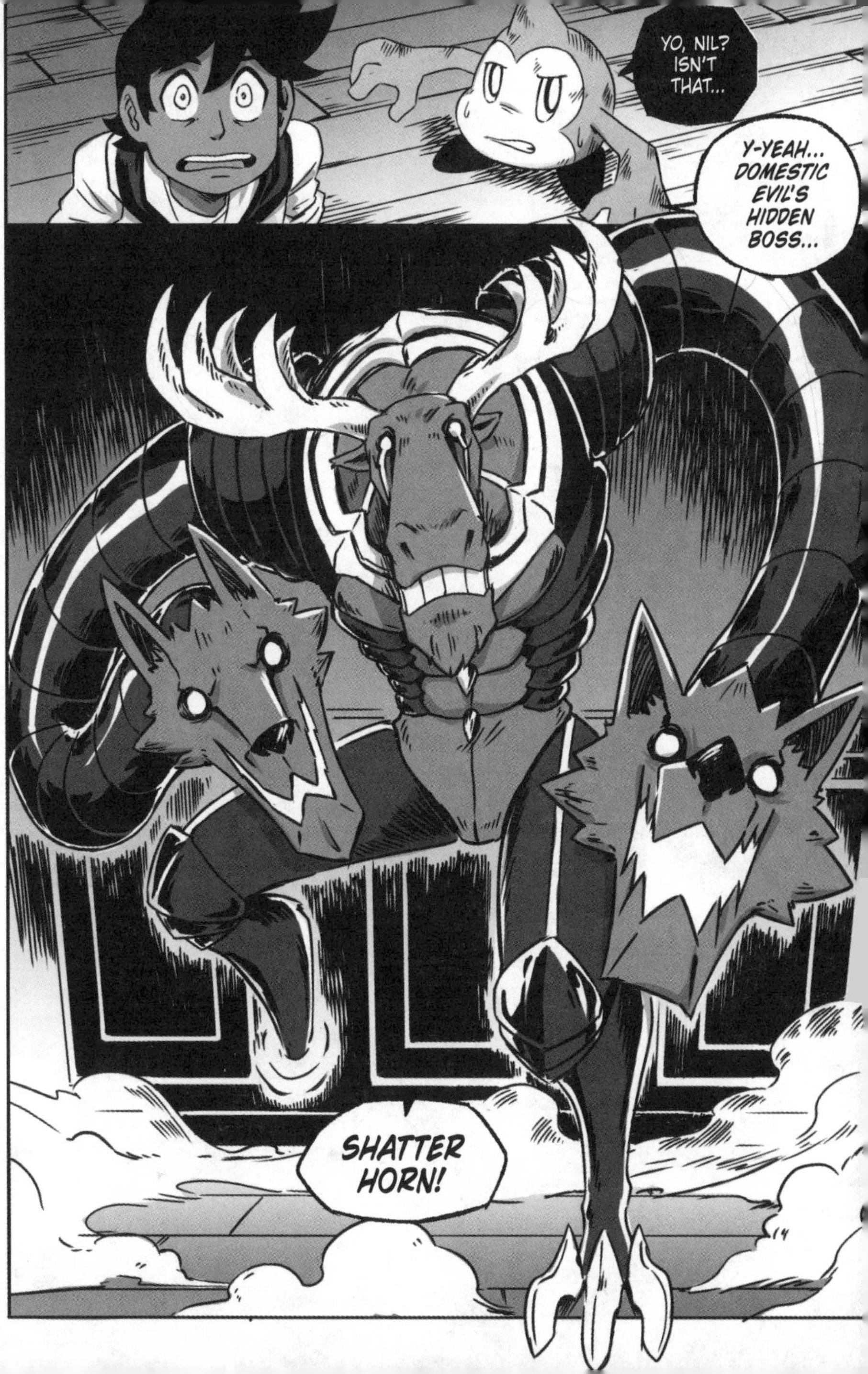
YO, NIL? ISN'T THAT...
Y-YEAH... DOMESTIC EVIL'S HIDDEN BOSS...
SHATTER HORN!

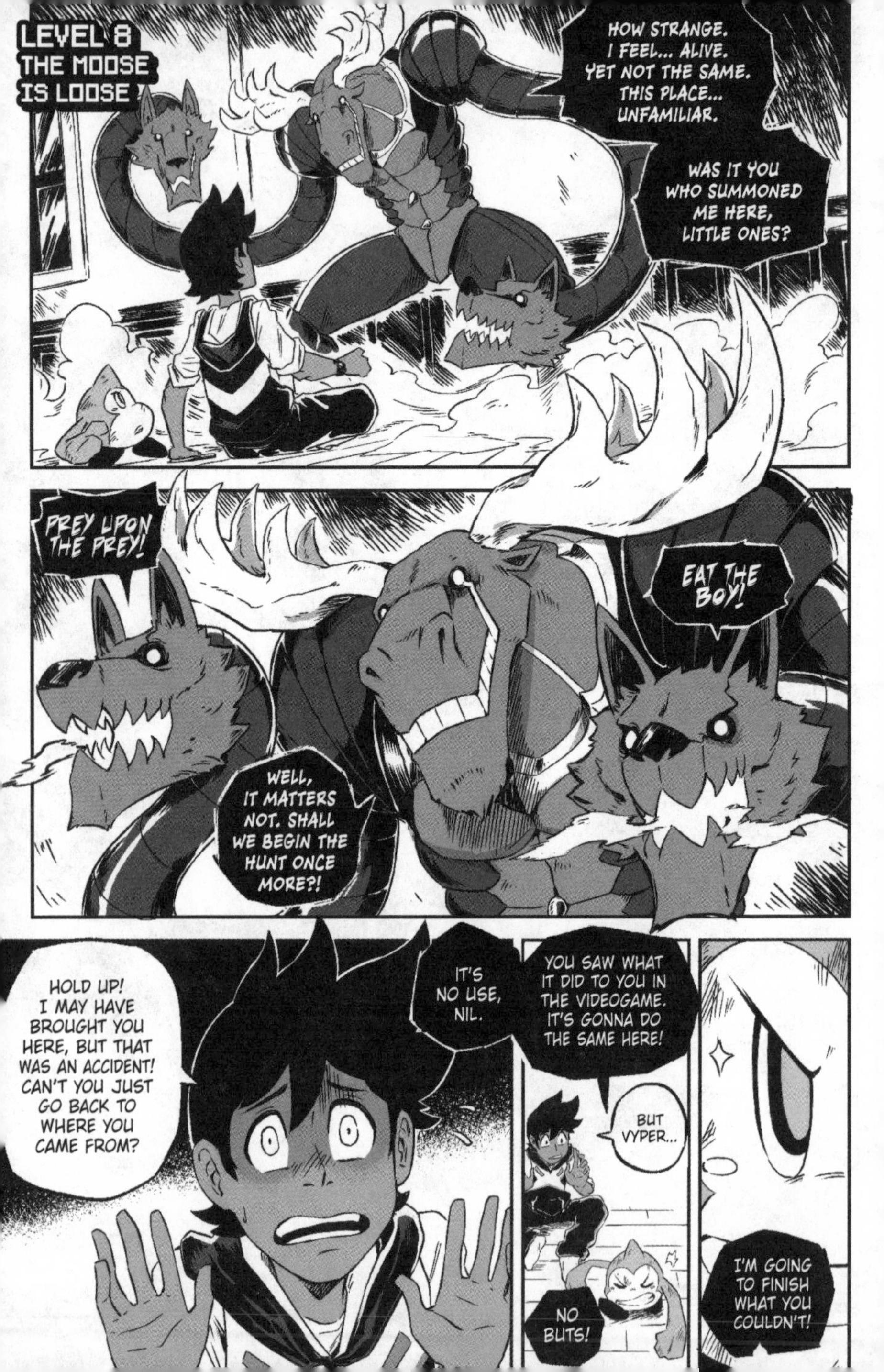
LEVEL 8
THE MOOSE IS LOOSE!
HOW STRANGE. I FEEL... ALIVE. YET NOT THE SAME. THIS PLACE... UNFAMILIAR.
WAS IT YOU WHO SUMMONED ME HERE, LITTLE ONES?
PREY UPON THE PREY!
EAT THE BOY!
WELL, IT MATTERS NOT. SHALL WE BEGIN THE HUNT ONCE MORE?!
HOLD UP! I MAY HAVE BROUGHT YOU HERE, BUT THAT WAS AN ACCIDENT! CAN'T YOU JUST GO BACK TO WHERE YOU CAME FROM?
IT'S NO USE, NIL.
YOU SAW WHAT IT DID TO YOU IN THE VIDEOGAME. IT'S GONNA DO THE SAME HERE!
BUT VYPER...
NO BUTS!
I'M GOING TO FINISH WHAT YOU COULDN'T!

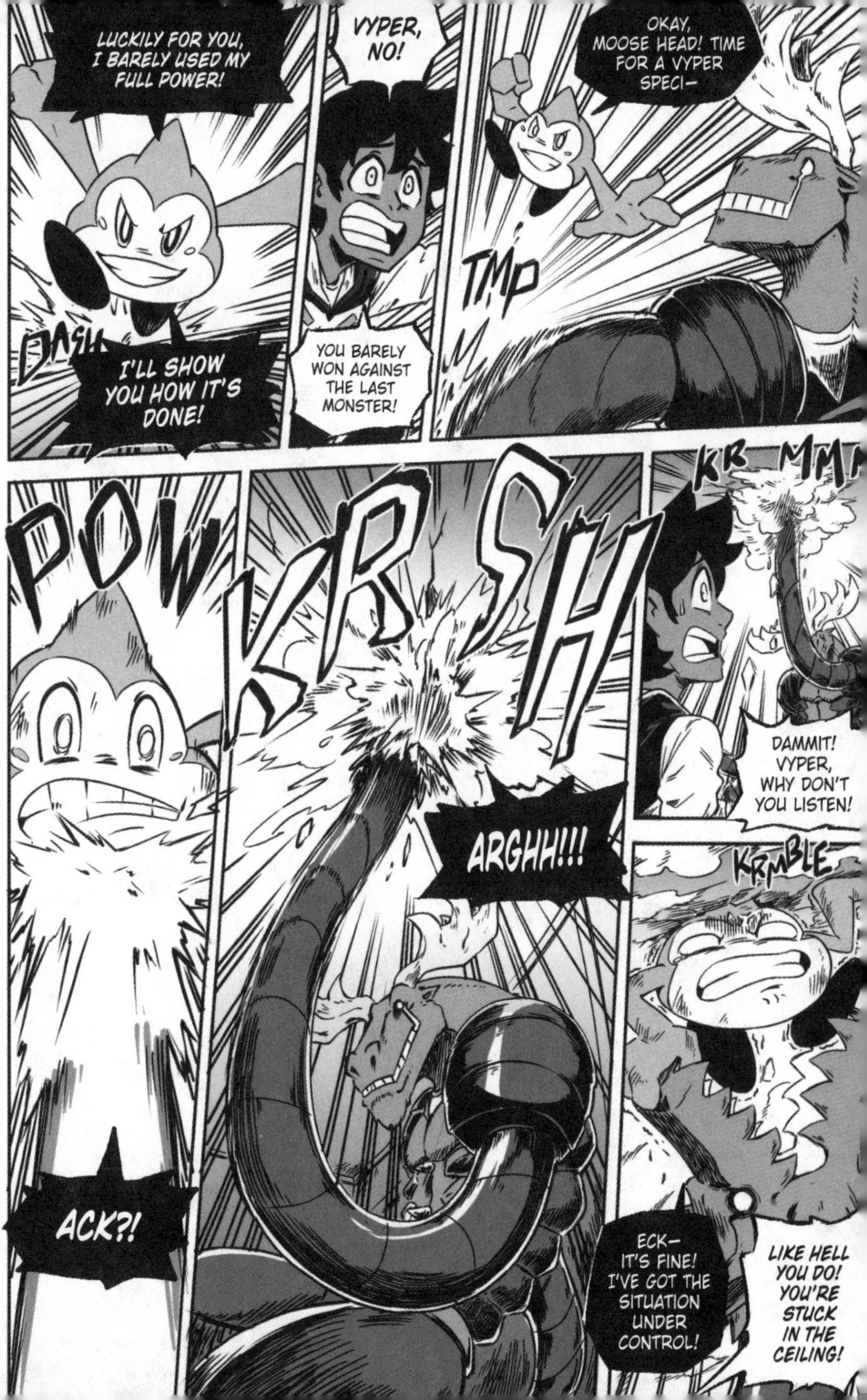

LUCKILY FOR YOU, I BARELY USED MY FULL POWER!
DASH
I'LL SHOW YOU HOW IT'S DONE!
VYPER, NO!
YOU BARELY WON AGAINST THE LAST MONSTER!
OKAY, MOOSE HEAD! TIME FOR A VYPER SPECI—
TMP
POW
ACK?!
KRSH
ARGHH!!!
KR MMM
DAMMIT! VYPER, WHY DON'T YOU LISTEN!
KRMBLE
ECK— IT'S FINE! I'VE GOT THE SITUATION UNDER CONTROL!
LIKE HELL YOU DO! YOU'RE STUCK IN THE CEILING!

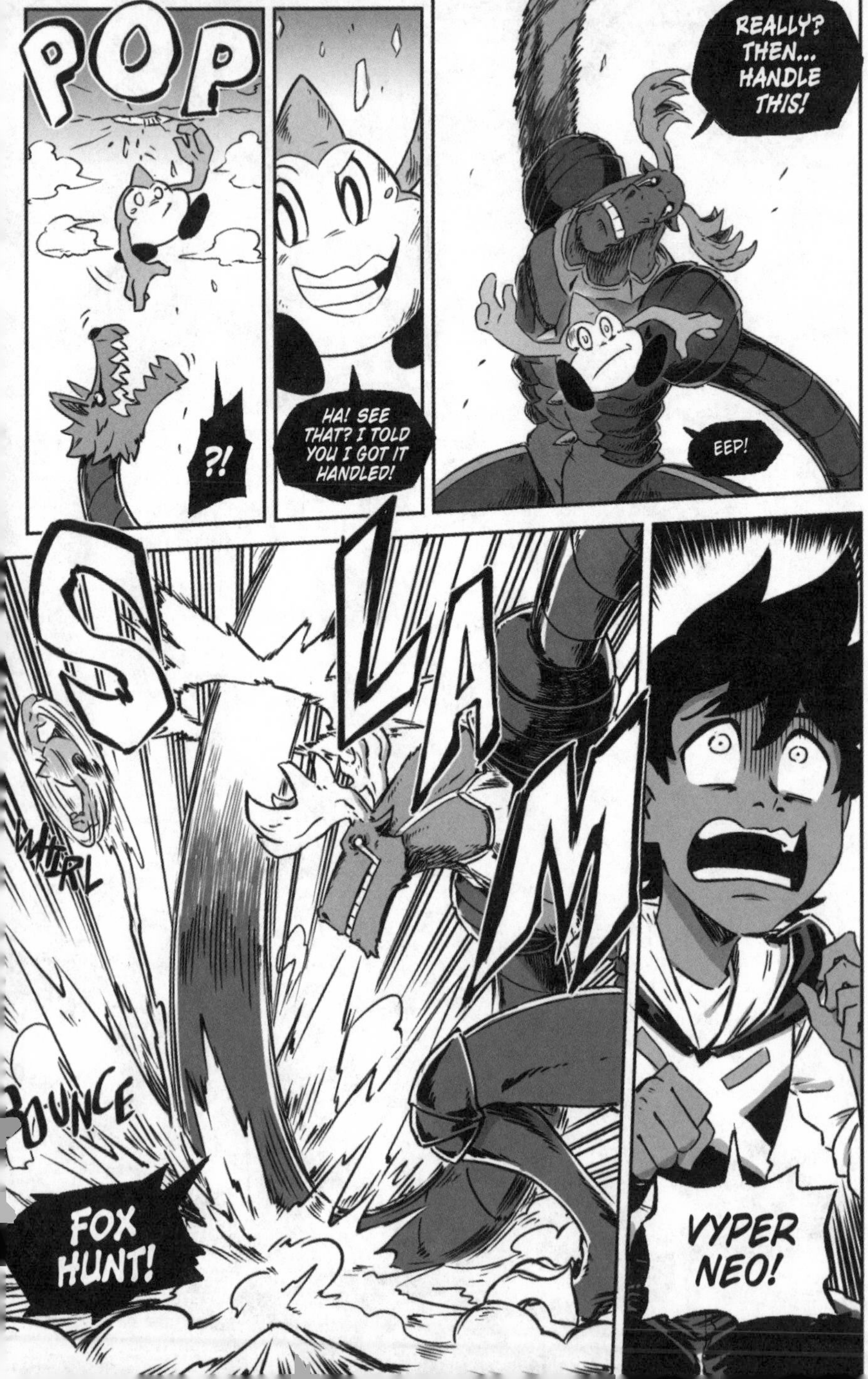
POP
?!
HA! SEE THAT? I TOLD YOU I GOT IT HANDLED!
REALLY? THEN... HANDLE THIS!
EEP!
SLAM
WHIRL
BOUNCE
FOX HUNT!
VYPER NEO!

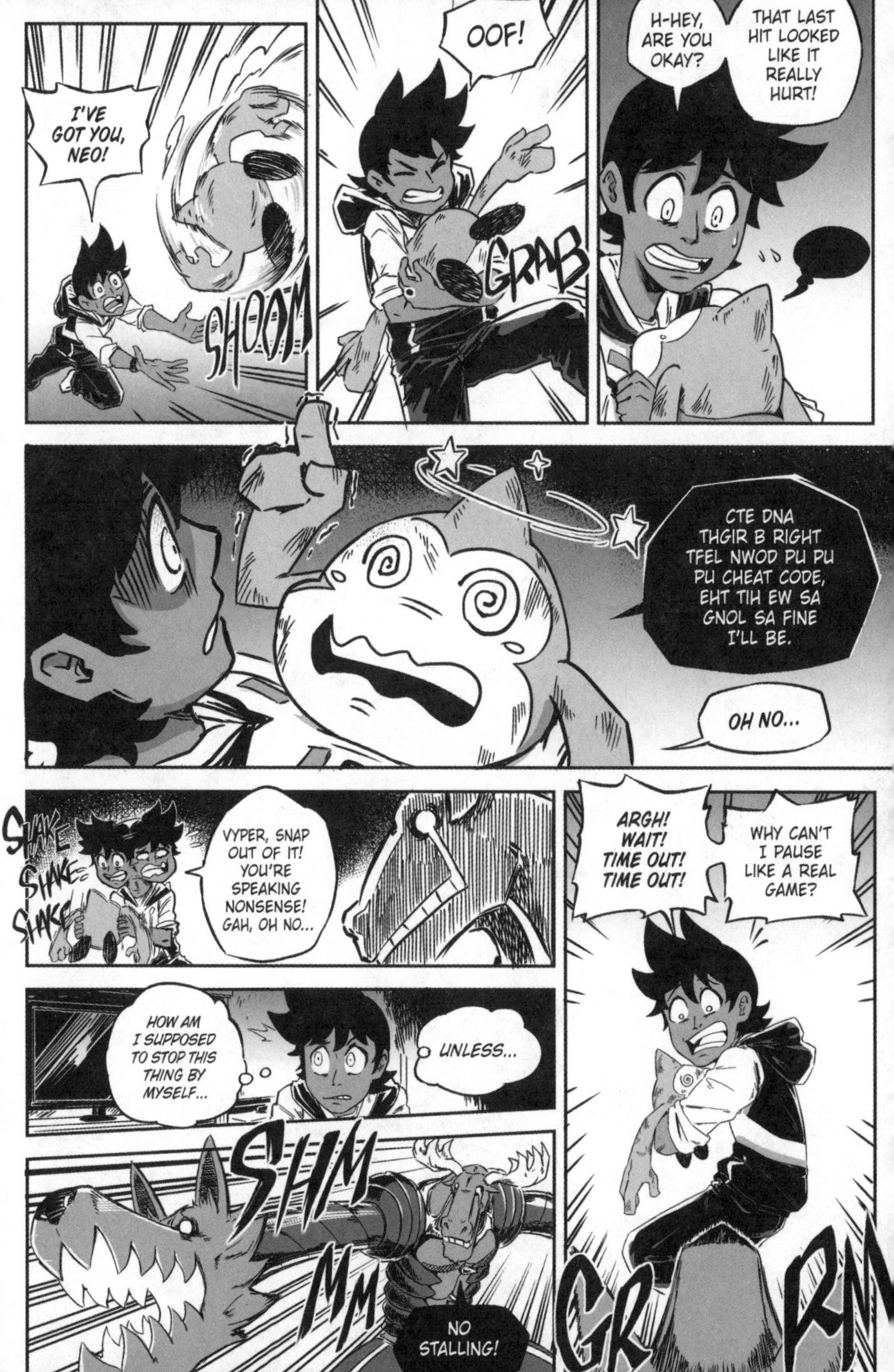

I'VE GOT YOU, NEO!
SHOOM
OOF!
GRAB
H-HEY, ARE YOU OKAY?
THAT LAST HIT LOOKED LIKE IT REALLY HURT!
CTE DNA THGIR B RIGHT TFEL NWOD PU PU PU CHEAT CODE, EHT TIH EW SA GNOL SA FINE I'LL BE.
OH NO...
SHAKE SHAKE SHAKE
VYPER, SNAP OUT OF IT! YOU'RE SPEAKING NONSENSE! GAH, OH NO...
HOW AM I SUPPOSED TO STOP THIS THING BY MYSELF...
UNLESS...
SHMMM
NO STALLING!
ARGH! WAIT! TIME OUT! TIME OUT!
WHY CAN'T I PAUSE LIKE A REAL GAME?
GRRM

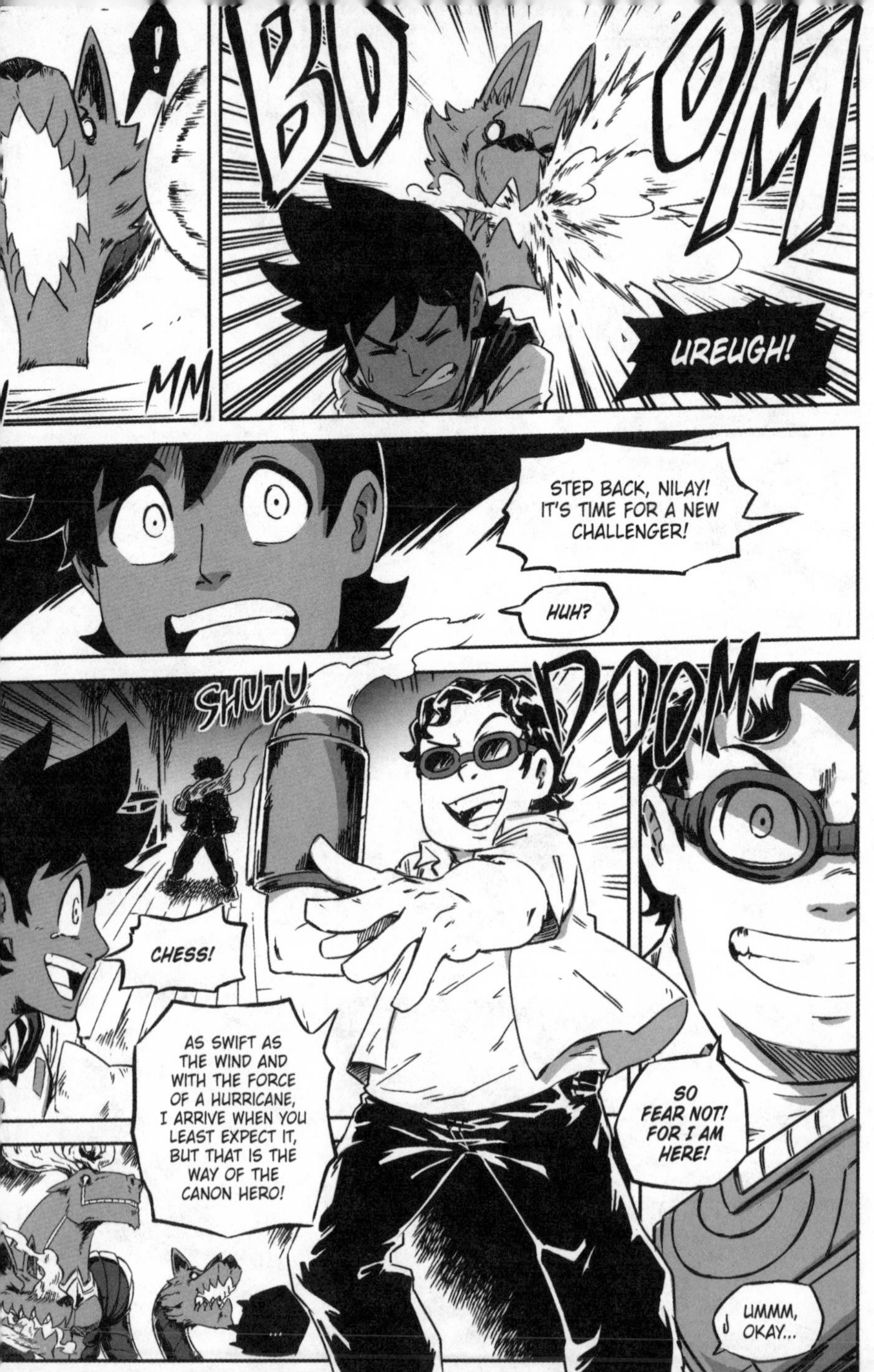
!
MM
BOOM
UREUGH!
STEP BACK, NILAY! IT'S TIME FOR A NEW CHALLENGER!
HUH?
SHUUU
DOOM
CHESS!
AS SWIFT AS THE WIND AND WITH THE FORCE OF A HURRICANE, I ARRIVE WHEN YOU LEAST EXPECT IT, BUT THAT IS THE WAY OF THE CANON HERO!
SO FEAR NOT! FOR I AM HERE!
UMMM, OKAY...
...

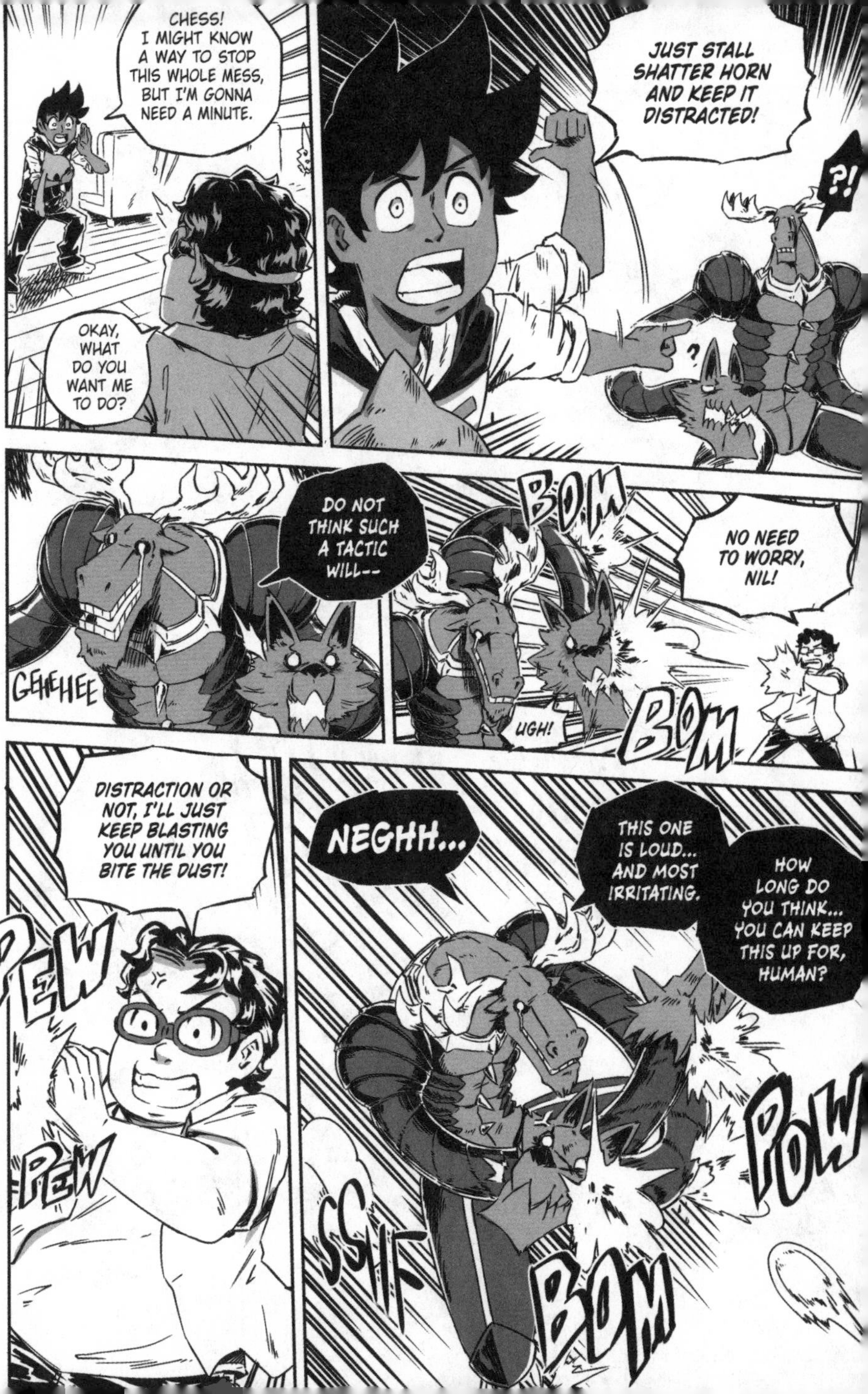

CHESS! I MIGHT KNOW A WAY TO STOP THIS WHOLE MESS, BUT I'M GONNA NEED A MINUTE.
OKAY, WHAT DO YOU WANT ME TO DO?
JUST STALL SHATTER HORN AND KEEP IT DISTRACTED!
?!
?
DO NOT THINK SUCH A TACTIC WILL--
GEHEHEE
BOM
NO NEED TO WORRY, NIL!
UGH!
BOM
DISTRACTION OR NOT, I'LL JUST KEEP BLASTING YOU UNTIL YOU BITE THE DUST!
PEW
PEW
NEGHH...
THIS ONE IS LOUD... AND MOST IRRITATING.
HOW LONG DO YOU THINK... YOU CAN KEEP THIS UP FOR, HUMAN?
POW
SSHF
BOM

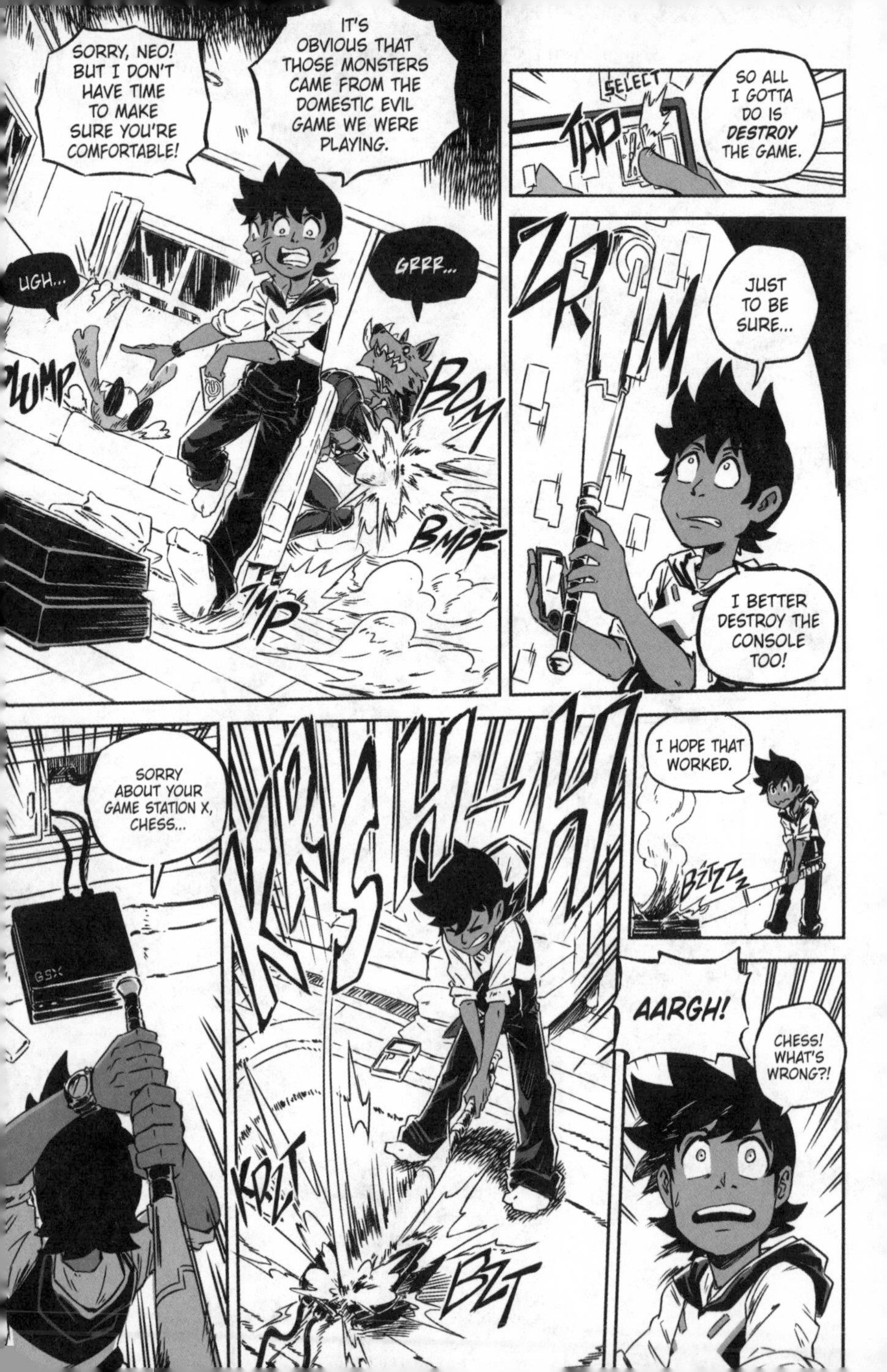
SORRY, NEO! BUT I DON'T HAVE TIME TO MAKE SURE YOU'RE COMFORTABLE!
IT'S OBVIOUS THAT THOSE MONSTERS CAME FROM THE DOMESTIC EVIL GAME WE WERE PLAYING.
UGH...
GRRR...
PLUMP
BOM
BMPF
TEMP
SELECT
TAP
SO ALL I GOTTA DO IS **DESTROY** THE GAME.
ZRIM
JUST TO BE SURE...
I BETTER DESTROY THE CONSOLE TOO!
SORRY ABOUT YOUR GAME STATION X, CHESS...
GSX
KRASH-H
KRZT
BZT
I HOPE THAT WORKED.
BZTZZ
AARGH!
CHESS! WHAT'S WRONG?!

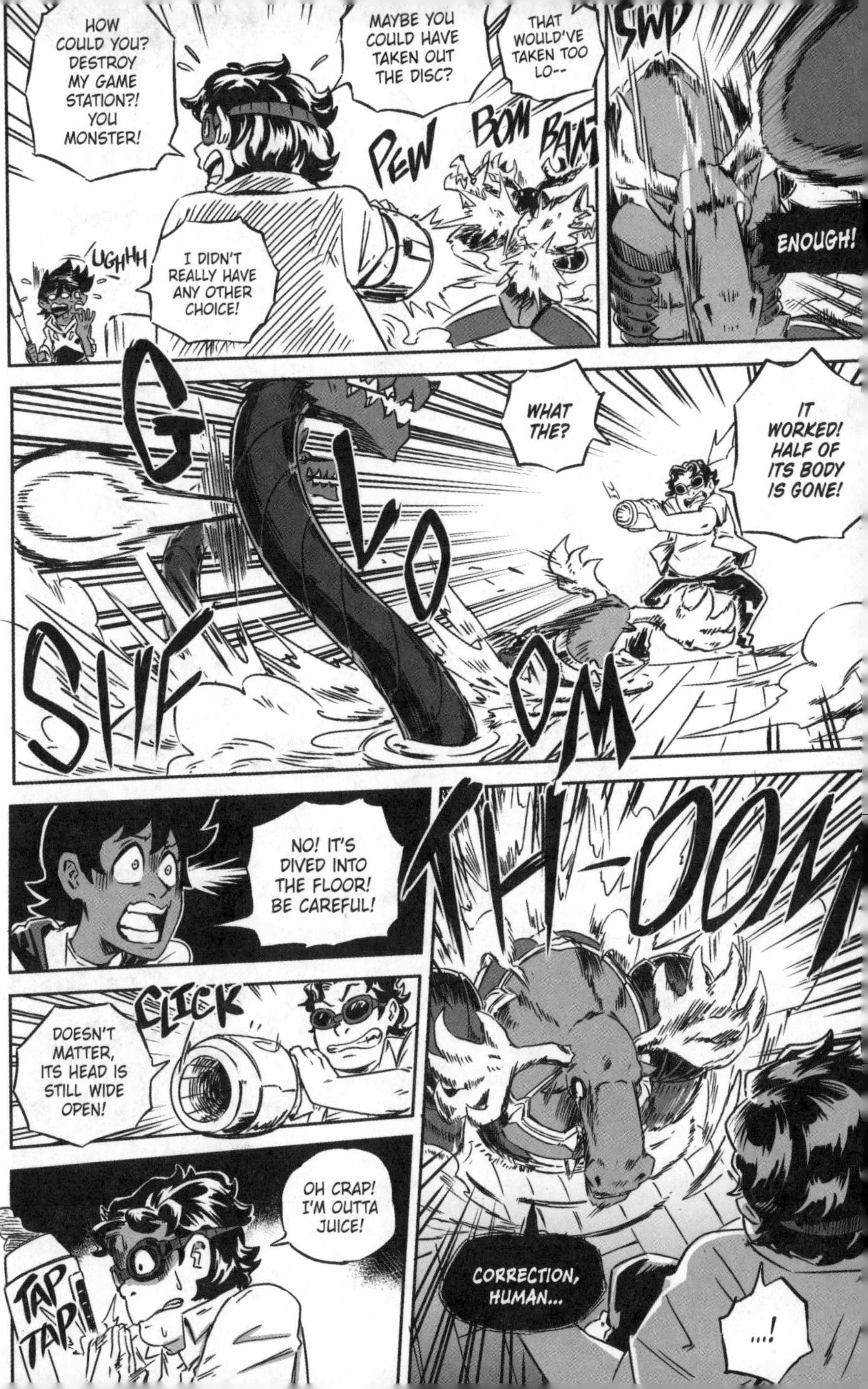
HOW COULD YOU? DESTROY MY GAME STATION?! YOU MONSTER!
MAYBE YOU COULD HAVE TAKEN OUT THE DISC?
THAT WOULD'VE TAKEN TOO LO--
PEW
BOM
BAM
UGHHH
I DIDN'T REALLY HAVE ANY OTHER CHOICE!
SWP
ENOUGH!
G
VO
OM
SHF
WHAT THE?
IT WORKED! HALF OF ITS BODY IS GONE!
NO! IT'S DIVED INTO THE FLOOR! BE CAREFUL!
CLICK
DOESN'T MATTER, ITS HEAD IS STILL WIDE OPEN!
OH CRAP! I'M OUTTA JUICE!
TAP
TAP
KH-OOM
CORRECTION, HUMAN...
...!

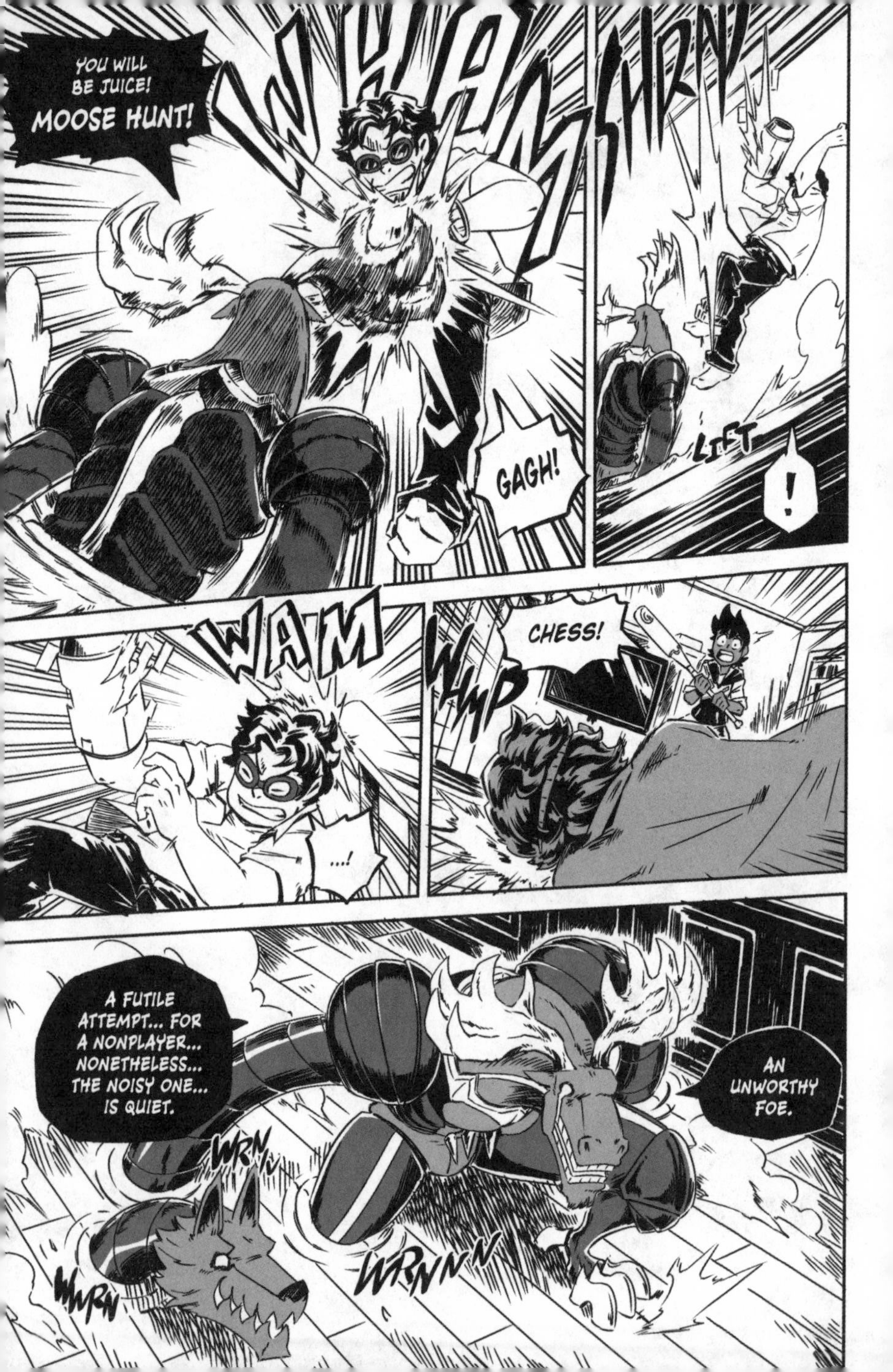
YOU WILL BE JUICE! MOOSE HUNT!
WHAM
GAGH!
SHRN
LIFT
!
WAM
...!
WMP
CHESS!
A FUTILE ATTEMPT... FOR A NONPLAYER... NONETHELESS... THE NOISY ONE... IS QUIET.
AN UNWORTHY FOE.
WRN
WRNNN
WWRN

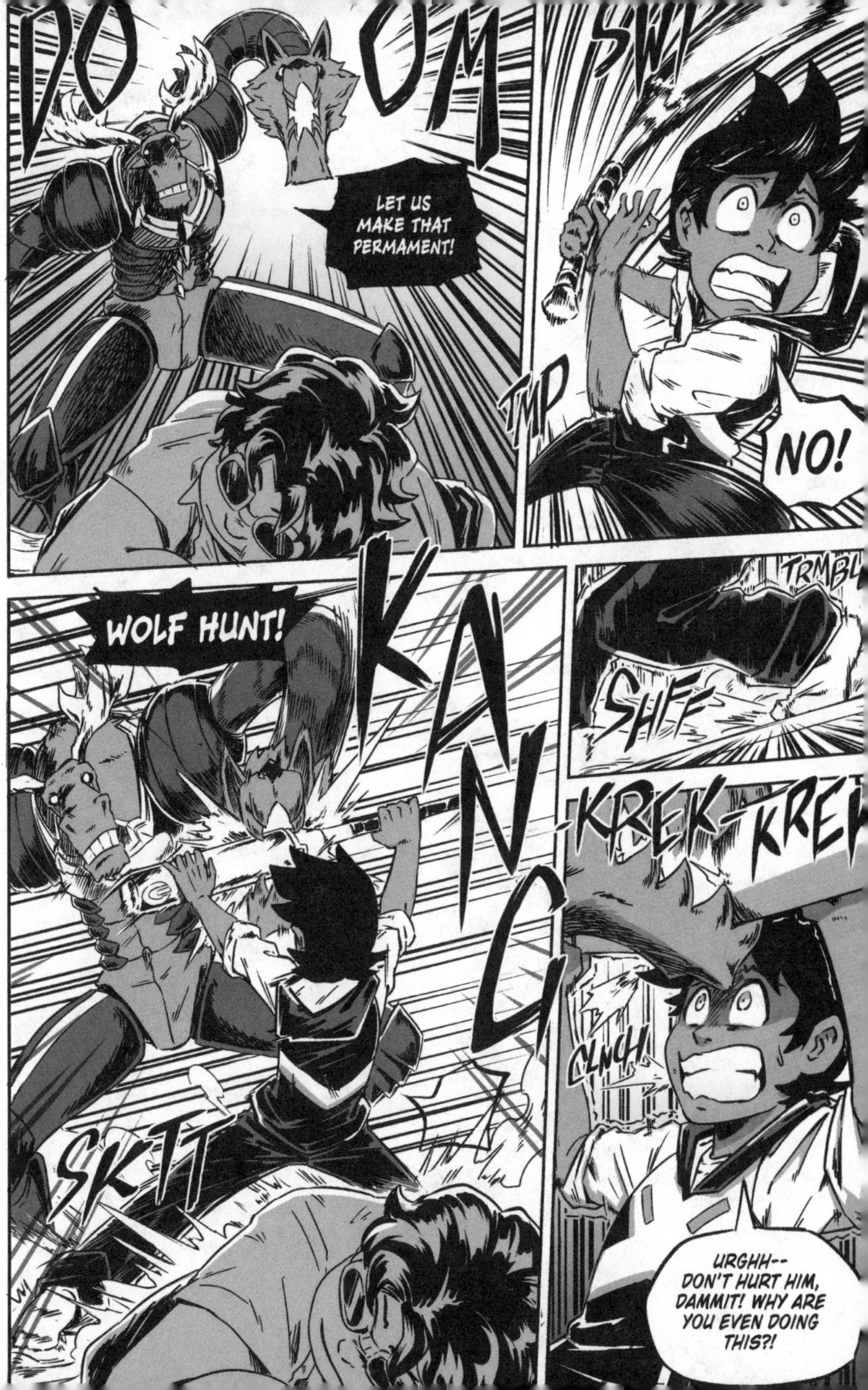
DOOM
LET US MAKE THAT PERMAMENT!
SWI
TMP
NO!
WOLF HUNT!
KANG
SKTT
TRMBL
SHFF
KREK KREK
CLNCH
URGHH-- DON'T HURT HIM, DAMMIT! WHY ARE YOU EVEN DOING THIS?!

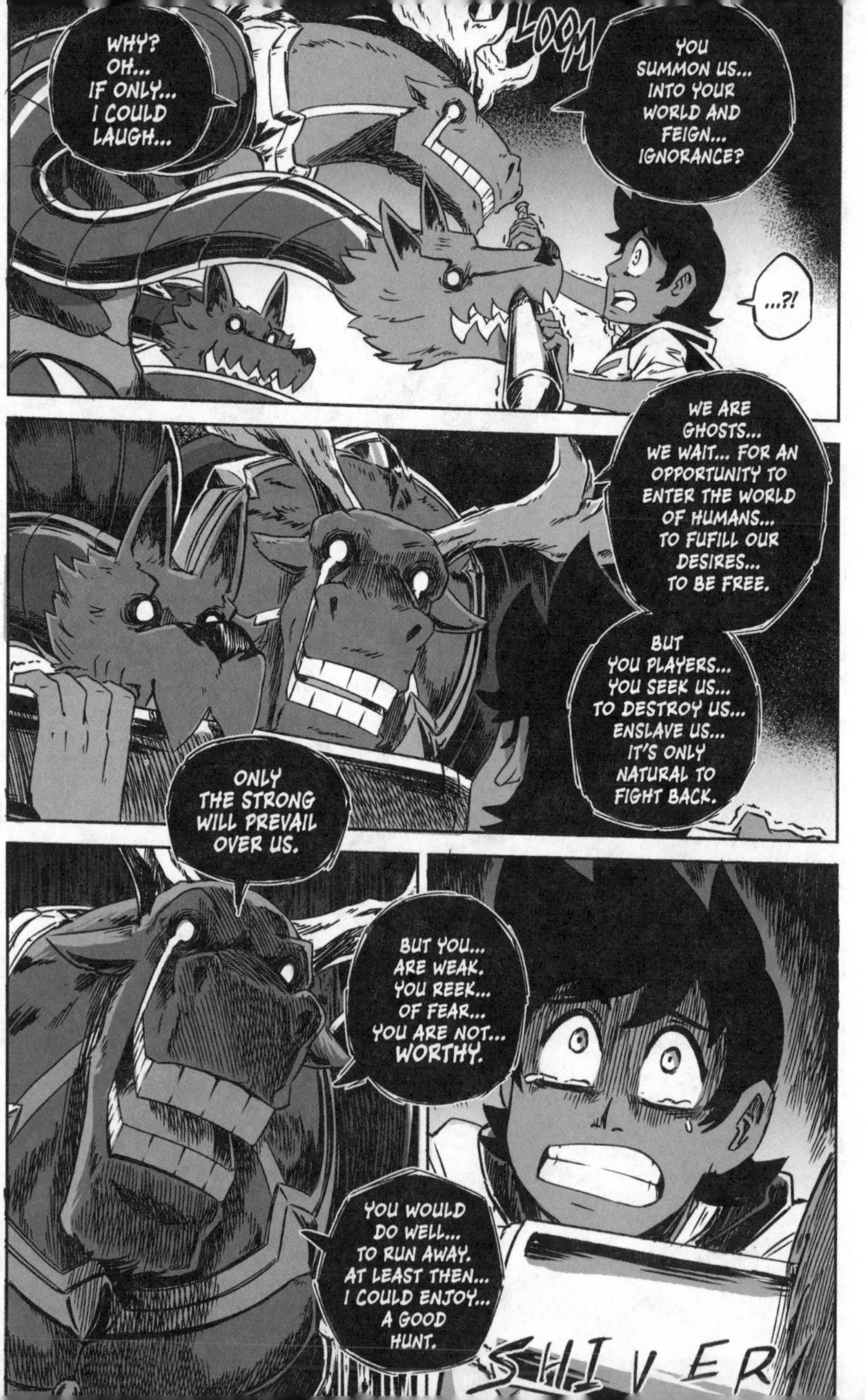
LOOM
WHY? OH... IF ONLY... I COULD LAUGH...
YOU SUMMON US... INTO YOUR WORLD AND FEIGN... IGNORANCE?
...?!
WE ARE GHOSTS... WE WAIT... FOR AN OPPORTUNITY TO ENTER THE WORLD OF HUMANS... TO FUFILL OUR DESIRES... TO BE FREE.
BUT YOU PLAYERS... YOU SEEK US... TO DESTROY US... ENSLAVE US... IT'S ONLY NATURAL TO FIGHT BACK.
ONLY THE STRONG WILL PREVAIL OVER US.
BUT YOU... ARE WEAK. YOU REEK... OF FEAR... YOU ARE NOT... WORTHY.
YOU WOULD DO WELL... TO RUN AWAY. AT LEAST THEN... I COULD ENJOY... A GOOD HUNT.
SHIVER

RUN AWAY? WHY DON'T YOU SHUT UP?

I DON'T UNDERSTAND WHAT YOU'RE RAMBLING ON ABOUT. I MAY BE WEAK AND SCARED, BUT...

KREK

I'M NOT A FOOL TO RUN AWAY AND LEAVE MY FRIENDS TO GET HURT! NO MATTER HOW SCARY IT ALL SEEMS! SO BACK OFF!

A BRAVE COWARD? HOW UNUSUAL IT IS... TO WITNESS ONE.

STILL... YOU HAVE... NO CHANCE... FOR VICTORY.

YOU CANNOT EVEN CONTROL... YOUR OWN GHOST...

UGH...

WHAT HAPPENED? I KIND OF FORGOT...

SOMETHING ABOUT A GAME AN--

NIL!!!

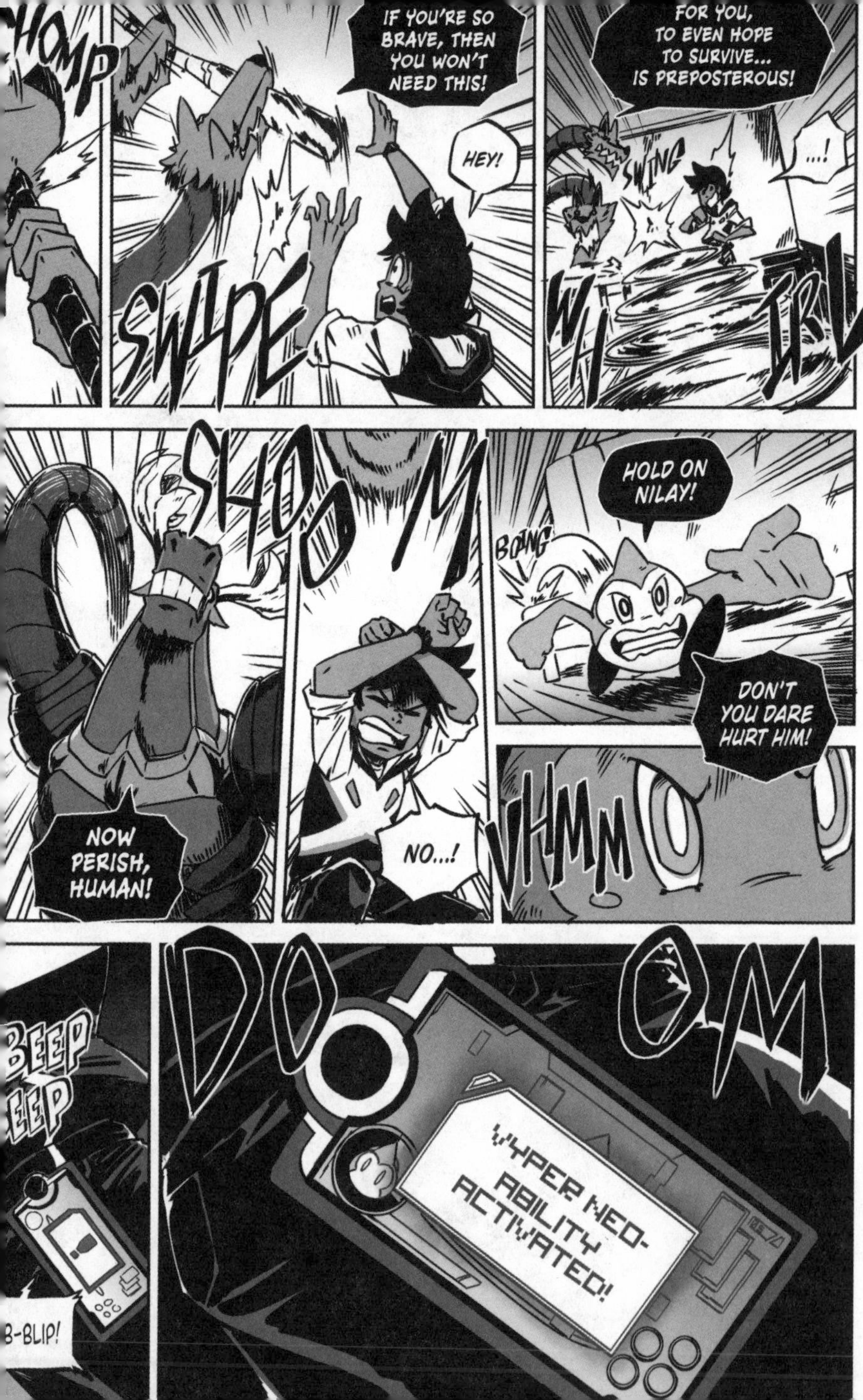
CHOMP
IF YOU'RE SO BRAVE, THEN YOU WON'T NEED THIS!
HEY!
SWIPE
FOR YOU, TO EVEN HOPE TO SURVIVE... IS PREPOSTEROUS!
...!
SWING
WHIRL
SHOOM
NOW PERISH, HUMAN!
NO...!
HOLD ON NILAY!
BOING
DON'T YOU DARE HURT HIM!
VHMM
DOOOM
BEEP
BEEP
VYPER NEO-ABILITY ACTIVATED!
B-BLIP!

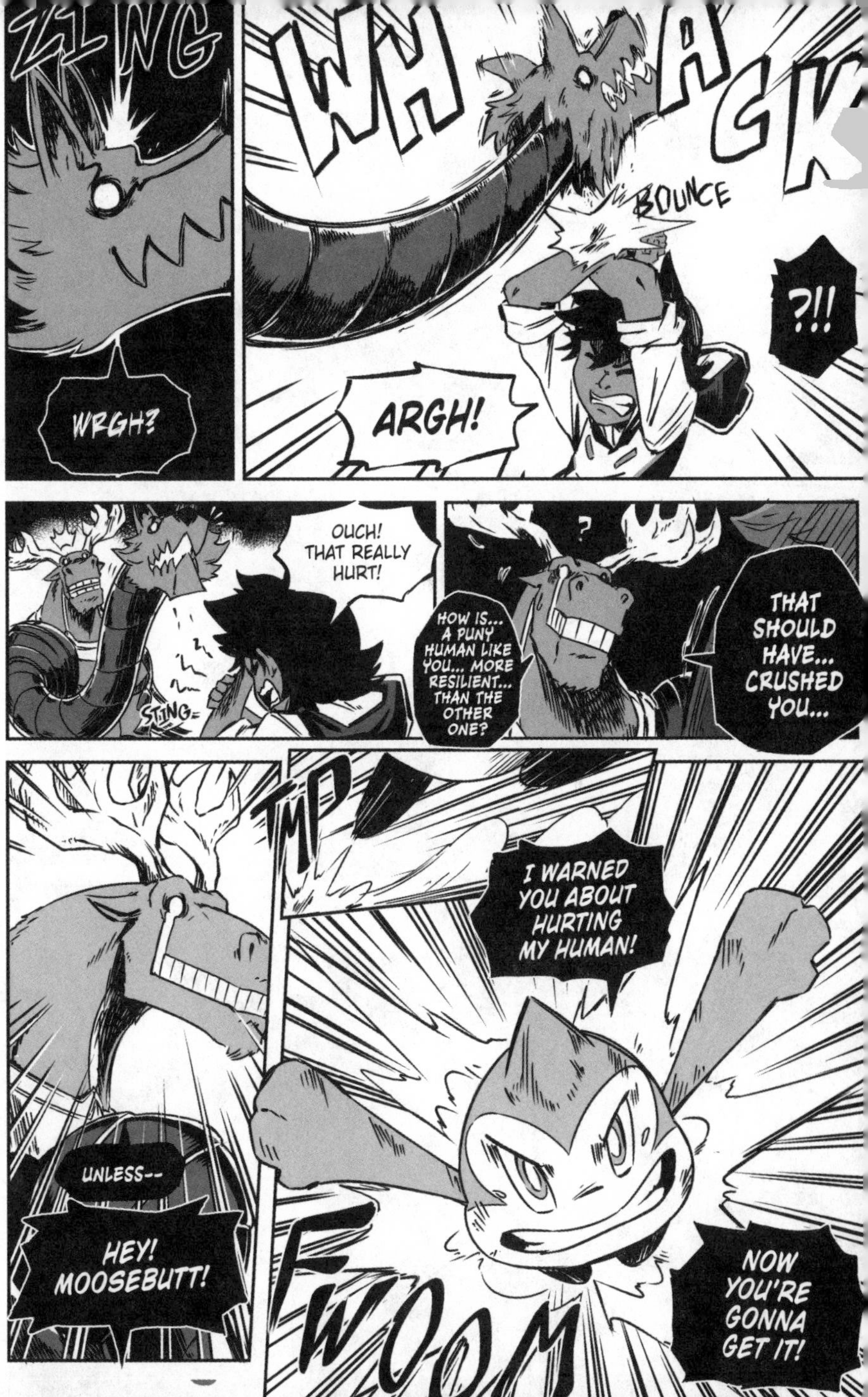
ZING
WRGH?
WHACK
BOUNCE
?!!
ARGH!
OUCH! THAT REALLY HURT!
STING
?
HOW IS... A PUNY HUMAN LIKE YOU... MORE RESILIENT... THAN THE OTHER ONE?
THAT SHOULD HAVE... CRUSHED YOU...
UNLESS--
HEY! MOOSEBUTT!
TMP
I WARNED YOU ABOUT HURTING MY HUMAN!
FWOOM
NOW YOU'RE GONNA GET IT!

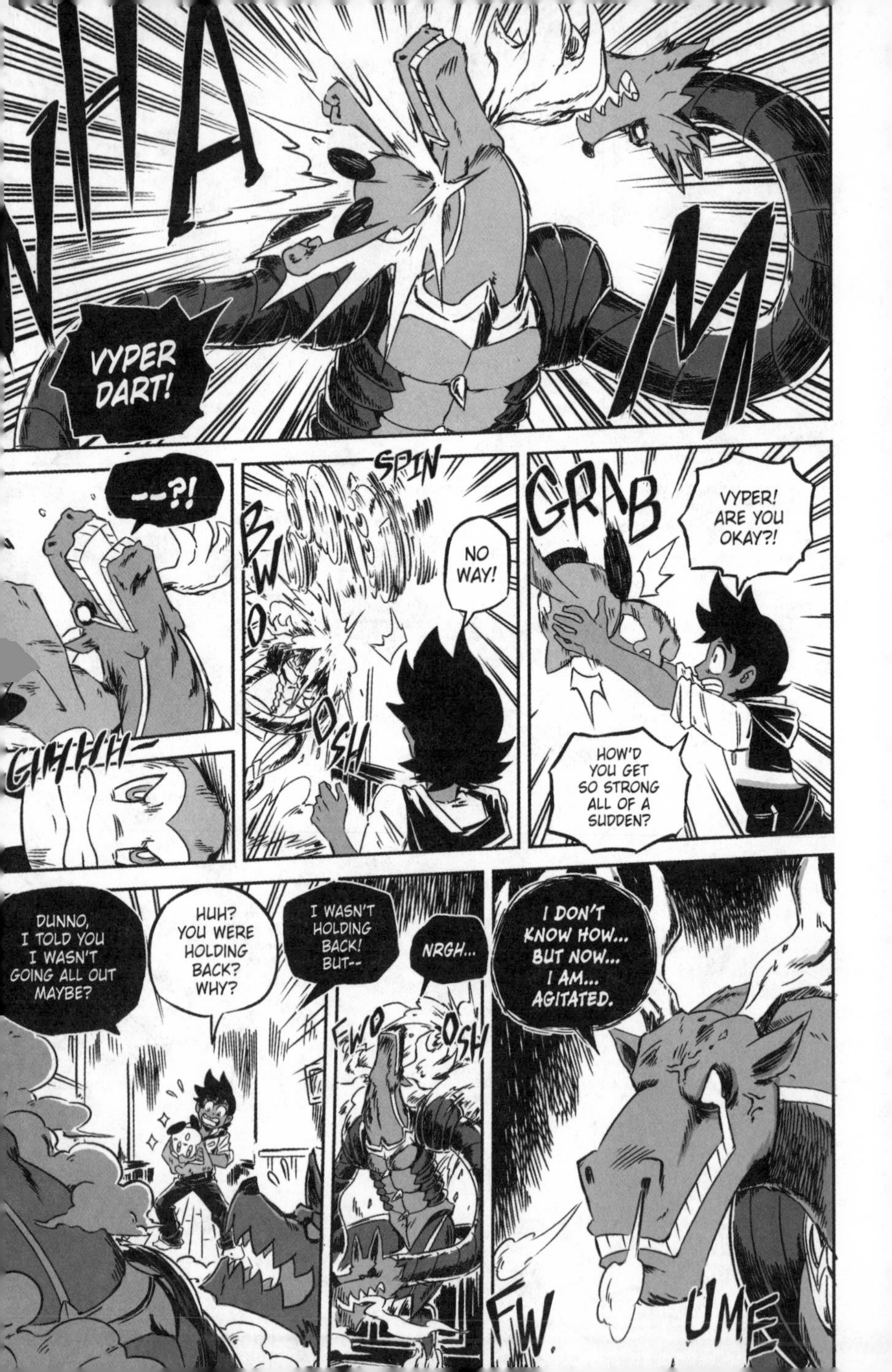

WHAM
VYPER DART!
--?!
GHHH--
SPIN
BWOOSH
NO WAY!
GRAB
VYPER! ARE YOU OKAY?!
HOW'D YOU GET SO STRONG ALL OF A SUDDEN?
DUNNO, I TOLD YOU I WASN'T GOING ALL OUT MAYBE?
HUH? YOU WERE HOLDING BACK? WHY?
I WASN'T HOLDING BACK! BUT--
NRGH...
FWOOSH
I DON'T KNOW HOW... BUT NOW... I AM... AGITATED.
FWUME

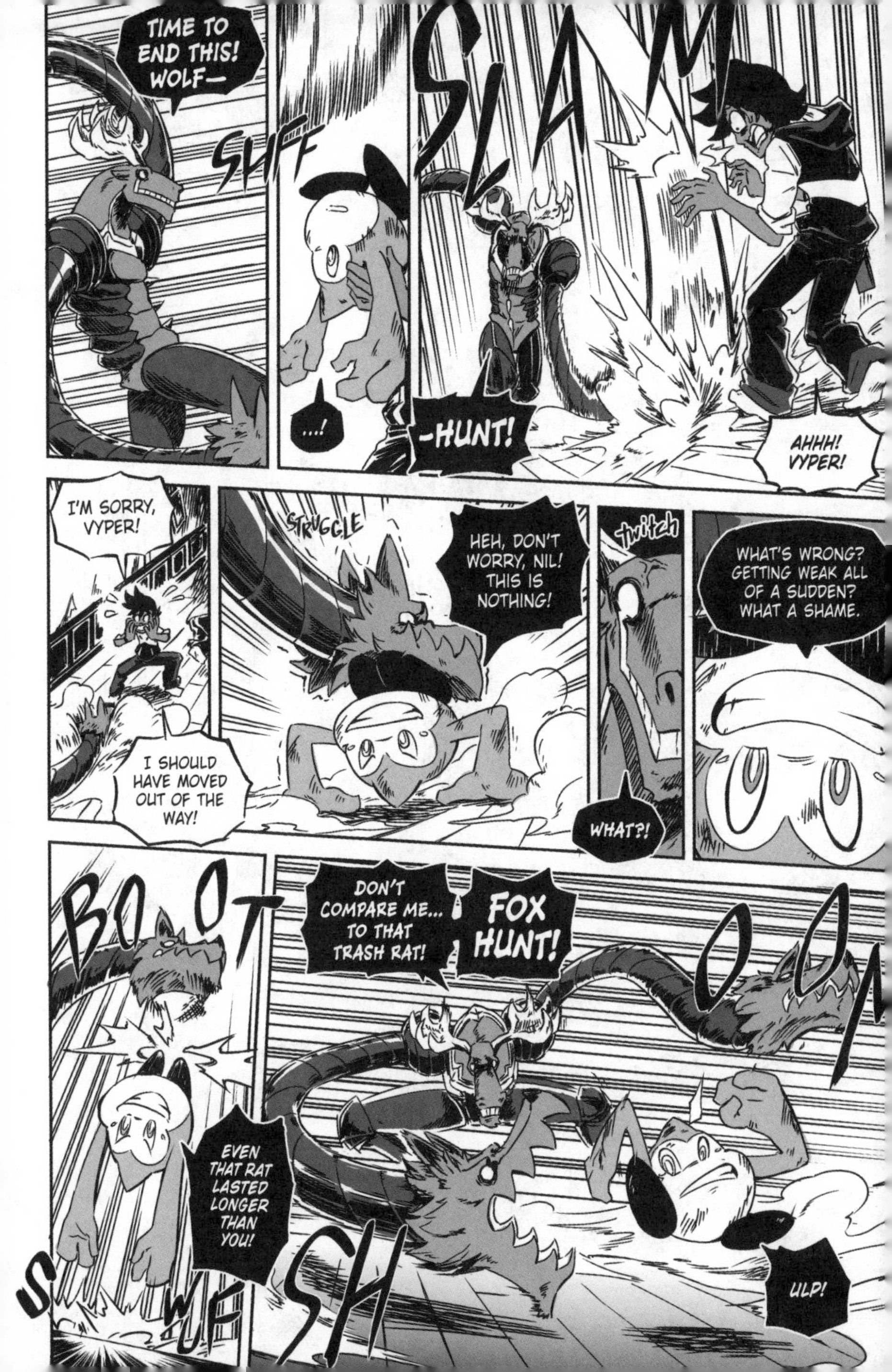
TIME TO END THIS! WOLF—
SHFF
...!
SLAM
-HUNT!
AHHH! VYPER!
I'M SORRY, VYPER!
I SHOULD HAVE MOVED OUT OF THE WAY!
STRUGGLE
HEH, DON'T WORRY, NIL! THIS IS NOTHING!
twitch
WHAT?!
WHAT'S WRONG? GETTING WEAK ALL OF A SUDDEN? WHAT A SHAME.
BOOT
DON'T COMPARE ME... TO THAT TRASH RAT!
FOX HUNT!
OOM
EVEN THAT RAT LASTED LONGER THAN YOU!
SWUF
SH
ULP!

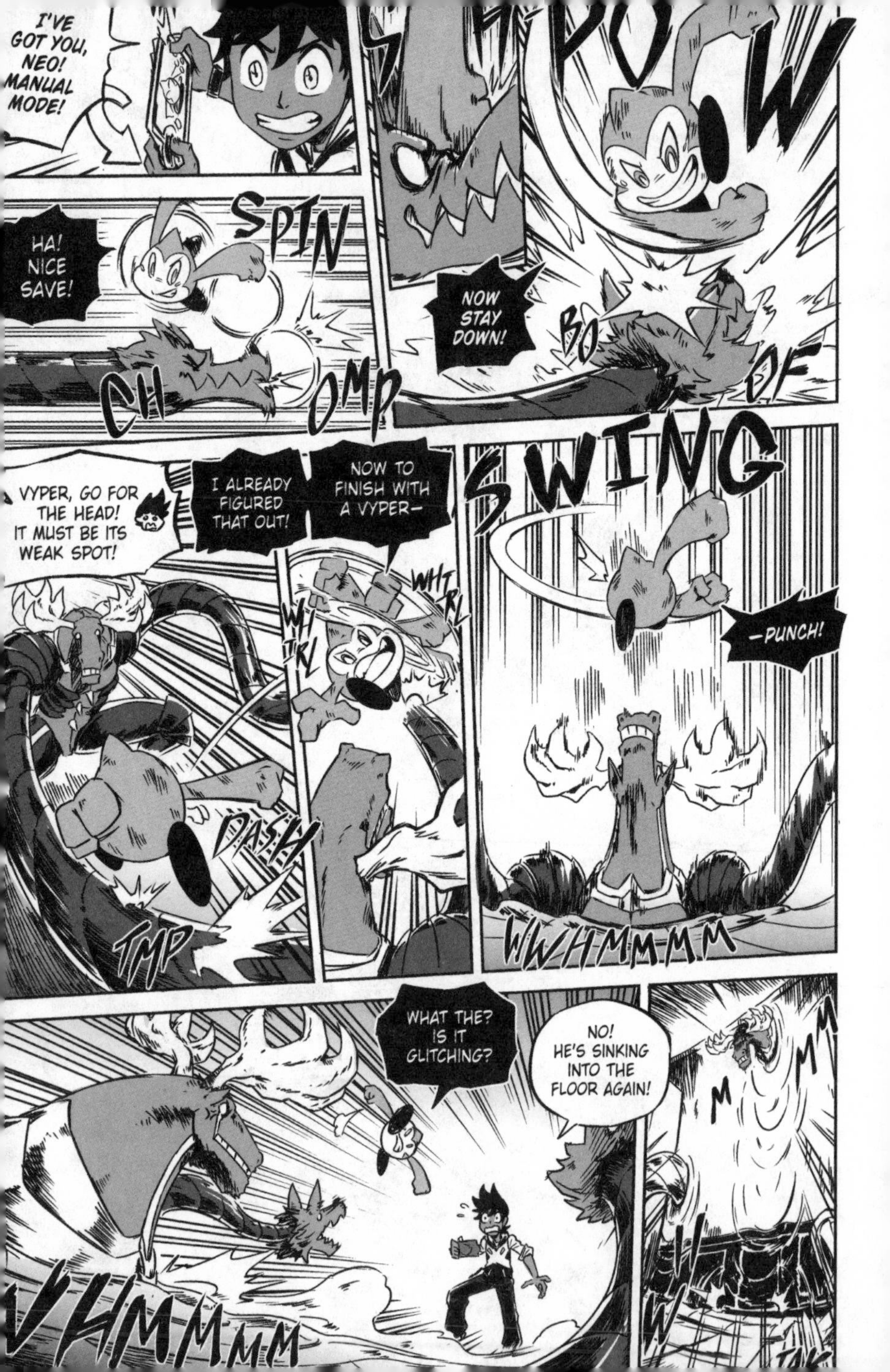
I'VE GOT YOU, NEO! MANUAL MODE!
SHPOW
HA! NICE SAVE!
SPIN
CHOMP
NOW STAY DOWN!
BOOF
VYPER, GO FOR THE HEAD! IT MUST BE ITS WEAK SPOT!
I ALREADY FIGURED THAT OUT!
DASH
TMP
NOW TO FINISH WITH A VYPER—
WHIRL
WHIRL
SWING
—PUNCH!
WWHMMMMM
VHMMMMM
WHAT THE? IS IT GLITCHING?
NO! HE'S SINKING INTO THE FLOOR AGAIN!

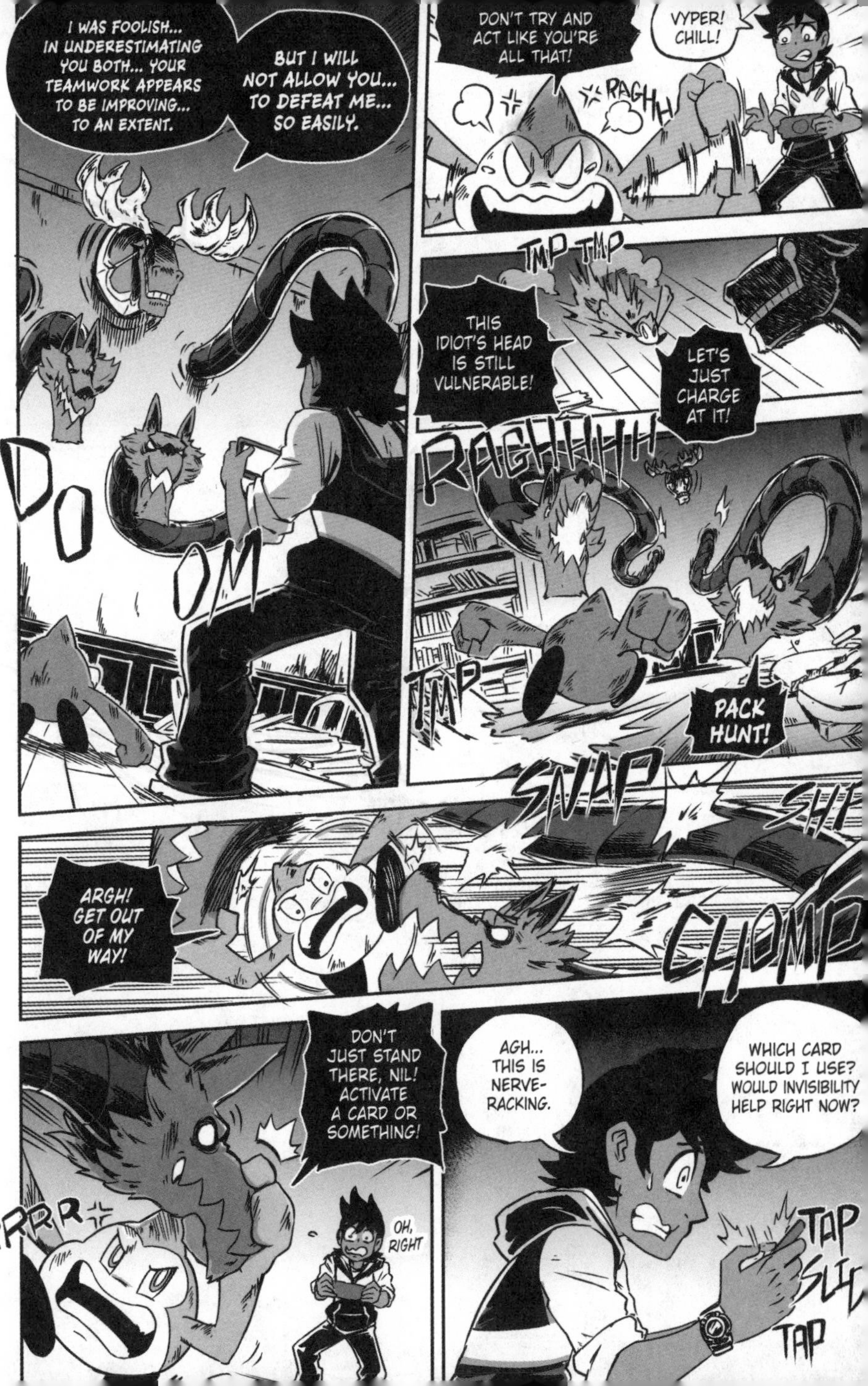

I WAS FOOLISH... IN UNDERESTIMATING YOU BOTH... YOUR TEAMWORK APPEARS TO BE IMPROVING... TO AN EXTENT.
BUT I WILL NOT ALLOW YOU... TO DEFEAT ME... SO EASILY.
DOOM
DON'T TRY AND ACT LIKE YOU'RE ALL THAT!
VYPER! CHILL!
RAGHH
TMP TMP
THIS IDIOT'S HEAD IS STILL VULNERABLE!
LET'S JUST CHARGE AT IT!
RAGHHHH
TMP
PACK HUNT!
SNAP
SHI
ARGH! GET OUT OF MY WAY!
CHOMP
DON'T JUST STAND THERE, NIL! ACTIVATE A CARD OR SOMETHING!
RRRR
OH, RIGHT
AGH... THIS IS NERVE-RACKING.
WHICH CARD SHOULD I USE? WOULD INVISIBILITY HELP RIGHT NOW?
TAP
SLI
TAP

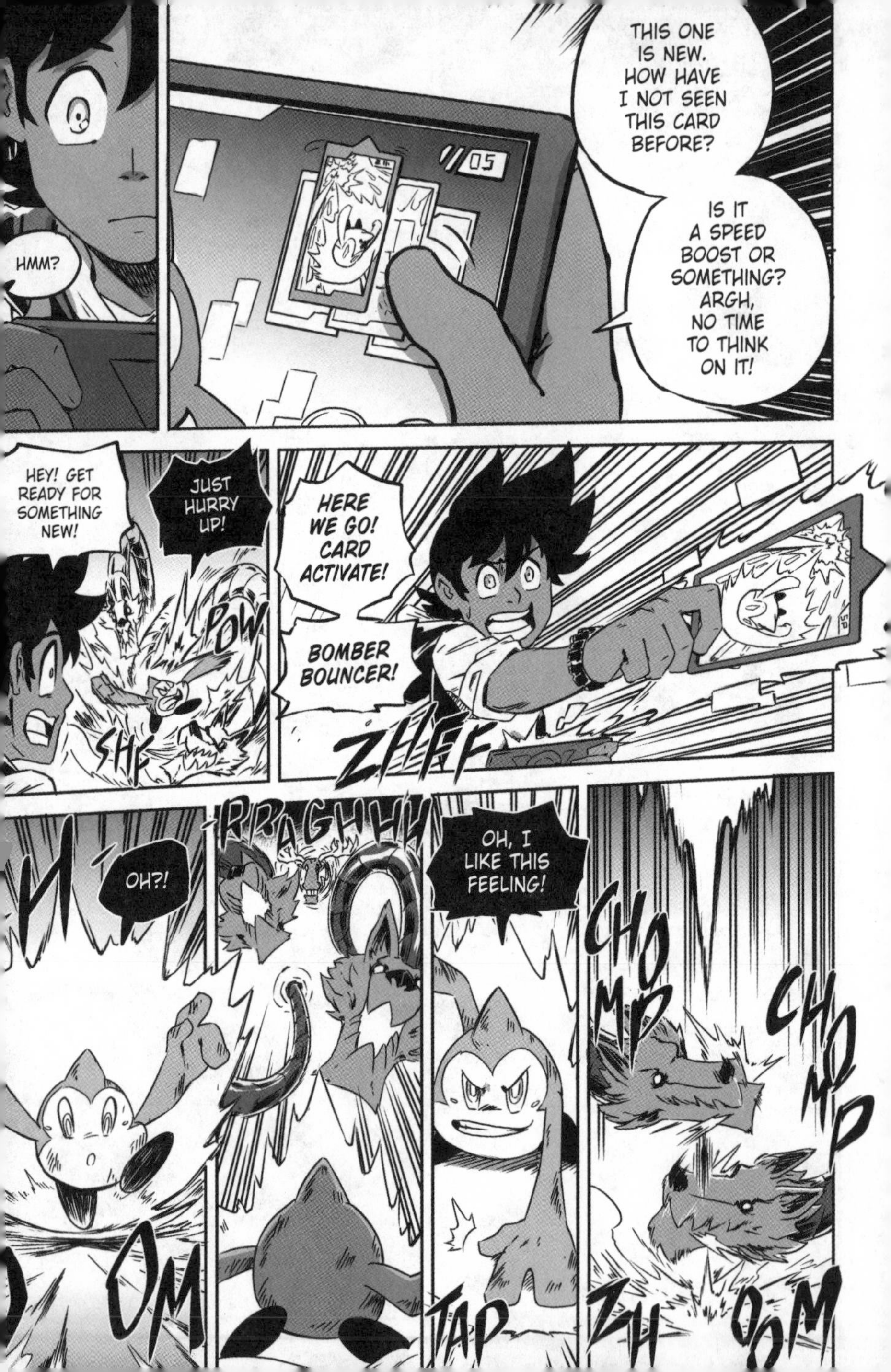
HMM?
THIS ONE IS NEW. HOW HAVE I NOT SEEN THIS CARD BEFORE?
IS IT A SPEED BOOST OR SOMETHING? ARGH, NO TIME TO THINK ON IT!
05
HEY! GET READY FOR SOMETHING NEW!
JUST HURRY UP!
POW
SHF
HERE WE GO! CARD ACTIVATE!
BOMBER BOUNCER!
ZHFF
OH?!
OM
RRAGHHH
OH, I LIKE THIS FEELING!
TAP
CHOMP
CHOMP
ZH
OOM

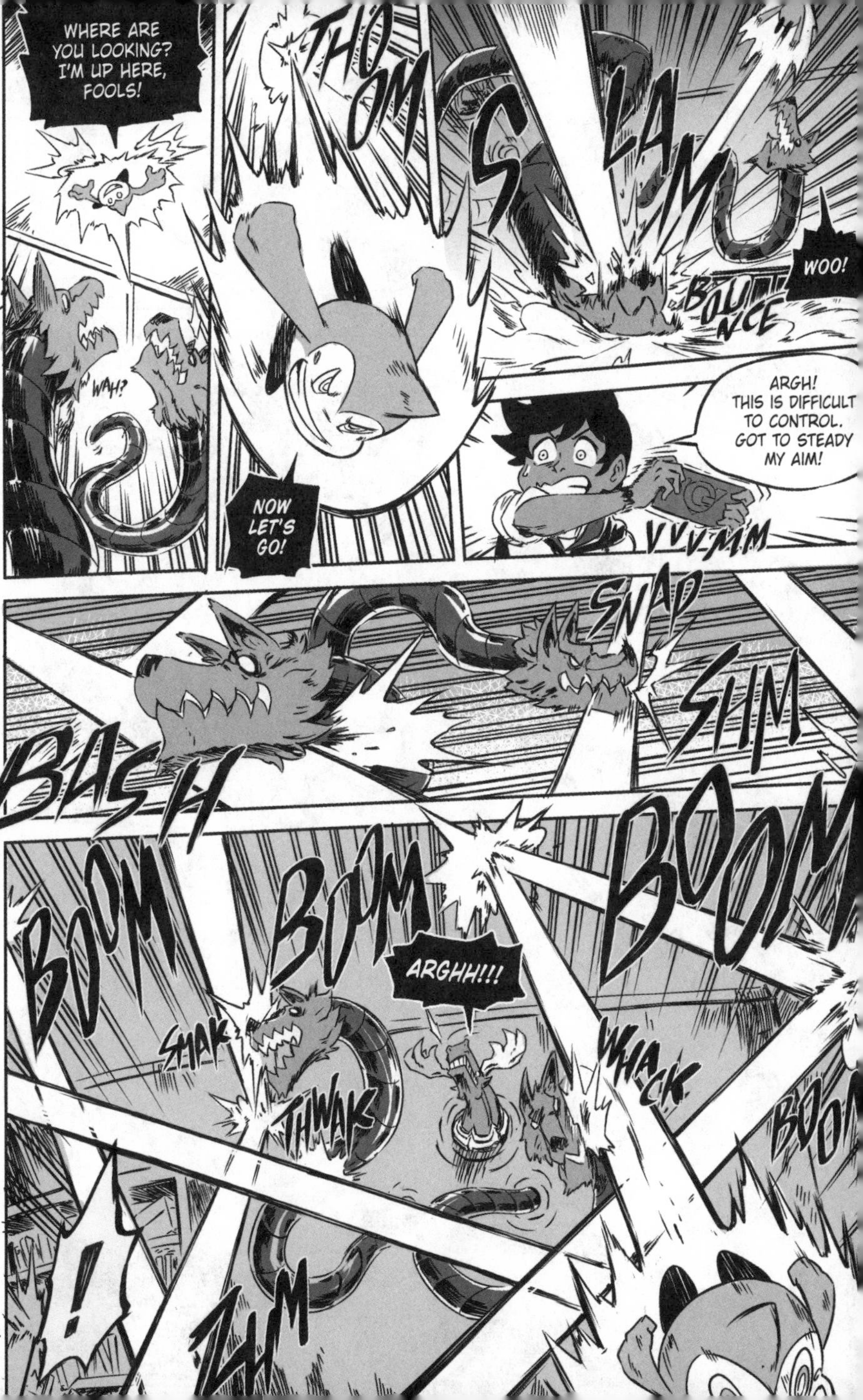
WHERE ARE YOU LOOKING? I'M UP HERE, FOOLS!
WAH?
THOOM
NOW LET'S GO!
SLAM
BOUNCE
WOO!
ARGH! THIS IS DIFFICULT TO CONTROL. GOT TO STEADY MY AIM!
VVVMM
SNAP
BASH
SHM
BOOM
BOOM
BOOM
ARGHH!!!
SMAK
THWAK
WHACK
BOOM
!
ZHM

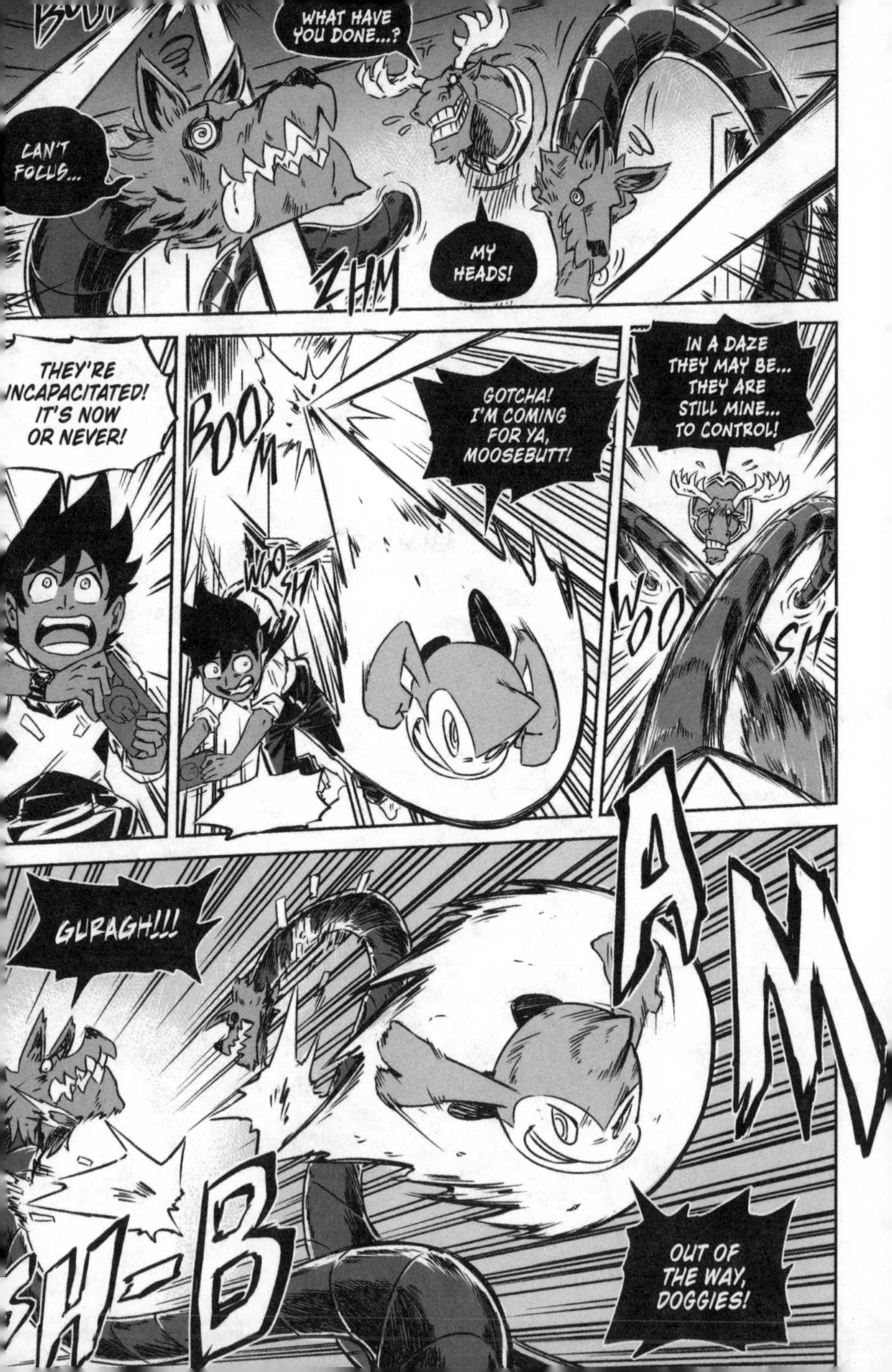
BOOM
WHAT HAVE YOU DONE...?
CAN'T FOCUS...
MY HEADS!
ZHM
THEY'RE INCAPACITATED! IT'S NOW OR NEVER!
BOOM
GOTCHA! I'M COMING FOR YA, MOOSEBUTT!
WOOSH
IN A DAZE THEY MAY BE... THEY ARE STILL MINE... TO CONTROL!
WOOSH
GURAGH!!!
SH-BAM
OUT OF THE WAY, DOGGIES!

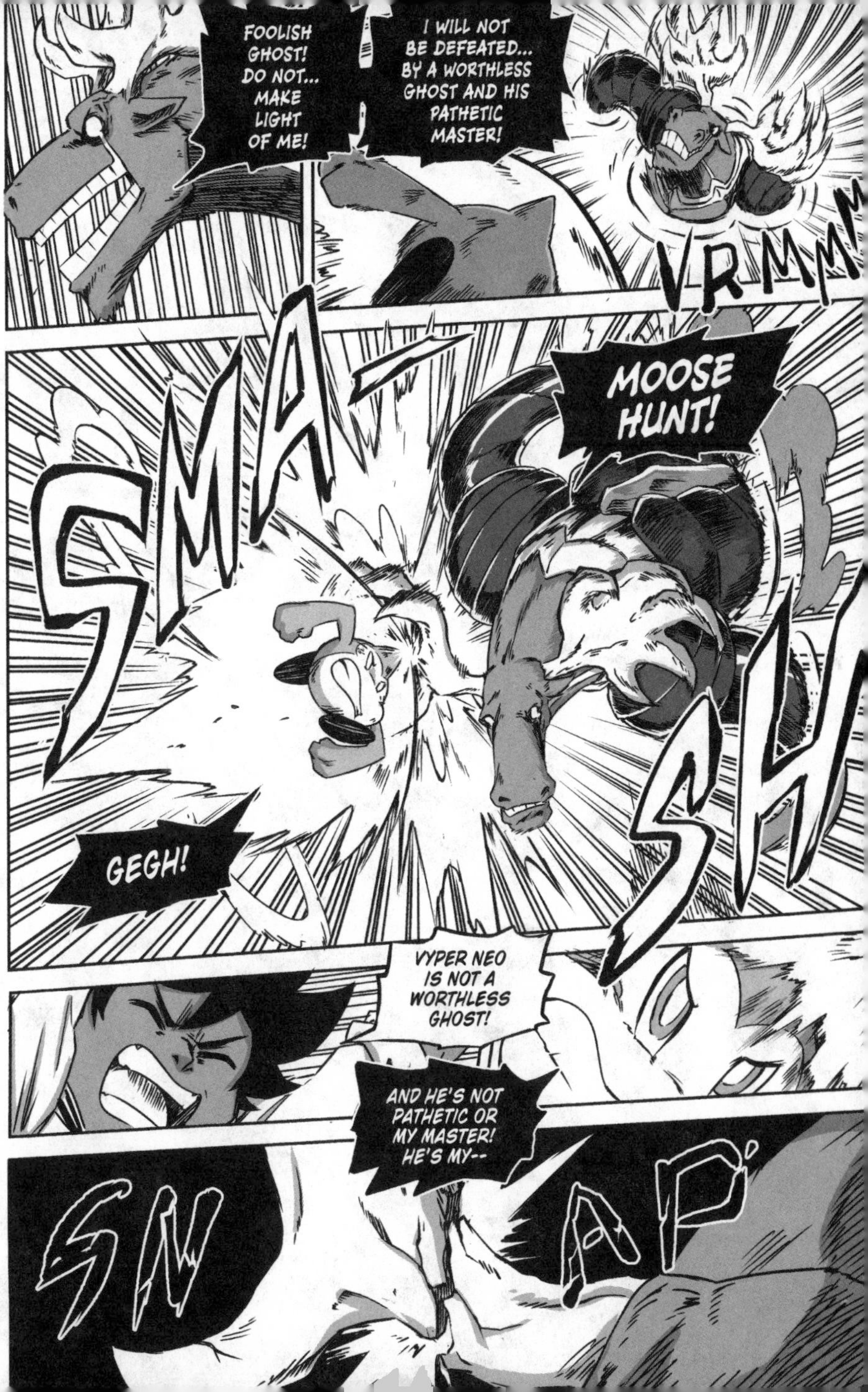
FOOLISH GHOST! DO NOT... MAKE LIGHT OF ME!
I WILL NOT BE DEFEATED... BY A WORTHLESS GHOST AND HIS PATHETIC MASTER!
VRMMM
SMA-
MOOSE HUNT!
SH
GEGH!
VYPER NEO IS NOT A WORTHLESS GHOST!
AND HE'S NOT PATHETIC OR MY MASTER! HE'S MY--
SNAP

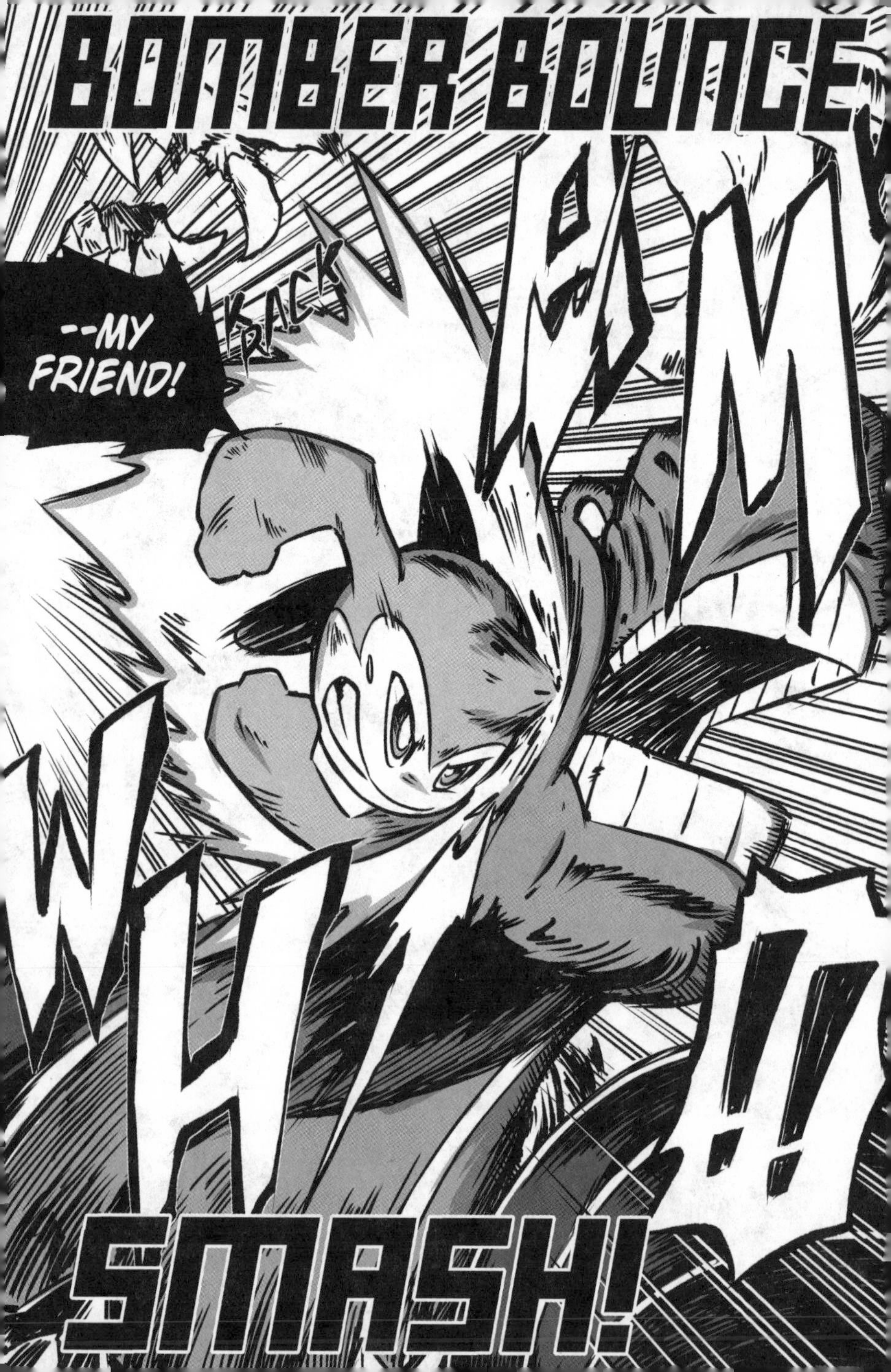
BOMBER BOUNCE
--MY FRIEND!
KRACK!
WHAM!!
SMASH!

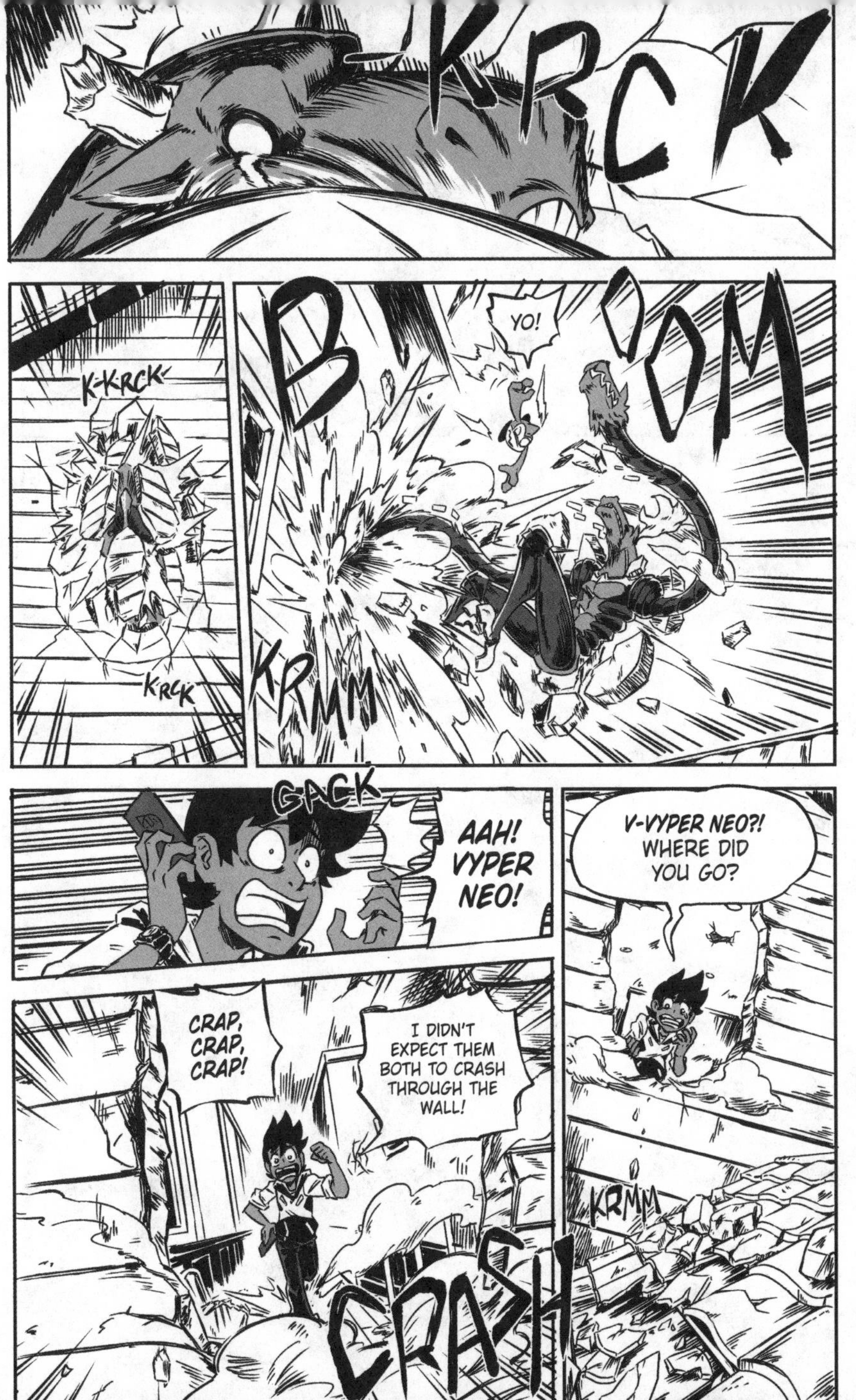

K-RCK
K-K-RCK
K-RCK
BOOM
YO!
KRMM
GACK
AAH! VYPER NEO!
V-VYPER NEO?! WHERE DID YOU GO?
CRAP, CRAP, CRAP!
I DIDN'T EXPECT THEM BOTH TO CRASH THROUGH THE WALL!
KRMM
CRASH

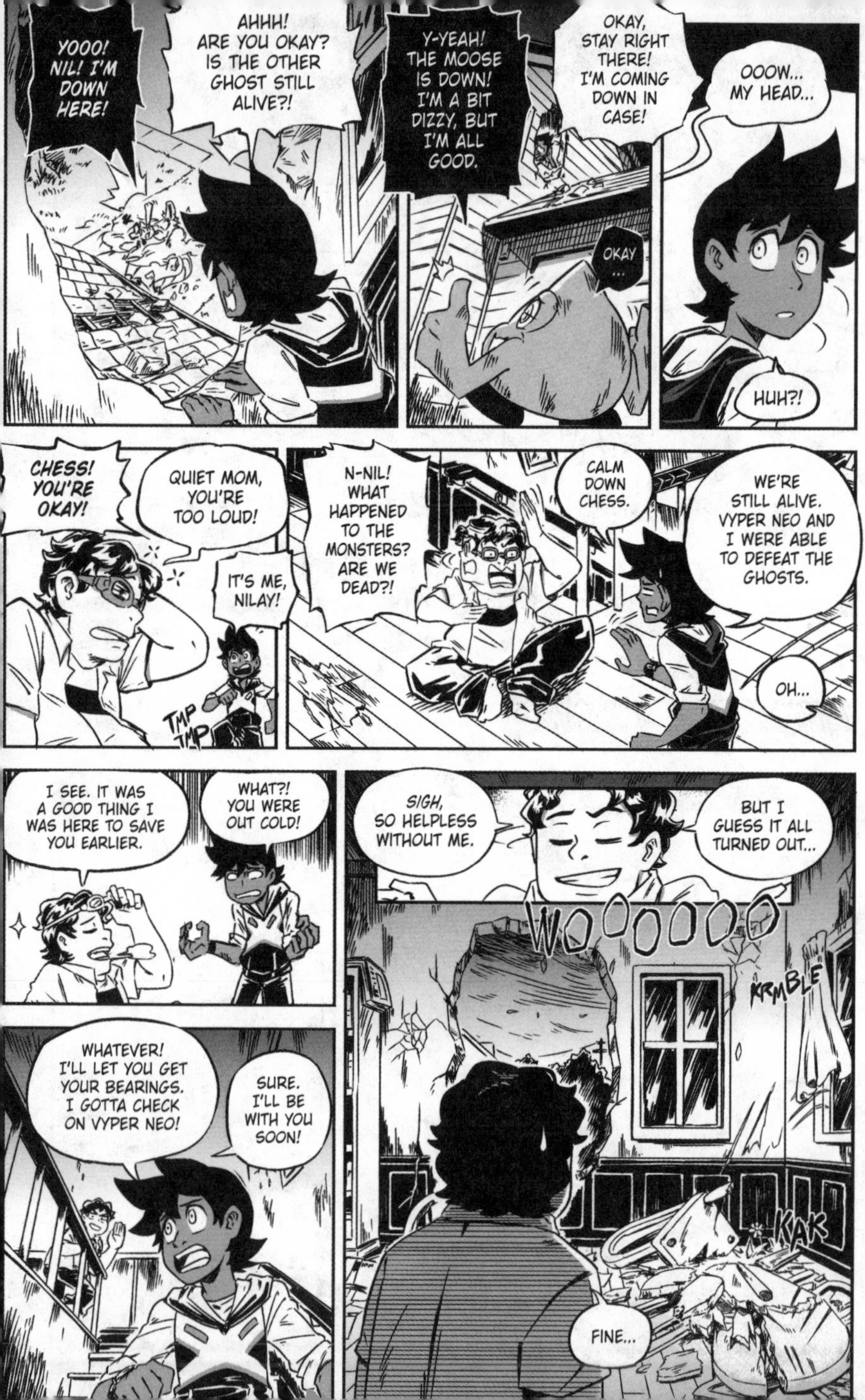
YOOO! NIL! I'M DOWN HERE!
AHHH! ARE YOU OKAY? IS THE OTHER GHOST STILL ALIVE?!
Y-YEAH! THE MOOSE IS DOWN! I'M A BIT DIZZY, BUT I'M ALL GOOD.
OKAY, STAY RIGHT THERE! I'M COMING DOWN IN CASE!
OKAY...
OOOW... MY HEAD...
HUH?!
CHESS! YOU'RE OKAY!
QUIET MOM, YOU'RE TOO LOUD!
IT'S ME, NILAY!
TMP TMP
N-NIL! WHAT HAPPENED TO THE MONSTERS? ARE WE DEAD?!
CALM DOWN CHESS.
WE'RE STILL ALIVE. VYPER NEO AND I WERE ABLE TO DEFEAT THE GHOSTS.
OH...
I SEE. IT WAS A GOOD THING I WAS HERE TO SAVE YOU EARLIER.
WHAT?! YOU WERE OUT COLD!
SIGH, SO HELPLESS WITHOUT ME.
BUT I GUESS IT ALL TURNED OUT...
WHATEVER! I'LL LET YOU GET YOUR BEARINGS. I GOTTA CHECK ON VYPER NEO!
SURE. I'LL BE WITH YOU SOON!
WOOOOOO
KRMBLE
KAK
FINE...

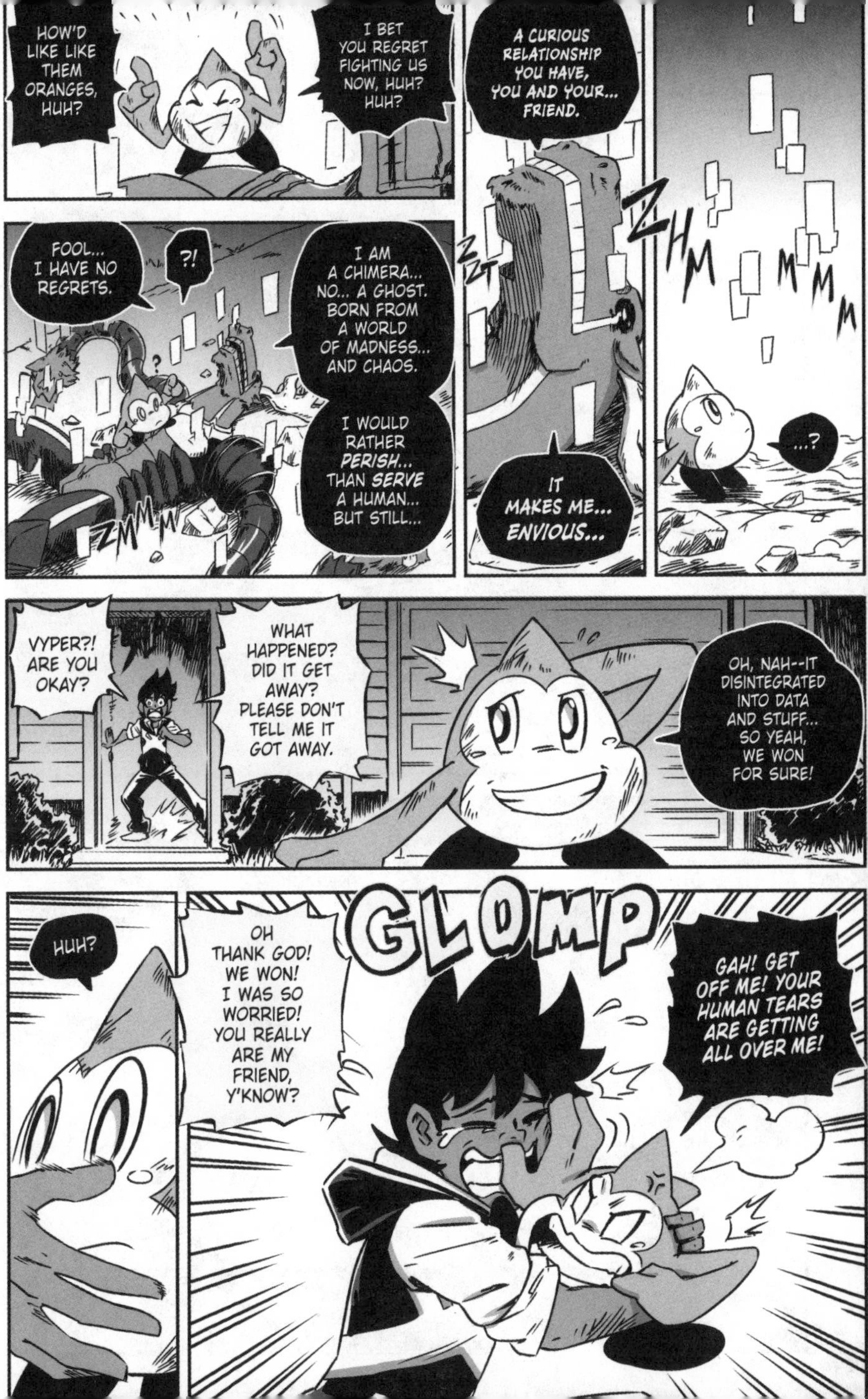
HOW'D LIKE LIKE THEM ORANGES, HUH?
I BET YOU REGRET FIGHTING US NOW, HUH? HUH?
A CURIOUS RELATIONSHIP YOU HAVE, YOU AND YOUR... FRIEND.
ZHMMMMMM
FOOL... I HAVE NO REGRETS.
?!
I AM A CHIMERA... NO... A GHOST. BORN FROM A WORLD OF MADNESS... AND CHAOS.
I WOULD RATHER PERISH... THAN SERVE A HUMAN... BUT STILL...
ZMMM
ZZT
IT MAKES ME... ENVIOUS...
...?
VYPER?! ARE YOU OKAY?
WHAT HAPPENED? DID IT GET AWAY? PLEASE DON'T TELL ME IT GOT AWAY.
OH, NAH--IT DISINTEGRATED INTO DATA AND STUFF... SO YEAH, WE WON FOR SURE!
HUH?
OH THANK GOD! WE WON! I WAS SO WORRIED! YOU REALLY ARE MY FRIEND, Y'KNOW?
GLOMP
GAH! GET OFF ME! YOUR HUMAN TEARS ARE GETTING ALL OVER ME!

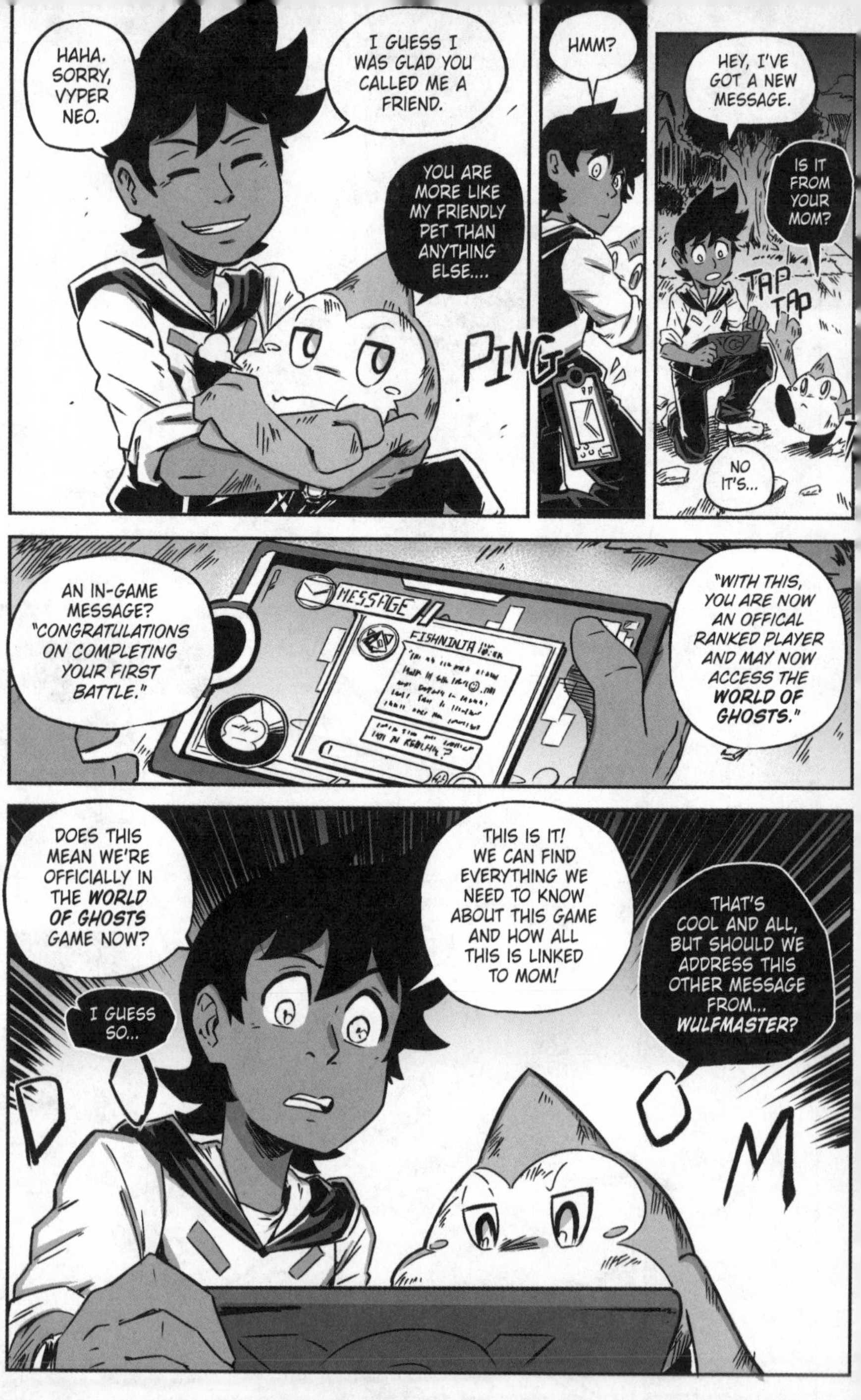

HAHA. SORRY, VYPER NEO.
I GUESS I WAS GLAD YOU CALLED ME A FRIEND.
YOU ARE MORE LIKE MY FRIENDLY PET THAN ANYTHING ELSE....
PING
HMM?
HEY, I'VE GOT A NEW MESSAGE.
IS IT FROM YOUR MOM?
TAP TAP
NO IT'S...
AN IN-GAME MESSAGE? "CONGRATULATIONS ON COMPLETING YOUR FIRST BATTLE."
MESSAGE
"WITH THIS, YOU ARE NOW AN OFFICAL RANKED PLAYER AND MAY NOW ACCESS THE WORLD OF GHOSTS."
DOES THIS MEAN WE'RE OFFICIALLY IN THE WORLD OF GHOSTS GAME NOW?
I GUESS SO...
THIS IS IT! WE CAN FIND EVERYTHING WE NEED TO KNOW ABOUT THIS GAME AND HOW ALL THIS IS LINKED TO MOM!
THAT'S COOL AND ALL, BUT SHOULD WE ADDRESS THIS OTHER MESSAGE FROM... WULFMASTER?
DOOM

THE MASSIVELY MULTIPLAYER WORLD OF GHOSTS

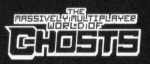

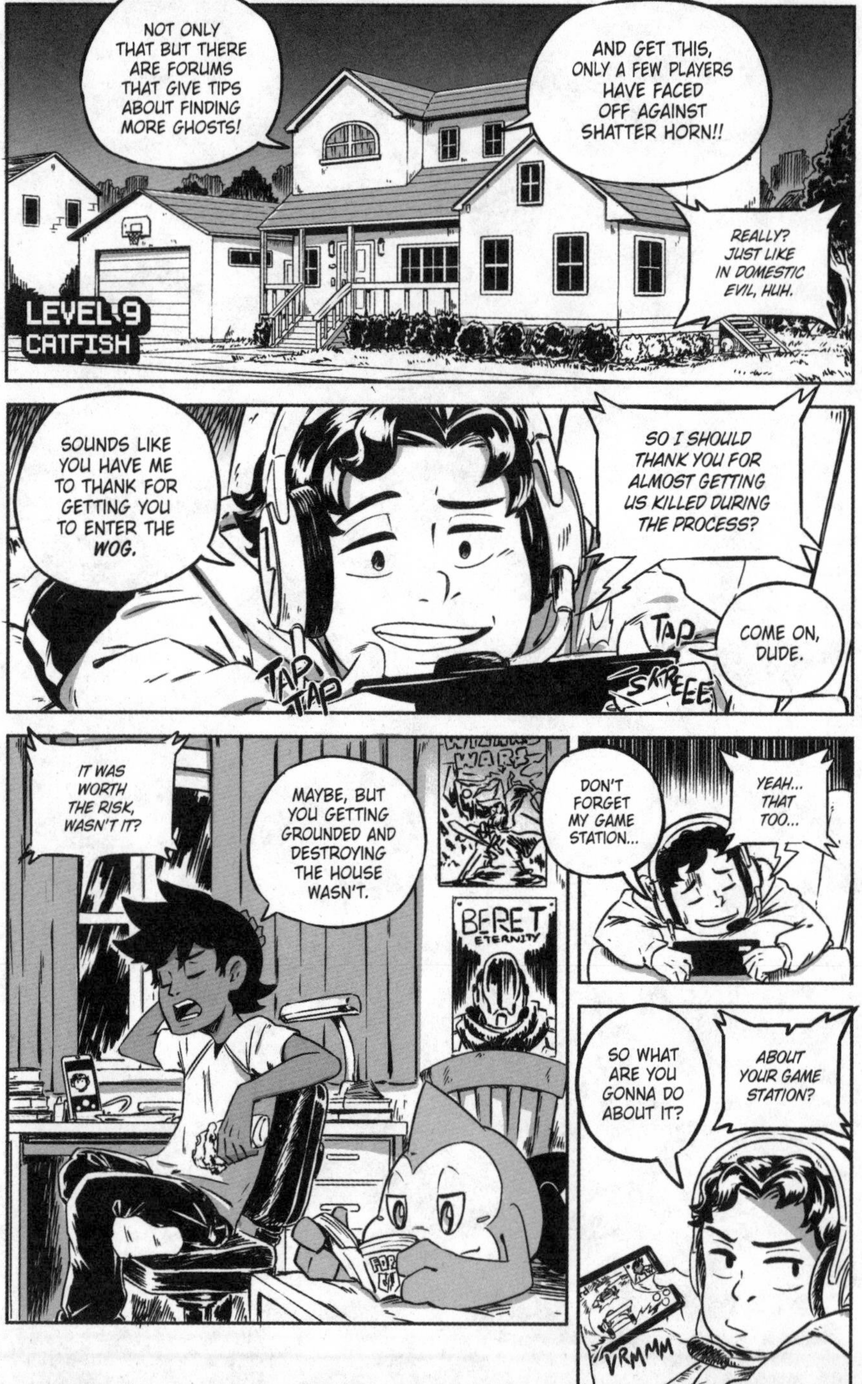
LEVEL 9
CATFISH
NOT ONLY THAT BUT THERE ARE FORUMS THAT GIVE TIPS ABOUT FINDING MORE GHOSTS!
AND GET THIS, ONLY A FEW PLAYERS HAVE FACED OFF AGAINST SHATTER HORN!!
REALLY? JUST LIKE IN DOMESTIC EVIL, HUH.
SOUNDS LIKE YOU HAVE ME TO THANK FOR GETTING YOU TO ENTER THE WOG.
SO I SHOULD THANK YOU FOR ALMOST GETTING US KILLED DURING THE PROCESS?
TAP TAP
TAP
SKREEE
COME ON, DUDE.
IT WAS WORTH THE RISK, WASN'T IT?
MAYBE, BUT YOU GETTING GROUNDED AND DESTROYING THE HOUSE WASN'T.
BERET ETERNITY
DON'T FORGET MY GAME STATION...
YEAH... THAT TOO...
SO WHAT ARE YOU GONNA DO ABOUT IT?
ABOUT YOUR GAME STATION?
VRMMM

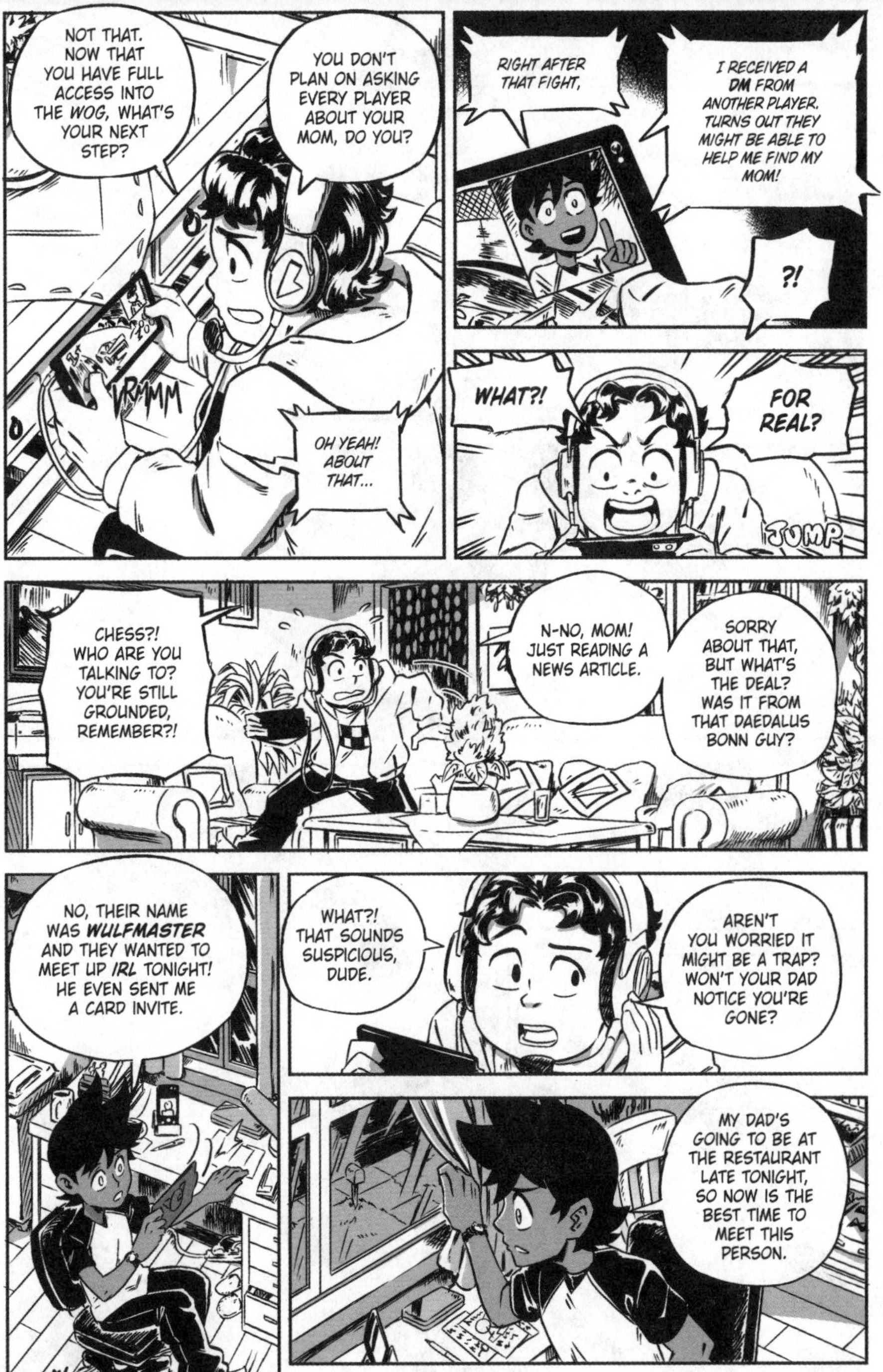
NOT THAT. NOW THAT YOU HAVE FULL ACCESS INTO THE *WOG*, WHAT'S YOUR NEXT STEP?
YOU DON'T PLAN ON ASKING EVERY PLAYER ABOUT YOUR MOM, DO YOU?
VRMMM
OH YEAH! ABOUT THAT...
RIGHT AFTER THAT FIGHT,
I RECEIVED A **DM** FROM ANOTHER PLAYER. TURNS OUT THEY MIGHT BE ABLE TO HELP ME FIND MY MOM!
?!
WHAT?!
FOR REAL?
JUMP
CHESS?! WHO ARE YOU TALKING TO? YOU'RE STILL GROUNDED, REMEMBER?!
N-NO, MOM! JUST READING A NEWS ARTICLE.
SORRY ABOUT THAT, BUT WHAT'S THE DEAL? WAS IT FROM THAT DAEDALUS BONN GUY?
NO, THEIR NAME WAS ***WULFMASTER*** AND THEY WANTED TO MEET UP *IRL* TONIGHT! HE EVEN SENT ME A CARD INVITE.
SHKK
WHAT?! THAT SOUNDS SUSPICIOUS, DUDE.
AREN'T YOU WORRIED IT MIGHT BE A TRAP? WON'T YOUR DAD NOTICE YOU'RE GONE?
MY DAD'S GOING TO BE AT THE RESTAURANT LATE TONIGHT, SO NOW IS THE BEST TIME TO MEET THIS PERSON.

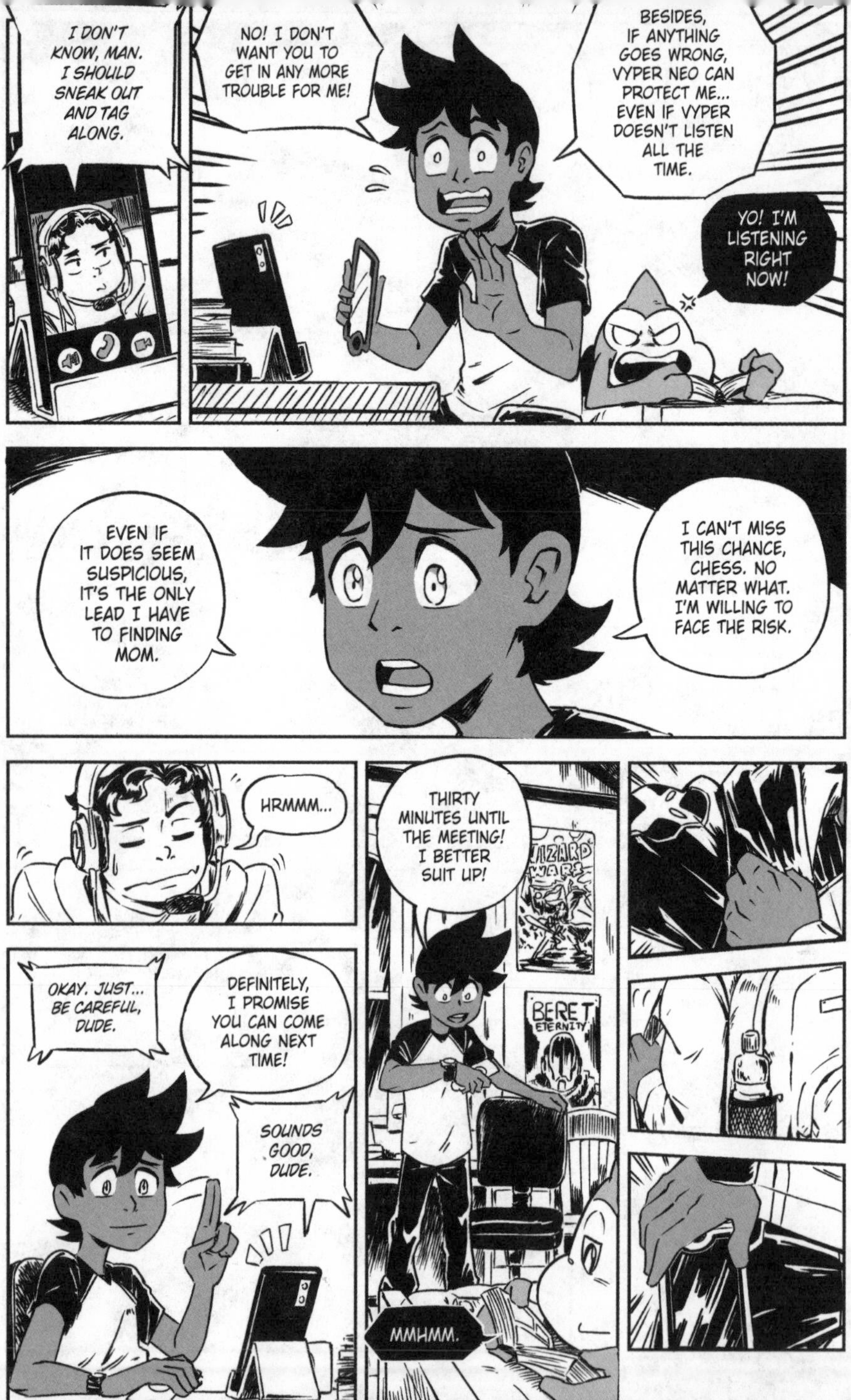
I DON'T KNOW, MAN. I SHOULD SNEAK OUT AND TAG ALONG.
NO! I DON'T WANT YOU TO GET IN ANY MORE TROUBLE FOR ME!
BESIDES, IF ANYTHING GOES WRONG, VYPER NEO CAN PROTECT ME... EVEN IF VYPER DOESN'T LISTEN ALL THE TIME.
YO! I'M LISTENING RIGHT NOW!
EVEN IF IT DOES SEEM SUSPICIOUS, IT'S THE ONLY LEAD I HAVE TO FINDING MOM.
I CAN'T MISS THIS CHANCE, CHESS. NO MATTER WHAT. I'M WILLING TO FACE THE RISK.
HRMMM...
OKAY. JUST... BE CAREFUL, DUDE.
DEFINITELY, I PROMISE YOU CAN COME ALONG NEXT TIME!
SOUNDS GOOD, DUDE.
THIRTY MINUTES UNTIL THE MEETING! I BETTER SUIT UP!
WIZARD WARS
BERET ETERNITY
MMHMM.

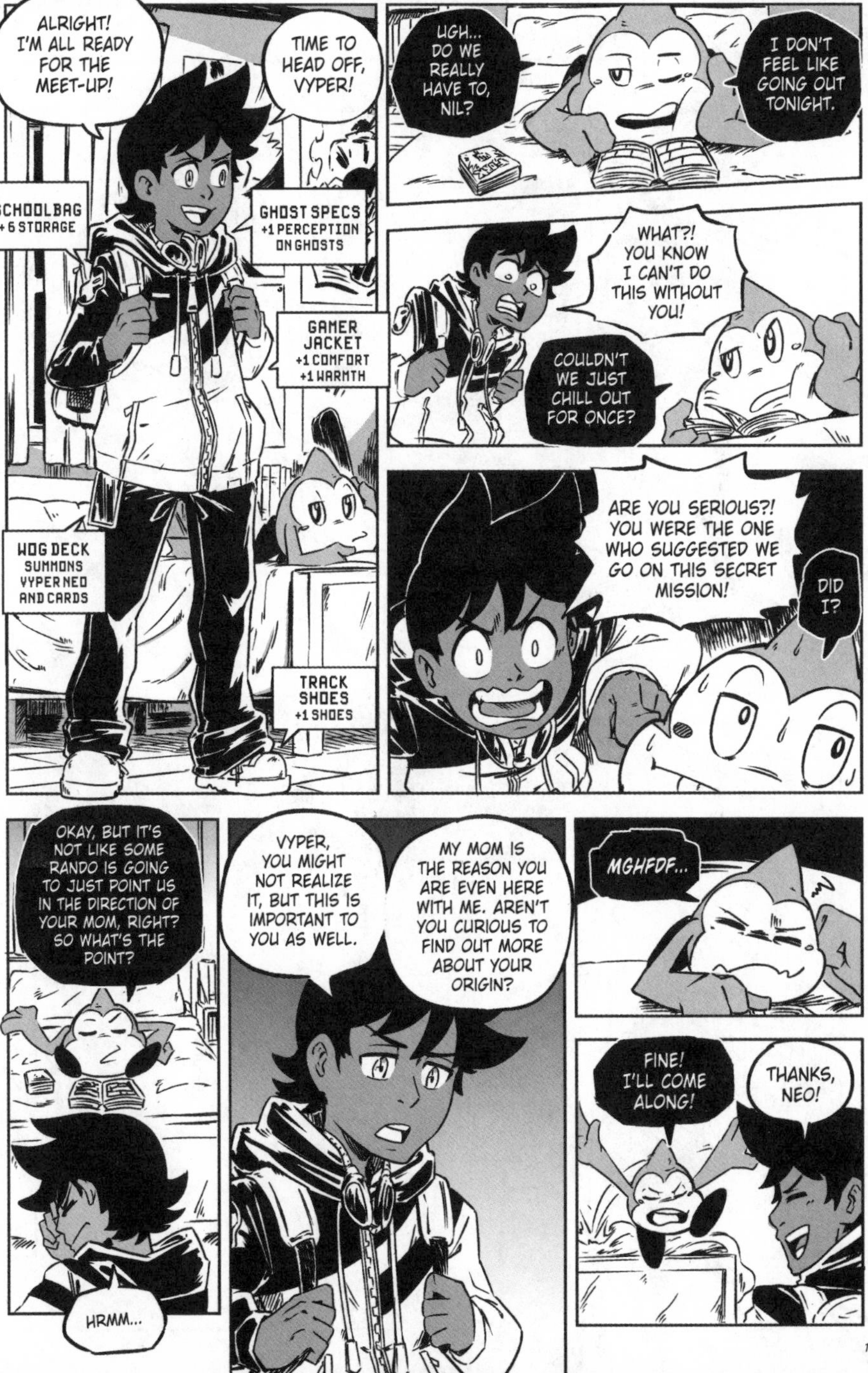
ALRIGHT! I'M ALL READY FOR THE MEET-UP!
TIME TO HEAD OFF, VYPER!
SCHOOLBAG +6 STORAGE
GHOST SPECS +1 PERCEPTION ON GHOSTS
GAMER JACKET +1 COMFORT +1 WARMTH
WOG DECK SUMMONS VYPER NEO AND CARDS
TRACK SHOES +1 SHOES
UGH... DO WE REALLY HAVE TO, NIL?
I DON'T FEEL LIKE GOING OUT TONIGHT.
WHAT?! YOU KNOW I CAN'T DO THIS WITHOUT YOU!
COULDN'T WE JUST CHILL OUT FOR ONCE?
ARE YOU SERIOUS?! YOU WERE THE ONE WHO SUGGESTED WE GO ON THIS SECRET MISSION!
DID I?
OKAY, BUT IT'S NOT LIKE SOME RANDO IS GOING TO JUST POINT US IN THE DIRECTION OF YOUR MOM, RIGHT? SO WHAT'S THE POINT?
HRMM...
VYPER, YOU MIGHT NOT REALIZE IT, BUT THIS IS IMPORTANT TO YOU AS WELL.
MY MOM IS THE REASON YOU ARE EVEN HERE WITH ME. AREN'T YOU CURIOUS TO FIND OUT MORE ABOUT YOUR ORIGIN?
MGHFDF...
FINE! I'LL COME ALONG!
THANKS, NEO!

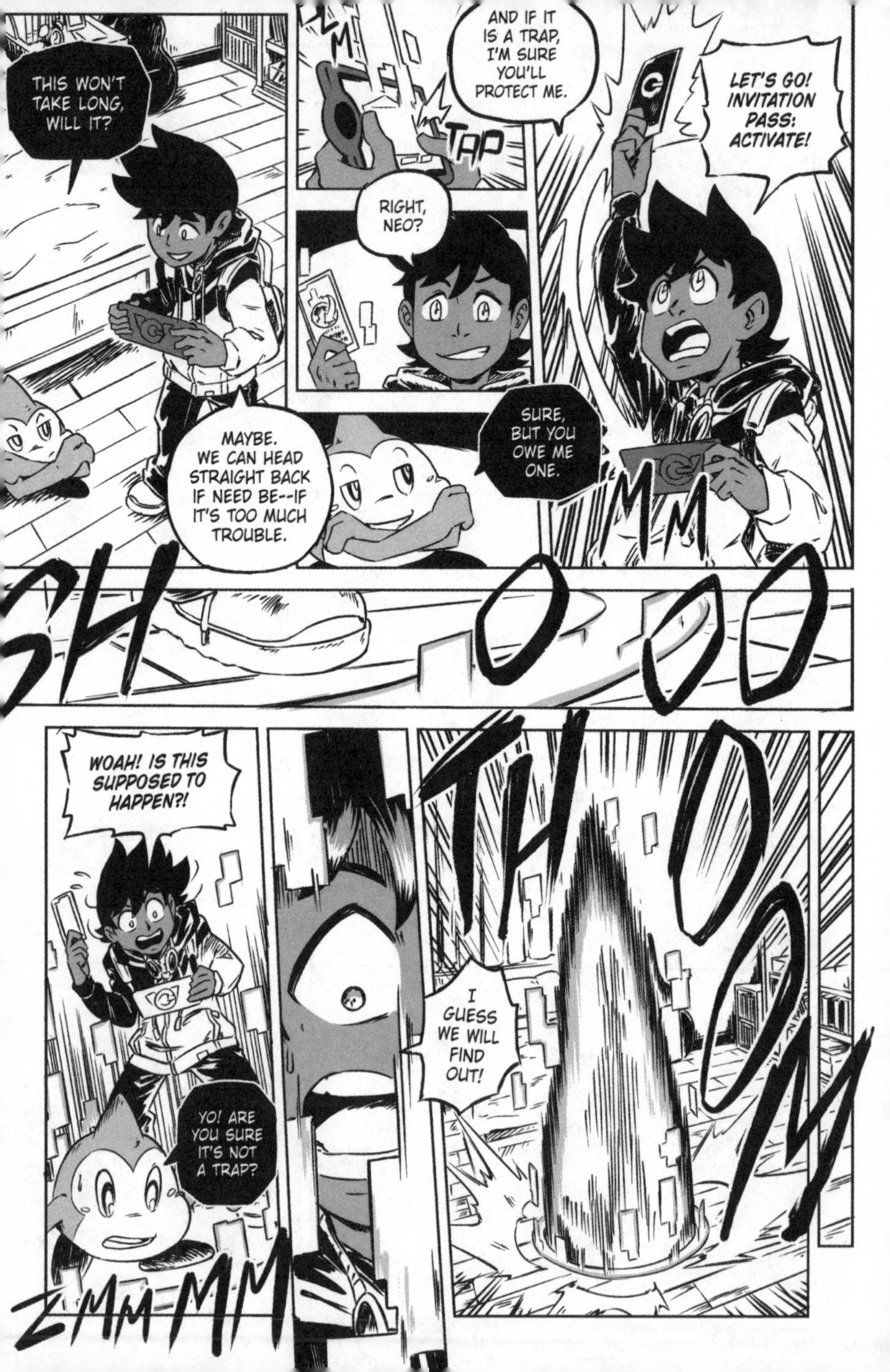
THIS WON'T TAKE LONG, WILL IT?
MAYBE. WE CAN HEAD STRAIGHT BACK IF NEED BE--IF IT'S TOO MUCH TROUBLE.
ZM
TAP
AND IF IT IS A TRAP, I'M SURE YOU'LL PROTECT ME.
RIGHT, NEO?
SURE, BUT YOU OWE ME ONE.
LET'S GO! INVITATION PASS: ACTIVATE!
MM
SHOOOO
WOAH! IS THIS SUPPOSED TO HAPPEN?!
YO! ARE YOU SURE IT'S NOT A TRAP?
ZMMMMM
I GUESS WE WILL FIND OUT!
THOOOM

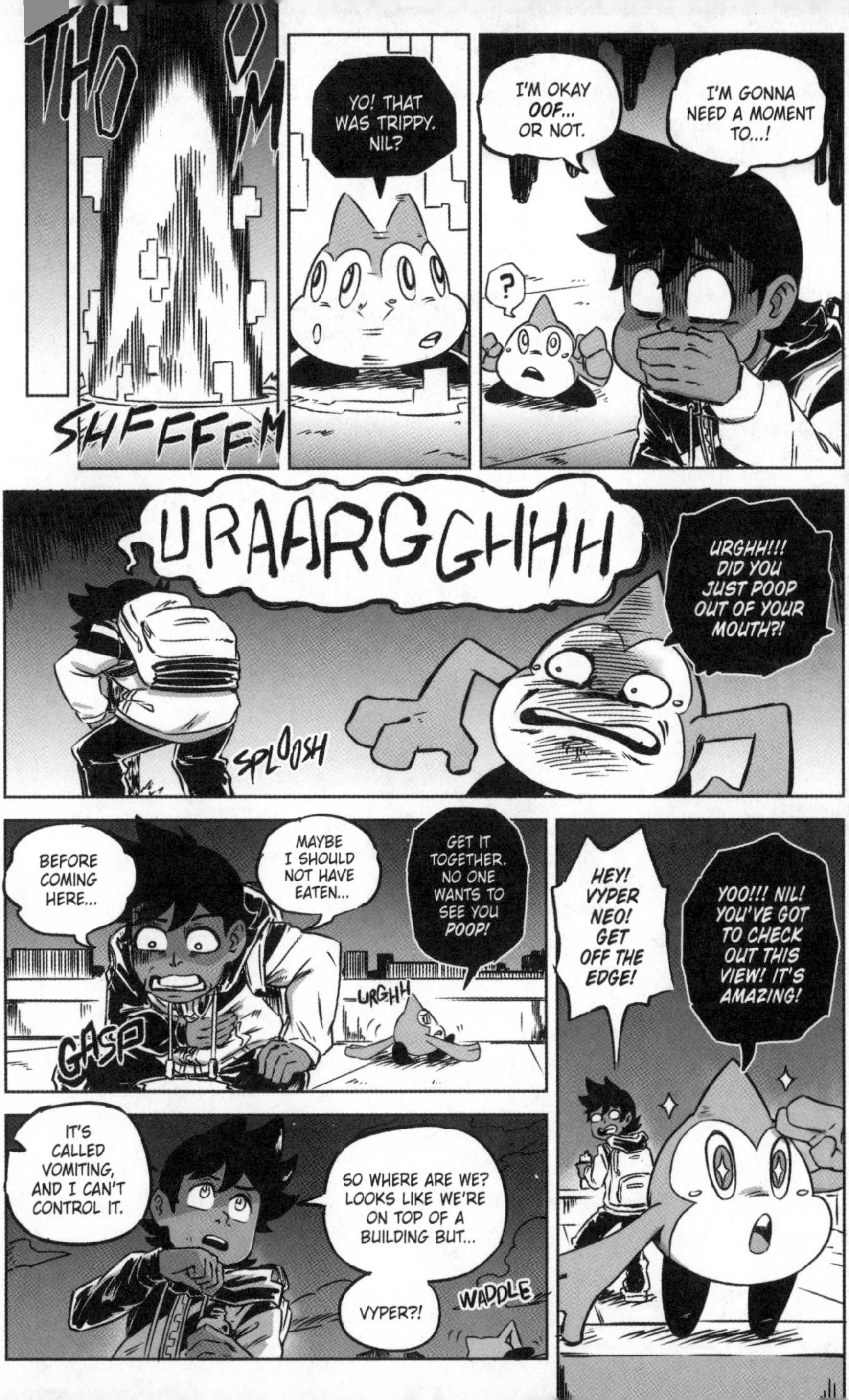
THOOM
SHFFFFM
YO! THAT WAS TRIPPY. NIL?
I'M OKAY *OOF*... OR NOT.
?
I'M GONNA NEED A MOMENT TO...!
URAARGGHHH
URGHH!!! DID YOU JUST POOP OUT OF YOUR MOUTH?!
SPLOOSH
BEFORE COMING HERE...
MAYBE I SHOULD NOT HAVE EATEN...
GET IT TOGETHER. NO ONE WANTS TO SEE YOU POOP!
URGHH
GASP
IT'S CALLED VOMITING, AND I CAN'T CONTROL IT.
SO WHERE ARE WE? LOOKS LIKE WE'RE ON TOP OF A BUILDING BUT...
VYPER?!
WADDLE
HEY! VYPER NEO! GET OFF THE EDGE!
YOO!!! NIL! YOU'VE GOT TO CHECK OUT THIS VIEW! IT'S AMAZING!

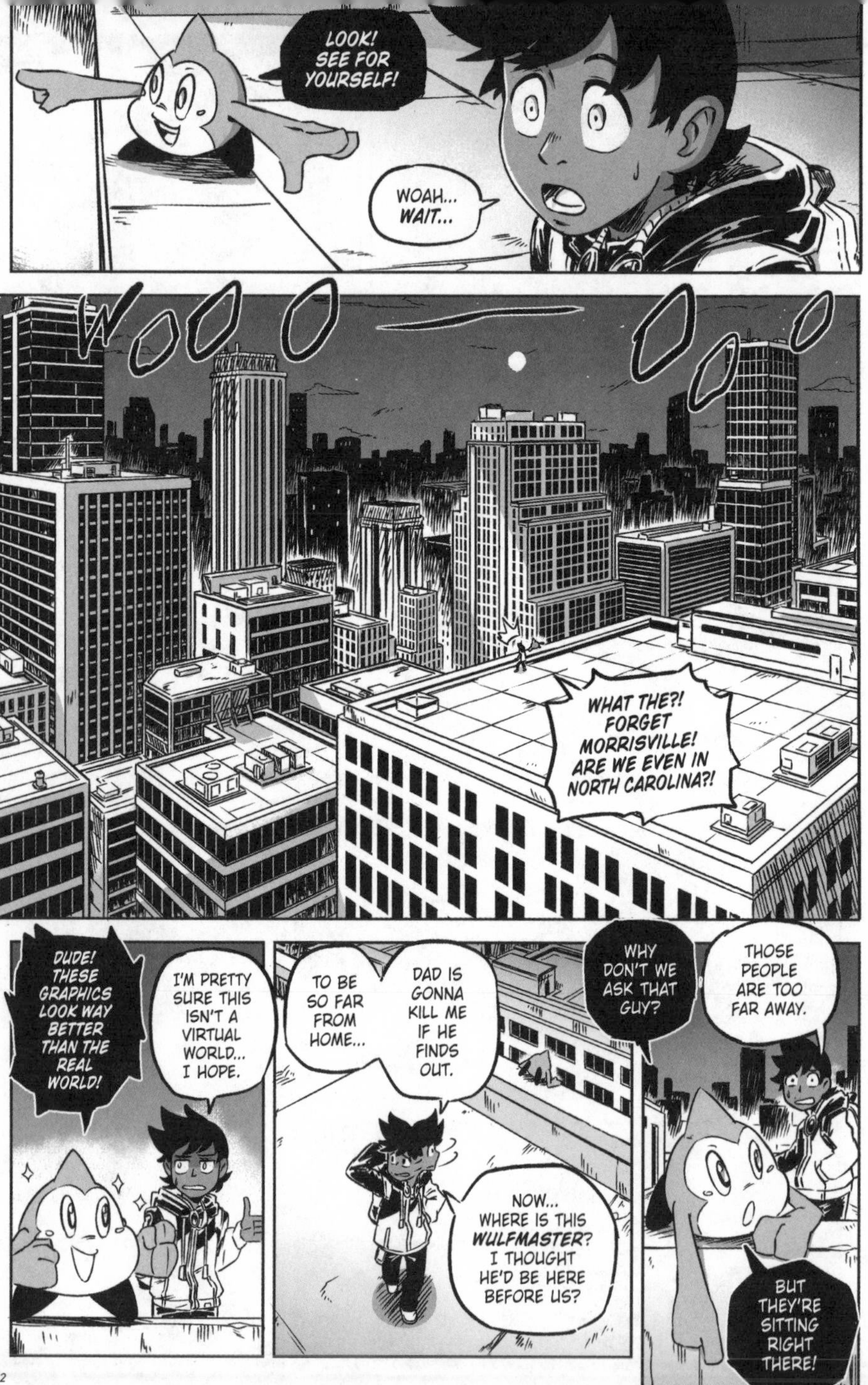
LOOK! SEE FOR YOURSELF!
WOAH... WAIT...
WOOO—OOOO
WHAT THE?! FORGET MORRISVILLE! ARE WE EVEN IN NORTH CAROLINA?!
DUDE! THESE GRAPHICS LOOK WAY BETTER THAN THE REAL WORLD!
I'M PRETTY SURE THIS ISN'T A VIRTUAL WORLD... I HOPE.
TO BE SO FAR FROM HOME...
DAD IS GONNA KILL ME IF HE FINDS OUT.
NOW... WHERE IS THIS WULFMASTER? I THOUGHT HE'D BE HERE BEFORE US?
WHY DON'T WE ASK THAT GUY?
THOSE PEOPLE ARE TOO FAR AWAY.
BUT THEY'RE SITTING RIGHT THERE!

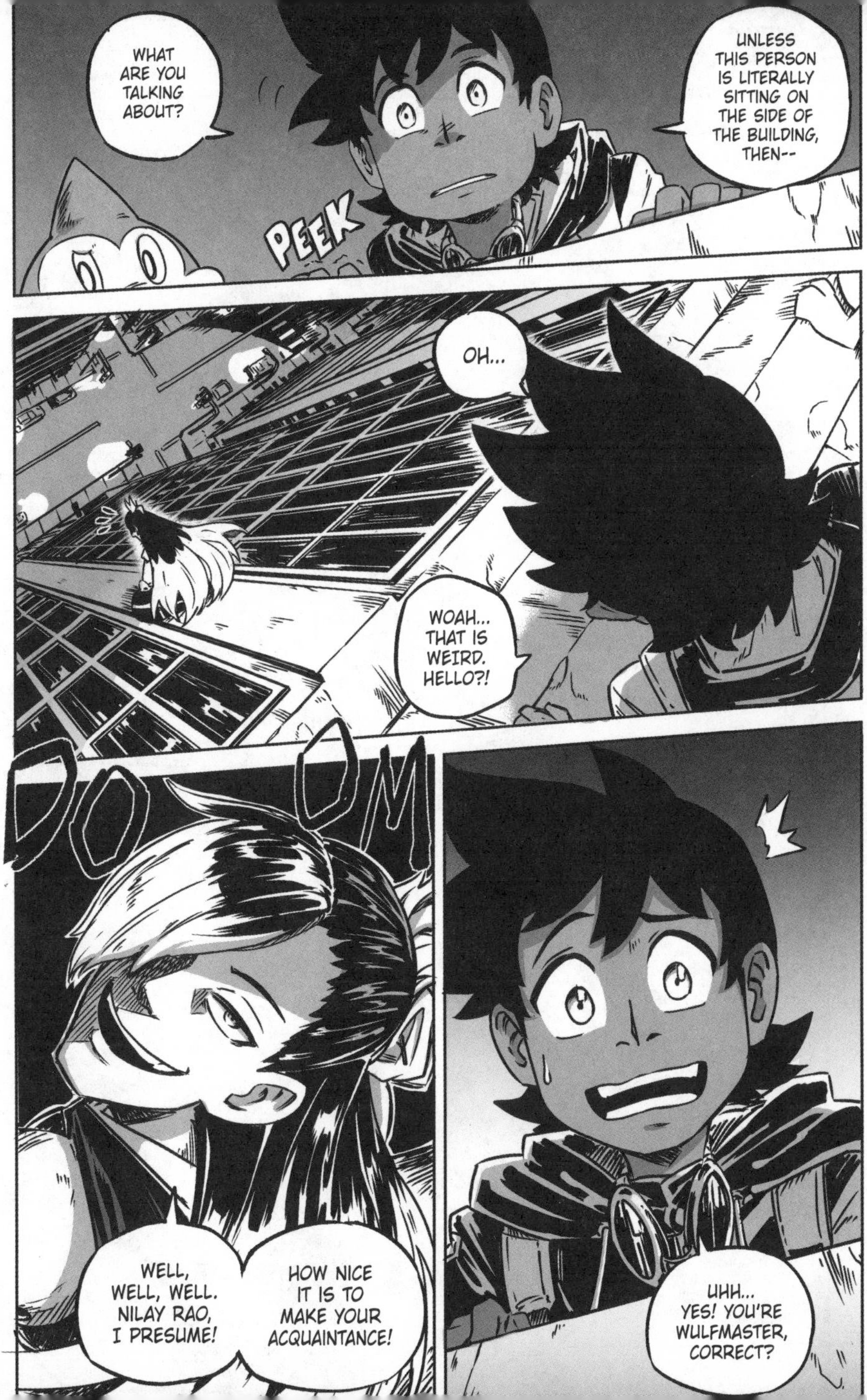
WHAT ARE YOU TALKING ABOUT?
UNLESS THIS PERSON IS LITERALLY SITTING ON THE SIDE OF THE BUILDING, THEN--
PEEK
OH...
WOAH... THAT IS WEIRD. HELLO?!
DOOM
WELL, WELL, WELL. NILAY RAO, I PRESUME!
HOW NICE IT IS TO MAKE YOUR ACQUAINTANCE!
UHH... YES! YOU'RE WULFMASTER, CORRECT?

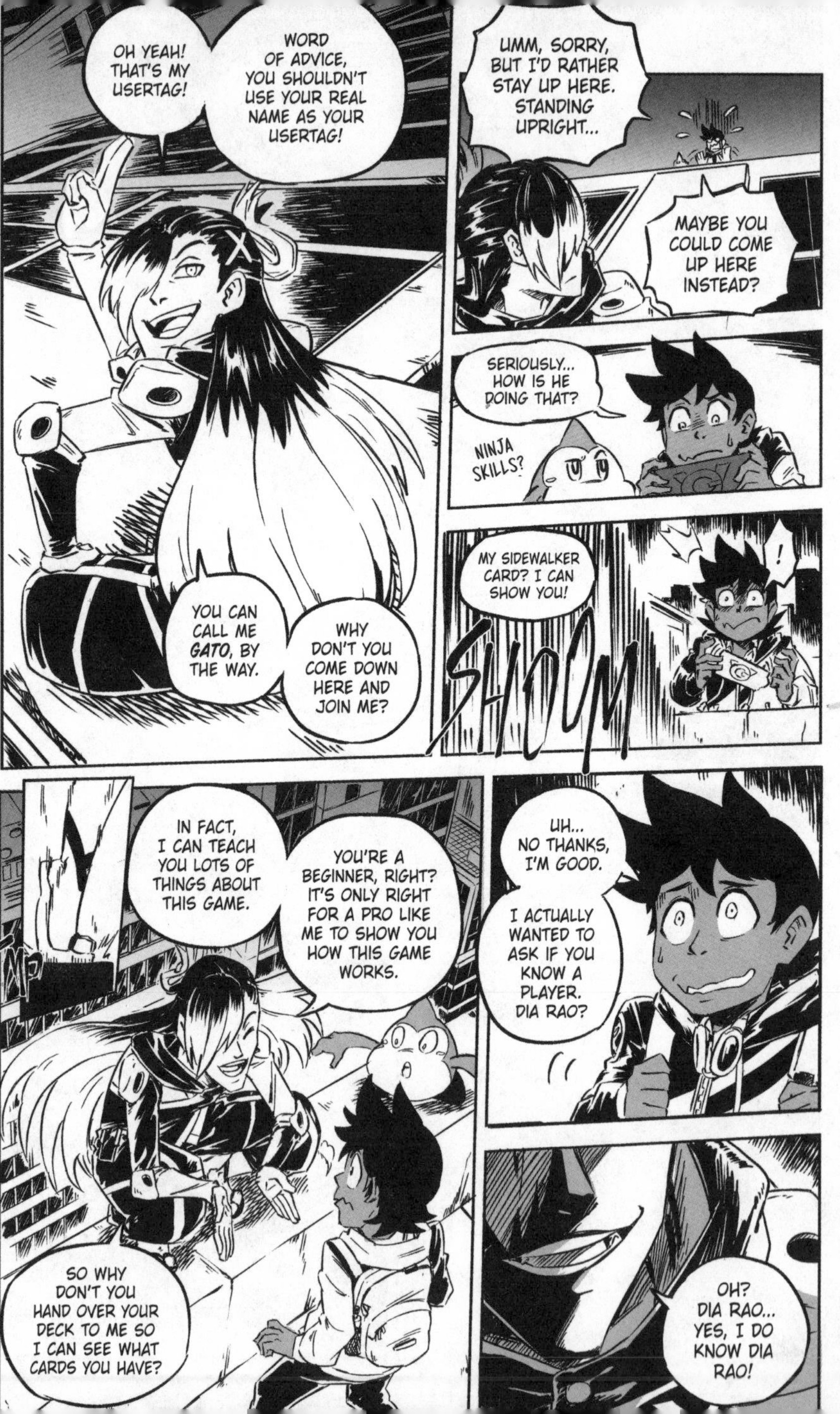
OH YEAH! THAT'S MY USERTAG!
WORD OF ADVICE, YOU SHOULDN'T USE YOUR REAL NAME AS YOUR USERTAG!
YOU CAN CALL ME GATO, BY THE WAY.
WHY DON'T YOU COME DOWN HERE AND JOIN ME?
UMM, SORRY, BUT I'D RATHER STAY UP HERE. STANDING UPRIGHT...
MAYBE YOU COULD COME UP HERE INSTEAD?
SERIOUSLY... HOW IS HE DOING THAT?
NINJA SKILLS?
MY SIDEWALKER CARD? I CAN SHOW YOU!
SHOOM
!
TMP
IN FACT, I CAN TEACH YOU LOTS OF THINGS ABOUT THIS GAME.
YOU'RE A BEGINNER, RIGHT? IT'S ONLY RIGHT FOR A PRO LIKE ME TO SHOW YOU HOW THIS GAME WORKS.
SO WHY DON'T YOU HAND OVER YOUR DECK TO ME SO I CAN SEE WHAT CARDS YOU HAVE?
UH... NO THANKS, I'M GOOD.
I ACTUALLY WANTED TO ASK IF YOU KNOW A PLAYER. DIA RAO?
OH? DIA RAO... YES, I DO KNOW DIA RAO!

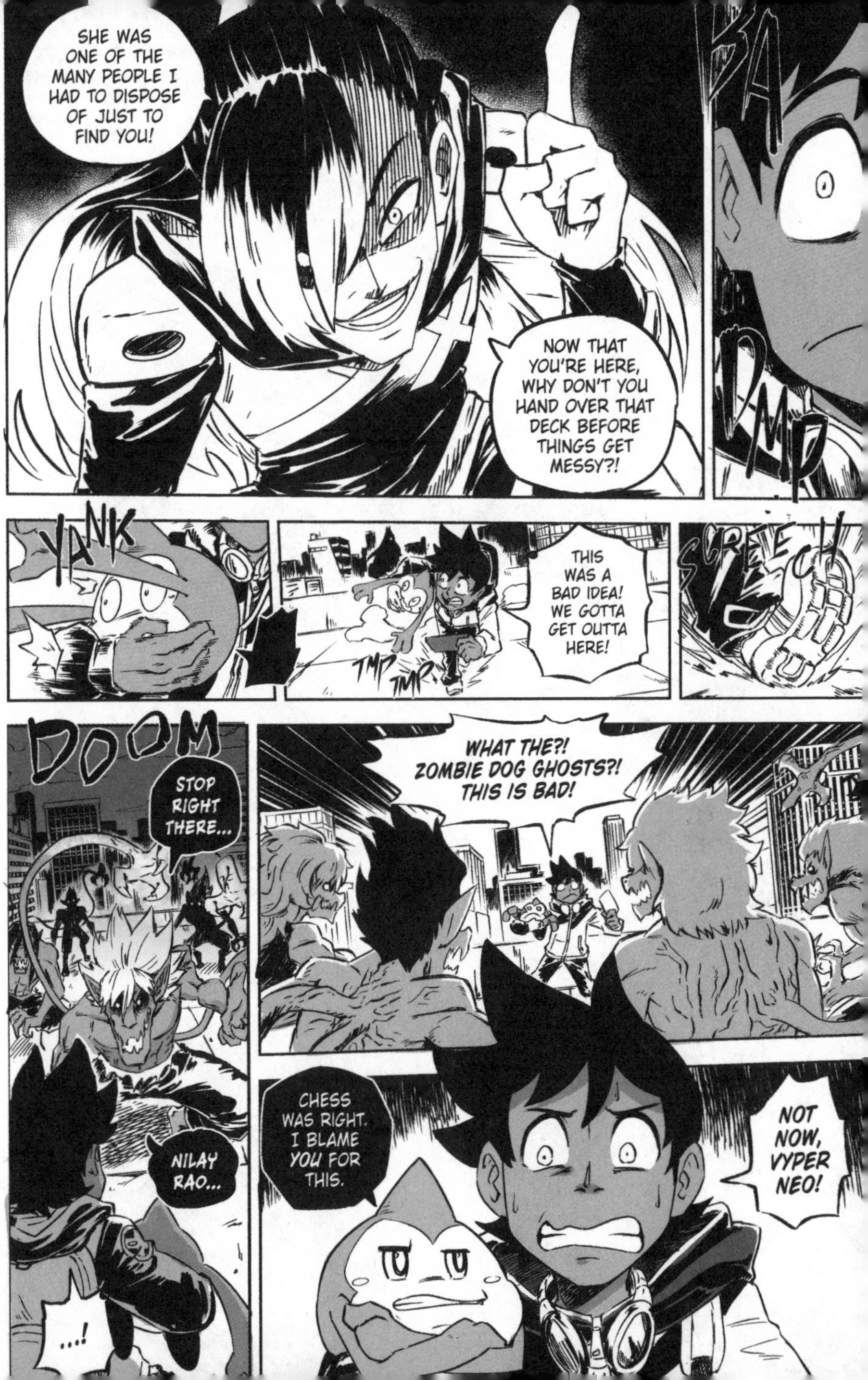
SHE WAS ONE OF THE MANY PEOPLE I HAD TO DISPOSE OF JUST TO FIND YOU!
NOW THAT YOU'RE HERE, WHY DON'T YOU HAND OVER THAT DECK BEFORE THINGS GET MESSY?!
BA
DMP
YANK
THIS WAS A BAD IDEA! WE GOTTA GET OUTTA HERE!
TMP TMP
SCREECH
DOOM
STOP RIGHT THERE...
NILAY RAO...
...!
WHAT THE?! ZOMBIE DOG GHOSTS?! THIS IS BAD!
CHESS WAS RIGHT. I BLAME YOU FOR THIS.
NOT NOW, VYPER NEO!

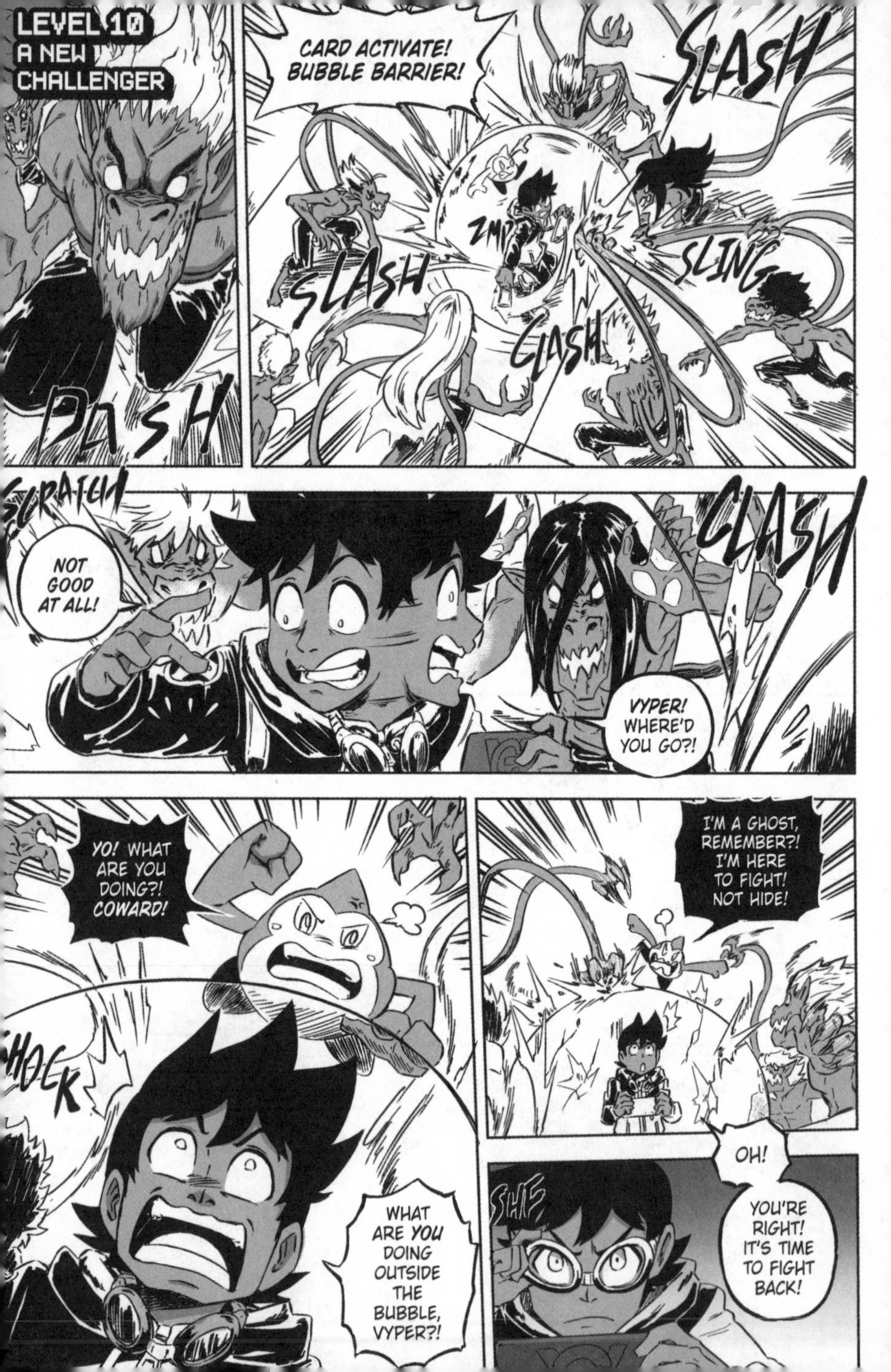
LEVEL 10
A NEW CHALLENGER
DASH
CARD ACTIVATE! BUBBLE BARRIER!
SLASH
SLASH
SLING
CLASH
SCRATCH
NOT GOOD AT ALL!
CLASH
VYPER! WHERE'D YOU GO?!
YO! WHAT ARE YOU DOING?! COWARD!
SHOCK
WHAT ARE YOU DOING OUTSIDE THE BUBBLE, VYPER?!
I'M A GHOST, REMEMBER?! I'M HERE TO FIGHT! NOT HIDE!
OH!
YOU'RE RIGHT! IT'S TIME TO FIGHT BACK!

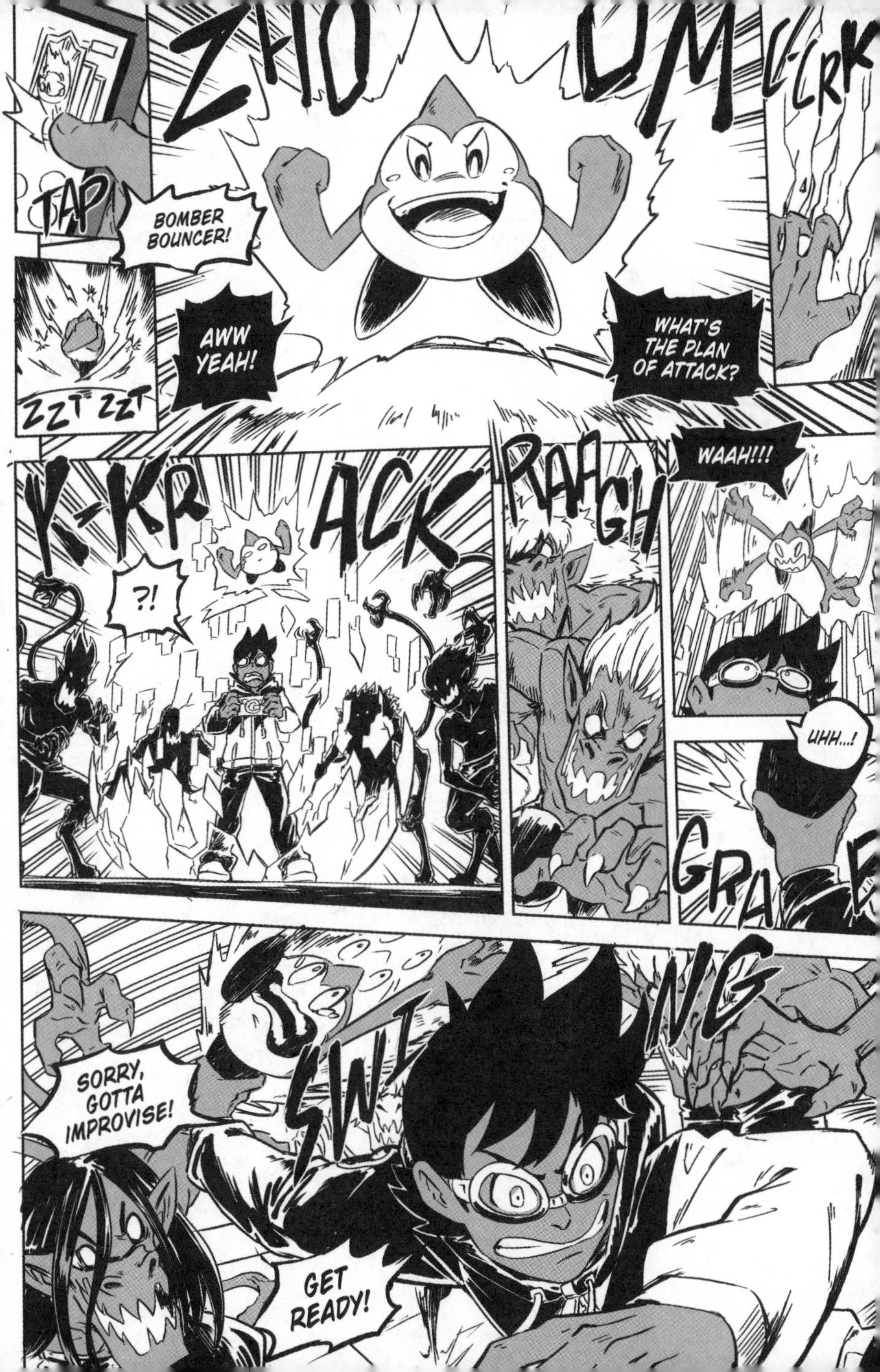
TAP
BOMBER BOUNCER!
ZZT ZZT
ZHO UM
AWW YEAH!
WHAT'S THE PLAN OF ATTACK?
C-CRK
Y-KR ACK
?!
RAAGH
WAAH!!!
UHH...!
GRA
SWI NG
SORRY, GOTTA IMPROVISE!
GET READY!

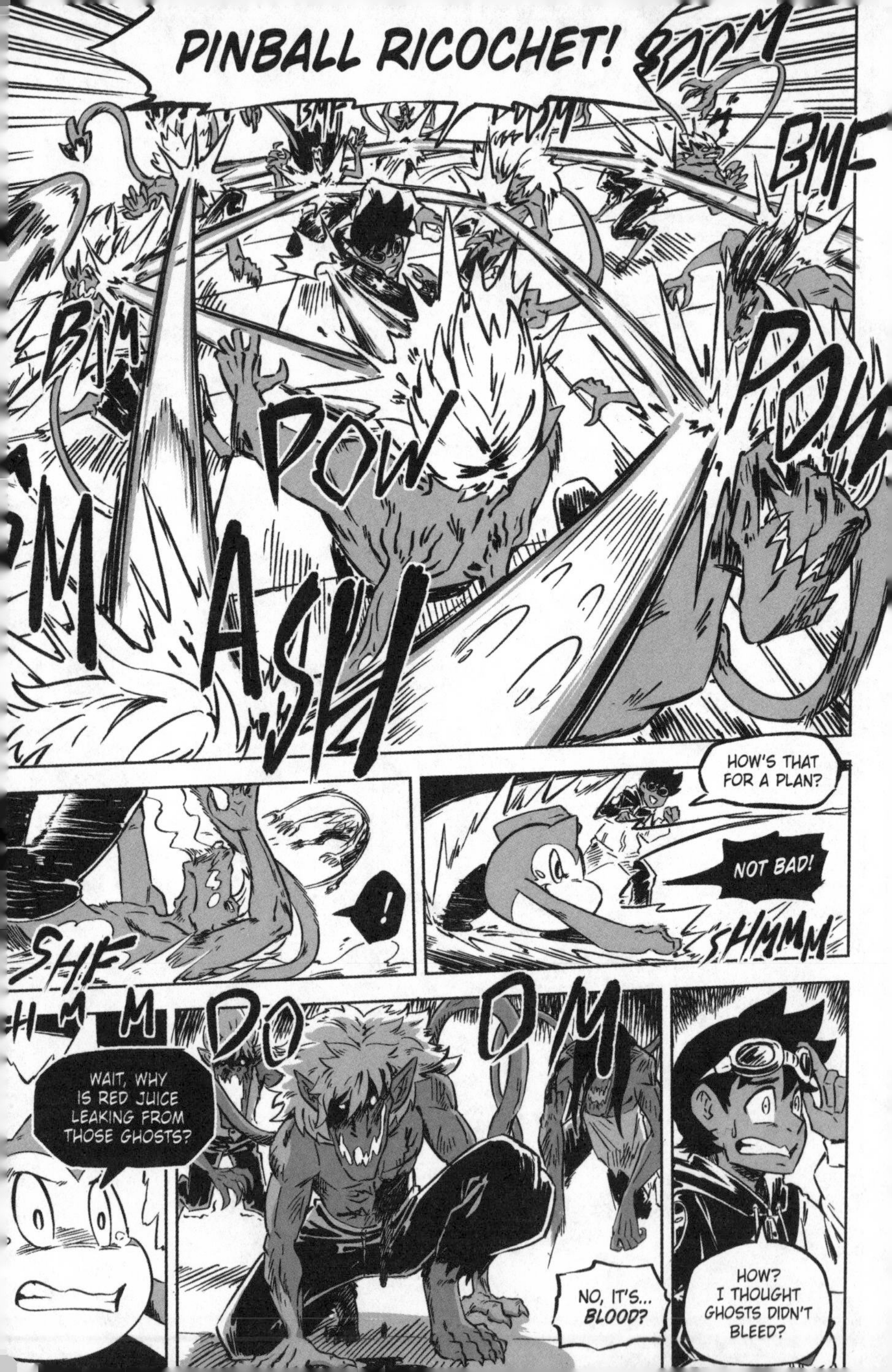
PINBALL RICOCHET!
BOOM
BMF
BAM
POW
POW
SMASH
!
SHF
HOW'S THAT FOR A PLAN?
NOT BAD!
SHMMM
DOOM
WAIT, WHY IS RED JUICE LEAKING FROM THOSE GHOSTS?
NO, IT'S... *BLOOD?*
HOW? I THOUGHT GHOSTS DIDN'T BLEED?

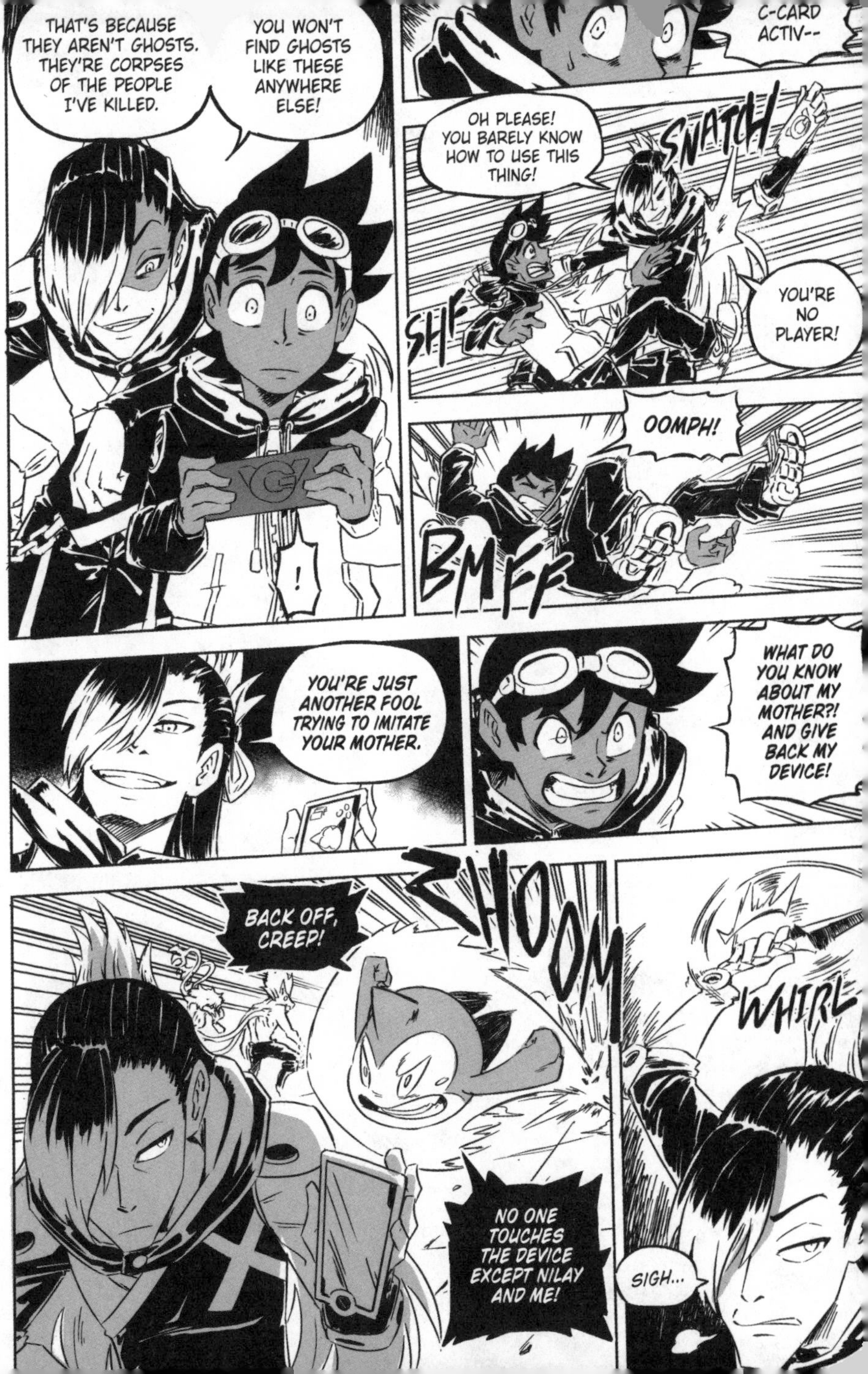
THAT'S BECAUSE THEY AREN'T GHOSTS. THEY'RE CORPSES OF THE PEOPLE I'VE KILLED.
YOU WON'T FIND GHOSTS LIKE THESE ANYWHERE ELSE!
!
C-CARD ACTIV--
OH PLEASE! YOU BARELY KNOW HOW TO USE THIS THING!
SNATCH
SHF
YOU'RE NO PLAYER!
OOMPH!
BMFF
YOU'RE JUST ANOTHER FOOL TRYING TO IMITATE YOUR MOTHER.
WHAT DO YOU KNOW ABOUT MY MOTHER?! AND GIVE BACK MY DEVICE!
BACK OFF, CREEP!
ZHOOM
NO ONE TOUCHES THE DEVICE EXCEPT NILAY AND ME!
WHIRL
SIGH...

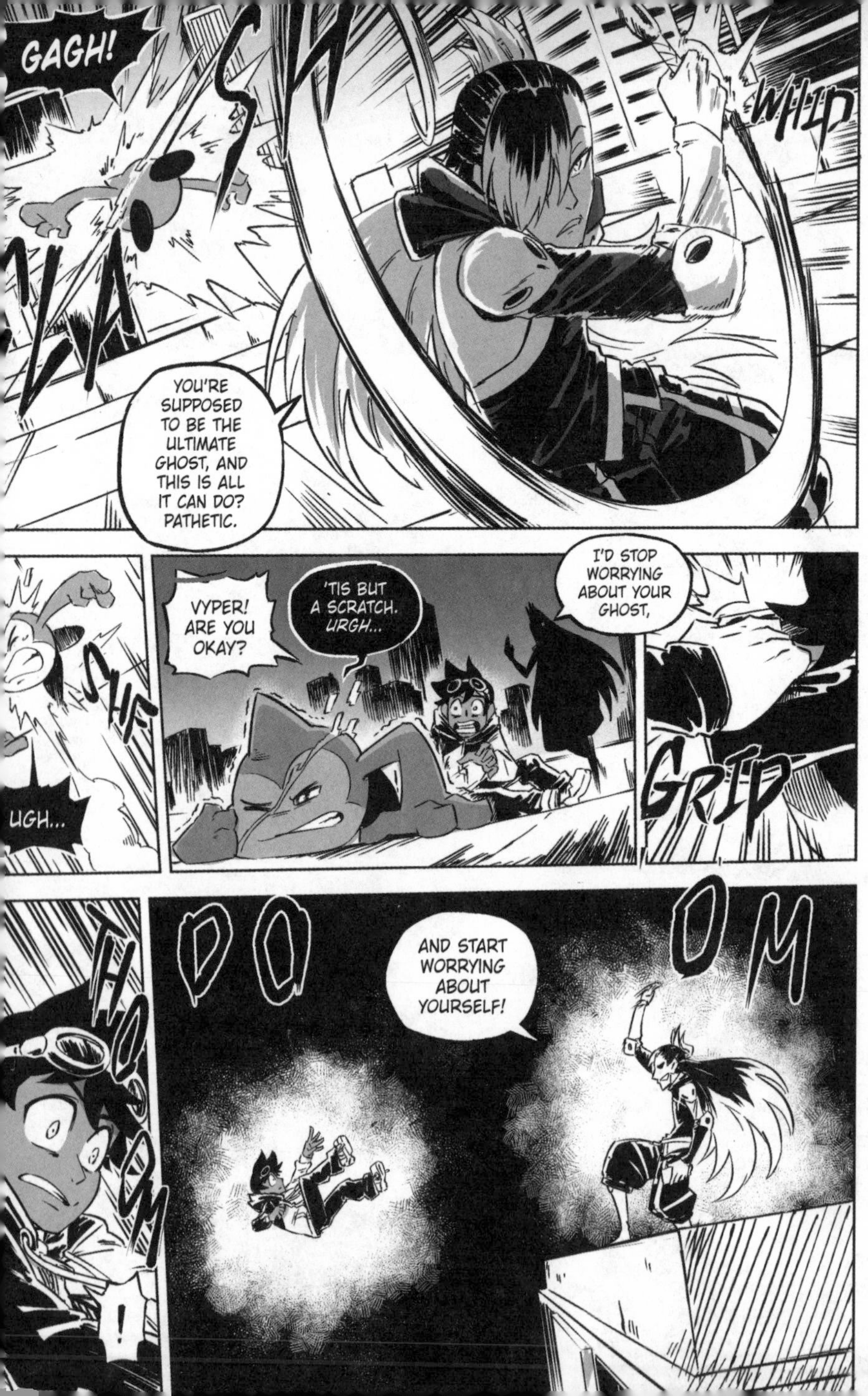
GAGH!
WHIP
YOU'RE SUPPOSED TO BE THE ULTIMATE GHOST, AND THIS IS ALL IT CAN DO? PATHETIC.
UGH...
VYPER! ARE YOU OKAY?
'TIS BUT A SCRATCH. URGH...
I'D STOP WORRYING ABOUT YOUR GHOST,
GRIP
DO
OM
AND START WORRYING ABOUT YOURSELF!
!

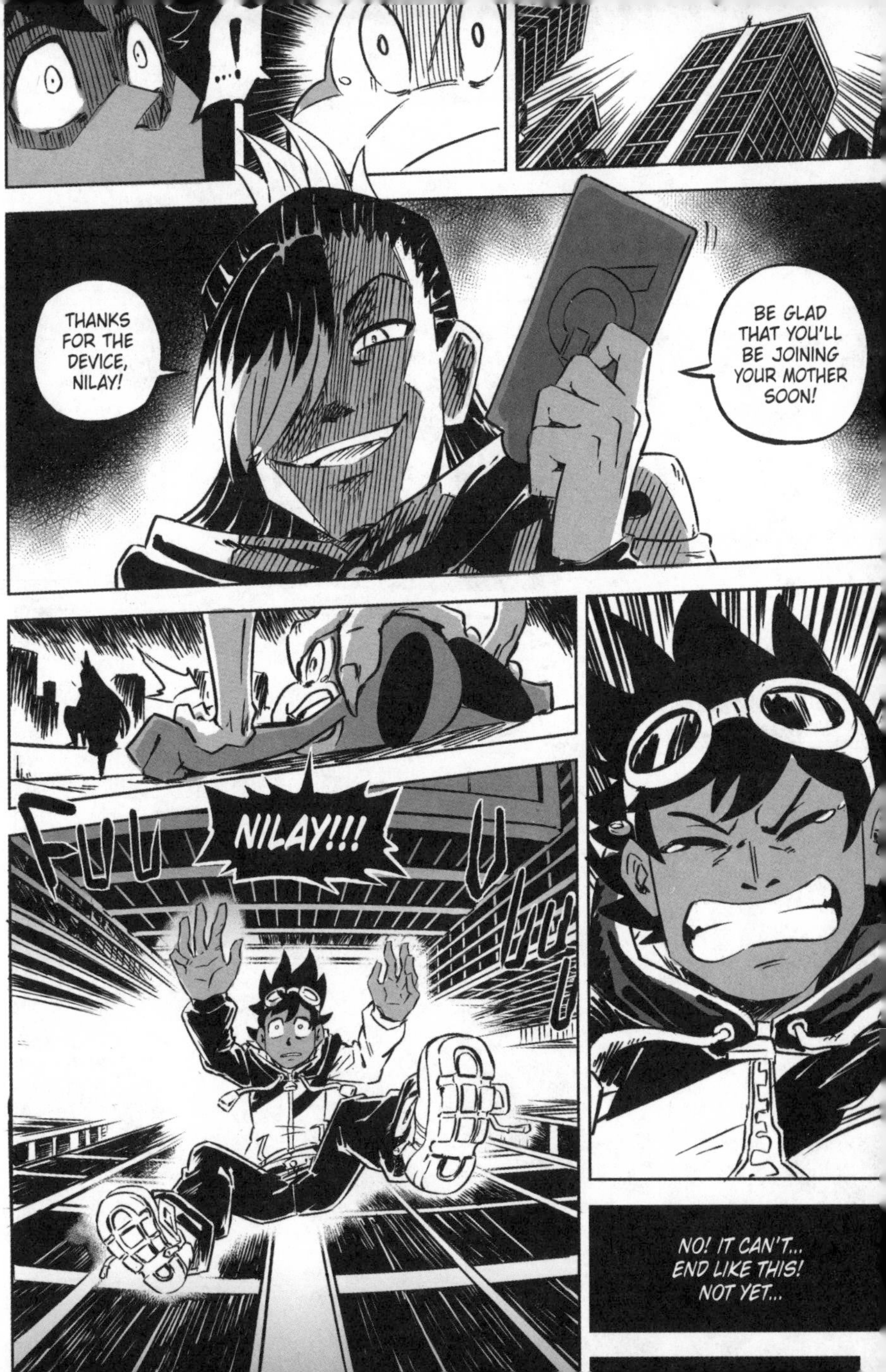
...!
THANKS FOR THE DEVICE, NILAY!
BE GLAD THAT YOU'LL BE JOINING YOUR MOTHER SOON!
NILAY!!!
NO! IT CAN'T... END LIKE THIS! NOT YET...

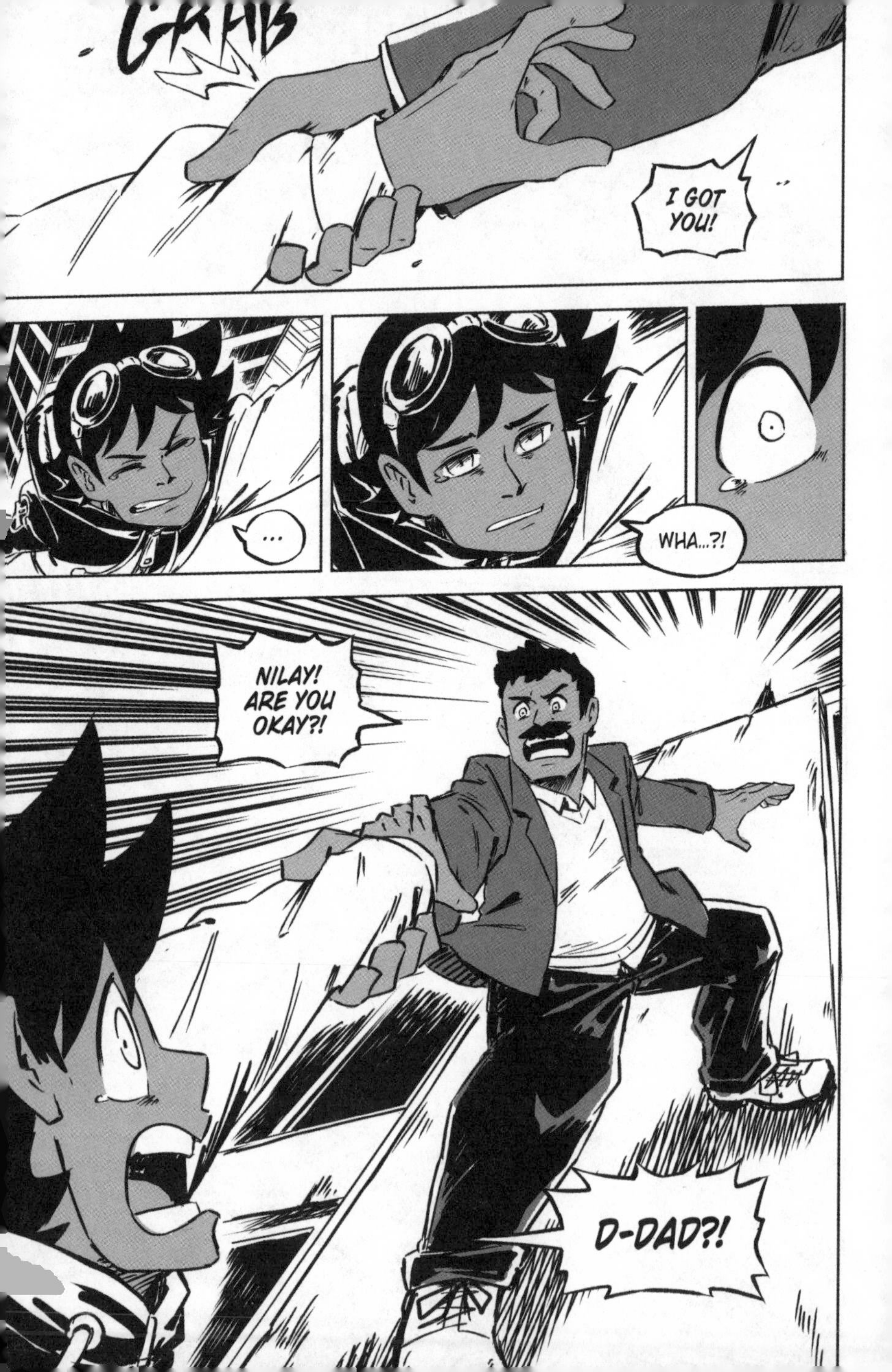
GRAB
I GOT YOU!
...
WHA...?!
NILAY! ARE YOU OKAY?!
D-DAD?!

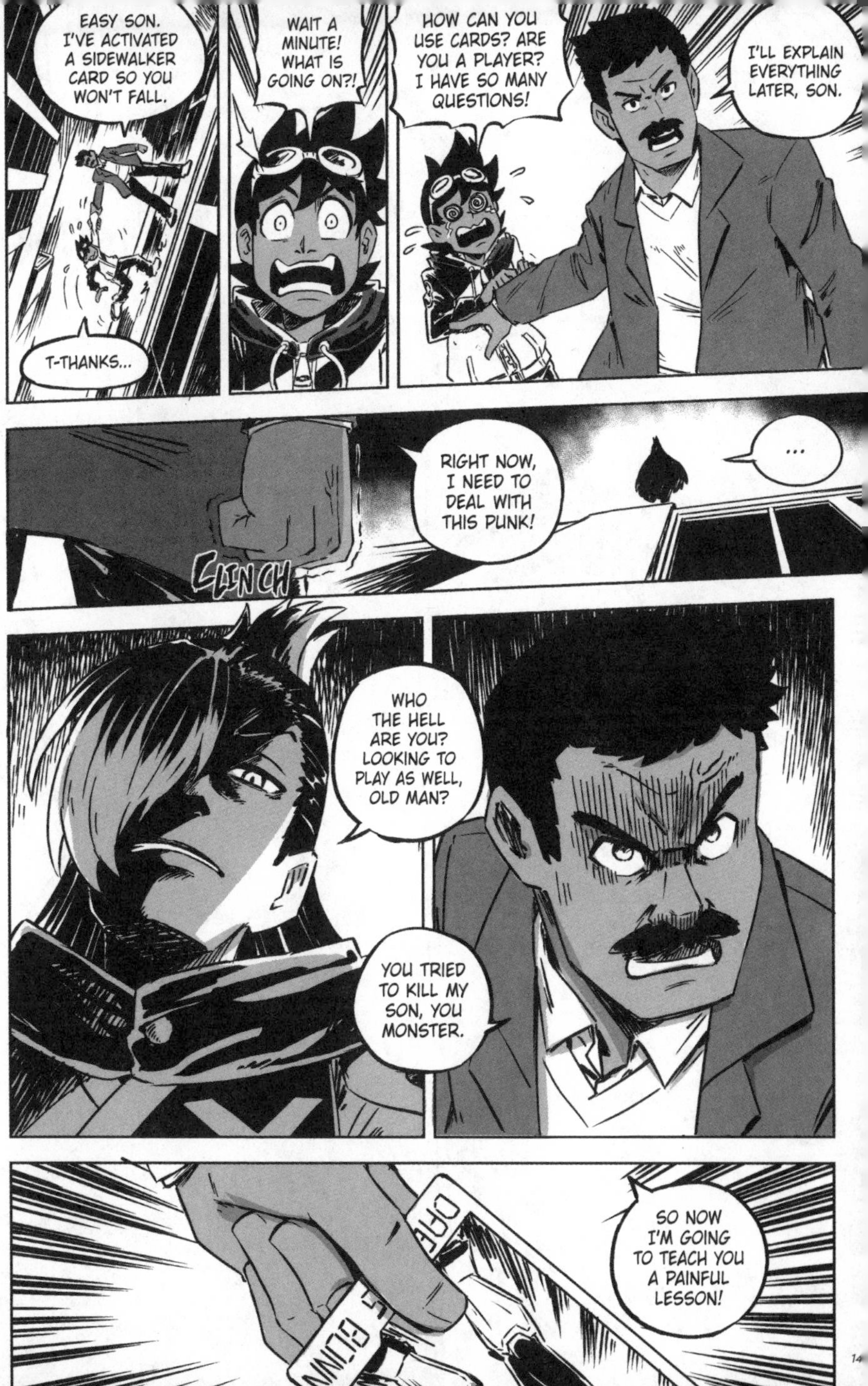
EASY SON. I'VE ACTIVATED A SIDEWALKER CARD SO YOU WON'T FALL.
T-THANKS...
WAIT A MINUTE! WHAT IS GOING ON?!
HOW CAN YOU USE CARDS? ARE YOU A PLAYER? I HAVE SO MANY QUESTIONS!
I'LL EXPLAIN EVERYTHING LATER, SON.
RIGHT NOW, I NEED TO DEAL WITH THIS PUNK!
CLINCH
...
WHO THE HELL ARE YOU? LOOKING TO PLAY AS WELL, OLD MAN?
YOU TRIED TO KILL MY SON, YOU MONSTER.
SO NOW I'M GOING TO TEACH YOU A PAINFUL LESSON!

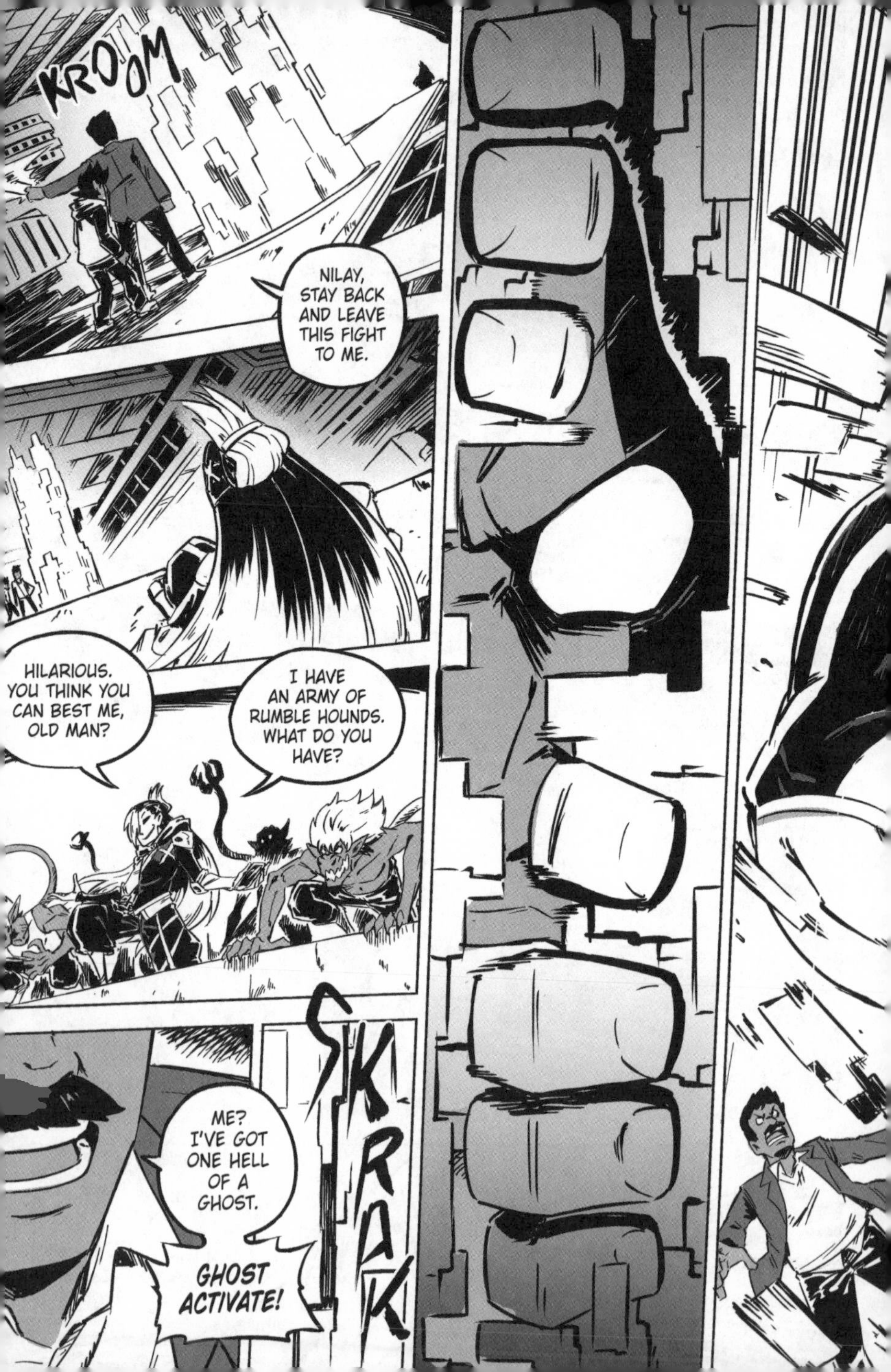
KROOM
NILAY, STAY BACK AND LEAVE THIS FIGHT TO ME.
HILARIOUS. YOU THINK YOU CAN BEST ME, OLD MAN?
I HAVE AN ARMY OF RUMBLE HOUNDS. WHAT DO YOU HAVE?
ME? I'VE GOT ONE HELL OF A GHOST.
GHOST ACTIVATE!
SKRAK

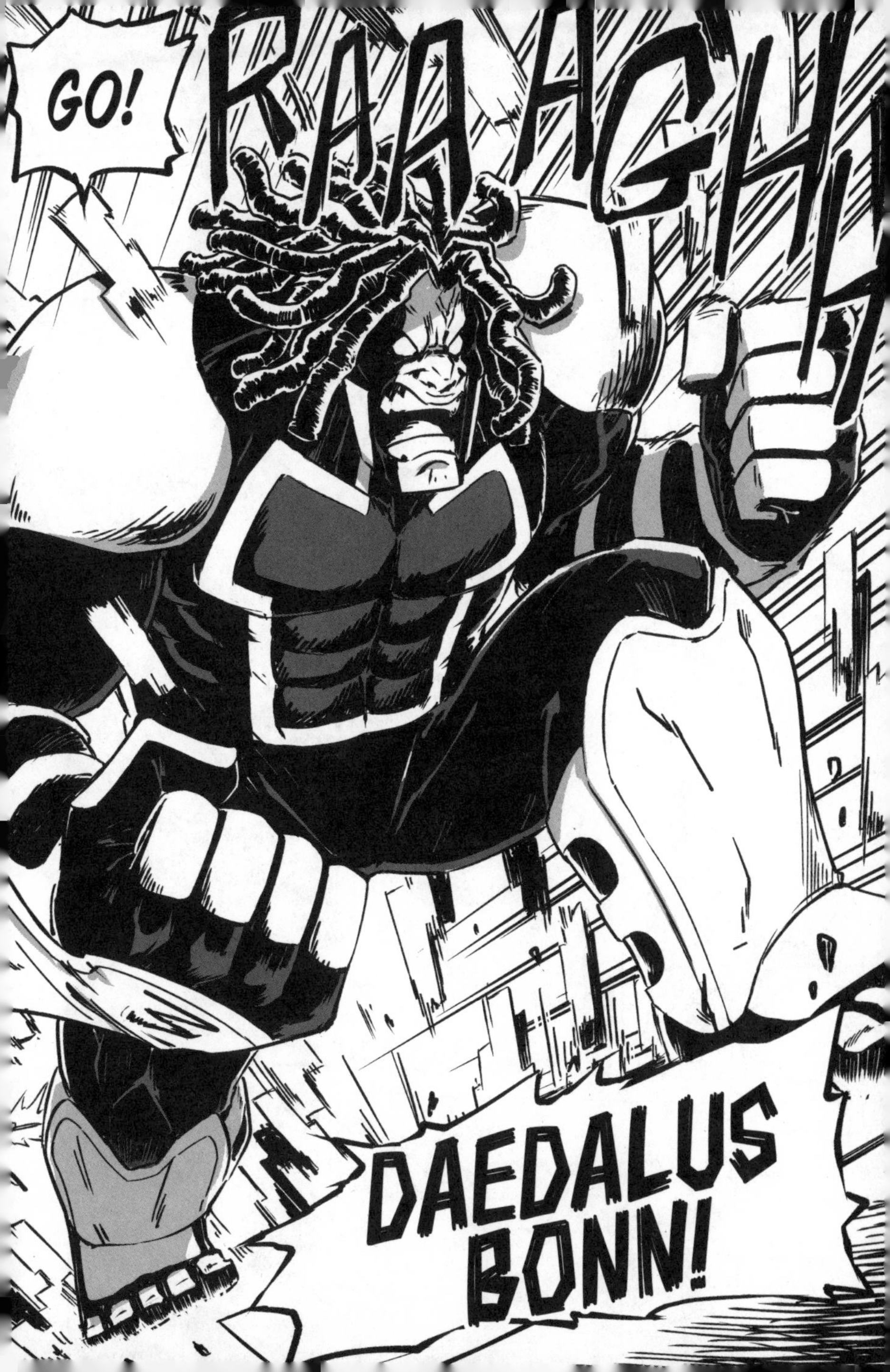
GO!
RAAAGH!!
DAEDALUS BONN!

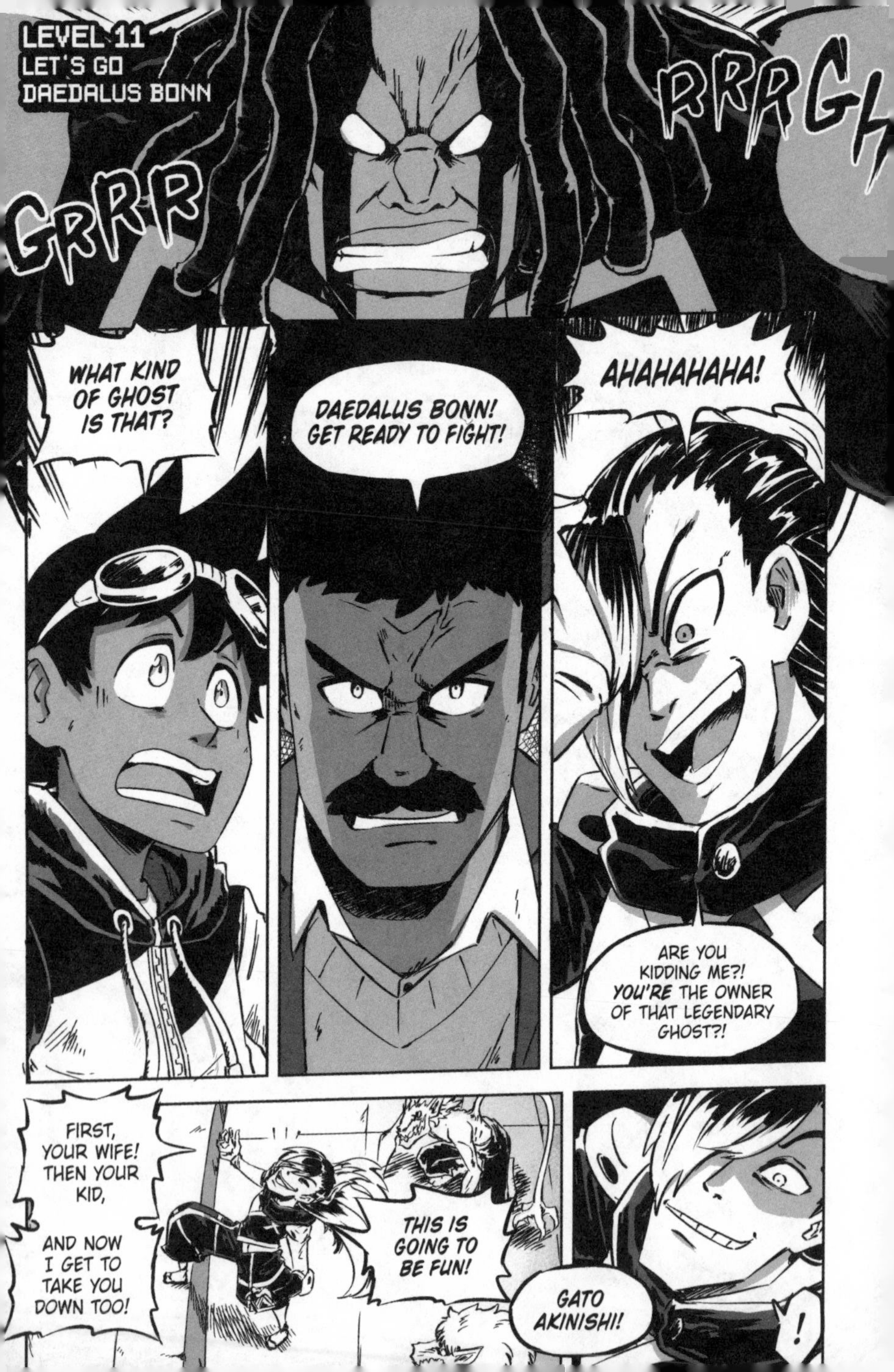
LEVEL 11
LET'S GO
DAEDALUS BONN
GRRR
RRRGH
WHAT KIND OF GHOST IS THAT?
DAEDALUS BONN! GET READY TO FIGHT!
AHAHAHAHA!
ARE YOU KIDDING ME?! YOU'RE THE OWNER OF THAT LEGENDARY GHOST?!
FIRST, YOUR WIFE! THEN YOUR KID,
AND NOW I GET TO TAKE YOU DOWN TOO!
THIS IS GOING TO BE FUN!
GATO AKINISHI!
!

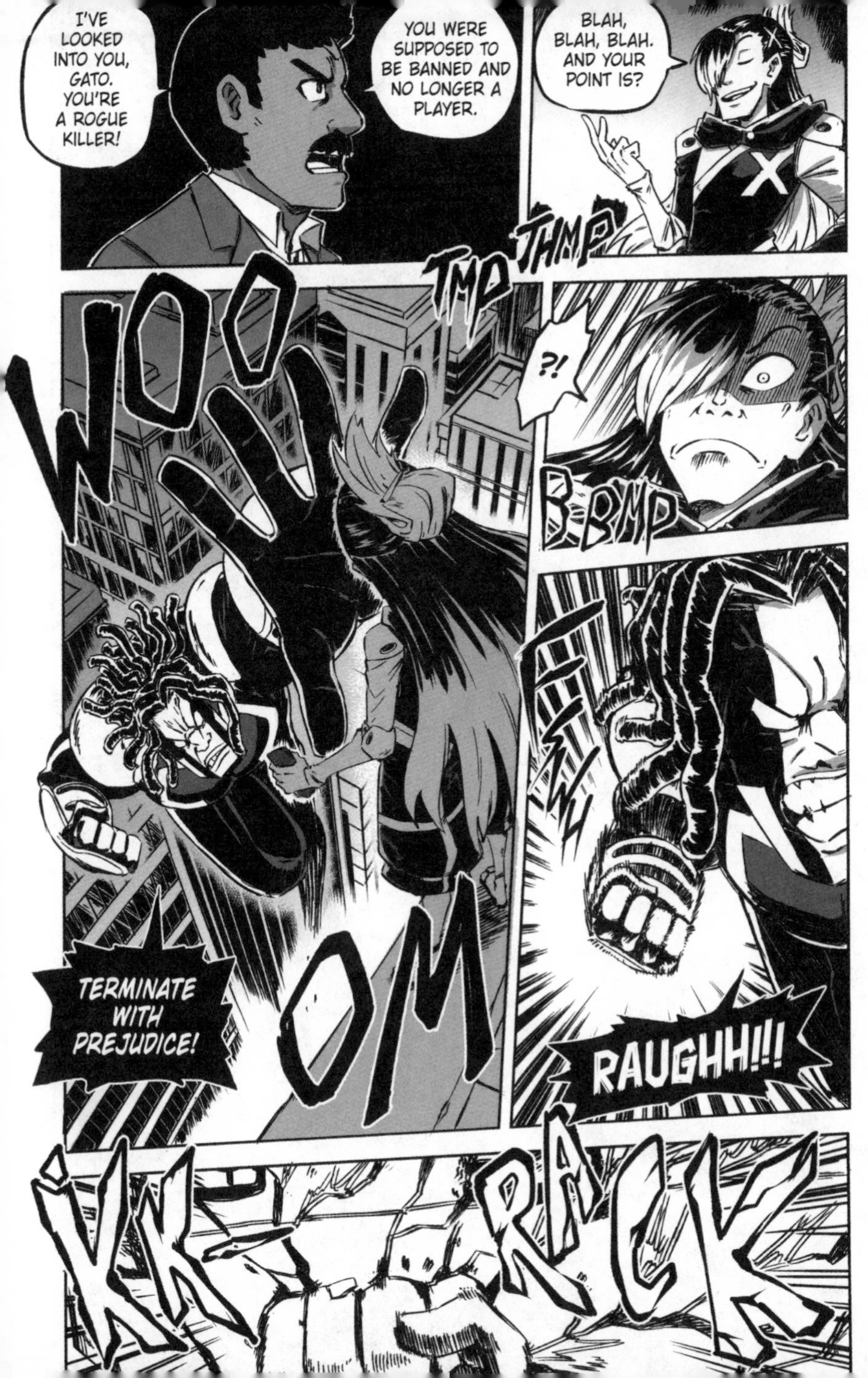

I'VE LOOKED INTO YOU, GATO. YOU'RE A ROGUE KILLER!
YOU WERE SUPPOSED TO BE BANNED AND NO LONGER A PLAYER.
BLAH, BLAH, BLAH. AND YOUR POINT IS?
THMP
TMP
WOOOM
TERMINATE WITH PREJUDICE!
?!
BBMP
FWW
RAUGHH!!!
KRACK

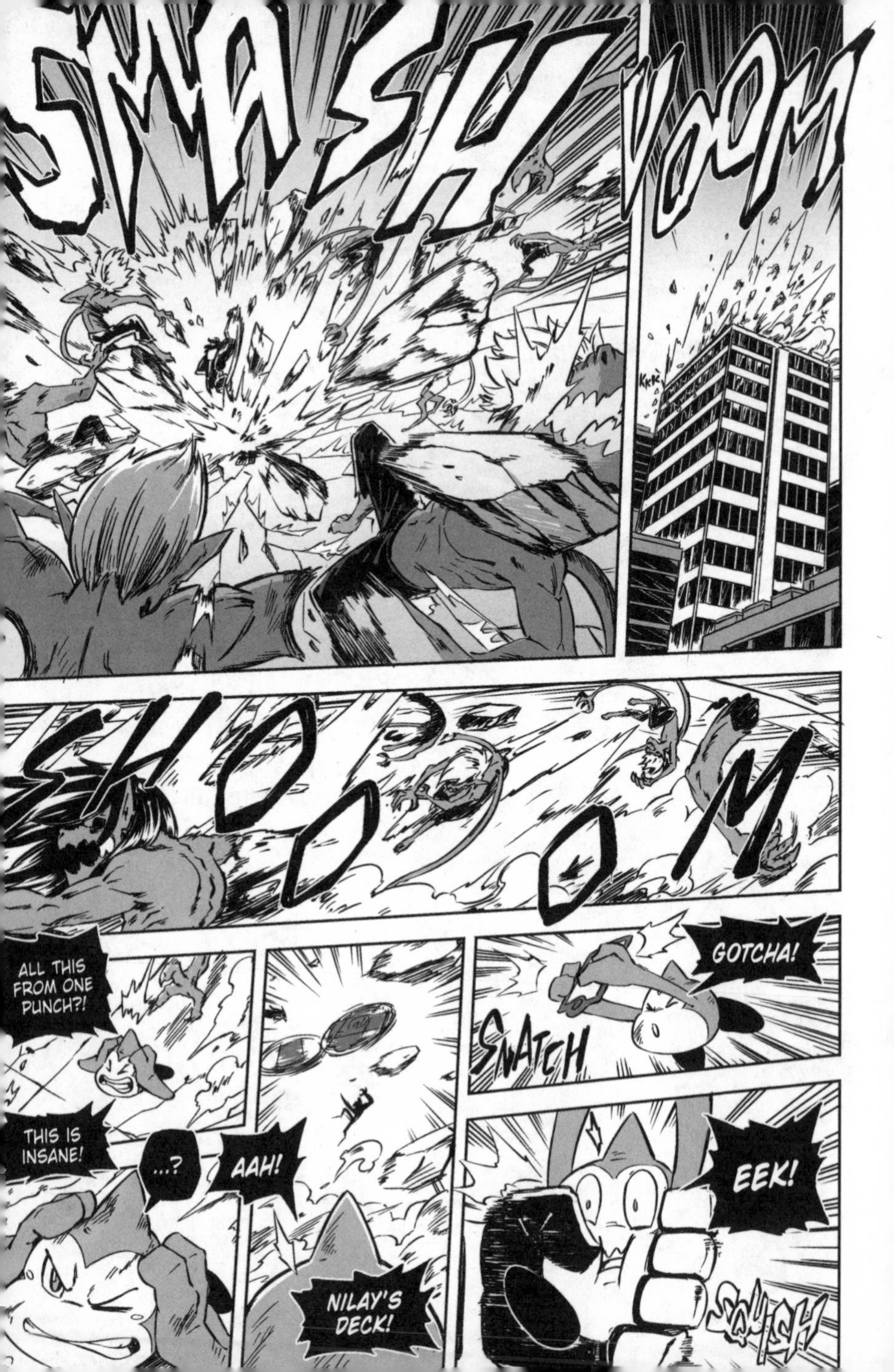
SMASH
VOOM
KKK
SHOOOM
ALL THIS FROM ONE PUNCH?!
THIS IS INSANE!
...?
AAH!
NILAY'S DECK!
SNATCH
GOTCHA!
EEK!
SQUISH

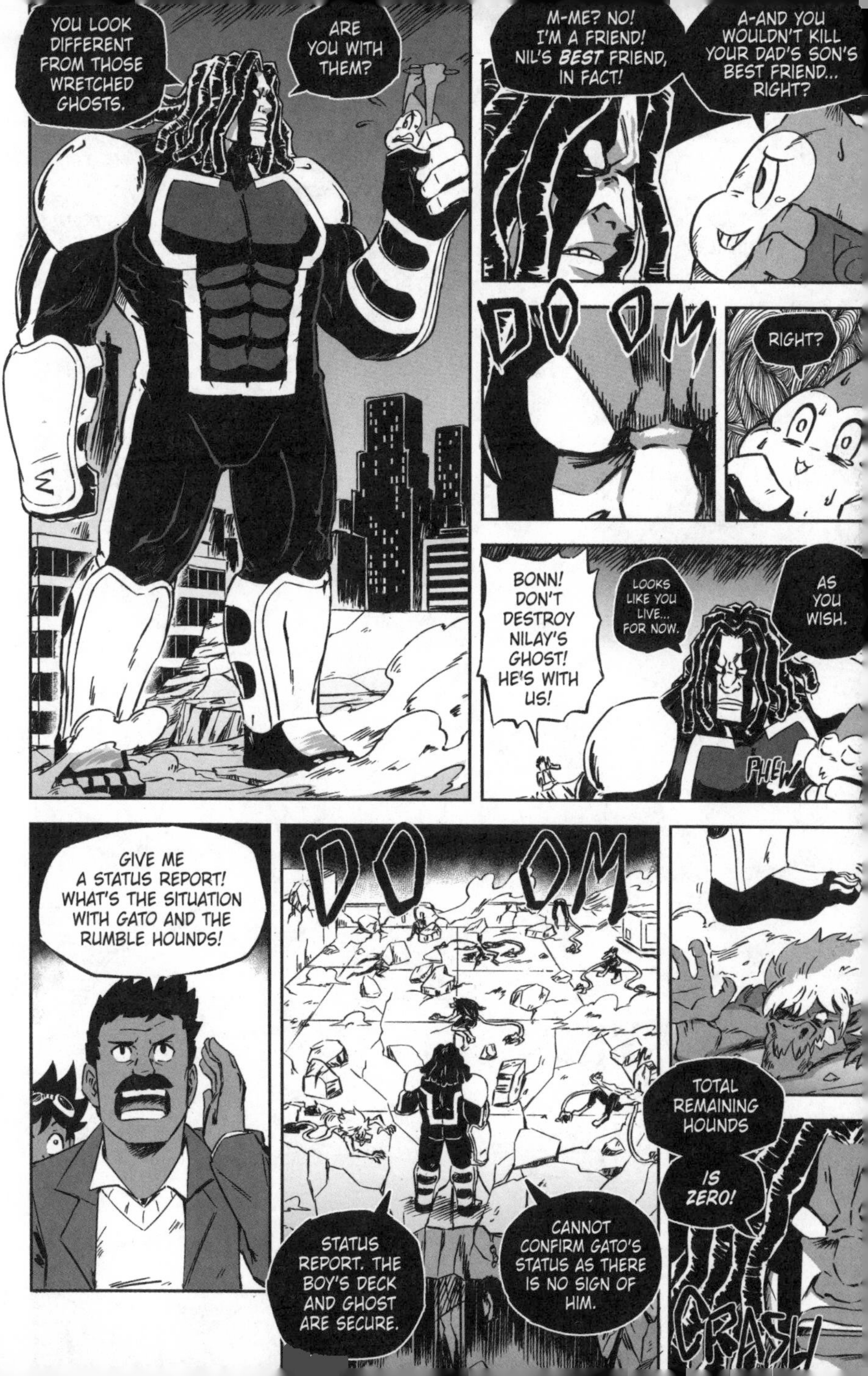
YOU LOOK DIFFERENT FROM THOSE WRETCHED GHOSTS.
ARE YOU WITH THEM?
M-ME? NO! I'M A FRIEND! NIL'S BEST FRIEND, IN FACT!
A-AND YOU WOULDN'T KILL YOUR DAD'S SON'S BEST FRIEND... RIGHT?
DOOM
RIGHT?
BONN! DON'T DESTROY NILAY'S GHOST! HE'S WITH US!
LOOKS LIKE YOU LIVE... FOR NOW.
AS YOU WISH.
PHEW
GIVE ME A STATUS REPORT! WHAT'S THE SITUATION WITH GATO AND THE RUMBLE HOUNDS!
DOOM
STATUS REPORT. THE BOY'S DECK AND GHOST ARE SECURE.
CANNOT CONFIRM GATO'S STATUS AS THERE IS NO SIGN OF HIM.
TOTAL REMAINING HOUNDS
IS ZERO!
CRASH

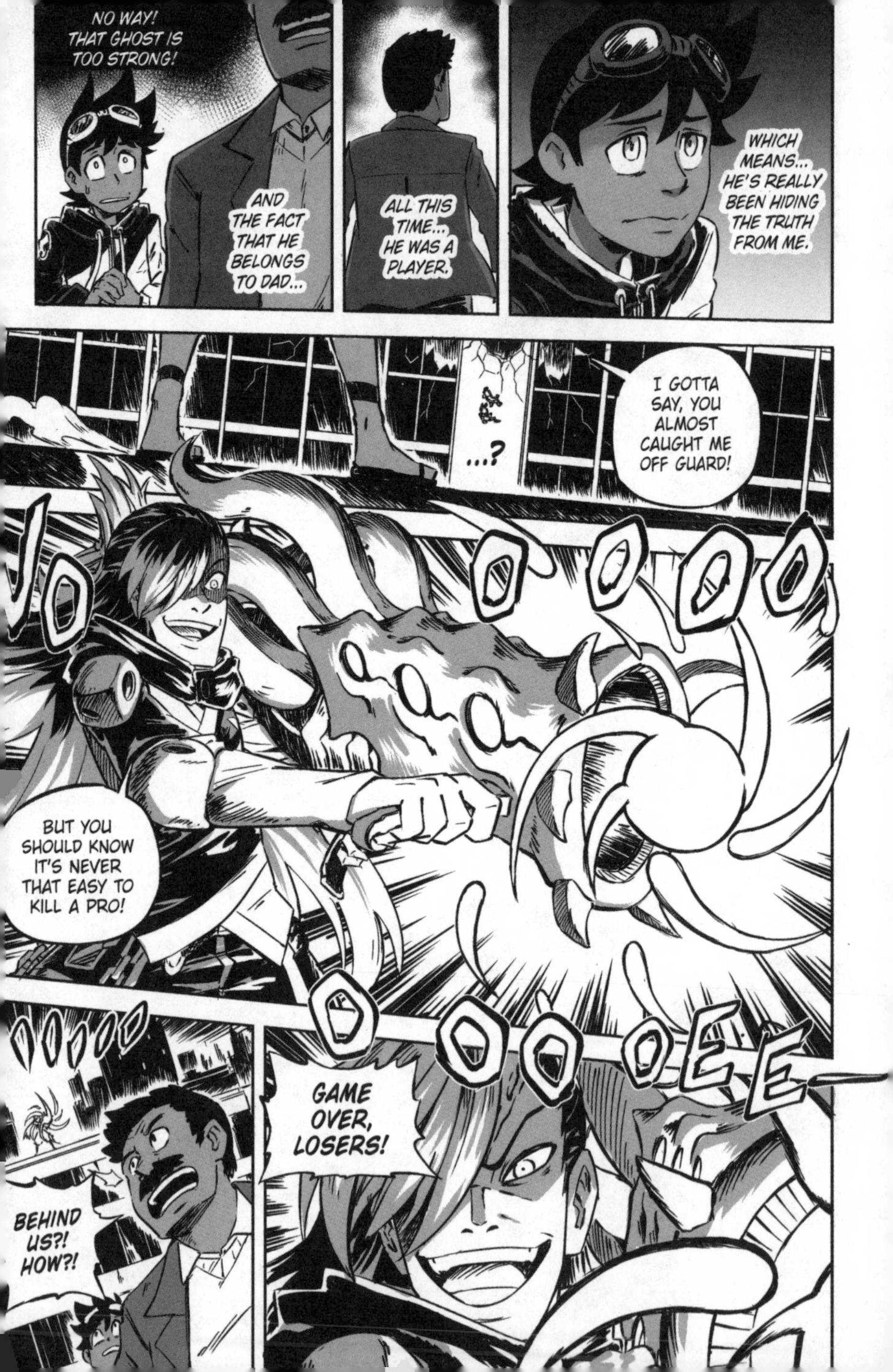
NO WAY! THAT GHOST IS TOO STRONG!
AND THE FACT THAT HE BELONGS TO DAD...
ALL THIS TIME... HE WAS A PLAYER.
WHICH MEANS... HE'S REALLY BEEN HIDING THE TRUTH FROM ME.
...?
I GOTTA SAY, YOU ALMOST CAUGHT ME OFF GUARD!
BUT YOU SHOULD KNOW IT'S NEVER THAT EASY TO KILL A PRO!
GAME OVER, LOSERS!
BEHIND US?! HOW?!

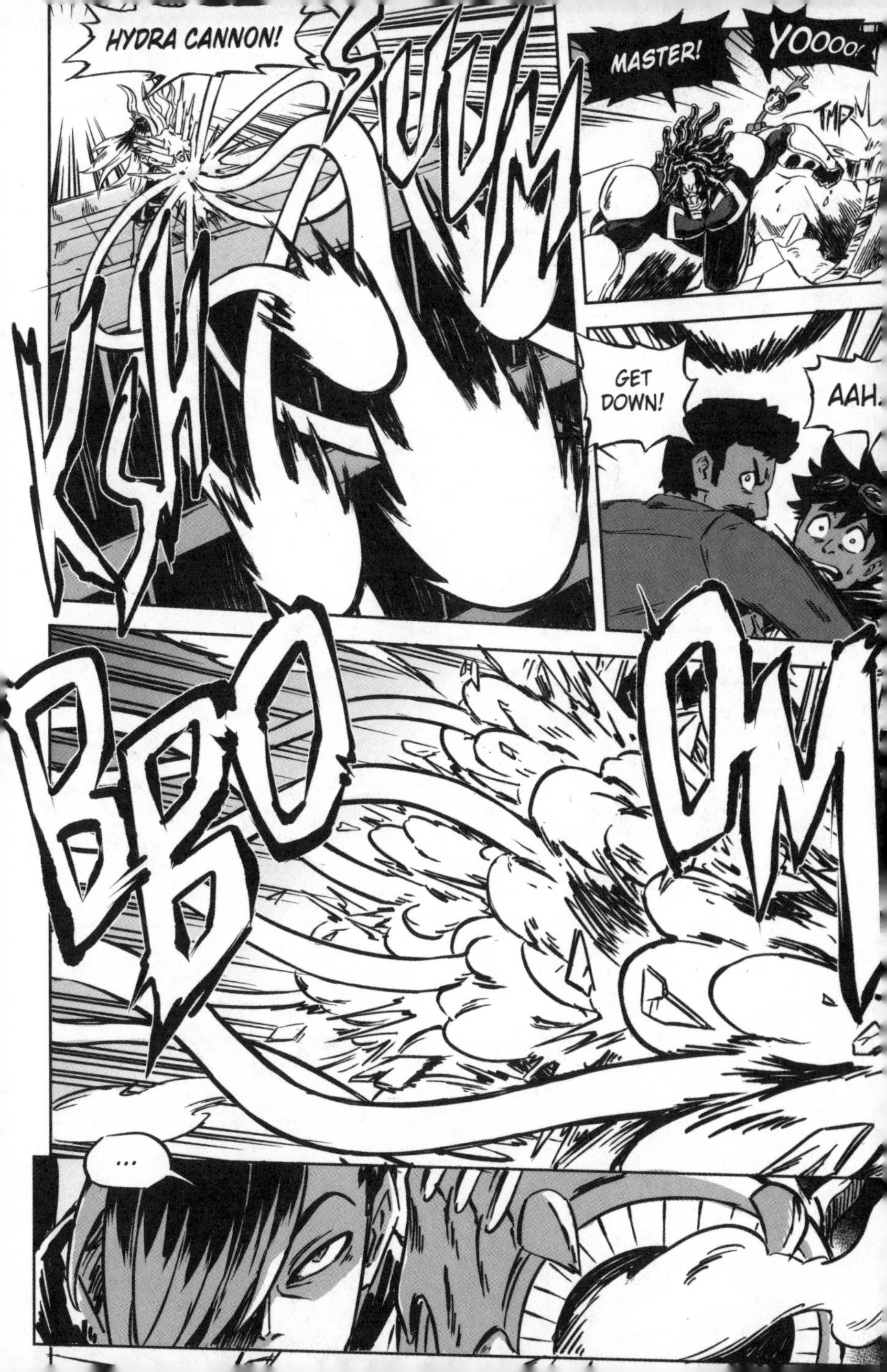
HYDRA CANNON!
MASTER!
YOOOO!
TMP
GET DOWN!
AAH.
...

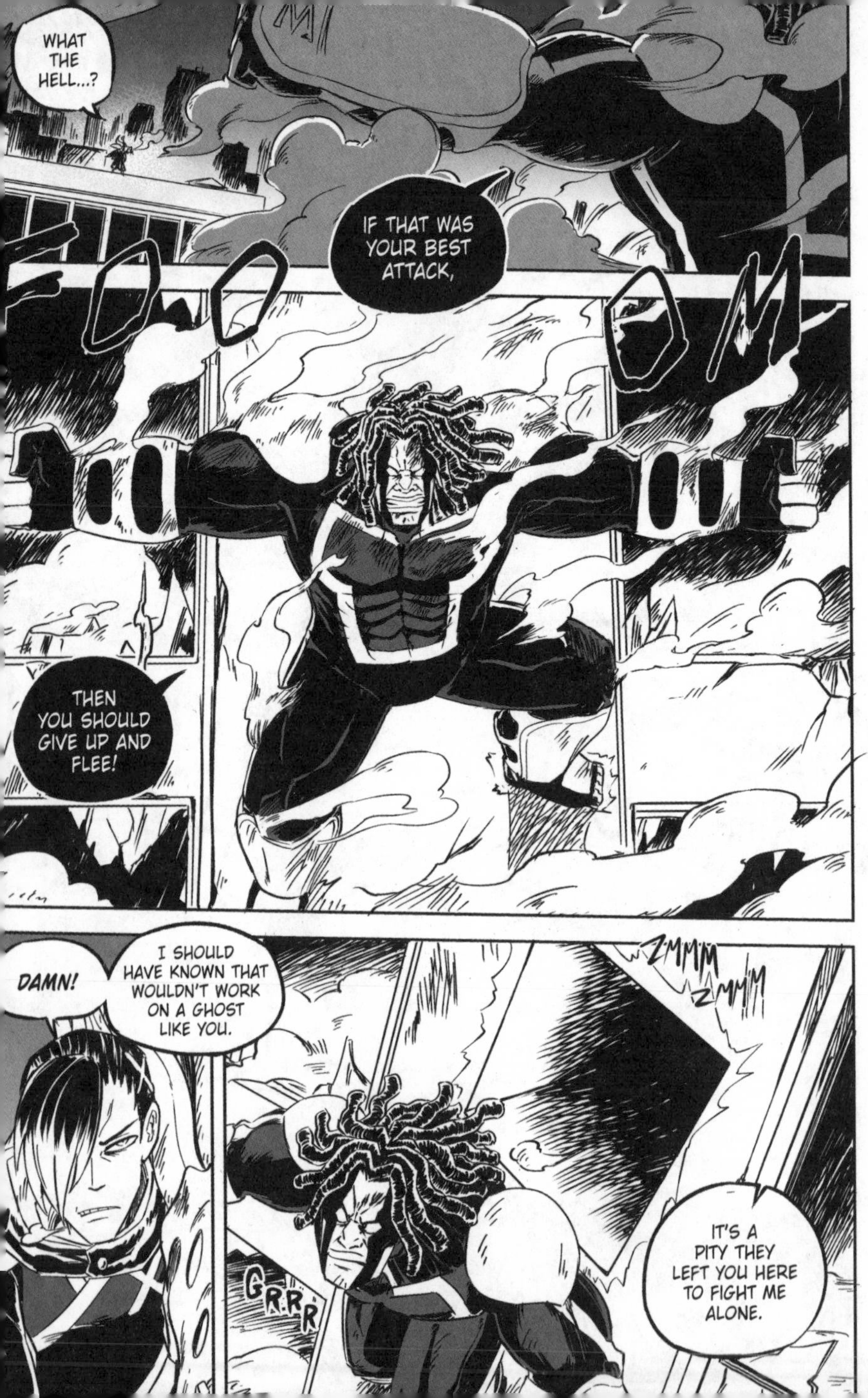
WHAT THE HELL...?
IF THAT WAS YOUR BEST ATTACK,
FOOOM
THEN YOU SHOULD GIVE UP AND FLEE!
DAMN!
I SHOULD HAVE KNOWN THAT WOULDN'T WORK ON A GHOST LIKE YOU.
ZMMM
ZMMM
GRRR
IT'S A PITY THEY LEFT YOU HERE TO FIGHT ME ALONE.

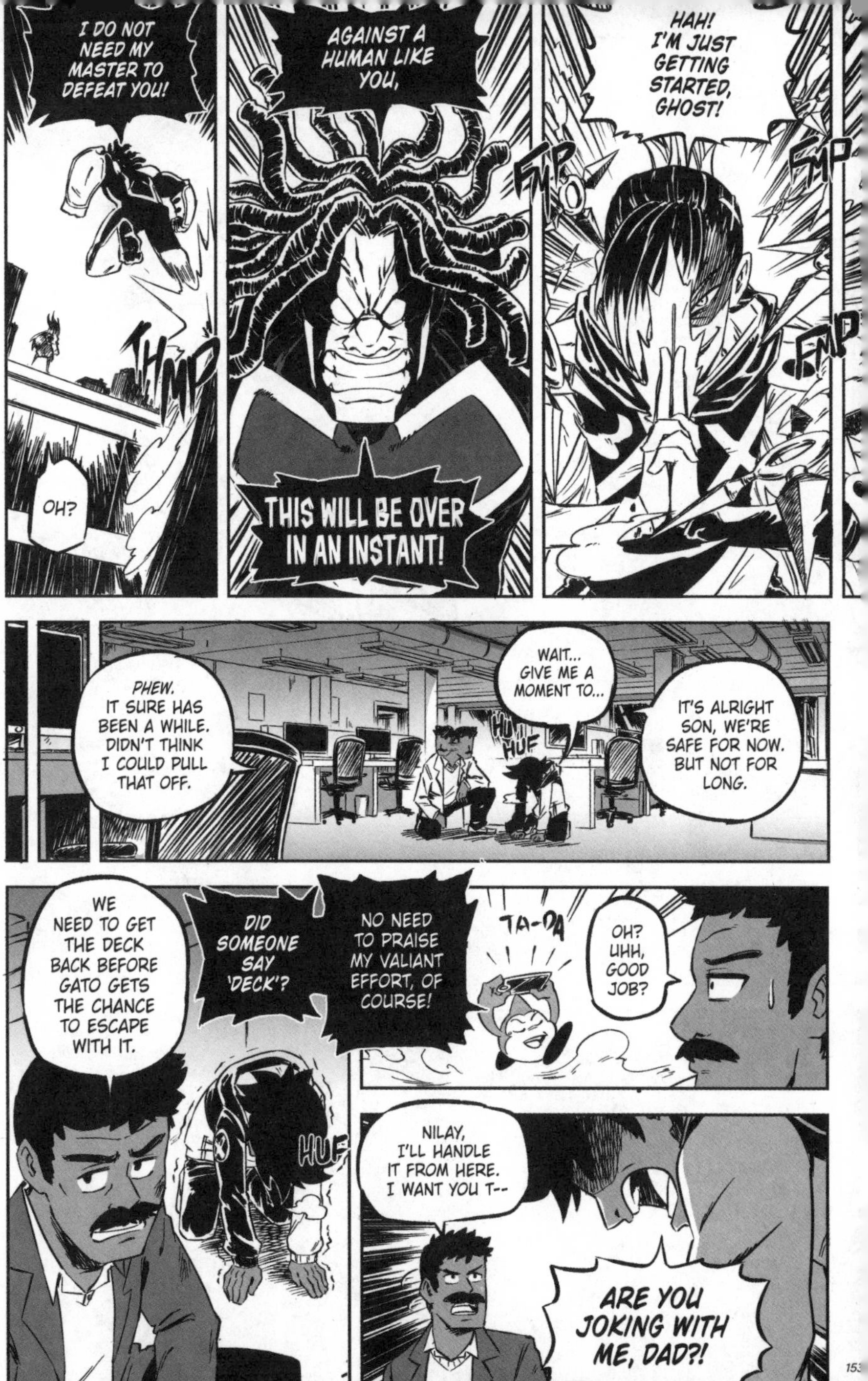
I DO NOT NEED MY MASTER TO DEFEAT YOU!
THMP
OH?
AGAINST A HUMAN LIKE YOU,
THIS WILL BE OVER IN AN INSTANT!
HAH! I'M JUST GETTING STARTED, GHOST!
FMP
FMP
FMP
PHEW. IT SURE HAS BEEN A WHILE. DIDN'T THINK I COULD PULL THAT OFF.
WAIT... GIVE ME A MOMENT TO...
HUF HUF
IT'S ALRIGHT SON, WE'RE SAFE FOR NOW. BUT NOT FOR LONG.
WE NEED TO GET THE DECK BACK BEFORE GATO GETS THE CHANCE TO ESCAPE WITH IT.
HUF
DID SOMEONE SAY 'DECK'?
NO NEED TO PRAISE MY VALIANT EFFORT, OF COURSE!
TA-DA
OH? UHH, GOOD JOB?
NILAY, I'LL HANDLE IT FROM HERE. I WANT YOU T--
ARE YOU JOKING WITH ME, DAD?!

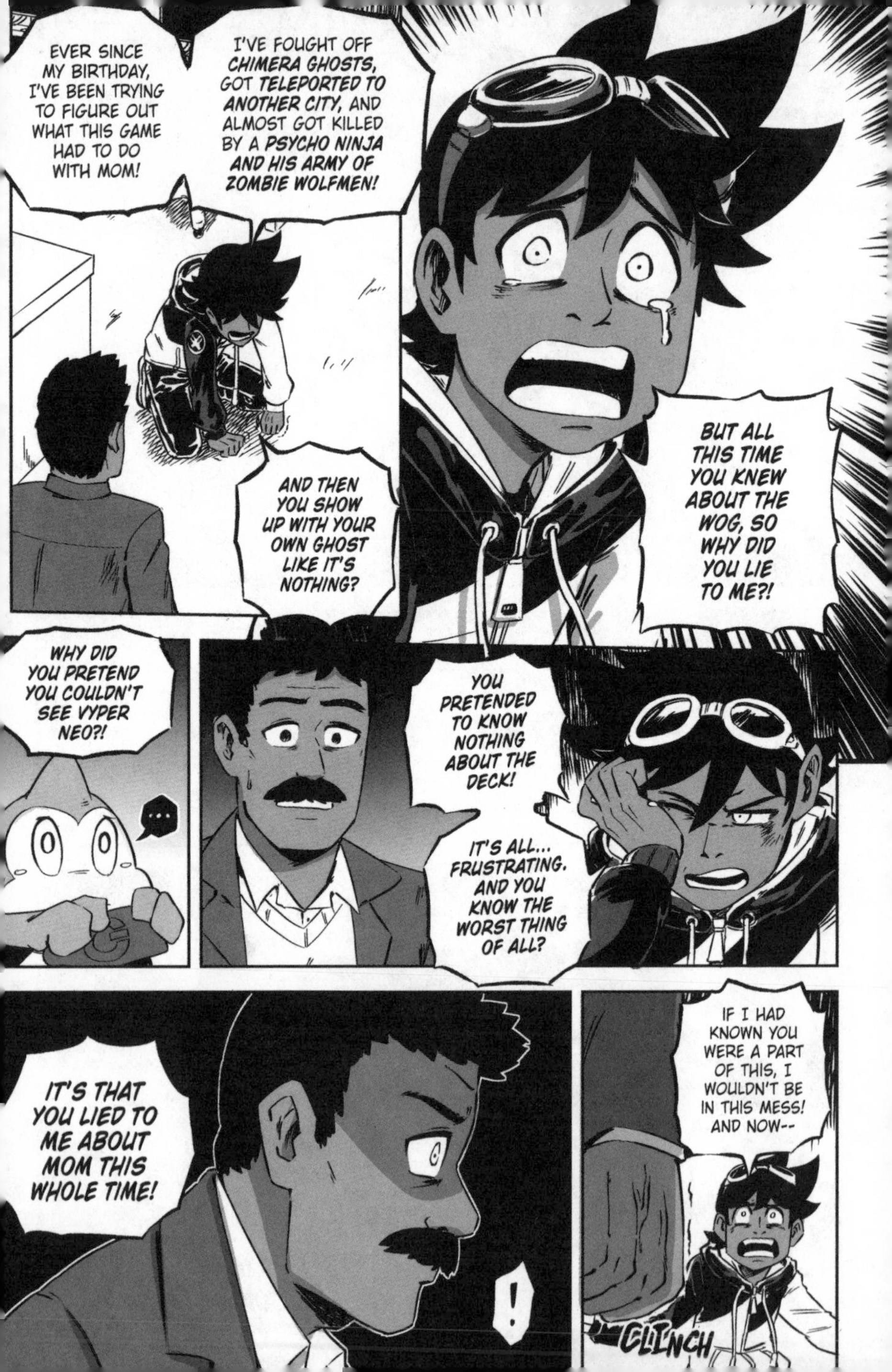

EVER SINCE MY BIRTHDAY, I'VE BEEN TRYING TO FIGURE OUT WHAT THIS GAME HAD TO DO WITH MOM!
I'VE FOUGHT OFF CHIMERA GHOSTS, GOT TELEPORTED TO ANOTHER CITY, AND ALMOST GOT KILLED BY A PSYCHO NINJA AND HIS ARMY OF ZOMBIE WOLFMEN!
AND THEN YOU SHOW UP WITH YOUR OWN GHOST LIKE IT'S NOTHING?
BUT ALL THIS TIME YOU KNEW ABOUT THE WOG, SO WHY DID YOU LIE TO ME?!
WHY DID YOU PRETEND YOU COULDN'T SEE VYPER NEO?!
YOU PRETENDED TO KNOW NOTHING ABOUT THE DECK!
IT'S ALL... FRUSTRATING. AND YOU KNOW THE WORST THING OF ALL?
IT'S THAT YOU LIED TO ME ABOUT MOM THIS WHOLE TIME!
!
IF I HAD KNOWN YOU WERE A PART OF THIS, I WOULDN'T BE IN THIS MESS! AND NOW--
CLINCH

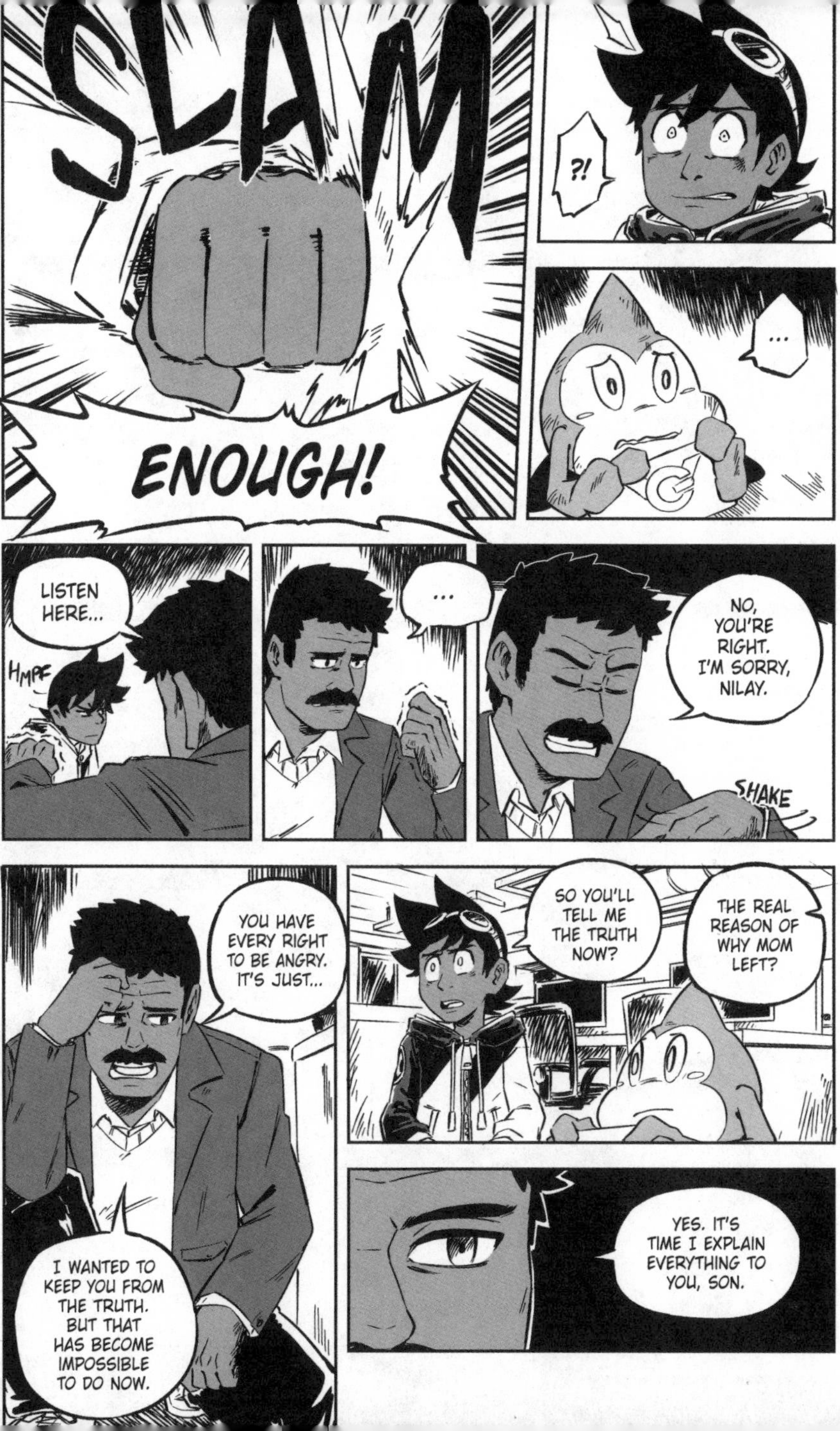
SLAM
ENOUGH!
?!
...
LISTEN HERE...
HMPF
...
NO, YOU'RE RIGHT. I'M SORRY, NILAY.
SHAKE
YOU HAVE EVERY RIGHT TO BE ANGRY. IT'S JUST...
I WANTED TO KEEP YOU FROM THE TRUTH. BUT THAT HAS BECOME IMPOSSIBLE TO DO NOW.
SO YOU'LL TELL ME THE TRUTH NOW?
THE REAL REASON OF WHY MOM LEFT?
YES. IT'S TIME I EXPLAIN EVERYTHING TO YOU, SON.

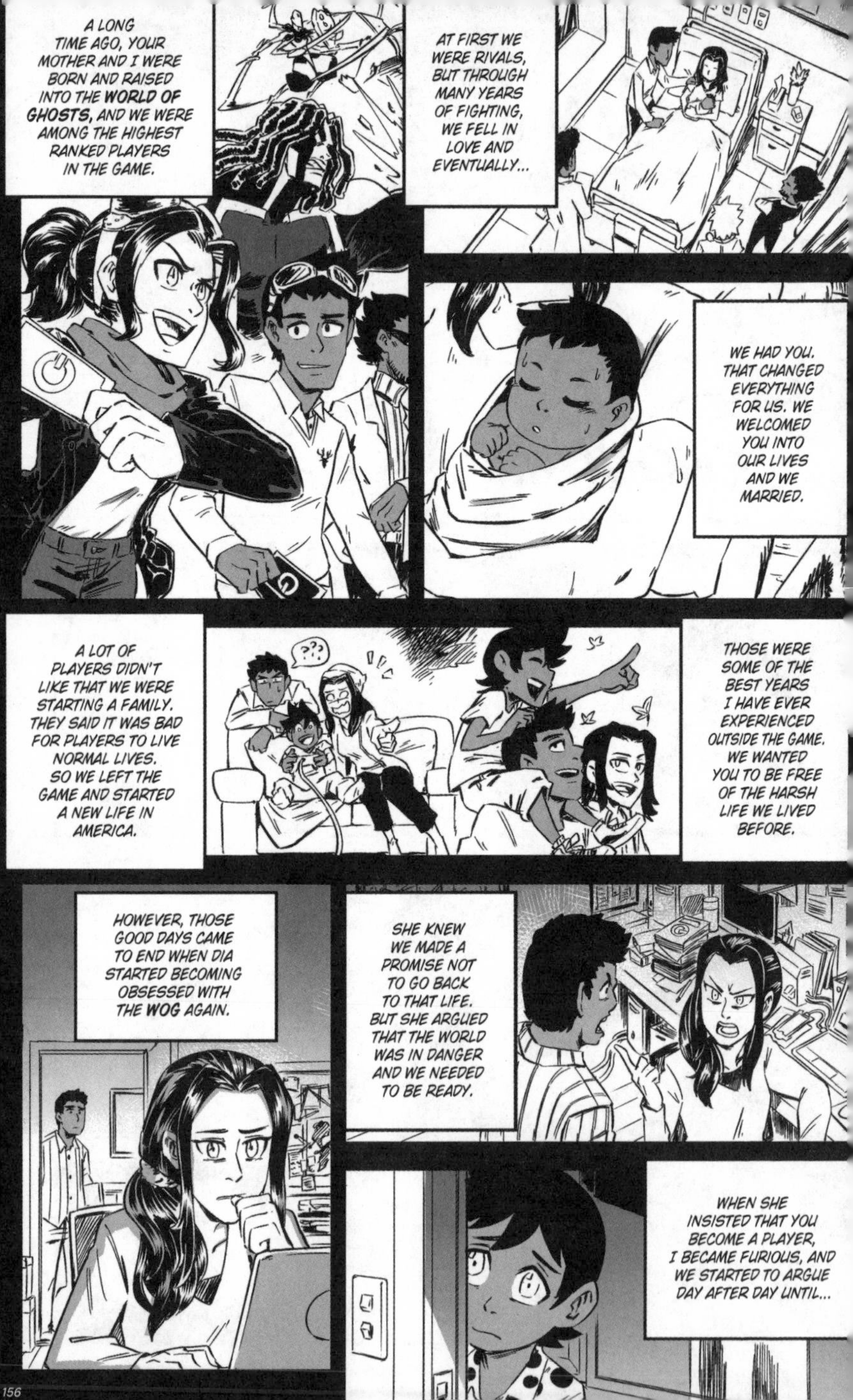
A LONG TIME AGO, YOUR MOTHER AND I WERE BORN AND RAISED INTO THE **WORLD OF GHOSTS**, AND WE WERE AMONG THE HIGHEST RANKED PLAYERS IN THE GAME.
AT FIRST WE WERE RIVALS, BUT THROUGH MANY YEARS OF FIGHTING, WE FELL IN LOVE AND EVENTUALLY...
WE HAD YOU. THAT CHANGED EVERYTHING FOR US. WE WELCOMED YOU INTO OUR LIVES AND WE MARRIED.
A LOT OF PLAYERS DIDN'T LIKE THAT WE WERE STARTING A FAMILY. THEY SAID IT WAS BAD FOR PLAYERS TO LIVE NORMAL LIVES. SO WE LEFT THE GAME AND STARTED A NEW LIFE IN AMERICA.
???
!
THOSE WERE SOME OF THE BEST YEARS I HAVE EVER EXPERIENCED OUTSIDE THE GAME. WE WANTED YOU TO BE FREE OF THE HARSH LIFE WE LIVED BEFORE.
HOWEVER, THOSE GOOD DAYS CAME TO END WHEN DIA STARTED BECOMING OBSESSED WITH THE **WOG** AGAIN.
SHE KNEW WE MADE A PROMISE NOT TO GO BACK TO THAT LIFE. BUT SHE ARGUED THAT THE WORLD WAS IN DANGER AND WE NEEDED TO BE READY.
WHEN SHE INSISTED THAT YOU BECOME A PLAYER, I BECAME FURIOUS, AND WE STARTED TO ARGUE DAY AFTER DAY UNTIL...

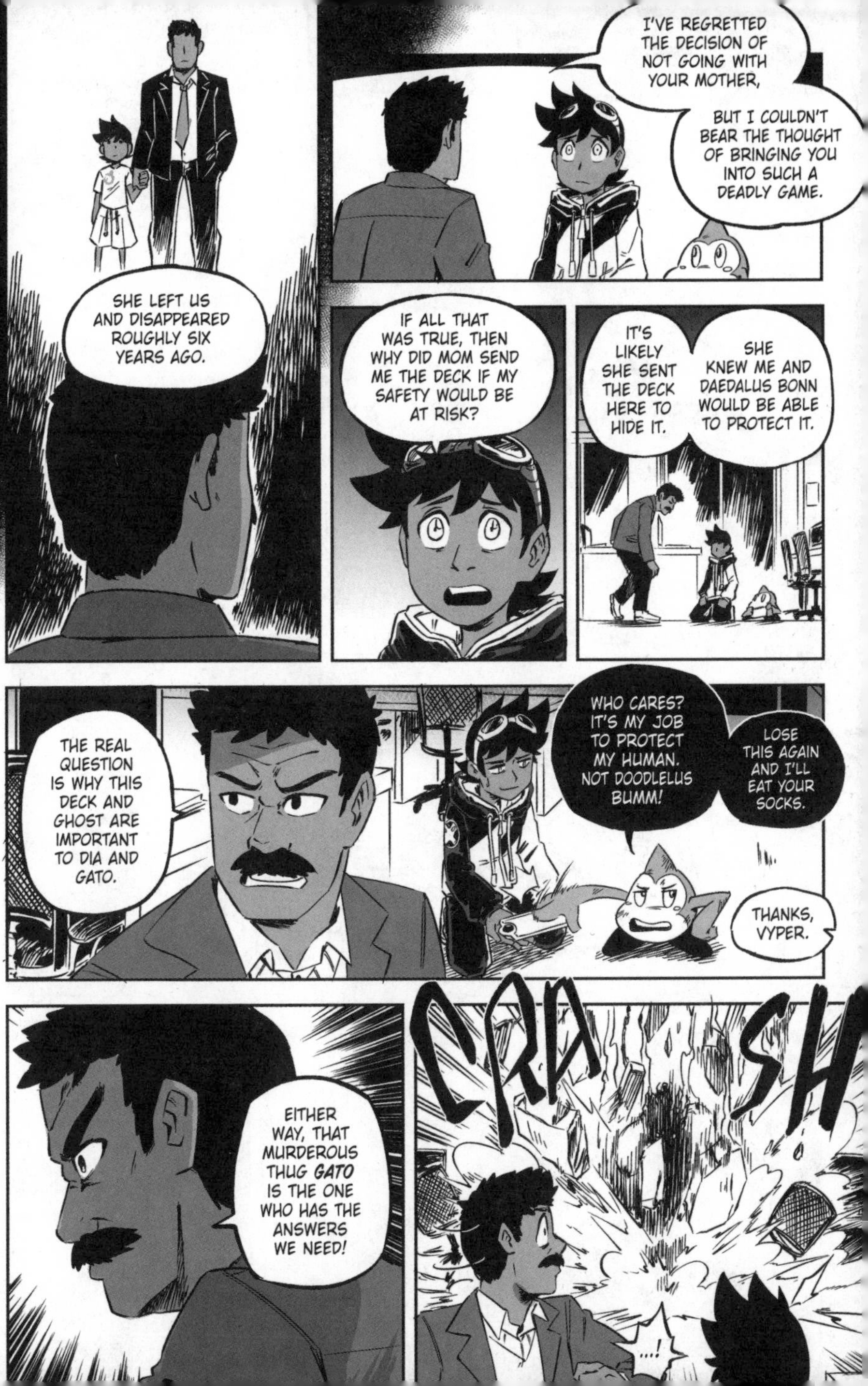
I'VE REGRETTED THE DECISION OF NOT GOING WITH YOUR MOTHER,
BUT I COULDN'T BEAR THE THOUGHT OF BRINGING YOU INTO SUCH A DEADLY GAME.
SHE LEFT US AND DISAPPEARED ROUGHLY SIX YEARS AGO.
IF ALL THAT WAS TRUE, THEN WHY DID MOM SEND ME THE DECK IF MY SAFETY WOULD BE AT RISK?
IT'S LIKELY SHE SENT THE DECK HERE TO HIDE IT.
SHE KNEW ME AND DAEDALUS BONN WOULD BE ABLE TO PROTECT IT.
THE REAL QUESTION IS WHY THIS DECK AND GHOST ARE IMPORTANT TO DIA AND GATO.
WHO CARES? IT'S MY JOB TO PROTECT MY HUMAN. NOT DOODLELUS BUMM!
LOSE THIS AGAIN AND I'LL EAT YOUR SOCKS.
THANKS, VYPER.
EITHER WAY, THAT MURDEROUS THUG ***GATO*** IS THE ONE WHO HAS THE ANSWERS WE NEED!
CRASH
...!

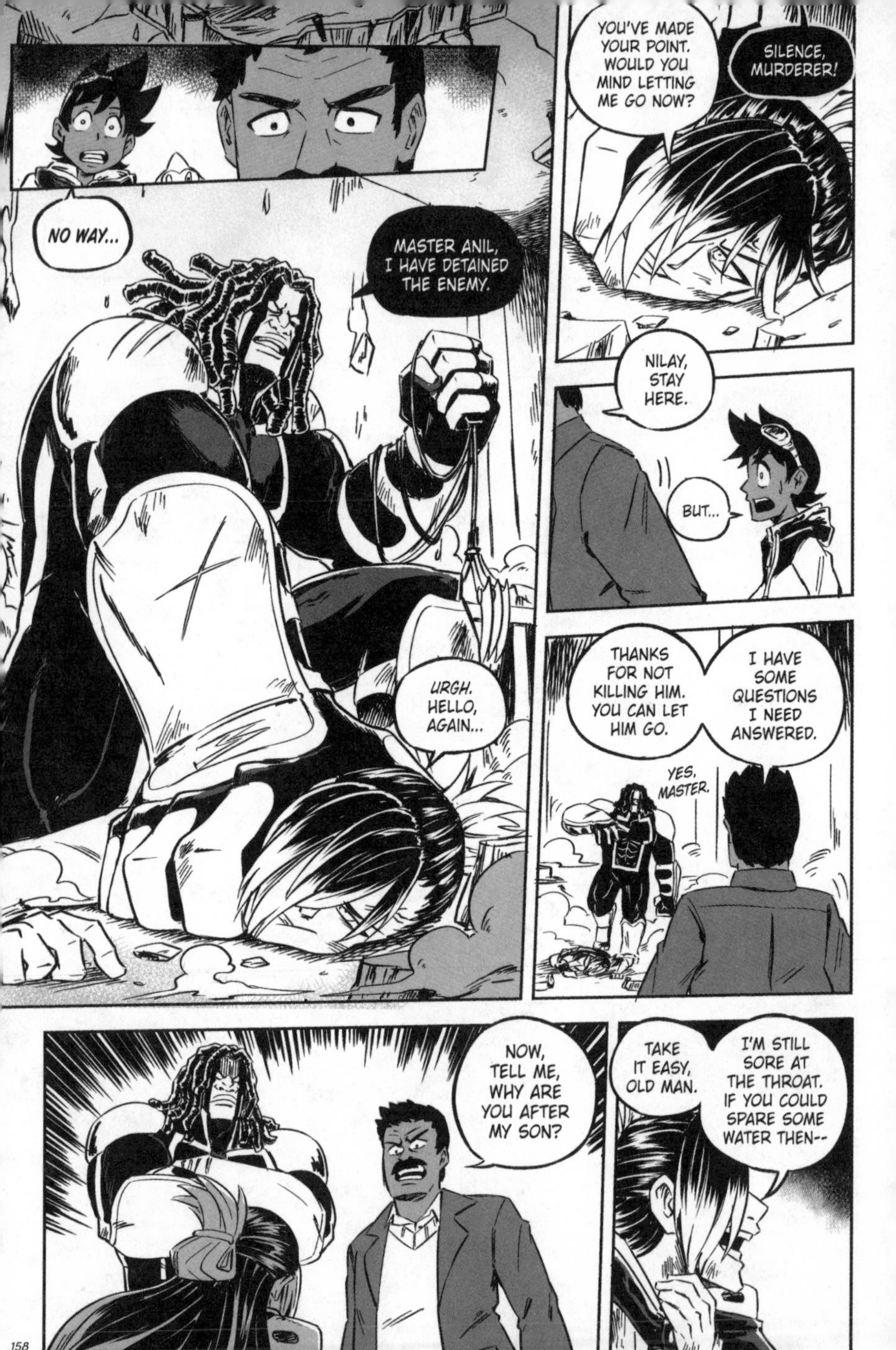
NO WAY...
MASTER ANIL, I HAVE DETAINED THE ENEMY.
URGH. HELLO, AGAIN...
YOU'VE MADE YOUR POINT. WOULD YOU MIND LETTING ME GO NOW?
SILENCE, MURDERER!
NILAY, STAY HERE.
BUT...
THANKS FOR NOT KILLING HIM. YOU CAN LET HIM GO.
I HAVE SOME QUESTIONS I NEED ANSWERED.
YES, MASTER.
NOW, TELL ME, WHY ARE YOU AFTER MY SON?
TAKE IT EASY, OLD MAN.
I'M STILL SORE AT THE THROAT. IF YOU COULD SPARE SOME WATER THEN--

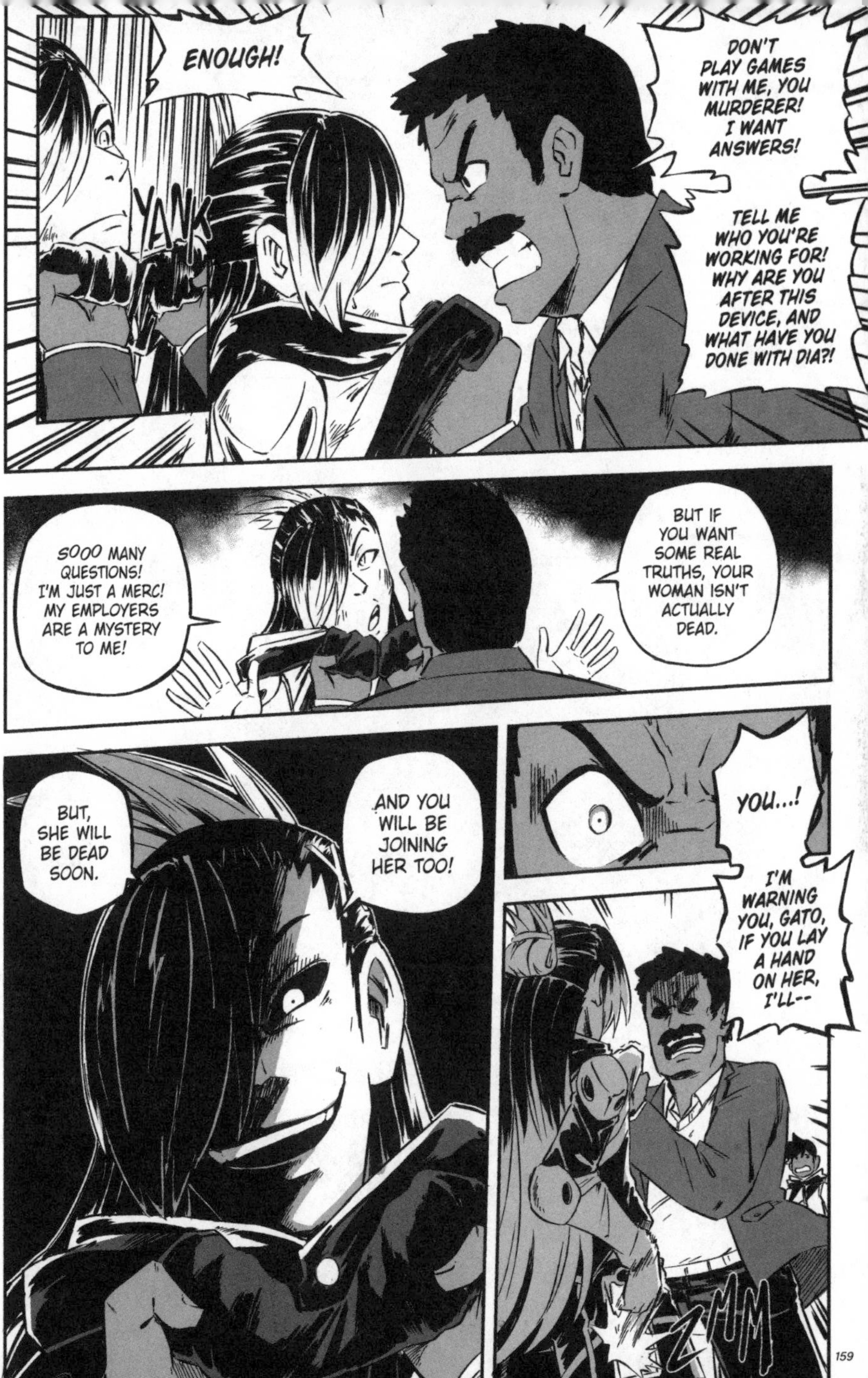
ENOUGH!
YANK
DON'T PLAY GAMES WITH ME, YOU MURDERER! I WANT ANSWERS!
TELL ME WHO YOU'RE WORKING FOR! WHY ARE YOU AFTER THIS DEVICE, AND WHAT HAVE YOU DONE WITH DIA?!
SOOO MANY QUESTIONS! I'M JUST A MERC! MY EMPLOYERS ARE A MYSTERY TO ME!
BUT IF YOU WANT SOME REAL TRUTHS, YOUR WOMAN ISN'T ACTUALLY DEAD.
BUT, SHE WILL BE DEAD SOON.
AND YOU WILL BE JOINING HER TOO!
YOU...!
I'M WARNING YOU, GATO, IF YOU LAY A HAND ON HER, I'LL--
ZMM

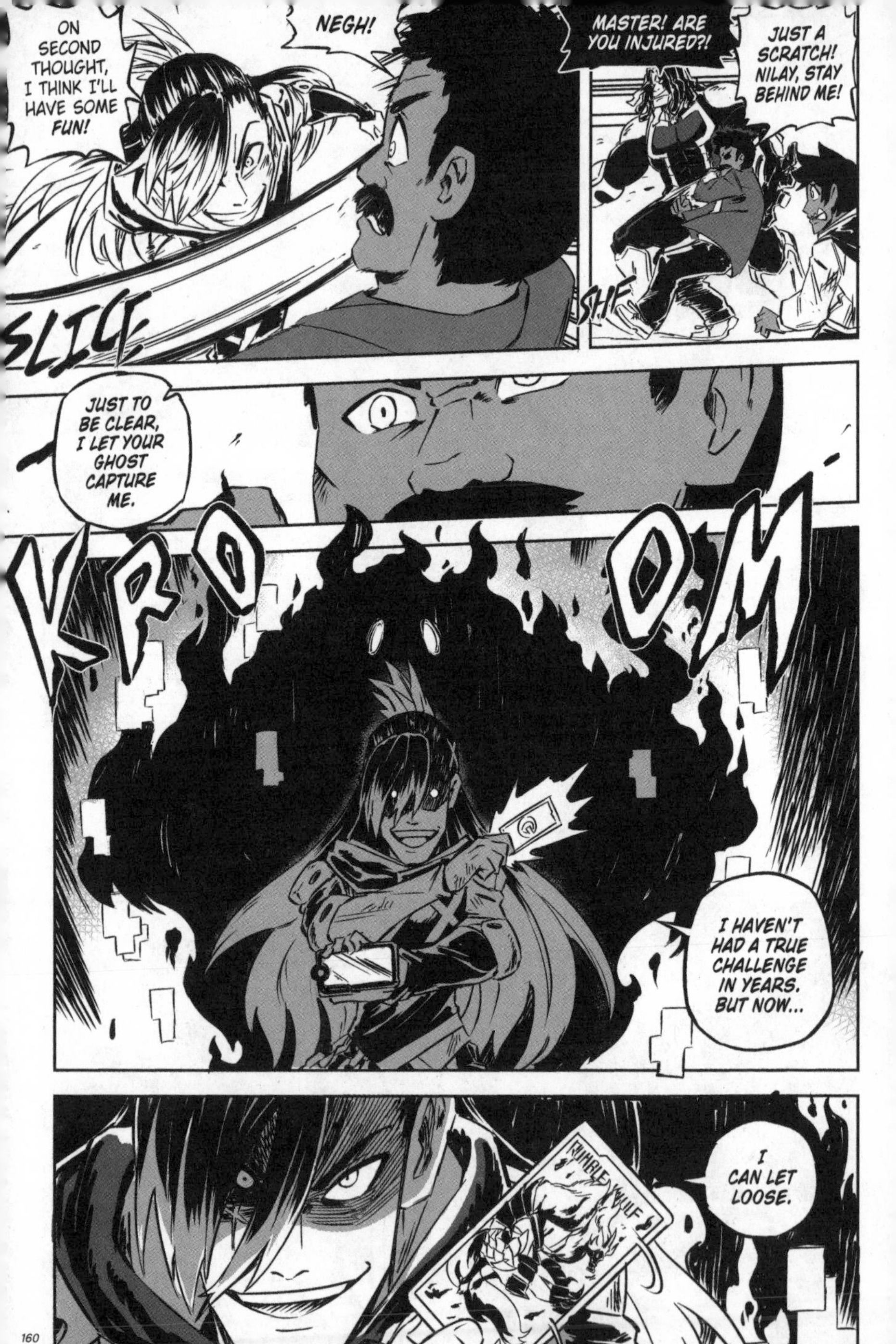

ON SECOND THOUGHT, I THINK I'LL HAVE SOME FUN!
NEGH!
SLICE
MASTER! ARE YOU INJURED?!
JUST A SCRATCH! NILAY, STAY BEHIND ME!
SHF
JUST TO BE CLEAR, I LET YOUR GHOST CAPTURE ME.
KROOM
I HAVEN'T HAD A TRUE CHALLENGE IN YEARS. BUT NOW...
I CAN LET LOOSE.

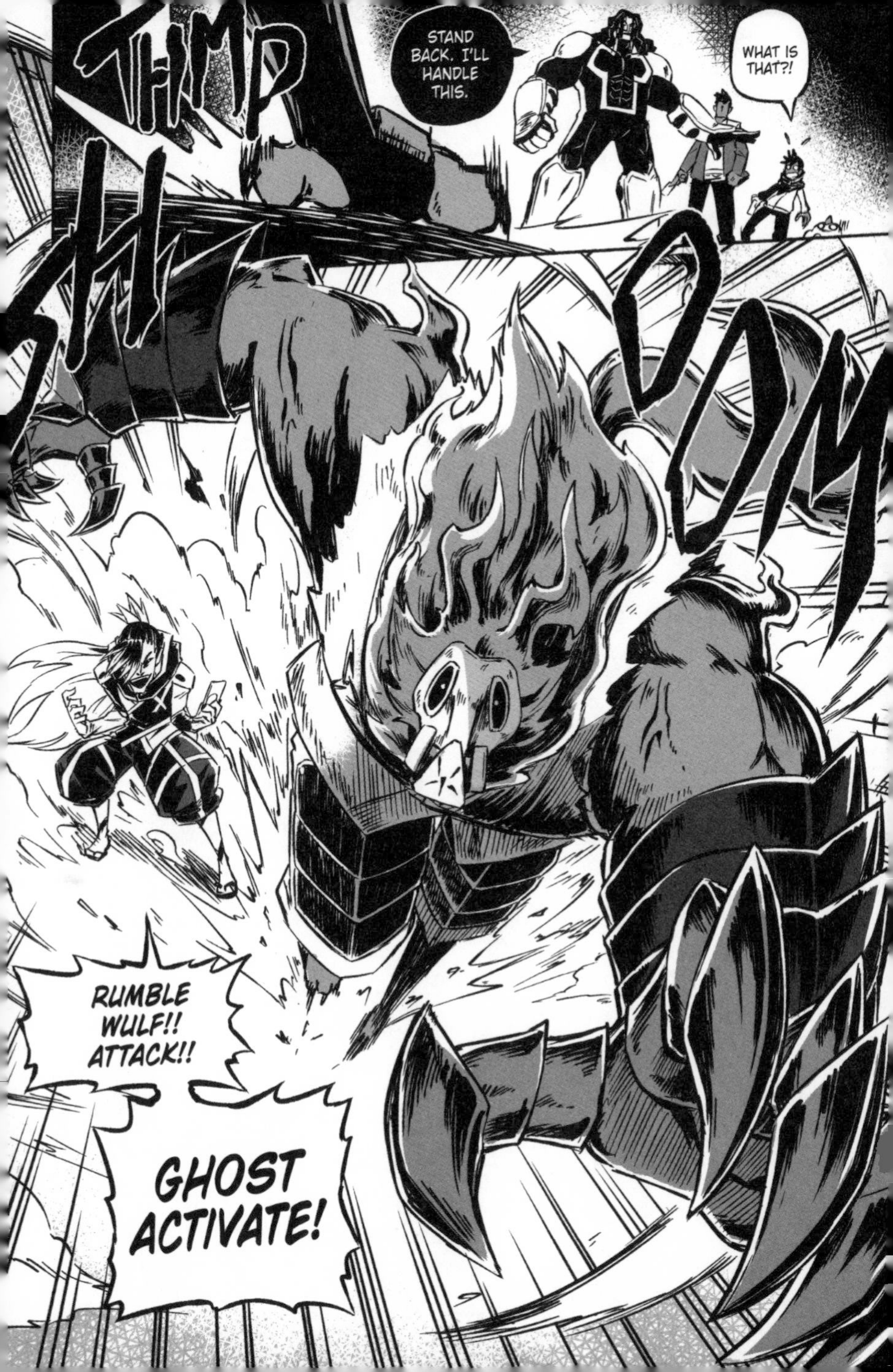
THMP
STAND BACK. I'LL HANDLE THIS.
WHAT IS THAT?!
RUMBLE WULF!! ATTACK!!
GHOST ACTIVATE!

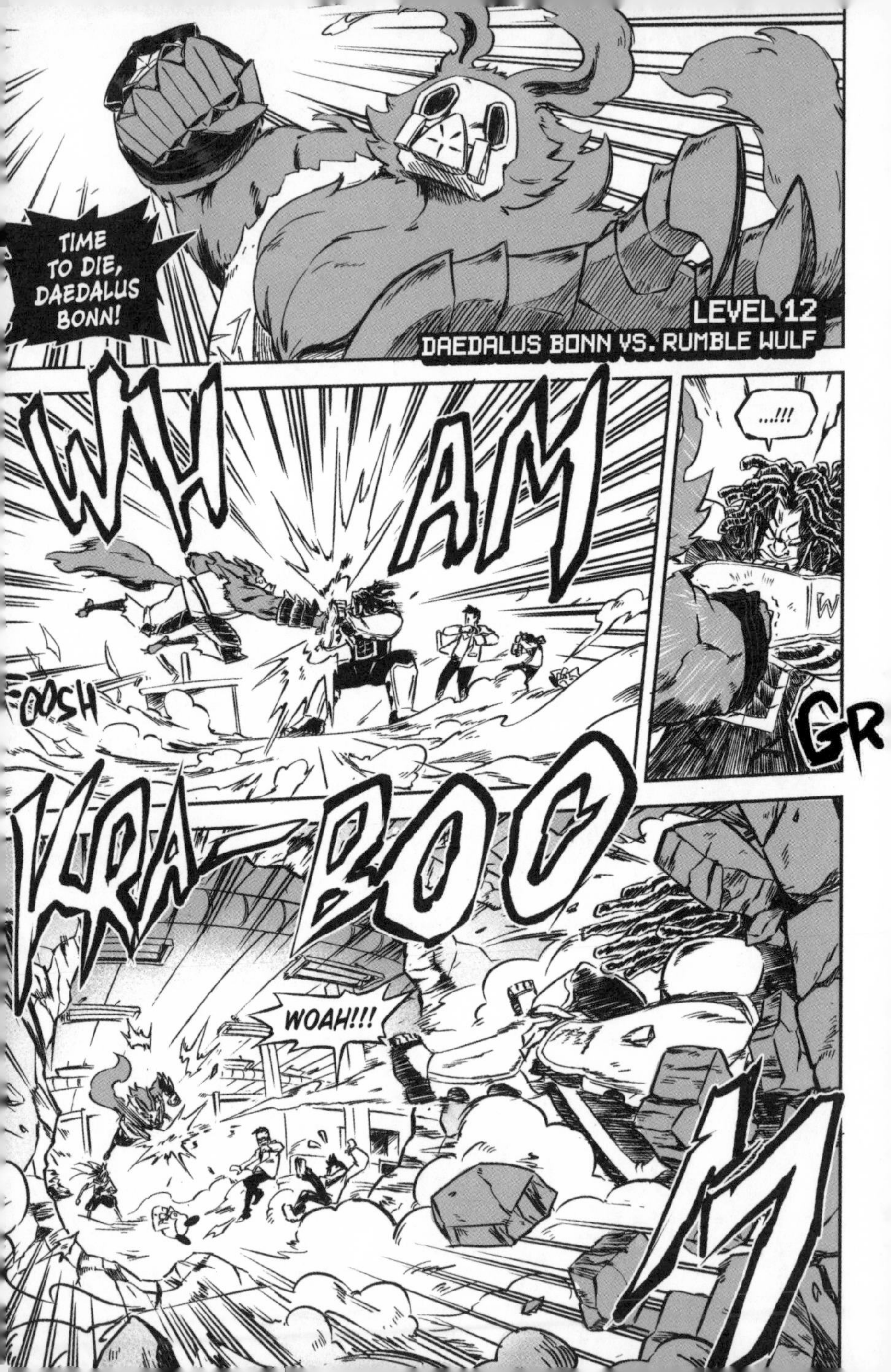
TIME TO DIE, DAEDALUS BONN!
LEVEL 12
DAEDALUS BONN VS. RUMBLE WULF
WHAM
FOOSH
...!!!
GR
KRA-BOOM
WOAH!!!

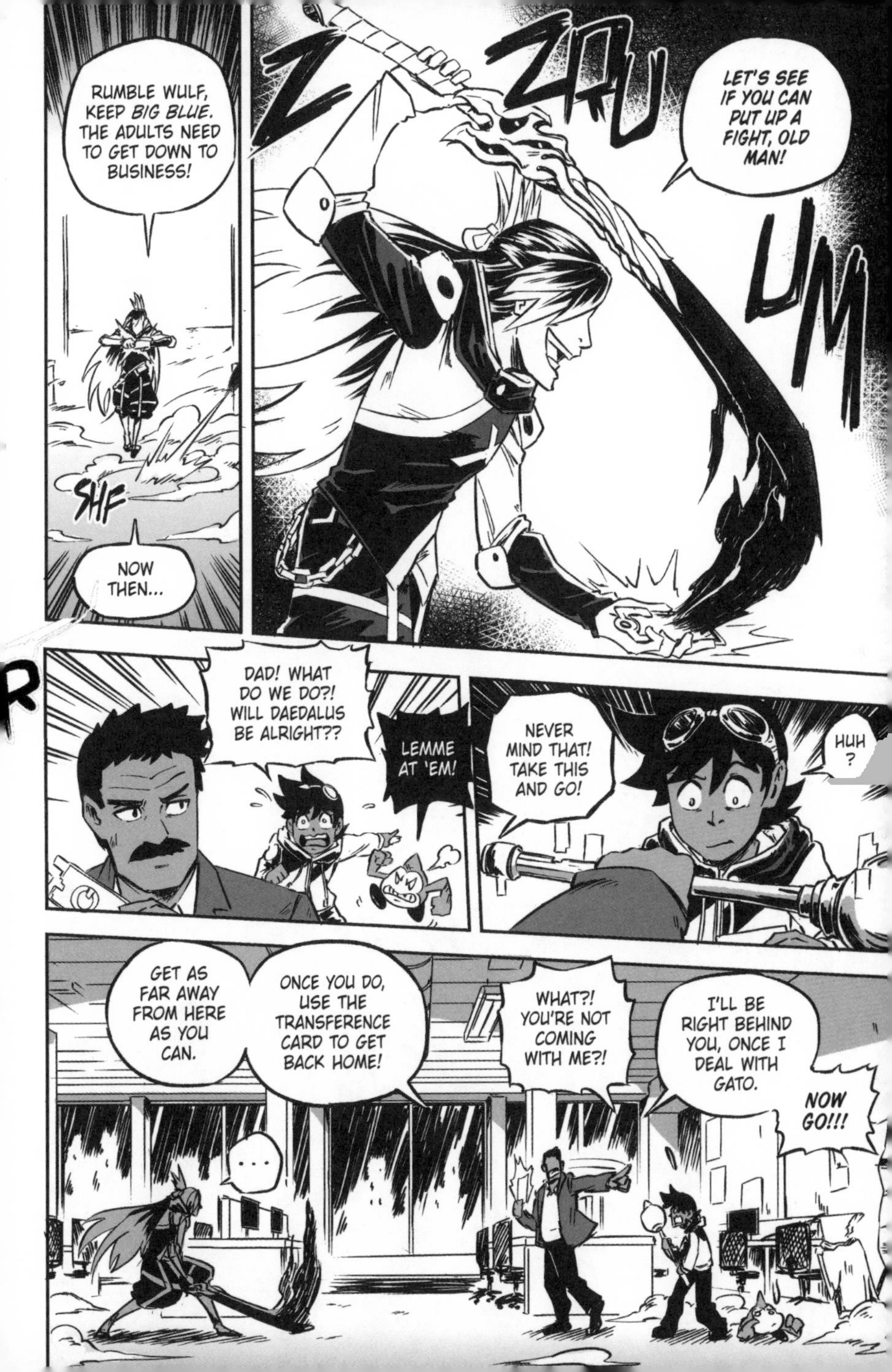

RUMBLE WULF, KEEP *BIG BLUE*. THE ADULTS NEED TO GET DOWN TO BUSINESS!
SHF
NOW THEN...
Z
ZRU
UM
LET'S SEE IF YOU CAN PUT UP A FIGHT, OLD MAN!
R
DAD! WHAT DO WE DO?! WILL DAEDALUS BE ALRIGHT??
LEMME AT 'EM!
NEVER MIND THAT! TAKE THIS AND GO!
HUH?
GET AS FAR AWAY FROM HERE AS YOU CAN.
ONCE YOU DO, USE THE TRANSFERENCE CARD TO GET BACK HOME!
WHAT?! YOU'RE NOT COMING WITH ME?!
I'LL BE RIGHT BEHIND YOU, ONCE I DEAL WITH GATO.
NOW GO!!!
...

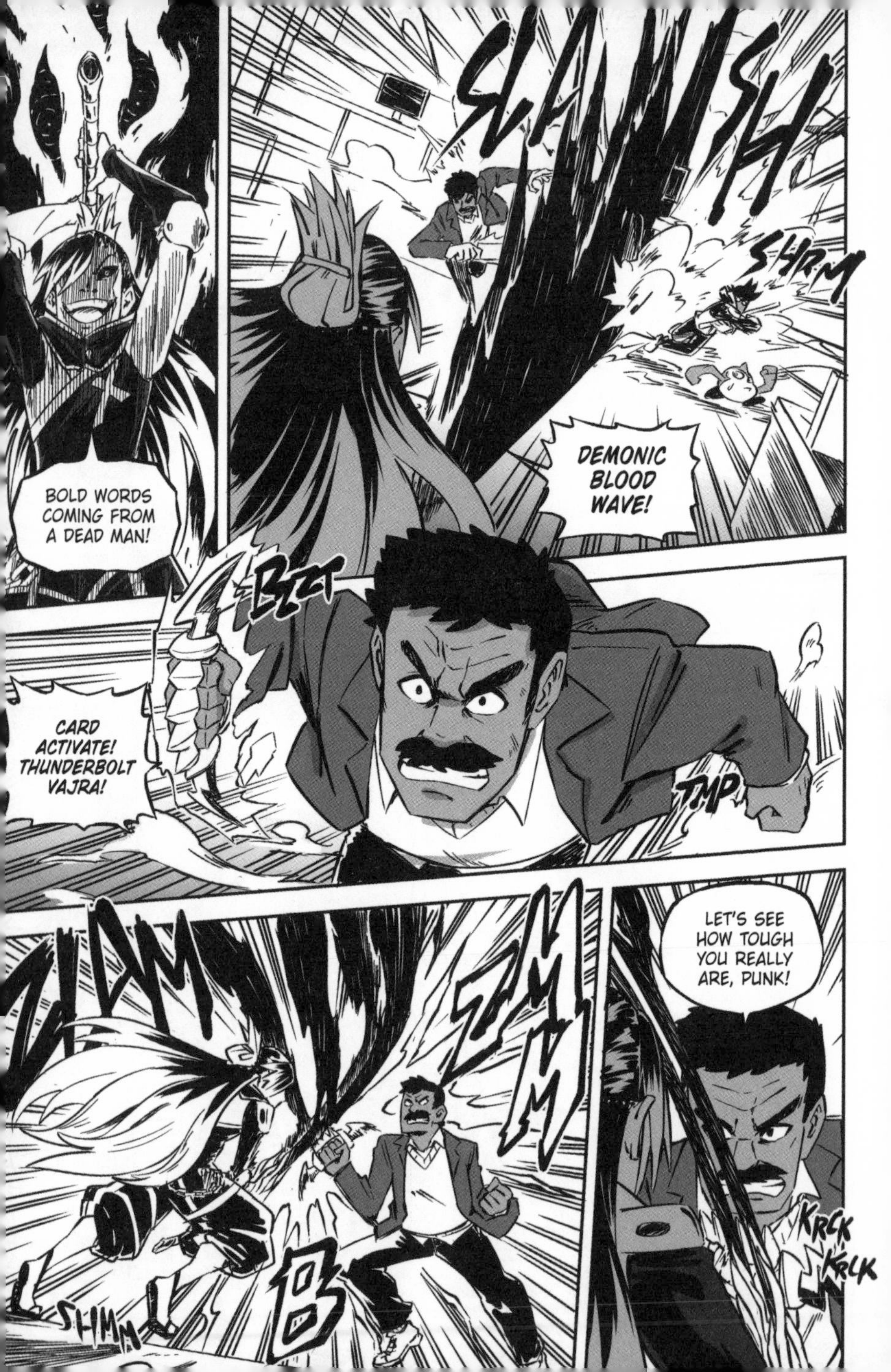

BOLD WORDS COMING FROM A DEAD MAN!
SLAMMSH
SHRM
DEMONIC BLOOD WAVE!
BZZT
CARD ACTIVATE! THUNDERBOLT VAJRA!
TMP
ZHMM
SHMM
B
LET'S SEE HOW TOUGH YOU REALLY ARE, PUNK!
KRCK
KRCK

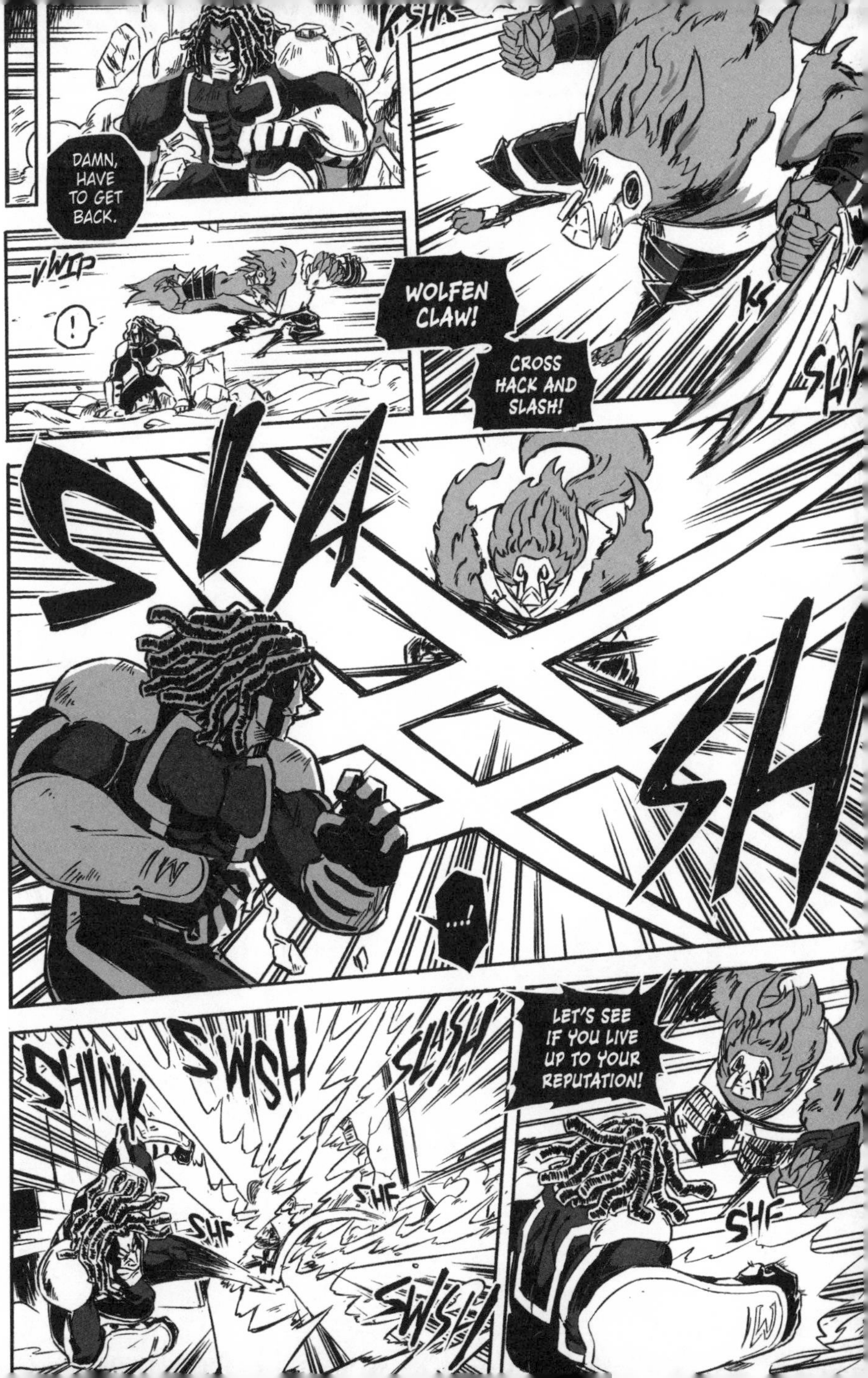
DAMN, HAVE TO GET BACK.
JWIP
!
WOLFEN CLAW!
CROSS HACK AND SLASH!
SLA
SH
...!
SHINK
SWSH
SLASH
SHF
SHF
SWSH
LET'S SEE IF YOU LIVE UP TO YOUR REPUTATION!
SHF

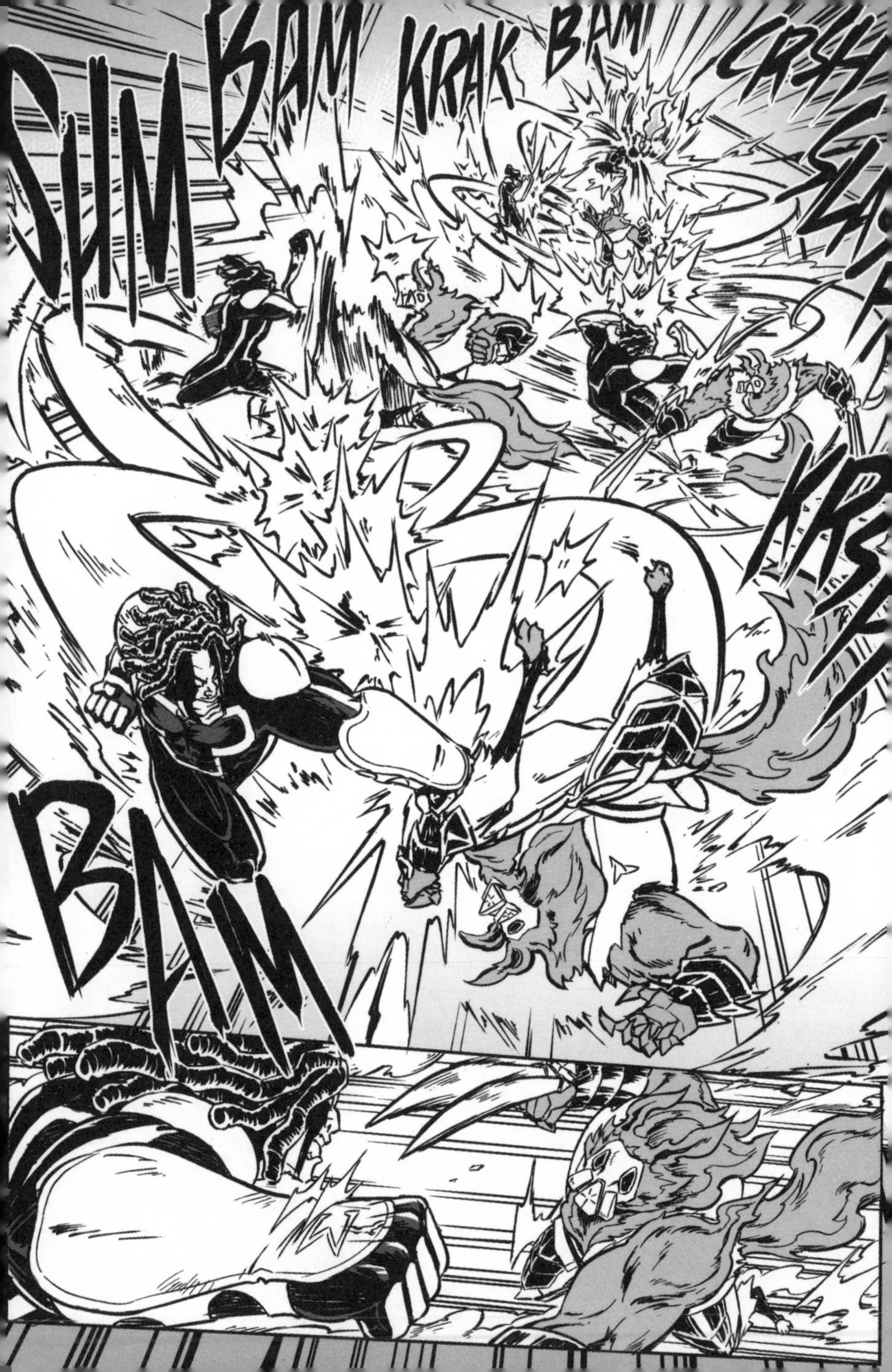
SLAM
BAM
KRAK
BAM
CRSH
SMASH
KRSH
BAM

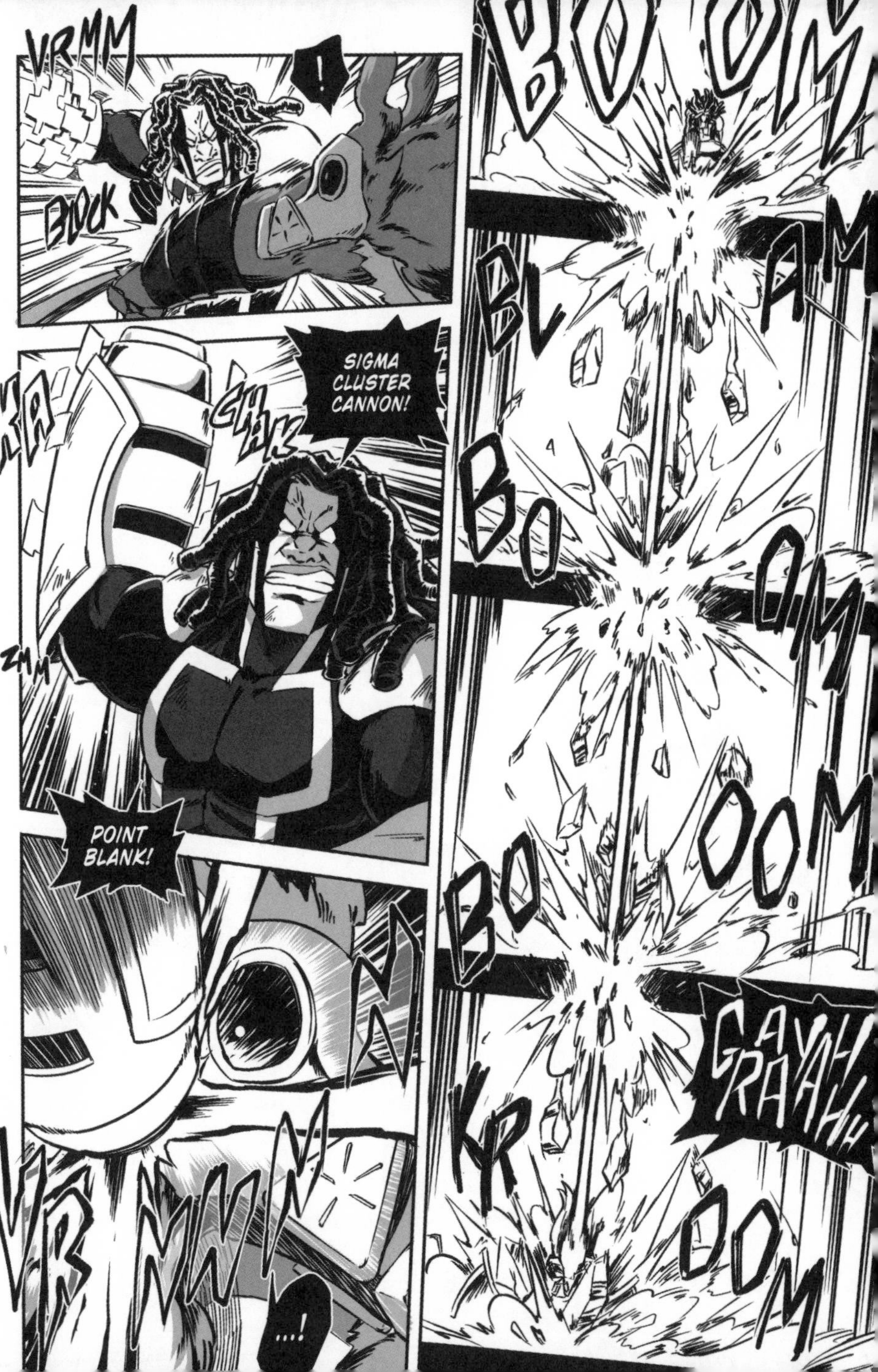
VRMM
!
BLOCK
KA
CHAK
SIGMA CLUSTER CANNON!
ZMM
POINT BLANK!
VRMMMN
...!
BOOM
BLAM
BOOM
BOOOM
KR
GAYAHH RAAHH
DOOM

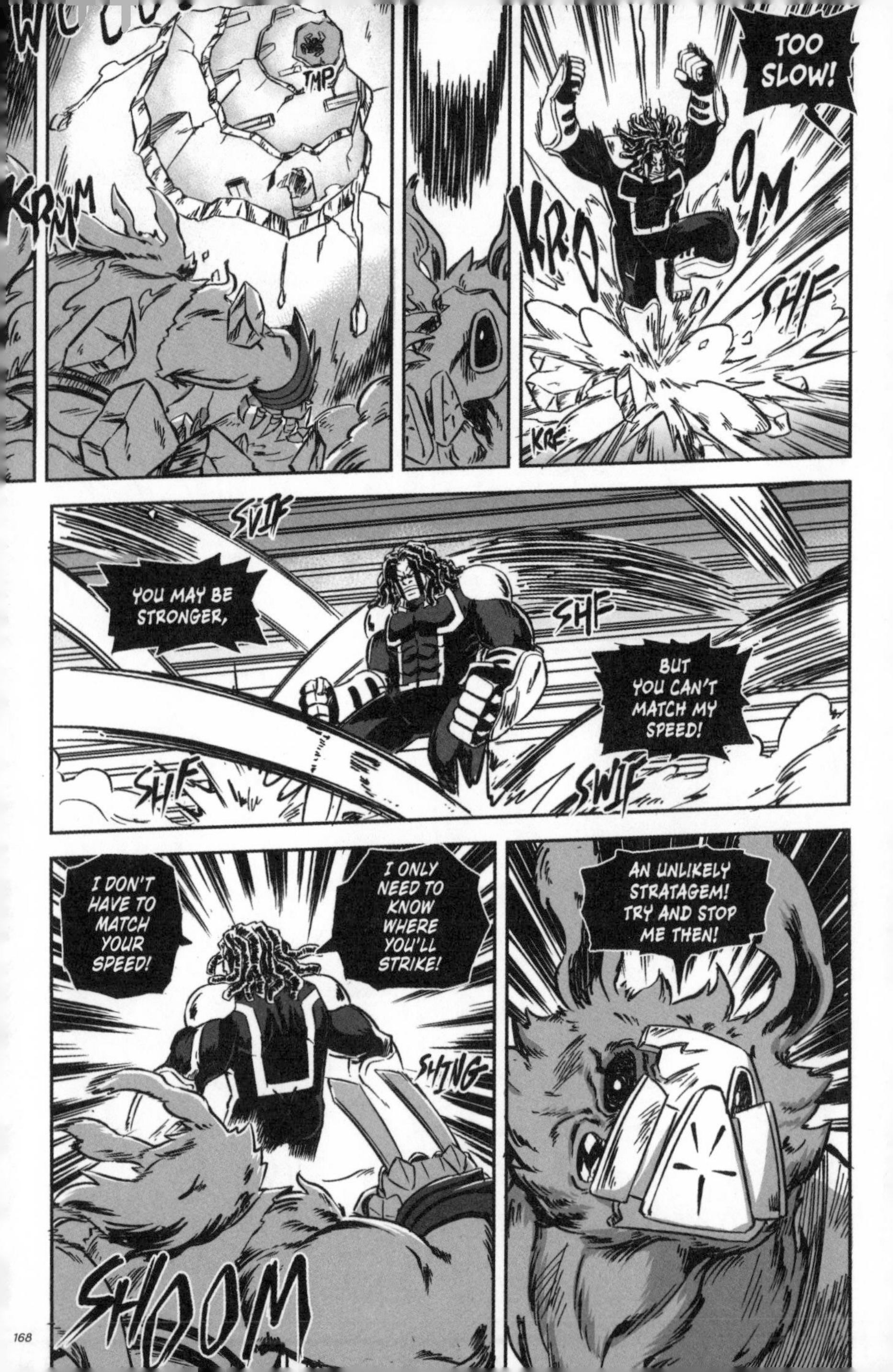
KRMM
TMP
TOO SLOW!
KROOM
SHF
KRF
SWIF
YOU MAY BE STRONGER,
SHF
BUT YOU CAN'T MATCH MY SPEED!
SHF
SWIF
I DON'T HAVE TO MATCH YOUR SPEED!
I ONLY NEED TO KNOW WHERE YOU'LL STRIKE!
SHING
SHOOM
AN UNLIKELY STRATAGEM! TRY AND STOP ME THEN!

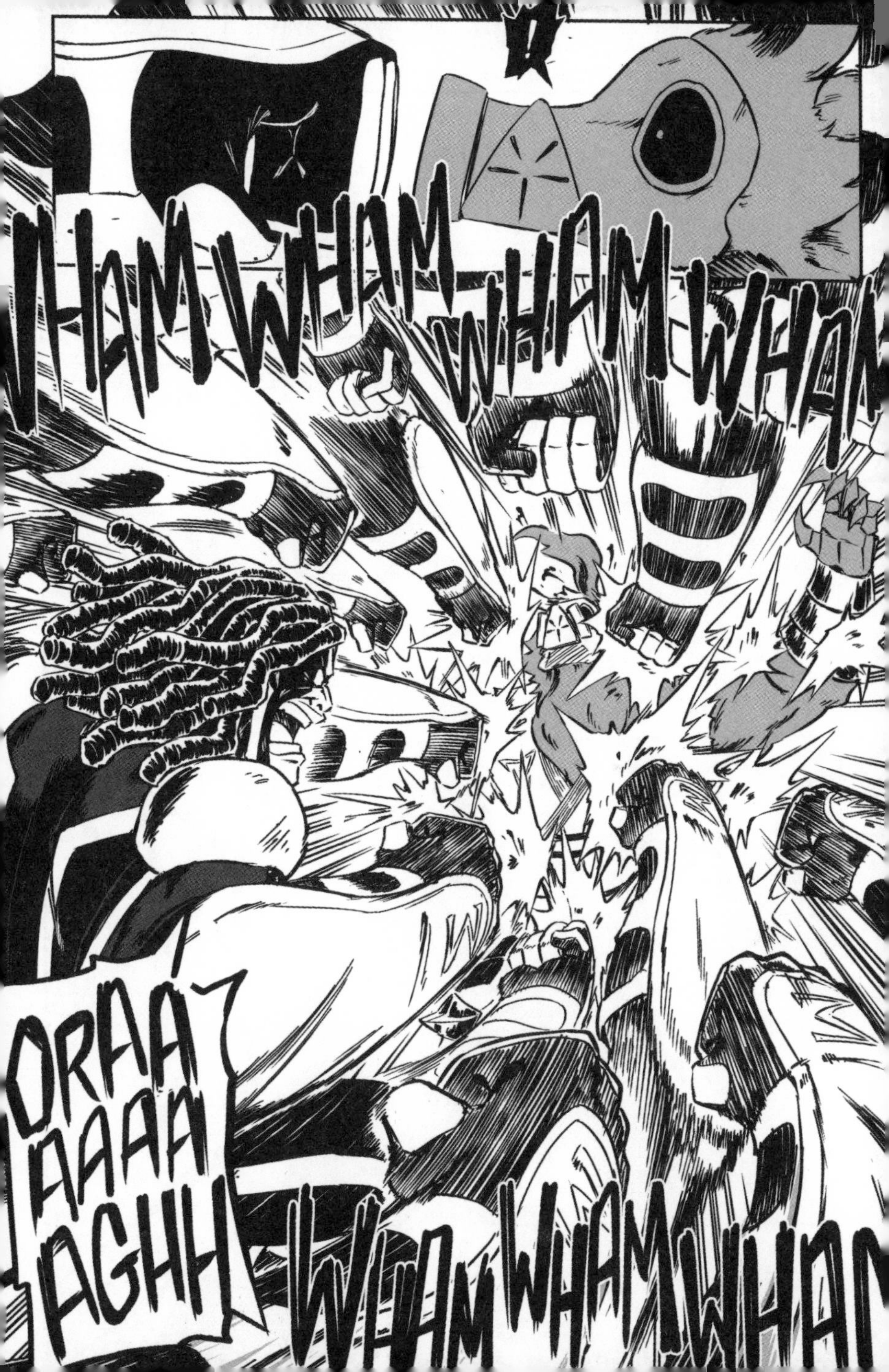
WHAM WHAM WHAM WHAM
ORAAAAAAAGHH
WHAM WHAM WHAM

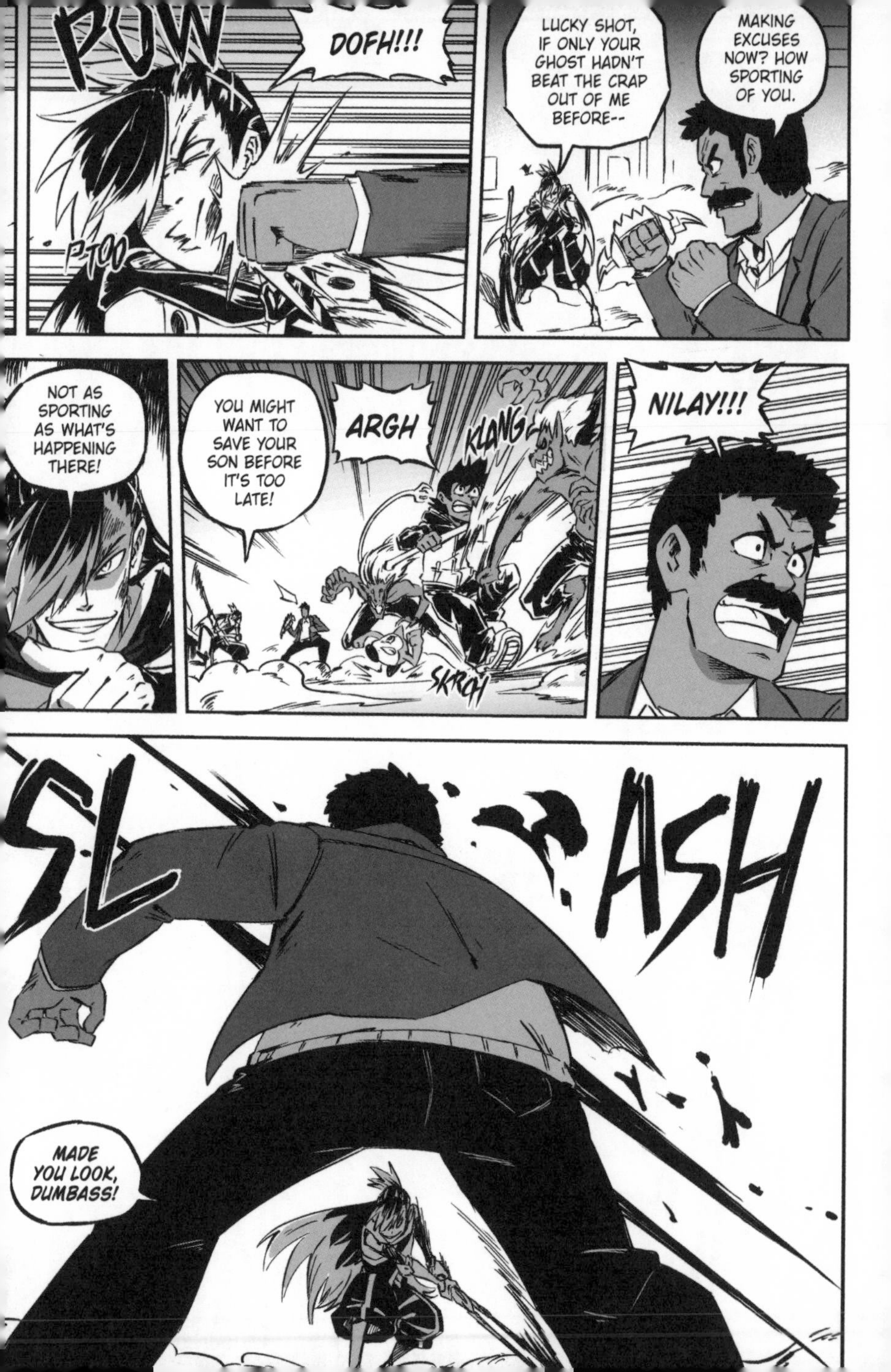
POW
DOFH!!!
P-TOO
LUCKY SHOT, IF ONLY YOUR GHOST HADN'T BEAT THE CRAP OUT OF ME BEFORE--
MAKING EXCUSES NOW? HOW SPORTING OF YOU.
NOT AS SPORTING AS WHAT'S HAPPENING THERE!
YOU MIGHT WANT TO SAVE YOUR SON BEFORE IT'S TOO LATE!
ARGH
KLANG
SKRCH
NILAY!!!
SLASH
MADE YOU LOOK, DUMBASS!

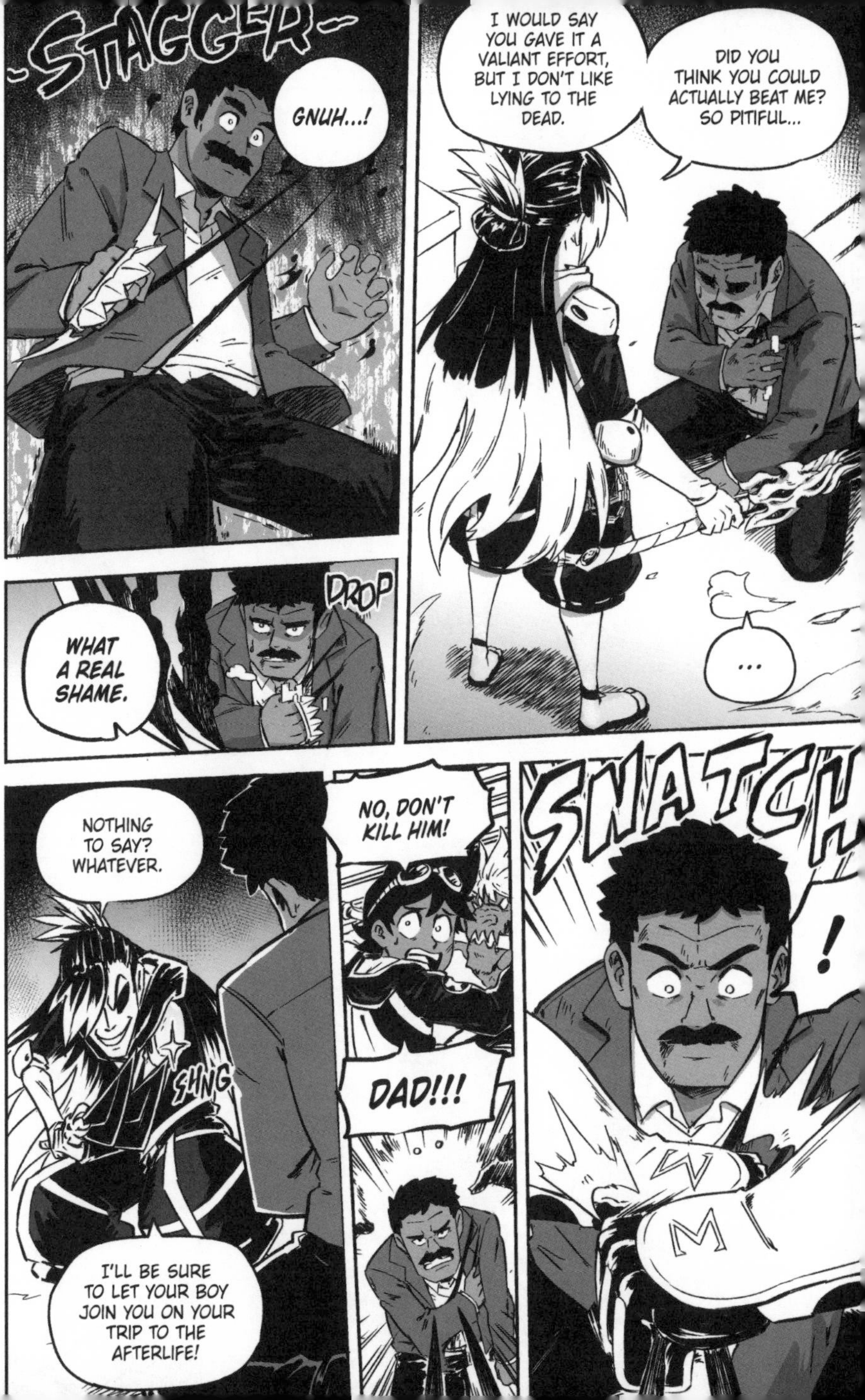

STAGGER
GNUH...!
I WOULD SAY YOU GAVE IT A VALIANT EFFORT, BUT I DON'T LIKE LYING TO THE DEAD.
DID YOU THINK YOU COULD ACTUALLY BEAT ME? SO PITIFUL...
DROP
WHAT A REAL SHAME.
...
NOTHING TO SAY? WHATEVER.
SHNG
I'LL BE SURE TO LET YOUR BOY JOIN YOU ON YOUR TRIP TO THE AFTERLIFE!
NO, DON'T KILL HIM!
DAD!!!
SNATCH
!

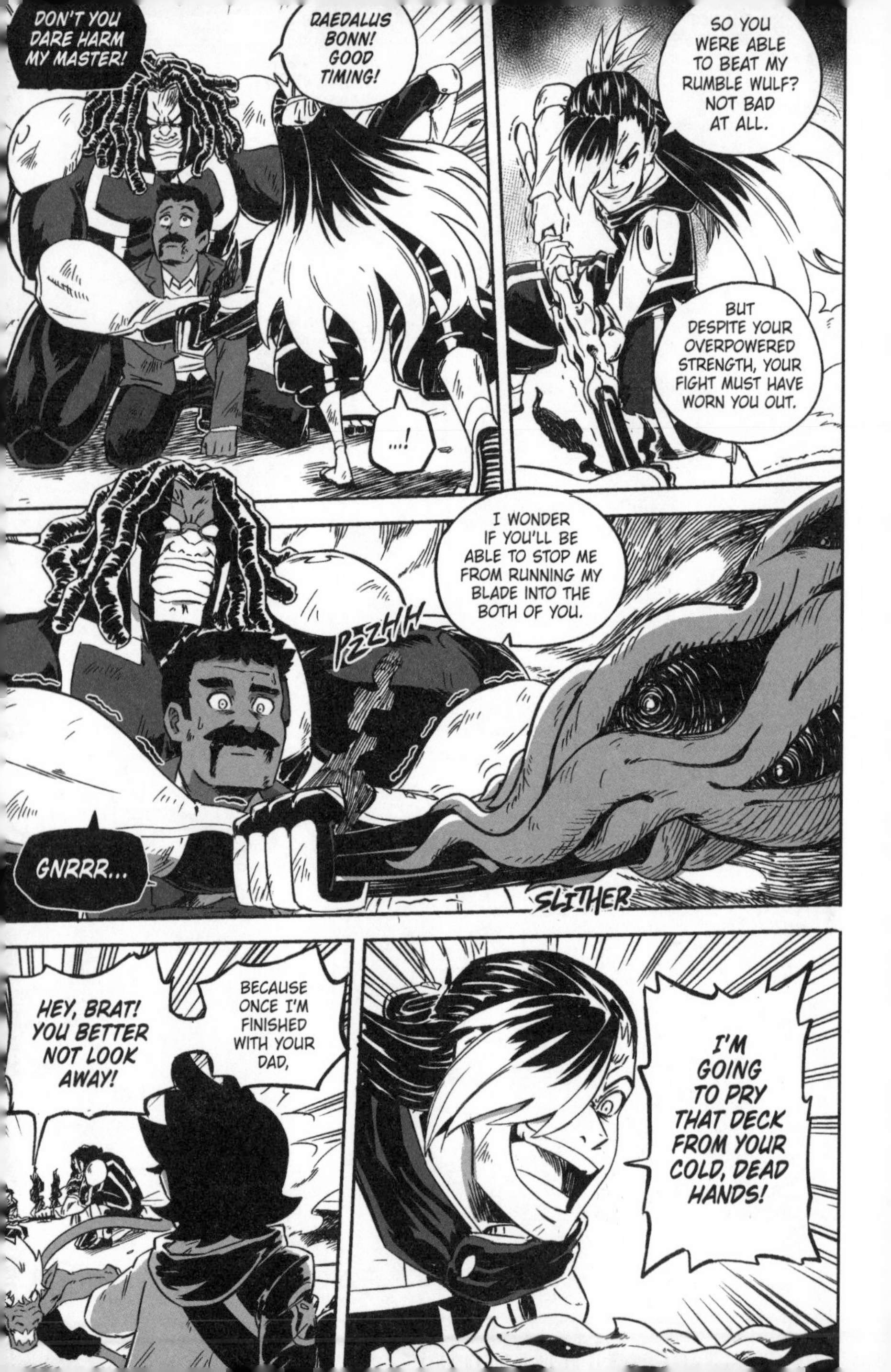
DON'T YOU DARE HARM MY MASTER!
DAEDALUS BONN! GOOD TIMING!
...!
SO YOU WERE ABLE TO BEAT MY RUMBLE WULF? NOT BAD AT ALL.
BUT DESPITE YOUR OVERPOWERED STRENGTH, YOUR FIGHT MUST HAVE WORN YOU OUT.
I WONDER IF YOU'LL BE ABLE TO STOP ME FROM RUNNING MY BLADE INTO THE BOTH OF YOU.
PZZHH
GNRRR...
SLITHER
HEY, BRAT! YOU BETTER NOT LOOK AWAY!
BECAUSE ONCE I'M FINISHED WITH YOUR DAD,
I'M GOING TO PRY THAT DECK FROM YOUR COLD, DEAD HANDS!

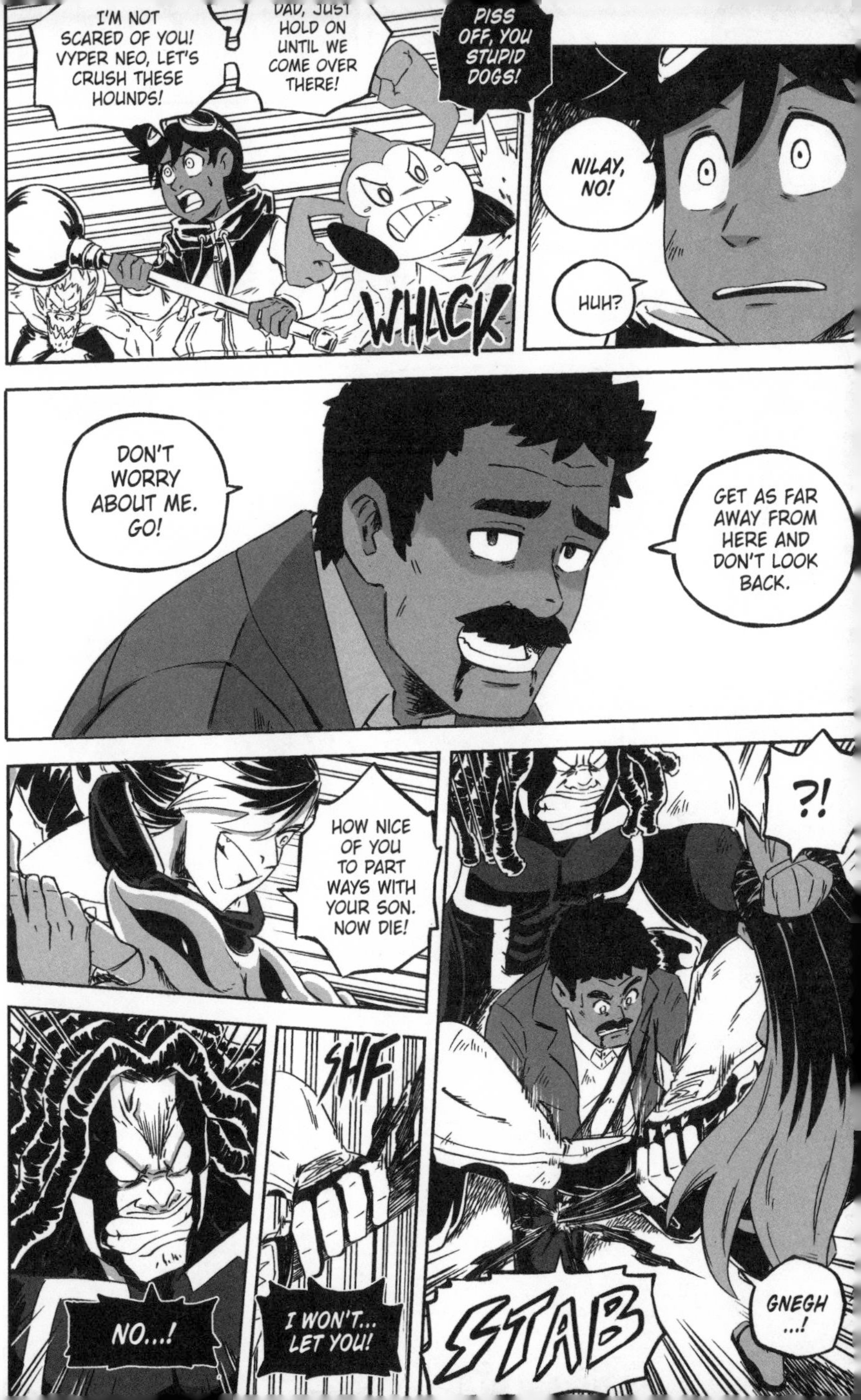
I'M NOT SCARED OF YOU! VYPER NEO, LET'S CRUSH THESE HOUNDS!
DAD, JUST HOLD ON UNTIL WE COME OVER THERE!
PISS OFF, YOU STUPID DOGS!
WHACK
NILAY, NO!
HUH?
DON'T WORRY ABOUT ME. GO!
GET AS FAR AWAY FROM HERE AND DON'T LOOK BACK.
HOW NICE OF YOU TO PART WAYS WITH YOUR SON. NOW DIE!
?!
NO...!
SHF
I WON'T... LET YOU!
STAB
GNEGH ...!

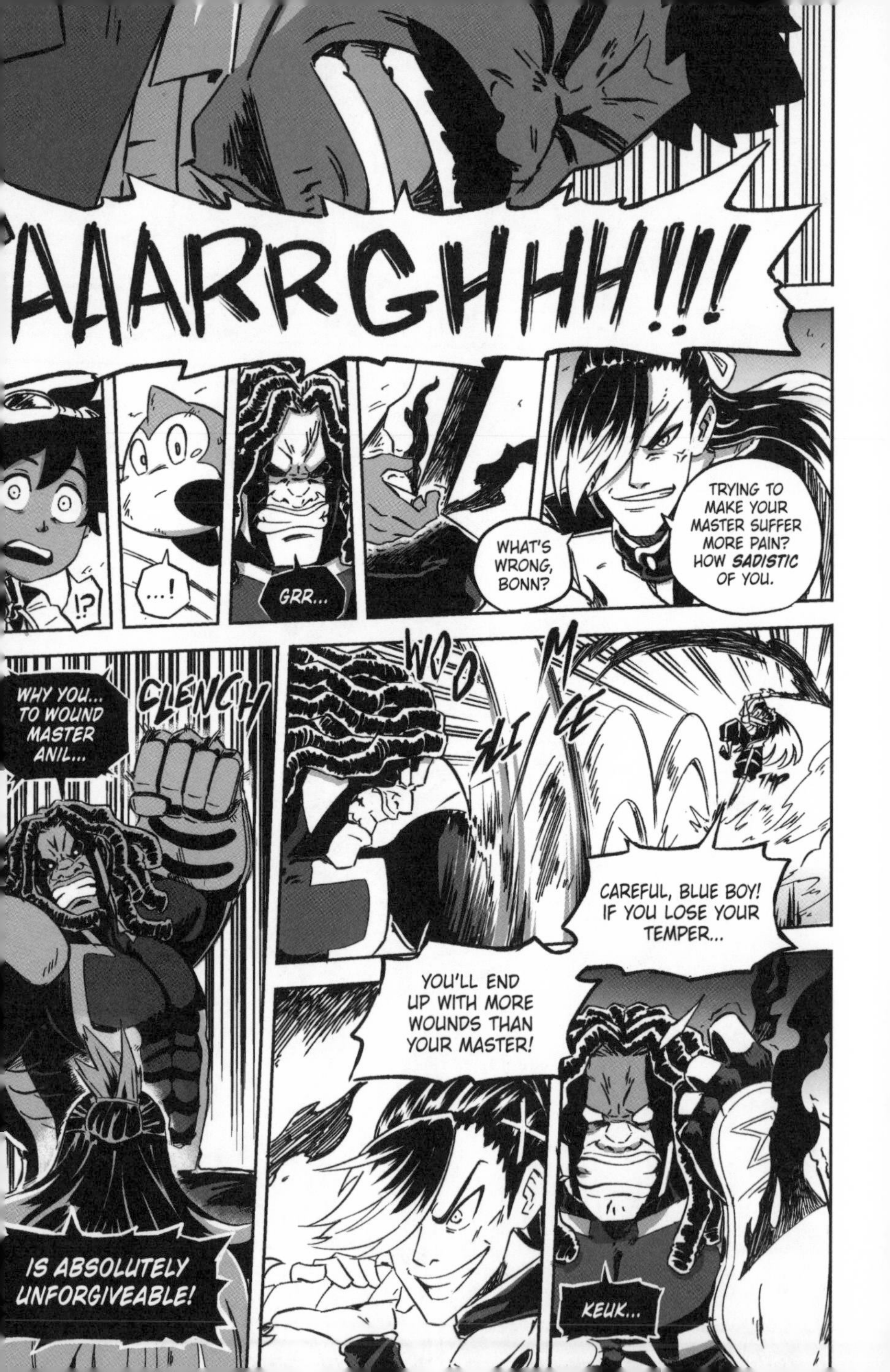

AAARRGHHH!!!
!?
...!
GRR...
WHAT'S WRONG, BONN?
TRYING TO MAKE YOUR MASTER SUFFER MORE PAIN? HOW SADISTIC OF YOU.
WHY YOU... TO WOUND MASTER ANIL...
CLENCH
WOOM
SLICE
CAREFUL, BLUE BOY! IF YOU LOSE YOUR TEMPER...
YOU'LL END UP WITH MORE WOUNDS THAN YOUR MASTER!
IS ABSOLUTELY UNFORGIVEABLE!
KEUK...

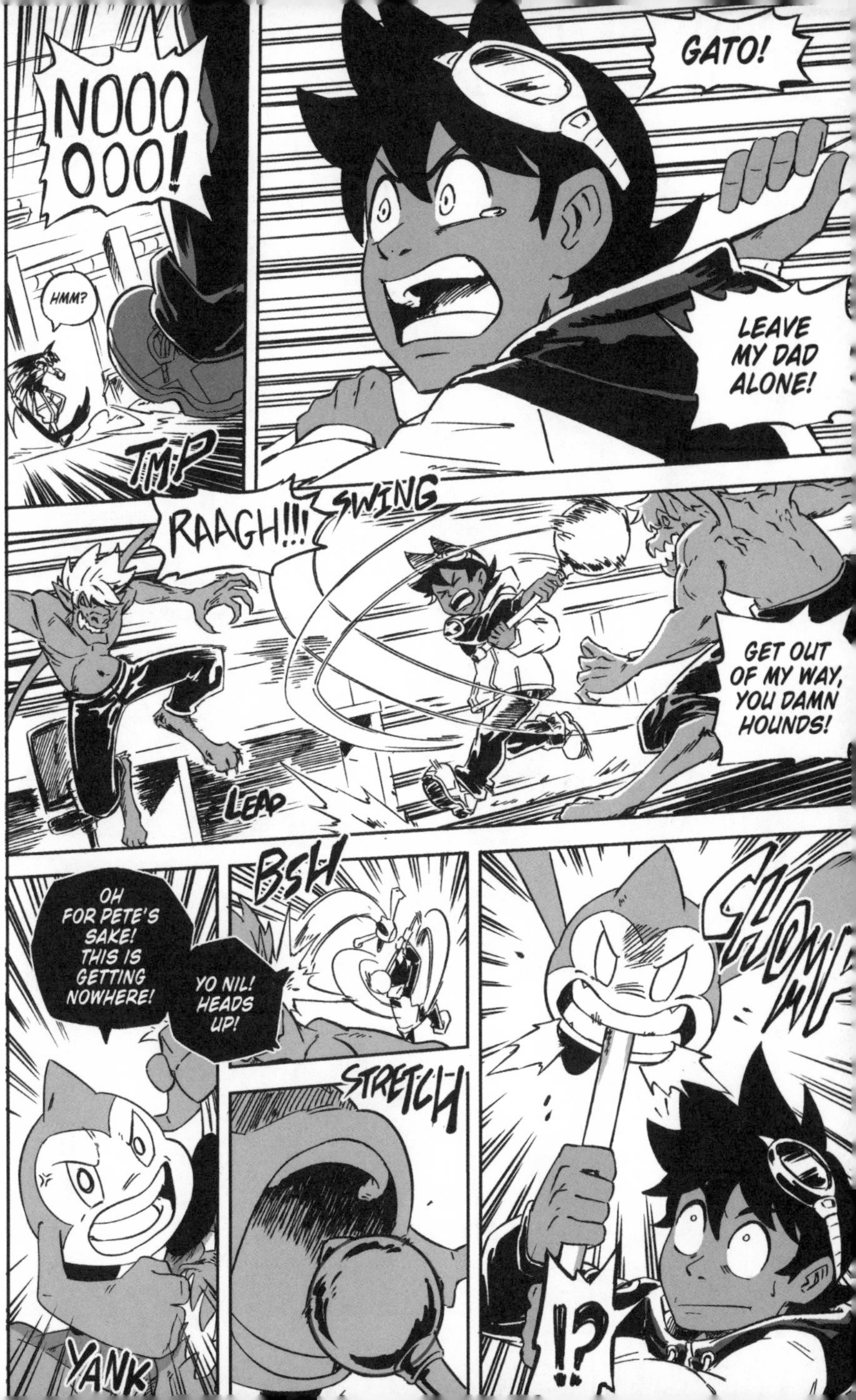
NOOO OOO!
HMM?
TMP
GATO!
LEAVE MY DAD ALONE!
RAAGH!!!
SWING
GET OUT OF MY WAY, YOU DAMN HOUNDS!
LEAP
OH FOR PETE'S SAKE! THIS IS GETTING NOWHERE!
YO NIL! HEADS UP!
BSH
YANK
STRETCH
CHOMP
!?

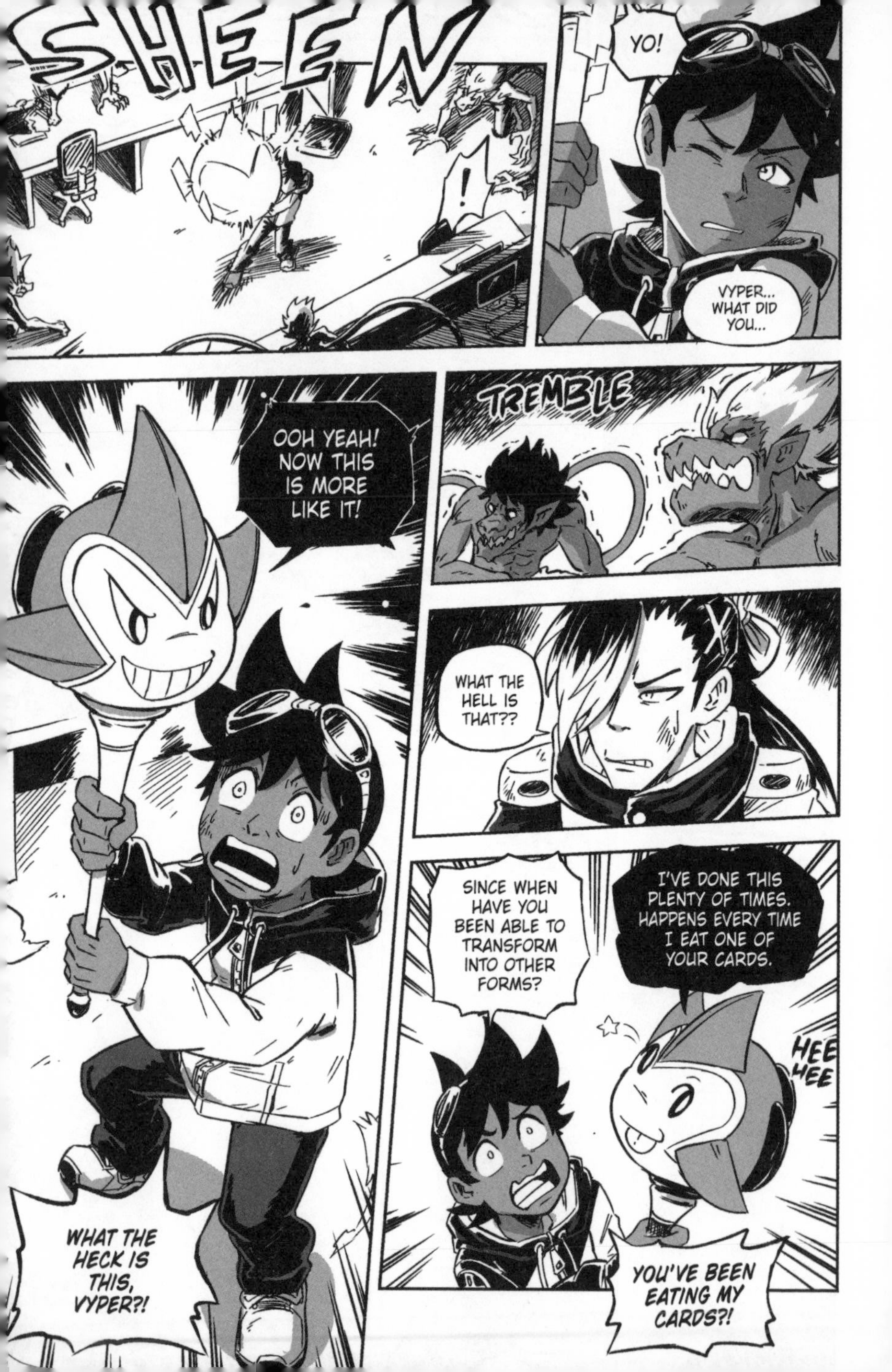
SHEEN
!
YO!
VYPER... WHAT DID YOU...
OOH YEAH! NOW THIS IS MORE LIKE IT!
WHAT THE HECK IS THIS, VYPER?!
TREMBLE
WHAT THE HELL IS THAT??
SINCE WHEN HAVE YOU BEEN ABLE TO TRANSFORM INTO OTHER FORMS?
I'VE DONE THIS PLENTY OF TIMES. HAPPENS EVERY TIME I EAT ONE OF YOUR CARDS.
HEE HEE
YOU'VE BEEN EATING MY CARDS?!

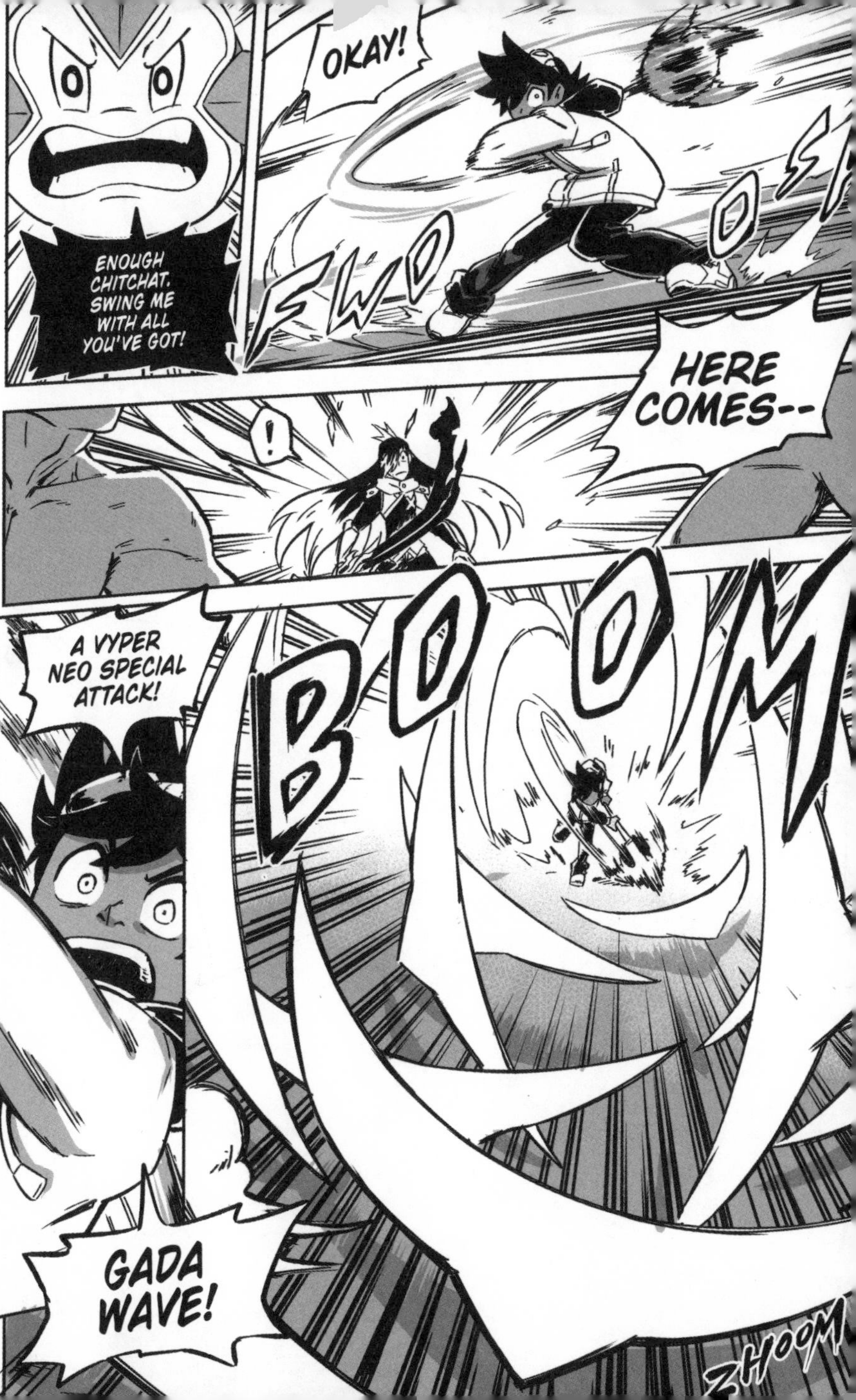

ENOUGH CHITCHAT. SWING ME WITH ALL YOU'VE GOT!
OKAY!
FWOOOSH
HERE COMES--
!
A VYPER NEO SPECIAL ATTACK!
BOOOM
GADA WAVE!
ZHOOM

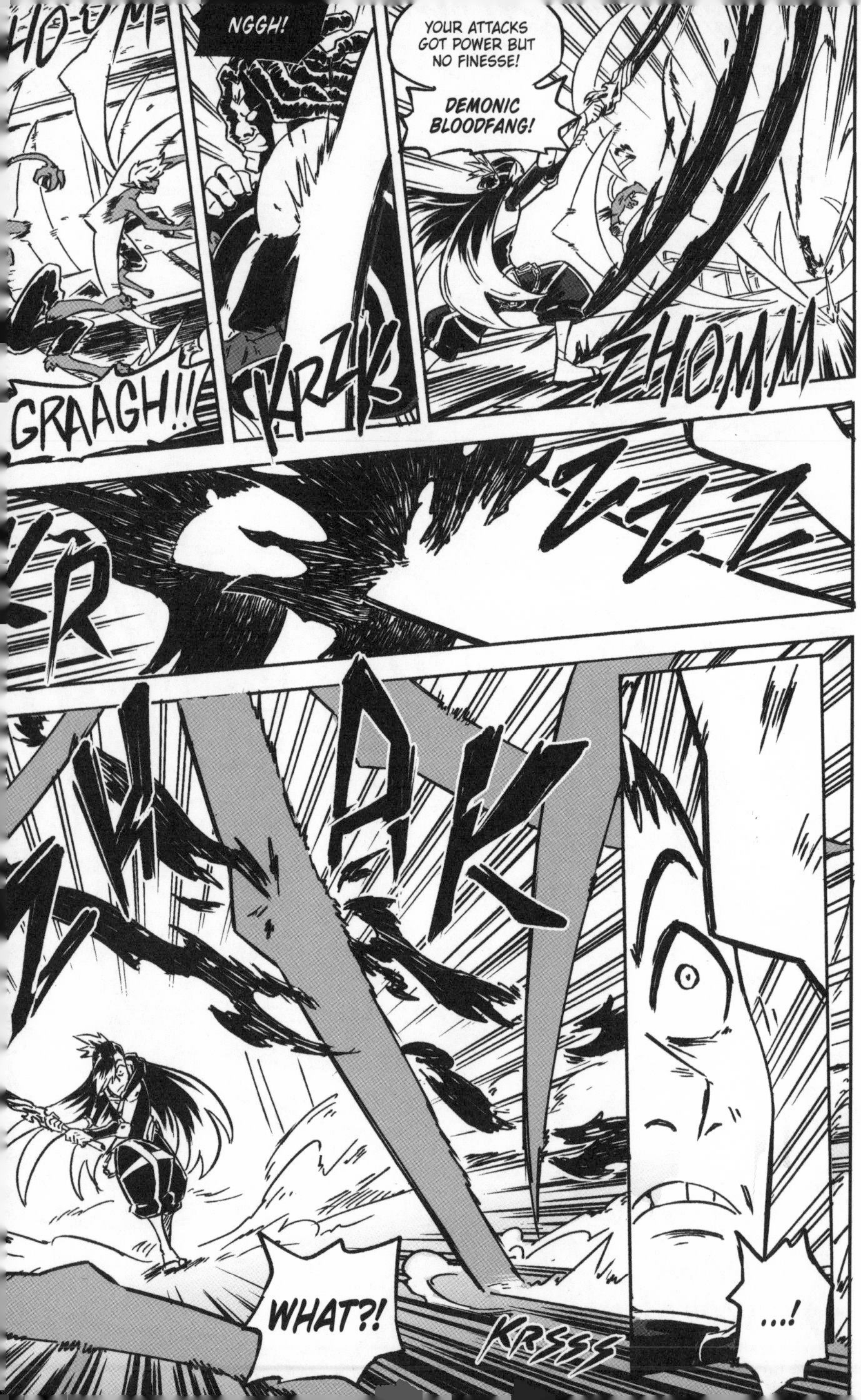
GRAAGH!!!
NGGH!
KRZZK
YOUR ATTACKS GOT POWER BUT NO FINESSE!
DEMONIC BLOODFANG!
ZHOMM
WHAT?!
KRSSS
...!

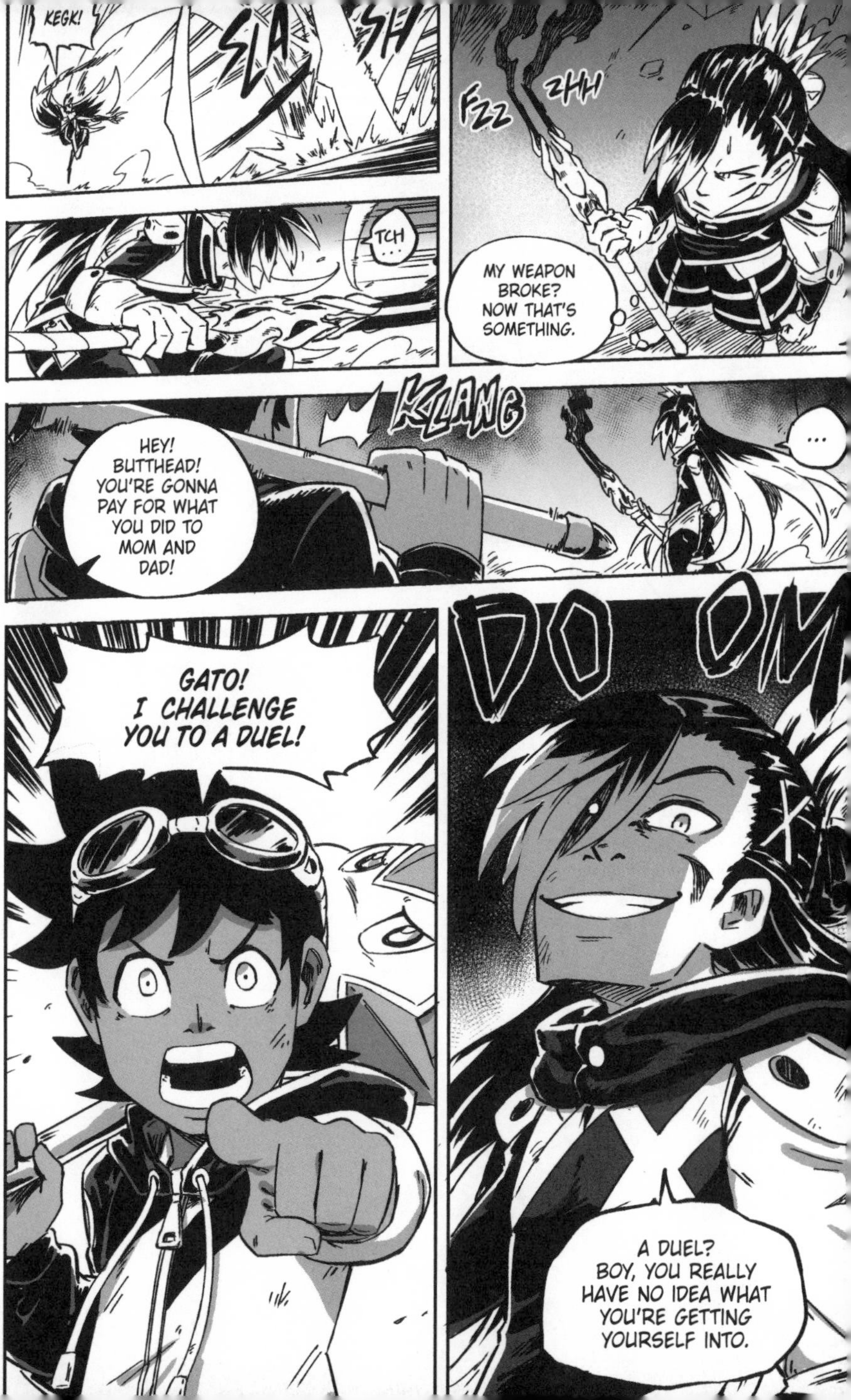
KEGK!
SLASH
FZZ ZHH
TCH...
MY WEAPON BROKE? NOW THAT'S SOMETHING.
KLANG
HEY! BUTTHEAD! YOU'RE GONNA PAY FOR WHAT YOU DID TO MOM AND DAD!
...
GATO! I CHALLENGE YOU TO A DUEL!
DOOM
A DUEL? BOY, YOU REALLY HAVE NO IDEA WHAT YOU'RE GETTING YOURSELF INTO.

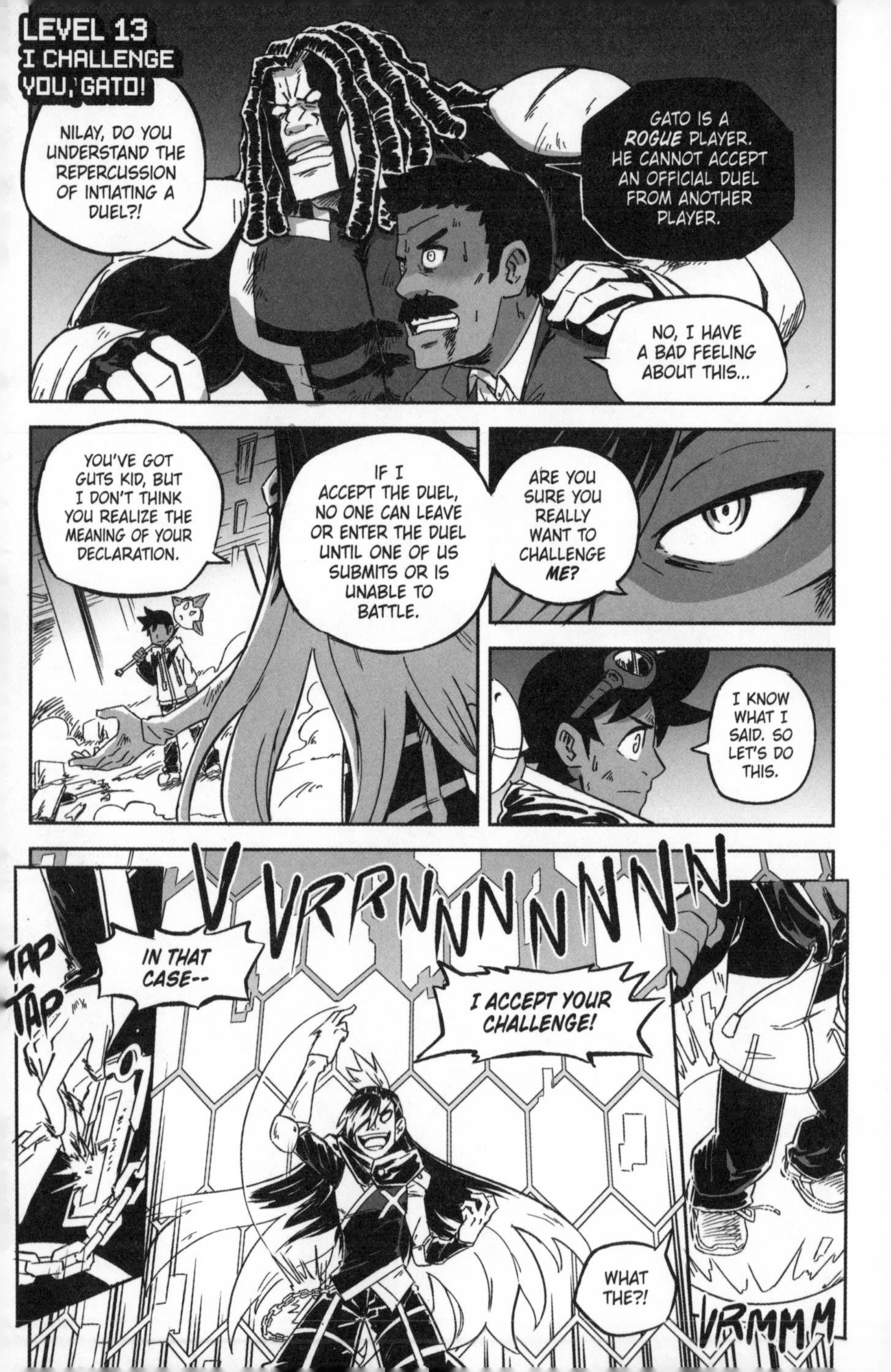
LEVEL 13
I CHALLENGE YOU, GATO!
NILAY, DO YOU UNDERSTAND THE REPERCUSSION OF INTIATING A DUEL?!
GATO IS A ROGUE PLAYER. HE CANNOT ACCEPT AN OFFICIAL DUEL FROM ANOTHER PLAYER.
NO, I HAVE A BAD FEELING ABOUT THIS...
YOU'VE GOT GUTS KID, BUT I DON'T THINK YOU REALIZE THE MEANING OF YOUR DECLARATION.
IF I ACCEPT THE DUEL, NO ONE CAN LEAVE OR ENTER THE DUEL UNTIL ONE OF US SUBMITS OR IS UNABLE TO BATTLE.
ARE YOU SURE YOU REALLY WANT TO CHALLENGE *ME*?
I KNOW WHAT I SAID. SO LET'S DO THIS.
TAP TAP
IN THAT CASE--
VVRRNNNNNNNN
I ACCEPT YOUR CHALLENGE!
WHAT THE?!
VRMMM

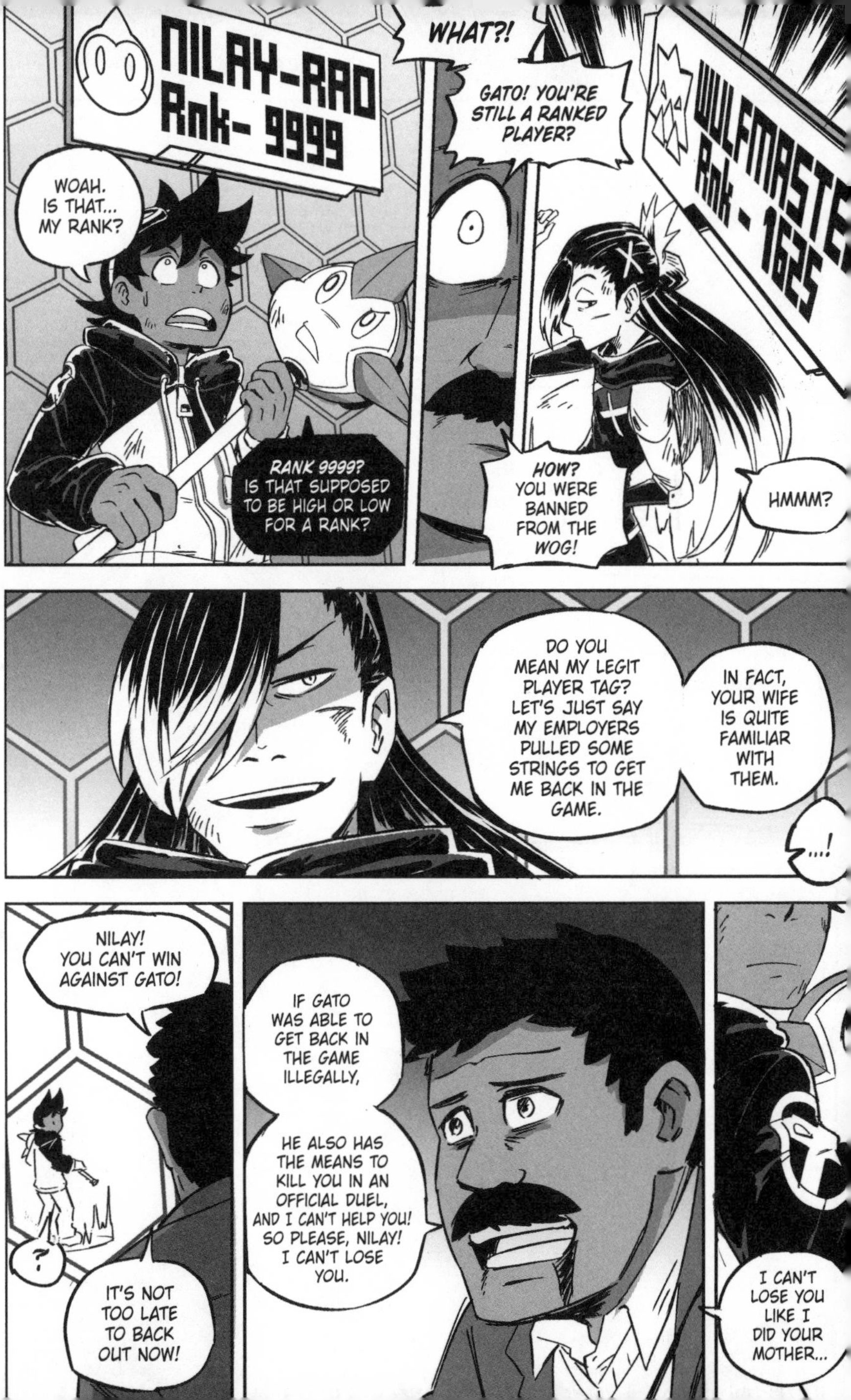
NILAY-RAD Rnk- 9999
WOAH. IS THAT... MY RANK?
RANK 9999? IS THAT SUPPOSED TO BE HIGH OR LOW FOR A RANK?
WHAT?!
GATO! YOU'RE STILL A RANKED PLAYER?
WULFMASTE Rnk - 1625
HOW? YOU WERE BANNED FROM THE WOG!
HMMM?
DO YOU MEAN MY LEGIT PLAYER TAG? LET'S JUST SAY MY EMPLOYERS PULLED SOME STRINGS TO GET ME BACK IN THE GAME.
IN FACT, YOUR WIFE IS QUITE FAMILIAR WITH THEM.
...!
NILAY! YOU CAN'T WIN AGAINST GATO!
?
IT'S NOT TOO LATE TO BACK OUT NOW!
IF GATO WAS ABLE TO GET BACK IN THE GAME ILLEGALLY,
HE ALSO HAS THE MEANS TO KILL YOU IN AN OFFICIAL DUEL, AND I CAN'T HELP YOU! SO PLEASE, NILAY! I CAN'T LOSE YOU.
I CAN'T LOSE YOU LIKE I DID YOUR MOTHER...

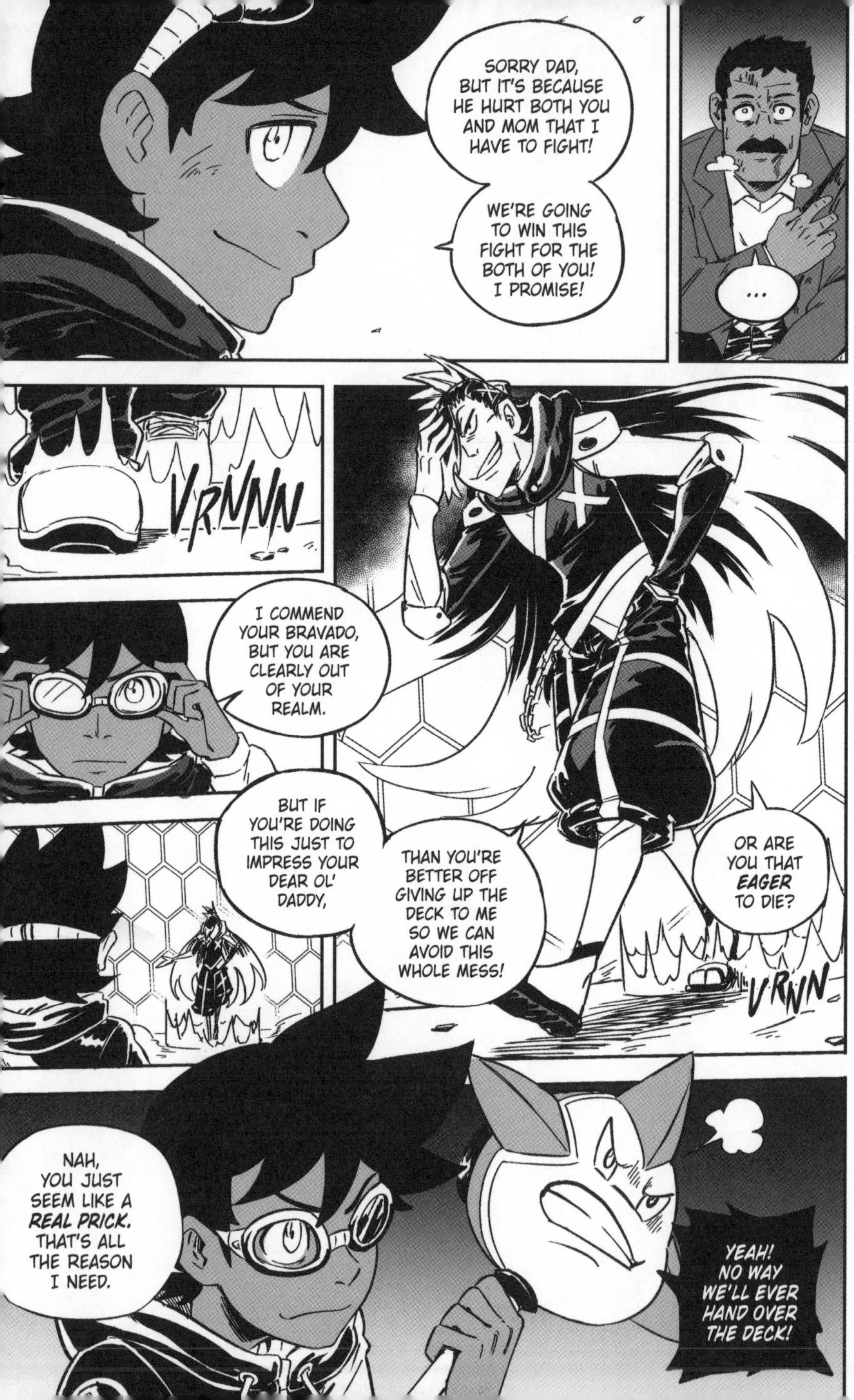
SORRY DAD, BUT IT'S BECAUSE HE HURT BOTH YOU AND MOM THAT I HAVE TO FIGHT!
WE'RE GOING TO WIN THIS FIGHT FOR THE BOTH OF YOU! I PROMISE!
...
VRNNN
I COMMEND YOUR BRAVADO, BUT YOU ARE CLEARLY OUT OF YOUR REALM.
BUT IF YOU'RE DOING THIS JUST TO IMPRESS YOUR DEAR OL' DADDY,
THAN YOU'RE BETTER OFF GIVING UP THE DECK TO ME SO WE CAN AVOID THIS WHOLE MESS!
OR ARE YOU THAT EAGER TO DIE?
VRNN
NAH, YOU JUST SEEM LIKE A REAL PRICK. THAT'S ALL THE REASON I NEED.
YEAH! NO WAY WE'LL EVER HAND OVER THE DECK!

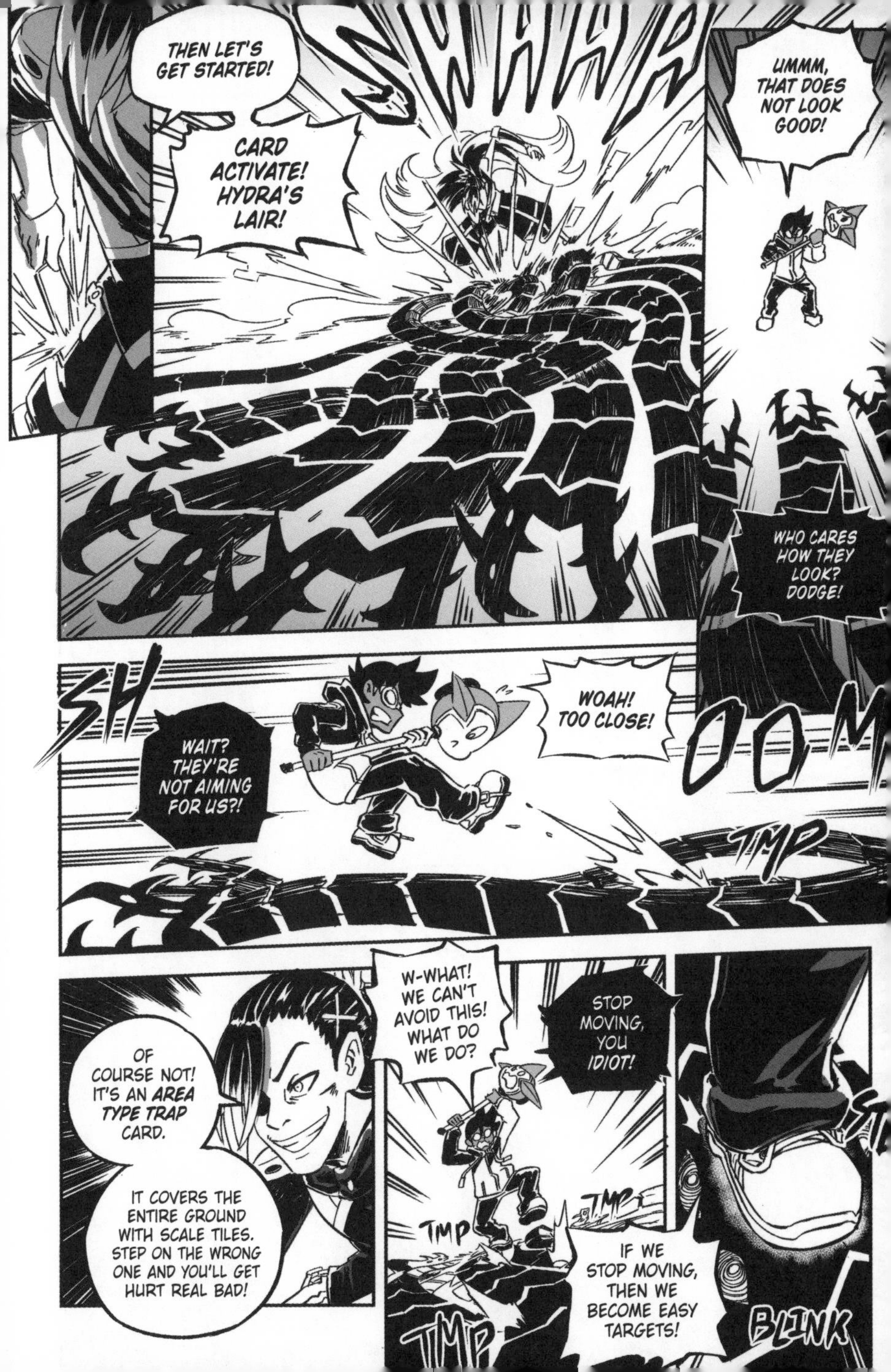
THEN LET'S GET STARTED!
SWHAAR
CARD ACTIVATE! HYDRA'S LAIR!
UMMM, THAT DOES NOT LOOK GOOD!
WHO CARES HOW THEY LOOK? DODGE!
SH
WAIT? THEY'RE NOT AIMING FOR US?!
WOAH! TOO CLOSE!
OOM
TMP
OF COURSE NOT! IT'S AN *AREA TYPE TRAP* CARD.
IT COVERS THE ENTIRE GROUND WITH SCALE TILES. STEP ON THE WRONG ONE AND YOU'LL GET HURT REAL BAD!
W-WHAT! WE CAN'T AVOID THIS! WHAT DO WE DO?
STOP MOVING, YOU IDIOT!
TMP
TMP
TMP
IF WE STOP MOVING, THEN WE BECOME EASY TARGETS!
BLINK

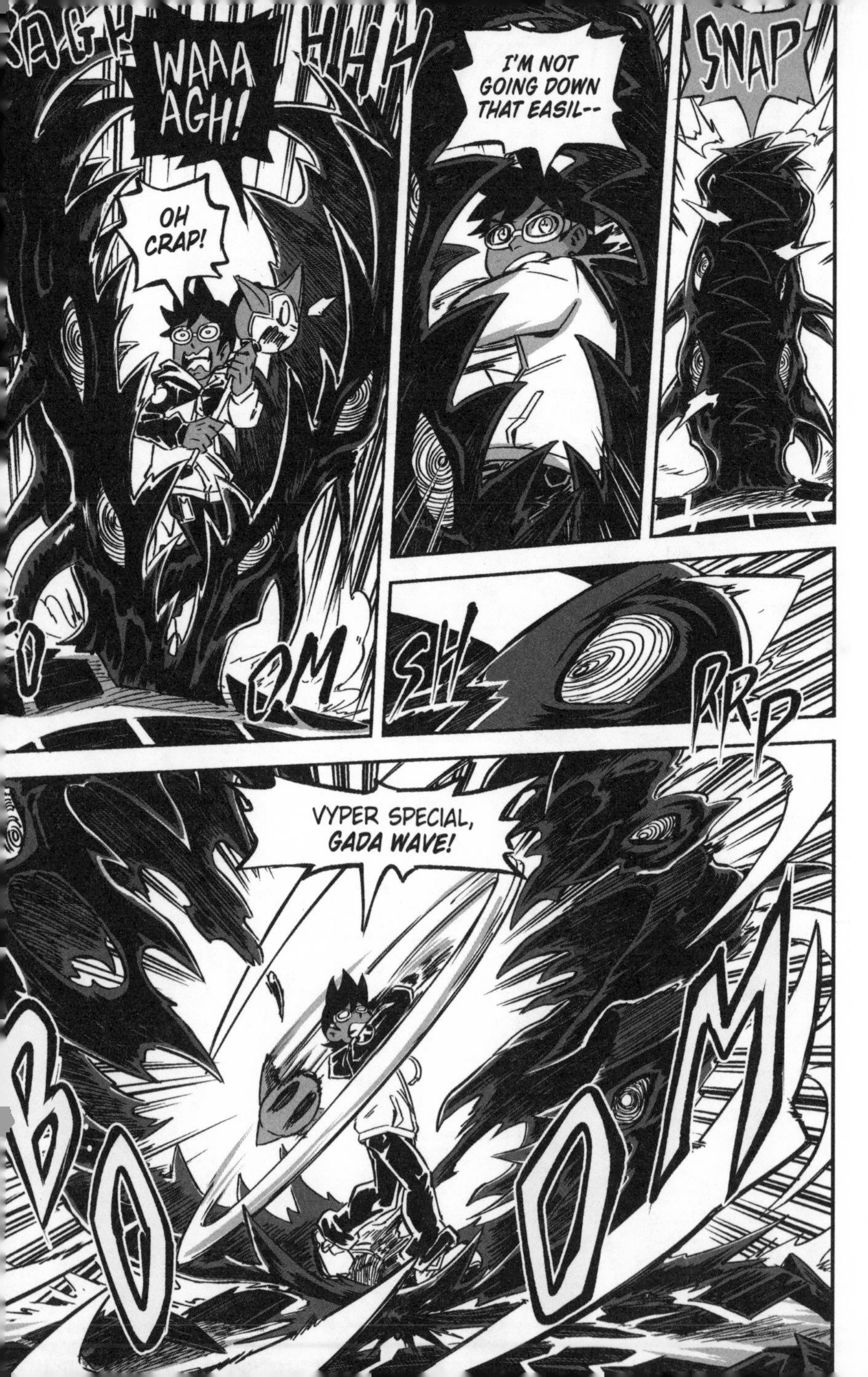
WAAA AGH!
OH CRAP!
I'M NOT GOING DOWN THAT EASIL--
SNAP
VYPER SPECIAL, GADA WAVE!
BOOOM

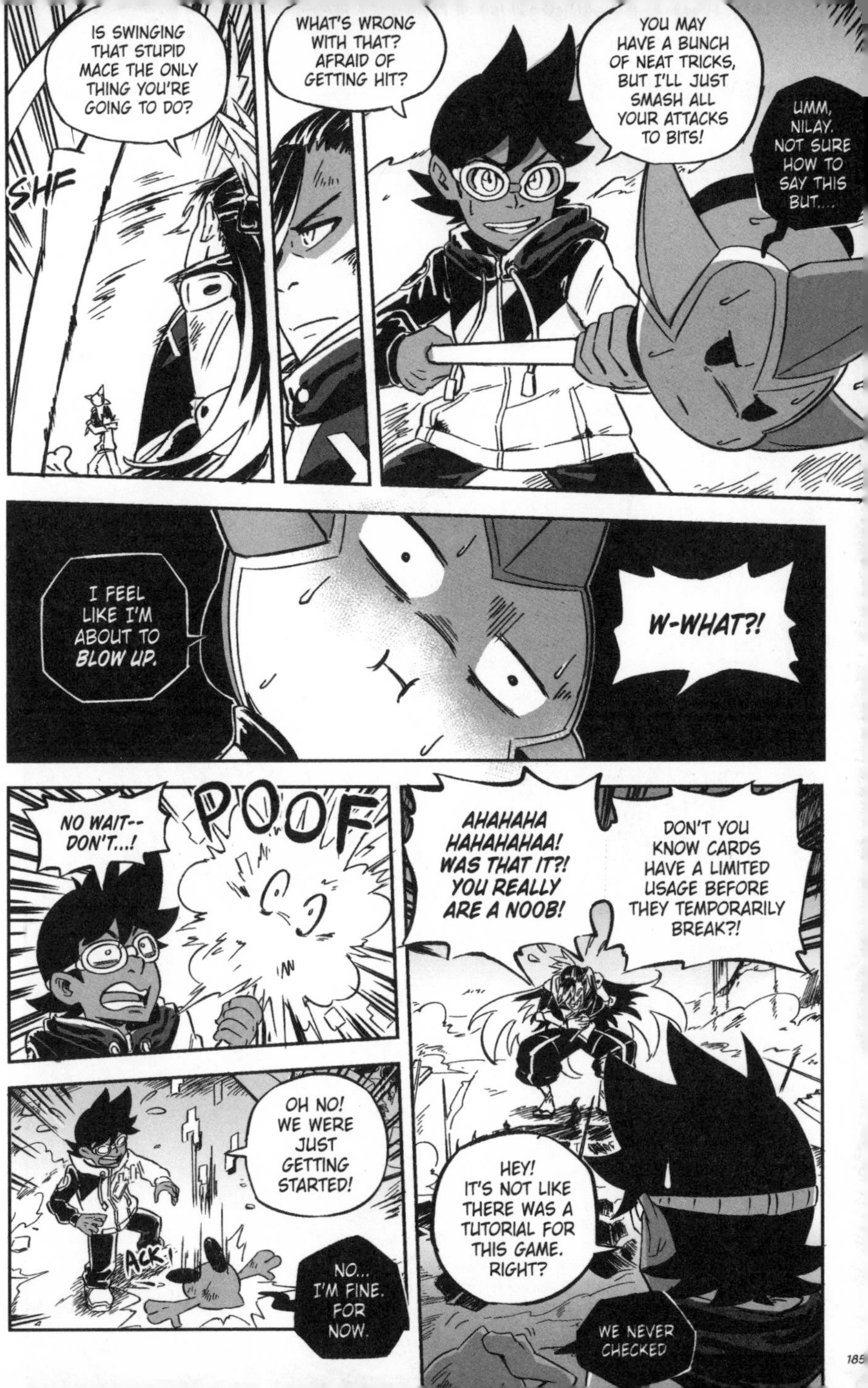

IS SWINGING THAT STUPID MACE THE ONLY THING YOU'RE GOING TO DO?
SHF
WHAT'S WRONG WITH THAT? AFRAID OF GETTING HIT?
YOU MAY HAVE A BUNCH OF NEAT TRICKS, BUT I'LL JUST SMASH ALL YOUR ATTACKS TO BITS!
UMM, NILAY. NOT SURE HOW TO SAY THIS BUT....
I FEEL LIKE I'M ABOUT TO BLOW UP.
W-WHAT?!
NO WAIT-- DON'T...!
POOF
AHAHAHA HAHAHAHAA! WAS THAT IT?! YOU REALLY ARE A NOOB!
DON'T YOU KNOW CARDS HAVE A LIMITED USAGE BEFORE THEY TEMPORARILY BREAK?!
OH NO! WE WERE JUST GETTING STARTED!
ACK
NO... I'M FINE. FOR NOW.
HEY! IT'S NOT LIKE THERE WAS A TUTORIAL FOR THIS GAME. RIGHT?
WE NEVER CHECKED

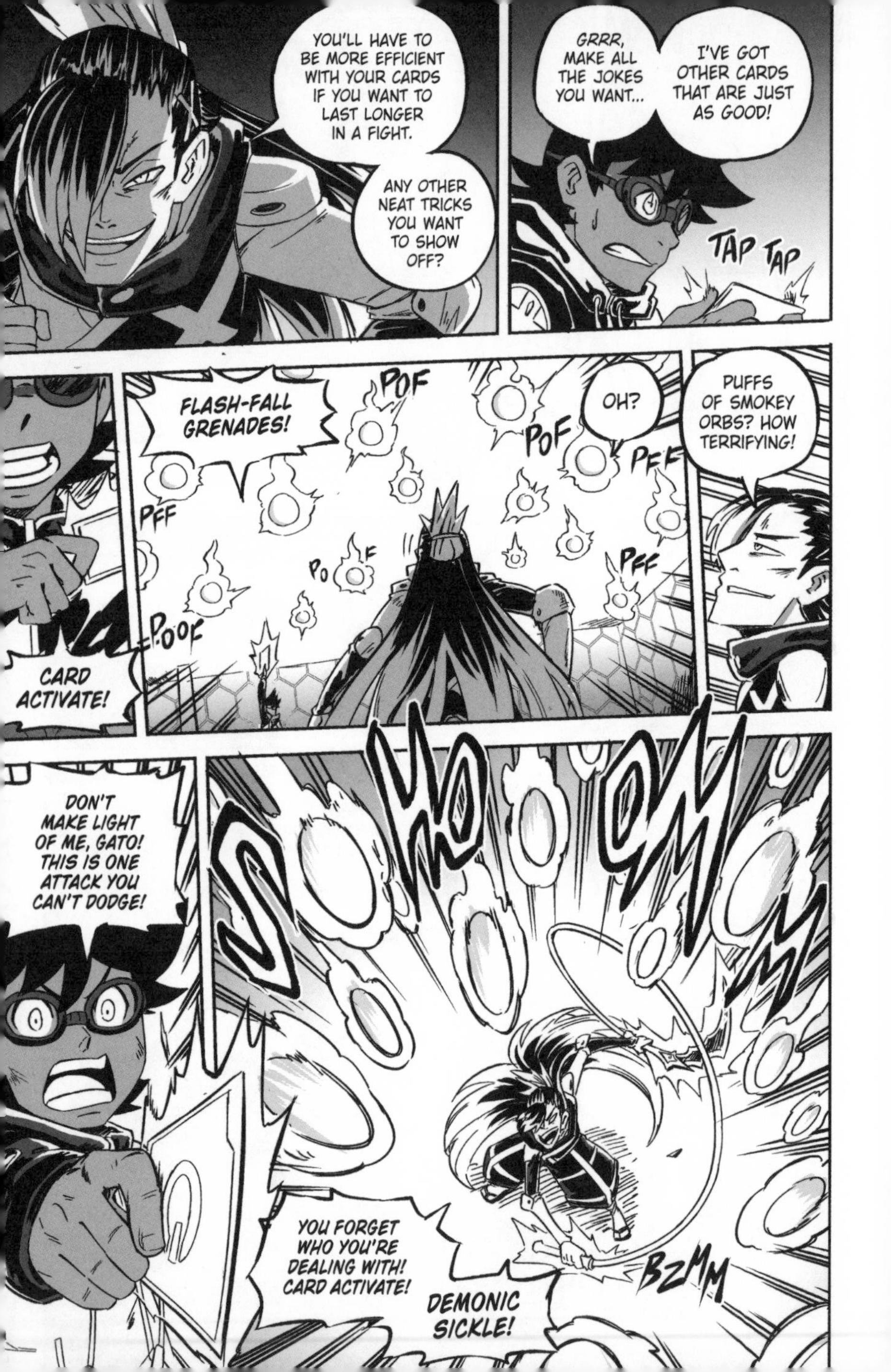
YOU'LL HAVE TO BE MORE EFFICIENT WITH YOUR CARDS IF YOU WANT TO LAST LONGER IN A FIGHT.
ANY OTHER NEAT TRICKS YOU WANT TO SHOW OFF?
GRRR, MAKE ALL THE JOKES YOU WANT...
I'VE GOT OTHER CARDS THAT ARE JUST AS GOOD!
TAP TAP
CARD ACTIVATE!
FLASH-FALL GRENADES!
POF
POF
PFF
PFF
OH?
PFF
POF
PFF
POOF
PUFFS OF SMOKEY ORBS? HOW TERRIFYING!
DON'T MAKE LIGHT OF ME, GATO! THIS IS ONE ATTACK YOU CAN'T DODGE!
YOU FORGET WHO YOU'RE DEALING WITH! CARD ACTIVATE!
DEMONIC SICKLE!
BZMM

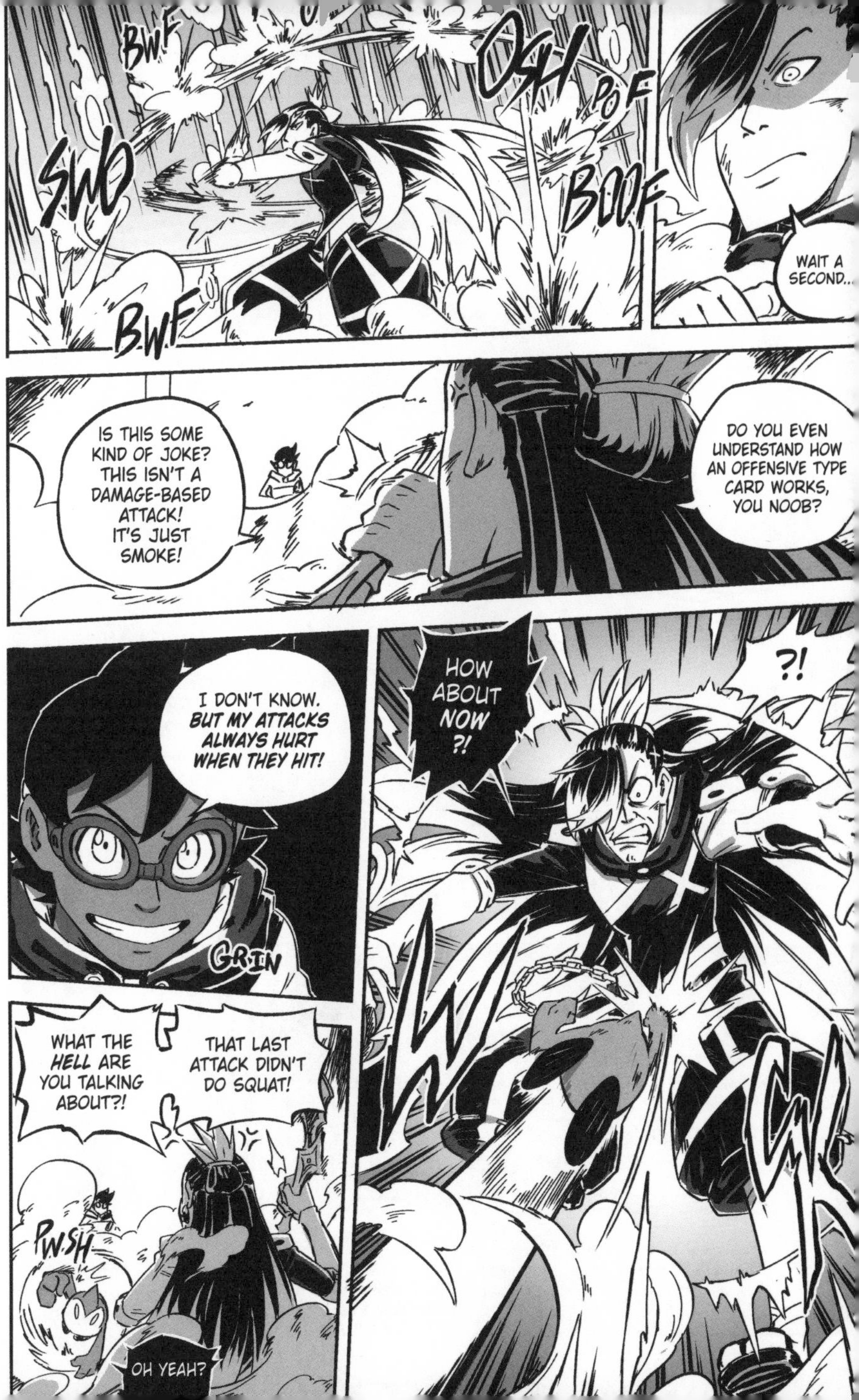
BWF
SWB
OSH
POF
BOOF
BWF
WAIT A SECOND...
IS THIS SOME KIND OF JOKE? THIS ISN'T A DAMAGE-BASED ATTACK! IT'S JUST SMOKE!
DO YOU EVEN UNDERSTAND HOW AN OFFENSIVE TYPE CARD WORKS, YOU NOOB?
I DON'T KNOW. BUT MY ATTACKS ALWAYS HURT WHEN THEY HIT!
GRIN
HOW ABOUT NOW ?!
?!
WHAT THE HELL ARE YOU TALKING ABOUT?!
THAT LAST ATTACK DIDN'T DO SQUAT!
PWSH
OH YEAH?

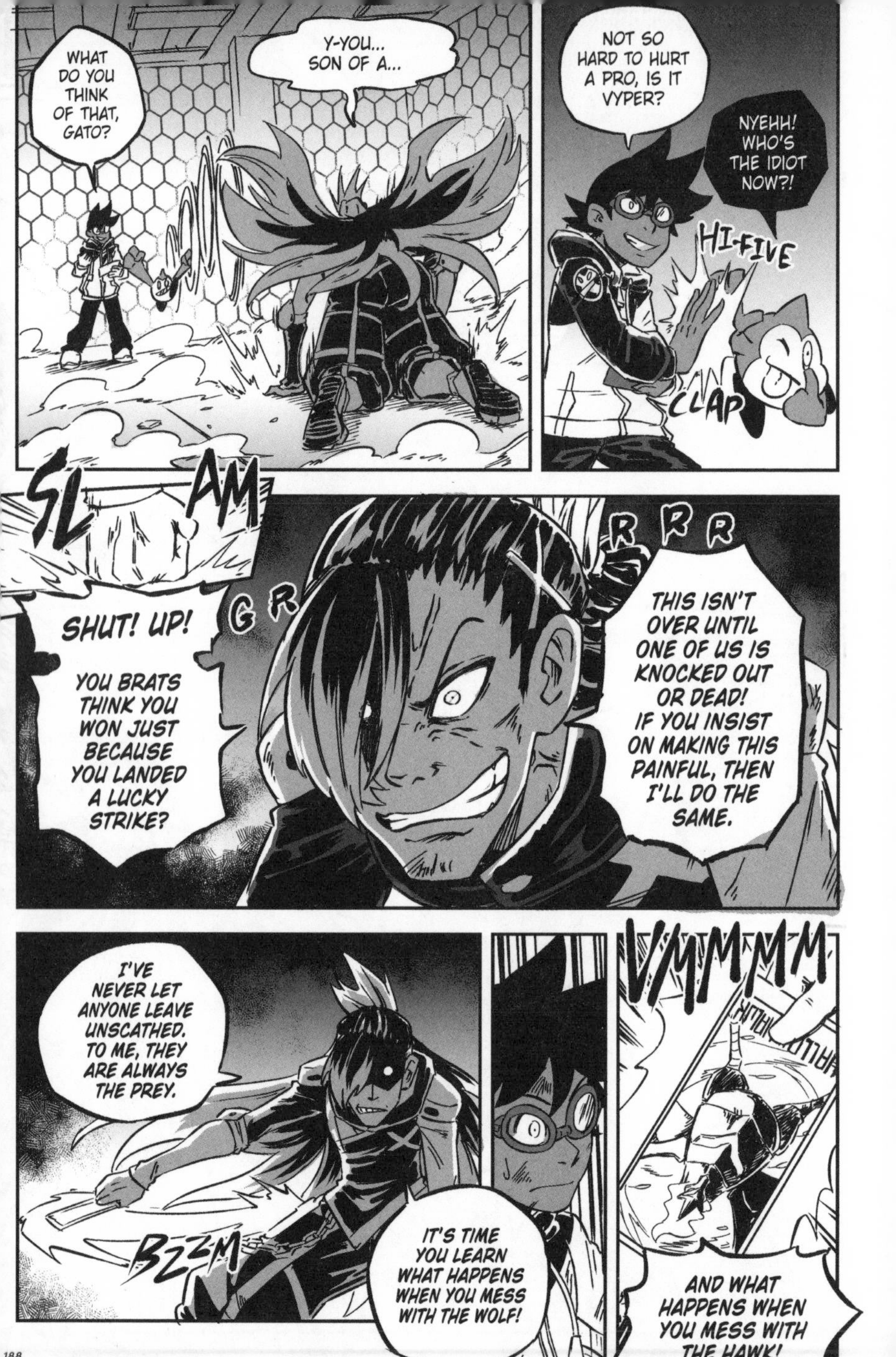
WHAT DO YOU THINK OF THAT, GATO?
Y-YOU... SON OF A...
NOT SO HARD TO HURT A PRO, IS IT VYPER?
NYEHH! WHO'S THE IDIOT NOW?!
HI-FIVE
CLAP
SLAM
SHUT! UP!
YOU BRATS THINK YOU WON JUST BECAUSE YOU LANDED A LUCKY STRIKE?
G R
R R R
THIS ISN'T OVER UNTIL ONE OF US IS KNOCKED OUT OR DEAD! IF YOU INSIST ON MAKING THIS PAINFUL, THEN I'LL DO THE SAME.
I'VE NEVER LET ANYONE LEAVE UNSCATHED. TO ME, THEY ARE ALWAYS THE PREY.
BZZM
IT'S TIME YOU LEARN WHAT HAPPENS WHEN YOU MESS WITH THE WOLF!
VMMMMM
AND WHAT HAPPENS WHEN YOU MESS WITH THE HAWK!

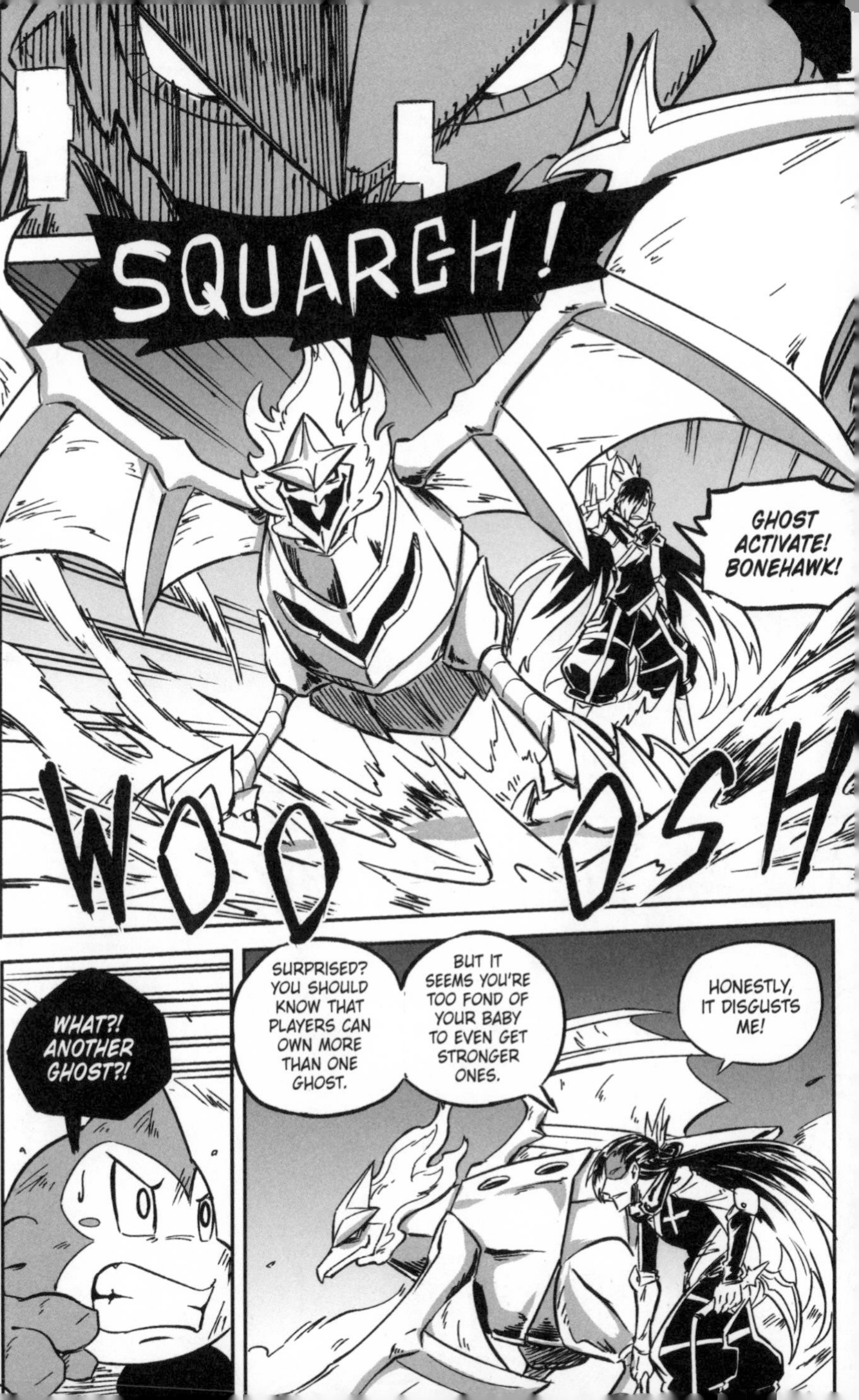
SQUARGH!
GHOST ACTIVATE! BONEHAWK!
WOOOSH
WHAT?! ANOTHER GHOST?!
SURPRISED? YOU SHOULD KNOW THAT PLAYERS CAN OWN MORE THAN ONE GHOST.
BUT IT SEEMS YOU'RE TOO FOND OF YOUR BABY TO EVEN GET STRONGER ONES.
HONESTLY, IT DISGUSTS ME!

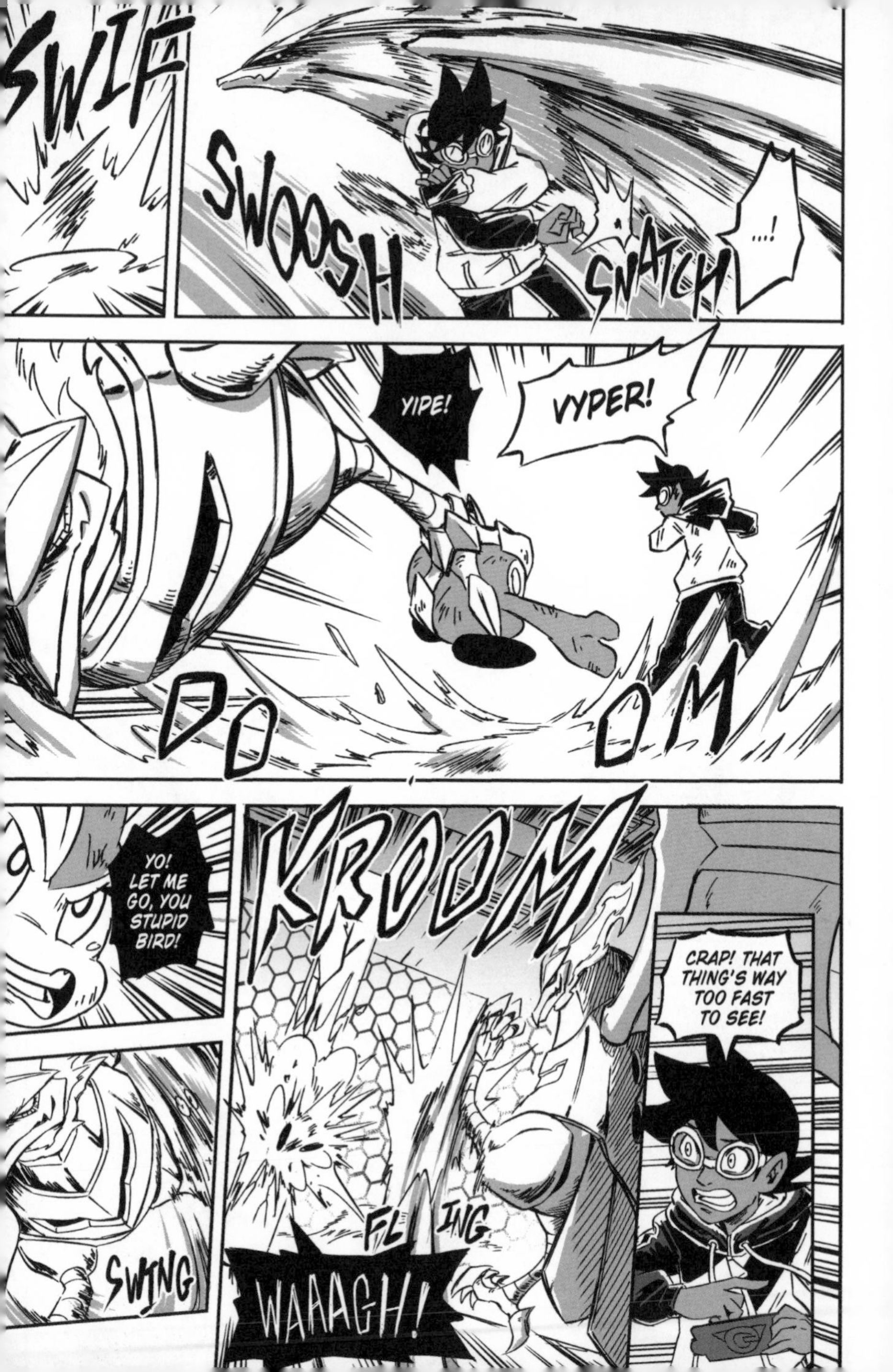
SWIF
SWOOSH
SNATCH
...!
YIPE!
VYPER!
DO OM
YO! LET ME GO, YOU STUPID BIRD!
SWING
KROOM
FL ING
WAAAGH!
CRAP! THAT THING'S WAY TOO FAST TO SEE!

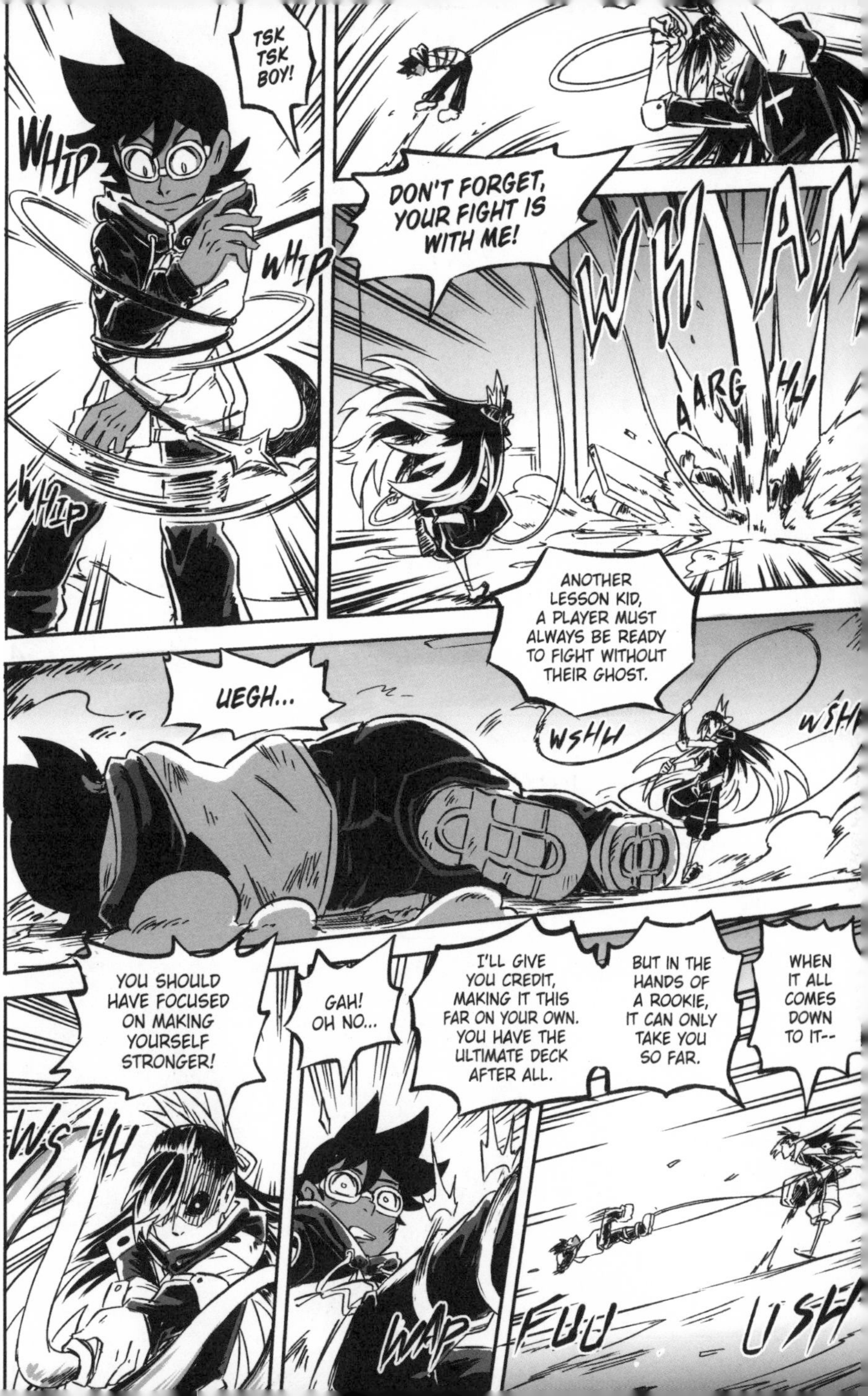
TSK TSK BOY!
WHIP
WHIP
WHIP
DON'T FORGET, YOUR FIGHT IS WITH ME!
WHYAM
AARGHH
ANOTHER LESSON KID, A PLAYER MUST ALWAYS BE READY TO FIGHT WITHOUT THEIR GHOST.
UEGH...
WSHH
WSH
YOU SHOULD HAVE FOCUSED ON MAKING YOURSELF STRONGER!
GAH! OH NO...
I'LL GIVE YOU CREDIT, MAKING IT THIS FAR ON YOUR OWN. YOU HAVE THE ULTIMATE DECK AFTER ALL.
BUT IN THE HANDS OF A ROOKIE, IT CAN ONLY TAKE YOU SO FAR.
WHEN IT ALL COMES DOWN TO IT--
WSHH
WAP
FUU
USH

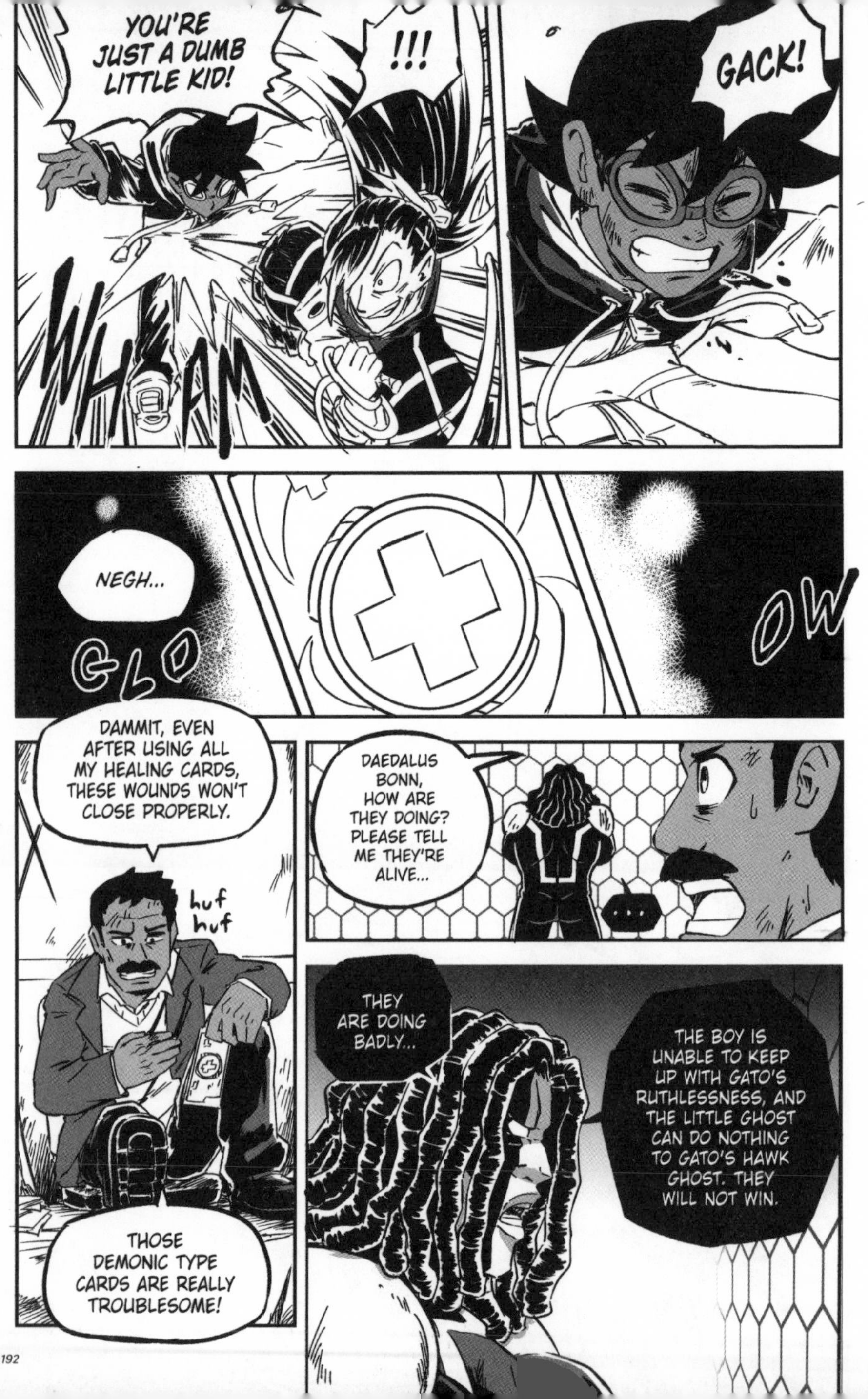
YOU'RE JUST A DUMB LITTLE KID!
!!!
WHAM
GACK!
NEGH...
GLO
OW
DAMMIT, EVEN AFTER USING ALL MY HEALING CARDS, THESE WOUNDS WON'T CLOSE PROPERLY.
huf huf
THOSE DEMONIC TYPE CARDS ARE REALLY TROUBLESOME!
DAEDALUS BONN, HOW ARE THEY DOING? PLEASE TELL ME THEY'RE ALIVE...
THEY ARE DOING BADLY...
THE BOY IS UNABLE TO KEEP UP WITH GATO'S RUTHLESSNESS, AND THE LITTLE GHOST CAN DO NOTHING TO GATO'S HAWK GHOST. THEY WILL NOT WIN.

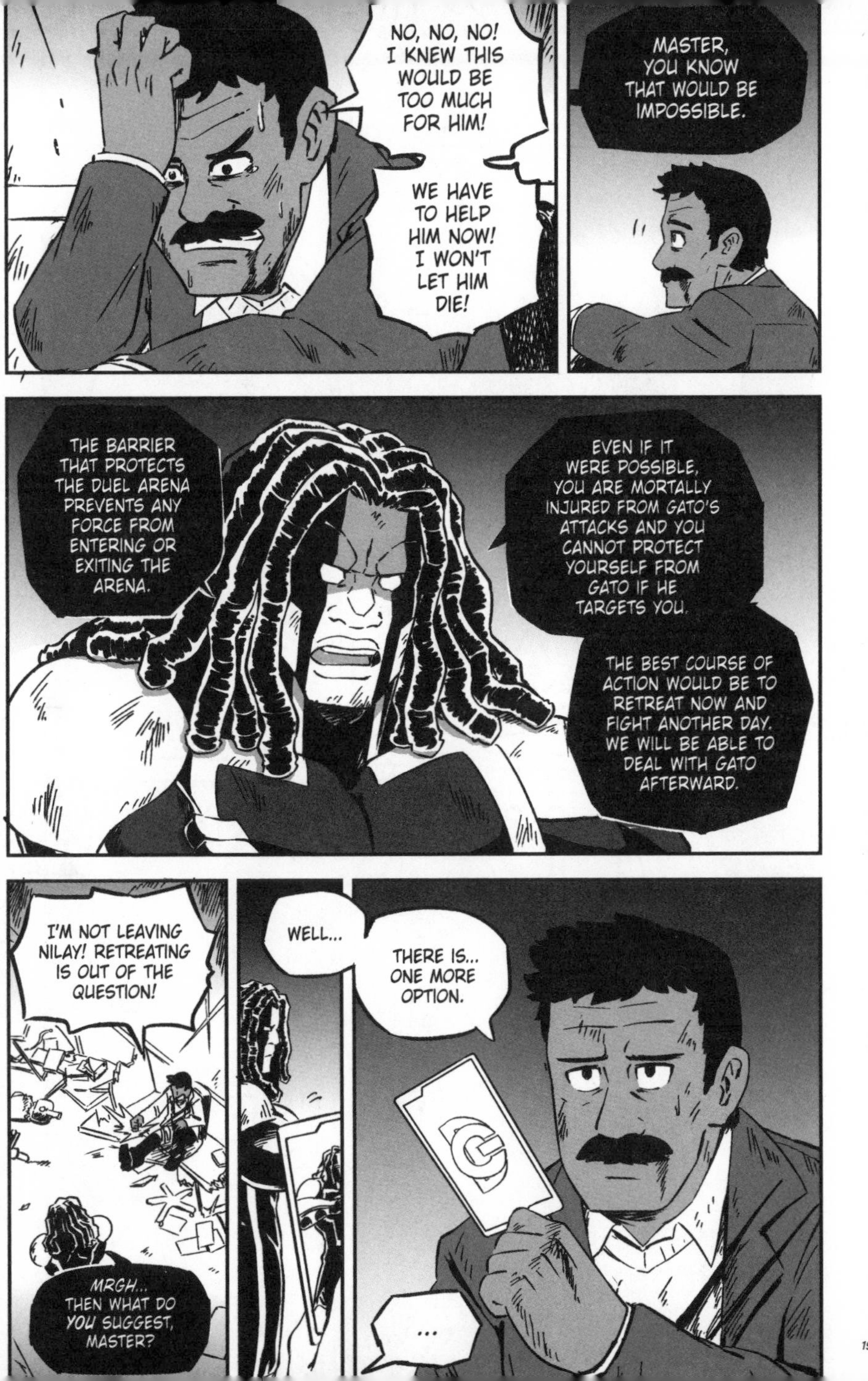
NO, NO, NO! I KNEW THIS WOULD BE TOO MUCH FOR HIM!
WE HAVE TO HELP HIM NOW! I WON'T LET HIM DIE!
MASTER, YOU KNOW THAT WOULD BE IMPOSSIBLE.
THE BARRIER THAT PROTECTS THE DUEL ARENA PREVENTS ANY FORCE FROM ENTERING OR EXITING THE ARENA.
EVEN IF IT WERE POSSIBLE, YOU ARE MORTALLY INJURED FROM GATO'S ATTACKS AND YOU CANNOT PROTECT YOURSELF FROM GATO IF HE TARGETS YOU.
THE BEST COURSE OF ACTION WOULD BE TO RETREAT NOW AND FIGHT ANOTHER DAY. WE WILL BE ABLE TO DEAL WITH GATO AFTERWARD.
I'M NOT LEAVING NILAY! RETREATING IS OUT OF THE QUESTION!
MRGH... THEN WHAT DO YOU SUGGEST, MASTER?
WELL...
THERE IS... ONE MORE OPTION.
...

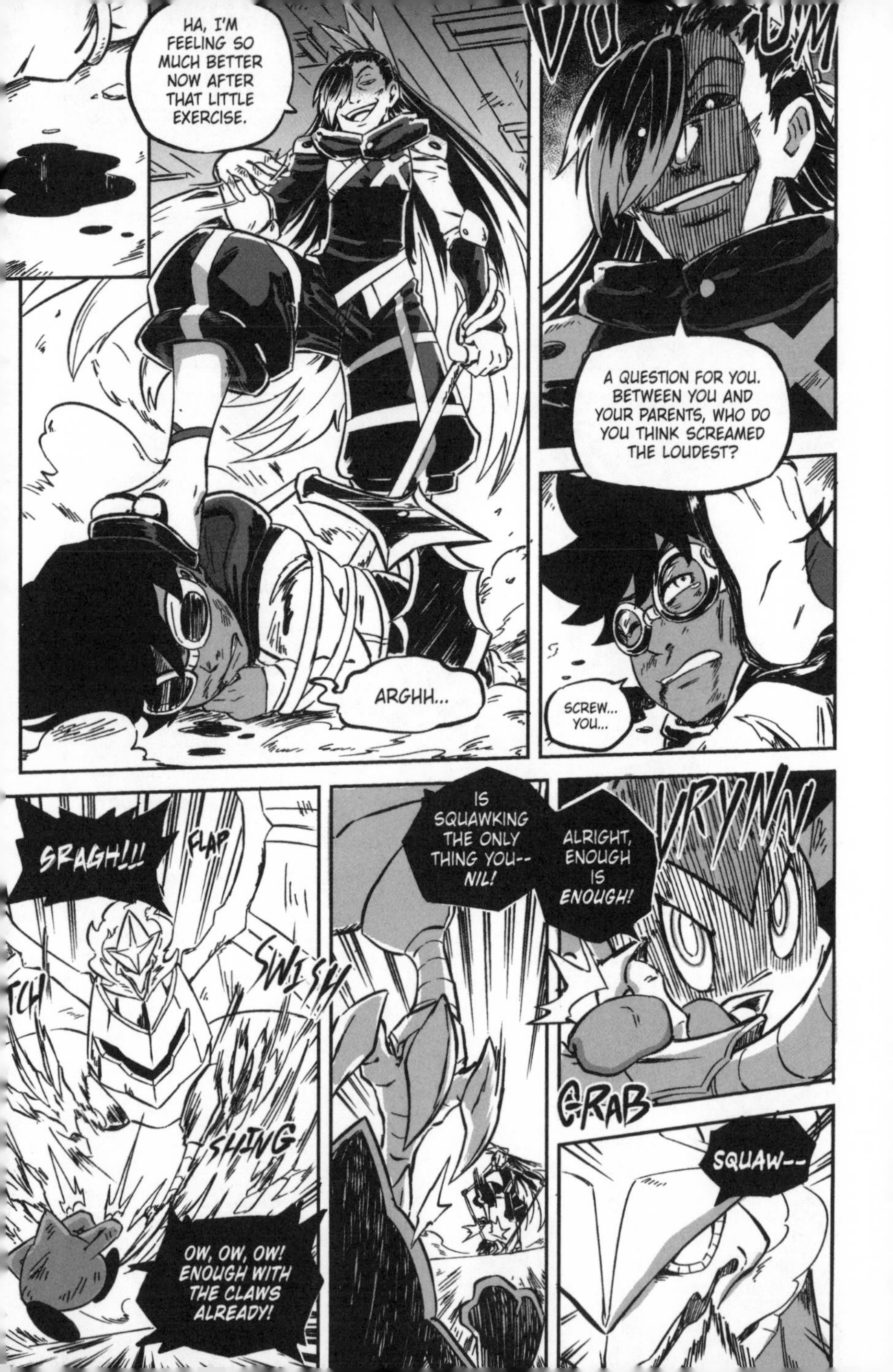

HA, I'M FEELING SO MUCH BETTER NOW AFTER THAT LITTLE EXERCISE.
ARGHH...
A QUESTION FOR YOU. BETWEEN YOU AND YOUR PARENTS, WHO DO YOU THINK SCREAMED THE LOUDEST?
SCREW... YOU...
SRAGH!!!
FLAP
TCH
SWISH
SHING
OW, OW, OW! ENOUGH WITH THE CLAWS ALREADY!
IS SQUAWKING THE ONLY THING YOU-- NIL!
ALRIGHT, ENOUGH IS ENOUGH!
VRYNN
GRAB
SQUAW--

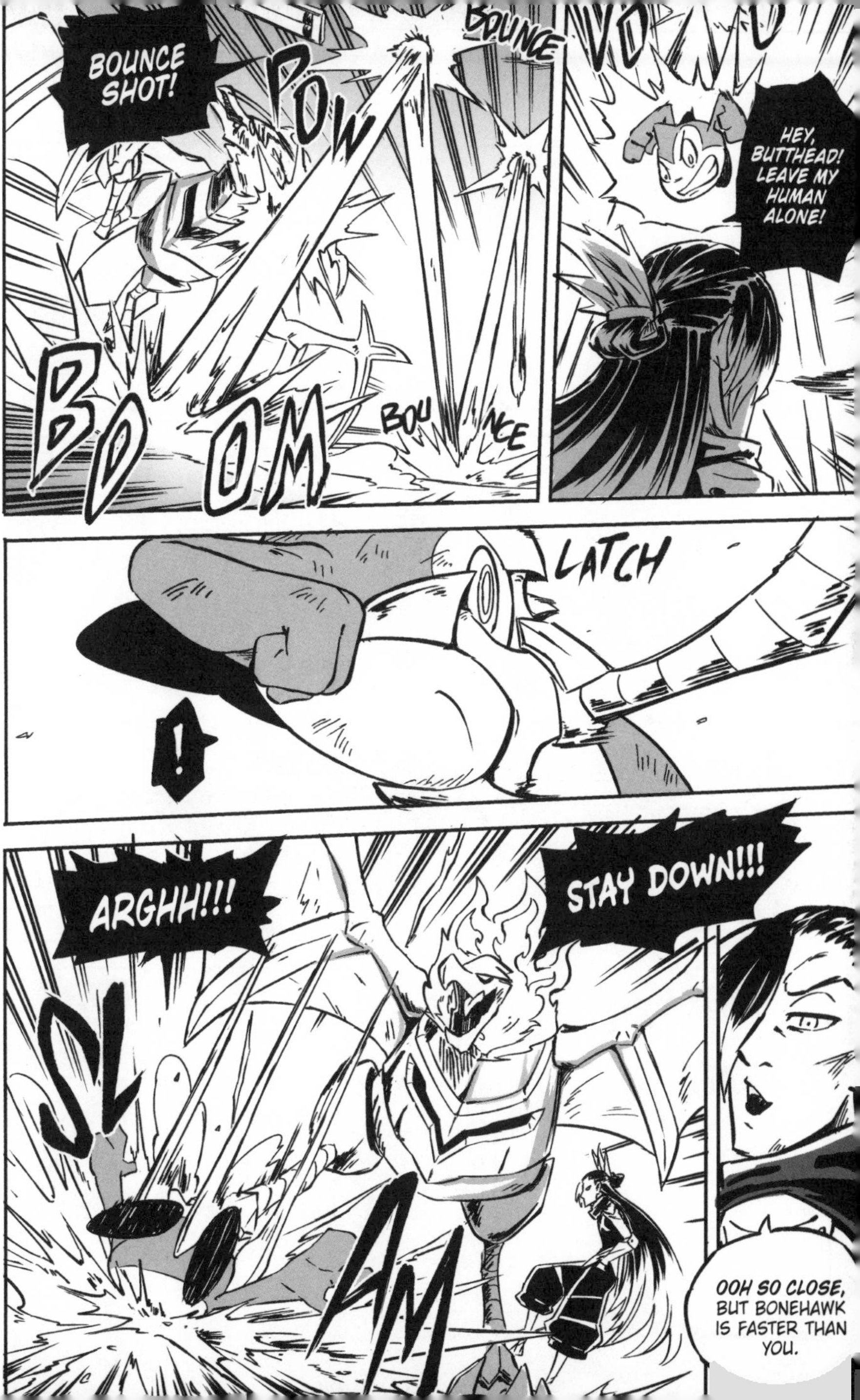
BOUNCE SHOT!
POW
BOUNCE
BOOM
BOUNCE
HEY, BUTTHEAD! LEAVE MY HUMAN ALONE!
LATCH
!
ARGHH!!!
STAY DOWN!!!
SLAM
OOH SO CLOSE, BUT BONEHAWK IS FASTER THAN YOU.

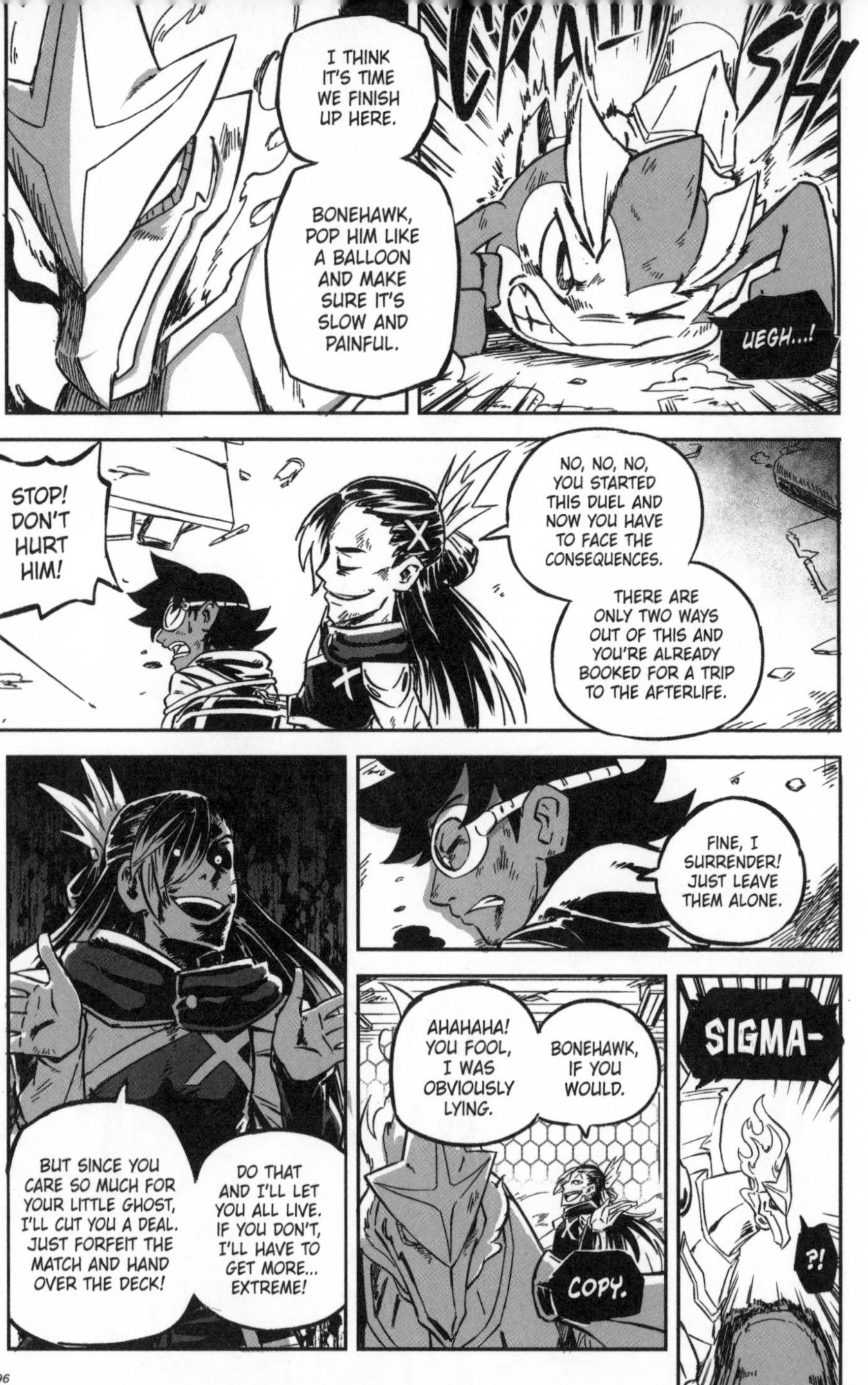
I THINK IT'S TIME WE FINISH UP HERE.
BONEHAWK, POP HIM LIKE A BALLOON AND MAKE SURE IT'S SLOW AND PAINFUL.
CRASH
UEGH...!
STOP! DON'T HURT HIM!
NO, NO, NO, YOU STARTED THIS DUEL AND NOW YOU HAVE TO FACE THE CONSEQUENCES.
THERE ARE ONLY TWO WAYS OUT OF THIS AND YOU'RE ALREADY BOOKED FOR A TRIP TO THE AFTERLIFE.
BUT SINCE YOU CARE SO MUCH FOR YOUR LITTLE GHOST, I'LL CUT YOU A DEAL. JUST FORFEIT THE MATCH AND HAND OVER THE DECK!
DO THAT AND I'LL LET YOU ALL LIVE. IF YOU DON'T, I'LL HAVE TO GET MORE... EXTREME!
FINE, I SURRENDER! JUST LEAVE THEM ALONE.
AHAHAHA! YOU FOOL, I WAS OBVIOUSLY LYING.
BONEHAWK, IF YOU WOULD.
COPY.
SIGMA-
?!

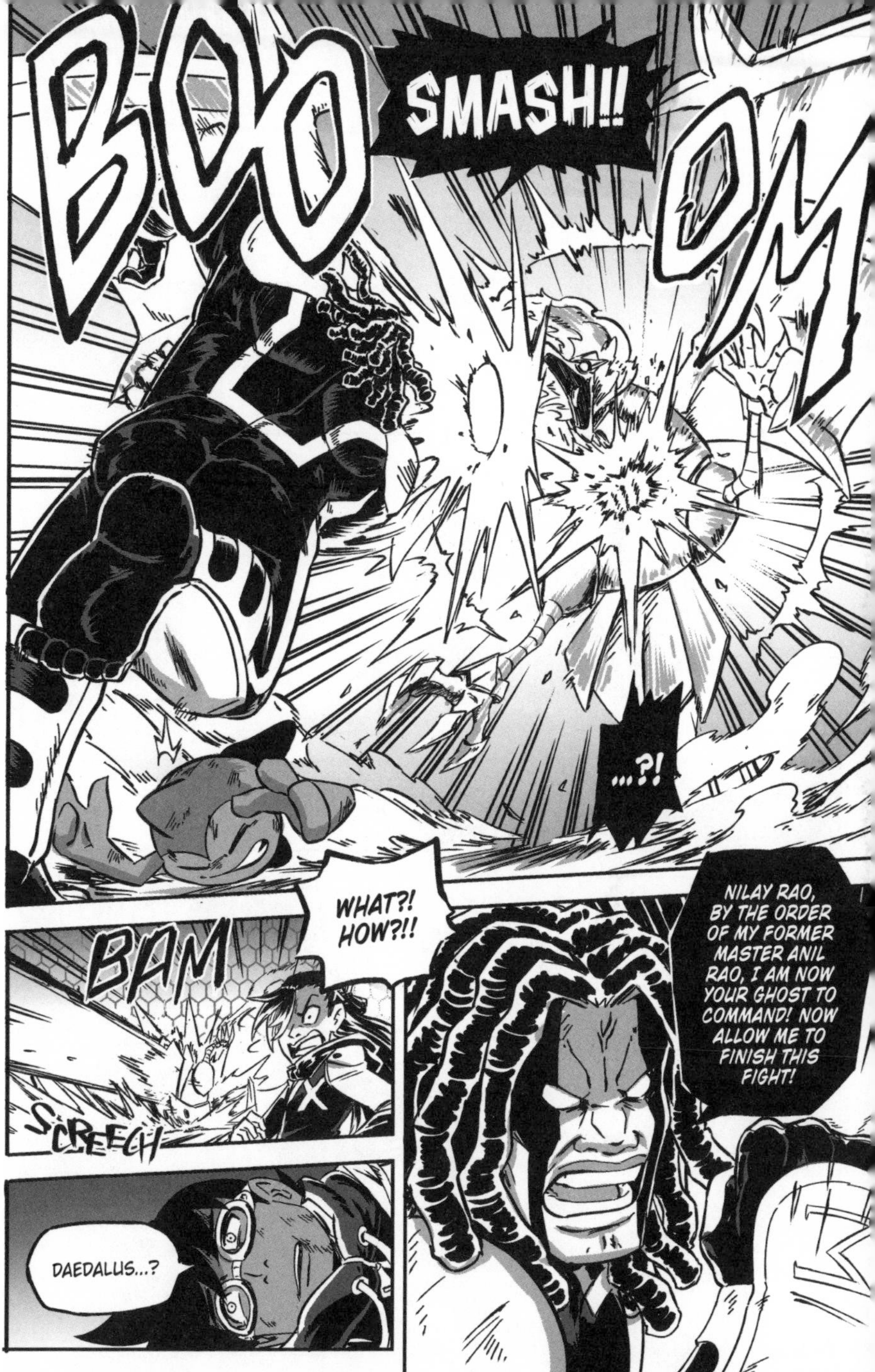
BOOOM
SMASH!!
...?!
WHAT?! HOW?!!
BAM
SCREECH
NILAY RAO, BY THE ORDER OF MY FORMER MASTER ANIL RAO, I AM NOW YOUR GHOST TO COMMAND! NOW ALLOW ME TO FINISH THIS FIGHT!
DAEDALUS...?

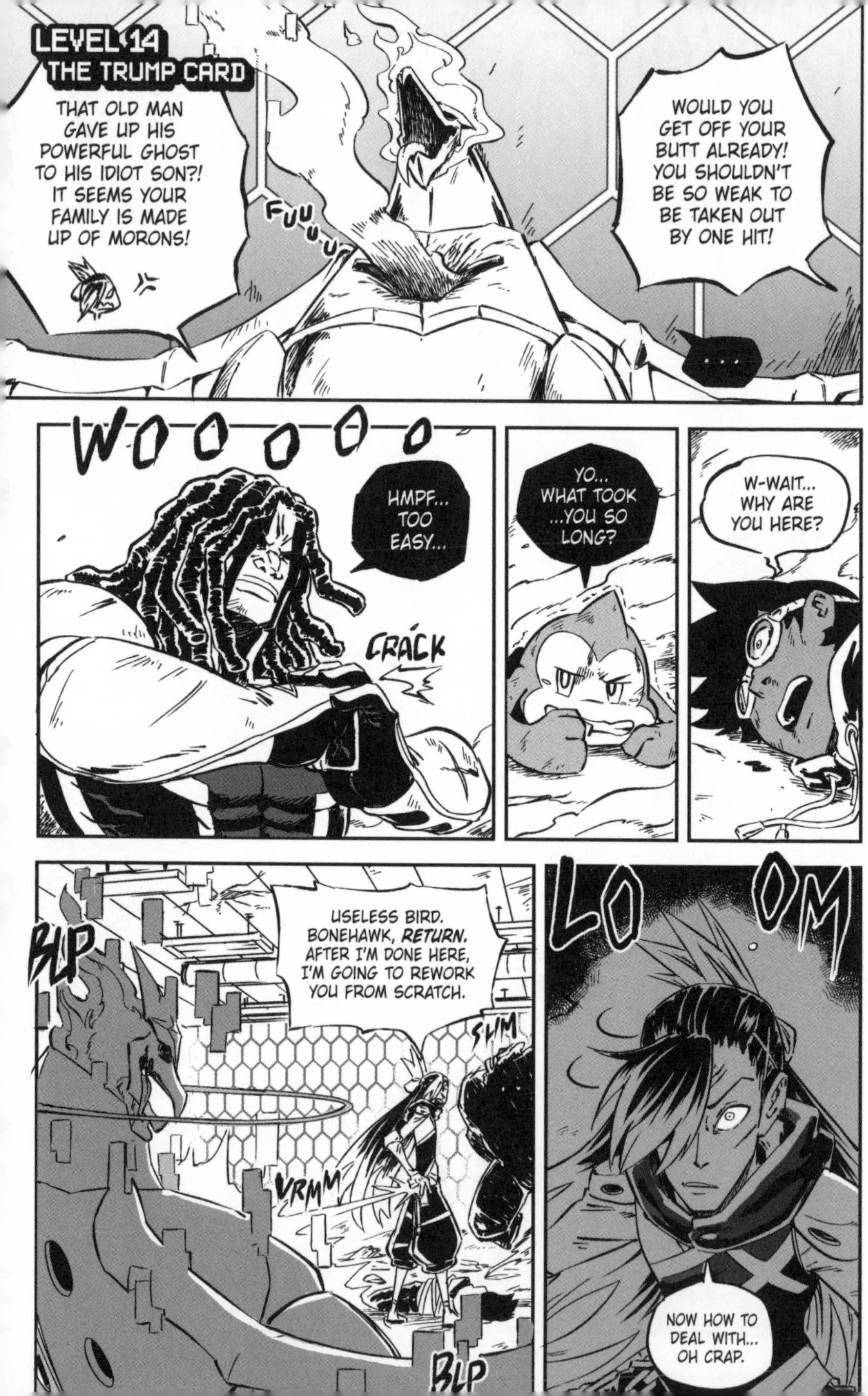
LEVEL 14
THE TRUMP CARD
THAT OLD MAN GAVE UP HIS POWERFUL GHOST TO HIS IDIOT SON?! IT SEEMS YOUR FAMILY IS MADE UP OF MORONS!
FUUUU
WOULD YOU GET OFF YOUR BUTT ALREADY! YOU SHOULDN'T BE SO WEAK TO BE TAKEN OUT BY ONE HIT!
...
WOOOOO
HMPF... TOO EASY...
CRACK
YO... WHAT TOOK ...YOU SO LONG?
W-WAIT... WHY ARE YOU HERE?
BLIP
USELESS BIRD. BONEHAWK, RETURN. AFTER I'M DONE HERE, I'M GOING TO REWORK YOU FROM SCRATCH.
SLIM
VRMM
BLIP
LOOM
NOW HOW TO DEAL WITH... OH CRAP.

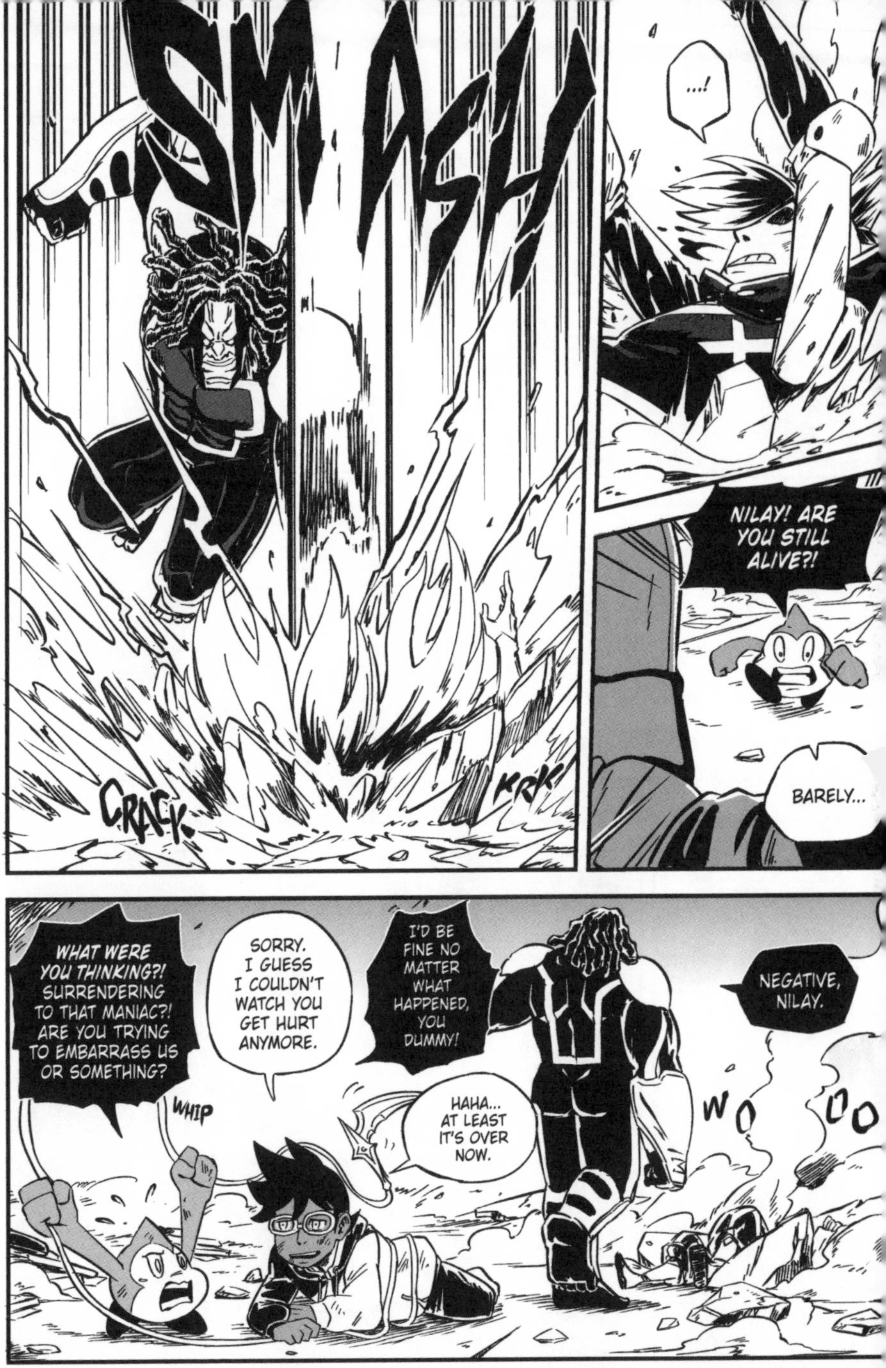
SMASH
CRACK
KRK
...!
NILAY! ARE YOU STILL ALIVE?!
BARELY...
WHAT WERE YOU THINKING?! SURRENDERING TO THAT MANIAC?! ARE YOU TRYING TO EMBARRASS US OR SOMETHING?
SORRY. I GUESS I COULDN'T WATCH YOU GET HURT ANYMORE.
I'D BE FINE NO MATTER WHAT HAPPENED, YOU DUMMY!
WHIP
HAHA... AT LEAST IT'S OVER NOW.
NEGATIVE, NILAY.
WOOO

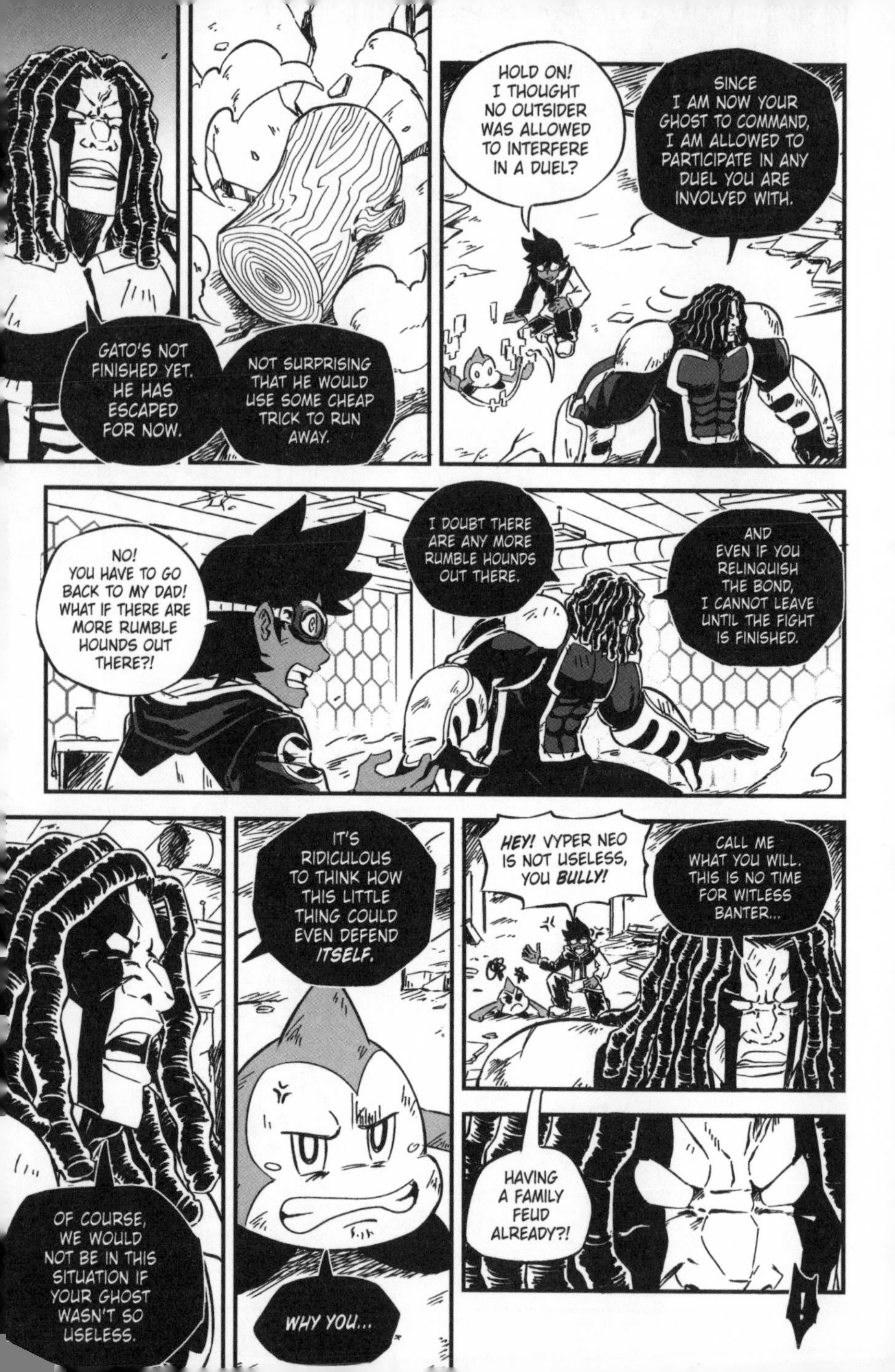
GATO'S NOT FINISHED YET. HE HAS ESCAPED FOR NOW.
NOT SURPRISING THAT HE WOULD USE SOME CHEAP TRICK TO RUN AWAY.
HOLD ON! I THOUGHT NO OUTSIDER WAS ALLOWED TO INTERFERE IN A DUEL?
SINCE I AM NOW YOUR GHOST TO COMMAND, I AM ALLOWED TO PARTICIPATE IN ANY DUEL YOU ARE INVOLVED WITH.
NO! YOU HAVE TO GO BACK TO MY DAD! WHAT IF THERE ARE MORE RUMBLE HOUNDS OUT THERE?!
I DOUBT THERE ARE ANY MORE RUMBLE HOUNDS OUT THERE.
AND EVEN IF YOU RELINQUISH THE BOND, I CANNOT LEAVE UNTIL THE FIGHT IS FINISHED.
OF COURSE, WE WOULD NOT BE IN THIS SITUATION IF YOUR GHOST WASN'T SO USELESS.
IT'S RIDICULOUS TO THINK HOW THIS LITTLE THING COULD EVEN DEFEND *ITSELF.*
WHY YOU...
HEY! VYPER NEO IS NOT USELESS, YOU *BULLY!*
CALL ME WHAT YOU WILL. THIS IS NO TIME FOR WITLESS BANTER...
HAVING A FAMILY FEUD ALREADY?!
!

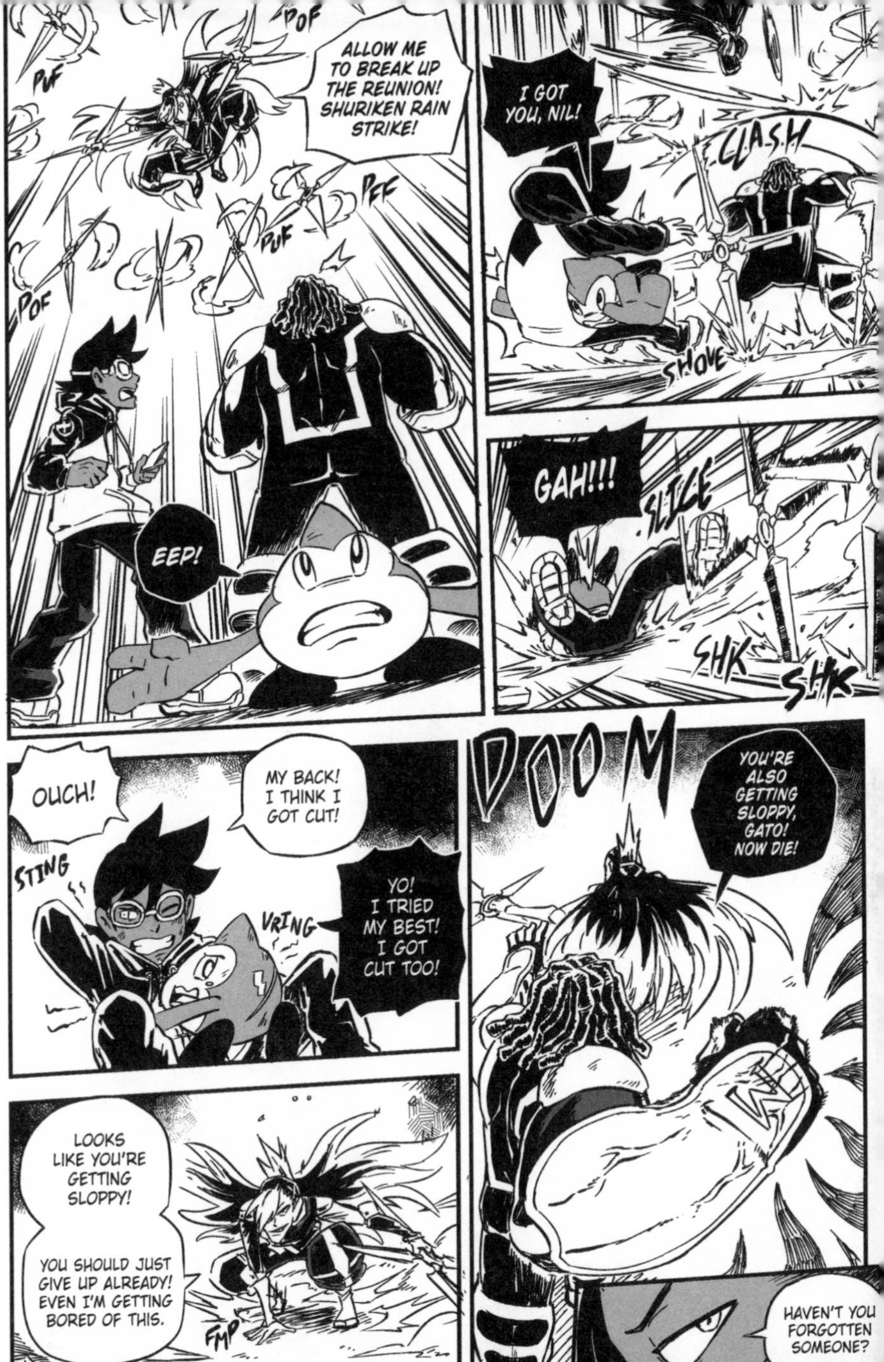
POF
PUF
ALLOW ME TO BREAK UP THE REUNION! SHURIKEN RAIN STRIKE!
PUF
PUF
POF
EEP!
I GOT YOU, NIL!
CLASH
SHOVE
GAH!!!
SLICE
SHK
SHK
OUCH!
MY BACK! I THINK I GOT CUT!
STING
VRING
YO! I TRIED MY BEST! I GOT CUT TOO!
LOOKS LIKE YOU'RE GETTING SLOPPY!
YOU SHOULD JUST GIVE UP ALREADY! EVEN I'M GETTING BORED OF THIS.
FMP
DOOM
YOU'RE ALSO GETTING SLOPPY, GATO! NOW DIE!
HAVEN'T YOU FORGOTTEN SOMEONE?

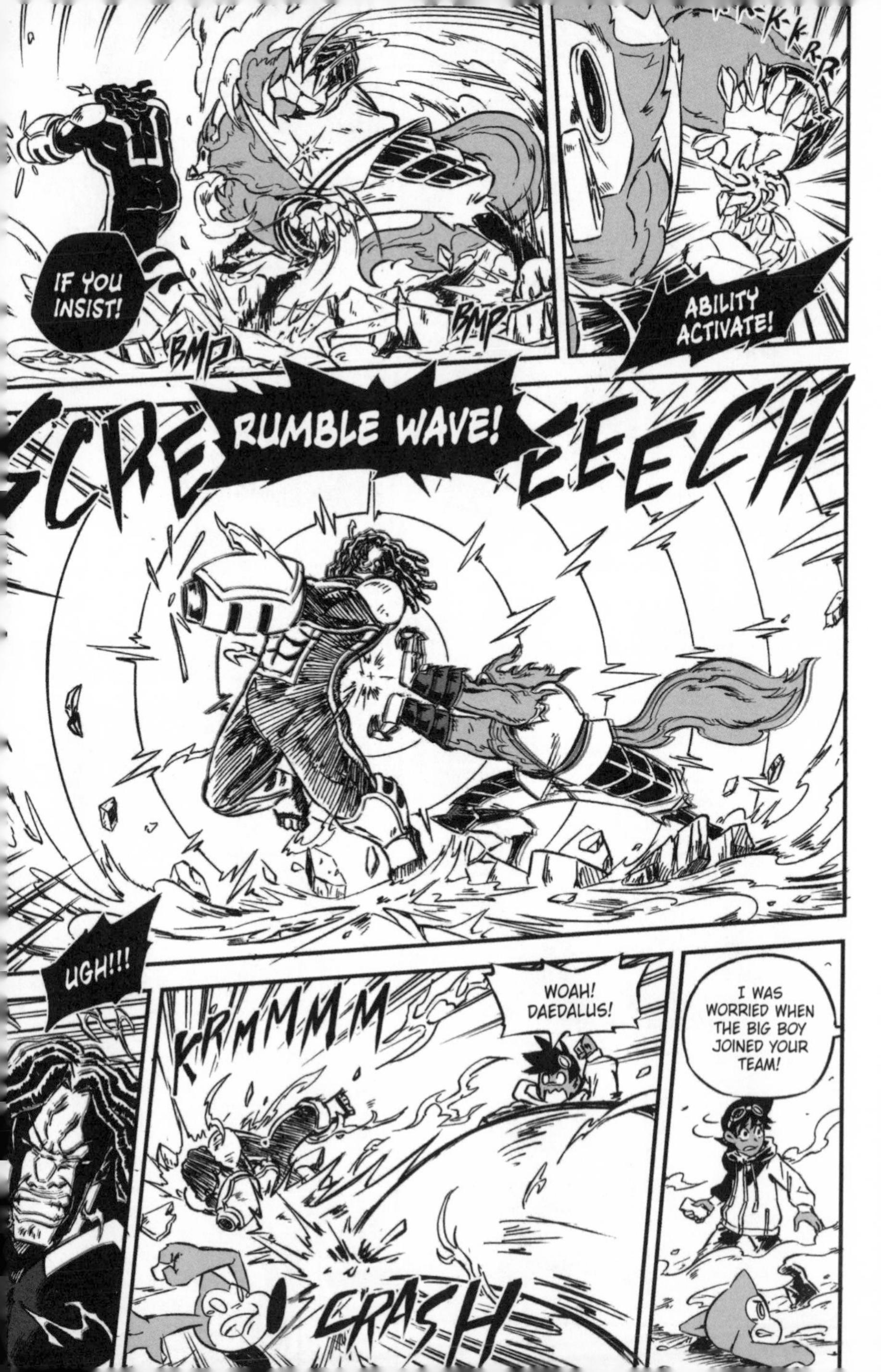

IF YOU INSIST!
BMP
BMP
ABILITY ACTIVATE!
SCRE
RUMBLE WAVE!
EEECH
UGH!!!
KRMMMM
WOAH! DAEDALUS!
CRASH
I WAS WORRIED WHEN THE BIG BOY JOINED YOUR TEAM!

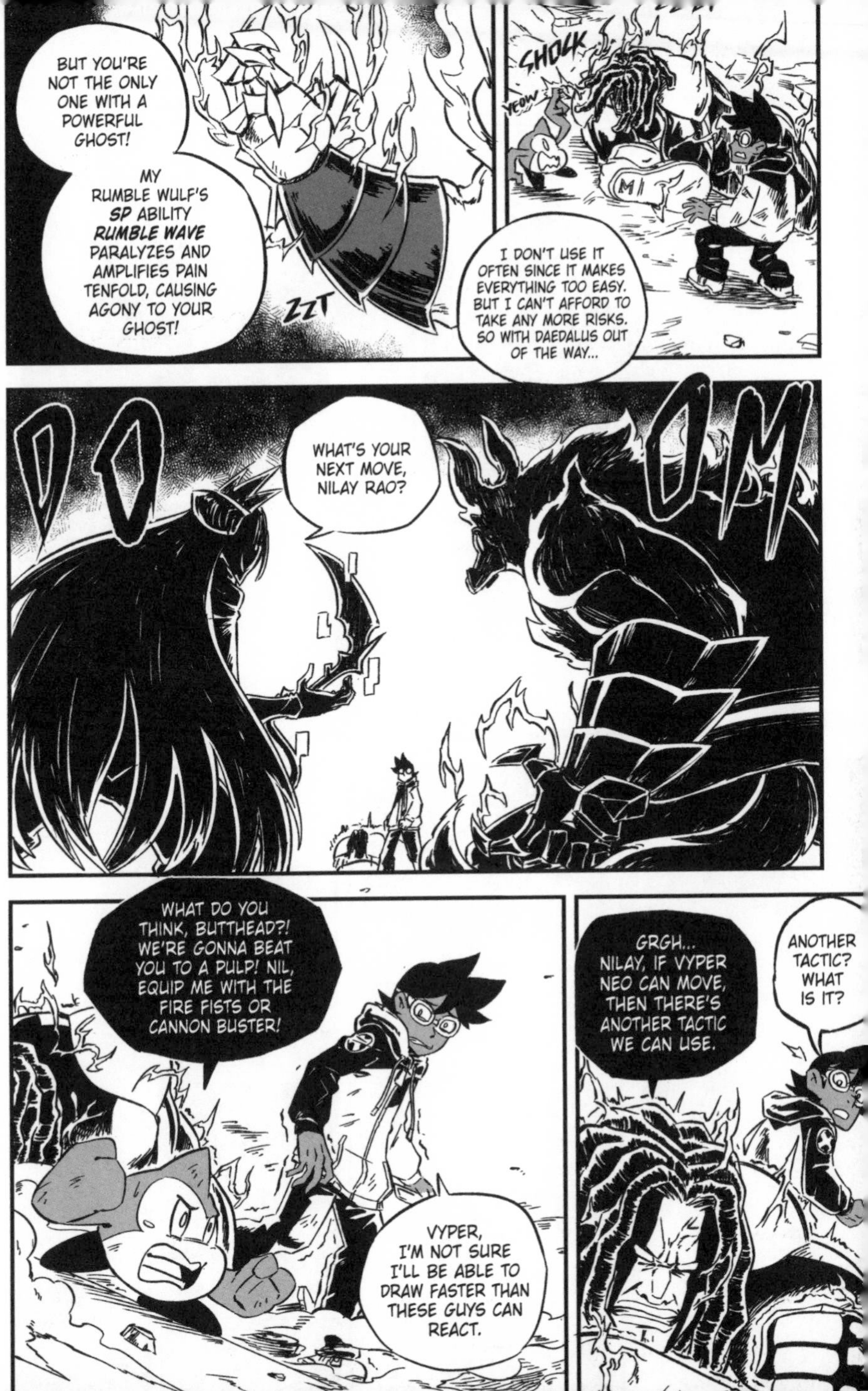
BUT YOU'RE NOT THE ONLY ONE WITH A POWERFUL GHOST!
MY RUMBLE WULF'S SP ABILITY RUMBLE WAVE PARALYZES AND AMPLIFIES PAIN TENFOLD, CAUSING AGONY TO YOUR GHOST!
ZZT
SHOCK
YEOW
I DON'T USE IT OFTEN SINCE IT MAKES EVERYTHING TOO EASY. BUT I CAN'T AFFORD TO TAKE ANY MORE RISKS. SO WITH DAEDALUS OUT OF THE WAY...
DOOM
WHAT'S YOUR NEXT MOVE, NILAY RAO?
WHAT DO YOU THINK, BUTTHEAD?! WE'RE GONNA BEAT YOU TO A PULP! NIL, EQUIP ME WITH THE FIRE FISTS OR CANNON BUSTER!
VYPER, I'M NOT SURE I'LL BE ABLE TO DRAW FASTER THAN THESE GUYS CAN REACT.
GRGH... NILAY, IF VYPER NEO CAN MOVE, THEN THERE'S ANOTHER TACTIC WE CAN USE.
ANOTHER TACTIC? WHAT IS IT?

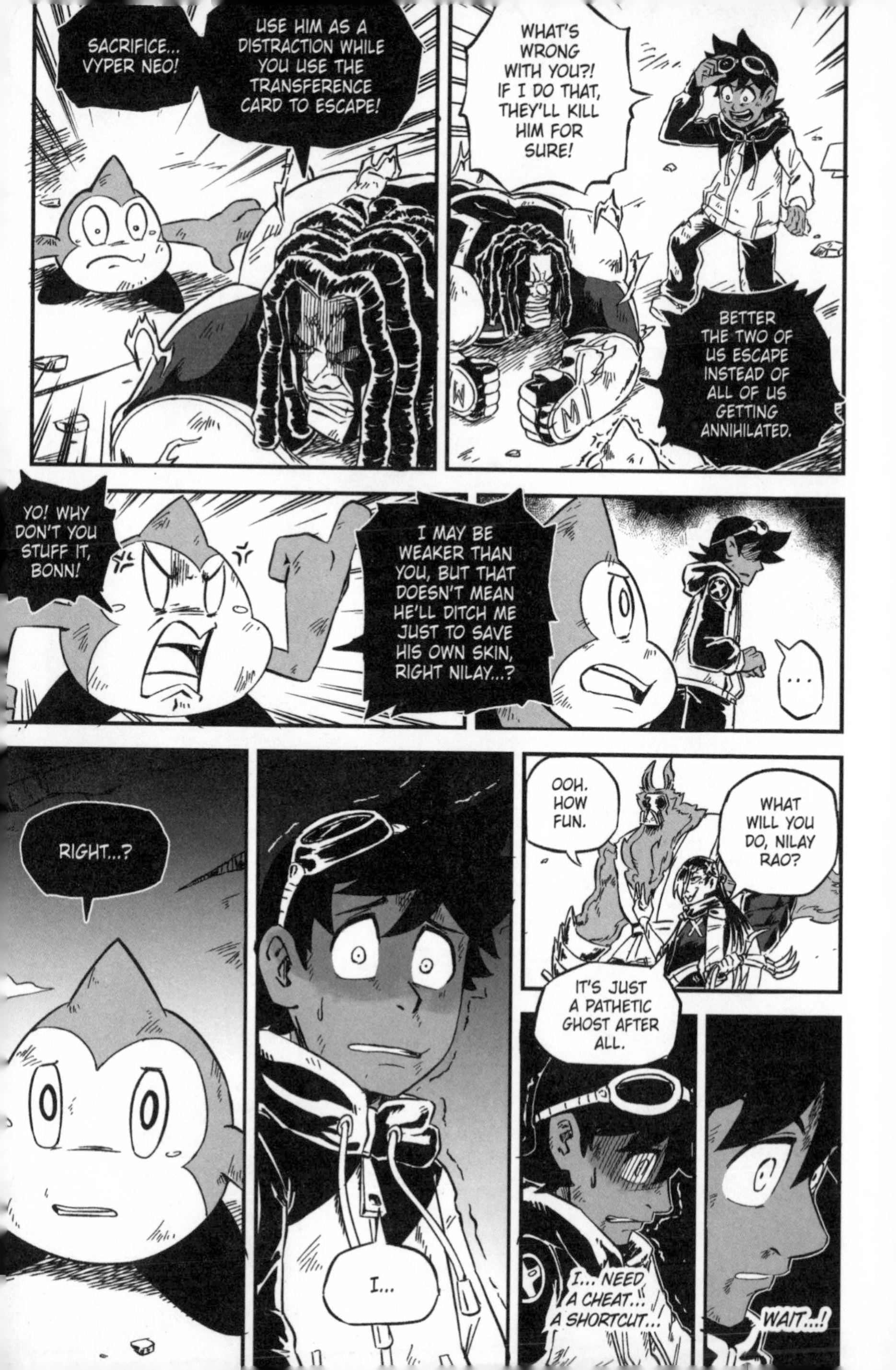
SACRIFICE... VYPER NEO!
USE HIM AS A DISTRACTION WHILE YOU USE THE TRANSFERENCE CARD TO ESCAPE!
WHAT'S WRONG WITH YOU?! IF I DO THAT, THEY'LL KILL HIM FOR SURE!
BETTER THE TWO OF US ESCAPE INSTEAD OF ALL OF US GETTING ANNIHILATED.
YO! WHY DON'T YOU STUFF IT, BONN!
I MAY BE WEAKER THAN YOU, BUT THAT DOESN'T MEAN HE'LL DITCH ME JUST TO SAVE HIS OWN SKIN, RIGHT NILAY...?
...
RIGHT...?
I...
OOH. HOW FUN.
WHAT WILL YOU DO, NILAY RAO?
IT'S JUST A PATHETIC GHOST AFTER ALL.
I... NEED A CHEAT... A SHORTCUT...
WAIT...!

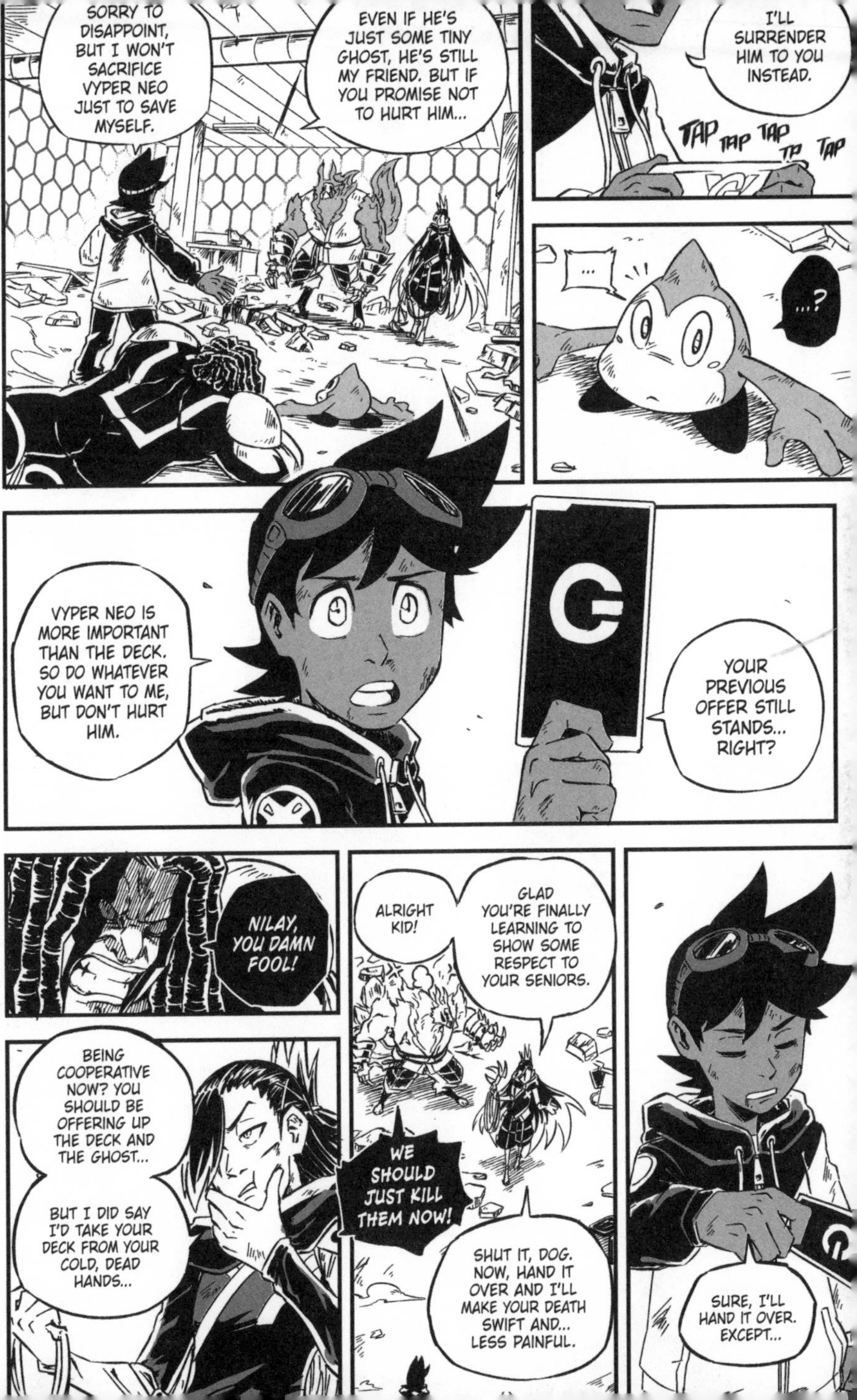
SORRY TO DISAPPOINT, BUT I WON'T SACRIFICE VYPER NEO JUST TO SAVE MYSELF.
EVEN IF HE'S JUST SOME TINY GHOST, HE'S STILL MY FRIEND. BUT IF YOU PROMISE NOT TO HURT HIM...
I'LL SURRENDER HIM TO YOU INSTEAD.
TAP TAP TAP TAP TAP
...
...?
VYPER NEO IS MORE IMPORTANT THAN THE DECK. SO DO WHATEVER YOU WANT TO ME, BUT DON'T HURT HIM.
YOUR PREVIOUS OFFER STILL STANDS... RIGHT?
NILAY, YOU DAMN FOOL!
ALRIGHT KID!
GLAD YOU'RE FINALLY LEARNING TO SHOW SOME RESPECT TO YOUR SENIORS.
BEING COOPERATIVE NOW? YOU SHOULD BE OFFERING UP THE DECK AND THE GHOST...
BUT I DID SAY I'D TAKE YOUR DECK FROM YOUR COLD, DEAD HANDS...
WE SHOULD JUST KILL THEM NOW!
SHUT IT, DOG. NOW, HAND IT OVER AND I'LL MAKE YOUR DEATH SWIFT AND... LESS PAINFUL.
SURE, I'LL HAND IT OVER. EXCEPT...

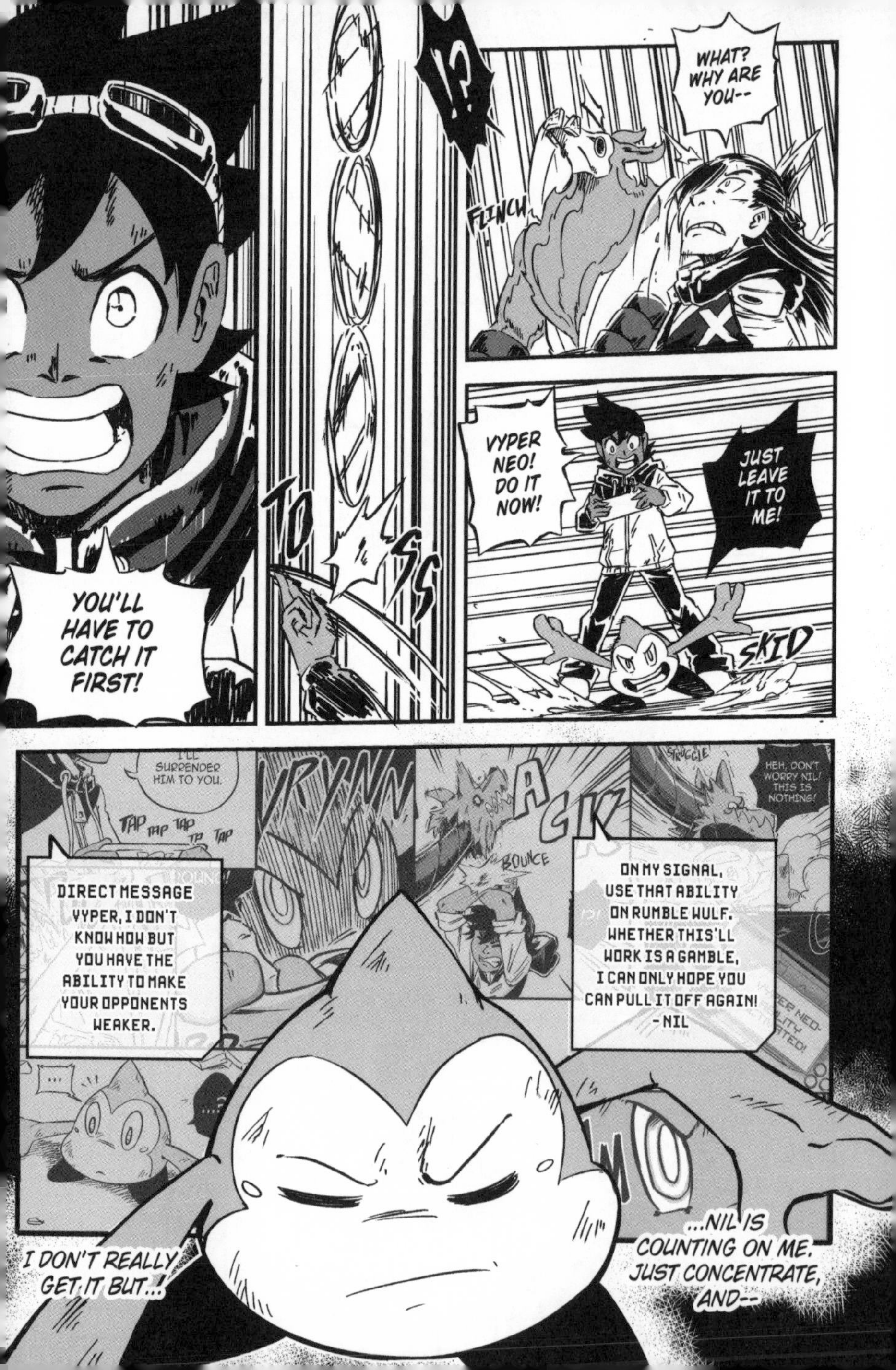
YOU'LL HAVE TO CATCH IT FIRST!
!?
TOSS
WHAT? WHY ARE YOU--
FLINCH
VYPER NEO! DO IT NOW!
JUST LEAVE IT TO ME!
SKID
I'LL SURRENDER HIM TO YOU.
TAP TAP TAP TP TAP
VRYNN
ACK
BOUNCE
STRUGGLE
HEH, DON'T WORRY NIL! THIS IS NOTHING!
DIRECT MESSAGE
VYPER, I DON'T KNOW HOW BUT YOU HAVE THE ABILITY TO MAKE YOUR OPPONENTS WEAKER.
ON MY SIGNAL, USE THAT ABILITY ON RUMBLE WULF. WHETHER THIS'LL WORK IS A GAMBLE, I CAN ONLY HOPE YOU CAN PULL IT OFF AGAIN!
- NIL
I DON'T REALLY GET IT BUT..!
...NIL IS COUNTING ON ME. JUST CONCENTRATE, AND--

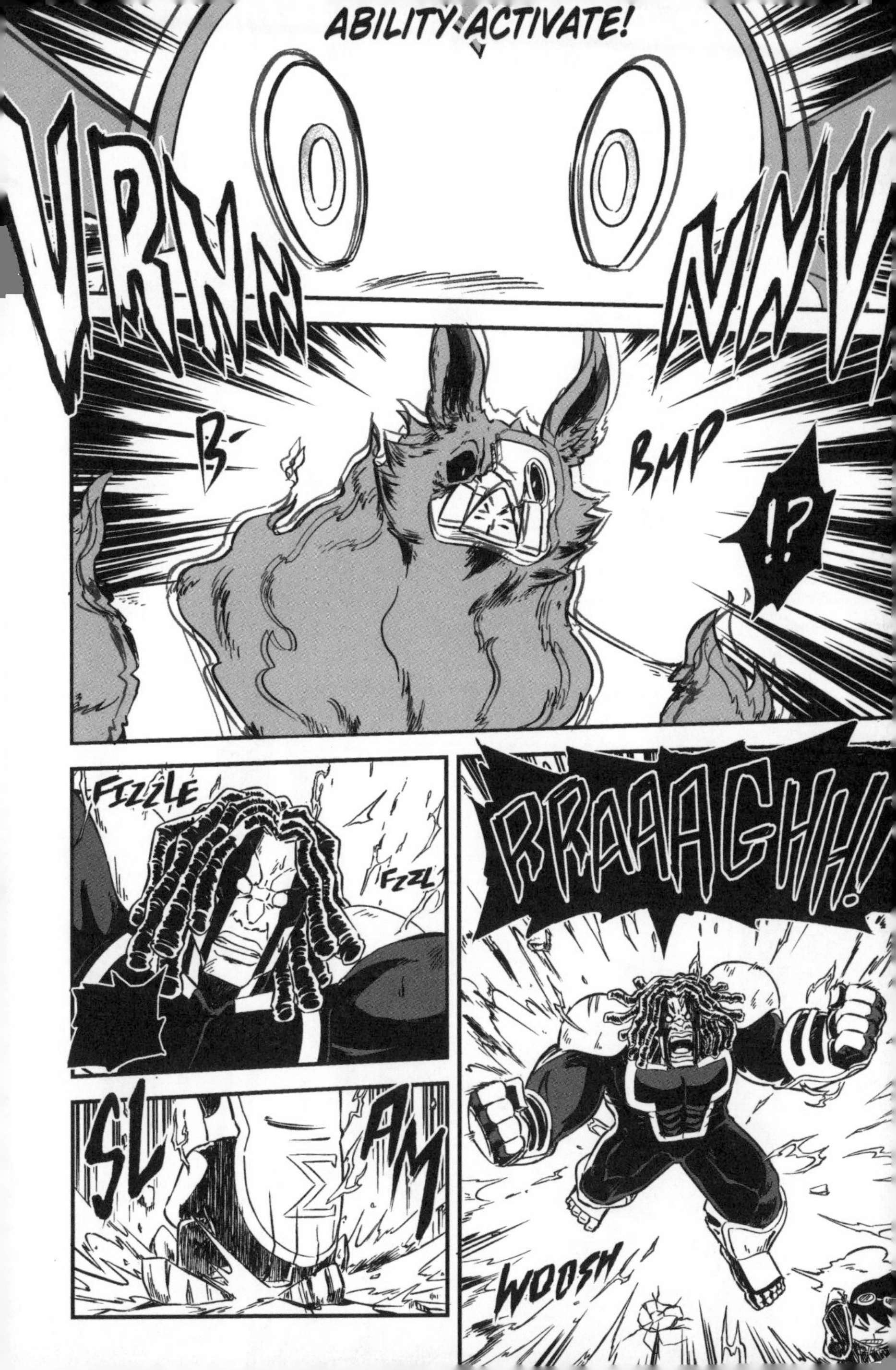
ABILITY ACTIVATE!
VRMM
NMMM
B-
BMP
!?
FIZZLE
FZZL
RRAAAGHH!!
SL
AM
WOOSH

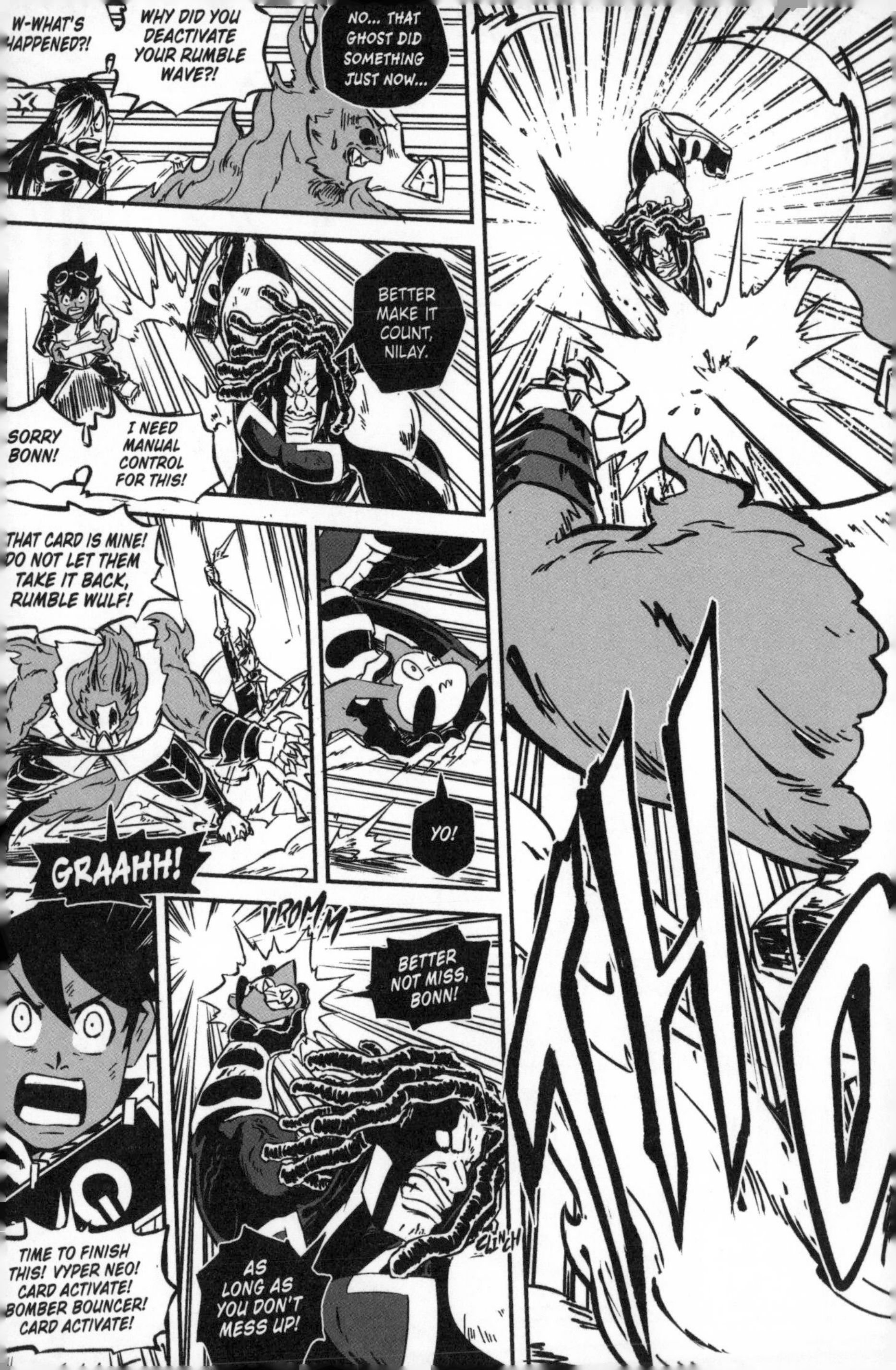
W-WHAT'S HAPPENED?!
WHY DID YOU DEACTIVATE YOUR RUMBLE WAVE?!
NO... THAT GHOST DID SOMETHING JUST NOW...
BETTER MAKE IT COUNT, NILAY.
SORRY BONN!
I NEED MANUAL CONTROL FOR THIS!
THAT CARD IS MINE! DO NOT LET THEM TAKE IT BACK, RUMBLE WULF!
GRAAHH!
YO!
TIME TO FINISH THIS! VYPER NEO! CARD ACTIVATE! BOMBER BOUNCER! CARD ACTIVATE!
VROOMM
BETTER NOT MISS, BONN!
AS LONG AS YOU DON'T MESS UP!
CLINCH

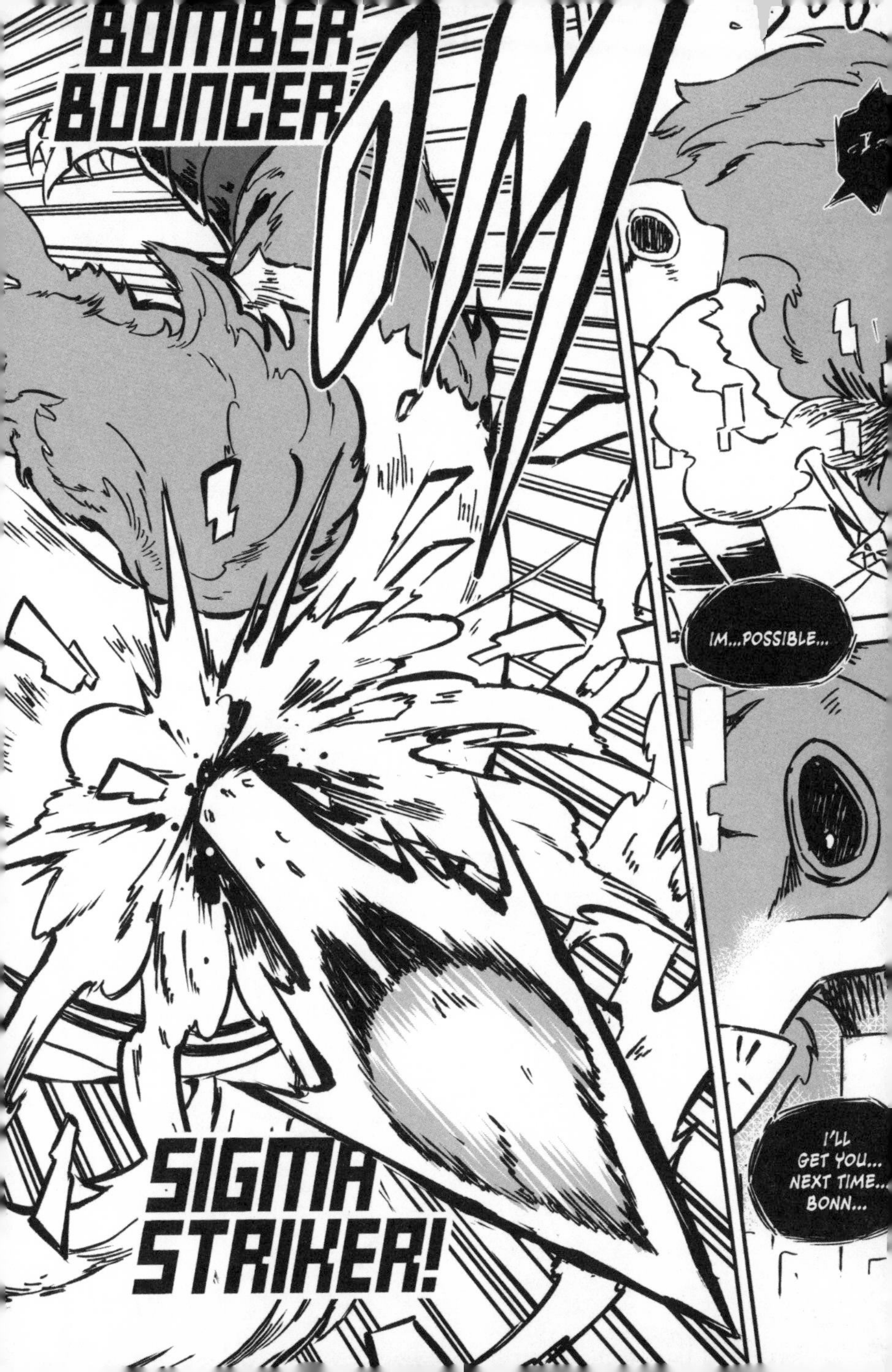
BOMBER BOUNCER
SIGMA STRIKER!
IM...POSSIBLE...
I'LL GET YOU... NEXT TIME... BONN...

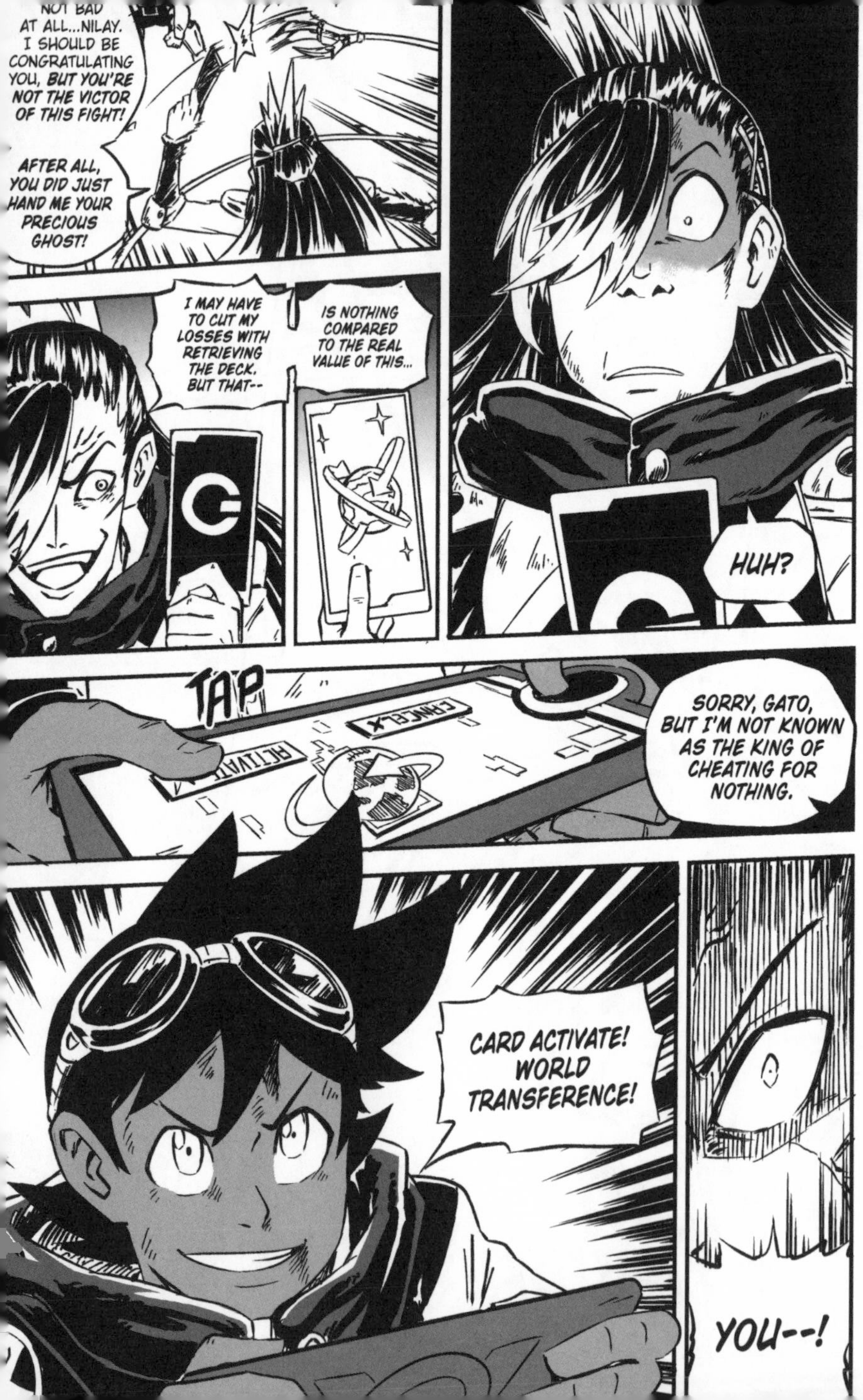
NOT BAD AT ALL...NILAY. I SHOULD BE CONGRATULATING YOU, BUT YOU'RE NOT THE VICTOR OF THIS FIGHT!
AFTER ALL, YOU DID JUST HAND ME YOUR PRECIOUS GHOST!
I MAY HAVE TO CUT MY LOSSES WITH RETRIEVING THE DECK. BUT THAT--
IS NOTHING COMPARED TO THE REAL VALUE OF THIS...
HUH?
TAP
SORRY, GATO, BUT I'M NOT KNOWN AS THE KING OF CHEATING FOR NOTHING.
CARD ACTIVATE! WORLD TRANSFERENCE!
YOU--!

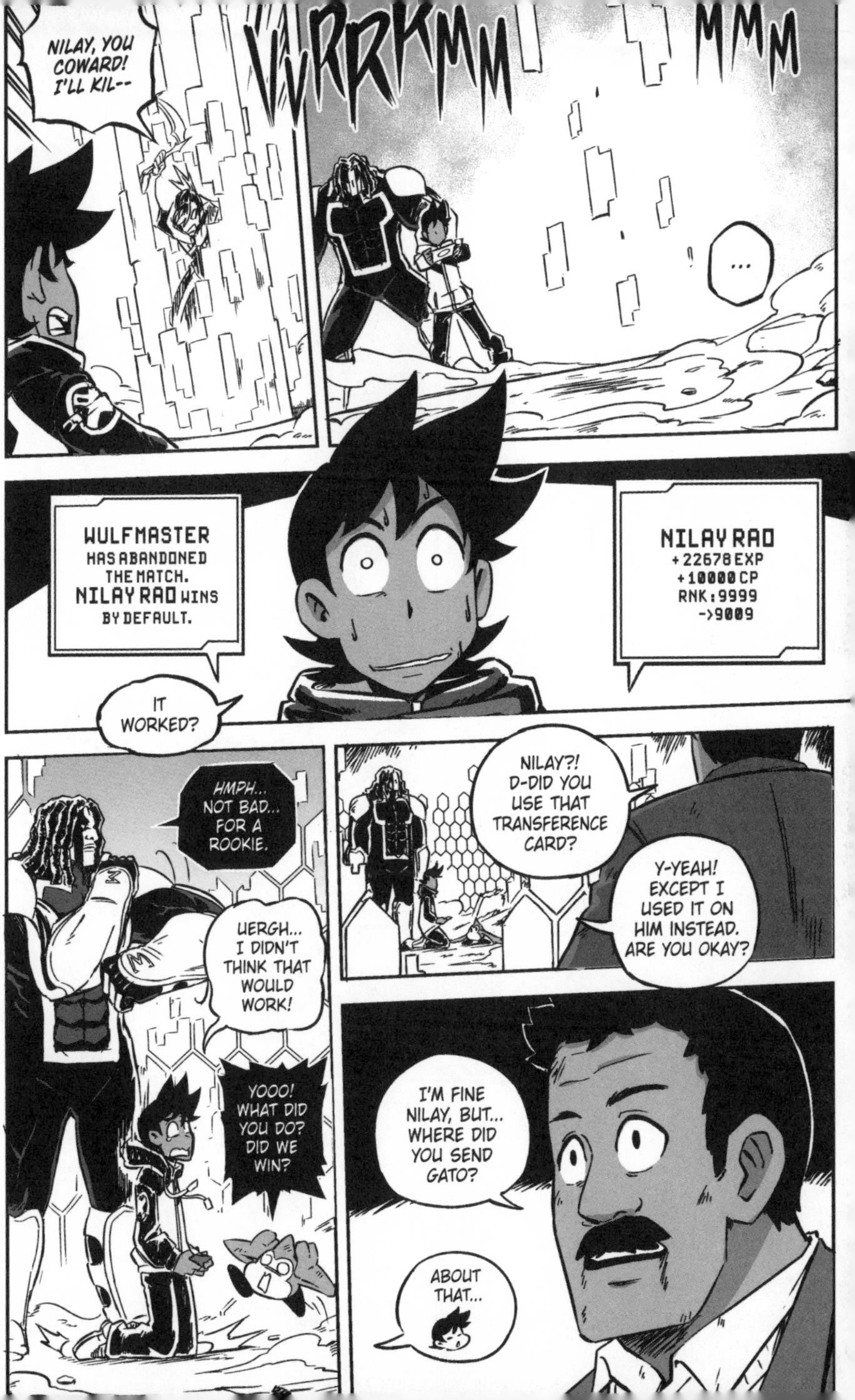
NILAY, YOU COWARD! I'LL KIL--
VRRRKMMM MMM
...
WULFMASTER HAS ABANDONED THE MATCH. NILAY RAD WINS BY DEFAULT.
NILAY RAD +22678 EXP +10000 CP RNK: 9999 ->9009
IT WORKED?
HMPH... NOT BAD... FOR A ROOKIE.
UERGH... I DIDN'T THINK THAT WOULD WORK!
YOOO! WHAT DID YOU DO? DID WE WIN?
NILAY?! D-DID YOU USE THAT TRANSFERENCE CARD?
Y-YEAH! EXCEPT I USED IT ON HIM INSTEAD. ARE YOU OKAY?
I'M FINE NILAY, BUT... WHERE DID YOU SEND GATO?
ABOUT THAT...

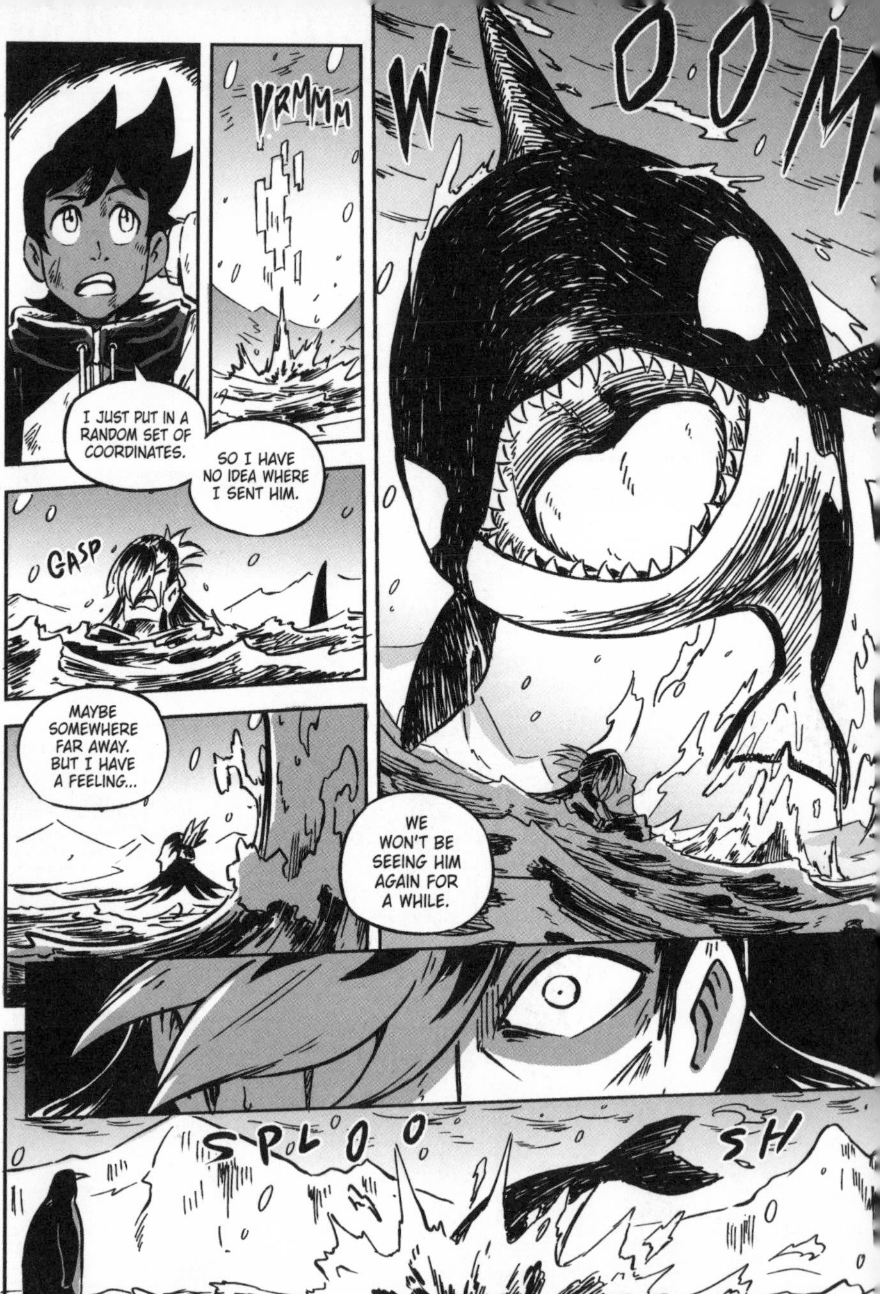
I JUST PUT IN A RANDOM SET OF COORDINATES.
VRMMMM
SO I HAVE NO IDEA WHERE I SENT HIM.
GASP
MAYBE SOMEWHERE FAR AWAY. BUT I HAVE A FEELING...
WE WON'T BE SEEING HIM AGAIN FOR A WHILE.
WOOOM
SPLOOOSH

THE MASSIVELY MULTIPLAYER WORLD OF GHOSTS

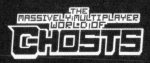

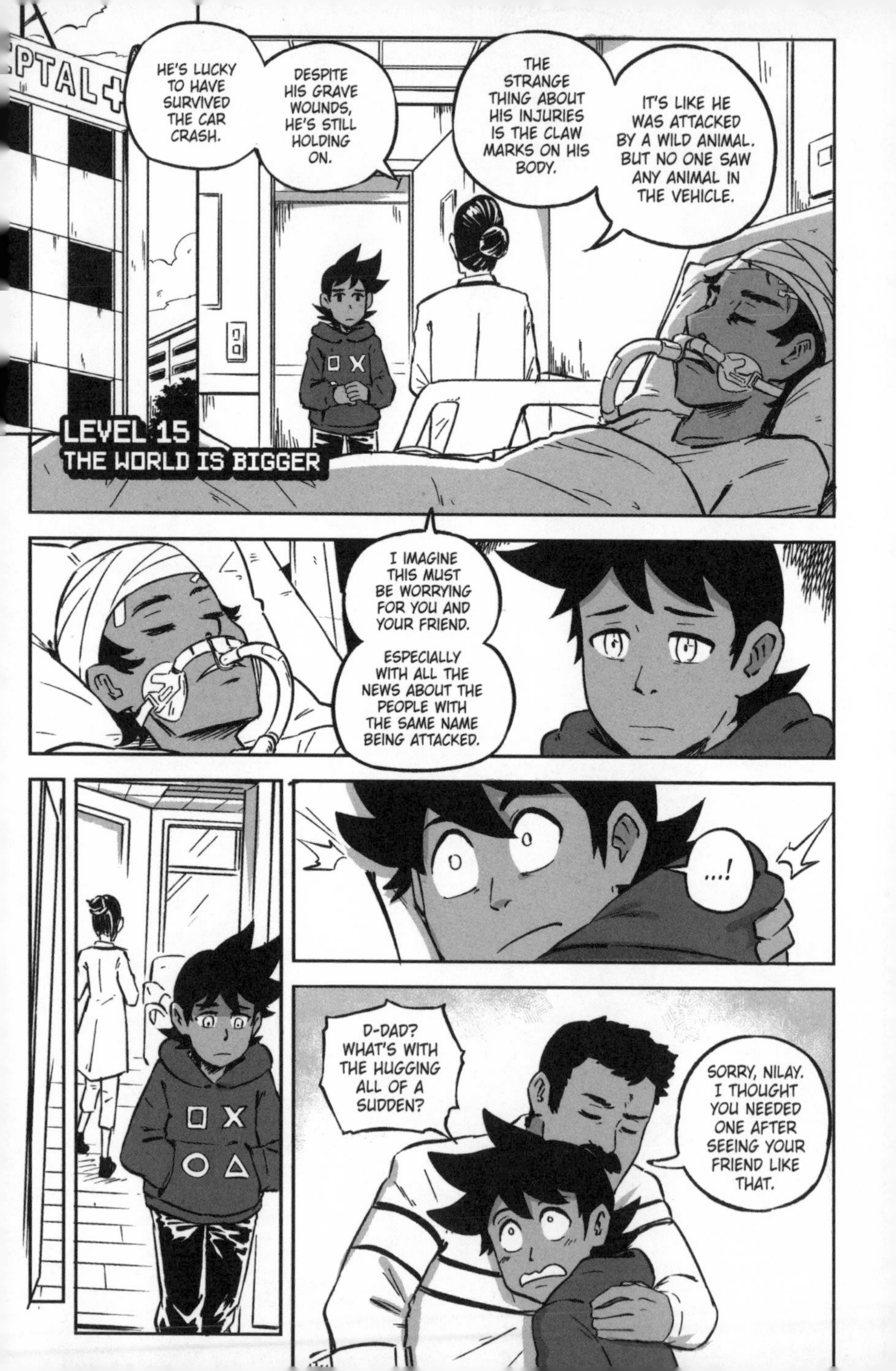

HE'S LUCKY TO HAVE SURVIVED THE CAR CRASH.
DESPITE HIS GRAVE WOUNDS, HE'S STILL HOLDING ON.
THE STRANGE THING ABOUT HIS INJURIES IS THE CLAW MARKS ON HIS BODY.
IT'S LIKE HE WAS ATTACKED BY A WILD ANIMAL. BUT NO ONE SAW ANY ANIMAL IN THE VEHICLE.
LEVEL 15
THE WORLD IS BIGGER
I IMAGINE THIS MUST BE WORRYING FOR YOU AND YOUR FRIEND.
ESPECIALLY WITH ALL THE NEWS ABOUT THE PEOPLE WITH THE SAME NAME BEING ATTACKED.
...!
D-DAD? WHAT'S WITH THE HUGGING ALL OF A SUDDEN?
SORRY, NILAY. I THOUGHT YOU NEEDED ONE AFTER SEEING YOUR FRIEND LIKE THAT.

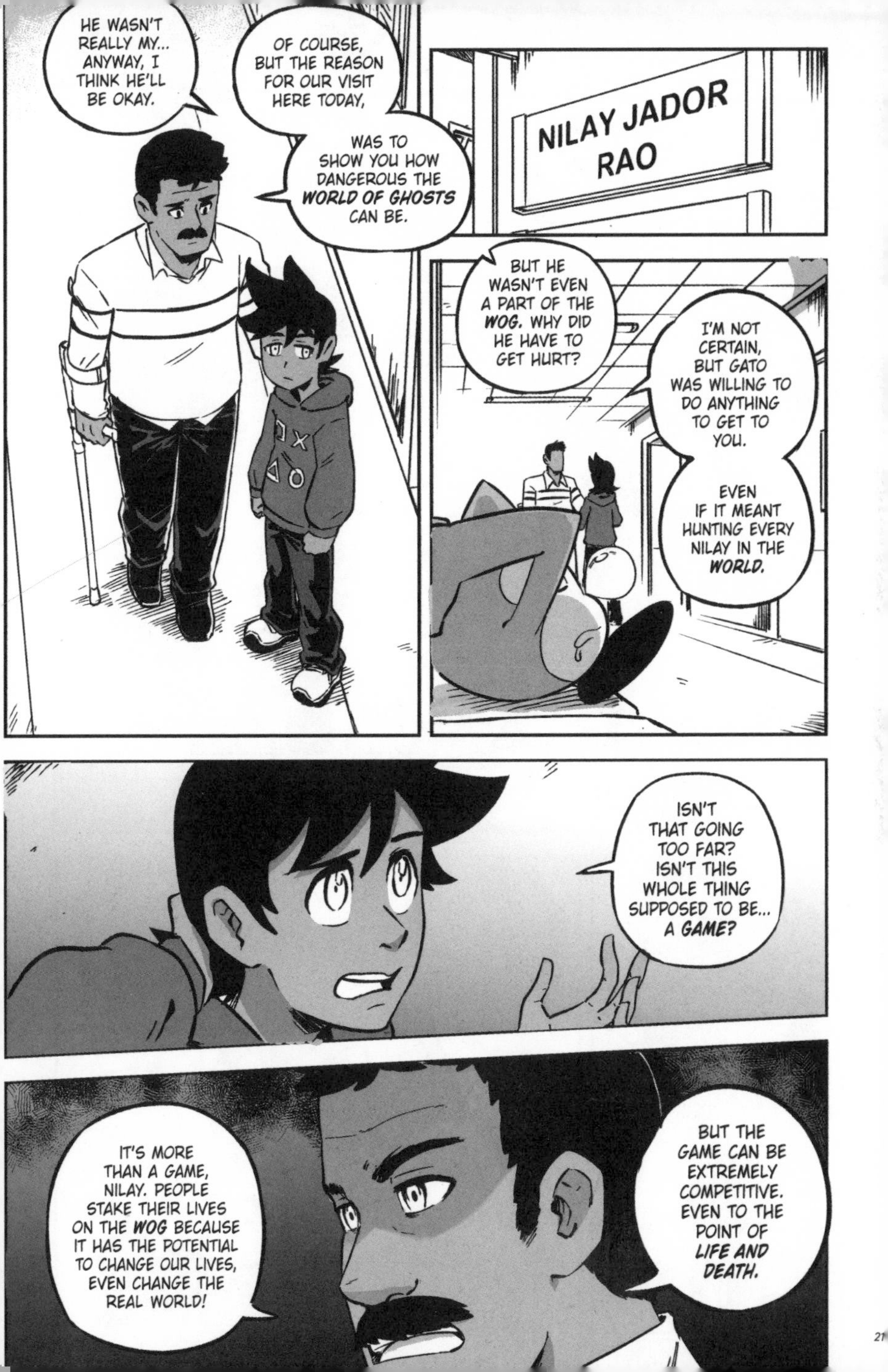
HE WASN'T REALLY MY... ANYWAY, I THINK HE'LL BE OKAY.
OF COURSE, BUT THE REASON FOR OUR VISIT HERE TODAY,
WAS TO SHOW YOU HOW DANGEROUS THE *WORLD OF GHOSTS* CAN BE.
NILAY JADOR RAO
BUT HE WASN'T EVEN A PART OF THE *WOG*. WHY DID HE HAVE TO GET HURT?
I'M NOT CERTAIN, BUT GATO WAS WILLING TO DO ANYTHING TO GET TO YOU.
EVEN IF IT MEANT HUNTING EVERY NILAY IN THE *WORLD*.
ISN'T THAT GOING TOO FAR? ISN'T THIS WHOLE THING SUPPOSED TO BE... A *GAME*?
IT'S MORE THAN A GAME, NILAY. PEOPLE STAKE THEIR LIVES ON THE *WOG* BECAUSE IT HAS THE POTENTIAL TO CHANGE OUR LIVES, EVEN CHANGE THE REAL WORLD!
BUT THE GAME CAN BE EXTREMELY COMPETITIVE. EVEN TO THE POINT OF *LIFE AND DEATH*.

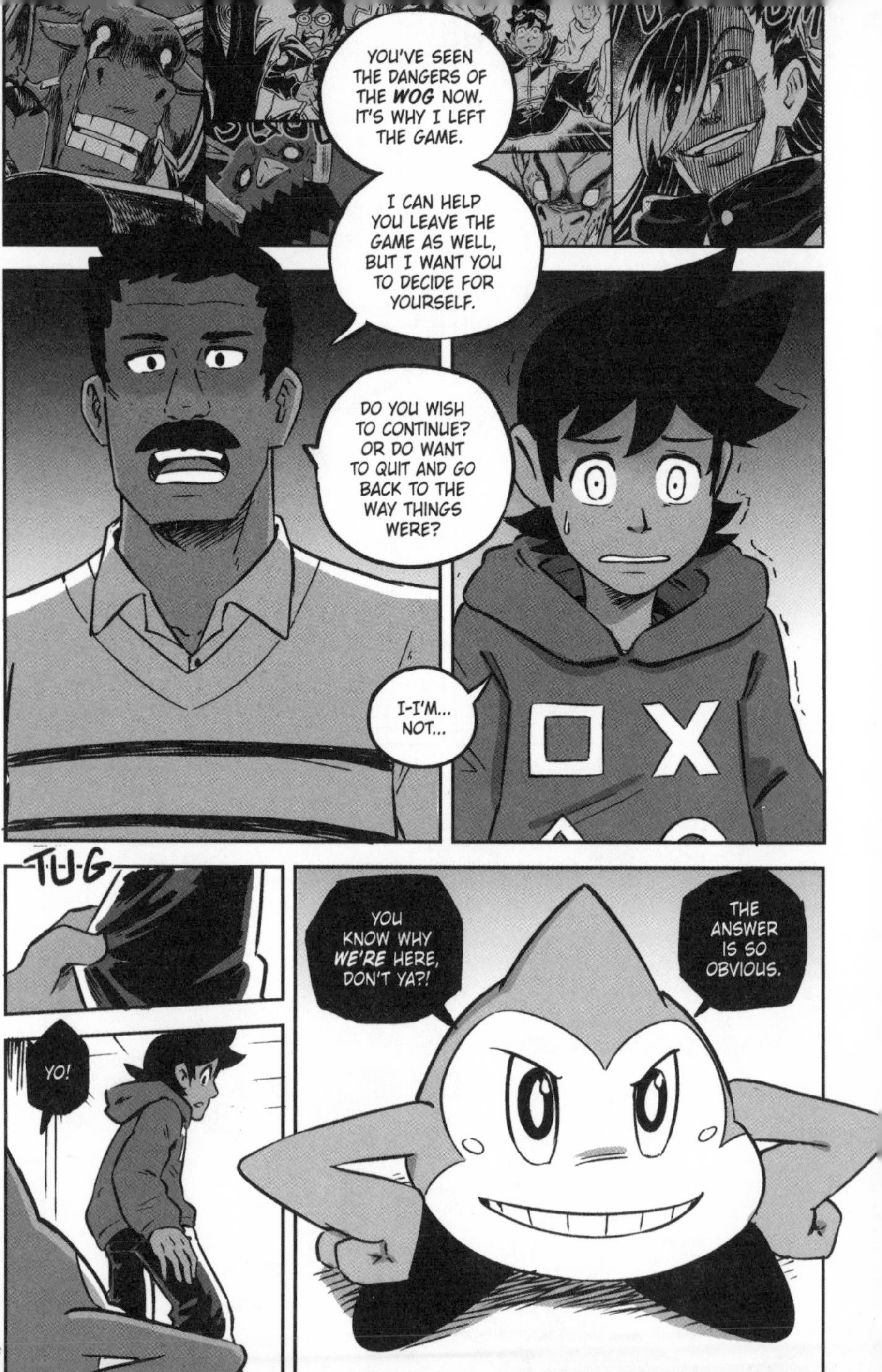
YOU'VE SEEN THE DANGERS OF THE WOG NOW. IT'S WHY I LEFT THE GAME.
I CAN HELP YOU LEAVE THE GAME AS WELL, BUT I WANT YOU TO DECIDE FOR YOURSELF.
DO YOU WISH TO CONTINUE? OR DO WANT TO QUIT AND GO BACK TO THE WAY THINGS WERE?
I-I'M... NOT...
TUG
YO!
YOU KNOW WHY WE'RE HERE, DON'T YA?!
THE ANSWER IS SO OBVIOUS.

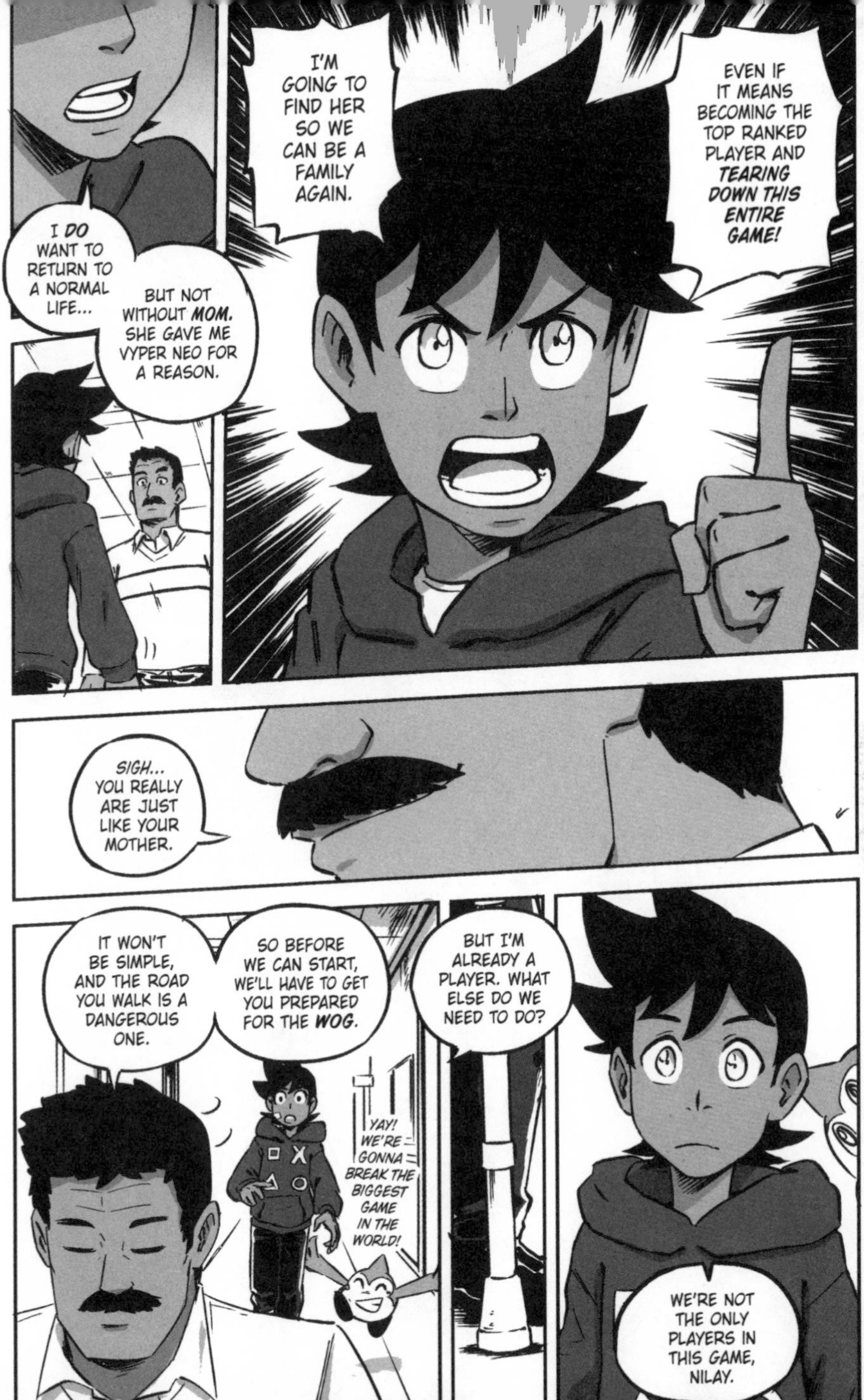
I *DO* WANT TO RETURN TO A NORMAL LIFE...
BUT NOT WITHOUT *MOM.* SHE GAVE ME VYPER NEO FOR A REASON.
I'M GOING TO FIND HER SO WE CAN BE A FAMILY AGAIN.
EVEN IF IT MEANS BECOMING THE TOP RANKED PLAYER AND ***TEARING DOWN THIS ENTIRE GAME!***
SIGH... YOU REALLY ARE JUST LIKE YOUR MOTHER.
IT WON'T BE SIMPLE, AND THE ROAD YOU WALK IS A DANGEROUS ONE.
SO BEFORE WE CAN START, WE'LL HAVE TO GET YOU PREPARED FOR THE ***WOG***.
YAY! WE'RE GONNA BREAK THE BIGGEST GAME IN THE WORLD!
BUT I'M ALREADY A PLAYER. WHAT ELSE DO WE NEED TO DO?
WE'RE NOT THE ONLY PLAYERS IN THIS GAME, NILAY.

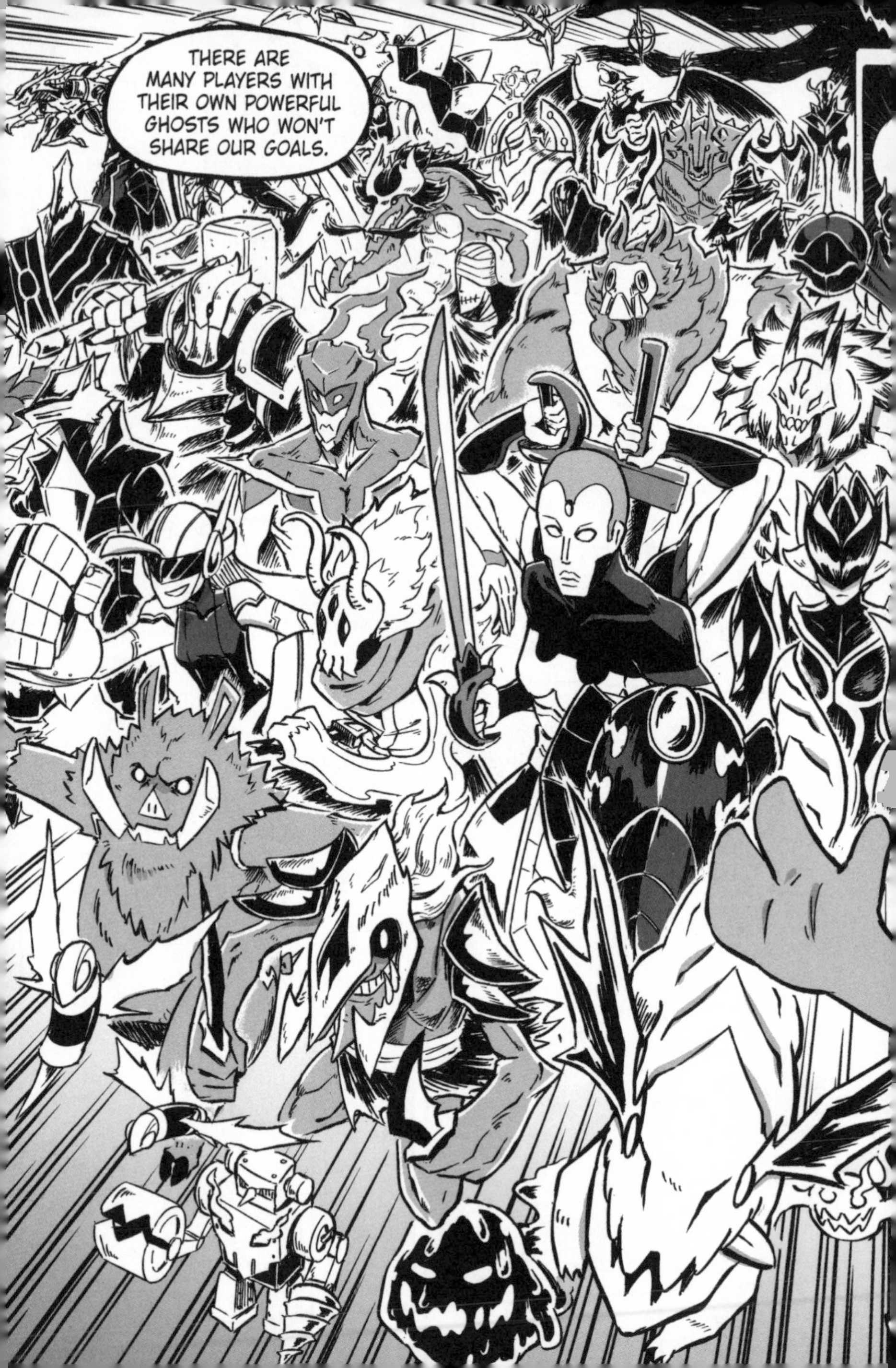
THERE ARE MANY PLAYERS WITH THEIR OWN POWERFUL GHOSTS WHO WON'T SHARE OUR GOALS.

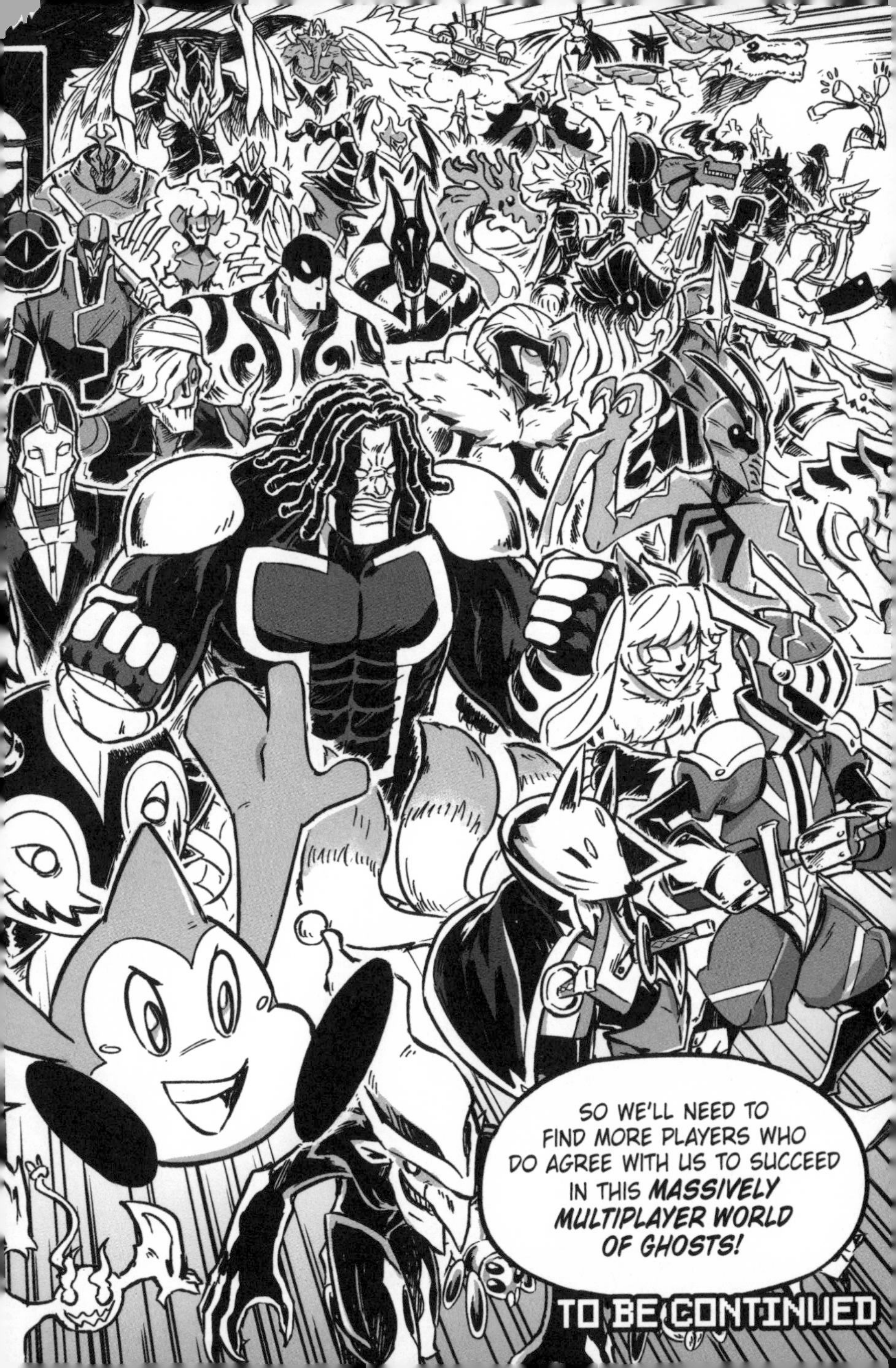
SO WE'LL NEED TO FIND MORE PLAYERS WHO DO AGREE WITH US TO SUCCEED IN THIS MASSIVELY MULTIPLAYER WORLD OF GHOSTS!
TO BE CONTINUED

THE MASSIVELY MULTIPLAYER WORLD OF GHOSTS

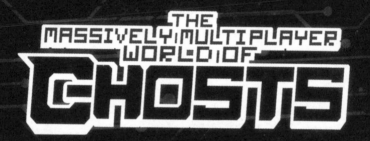

END OF VOLUME 1

BY OSCAR FONG WITH FREDERICK L. JONES

ABOUT THE AUTHORS

OSCAR FONG

Oscar Fong is known online as Fongfumaster and hails from the Auckland Region of New Zealand. While he has a background in animation and digital design, Oscar focuses on illustrative projects and is fond of tabletop role-playing games and crafting.

FREDERICK L. JONES

Frederick L. Jones graduated from the University of North Carolina at Chapel Hill with a BA in communication studies. After a decade as an executive in the video game industry, Frederick combined his experiences in product marketing, product development, and brand management with his lifelong love of anime to create the diverse manga brand Saturday AM in 2013.

ACKNOWLEDGMENTS

I WISH TO OFFER MY DEEPEST GRATITUDE TO MY FAMILY FOR GIVING ME THEIR SUPPORT TO ALLOW ME TO PURSUE MY DREAMS AND APPRECIATION TO THE STAFF OF SATURDAY AM AND FANS FOR HELPING ME ACHIEVE THAT GOAL!

—Oscar Fong

THIS BOOK IS VERY SPECIAL FOR THE LEGACY OF SATURDAY AM. IT'S THE FIRST TITLE DEVELOPED FOR THE BRAND AND IS THE FIRST MANGA-INSPIRED SERIES WITH AN INDIAN LEAD CHARACTER. AS A KID GROWING UP AND AN ADULT LIVING IN RALEIGH-DURHAM, NORTH CAROLINA, THE BROADER ASIAN COMMUNITY IS A SIGNIFICANT PART OF MY FRIEND GROUP. HAVING CHARACTERS OF THAT ETHNICITY WHO ARE THE HEROES AND MAIN PROTAGONISTS OF OUR STORIES IS REWARDING.

TO THAT END, I HAVE TO THANK MY FRIENDS; FAMILY; DOG, ALLIE; AND MY CREATIVE PARTNER, OSCAR FONG. THIS TALENTED YOUNG ARTIST WAS EYE-CATCHING WHEN HE FIRST APPROACHED US YEARS AGO, AND TO SEE HIS DEVELOPMENT IS IMPRESSIVE. HE'S ALSO ONE OF THE SWEETEST PEOPLE YOU'LL MEET (IF NOT INCREDIBLY INQUISITIVE 99 PERCENT OF THE TIME). LIKEWISE, WE ARE THANKFUL TO HAVE THIS OPPORTUNITY COURTESY OF OUR PARTNERS AT THE QUARTO GROUP, INCLUDING JOY, KRISTINE, MEL, THE ANNES, AND WINNIE!

I HOPE YOU WILL ENJOY THIS BOOK WITH SO MANY IDEAS FORTHCOMING THAT WE PLEAD FOR YOUR PATIENCE AS WE SET UP THIS EPIC TALE ACROSS THIS AND FUTURE VOLUMES.

—Frederick L. Jones

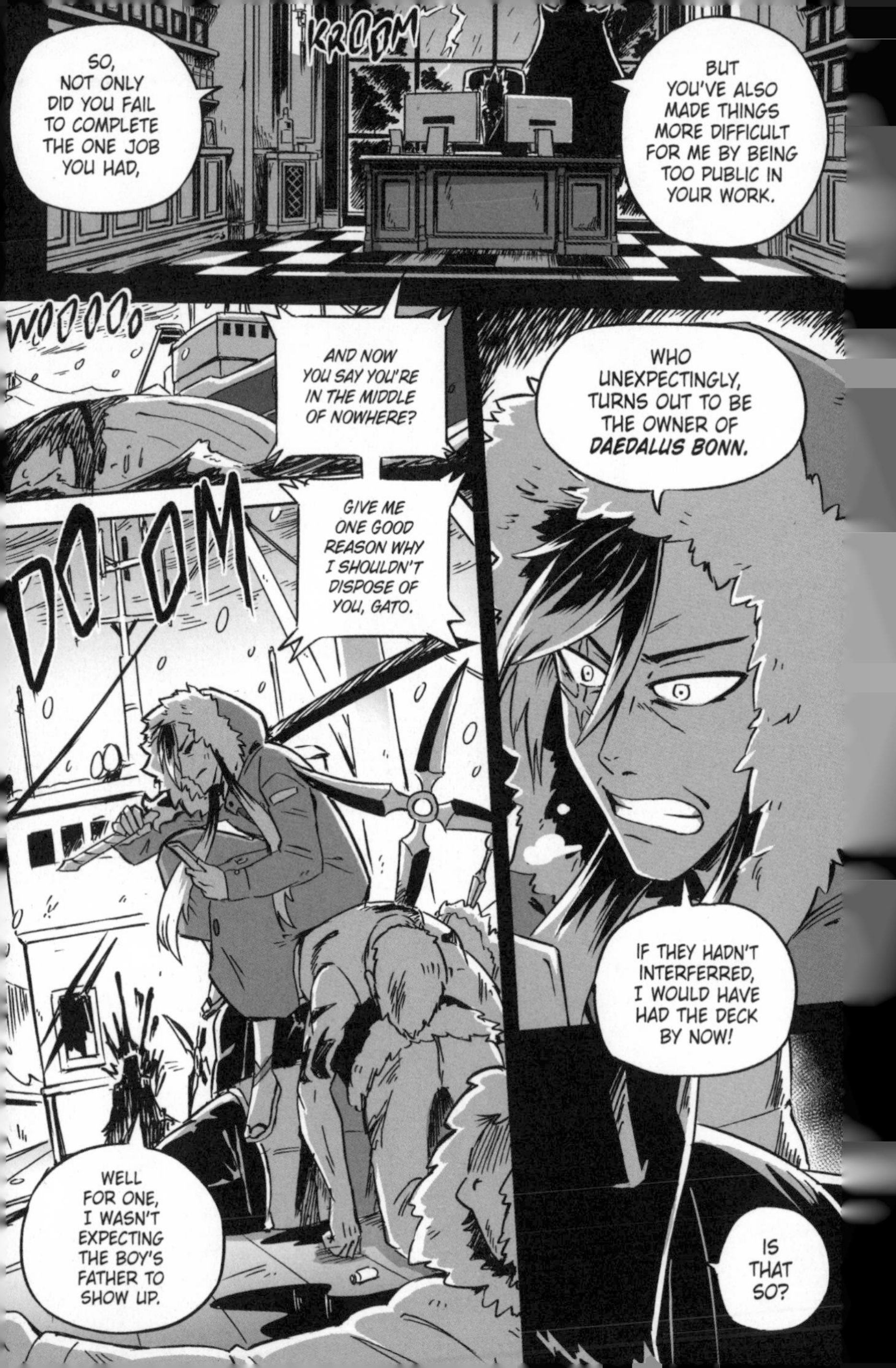
KROOM
SO, NOT ONLY DID YOU FAIL TO COMPLETE THE ONE JOB YOU HAD,
BUT YOU'VE ALSO MADE THINGS MORE DIFFICULT FOR ME BY BEING TOO PUBLIC IN YOUR WORK.
WOOOOO
AND NOW YOU SAY YOU'RE IN THE MIDDLE OF NOWHERE?
DOOM
GIVE ME ONE GOOD REASON WHY I SHOULDN'T DISPOSE OF YOU, GATO.
WELL FOR ONE, I WASN'T EXPECTING THE BOY'S FATHER TO SHOW UP.
WHO UNEXPECTINGLY, TURNS OUT TO BE THE OWNER OF DAEDALUS BONN.
IF THEY HADN'T INTERFERRED, I WOULD HAVE HAD THE DECK BY NOW!
IS THAT SO?

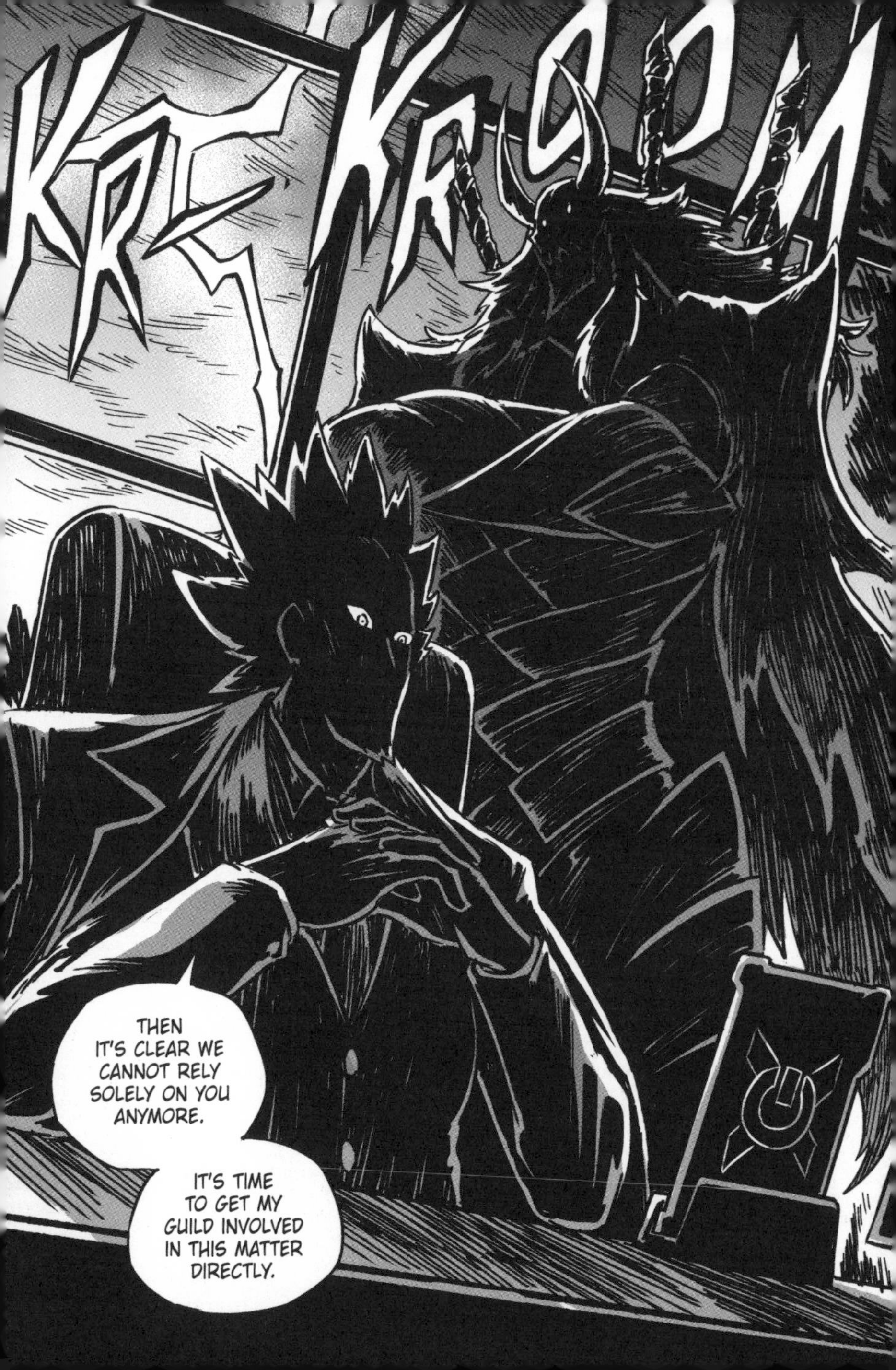
THEN IT'S CLEAR WE CANNOT RELY SOLELY ON YOU ANYMORE.
IT'S TIME TO GET MY GUILD INVOLVED IN THIS MATTER DIRECTLY.

Brimming with creative inspiration, how-to projects, and useful information to enrich your everyday life, quarto.com is a favorite destination for those pursuing their interests and passions.

First published in 2022 by Rockport Publishers, an imprint of The Quarto Group, 100 Cummings Center, Suite 265-D, Beverly, MA 01915, USA. T (978) 282-9590 F (978) 283-2742 Quarto.com

Rockport Publishers titles are also available at discount for retail, wholesale, promotional, and bulk purchase. For details, contact the Special Sales Manager by email at specialsales@quarto.com or by mail at The Quarto Group, Attn: Special Sales Manager, 100 Cummings Center, Suite 265-D, Beverly, MA 01915, USA.

10 9 8 7 6 5 4 3 2 1

ISBN: 978-0-7603-7688-1

Library of Congress Cataloging-in-Publication Data is available.

Created by: Frederick L. Jones
Story by: Frederick L. Jones and Oscar Fong
Art by: Oscar Fong
Lettering: Evan Hayden
Design and additional lettering: Mitch Proctor
Editors: Frederick L. Jones, Peter Doney and Austin Harvey

Printed in USA

The Massively Multiplayer World of Ghosts, Volume 1, is rated T for Teens and is recommended for ages 13 and up. It contains mild profanity and some violent action scenes.